Women in Sociology

A BIO-BIBLIOGRAPHICAL SOURCEBOOK

Edited by
Mary Jo Deegan

Greenwood Press

New York
Westport, Connecticut
London

Library of Congress Cataloging-in-Publication Data

Women in sociology : a bio-bibliographical sourcebook / edited by Mary
    Jo Deegan.
        p. cm.
    Includes indexes.
    ISBN 0–313–26085–0 (lib. bdg. : alk. paper)
    1. Women sociologists—Biography.   I. Deegan, Mary Jo.
HM19.W59   1991
016.301'092'2—dc20
    [B]   90–43376

British Library Cataloguing in Publication Data is available.

Library of Congress Catalog Card Number: 90–43376
ISBN: 0–313–26085–0

First published in 1991

Greenwood Press, 88 Post Road West, Westport, CT 06881
An imprint of Greenwood Publishing Group, Inc.

Printed in the United States of America

The paper used in this book complies with the
Permanent Paper Standard issued by the National
Information Standards Organization (Z39.48–1984).

10 9 8 7 6 5 4 3 2 1

Women in Sociology

THIS BOOK IS DEDICATED TO ALL WOMEN IN SOCIOLOGY

WOMEN, DISEASE, AND WORK IN SOCIOLOGY

CONTENTS

TABLES AND FIGURE

TABLES

FIGURE

PREFACE

This book is a dream fulfilled. I first discovered the vast work done by early women sociologists when I was standing in the basement stacks at Regenstein Library at the University of Chicago in 1975. In front of me were row upon row, from floor to ceiling, of dozens and dozens of books written on women's work in the marketplace, and almost all were written before 1925. Who were these female authors? Were they sociologists? Why had I been led to believe that feminists raised similar questions only since 1965 or 1970? I started to examine these questions then and continue to ask them today. This volume is the first extensive reference book on great female sociologists. It has been a long journey from that beginning to completing it.

I have had so much help from so many people over the past sixteen years that it is literally impossible to remember and to thank them all. I will try to reconstruct only the most immediate helpers who aided me in determining the list of women to be included. They are Jessie Bernard, Valerie Malhotra Bentz, Steven M. Beuchler, Nancy Brooks, Kay Broschart, Miguel Carranza, Irene Diggs, Virginia Fish, Jan Fritz, Jacquelyne Jackson, Louise Haller, Beth Hess, Michael R. Hill, Irving Louis Horowitz, Joan Huber, Helen MacGill Hughes, Al Lee, Elizabeth Briant Lee, Judy Long, Virginia Olesen, Shula Reinharz, Alice Rossi, Guenther Roth, Ronni Rothman, Vicki Ruiz, Mary Kay Schleiter, Ethel Shanas, John Stanfield, Peter T. Suzucki, and Norma Williams. Wilbur Watson first suggested Irene Diggs to me as an eminent sociologist, and Laurel R. Walum supported my interest in Mary E.B.R.S. Coolidge through inviting me to speak on a panel at the North Central Sociology Association in 1989. Norma Sue Griffin organized an excellent conference on Leta Hollingworth in the fall of 1989 at the University of Nebraska-Lincoln. Here I met with several helpful colleagues, especially Ludy

T. Benjamin and Stephanie Shields. Archivists who have provided advice on this project include Lynn Beideck-Porn, Mary Bomberger, Jim Gulich, Gretchen Laguna, Linda Long, Dan Meyer, Wilma Slaight, and Joseph Svoboda. Patricia and Scott Wendt of Bluestem Books obtained many "obscure" books for me at minimal cost. Jen and Larry Sutter aided me in completing my Irene Diggs interview by providing both a place to stay and an interested ear. The helpful environment at the Women's Studies Program at the University of Michigan-Ann Arbor gave me the courage to take on this task in the spring of 1987. I had cheerful and competent secretarial help from Kathy Borman, Joleen Deets, Roxann Roggenkamp, and Sharon Selvage at the University of Nebraska-Lincoln. My last weeks of preparation were eased by the assistance of Jian Wu. Agnes Riedmann helped to edit several entries and the introduction in addition to her support throughout the project.

Two teaching experiences were helpful during the course of preparing this book. A graduate seminar in the fall of 1987 on "The History of Sociological Theory" sparked a deep interest in this subject between myself, Michael R. Ball, Michael R. Hill, and Bruce Keith. My undergraduate "History of Feminist Theory" course in the spring of 1989 was a rewarding teaching experience, too, allowing me to teach about great women in sociology for fifteen weeks. This was an intellectually exciting atmosphere for the twenty-five class members and for me.

In addition to these particularly helpful colleagues, friends, and students, all the entrants and their biographers are due heartfelt appreciation. Many of the latter wrote the first comprehensive analysis of their subject's sociological corpus, and they became pioneers in their own way. Many of the contributors who studied contemporary great women engaged in intensive correspondence, interviews, and analyses with their biographees. One contributor cried after she finished her entry on a deceased woman because it was too late to ever meet and get to know her in person. I look forward to their publishing other articles and books on great female sociologists in the future.

I am very grateful to Mary Sive, who initiated this project with me, to Loomis Mayer, who continued it, and to Mildred Vasan, who helped to complete it, for their editorial interest, support, and work for Greenwood Press. The final manuscript was carefully clarified through the skills of Kathy Johnson of Love Library at the University of Nebraska-Lincoln. She unearthed missing data on pamphlets, government reports, and obscure books. Barbara Hodgson of Greenwood Press undertook the arduous task of copyediting the manuscript. She noted contradictory passages and references that had escaped my weary brain. Penny Sippel, also of Greenwood Press, helped put the whole volume together as production coordinator. The accuracy and appearance of this book were greatly enhanced by Kathy's, Barbara's, and Penny's labor.

Despite this outpouring of support and help, this has not been an easy task to complete. Structural barriers to an enterprise such as this volume exist within the academy. Rewards for writing and teaching about women intellectuals are still problematic. For example, when I was reviewed for meritorious work in 1988 at the University of Nebraska-Lincoln to determine my salary for 1988–1989, I was informed by a committee consisting of my department chair and three of our professorial staff: "We did not give much weight to the editing of volumes, either actual or prospective." Indeed, when I assigned my volume on *Jane Addams and the Men of the Chicago School, 1892–1918* (1988) for four weeks of a fifteen-week course, "History of Sociological Theory," I was informed by the department's merit committee: "Although academic freedom gives you the right to talk about whatever you want, the institution does not need to reward you for it." My salary for that year was lowered as a result of my daring to research and teach about female sociologists in any way.

Another stressful problem was that several entries were not completed as promised by scholars who originally agreed to write biographies. This situation necessitated my stretching my own areas of expertise to fill in the gaps and complete the task at hand. My work, like that of all other contemporary academic sociologists, still emphasizes our vastly male-dominated corpus and overspecialization. These bastions of ignorance are being eroded, however, as this volume documents.

My partner, Michael R. Hill, totally donated three months to checking bibliographies, reentering them on our personal computer, and encouraging me to continue. When I had deep reservations about taking on this project because of the time and work involved and facing the hazards on an uncharted sea of knowledge, he unequivocally urged me to take the challenge.

I wrote more than 250 letters in the course of this project, without a graduate assistant or grant money. This type of intensive labor is the lot of women in this field, even in our more liberated era. I felt highly rewarded, however, in being able to help the great women in sociology be remembered and honored. I am pleased with our "labor of love," and privileged to study these brilliant founders and to help establish a professional network of biographical work on women in sociology. I hope you, the reader, enjoy it, learn from it, and are encouraged to contribute to future studies of women in sociology.

Mary Jo Deegan
University of Nebraska-Lincoln

Women in Sociology

INTRODUCTION

Female sociologists have shaped and changed the world. This volume documents the major outlines of their work and their profound impact during the past 150 years, from 1840 to 1990. The expertise and influence of these women are of such magnitude that it should have been impossible to forget or neglect them in the discipline of sociology; yet far too frequently their connections to sociology and to sociological labor have been buried. Thus, as word of the current project made its way through the sociological grapevine, several colleagues wrote or called to tell me that this project could not be done because women did not enter the profession until after 1930. Many—but not all—reported this "fact" with regret and resignation. This significant group of predominantly white, male experts is being challenged by a larger and, in my opinion, more significant group of colleagues of all colors, both genders, and all areas of specialization. This latter group wrote and called, asking for more information on founding women in sociology. This book is dedicated to these progressive colleagues and others who share this spirit of inquiry and openness.

The lack of knowledge about the women who helped to found the profession is reflected in this volume through the sometimes minimal professional critiques of their writings. How did some of the greatest women in the world get separated from their professional roots as sociologists? Unfortunately this fascinating, epistemological question cannot be answered here, but a number of other, vital questions can be dealt with for the first time. The information in this volume can answer these questions: Who were or are the female founders in sociology? Where were they born and when? What were their most important writings? What were their major accomplishments? How have they been honored? What are their connections to the discipline of sociology?

In this introduction I share my decision making with you, the reader, and unravel a few of the underlying patterns. My greatest hope is that this book will soon be outdated by the research it generates.

DEFINING THE CONCEPT: "FOUNDING SISTERS"

Male sociologists celebrate themselves with great frequency. The gendered nature of this scholarly project is seen in their naming of male founders as "masters of ideas," "great men of ideas," and "founding fathers." None of these terms fit women founders. Indeed, none of these terms are applied to women, despite their eminence. "Masters of ideas" has a terrible female counterpart: "mistresses of ideas." This objectionable phrase evokes sexual associations, of women bought and commoditized by men.

"Great men of ideas" has a more congenial female form: "great women of ideas." This latter, melodious phrase certainly can be useful, but it does not have the political and emotional anchor that "founding sisters" has for me. So I take a moment to explain my favoring the words "founding sisters."

The most common term used to refer to male founders in sociological texts, classrooms, and discourse is "founding fathers." I do not define the most powerful women in sociology as "founding mothers," although other scholars (whom I admire generally) are beginning to use this terminology (e.g., Hess, Markson, and Stein 1988). I do not favor the imagery and meaning of maternity in the context of brilliant women. Many of these women dedicated their lives to the elimination of traditional female roles, particularly the oppressiveness surrounding mothering. The symbol of motherhood, furthermore, often is rooted in emotional rather than intellectual care. In addition, mothers are nurturant but often subservient to men—fathers, husbands, and sons—in the family (Bernard* 1968, 1972; N.B. names of founding sisters who are included in this sourcebook are followed by an asterisk, on first mention). The founding sisters of sociology are not in this subservient relationship to founding fathers. Finally, mothers are powerful in the home, but not in the public realm of ideas, the academy, and social institutions like hospitals and the military (Bernard 1964, 1981; Rossi* 1974; Rossi and Calderwood 1974; Smith* 1987, 1988). Founding sisters speak with authority on both public and private worlds, engaging both sexes, and transcending traditional limits of sociology and women.

The phrase "founding sisters of sociology" is connected politically to the feminist meaning of "sisterhood."

It is in sisterhood that we discover the objectivity of our oppression. That discovery is made in the relation to other women, in our discussion with other women, in our exploring with other women the dimensions of the oppression. For we discover oppression in learning to speak of it as such, not as something which is an inner weakness, nor as estrangement from yourself, but as something which is indeed imposed upon you by the society and which is experienced in common with others. . . . But what it also means is the discovery of women as your own people . . . as my people . . . as the people I stand with . . . as the people whose part I take. (Smith 1977, 10–11)

"Sisters" and an all-encompassing sisterhood including race and class issues (Dill 1987) are part of this project. "The spirit of sisterhood," to paraphrase Jane Addams* (1912), permeates the lives of the founding sisters, the contributors to this volume, and the editor.

The term "founding" may need some explanation, too, in light of the 150 years of sociological history considered. Although men who founded the profession are historically clustered around the turn of the century, women remain marginal to the profession. As I discuss further in a later section, women in sociology have been admitted only recently to a dual sexual division of labor after a struggle initiated around 1970 with the establishment of Sociologists for Women in Society (SWS). The eminent contemporary women studied in this volume helped to found this professional organization. The dozens of women who were denied tenure in the intervening years and the unchanging demographic data on women in prestigious, graduate training institutions reveal how radical and fragile these innovations are. All the women honored in this volume are on the frontier of establishing women in a patriarchal profession.

"Founding sisters" may sound weaker today than the term "founding fathers." I hope that the feminist intention underlying sisterhood and the patriarchal intention underlying both fatherhood and motherhood become clearer over time. "Founding sisters" will then sound not only more harmonious to the ear, but also more powerful in its message.

DISCOVERING THE FOUNDING SISTERS

I first grasped the magnitude of women's sociological achievements in the mid–1970s, through my studies of Jane Addams and her cohort who worked at the University of Chicago and at the social settlement Hull-House (Deegan 1978). I dreamt of the day when they and women like them would be included in the annals of the profession. Because of the deep abyss of knowledge about them and often harsh hostility to accepting them as sociologists (e.g., Bulmer 1989), I suspected that this inclusion would not occur in my lifetime. As I gradually found other scholars working on early women sociologists (many of the former are contributors to this volume), along with published articles in the area (e.g., Deegan 1983, 1986), and as I finished my book on Jane Addams (Deegan 1988a), a small body of legitimating knowledge on the lives and writings of founding women in sociology emerged. Since 1985 this group of scholars and the knowledge we generated have snowballed: many sociologists are eager to know more about their female founders. Imagine my pleasure, and theirs, in completing this volume! We have accomplished what I thought only decades of work could do:

Figure 1.1
Great Women in Sociology: 1840–1990

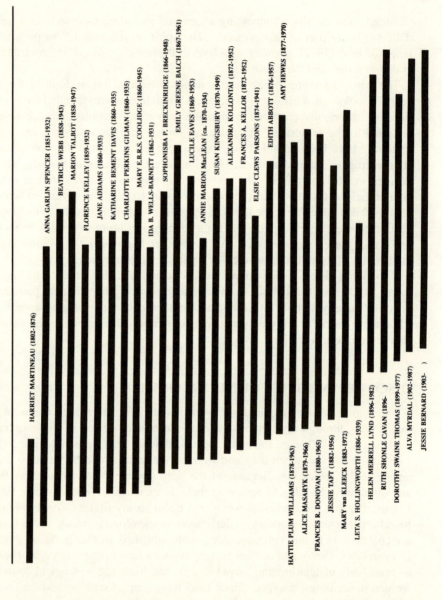

HARRIET MARTINEAU (1802-1876)

ANNA GARLIN SPENCER (1851-1932)

BEATRICE WEBB (1858-1943)

MARION TALBOT (1858-1947)

FLORENCE KELLEY (1859-1932)

JANE ADDAMS (1860-1935)

KATHARINE BEMENT DAVIS (1860-1935)

CHARLOTTE PERKINS GILMAN (1860-1945)

MARY E.B.R.S. COOLIDGE (1860-1945)

IDA B. WELLS-BARNETT (1862-1931)

SOPHONISBA P. BRECKINRIDGE (1866-1948)

EMILY GREENE BALCH (1867-1961)

LUCILE EAVES (1869-1953)

ANNIE MARION MacLEAN (ca. 1870-1934)

SUSAN KINGSBURY (1870-1949)

ALEXANDRA KOLLONTAI (1872-1952)

FRANCES A. KELLOR (1873-1952)

ELSIE CLEWS PARSONS (1874-1941)

EDITH ABBOTT (1876-1957)

AMY HEWES (1877-1970)

HATTIE PLUM WILLIAMS (1878-1963)

ALICE MASARYK (1879-1966)

FRANCES R. DONOVAN (1880-1965)

JESSIE TAFT (1882-1956)

MARY van KLEECK (1883-1972)

LETA S. HOLLINGWORTH (1886-1939)

HELEN MERRELL LYND (1896-1982)

RUTH SHONLE CAVAN (1896-)

DOROTHY SWAINE THOMAS (1899-1977)

ALVA MYRDAL (1902-1987)

JESSIE BERNARD (1903-)

4

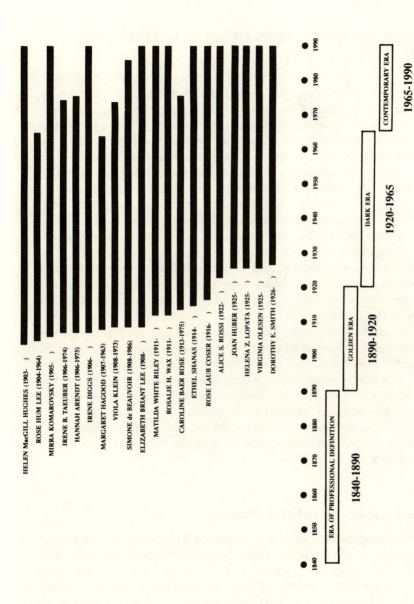

Source: Compiled by Mary Jo Deegan. Graphics by Michael R. Hill. Copyright 1990 by Mary Jo Deegan.

a reference book documenting the lives and work of founding women in sociology.

THE SOCIAL CONSTRUCTION OF A FIELD: SELECTING THE LIST

Women in sociology have never before been systematically recognized. Mapping out their contributions has been a challenge and an exploration. A few comments on my criteria for compiling the list of names are, therefore, in order. First, as an editor, I wanted entries that were long enough to reflect on the women's lives and social thought, yet short enough to be read quickly. Fifty-one entries, many the first analyses of these women from a sociological perspective, seemed like a difficult but manageable goal. Second, I wanted to cover the entire era of women's sociological influence from the 1840s to the present. Third, I selected women who were born before 1927. The list includes substantial leaders among contemporary women sociologists. They have spent their lives building a literature and a practice within sociology and the everyday world. This decision also gave me the freedom to analyze the generations who were trained primarily before the second wave of feminism developed after 1965. Many contemporary women included in this volume started this second wave within sociology. They were the founders and leaders of this change.

The list of names of the women included in this volume (see Figure 1.1) was generated through (a) recommendation by experts in sociology; (b) a search of other reference books that include leading women in the profession; and (c) the application of a formal set of criteria emphasizing achievement; chronological eras, from about 1840 to the present; international leaders; national and regional leaders in the United States, the earliest institutional center favorable to both sociology's development and the training of female professionals; ethnic, political, and racial diversity; and institutional variations in their employment. Each criterion is discussed briefly below.

Recommendations by Other Authorities

Because so many women have been neglected as scholars in sociology, I depended heavily on other experts' knowledge. I corresponded and spoke with dozens of sociologists who were experts in the study of women, the history of sociology, or a particular subfield. Although many of these experts suggested that I abandon the project or only study contemporary women, the suggestions and support of many others were invaluable. As mentioned earlier, most sociologists do not know about many of the women discussed here or about their elaborate alternate network of scholarship and support.

A Search of Other References

I systematically consulted standard reference books on outstanding women, sociologists, and intellectuals: *Notable American Women*; *White's Conspectus on Biography*; *The National Cyclopedia of Biography*; *The International Encyclopedia of the Social Sciences*; various *Who's Who* volumes—regional, national, and international; and *Outstanding Men and Women in the Social Sciences*. The computerized "Sociofile" for sociological abstracts also was used. All were valuable sources of information and names.

In addition, two female sociologists have done yeowoman's service on biography, social theory, and feminism: Dale Spender (1983, 1988) and Alice Rossi (1973). I frequently consulted their writings on founding sisters.

The Application of Formal Criteria

Käsler's Criteria for Determining Sociologists

Because of the lack of scholarship on women in sociology, some formal criteria were needed to determine the pool of possible entrants. Dirk Käsler (1981), who studies early German sociologists, determined that if one of the following five criteria was met by a person, then she or he was a member of the profession. He wrote:

As *sociologist* I define those who fulfill at least one of the following five criteria:
—occupy a chair of sociology and/or teach sociology
—membership in the German Sociological Society (changed here to membership in any national sociological society—MJD)
—coauthorship of sociological articles or textbooks
—self-definition as a "sociologist"
—definition by others as a sociologist.

All the founding sisters meet at least one of Käsler's criteria. Most of the entrants far surpass these five minimal requirements. Using these criteria generated a systematic basis for making decisions on subjects to be included (Deegan 1988: 9–13).

Women Who Set Precedents in Sociology

Many women who were the "first" in a variety of structural positions in sociology are included here. They provided leadership in the academy and in professional organizations. They broke racial barriers, and they were role models. Table 1.1 is a chart of their pathbreaking accomplishments in the discipline.

Table 1.1
Professional Precedents of Founding Sisters

"Firsts"	Women Sociologists
Sociologist/methodologist (1838)	Martineau, Harriet
Doctorate (1887)	Rose P. Firestone *
Assistant Professor (1894)	Coolidge, Mary Elizabeth Burroughs Roberts Smith
Black American Sociologist (1892)	Wells-Barnett, Ida B.
Chicago Sociologist (1892)	Talbot, Marion
Author of the U.S.A. Equal Rights Amendment (1923)	Paul, Alice *
Chair of Coeducational Doctoral Sociology Program (1923)	Williams, Hattie Plum
Chinese American (1940)	Lee, Rose Hum
President of the American Sociological Association (1948)	Thomas, Dorothy Swaine

* See Appendix

Table 1.2
Nobel Peace Prize Winners Who Are Founding Sisters

Nobel Prize	Women Sociologists
1931	Addams, Jane
1946	Balch, Emily Greene
1982	Myrdal, Alva

Emphasizing Achievement

These women's contribution to ideas is evident in their bibliographies. With few exceptions, the founding sisters dramatically influenced the world. The powerful application of their ideas is reflected in the three who were awarded Nobel Peace Prizes (see Table 1.2). Their cumulative power is far beyond this single, prestigious award. Founding sisters helped earthquake victims (e.g., Mary Elizabeth Burroughs Roberts Smith Coolidge,* Lucile Eaves,* and Katharine Bement Davis*), fought for women's suffrage and helped to wrest it from men (e.g., Edith Abbott,* Sophonisba Breckinridge,* and Charlotte Perkins Gilman*), organized large voluntary associations (e.g., Marion Talbot,* who co-founded the American Association of University Women, and Alice Rossi, who cofounded the National Organization of Women), and articulated women's rights to equal work (e.g., Edith Abbott and Helen MacGill Hughes*), activism (e.g., Jessie Taft* and Dorothy E. Smith*), and peace (e.g., Hannah Arendt* and Alvah Myrdal*). The founding sisters are outstanding women of achievement.

Table 1.3
Founding Sisters Who Were Presidents of the American Sociological Association

Year of Presidency	Women Sociologists
1948	Thomas, Dorothy Swaine
1973	Komarovsky, Mirra
1978	Rossi, Alice
1986	Riley, Matilda White
1989	Huber, Joan

Within the profession of sociology they have struggled to make inroads as administrators (Hattie Plum Williams*), officers in professional associations (see Table 1.3), theorists, and scholars.

Covering Chronological Eras, from 1840 to 1990

The peak of power and visibility for female sociologists born before 1927 occurred between 1890 and 1920, especially in the city of Chicago (Deegan 1987, 1988b). The viability of early women in sociology and the extreme attractiveness of it as a career for women are reflected in Graham Morgan's article on women who studied sociology at American universities during the nineteenth century (1980). He has compiled a list of other 100 women. I expanded my scope and time line beyond this absorbing golden era. My more broadly defined, intergenerational analysis over several eras is summarized later in this chapter.

Examining International Women

International women, ideas, work, and networks are emphasized. Several factors made this international examination problematic. First, the major structural development of the profession occurred in the United States from 1890 to about 1950. This institutional reality is reflected in the overrepresentation of women from this country (see next section). Second, the research on founding sisters in sociology is weaker in other countries today than it is in the United States. Third, as a group, American scholars (including myself) are extremely ignorant of international sociology, other languages, and different cultures. Our training seldom includes more than ''founding fathers'' from France and Germany. Thus patriarchal practice is connected to American nativism. An attempt to transcend this bias and acknowledge a worldwide sisterhood is made here.

Fourth, knowledge about founding sisters from Africa, Latin America, and Central America is sorely lacking. Olive Schreiner, a noted feminist and an antiapartheid author, represents an important intellectual contribution from Africa. Because this entire continent is severely underrepresented here, I considered including Schreiner as a small recognition of a major political and intellectual issue. I could not find that she had any connection to the profession of sociology, nonetheless, and I could not justify her inclusion here. The most notable sociological scholar on Africa included here is Irene Diggs,* and her interest in this area of the world was considerably more supported in anthropology than in sociology. Thus there are two epistemological problems for women who study Africa from a sociological perspective: lack of recognition in the profession and a lack of mentors for women.

The amazing Indian scholar and religious leader Pandita Ramabai also was considered at length for inclusion. (Her name is in the Appendix, which lists eminent female sociologists who were not selected for inclusion here.) Her book on *The High-Caste Hindu Woman* is an especially fine piece of scholarship. On the one hand, one scholar, Gupti, considers Ramabai a founder of the sociology of marriage and the family in India. On the other hand, dozens of English texts on Ramabai are religious books. It was difficult to separate the voice of Ramabai from the problems of translations, religious interpretations, and the borders between "charity," "sociology," "social work," "religion," and theology. These Western categories do not fit many non-Western careers, and I opted for a disciplinary boundary that was more defined in this case, too.[1]

I believe that there are Hispanic founding sisters; but despite an exhaustive effort to find them, I was unsuccessful. Clearly I was hampered by my own limited North American network, my weak Spanish language skills, and the barriers against women scholars operative in these countries. At this time, however, such women are unknown to the Latin and Central American scholars I contacted.

Founding sisters from the U.S.S.R. and Eastern Europe are underrecognized, too, because of the previous intellectual and political barriers between these countries and the United States. It was with deep regret that I read of the death of Magdalena Sokolowska in 1989. I learned of her crucial role in establishing medical sociology in Poland through her eulogies that were published after this book was completed. This information arrived in the spring of 1990, although it carries a 1989 publication date (Archer 1989; Bottomore 1989; Elling and Elinson 1989).

Seeking out women sociologists from around the world provided a coherence to women's work in sociology that is lacking when the United States is the only focus of study. This work was intellectually challenging and exciting to watch as it unfolded. The nations represented here are noted in Table 1.4.

National and Regional Influence in the United States

The United States has a clear international lead in the legitimation, training, hiring, and funding of sociologists. Great Britain, Russia, and Europe shared, if not excelled, in developing the profession. But World War I and World War II had devastating effects on these nations' sociological development. The train-

Table 1.4
Nationalities of Founding Sisters Other Than the United States of America

Nationality	Founding Sisters
Austria	Klein, Viola
Canada	Hughes, Helen MacGill * MacLean, Annie Marion * Smith, Dorothy E.
Czechoslovakia	Masaryk, Alice
Great Britain	Martineau, Harriet Webb, Beatrice
France	de Beauvoir, Simone
Germany	Arendt, Hannah * Coser, Rose Laub *
Poland	Lopata, Helena Znaniecka *
Soviet Union	Kollontai, Alexandra Komarovsky, Mirra *
Sweden	Myrdal, Alva

* Naturalized citizens of the United States of America

ing of female professionals appears to have been more limited as well, although the lack of scholarship on founding sisters makes this point difficult to determine. Thus many women may have had flourishing careers during their lifetimes, and it may be discrimination against them after their death that is the severer problem. Contemporary ignorance may make discrimination against founding sisters appear to be severer in the present than it was in the past. The regional representation of women from the United States is noted in Table 1.5.

Covering Ethnic, Political, and Ideological Diversity

White, Anglo-Saxon, Protestant women (see Helen MacGill Hughes on her experience as a WASP, 1972) from the middle and upper middle classes predominate in the marginal world of women sociologists. Mainstream ideas representing, first, the patriarchal profession and, second, the world view of WASP women are powerful within the networks of women in the profession. To address the patriarchal ideology discriminating against women of color, political radicals, and scholars of less popular theories and methodologies, I sought out women who represented this diversity. They are less clearly anchored to formal criteria and networks; but like their more privileged sisters, they accomplished great

Table 1.5
Founding Sisters Born in the United States of America by Region

Region	Founding Sisters
Eastern	Balch, Emily Greene Coser, Rose Laub * Diggs, Irene Hewes, Amy Hollingworth, Leta S. Lee, Elizabeth Bryant Lynd, Helen Merrell Taft, Jessie Taeuber, Irene van Kleeck, Mary
Great Plains	Williams, Hattie Plum
Midwest	Abbott, Edith Addams, Jane Arendt, Hannah * Breckinridge, Sophonisba P. Cavan, Ruth Shonle Davis, Katharine Bement Donovan, Frances Huber, Joan Komarovsky, Mirra * Lee, Rose Hum Lopata, Helena Znaniecka Shanas, Ethel Talbot, Marion Wells-Barnett, Ida B.
South	Hagood, Margaret
West	Coolidge, Mary Elizabeth Burroughs Roberts Smith Olesen, Virginia
Multiregional **	Bernard, Jessie Eaves, Lucile Gilman, Charlotte Perkins Hughes, Helen MacGill * Kelley, Florence Kellor, Frances Kingsbury, Susan MacLean, Annie Marion * Parsons, Elsie Clews Riley, Matilda White Rose, Caroline Rossi, Alice Thomas, Dorothy Swaine Wax, Rosalie Wells-Barnett, Ida B.

* Naturalized citizens of the United States of America
** Over ten years lived in more than one region of the country

tasks. Because these women are doubly discriminated against, they fought particularly difficult battles and reflect a unique heritage.

As noted above, I contacted more than a dozen scholars in my search for a Hispanic founding sister, but without success. Once again, I am unsure whether this lack of representation reflects the deep bias against founding sisters in the past or in the present.

Encompassing Institutional Variation

Prestigious universities and research moneys have been riddled by discrimination against women in sociology. Professional societies, schools of thought, and informal networks also posed barriers for women. In this context of bigotry founding sisters found employment in other types of institutional settings (e.g., social settlements and governmental agencies) and in marginal professional niches. They triumphed over their restrictions, but these constraints forced the founding sisters to seek employment where they could find it. Discovering how they practiced sociology in settings outside the academy was essential to the documentation of their contributions.

Applying the criteria above to generate a list of eminent women was only the first step in completing this project. The entries themselves are the core contributions. Analyzing the generational patterns that emerged illustrates how these individual entries reveal complex patterns of women's work in sociology.

THE ERAS OF WOMEN IN SOCIOLOGY

Founding Sisters in an Era of Professional Definition (1840–1890)

The earliest women, those working professionally before 1890, were part of an emerging feminist consciousness. They were pioneers in creating an opportunity structure for women to work as public lecturers, as authors of nonfiction, and as women struggling to break down the barriers to women's higher education. In addition, they were opening the doors to a new profession: sociology. They often battled with religious definitions of the world and women's place in it. For male sociologists, this religious battle emerged from their clerical training. For female sociologists, this religious battle emerged from women's role as symbolic angels, embodiments of the moral order.

Harriet Martineau* is the earliest founding sister included here. She is one of the major founders of sociology as a legitimated area of study. Her preeminence in this regard is equal to, if not greater than, that of any man in her era, including the relatively overpraised Comte and de Tocqueville. Martineau's lucid translation of Comte's work contributed significantly to his recognition as a founding sociologist. She condensed his voluminous *Cours de Philosophie Positiv* and made it more accessible to those who later established sociology in the English-speaking world. In addition, her travels in the United States were more insightful, comprehensive, and methodologically creative than those of de Tocqueville. Martineau is a giant in sociology, and her undisputed leadership is recognized here.

A view of her remarkable transcendence of the limits on women's mind is captured in this passage from her autobiography:

When I was young, it was not thought proper for young ladies to study very conspicuously; and especially with pen in hand . . . Jane Austen herself . . . was compelled by the feelings of her family to cover up her manuscripts with a large piece of muslin work, kept on the table for the purpose, whenever any genteel people came in. (Martineau 1877: 100)

Not only did Martineau dare to write; she dared to write about her views on society and in support of a daring young discipline: sociology.

Other women from this era who were more tenuously associated with sociology include Madame de Staël, Josephine Butler, and Rose P. Firestone. Madame de Staël was a social analyst of Napoleanic France whose writings preceded Martineau's. Madame de Staël had no relation, therefore, to the formal discipline of sociology, but she was an important female theorist on society. Josephine Butler also lacked ties to the emerging discipline of sociology. Her work for women in England, particularly on behalf of prostitutes, and her writings on society influenced other women sociologists, including her contemporary Harriet Martineau. Thus Jane Addams, Anna Garlin Spencer,* and the contemporary sociologist Kathleen Barry (1984) have analyzed and critiqued Butler's life and writings.

A number of early feminist theorists, like Mary Wollstonecraft, Lucy Stone, and Matilda Joslyn Gage (see Rossi 1973; Spender 1983), laid vital foundations for feminist theory that are precursors to feminist sociology. Connecting their writings to the profession of sociology is at a rudimentary stage, and still remains outside the professional structure that the founding sisters helped to erect.

Finally, Rose P. Firestone was awarded a doctorate in the sociology of the family in 1887 at University of Wooster in Wooster, Ohio (Eells 1956: 651). She was the first woman to earn a doctorate in sociology, and perhaps she was the first doctorally trained sociologist in the world. The University of Wooster disbanded its doctoral program in 1900. Hence no ''school'' developed there, nor any powerful sociological network. Firestone has left little trace of her life other than this one, outstanding achievement.[2] Given the paucity of information on her, I decided that her precedent is worthy of a comment here but not an entry.

The earliest founding sisters worked independently in their labor as sociologists, although many were well known in literary or political circles. They were strong people who supported a separate profession to study society and human relations.

The Golden Era of Women in Sociology (1890–1920)

The second group of founding sisters, working primarily from 1890 to 1920, were part of a "golden era for women in sociology." This amazing cohort entered sociology with a new vision for the disenfranchised in general, and for women in particular. They wanted to establish a new profession in a transformed, more humane society. They worked primarily in a woman-centered, separate institutional world (Deegan 1987, 1988a, 1988b).

Sociology was recognized as a distinct profession in academia with the founding of the first graduate department of sociology at the University of Chicago in 1892. (I have used 1892 as the beginning year for this era elsewhere [Deegan 1987, 1988b] because I was concentrating on the United States.) There were two generations of women in sociology during this golden era. The first generation, born between 1855 and 1870, were "pioneers" who helped to build a place for "women's work" in a society with distinct spheres for each sex. This gender ideology, the doctrine of the separate spheres, allowed for the growth of a women's network in sociology. It was led by women and emphasized the study of the home, women, children, and the family. Because of women's "emotional and cultural sensitivity," they were deemed ideal professionals to use knowledge to improve society: to make society more humane. The men's network was more abstract, intellectual, and academic. I have analyzed this gendered division of labor in depth elsewhere (1978, 1981, 1987, 1988a, 1988b). The second generation of women in the golden era of sociology were "professionals" who obtained male credentials in the academy, but who sometimes chose and sometimes were forced to operate in the distinct women's world within sociology (Deegan 1987, 1988a, 1988b).

A powerful network of founding sisters flourished during these years. They recruited one another into the profession, helped one another find employment, stayed with one another through hard times, documented women's lives, shared a vision of a more equalitarian society, lobbied for legislation, founded massive social organizations, and wrote books, pamphlets, articles, and broadsides together. They were friends, allies, sometimes lovers, and colleagues in a new profession. They critiqued one another's work, elaborating and extending their intellectual corpus. They were part of the "first wave of feminism," and sociology was integral to their work and lives. Their network was international in scope and linked to women's demands for higher education. Changing women's roles in society were linked to the emerging social science, especially sociology (Klein* 1948). These women encompassed two generations from 1890 to 1920: the pioneers and the first professionals.

The Pioneers

The pioneers in the golden era battled for women's right to higher education, suffrage, work outside the home, and the use of social science to document women's restricted lives and opportunities. Jane Addams was a central figure in this sociological drama, especially in the areas of applied sociology and the social thought generated by the Chicago school of sociology. Hull-House, which she headed, was the major women's sociological institution. It generated a new model of professional work, in which the home and the workplace were combined. It was a kind of intellectual commune and salon.[3] Some of the brilliant female sociologists who lived and worked there were Edith Abbott, Emily Greene Balch,* Sophonisba Breckinridge, Charlotte Perkins Gilman, Florence Kelley,* Frances Kellor,* Julia Lathrop, Mary McDowell, and Annie Marion MacLean.* Dozens of other women sociologists, including Beatrice Webb,* Ida B. Wells-Barnett,* and Alice Masaryk,* visited it.

The sociology of Addams as an intellectual legacy is a function of two major streams of thought: cultural feminism and critical pragmatism. "Cultural feminism" is a theory of society that assumes that traditionally defined feminine values are superior to traditionally defined male values. "Critical pragmatism" (Deegan 1988a) is a theory of science that emphasizes the need to apply knowledge to everyday problems based on radical interpretations of liberal and progressive values. Addams' work was firmly grounded in that of men in the "Chicago School" of pragmatism and of sociology, especially that developed by John Dewey, George Herbert Mead, and W. I. Thomas. In addition, Addams' critical pragmatism was based on reanalyses of sociological traditions in Britain (especially that developed by Beatrice Webb, Charles Booth, Patrick Geddes, and Canon Barnett), in Russia (especially that developed by Leo Tolstoy and Petr Kropotkin), and in the Germanic tradition (especially that developed by Karl Marx and Friedrich Engels).

Addams assumed that feminine values would be adopted by the general public; for many years her sociological thought and practice supported this assumption. With the advent of World War I, however, her pacifism conflicted with the popular support of the war. She was forced to choose between her female vision of a cooperative society and her democratic commitment to a society at war. At great personal and intellectual cost she opted for an antimilitarism stance. The incompatibility between cultural feminism and critical pragmatism was not addressed by Addams during her major era of influence in sociology, from 1892 to 1918. The internal inconsistency of her work was partly responsible for her decline in sociological leadership. Clearly, however, her choice to emphasize cultural feminism, with its preference for feminine values over masculine ones, was the major reason for her "fall from grace." Her national censure as a pacifist coincided with her "failure" as a sociologist, and for many years she remained a social outcast in society and the profession (Deegan 1988; see also my entry on Addams here).

The elimination of Addams as a leading sociologist was tied to the elimination and erasure of her cohort. The power of the flourishing separatist world of the golden era also brought about its dramatic erasure. Few students, colleagues, institutions, and texts championed their sociology after 1920. Two women in particular were removed from their sociological positions: Emily Greene Balch, in 1919, and Anna Garlin Spencer, in 1920. "Founding fathers," such as George H. Mead and E. A. Ross, eschewed many of their previous ideas and values associated with the founding sisters.

Many similar patterns of pioneer women in sociology emerged in other countries. Alice Masaryk's life was torn asunder by World War I, including her imprisonment. Alexandra Kollontai* was in the turmoil of the Bolshevik Revolution, and during its aftermath she, too, was imprisoned on several occasions. Beatrice Webb was involved in Fabian governmental changes throughout these years, and the work of the London Sociological Society, in which she was active, was similarly interrupted. A future generation of founding sisters were children during these years, and their lives also were dramatically changed by the Great War. For example, Helena Znaniecka Lopata* fled Poland as a child, while Mirra Komarovsky* fled Russia as a young girl.

The pioneers saw the end of their powerful, separatist network in sociology after 1920. They survived in a narrowly defined patriarchal profession, if at all. The first wave of feminism receded in power in sociology and in society at large.

The Earliest Professionals

The young women drawn to sociology during the golden era combined the role established by the pioneers with formal training in the academy. Many of these professionals were mentored by the pioneers and by sympathetic male sociologists such as George H. Mead and W. I. Thomas at the University of Chicago, Franklin Giddings at Bryn Mawr College and Columbia University, and George E. Howard and E. A. Ross at Stanford University and the University of Nebraska. Female students were not accepted as equal members in the male academy, however. The women struggled on the margins of sociology departments. These professional women all earned advanced degrees in the social sciences: Edith Abbott, Sophonisba Breckinridge, Katharine Bement Davis,* Amy Hewes,* and Jessie Taft at the University of Chicago; Emily Greene Balch at Bryn Mawr College; Leta Stetter Hollingworth* and Elsie Clews Parsons* at Columbia University; Mary Elizabeth Burroughs Roberts Smith Coolidge, Susan Kingsbury,* and Lucile Eaves* at Stanford University; and Hattie Plum Williams at the University of Nebraska. Some willingly turned to social work as a more inviting profession for women. Others entered social work because they felt pressured by unemployment and limited professional opportunities in sociology. Thus the female faculty in sociology at the University of Chicago (Edith Abbott, Sophonisba Breckinridge, Mary McDowell, and Marion Talbot) was transferred from sociology to social work in 1920 (Deegan 1978), and they were relieved to be rid of their second-class status as sociologists. Hattie Plum Williams, however, was pushed out of the sociology department at the University of Nebraska somewhat later, in 1928.

Other professional founding sisters from this era turned to anthropology (e.g.,

Elsie Clews Parsons) or psychology (e.g., Leta S. Hollingworth), and established outstanding careers in those more congenial disciplines. (These two women were trained at Columbia University, reflecting a different institutional pattern than that of the women at the University of Chicago, who tended to enter social work.) A few women worked in women's colleges (e.g., Amy Hewes at Mount Holyoke College and Mary Elizabeth Burroughs Roberts Smith Coolidge at Mills College) after several years of sporadic funding and jobs.

Powerful founding sisters—doctorally trained, prolific writers, and active in the American Sociological Society—virtually disappeared from male academies in sociology departments after 1920. Male sociologists erased their ties to these founding sisters and began a new era.

FOUNDING SISTERS IN THE DARK ERA OF PATRIARCHAL ASCENDANCY (1920–1965)

The Professionals Trained in a Redefined Male Profession (1920–1929)

In the United States a systematic opposition to the work and writings of the female sociologists who worked and trained during the golden era began after World War I. With the dispersion and destruction of the women's network in sociology there was a dramatic, international loss of power and visibility of women in the profession. England, France, Germany, Czechoslovakia, and the Soviet Union, major sociological centers before the Great War, were in turmoil. European countries were devastated by the war, and most sociology programs were greatly undermined. Social reconstruction became an international priority. Restoring peace and order absorbed social energies and minds, and many of the founding sisters turned to international social problems and away from the new vision of sociology being developed by male sociologists in the academy. With millions of men who would have been recruited into sociology dead or seriously injured, the optimistic change-oriented applied sociology of the prewar era did not survive the carnage of world conflict.

Despite this upheaval, the Chicago School of Sociology flourished with renewed vigor. It dominated the profession worldwide from the end of World War I until the beginning of World War II (Faris 1967; Kurtz 1984). It also spearheaded the elimination of women in sociology. Women who were trained in sociology in the 1920s entered a male world, discourse, and institutional structure. They were second-class citizens without a powerful women's network. This was the world of Jessie Bernard, Ruth Shonle Cavan,* Frances Donovan,* Helen MacGill Hughes, Dorothy Swaine Thomas,* Fay Berger Karpf, Harriet E. Mowrer, Mabel Elliot, Belle Boone Beard, Ellen Winston Black, Pauline Young, and Vivien Palmer, among others. These women needed a powerful male sponsor, or suffered professionally. Founding sisters from this dark age of patriarchal ascendancy learned to survive in a male world with male rules. They wrote textbooks, taught at less prestigious colleges, and received minimal research funds. In short, they had a "back seat" in the discipline.

During the 1920s the women who had flourished during the golden age were thrust out of professional networks, recognition, and legitimation. Most of them realigned professionally with another field, especially with social work. Their years of struggle are documented in the entries here.

The Professionals Trained During the Great Depression (1929–1939)

The grim, worldwide economic collapse that characterized the 1930s had a profound impact on sociology. Sociologists increasingly justified their withdrawal from the study of a society in despair by claiming that it was "natural" for scientists who studied "facts" to search for "social regularities" outside and unaffected by the turmoil in the economic order. They retreated into "value-free" scientific rhetoric, a popular political position that continues in the United States into the 1990s.

Mathematical work was originally defined as part of women's work in sociology. It was "technical," and defined as repetitive and uninteresting. Men's work required "creativity" and the power to analyze patterns of social action. After the Great Depression mathematical work was redefined as "sophisticated" male labor and claimed as men's special interest. One type of statistical work that was still legitimated for women was demography. Counting births and death was defined as more "feminine" than counting armaments, industrial stockpiles, and the numbers of friends in social networks. Margaret Jarman Hagood,* Alva Myrdal, Dorothy Swaine Thomas, and Irene Taeuber* became leaders in demography, a "women's corner" of statistical work. (Lee [1988], notes other women superstars in demography: Elinor Lansing Dulles, Hope Eldridge, and Faith Williams.)

Despite the men's redefinition of sociology and quantitative methods, most women trained in sociology in the 1930s were oriented to the community and solving social problems. Irene Diggs, for example, was studying black people, especially young black delinquents. Alva Myrdal, living in Sweden and thousands of miles away from Diggs, came of age witnessing the association between poverty, society, children, and violence. Elizabeth Briant Lee* was beginning a career of social activism and critique, especially of the fascist American Father Coughlin (Lee and Lee 1939). Almost all the women pioneers from the golden era had died or retired. The first professionals were seldom active in sociology during the 1930s, although they often did ground-breaking work in other disciplines and outside the academy. Thus they seldom mentored the next generation of women in sociology.

Within the dark era two academies trained a number of women in sociology: the University of Chicago and Columbia University in New York City. The latter institution, moreover, gained ascendancy over the training of women in sociology in the 1940s. Robert Merton, Robert Lynd, and C. Wright Mills worked at Columbia, where they established a relatively open context for women in sociology.

The Professionals Trained During World War II and After Its Immediate Aftermath (1939–1950)

World War II started in the mid–1930s for some European women, such as Alice Masaryk. She suffered terribly during this war and its immediate aftermath, especially after the death of her brother and the prime minister of Czechoslovakia, Jan Masaryk. Viola Klein fled Austria and emigrated to Great Britain. In France, Simone de Beauvoir* was beginning her intellectual odyssey, however. Supported and encouraged by Jean Paul Sartre, she remained in a patriarchal enclave, succeeding as a woman in a male world located outside the development of sociology in the French academy.

A number of outstanding women sociologists were trained or being trained at Columbia University during this era (e.g., Grace Coyle, Mirra Komarovsky, Gladys Meyer, and Alice Rossi). In the 1940s Rose Hum Lee,* Ethel Shanas,* and Helena Znaniecka Lopata were being trained at the University of Chicago. Unlike the women in the golden era of sociology, this new cohort tended to marry. Many of the husbands of these eminent women became or were eminent sociologists (e.g., Jessie Bernard and L. L. Bernard; Helen MacGill Hughes and Everett C. Hughes; Elizabeth Briant Lee and Al Lee; Carolyn Rose* and Peter Rose; Alice S. Rossi and Peter Rossi). In a juggling act that continued until the mid–1960s the new generation of founding sisters combined marriage, motherhood, and careers in a hostile discipline. They did not operate within a strong female-supported network, however. In fact, during different interviews and conversations with me over the years, Helen MacGill Hughes, Jessie Bernard, Elizabeth Briant Lee, and Irene Diggs have mentioned the tension between female professionals, particularly at professional meetings.

The Professionals Trained During the Years When "the Woman Problem" Had No Name (1950–1965)

Between 1950 and 1965 women's proper place was in the home, "together" with her family. During these years few women entered sociology. Betty Friedan sparked a tinderbox of unrest in 1963 when she critiqued women's status as "the problem that has no name." This haunting yet unspoken problem permeated the lives of Helena Znaniecka Lopata, Helen MacGill Hughes, and Caroline Rose. Although a number of founding sisters were writing and surviving, they were not flourishing professionally. Virginia Olesen* was one of the few young scholars to survive this age of repression. Perhaps more founding sisters trained during this period will emerge in the near future. As this cohort enters their sixties and seventies they may experience the spurt of creativity reflected in the lives of several women trained in the 1930s and 1940s (e.g., Matilda White Riley*).

THE CONTEMPORARY ERA: THE BATTLE FOR WOMEN'S EQUAL OPPORTUNITY IN SOCIOLOGY (1965–1990)

In 1964 Alice Rossi raised one of the first voices in sociology calling for "an immodest proposal": equality between the sexes. From this ideal and a snow-balling women's movement in the wider society the famous 1969 caucus of women in sociology established a new organization: Sociologists for Women in Society (SWS). A new era for women in sociology emerged. Their protests have met with mixed success, however. Clearly individual women are flourishing and establishing precedents. For example, women have been elected increasingly to serve as president of the American Sociological Association (see Table 1.3). But the many years between the election of the first woman (1948) and the second woman (1973) in this position points to the need for cautious statements about women's precedents. Women's acceptance as "tokens" is vastly different from their inclusion in everyday patterns of legitimation as professionals. Women in sociology currently are organized, vocal, and visible; but as a group they remain on the margins. Women in sociology have not made significant inroads in tenured positions in prestigious graduate institutions, in obtaining well-funded grants and fellowships, or in pay and promotions (Hughes 1973; Rossi and Calderwood 1974; Smith 1977, 1988).

The generation of women who have come of age in this more open era are providing a wide range of leadership activities: as scholars, mentors, professional leaders, journal editors, and community voices. The recent proliferation of women in sociology has generated a number of outstanding women whose lives need to be documented and shared. This younger cohort built on the base established by the founding sisters, but many of us in this newer generation are ignorant of this foundation. We need to retrain and reconnect ourselves to our hidden and powerful heritage. We need to share it with one another, our students, and our successors (Deegan 1988b).

Unfortunately, as great as our current numbers are, Helen MacGill Hughes' ground-breaking documentation of how women were kept out of tenured positions in prestigious graduate institutions until 1977 is a pattern that we can now document as operative in 1990. Stinging blows to affirmative action programs were delivered by the Supreme Court in 1989, and many women did not receive tenure during the economically constrained years in the academy from the late 1970s and throughout the 1980s. So the founding sisters continue to lead a struggle for a permanent place for women in the profession of sociology. For their courage and vision, we honor them in this volume. For their intellectual heritage and power, we critique and build on their foundations.

THE EPISTEMOLOGY OF THE FOUNDING SISTERS

Although the founding sisters tend to actively support women's issues, not all of them are feminists (e.g., Hannah Arendt). They do share a fundamental world view and social location, however. Regardless of their different generations, interests, and nationalities they are women in a man-made world (Gilman 1911). They share a major system of relevance that constructs their life world (Schutz 1970). This gendered location has led to a particular body of knowledge that is identifiably female. This gender-specific knowledge was both chosen by them and shaped by others. It dialectically emerged from a process of choice and coercion.

"Women" are a topic of study that runs throughout their bibliographies. "Women's issues," such as children, marriage, family, divorce, childbirth, paid labor outside the home, and the social construction of women's lives, are analyzed repeatedly through various voices. "Minority issues," such as people of color, the aged, and the poor, are emphasized too. "Biology" is another echoing refrain, for women are shaped and categorized by biology as men are not. "Nonviolence" is a recurring, radical thread, an epistemological assumption that crosses national and generational boundaries.

"Men's topics," such as the institutional church, military, bureaucratic organizations, governmental politics, nation states, violent crime, technology, international markets, and suicide, are more rarely found in this corpus than in that of comparable "founding fathers." "Conflict" theories and "systems" theories supporting the status quo are likewise less in evidence. After all, women see the underside of public life and history more than men do, even elite women like many of the founding sisters.

The founding sisters are profoundly more critical of education and the discipline of sociology than are male sociologists. Because of historical barriers against women in the academy, founding sisters have tended to work outside the academy or on its margins. Applied sociology is one of their most viable options, and this emphasis on practical community uses of sociology structures their work as a group. Similarly, founding sisters have careers shaped by husbands' careers, childbirth, and children's needs. It appears from my reading of all these women's lives, especially the contemporary lives, that as they age, their freedom tends to increase. Professional women use their years after child rearing as an exciting time for growth to a far greater degree than men in their same age cohort do.

These women's lives are characterized by extreme struggle and triumph. These fascinating lives, often particularly unusual for women, encouraged the founding sisters to be reflective about their experiences and use of knowledge. These women have built a literature of biography and autobiography based on their lived experience of social change and professional challenges. They have tried to unite ideas, experiences, and views that are dichotomized, sanitized, and simplified by a predominantly white male elite in sociology. The extent of all these women's epistemology and work in the realm of ideas is more readily discernible because of the bio-bibliographies provided in this book. I believe that the women were part of "invisible colleges" and networks—such as one uniting Alexandra Kollontai, Rosa Luxemburg, and Klara Zetkin—that have yet to be fully discovered.

Feminist epistemology requires a new vision of doing theory: an approach that is more discursive and convoluted. Josephine Donovan has written one of the most serious theoretical analyses of feminist theories (1985), but she has used a patriarchal world view that divides women into competing schools with different epistemologies. Thus she characterizes distinct categories as often in opposition. Instead of this "Marxist," versus this "contemporary moral vision," versus "existentialist," versus "enlightenment liberal," as distinct steps in a process of conflict or "progress" in ideas, I see more commonalities and variations on common themes. Jane Addams is an example of these continuities and changes.

Donovan categorizes Addams as a "cultural feminist," and has a different category for a "new feminist moral vision." This "new" vision is a direct extension of Addams's cultural feminism. The "enlightenment liberal feminist vision," which preceded Addams's cultural feminism, also is interpreted by Donovan as a distinct theoretical stage. I interpret this earlier work by women as an inspiration and basis for cultural feminism. Although Donovan notes some of these interconnections, most of the continuities are made invisible by her underlying model of "progress" and emphasis on distinctions between theorists. Similarly, Addams valued experience, as do the existentialists and the new moral visionaries. Clearly new theorists and historical changes alter the work of feminist theorists, which Donovan correctly notes, but there is a "deep epistemological" continuity that she ignores. My epistemology involves a break with patriarchal dichotomization and categorization that underlies most of the formal theorizing done in the sociology of sociology (Deegan 1980).

Without a new epistemological framework, each new "school" of feminism may divorce itself from founding sisters and give the appearance of theoretical discontinuities and innovations that are at odds with our rich heritage. Thus the "new moral vision" discussed by Donovan does not acknowledge its indebtedness to earlier feminist theories. Instead, patriarchal visions are critiqued, while "new" feminist theorists act as if they are isolated people or isolated generations. In this way, contemporary feminists help to erase and to separate themselves from their own rich traditions. Clearly this impoverished feminist work emerges from a system of patriarchal education that erases each feminist generation's ties and continuities. Feminism is, by definition, a transcendence of patriarchal boundaries (Deegan 1988b). It incorporates sisterhood into its epistemology and praxis.

The thought of great female scholars seldom fits patriarchal "paradigms" or dichotomies. The women's fundamental divergence from patriachal ways of thinking partially accounts for their general failure to be included in the annals of sociology. Their work, to greater and lesser degrees, only approximates the world view of men. I have recently suggested that critiques of scholarly work be considered "conversations" rather than antagonistic "comments" (Deegan 1989), and I have offered a "multilectic" rather than dialectic model elsewhere (Deegan 1980). A multilectic model assumes that ideas, practices, and groups are sometimes complementary and supportive of one another, sometimes in conflict, and sometimes isolated or indifferent to one another. This more flexible, open, and complex concept fits women's epistemologies better than more compartmentalized distinctions, and it challenges traditional ways of defining knowledge. I see this type of epistemological assumption in most of the thought of the founding sisters. When I began this introduction, I stated that these sociology of knowledge questions cannot be fully answered here; but a crucial tool for finding the answers is available for the first time through the collected information provided in these entries.

CONCLUSION: FOUNDING SISTERS OF SOCIOLOGY

Female sociologists have changed the world. This book celebrates their power and lives. Despite their overwhelming achievements, many of these women remain unknown in sociology. Regrettably, professional barriers against women often are an invisible thread weaving together their various approaches and times. These women were not powerless victims, however. They used the power of knowledge to observe themselves and the world around them. Many of them applied this knowledge, and they often met with remarkable success.

Their situation as women generated a perspective that frequently emphasized the study of women, children, oppressed people, practice, and social justice. During the golden era of women in sociology, this intellectual commonality often was acknowledged and overtly coordinated. Critical pragmatism and cultural feminism created a common intellectual heritage. Later eras show both more diversity and less *shared* intellectual power. Nonetheless, as individual scholars, many contemporary women in sociology have made major contributions to society throughout the world.

An anomalous situation has emerged in contemporary sociology: some of the most influential women in the world have been sociologists, yet few sociologists know this! The situation is particularly ironic for a profession that has an epistemological intention to study the world with sophisticated reflexivity about biases and the social construction of labels and minorities.

To uncover a hidden past, I used numerous criteria. These criteria yielded the list of "founding sisters" included here. Applying this criteria does not mean that a final, "closed" list has been determined. To meet the intent of this volume—including international, regional, ideological, and professional criteria—I had to exclude some of my "favorite women" from Chicago or Great Britain; some women whom I personally admire; and some women who have left so little information about their lives that documenting their eminence in sociology is difficult. I see the founding sisters included here as part of a large group of sisters who will reshape the profession and practice of sociology in the future.

This entire text is limited by the distorted lens of a patriarchal profession, a discourse and world view we "experts" successfully internalized to become credentialed sociologists. We have been further limited by the fact that few critical analyses have been written about the majority of these women as sociologists. The loss of an entire group's heritage is an abysmal sign of the patriarchal dominance of the profession. This biographical reference guide documents the overwhelming richness and power of women's work in sociology, yet it remains the tip of the proverbial iceberg. A few of these general shapes are now discernible. For example, we now have an enhanced understanding of the effects of social changes on different generations of women in sociology from 1840 to 1990. We also know that an identifiable gendered body of knowledge and career has emerged. In many ways, women have benefited from their ostracism from patriarchal sociology: they have been forced to be in the world of everyday people and to justify their lives and ideas in a public arena in a way that their frequently "ivory-tower" male colleagues have not.

The founding sisters of sociology often were forgotten by their male colleagues who control the profession. This situation is changing, and it has been my privilege to watch part of this new consciousness emerge during the coauthoring and editing of this book. It is intended to stimulate new research and more in-depth analyses of women in sociology. This will lead to the discovery of new information, the uncovering of forgotten contributions, and the recovery of more founding sisters. In this way, I hope this biobibliography is part of a new, more liberated history of sociology. In this new corpus, race, sex, religion, politics, and sexual preference will not be barriers to professional recognition, but mirrors reflecting the rich human lives found in our communities.

NOTES

1. I corresponded with the staff at the college archives at Wooster College (formerly the University of Wooster), but they could not provide any more information on Rose P. Firestone beside her name, thesis title, graduation with a doctorate, and birth in Peru, Ohio.

2. Pandita Ramabai's most important sociological contribution was *The High-Caste Hindu Woman* (Philadelphia: J. B. Rogers Co., 1887; new edition, 1901; reprinted, Westport, CT: Hyperion Press, 1976). Biographical information is found in C. F. Andrews, "Ramabai, Pandita," *Encyclopaedia of the Social Sciences*, Vol. 13, ed. E.R.A. Seligman and Alvin S. Johnson. (New York: Macmillan, 1934), p. 100. The major work crediting Ramabai with sociological import has been done by Kuntesh Gupta, "Family Patterns and Role Definitions in Jodhpur City" (Ph.D. diss., Department of Sociology, Mecrut University, 1982); "Female Sociologists and Family Sociology in India: Theoretical and Empirical Concerns," *Indian Journal of Social Research* 23 (December 1982): 229–44.

3. Major statements on the "school" can be found in Steven Diner, "Department and Discipline," *Minerva* 8 (Winter 1975): 514–53; Robert E. L. Faris, *Chicago Sociology: 1920–1932* (Chicago: University of Chicago Press, 1967); Ernest W. Burgess and Donald J. Bogue, *Contributions to Urban Sociology* (Chicago: University of Chicago Press, 1964); James F. Short, Jr., *The Social Fabric of the Metropolis* (Chicago: University of Chicago Press, 1971); and Mary Jo Deegan, *Jane Addams and the Men of the Chicago School*, *1892–1918* (New Brunswick, NJ: Transaction Press, 1988).

4. Addams documents her life and era best. See her *Twenty Years at Hull-House* and *The Second Twenty Years* (New York: Macmillan, 1910 and 1930, respectively).

REFERENCES

Addams, Jane. 1910. *Twenty Years at Hull-House*. New York: Macmillan.

———. 1912. *The Spirit of Youth and City Streets*. New York: Macmillan.

———. 1930. *The Second Twenty Years*. New York: Macmillan.

Andrews, C. F. 1934. "Ramabai, Pandita." In *Encyclopaedia of the Social Sciences*, vol. 13, edited by E.R.A. Seligman and Alvin S. Johnson, p. 100. New York: Macmillan.

Archer, Margaret. 1989. "In Memoriam: Magdalena Sokolowska 1922–1989." *ISA Bulletin* 50 (Summer): 3.

Barry, Kathleen. 1984. *Female Sexual Slavery*. With a new introduction by Kathleen Barry. New York: New York University Press.

Bernard, Jessie. 1964. *Academic Women*. University Park: Pennsylvania State University Press.

———. 1968. *The Sex Game*. Englewood Cliffs, NJ: Prentice-Hall,

———. 1972. *The Future of Marriage*. New York: World Publishers.

———. 1981. *The Female World*. New York: Free Press.

Bottomore, Tom. 1989. "In Memoriam: Magdalena Sokolowska 1922–1989." *ISA Bulletin* 50 (Summer): 4.

Bulmer, Martin. 1989. "Review of *Jane Addams and the Men of the Chicago School*, *1892–1918*." *American Journal of Sociology* 94 (May): 1479–81.

Burgess, Ernest W., and Donald J. Bogue. 1964. *Contributions to Urban Sociology*. Chicago: University of Chicago Press.

Deegan, Mary Jo. 1978. "Women in Sociology: 1890–1930." *Journal of the History of Sociology* 1 (Fall): 11–34.

———. 1980. "Feminist Sociological Theory." Midwest Sociology Society, Milwaukee, Wisconsin, April.

———. 1981. "Early Women Sociologists and the American Sociological Society." *The American Sociologist* 16 (February): 14–34.

———. 1983. "Sociology at Wellesley College, 1900–1919." *Journal of the History of Sociology* 6 (December): 91–115.

———. 1986. "The Clinical Sociology of Jessie Taft." *Clinical Sociology Review* 4: 33–45.

———. 1987. "An American Dream: The Historical Connections Between Humanism, Women, and Sociology." *Humanity and Society* 11 (August): 553–65.

———. 1988a. *Jane Addams and the Men of the Chicago School, 1892–1918*. New Brunswick, NJ: Transaction Press.

———. 1988b. "Transcending a Patriarchal Past: Teaching the History of Early Women Sociologists." *Teaching Sociology* 16 (April): 141–59.

———. 1989. "Sociology and Conviviality: A Conversation with Ellenhorn on Convivial Sociology." *Humanity and Society* 13 (February): 85–88.

Deegan, Mary Jo, and Michael R. Hill, eds. 1987. *Women and Symbolic Interaction*. Boston, MA: Allen & Unwin.

Dill, Bonnie Thornton. 1987. "Race, Class and Gender: Prospects for an All Inclusive Sisterhood." In *Women and Symbolic Interaction*, edited by Mary Jo Deegan and Michael R. Hill, pp. 159–75. Boston, MA: Allen & Unwin.

Diner, Steven. 1975. "Department and Discipline." *Minerva* (Winter): 514–53.

Donovan, Josephine. 1985. *Feminist Theory: The Intellectual Traditions of American Feminism*. New York: Frederick Ungar.

Eells, Walter Crosby. 1956. "Earned Doctorates for Women in the Nineteenth Century." *AAUP Bulletin* 42 (Winter): 644–51.

Elling, Ray, and Jack Elinson. 1989. "In Memoriam: Magdalena Sokolowska 1922–1989." *ISA Bulletin* 50 (Summer): 5–6.

Faris, Robert E. L. 1967. *Chicago Sociology: 1920–1932*. Chicago: University of Chicago Press.

Friedan, Betty. 1963. *The Feminine Mystique*. New York: W. W. Norton.

Gilman, Charlotte Perkins. 1911. *The Man-Made World, or, Our Androcentric Culture*. New York: Charlton Co.

Gupta, Kuntesh. 1982a. "Family Patterns and Role Definitions in Jodhpur City." Ph.D. diss., Department of Sociology, Mecrut University.

———. 1982b. "Female Sociologists and Family Sociology in India: Theoretical and Empirical Concerns." *Indian Journal of Social Research* 23 (December): 229–44.

Hess, Elizabeth, Elizabeth Markson, and Peter Stein. 1988. *Introductory Sociology*. 3rd ed. New York: Macmillan.

Hughes, Helen MacGill. 1977. "Wasp/Woman/Sociologist." *Society* 14 (July–August): 69–80.

Hughes, Helen MacGill, ed. 1973. *The Status of Women in Sociology, 1968–1972*. Washington, DC: American Sociological Association.

Kasler, Dirk. 1981. "Methodological Problems of a Sociological History of Early German Sociology." Paper presented at the Department of Education, University of Chicago, November 5.

Klein, Viola. 1948. *The Feminine Character: The History of an Ideology*. New York: International Universities Press.

Kurtz, Lester R. 1984. *Evaluating Chicago Sociology: A Guide to the Literature, with An Annotated Bibliography*. Chicago: University of Chicago Press.

Lee, Al, and Elizabeth Briant Lee. 1939. *The Fine Art of Propaganda: A Study of Father Coughlin's Speeches*. New York: Institute for Propaganda Analysis and Harcourt, Brace and Co.

Lee, Ann S. 1988. "Early Women Superstars in PAA." *PAA Affairs* n.v. (Fall): 4–5.

Morgan, Graham. 1980. "Women in American Sociology in the Nineteenth Century." *Journal of the History of Sociology* 2 (Spring): 1–34.

Nebraska Feminist Sociology Collective, eds. 1983. "A Feminist Ethic for Social Science Research." *International Women's Studies Quarterly* 6 (December): 535–43.

————, eds. 1989. *Feminist Ethics and Social Science Research*. Lewiston, NY: Mellen Press.

Ramabai, Pandita. 1976. *The High-Caste Hindu Woman*. Philadelphia: Press of the J. B. Rogers Co., 1887; new edition, 1901; reprinted Westport, CT: Hyperion Press.

Rossi, Alice, ed. 1973. *The Feminist Papers: From Adams to de Beauvoir*. New York: Columbia University Press.

Rossi, Alice, and Ann Calderwood, eds. 1973. *Academic Women on the Move*. New York: Russell Sage.

Rossiter, Margaret. 1982. *Women Scientists in America*. Baltimore: Johns Hopkins University Press.

Short, James F., Jr. 1971. *The Social Fabric of the Metropolis*. Chicago: University of Chicago Press.

Schutz, Alfred. 1970. *Reflections on the Problems of Relevance*, edited, annotated, and introduced by Richard M. Zaner. New Haven, CT: Yale University Press.

Schwendinger, Herman, and Julia Schwendinger. 1974. *The Sociologists of the Chair*. New York: Basic Books.

Smith, Dorothy E. 1977. *Feminism and Marxism—A Place to Begin, A Way to Go*. Vancouver: New Star Books.

————. 1987. *The Everyday World As Problematic: A Feminist Sociology*. Boston: Northeastern University Press.

————. 1988. ''The Deep Structure of Gender Antithesis: Another View of Capitalism and Patriarchy.'' In *A Feminist Ethic for Social Science Research*, edited by the Nebraska Feminist Sociology Collective, pp. 23–36. Lewiston, NY: Edwin Mellen.

Spender, Dale. 1983. *Feminist Theorists: Three Centuries of Key Women Thinkers*. New York: Pantheon.

————. 1988. *Women of Ideas (and What Men Have Done to Them): From Aphra Behn to Adrienne Rich*. Boston: Pandora.

EDITH ABBOTT (1876–1957)

Abbott was the first woman dean of a graduate school in an American university and, simultaneously, the first dean of the first graduate school of social work in the nation. Her leading role in social work overshadowed her deep roots in sociology, in which she was a major scholar of her day. She was a prolific author (Marks 1958) and specialized in the study of women's rights and wages. Her life was dedicated to the eradication of social inequality facing blacks, immigrants, people in poverty, and laborers. Abbott championed the use of statistical data at the University of Chicago during an era when this activity was considered "women's work" in sociology.

BIOGRAPHY

Edith Abbott was born on September 26, 1876, into a well-established, argumentative, and honorable family that moved to the Nebraska frontier just before her birth. She was encouraged to be independent and to follow intellectual pursuits. Her parents, Elizabeth Griffin and Othman Abbott, moved to Grand Island, Nebraska, after their own pioneer childhoods in Illinois. Edith's mother was a feminist, abolitionist, republican, and Quaker who was part of the movement for women's higher education (she graduated from Rockford Seminary in 1868). Her remarkable background was matched by her husband, a soldier in the Civil War, a frontier lawyer and banker, and the first lieutenant governor of the new state of Nebraska. His feisty struggle for survival is recounted in his autobiography (O. Abbott 1929), an account that Edith urged him to write. The Abbotts had four remarkable children of which Edith was the second. Two years after Edith's birth, her equally talented sister, Grace Abbott, was born (November 17, 1878). The family's politically exciting life was visible as early as 1882 when six-year-old Edith "helped suffrage" by sharing her bed with Susan B. Anthony when Anthony stayed with the Abbotts on her national campaign for women's suffrage.

Edith was sent to Brownell Hall, a private school in Omaha, in the autumn of 1888. She graduated from Brownell with honors, as the valedictorian and winner of a gold medal for achievement, in 1893. This upper-middle-class training halted abruptly with the economic depression of 1893. Heavy losses at the Citizens National Bank, where her father was a director, stockholder, and attorney, caused the collapse of the bank and the Abbotts's finances. Honorably, Othman Abbott and his children worked for years to repay all the depositors who lost their savings when the bank failed. This difficult effort sharply curtailed the schooling of Edith and Grace. When they visited the Columbian World's Fair in Chicago and first saw the fledgling University of Chicago in the summer of 1893, it was one of their last fun expeditions as students, but it foreshadowed their future work.

From 1893 to 1895 Edith Abbott taught at Grand Island High School in Nebraska. From 1893 to 1901 she also struggled to continue her higher education. She enrolled in correspondence courses, summer sessions, and then full-time study at the University of Nebraska. Finally, in 1901, she graduated with a bachelor of arts degree. The University of Nebraska was then at a high point intellectually. She studied with Louise Pound, a noted linguist; Roscoe Pound, Louise's brother and the founder of sociological jurisprudence; and E. A. Ross, an eminent sociologist. Her friends included Willa Cather, later a major novelist. From 1901 to 1903 Abbott enrolled in graduate classes and taught at Lincoln High School.

During 1902 she attended summer school at the University of Chicago and was noticed by political economists J. L. Laughlin and Thorstein Veblen. With their backing, she received a fellowship in political economy from the University of Chicago in the fall of 1903. At Chicago she studied with W. I. Thomas and Sophonisba Breckinridge* in sociology, and graduated with honors and a Ph.D. in political economy in the spring of 1905.

After graduation Abbott took jobs in Boston with the Women's Trade Union League and the Carnegie Institution. In the latter position she worked with sociologist Carroll D. Wright and continued her statistical studies of women's work. She lived at Dennison House (cofounded by Emily Greene Balch*), and in 1906 went to London (on a Carnegie fellowship) where she attended the University of London's University College and the London School of Economics and Political Science. She studied with Beatrice Webb* and Sydney Webb, the Fabian Socialists, lived at St. Hilda's Settlement, and observed militant English suffragists (Abbott 1906b). Her favorite course, taught by Beatrice Webb, was "Methods of Social Investigation." Abbott reproduced this training at the University of Chicago when she subsequently offered a sociology course with the same title and structure from 1913 to 1920. The Webbs' studies of the poor laws and advisory commissions also were incorporated in Abbott's later writings (e.g., Abbott 1929).

Abbott returned to Boston in 1907 to work with Emily Greene Balch* in the then eminent Department of Economics and Sociology at Wellesley College. Abbott's female friends in Chicago did not forget her, however, and she was invited to take on a new role in a basically new institutional structure amid her former allies. To the shock of her Boston friends, Abbott accepted the untried Chicago job. In the fall of 1908 she began work as director of social research in the Chicago School of Civics and Philanthropy, then sponsored by the Department of Sociology at the University of Chicago. She resided at Jane Addams's* Hull-House until 1920 with her lifelong friend, faculty colleague, and mentor, Sophonisba Breckinridge. Other residents included Grace Abbott (Edith's younger sister) and many other notable women.

This trio (Breckinridge and the two Abbotts) became a research and administrative powerhouse for one another, for other women scholars, and for oppressed people. Chicago and Hull-House were the scene of many controversies in which Edith Abbott was in the forefront. She worked, for example, to support the women workers who went on strike against the Chicago garment industry in 1910; joined the Progressive party in 1912; became a board member of a black social settlement (the Wendell Phillips Settlement); and fought Chicago's corrupt political machine. Breckinridge and Abbott (1912), with the support of Jane Addams, opposed the antisuffragist Minnie Bronson in national debate. Further, Abbott and Breckinridge organized a major conference in 1912 that recognized the plight of urban children as a scholarly and political issue. Abbott was labeled a "radical" as a result of these activities, and was plagued by red-baiting, as were her activist friends, including Jane Addams, Emily Greene Balch, Sophonisba Breckinridge, and Florence Kelly* (Lemons 1975).

From 1908 until she retired in 1943, Abbott was an industrious and illustrious member of the faculty of the University of Chicago. She worked from 1908 to 1920 under the administration of the Department of Sociology at the University of Chicago. She taught as a lecturer in social statistics in sociology from 1913 until 1920. When the School of Social Service Administration was founded in 1920, she was appointed associate professor of social economy, and from 1924 to 1942 she was the dean of the School of Social Service Administration.

Abbott pressed for administrative positions for women, and thus established the female control of social work that endures to the present (Bernard* 1964). Abbott, her sister Grace, and Breckinridge were major leaders in the formation of public policy affecting women, children, industrial relations, and immigration. They helped to establish the profession of social work as an academic occupation, raising its prestige and power to act as a force for social change. Abbott and Breckinridge cofounded the *Social Service Review* in 1927, and it soon became (and remains today) the leading journal in social work. They established a tradition of sound research and political advocacy on behalf of the powerless, especially women. Unfortunately this tradition lost its momentum among today's more conservative social workers. Ironically, Abbott is, at times, considered part of this conservative, status quo outlook (e.g., Platt 1977), even though she spent her life opposing the reification of elitist social structures.

Abbott assumed many public roles as an adviser and consultant (Costin 1983). She worked to establish the Social Security Act, for example, in 1934. She also maintained her many international ties, especially her British connections to Fabian socialism.

Abbott was professionally active in the American Statistical Association, the American Economic Association (serving as vice-president in 1918–1919), the Women's Trade Union League, the American Sociological Society, the National Consumer's League, the National American Women's Suffrage Association, the National Association for the Advancement of Colored People, the National Urban League, and the Women's City Club of Chicago. She served as president of the National Conference of Social Work and as president of the American Association of Schools of Social Work.

Edith's younger sister, Grace, died in June 1939. Edith, who nursed her until the end, experienced profound grief. She continued to work, however. From 1942 to 1953 Abbott was dean emeritus of the School of Social Service Administration. Officially retired, she continued her work (e.g., Abbott 1943) but slowed the pace of her commitments. A marked decline in her activities was precipitated in 1948 when Sophonisba Breckinridge died. Abbott moved back into Hull-House in 1949, and red-baiting began anew with the McCarthy era. She was not personally attacked as viciously as before, but her hopes and ideas were severely undermined by this new threat. She was, moreover, an elderly outsider to the diminished life that now characterized Hull-House. She returned in 1953 to Grand Island, Nebraska, where she lived with her brother, Arthur, until her death on July 28, 1957. Her last years were painful. Physically, she became blind. Professionally, she was the last of her generation of progressive women sociologists. She was enrolled in the Women of Nebraska Hall of Fame in 1975, an honor she would have relished.

MAJOR THEMES

Women's wages and occupations were powerful, organizing themes in Abbott's writings. She early critiqued Harriet Martineau's* account of women's occupations in the United States (Abbott 1906a). Abbott's (1910) first book, *Women in Industry*, is a massive, comprehensive statement on women's work in the marketplace. Evolving from earlier work with Sophonisba Breckinridge on census data on the employment of women, Abbott developed a complex, thorough analysis of women in various industrial areas: factories, cotton mills, and the clothing and printing industries. She recorded the historical antecedents of women's industrial labor as well as relevant contemporary public opinion. She produced an invaluable history of early labor movements and occupational structures, as well as the more specialized topic of women and industry. Abbott's concern with women in the marketplace echoes that of other Chicago female sociologists (for example, Amy Hewes*).

Abbott embraced a pragmatic agenda for improving the lives of other oppressed people: immigrants, blacks, juvenile delinquents, children, the poor, and laborers. She typically explored institutional inequities that could be documented statistically.

Breckinridge and Abbott (1912) coauthored *The Delinquent Child and the Home*. This work systematically documented the myriad problems faced by urban youths. Abbott and Breckinridge (1916) again collaborated to write *Truancy and Non-Attendance in the Chicago Schools*. They were committed to a policy of education until age sixteen, and they examined the many factors that lead to school absence, such as poverty, mental and physical defects, lack of knowledge of the immigrant parents and child, and delinquency. Documenting the existence and extent of missed school days and the historical development of compulsory education, Abbott and Breckinridge suggested pragmatic remedies. Their arguments are still timely and the controversy is still lively.

Abbott, Breckinridge, and their associates (1936) documented the problems of inadequate housing over a period of decades. *The Tenements of Chicago, 1908–1935* is a massive study of housing conditions and poverty in Chicago. The book resulted from twenty-five years of study and cooperative research with dozens of students (cf., Lucile Eaves*) and is based on house-to-house canvassing of 151 city blocks, including visits to 18,225 apartments. The problems Abbott and Breckinridge noted, such as unenforced housing regulations, understaffed city inspection services, high rents for substandard housing, and large numbers of unemployed people suffering from the social stresses of broken families, ill health, and lack of education, are as relevant today as they were more than forty years ago. The careful documentation of these problems provides an excellent basis for understanding the historical dimensions of these same issues today.

Abbott's (1931b) vision of social work as an aggressive, policy making, and controversial profession is clearly specified in *Social Welfare and Professional Education*. Written partially during the Great Depression, the book advocates government-sponsored, guaranteed employment centralized and organized through public agencies. Abbott authored several writings on social work training, history, and professionalization (e.g., Abbott 1937).

Abbott (e.g., 1924, 1926, 1941) wrote a series of books on immigrants in which she used a documentary method keyed to case histories, social history, and statutory legislation (for further discussion, see the entry on Sophonisba Breckinridge). Finally, Abbott also specialized in the study of crime and juvenile delinquency. Her work for the National Commission on Law Observance and Enforcement resulted in one of the earliest and most comprehensive analyses of Mexican immigrants and their encounters with the criminal justice system (Abbott 1931a).

CRITIQUES OF EDITH ABBOTT

The major biography of the Abbott sisters, Edith and Grace, is by Lela B. Costin (1983). Costin provides a useful narrative of these remarkable sisters who aided and reciprocally supported each other as people, friends, and colleagues. Costin greatly expands the information known about their lives and influence, but does not analyze their intellectual contributions, their work in sociology, or their complex mixture of conservative and radical practices. Costin omits the women-centered focus of the Abbotts's lives and leaves untouched the growth of that focus from a network of vital women who worked cooperatively together for decades.

Sandra Stehno's (1988) analysis of Abbott and Breckinridge's work with black children in Chicago provides the complexity and depth needed to explicate the intellectual features of Abbott's work. Stehno's archivally based study details the commitment of Abbott and Breckinridge to children of color and to the generation of public responsibility in an often heartless capitalist society.

Steven Diner (1977) wrote a meticulous analysis of the work and role of *The Social Service Review*. Although his study is oriented to social work historians, it is helpful to all scholars studying Abbott and Breckinridge. Hill (1989, 557– 665) documents Abbott's relatively more powerful position vis-à-vis Hattie Plum Williams* in the world of "women's work" in sociology.

Abbott was a talented, conscientious scholar, educator, and social reformer who often was overshadowed by the fame and writings of her close friends and colleagues at Hull-House, especially Jane Addams, Sophonisba Breckinridge, and her sister, Grace Abbott. Today, Edith Abbott remains little known outside the field of social work, but her writings are a witness and a tribute to her sociological talents and contributions.

BIBLIOGRAPHY

Selected Writings by Edith Abbott

1905. "Wages of Unskilled Labor in the United States, 1850–1900." *Journal of Political Economy* 13 (June): 321–367. Ph.D. diss., University of Chicago.
1906a. "Harriet Martineau and the Employment of Women in 1836." *Journal of Political Economy* 14 (December): 614–626.
1906b. "Woman Suffrage Militant: The New Movement in England." *The Independent* 61 (November 29): 1276–1278.
1907. "Municipal Employment of Unemployed Women in London." *Journal of Political Economy* 15 (November): 513–530.
1908. "A Study of Early History of Child Labor in America." *American Journal of Sociology* 14 (November): 15–37.

1909. "Women in Industry: The Manufacture of Boots and Shoes." *American Journal of Sociology* 15 (November): 335–360.

1910. *Women in Industry: A Study of American Economic History*. New York: D. Appleton.

1915. *The Real Jail Problem*. Chicago: Juvenile Protective Association.

1916. *One Hundred and One County Jails of Illinois and Why They Ought to Be Abolished*. Chicago: Juvenile Protective Association.

1917a. "Charles Booth, 1840–1916." *Journal of Political Economy* 15 (July): 641–678.

1917b. "The War and Women's Work in England." *Journal of Political Economy* 25 (July): 641–678.

1918. *Democracy and Social Progress in England*. University of Chicago War Papers, No. 8. Chicago: University of Chicago Press.

1924. *Immigration: Select Document and Case Records*. Chicago: University of Chicago Press.

1926. *Historical Aspects of the Immigration Problem: Select Documents*. Chicago: University of Chicago Press.

1929. "The Webbs on the English Poor Law." *Social Service Review* 3 (June): 252–269.

1931a. *Report on Crime and the Foreign Born*. National Commission on Law Observance and Enforcement, Vol. 3, No. 10. Washington, D.C.: U.S. Government Printing Office.

1931b. *Social Welfare and Professional Education*. Chicago: University of Chicago Press; revised and enlarged, 1942.

1935. "Jane Addams Memorial Service." *Proceedings of the National Conference of Social Work*, pp. 3–5.

1937. *Some American Pioneers in Social Welfare: Select Documents with Editorial Notes*. Chicago: University of Chicago Press.

1939. "Grace Abbott: A Sister's Memories." *Social Service Review* 13 (September): 351–408.

1941. *Public Assistance*. Chicago: University of Chicago Press.

1943. *Twenty-One Years of University Education for Social Service, 1920–1941*. Chicago: University of Chicago Press.

1948. "Sophonisba P. Breckinridge: Over the Years." *Social Service Review* 22 (December): 417–423.

1950. "Grace Abbott and Hull-House, 1908–21. Parts I and II." *Social Service Review* 24 (September): 374–394; 24 (December): 493–518.

1952. "The Hull-House of Jane Addams." *Social Service Review* 26 (September): 334–338.

Coauthored Works

Abbott, Edith, and Sophonisba Breckinridge. 1906. "Employment of Women in Industries: Twelfth Census Statistics." *Journal of Political Economy* 14:14–40.

1910. "Chicago's Housing Problems: Families in Furnished Rooms." *American Journal of Sociology* 16 (November): 289–308.

1910–1912. *The Housing Problem in Chicago*. Chicago: University of Chicago Press.

1911a. "Housing Conditions in Chicago. III: Back of the Yards." *American Journal of Sociology* 16 (January): 433–468.

1911b. "Chicago Housing Conditions. IV: The West Side Revisited." *American Journal of Sociology* 17 (July): 1–34.

1911c. "South Chicago at the Gates of the Steel Mills." *American Journal of Sociology* 17 (September): 145–176.

1911d. "Women in Industry: The Chicago Stockyards." *Journal of Political Economy* 19 (October): 632–654.

1912. *Wage-Earning Women and the State: A Reply to Miss Minnie Bronson*. Boston: Equal Suffrage Association for Good Government.

1916. *Truancy and Non-Attendance in the Chicago Schools*. Chicago: University of Chicago Press.

1936. *Truancy and Non-Attendance in the Chicago Schools: A Study of the Social Aspects of the Compulsory Education and Child Labor Legislation of Illinois*. Chicago: University of Chicago Press.

Abbott, Edith, assisted by Sophonisba Breckinridge and other associates. 1936. *The Tenements of Chicago: 1908–1935*. Chicago: University of Chicago Press.

Abbott, Edith, Mabel Gillespie, and Anne Withington. 1906. *History of Trade Unionism Among Women in Boston*. Boston: Women's Trade Union League.

Breckinridge, Sophonisba, and Edith Abbott. 1912. *The Delinquent Child and the Home*. New York: Charities Publication Committee.

Studies About Edith Abbott and Supplemental References

Abbott, Othman A. 1929. *Recollections of a Pioneer Lawyer*, edited by Addison E. Shelton. Lincoln, NE: Nebraska State Historical Society.

Bernard, Jessie. 1964. *Academic Women*. University Park: Pennsylvania State University Press.

Costin, Lela B. 1983. *Two Sisters for Social Justice: A Biography of Grace and Edith Abbott*. Urbana: University of Illinois Press.

Deegan, Mary Jo. 1979. "Edith Abbott." In *American Women Writers*, vol. 1, edited by Lina Mainiero, pp. 3–5. New York: Ungar.

Diner, Steven J. 1977. "Scholarship in the Quest for Social Welfare: A Fifty-Year History of the *Social Service Review*." *Social Service Review* 51 (March): 1–66.

Lemons, J. Stanley. 1975. *The Woman Citizen: Social Feminism in the 1920s*. Urbana: University of Illinois Press.

McMillen, Wayne. 1953. "The First Twenty-Six Years of the *Social Service Review*." *Social Service Review* 25 (March): 1–14.

Marks, Rachel. "The Published Writings of Edith Abbott: A Bibliography." *Social Service Review* 32 (March 1958): 51–56.

Platt, Anthony M. 1977. *The Child Savers: The Invention of Delinquency*. 2nd ed. Chicago: University of Chicago Press.

Stehno, Sandra M. 1988. "Public Responsibility for Dependent Black Children: The Advocacy of Edith Abbott and Sophonisba Breckinridge." *Social Service Review* 62 (September): 495–503.

Wisner, Elizabeth. 1958. "Edith Abbott's Contributions to Social Work Education." *Social Service Review* 32 (March): 2–4

Unpublished Material

Hill, Michael R. 1989. "Roscoe Pound and American Sociology: A Study in Archival Frame Analysis, Sociobiography, and Sociological Jurisprudence." Ph.D. diss., Department of Sociology, University of Nebraska-Lincoln.

MARY JO DEEGAN AND MICHAEL R. HILL

JANE ADDAMS (1860–1935)

Jane Addams is the most important female sociologist for several reasons. From 1890 to 1920, she was a leader of dozens of women in sociology. Her social settlement, Hull-House, was the institutional anchor for this network, serving as a focus for women's work and as a liaison with the most important male sociological center during this era, the University of Chicago. Addams's ideas of cultural feminism and critical pragmatism guided the work of many other women and articulated their ideas as well.

BIBLIOGRAPHY

More books and articles have been written about Jane Addams than any other American woman. She captured the dreams, ideals, and imagination of a generation. In the process, her intellectual significance was obscured in light of her popular image as a "saint" or a "villain," a woman who was larger than life and often portrayed as a simple follower of her convictions (Davis, 1973).

Born in 1860, she was a contemporary of the early Chicago men. Profoundly influenced by her father, John H. Addams, a Quaker, state senator, and mill owner, Jane Addams was raised in a small Midwestern town. Her mother, Sarah Weber Addams, died when Addams was two years old. Her family background was based on several generations of Americans. In 1849 she entered Rockford Female Seminary, in Rockford, Illinois, which was one of the pioneering colleges for women. Unresponsive to the religious message of the school, Addams sought to get "back to a great Primal cause—not nature, exactly, but a fostering Mother, a necessity, brooding, and watching over all things, above every human passion" (Jane Addams to Ellen Gates Starr, August 11, 1879, cited in Davis 1973:16). After she graduated in 1881, she entered an extended period of unhappiness, nervous strain, and depression. Like many of her colleagues, notably George Herbert Mead and William James, Addams sought a meaning for her life but rejected traditional religion as an answer to her questions.

This year, 1881, was crucial in her search for a place in the world. In August her father died, and his absence left her confused and despairing. But she also entered the Women's Medical College in Philadelphia. Before the year was out, she dropped out of medical training and returned home to Illinois. There she was caught between the demands of her stepmother, a pressing suitor, and her ambition to have a career. Ill and surrounded by family problems, Addams drifted for a year. Finally taking some action, in 1883 she traveled to Europe. Although she was interested in the problems of the poor at this time, she was not too troubled by their plight.

Her family attempted to "enter her" into society, like Elsie Clews Parsons* and Mary van Kleeck,* but she rejected their plans. She remained frustrated and depressed for the next two years. Then, once again, she traveled to Europe. On this journey, accompanied by her college friend Ellen Gates Starr, she finally found a direction for her life. When she visited Toynbee Hall in London's East End, she was impressed with the work being done there for the poor. This social settlement was associated with Oxford University and was designed to provide leadership to a district populated by the exploited working classes. Emphasizing urban disorganization as a barrier to needed education and "culture," Toynbee Hall provided a model for Addams's resolution of her personal and occupational crisis.

Years later she theorized that one of the most difficult tasks for women was managing the conflicting demands between their "family" and "social" claims. For Addams, this resolution occurred through social settlements where she could be a "lady" while making a social and political impact. Simultaneously, she was independent of traditional female roles and responsibilities in the family and home. Because of these self-benefits for those who helped others, she always emphasized both the "subjective" and the "objective" needs for social settlements. This stress on the dual functions of settlements prevented her from becoming the sentimental or insensitive "matrician" she often is portrayed as being. With her internal battle in abeyance, she quickly succeeded in assuming leadership of the American social settlement movement and subsequently altered the course of American thought and politics.

This dramatic public role began soon after she returned to the United States in January 1889. Addams and Starr moved to Chicago, and within a few months they moved to one floor of a house owned by Helen Culver of the Hull family. "Hull-House," as it was called, quickly abandoned the British Toynbee Hall model and became more egalitarian, more female-oriented, and less religious. These changes were important intellectual innovations, often implemented by Addams but frequently instigated by the women with whom she surrounded herself, particularly Florence Kelley.* Moreover, in 1892 the University of Chicago opened its doors, bringing many faculty members, predominantly men, as visitors and lecturers to Hull-House. Although the University of Chicago is frequently depicted as the most influential sociological center in the world before 1930, it was Addams and Hull-House that were the leader and leading institution in Chicago in the 1890s and early 1900s. Not only was she the charismatic head of a rapidly expanding social movement, but she also was one of the leading sociologists of her day.

The 1890s were lively and controversial years at Hull-House. Anarchists, Marxists, socialists, unionists, and leading social theorists congregated there. John Dewey and George Herbert Mead, among others, were frequent visitors, lecturers, and close friends of Addams. Chicago pragmatism was born through their collegial contacts and intellectual exchanges. They wanted to combine scientific and objective observation with ethical and moral values to generate a just and liberated society. A ground-breaking sociological text, *Hull-House Maps and Papers*, was published by Hull-House residents in 1893, predating and establishing the interests of the early Chicago male sociologists. During this time, Hull-House and Addams gained both a national and an international reputation for being radical, innovative, and successful. Oriented toward social change, they articulated an American dream, particularly adapted to bright, educated Anglo women who wanted a new role in life and society.

Addams surrounded herself with brilliant and dedicated people, particularly women. These women formed a core group who lived at the settlement, wrote together, gathered statistics, investigated factories and industries, conducted health examinations, examined sanitary conditions, lobbied for legislative and political reform, and organized for social betterment in their congested, immigrant working-class district. Out of this welter of activity, Addams was the charismatic leader who translated the "facts" into everyday language, articulating the problems and needs of the community and forming American ideals and social thought.

Author of eleven books and hundreds of articles, Addams continued her teaching and educating efforts through lectures across the country and at Hull-House. She became the spokesperson of her era and, in particular, for women and the working-class immigrant. She led social reform organizations, campaigned for the Progressive party, and helped to found numerous government agencies, notably the Children's, Women's, and Immigration Bureaus. She practiced and advocated free speech for all, and "radical democracy"; that is, she believed that the equality must extend beyond citizenship rights and pervade all aspects of economic and social life. A "critical pragmatist" (defined and discussed in Deegan 1988: 247–308), she sought not only answers to problems, but also those answers that were in the best interests of all, including the poor and the disenfranchised.

Addams was a cultural feminist, and her views on women were little understood then or now. Having a popular image as a "saintly" woman who worked for the poor, Addams in fact believed that female values were superior to those of males and that a society built on the former would be more productive, peaceful, and just. Despite the lack of complete understanding of her intellectual thought, her innovative and critical ideas were accepted by the public for more than two decades, when she was the "Saint Jane" of the popular press. Simultaneously, she was an intellectual leader in sociology as well as in related disciplines.

Only her pacifist ideas were truly understood in terms of their radical import. As a pacifist before World War I, Addams was lauded as a "good woman." However, with the building of patriotic feeling from 1913 until America's entry into the war in 1917, she became the target of animosity and personal attack. By 1917 she was socially and publicly ostracized. She went from being a saint to being a villain. Booed off speaking platforms and abandoned by her friends, colleagues, and, most notably here, other sociologists, Addams was a social pariah.

This was an agonizing time for her. Committed to her values, based on "feminine" ideals, she maintained her pacifist position. The culmination of her politically untouchable status occurred in 1919 when she was labeled by the U.S. government as the most dangerous woman in America. At this point her major role as a sociologist diminished. After 1919 Addams was ostracized by succeeding generations of sociologists until the present.

In 1920 women were granted the franchise, and for Addams and many other suffragists, this was a major victory. Contrary to expectations of a powerful women's vote, the 1920s led to an eclipse of the former power of women activists, including that of Addams. In addition, Progressive leadership was squelched after World War I, and the liberal vision of a changing, optimistic, and scientifically rational society was doomed. Addams gradually resumed leadership in American thought during this decade, but it was primarily the impact of the Depression that restored her to the forefront of American leadership. Winner of the Nobel Peace Prize in 1931, Addams became the spokesperson for many of the values and policies adopted during the New Deal. She and her female colleagues were instrumental in establishing social security and many other government programs that altered the nature of American capitalism. Dying in 1935, she was mourned worldwide as a great leader and interpreter of American thought.

MAJOR THEMES

Addams was a central figure in applied sociology, especially in the Chicago School of Sociology. Hull-House generated a new model of professional work in which the home and workplace were combined. It was a home, an intellectual commune, and a salon. Some of the brilliant female sociologists who lived and worked there are Florence Kelley, Emily Greene Balch,* Edith Abbott,* Charlotte Perkins Gilman,* Annie Marion MacLean,* Mary McDowell, Sophonisba Breckinridge,* and Julia Lathrop. Dozens of other women sociologists visited it, including Beatrice Webb,* Ida B. Wells-Barnett,* and Alice Masaryk.* The influence of a core group of residents at Hull-House on the School of Chicago Sociology is dramatically revealed in the cooperatively produced and critical text *Hull-House Maps and Papers*. This book, drawing on detailed maps of social life on the South Side of Chicago, analyzed the effects of social disorganization, immigration, and the economy on the everyday life of an urban neighborhood. In other words, this book established the major substantive interests and methodological technique of the Chicago School of Sociology that defined the school for the next forty years.

The sociology of Addams as an intellectual legacy is a function of two major streams of thought: cultural feminism and critical pragmatism. Cultural feminism is a theory of society that assumes that traditionally defined feminine values are superior to traditionally defined masculine values. Critical pragmatism, a term coined by me, is a theory of science that emphasizes the need to apply knowledge to everyday problems based on radical interpretations of liberal and progressive values. Addams's critical pragmatism was based on reanalyses of many sociological traditions in Britain (especially those of Beatrice Webb, Charles Booth, Patrick Geddes, and Canon Barnett), in Russia (especially those of Leo Tolstoy and Petr Kropotkin), and in Germany (especially those of Karl Marx and Friedrich Engels). The incompatibility between cultural feminism and critical pragmatism was not addressed by Addams during her major era of influence in sociology, from 1892 to 1918. A major axis of internal conflict arises when the democratic or majority opinion opposes feminine values. This contrast was stark for pacifists during World War I, an international conflagration supported by the popular press and the public. This internal inconsistency of her work is partially responsible for the decline in her sociological leadership. Clearly, her choice of emphasizing cultural feminism, with its preference of feminine values over masculine values, was the major reason for her "fall from grace." Her national censure as a pacifist coincided with her "failure" as a sociologist, and for many years she remained a social outcast.

WRITINGS ABOUT JANE ADDAMS

There is a vast literature on Addams; most of it is interesting for background information, interpretations of her social work, and documentation of her public role in American society. One of the best and most available bibliographies on Addams and her era can be found in John C. Farrell's *Beloved Lady* (1967). His work is an excellent overview of Addams's life, public career, and applied ideas. Most of these writings do not reveal her sociological legacy and influence, which is of primary interest here.

A few books and articles are central for understanding her life and intellectual legacy. One of the most scholarly general introductions to Addams is Allen Davis's (1973) biography of her. His work is critical, well documented, and handled with insight and sophistication. He does not examine sociology or Addams's intellectual heritage in any depth, however.

Lasch has examined Addams's intellectual work in an important collection of her writings (1965), although he considers her an "anti-intellectual" elsewhere (1965). Curti (1961) and Lynd (1961) provide two of the rare evaluations of Addams as a scholar and force in American social thought.

Addams was originally highly integrated into sociological literature. Evidence of this are her well-received books that were reviewed in the *American Journal of Sociology*, often by famous sociologists such as William James, George H. Mead, and Florence Kelley. Another indication is the impact of *Hull-House Maps and Papers* on the Chicago School of Sociology and on the work of the noted black sociologist W.E.B. DuBois (Deegan 1988c). This leadership in sociology was erased, however, until her sociological legacy had virtually vanished from contemporary consideration.

My book (1988a) and a series of articles on Addams (1978, 1981, 1987, 1988b) are the first serious attempt to reconsider Addams as a sociologist. Most of my major points are included here and serve as an introduction to my larger enterprise. Rediscovering her role and influence in sociology took thirteen years to document, but her legacy can now be seen, given my interpretive framework Her effect on the most influential male school of sociology, the Chicago School, during her era is documented there (see Faris, 1967, for a discussion of this male sociological tradition).

Surrounded by the imagery of a "good and noble woman," Addams articulated radical changes in American life and politics, altering the possibilities for human growth and action for the working class, immigrants, youth, the aged, and women. On the one hand, her significant contributions to public life are well known and lauded. On the other hand, her intellectual stature is barely appreciated, and her contributions to sociology were obscured for decades. Her profound influence on the course and development of sociology is only suggested in the literature. My book is a beginning analysis of a little examined, alternative heritage and tradition in American sociology.

BIBLIOGRAPHY

Selected Writings by Jane Addams

1880. "Bread Givers." In *Jane Addams: A Centennial Reader*, edited by Emily Cooper Johnson, pp. 103–104. Reprint. New York: Macmillan, 1960.

1893. "The Subjective Necessity of Social Settlements." 1–26 In *Philanthropy and Social Progress: Seven Essays by Miss Jane Addams, Robert A. Woods, Father J.O.S. Huntington, Professor Franklin H. Giddings, and Bernard Bosanquet Delivered Before the School of Applied Ethics at Plymouth, Mass., During the Session of 1892*, introduction by Henry C. Adams, pp. 1–26. Reprint. New York: Books for Libraries Press, 1969.

1895. "Prefatory Note" and "The Settlement as a Factor in the Labor Movement." In *Hull-House Maps and Papers, by Residents of Hull-House, a Social Settlement, a Presentation of Nationalities and Wages in a Congested District of Chicago,*

Together with Comments and Essays on Problems Growing Out of the Social Conditions, pp. vii–viii, 183–204. New York: Crowell.

1896. "A Belated Industry." *American Journal of Sociology* 1 (March): 536–550.

1899. "Trade Unions and Public Duty." *American Journal of Sociology* 4 (January): 448–462.

1902. *Democracy and Social Ethics*. New York: Macmillan.

1905a. "Problems of Municipal Administration." *American Journal of Sociology* 10 (January): 425–444.

1905b. "Recent Immigration: A Field Neglected by the Scholar." *University Record* 9 (January): 274–284.

1907. *Newer Ideals of Peace*. New York: Macmillan.

1908a. "Comment on an article by John R. Commons, 'Class Conflict in America.' " *American Journal of Sociology* 13 (May): 770–773.

1908b. "The Chicago Settlements and Social Unrest." *Charities and the Commons* 20 (May 2): 155–166.

1909. *The Spirit of Youth and the City Streets*. New York: Macmillan.

1910. *Twenty Years at Hull-House*. New York: Macmillan.

1911. "The Social Situation." *Religious Education* 6 (June): 145–152.

1912a. "Recreation as a Public Function in Urban Communities." *American Journal of Sociology* 17 (March): 615–619.

1912b. "A Modern Lear." *Survey* 29 (November 2): 131–137.

1913. "If Men Were Seeking the Franchise." In *Jane Addams, A Centennial Reader*, edited by Emily Cooper Johnson, pp. 107–113. Reprint. New York: Macmillan, 1960.

1914a. *A New Conscience and an Ancient Evil*. New York: Macmillan.

1914b. "A Modern Devil Baby." *American Journal of Sociology* 20 (July): 117–118.

1916a. "War Times Challenging Woman's Traditions." *Survey* 36 (August): 475–478.

1916b. *The Long Road of Woman's Memory*. New York: Macmillan.

1920. "Americanization." *Papers and Proceedings of the American Sociological Society* 14: 206–214.

1922. *Peace and Bread in Time of War*. New York: Macmillan.

1927. "A Book That Changed My Life." *Christian Century* 44 (October 13): 1196–1198.

1930a. *The Second Twenty Years at Hull-House*. New York: Macmillan.

1930b. "Aspects of the Woman's Movement." *Survey* 8 (August): 113–123.

1931. "Tolstoy and Gandhi." *Christian Century* 48 (November 25): 1485–1488.

1932a. *The Excellent Becomes Permanent*. New York: Macmillan.

1932b. *My Friend, Julia Lathrop*. New York: Macmillan.

1960. *Jane Addams: A Centennial Reader*, edited by Emily Cooper Johnson. New York: Macmillan.

1965. *The Social Thought of Jane Addams*, edited an introduced by Christopher Lasch. Indianapolis: Bobbs-Merrill.

Coauthored Works

Addams, Jane, Emily Greene Balch, and Alice Hamilton. 1915. *The Women at the Hague*. New York: Macmillan.

Studies About Jane Addams and Supplemental References

Curti, Merle. 1961. "Jane Addams on Human Nature." *Journal of the History of Ideas* 22 (April-June): 240–253.

Davis, Allen F. *American Heroine*. 1973. New York: Oxford University Press.

Davis, Allen F., and Mary Lynne McCree. 1969. *Eighty Years at Hull-House*. Chicago: Quadrangle Books.

Deegan, Mary Jo. 1978. "Women in Sociology: 1890–1930." *Journal of the History of Sociology* 1 (Fall): 11–34.

————. 1981. "Early Women Sociologists and the American Sociological Society." *The American Sociologist* 16 (February): 14–24.

————. 1987. "An American Dream: The Historical Connections Between Women, Humanism, and Sociology." *Humanity and Society* 11 (August): 553–565.

————. 1988a. *Jane Addams and the Men of the Chicago School, 1892–1918*. New Brunswick, NJ: Transaction Books.

————. 1988b. "Transcending a Patriarchal Past: Teaching the History of Women in Sociology, 1892–1920." *Teaching Sociology* 16 (April): 141–150.

————. 1988c. "W.E.B. DuBois and the Women of Hull-House, 1898–1899." *American Sociologist* 19 (Winter): 301–311.

Faris, Robert E. L. 1967. *Chicago Sociology: 1920–1932*. Chicago: University of Chicago Press.

Farrell, John C. 1967. *Beloved Lady*. Baltimore: Johns Hopkins University Press.

Henderson, Charles R. 1902. "Review of *Democracy and Social Ethics*." *American Journal of Sociology* 8 (July): 136–138.

Kelley, Florence. 1912. "Review of *A New Conscience and an Ancient Evil*." *American Journal of Sociology* 18 (September): 271–272.

Lasch, Christopher. 1965. *The New Radicalism in America, 1889–1963*. New York: Knopf.

Linn, James. 1935. *Jane Addams*. New York: Appleton-Century Crofts.

Lynd, Staughton. 1961. "Jane Addams and the Radical Impulse." *Commentary* 32 (July): 54–59.

Mead, George H. 1907. "Review of *The Newer Ideals of Peace*." *American Journal of Sociology* 13 (July): 121–128.

Mills, C. Wright. 1964. *Sociology and Pragmatism*, edited by Irving Louis Horowitz. New York: Paine-Whitman.

Ravitch, Jessie S. 1925. "Review of *The Child, the Clinic and the Court*." *American Journal of Sociology* 31 (July): 834–835.

Thomas, Harriet, and William James. 1910. "Review of *The Spirit of Youth City Streets*." *American Journal of Sociology* 15 (January): 550–553.

Thompson, Walter S. 1920. "Comment on 'Americanization.'" *Papers and Proceedings of the American Sociological Society* 14: 214–215.

MARY JO DEEGAN

HANNAH ARENDT (1906–1975)

Hannah Arendt was a political theorist: her fundamental project was not involvement in political life, but thinking about it. She spoke out and took action on issues of importance to her, nonetheless, such as Jewish military resistance to the Nazis. Arendt severely criticized analyses of intellectual accomplishments as rooted in the gender of the writer, and she abhorred all biological determinism at the individual and societal levels. Nevertheless, as a woman who is one of the giants of political and social theory, she advanced the feminist cause.

BIOGRAPHY

Hannah Arendt was born in Hanover, Germany, on October 14, 1906, to middle-class parents who were members of the Social Democrat party. Although her parents were Jewish, they maintained an ethnic, rather than religious, identity with Jewish culture. Hannah attended the synagogue only as a courtesy when visiting one of her grandmothers. She had, nonetheless, a deep sense of Jewish identity that shaped her writings and world view.

Hannah's father and grandfather (a second father figure) both died when she was seven, and she fled with her mother to Berlin in 1914 when World War I began. They returned to Hanover before the end of the year, and her mother, Martha, married a widower with two grown daughters. In 1924, at eighteen, Hannah went to Marburg to study with Martin Heidegger, with whom she had a brief love affair.

This relationship lasted for three months, and in 1925 Hannah moved to Heidelberg, where she met Karl Jaspers, who later guided her doctoral dissertation on St. Augustine's idea of love. In 1929 she married Gunther Stern, a German Jew, and they moved to Frankfurt, where she began associating with members of the Frankfurt School, including Theodor Adorno, Max Horkheimer, and Herbert Marcuse. When Hitler came to power in 1933, Hannah and Gunther separated, and she turned her Berlin flat into a refuge for fleeing Communists. She was arrested in the spring for this activity and imprisoned eight days. On gaining her freedom, she and her mother escaped to Czechoslovakia and traveled to Paris, where they settled. There Arendt became acquainted with Jean-Paul Sartre, an existentialist philosopher and activist and the partner of Simone de Beauvoir.*

In 1936 she and Stern were formally divorced, and he left for New York. At this point Hannah began examining "statelessness," since Paris was a huge clearing ground for refugees (including Hannah) with uncertain futures. This line of inquiry formed the basis of what would later become *The Origins of Totalitarianism*. She wrote: "To be uprooted means to have no place in the world, recognized and guaranteed by others; to be superfluous means not to belong to the world at all" (1951, 475). She continued this inquiry throughout her life, examining relationships and their workability at all levels: individual, community, national, and international.

Her work in Paris consisted of reeducating orphaned Jewish children for their emigration to Palestine. Although she admired the vigor and enthusiasm displayed by kibbutz workers in Palestine, she had misgivings about the new Jewish state. "She feared a new Jewish nationalism would emerge in a Jewish state with its own intolerance towards other races" (May 1986, 42). She believed that this attitude was the antithesis of the proper destiny for Jews. She later envisioned Palestine as a member of the British Commonwealth—like India— where Jews and Arabs were equal citizens.

She constantly wrestled in the *Origins of Totalitarianism* with the idea of the "proper" place in society for Jews. She saw two options for German Jews. They could be either pariahs and excluded from German society, or parvenus, showing qualities of inhumanity, greed, insolence, and determination to survive (her idea of "mass man"). Neither option satisfied her, and she chose instead to be a "conscious pariah," a thinking, acting human being (1951, 66–67).

In the spring of 1936 she met Heinrich Blucher, whom she married in 1940 and with whom she remained until his death in 1970. Meanwhile the increased influx of Jews into France between 1936 and 1938 created a growing mood of anti-Semitism in France. The French government began limiting Jews' right to work and expelling those without proper papers. Jewish immigrants responded by moving into ghetto communities, which Hannah considered "ostrich" behavior in the face of the Nazi influence in Europe. In May 1940 Hannah was taken to a labor internment camp at Gurs on the Spanish border along with many other German refugees. She was released a month later when France fell, and in January 1941 she and Heinrich obtained visas to leave France for Lisbon. They arrived in New York by boat in May 1941. In November she got a job as a columnist for *Aufbau*, a German émigré newspaper, and began her career as a journalist/writer.

In 1944 she became research director for the Commission on European Cultural Reconstruction, an organization devoted to recording and retrieving Jewish cultural treasures held in countries under Nazi rule. In 1948 she became the executive director of the Commission, and in the same year her mother died.

The next years were filled with many triumphs and changes. For example, in 1951 Arendt became an American citizen. In 1953 she gave a lecture series at Princeton on Marx and the Great Tradition and another series at Berkeley in 1955 on political history. By 1967 Hannah was financially well-off, and supported Israeli charities and helped with the education of children of her surviving relatives and old friends.

The final years of Hannah's life were devoted to philosophical pursuits rather than the social issues characteristic of her youth. She gave the Gifford lectures at Aberdeen University in 1973 on "Thinking." These lectures became the first volume of her posthumously published work, *The Life of the Mind*. She gave a second lecture series on the topic of "Willing," which became the second volume of *The Life of the Mind*. She never completed this lecture series because she had a heart attack after her first presentation. Hannah had a second heart attack during a dinner party in December 1975 and died several days later without regaining consciousness. In her typewriter was a sheet of paper with one word, "Judging," which was to be the third volume of *The Life of the Mind*.

MAJOR THEMES

Arendt's complex writings are organized here under several topics: history and action; good government; nonviolence, upheaval, and social order; politics; the community; economics; science; education; and the family.

History and Action

Arendt believed in multicausal explanations of history and believed that events created a predisposition in people to act a certain way or to make it easier for them to do so (May 1986, 61). She saw the appearance of "mass man" in Europe as a fundamental precondition for the success of Nazism (1951, 315). She expressed her vision of hope for humanity in this way:

Every end in history necessarily contains a new beginning, this beginning is the promise, the only "message" which the end can ever produce. Beginning, before it becomes a historical event, is the supreme capacity of man; politically, it is identical with man's freedom. This beginning is guaranteed by each new birth; it is indeed every man. (Arendt 1951, 478–479)

The embodiment of this ideal of political freedom became the subject of *The Human Condition*, published in 1958.

Good Government

Arendt defined good government as pluralistic, cooperative, and dependent on many participants. For Arendt, this was the only possible form of an enduring government. Rule by force is not only inherently unstable, but also legitimates, institutionalizes, and perpetuates violence. "The seizure of power through the means of violence is never an end in itself but only the means to an end" (1951, 326). She saw "promises, made mutually, are what keep a body of people together, acting in concert, enabling them to dispose of the future as though it were the present" (May 1986, 87).

Between Past and Future was published in 1961, the same year she traveled to Jerusalem to cover the trial of Adolph Eichmann, whom she saw as a feeble-minded clown, unable to distinguish between good and evil (1963, 252). Eichmann embodied her idea of the parvenu as well as the worst possible consequences of the "mass man." In her role as a conscious pariah, she questioned the rationalizations necessary to produce the type of thinking that allowed people to participate in or resist Nazi ideology:

What enabled some people to resist cooperation with the Nazis was a particular way of thinking and judging that they had. [They] asked themselves: to what extent they would still be able to live in peace with themselves after having committed certain deeds. . . . Therefore, they chose to die when they were forced to participate. (Arendt in May 1986, 112)

Nonviolence, Upheaval, and Social Order

To Arendt, the concept of a revolution was "inextricably bound up with the notion that the course of history suddenly begins anew, that an entirely new story, a story never known or told before, is about to unfold" (1963, 21). Her book *Men in Dark Times* (1968) was a collection of essays about public figures who concealed the truth at crucial points in history. In *On Violence* (1970) she argued that in times of rebellion, the use of violence is always self-defeating. She saw "true and lasting power only manifested when men act in concert. When there is no longer agreement between men who originally set out to fight a common foe . . . commands [are] no longer obeyed . . . the means of the violence [are] useless" (May 1986, 123). Arendt's views on nonviolence echo the concerns of Jane Addams,* Emily Greene Balch,* Alva Myrdal,* and other women in sociology.

Politics

To Arendt, the political is the hub of all important human events. The existence of a "world" that humans share and in which they act meaningfully depends on a public realm (polis). Without shared political life, the outcomes of human action, which are always capricious, could never be represented as purposeful. The means for interpreting the motives of past acts, and thus rendering them culturally significant (or insignificant), are created and maintained in the context of an active political life. The crises of the modern age are precisely related to a decline in public political life.

The loss of authority is an evil to Arendt because it means that humans lose their bearings (i.e., senses of meaning) in the world. Authority is not synonymous with either force or persuasion. It rests on recognition of the right to be obeyed by virtue of respect for the office and/or its embodied representative. Liberals typically err, she says, when they identify authority with totalitarianism and despotism. Conservatives, on the other hand, are too willing to substitute force for authority, believing them functionally equivalent and, therefore, the same. The "authoritarian personality" is thus a liberal misnomer for the "totalitarian" or "tyrannical" personality. Arendt's great love for the Greek political system helped to shape her view of an "ideal" type of government. She fully supported a participatory form of government in which each citizen's voice could be heard.

The Community

Power is rooted in free communities of people in symbolic communication. It protects a life world in which adult citizens preserve, protect, and extend their social world. Violence interrupts and violates these relations. Violence is the rape of the intersubjective life world. Free, interacting communities must defend themselves from such onslaughts. Ultimately the state controls the means of legitimated violence. Unlike power, authority can rest in a person, parents, or teachers. The hallmark of authority is "unquestioning recognition by those asked to obey." Contempt and laughter undermine authority. The modern world is violent. Authority has all but vanished from the modern world. Violence has ripped apart the fabric of the intersubjective world, from the level of the family on up to the international level.

Economics

In *The Human Condition* (1958) Arendt distinguishes three types of human activity (Vita Activa): labor, work, and action. Labor corresponds to functions necessary for biological activities. She wanted to "free" people from labor to pursue other activities. Work, Arendt's second activity, generates our material culture, and artificial world of things distinctly different from our natural sur-roundings. Work imposes permanence and durability on mortal life and human time. The third activity, action, is the only one that occurs directly between men. Action is the human condition of plurality and creates the condition for history.

Like Marx, Arendt explored the question of alienation. The conditions that gave rise to alienation for Marx, however, involved the lack of "voice" of the working classes over the use of their productive labor. Arendt also thought "voicelessness" promoted alienation, but she was concerned with the lack of political voice or voting rights. For Arendt, displaced refugees experienced alienation because of their stateless condition; they therefore had no sense of belonging to a nation. Arendt's theory of alienation is applicable today. The Palestinians in Israel, the blacks in South Africa, the campesinos in Central American nations, and the homeless in the United States all represent people whose nationhood has been denied them, even while living in their indigenous countries.

Science

Arendt traces problems and concerns for objectivity in the sciences (social, historical, and physical sciences) to the decay of political life. Scientific objectivity has roots in Aristotelian "extinction of the self," Homeric "impartiality," and Thucydidean "objectivity." In the nineteenth-century view of science, the distinction between objectivity and impartiality was lost. Conditions for impartiality and objectivity do not exist in the modern world because of the cultural emphasis on self-interest and private goals. Impartial disinterest thrives only where the polis defines a shared world, transcendent of the physical survival of each member. In Arendt's words: "Since we have made life our supreme and foremost concern, we have no room left for an activity based on contempt for one's own life interest" (1961, 52–53).

A focus on the individual strips human conduct of its social meaning. When nineteenth-century thinkers such as Karl Marx, Martin Heidegger, and Feodor Dostoyevsky turned Hegelian philosophy on its head, they generated a belief that people can consciously "make" history as one makes a product, or builds a model to be implemented. Such a viewpoint destroys the process of discovering meaning reflectively in history. Humans can create a technology of behavior if they are willing to destroy freedom, meaning, and a social world. Significantly, the greatest advances in this type of social engineering take place in totalitarian regimes. An Arendtian sociological theory, therefore, would not be a basis for interference in the world. It would be world-building in its focus on the meaningful qualities in the action of predecessors and contemporaries.

The crisis of meaning is intensified by an epistemology of the sciences, which elucidates the relation between hypothesis and discovery (see Bernstein 1983). We are presented with a world in which we can create any meaning, or none at all. This ahistorical theorizing allows us to disconnect ideas from their roots in the life world. In Arendt's words: "The moment one separates an idea entirely from its basis in real experience it is not difficult to establish a connection between it and almost any other idea" (1961, 69).

The age of the experiment emerged because devices such as the telescope necessarily caused doubt about the human ability to discern truth through sensory observation. Even British empiricists temper their argument with statements of doubt about all observations. The interpretation of their sensory-observed "facts" admittedly depends on the world of common sense. When truth and power conflict, Arendt says, truth is suppressed. The possibility for order, however, ultimately depends on at least some institutions defending the truth. If the judiciary and the universities, two such institutions, pervert truth, the price is impotency for the culture and loss of true power.

The new Archimedean point for viewing human life on earth is Einstein's "observer freely poised in space." Arendt cautions us that such a perspective becomes antihuman whenever it makes human action and human culture appear to be manifestations of merely biological processes. In this way, Arendt warns, science and the conquest of space may destroy the stature of humanity.

Education

Current trends in schools and pedagogical techniques are symptoms of the loss of true political power and authority. Arendt believes that they amount to an abdication of responsibility for the education of children. The belief in a "child's world" of reality devalues the wider cultural world that the child enters. The child does not have adequate understanding to thrive in and create anew this world. This world must be protected from the onslaught of a new generation that can destroy it by attack or through unappreciative or imperceptive discounting. Education to Arendt does not simply mean training or imparting knowledge. It involves conservation of the cultural world. It ought not involve teaching the art of living, however. Equalization between teacher and student can only result in a loss of the teacher's authority. It proceeds at the expense of the gifted. One cannot speak of education in the realm of politics; politics is for adults who are already educated. Attempts to change a political system through "education" are really attempts to depoliticize, persuade, or coerce dissenting adults.

To advocate the autonomy of the children's world is to expose children to the peer group before they have the necessary protection of an environment in which they can firmly establish themselves. It is unlikely that a group of seedling pine trees could survive, even collectively, if taken out of the protective shade of the forest. If one lets them grow strong, they can be transplanted elsewhere, adapting to and changing in a new environment. This metaphor of cultivation (prominent also in the work of Heidegger) underlies Arendt's view of the responsible person who would preserve and change the world. Only such an educated and caring person can be trusted to seek truth and teach.

The Family

The parent-child relationship without authority tends to be violent. Studies of the intergenerational transmission of violence in families indicates that violence begets violence. Studies of the loss of authority in parent-child relationships (see Malhotra Bentz 1989; Malhotra and Deneen 1984) indicate that neither appreciation of each other nor increased understanding of the world occurs when parent-child relationships degenerate into a power struggle. Arendt does not mince words about the obligation of parents and the community to children. The family must provide children with a secure and secluded place in which to grow, away from the public eye. Too much exposure too early is disastrous to the child. The child must not be left in the hands of the tyrannical bullies among the children. Children cannot fight their own battles and should not be forced to do so. Finally, Arendt strongly contends that any adult who does not participate as a responsible citizen has no right to bring children into the world or have anything to do with their upbringing or education.

Through education we decide whether we love the world enough to assume responsibility for it and save it from the ruin that would be inevitable without renewal, the new, and the young. Education, too, is where we decide whether we love our children enough not to expel them from our world and leave them to their own devices, to allow them their chance of undertaking something new, something unforeseen by us, while preparing them in advance for the task of renewing a common world (1954, 196).

CRITIQUES OF HANNAH ARENDT

Major sociological theory texts ignore Arendt. This intellectual matricide cannot be explained by her disciplinary affiliation. If formal academic ties were crucial, then Thorstein Veblen, George H. Mead, Georg Simmel, and many other men would have to be stricken from the texts. Is she excluded because she is a woman who cannot and will not be packaged into a chapter on "feminist theory"? Or is it because of the unique challenges that she poses to sociologists of the positivist, functionalist, and Marxist traditions?

Fortunately Arendt has been seriously critiqued by many sociological theorists in scholarly publications (e.g., Wolff 1961). An important sociological literature concerns Arendt's relations to the work of Jurgen Habermas (1977, 1983), who finds Arendt's ideas basic to his model of communicative competence and the discovery and implementation of human interests. Habermas's warning about the predominance of rational-purposive thought and action in technological society is congruent with Arendt's warnings about the possible human consequences of the conquest of space. He argues that Arendt's concept of power is the opposite of Max Weber's in which power is defined as the ability to accomplish one's ends despite resistance. To Arendt, power is the human ability to act in concert (Habermas 1977). Margaret Canovan critiques both Arendt and Habermas (1983), while Walter Adamson compares their joint work to that of Gramsci (1978).

Her books have been critiqued by major theorists such as Lewis Coser, Daniel Bell, and Irving Louis Horowitz as well (see references to these and other reviews in Nordquist 1989), and her ideas have been examined in depth in two special journal issues devoted entirely to her work ("Arendt, Politics, and the Self"

1988; "Hannah Arendt" 1977) and an anthology of critiques (Hill 1979). In addition, several biographies are quite useful (see Canovan 1974; Kateb 1984; May 1986; Young-Bruehl 1982; Whitfield 1980; Tolle 1982; Tlaba 1987). The major book on Arendt's work that is interpreted from primarily a sociological framework is Natalie Moehle's (1978).

Arendt was never simplistic. She demanded that one stretch the limits of thought about the human condition into the farthest knowable reaches of the past and future. She illuminates the paths that the mind travels in its political and social journey from the past into the future. People who "know well how to choose company among persons, among things, among thought, in the present as well as in the past" (1961, 226) will choose the company of Hannah Arendt's profound thought.

BIBLIOGRAPHY

Selected Writings by Hannah Arendt

1951. *The Origins of Totalitarianism*. New York: Harcourt, Brace.

1958a. *The Human Condition*. Chicago: University of Chicago Press.

1958b. *Rahel Varhnhagen: The Life of a Jewish Woman*. Reprint. New York: Harcourt Brace Jovanovich, 1974.

1961. *Between Past and Future: Six Exercises in Political Thought*. New York: Viking. Rev. ed., *Eight Exercises in Political Thought*, 1968.

1963. *Eichmann in Jerusalem: A Report on the Banality of Evil*. New York: Viking.

1965. *On Revolution*. New York: Viking.

1968. *Men in Dark Times*. New York: Harcourt Brace & World.

1970. *On Violence*. New York: Harcourt Brace & World.

1972. *Crises of the Republic*. New York: Harcourt Brace Jovanovich.

1977. *The Life of the Mind*. Vol. 1, *Thinking*; Vol. 2, *Willing*, edited by Mary McCarthy. New York: Harcourt Brace Jovanovich.

1978. *The Jew as Pariah: Jewish Identity and Politics in the Modern Age*. New York: Grove Press.

Studies About Hannah Arendt and Supplemental References

Adamson, Walter. 1978. "Beyond 'Reform and Revolution': Notes on Political Education in Gramsci, Habermas and Arendt." *Theory and Society* 6 (November): 429–460.

1988. "Arendt, Politics, and the Self." Symposium. *Political Theory* 16 (February): 29–98.

Bentz, Valerie Malhotra. 1989. *Becoming Mature: Childhood Ghosts and Spirits in Adult Life*. New York: Aldine deGruyter.

Bernstein, Richard J. 1983. *Beyond Objectivism and Relativism: Science Hermeneutics and Praxis*. Philadelphia: University of Pennsylvania Press.

Bottomore, Tom. 1973. "Is There a Totalitarian View of Human Nature?" *Social Research* 40 (Autumn): 47–73.

Canovan, Margaret. 1974. *The Political Thought of Hannah Arendt*. New York: Harcourt
    Brace Jovanovich.
————. 1983. "A Case of Distorted Communications: A Note on Habermas and Arendt."
    Political Theory 11 (February): 105–116.
Habermas, Jurgen. 1977. "Hannah Arendt's Communications Concept of Power." *Social
    Research* 44 (Spring): 3–24.
————. 1983. "Hannah Arendt: On the Concept of Power." In *Philosophical-Political
    Profiles*, by Jurgen Habermas, pp. 171–187. Cambridge, MA: MIT Press.
"Hannah Arendt." 1977. Special issue. *Social Research* 44 (Spring): 1–190.
Hill, Melvyn A., ed. 1979. *Hannah Arendt: The Recovery of the Public World*. New
    York: St. Martin's Press.
Jegstrup, Elsebet. 1986. "Spontaneous Action: The Rescue of the Danish Jews from
    Hannah Arendt's Perspective." *Humboldt Journal of Social Relations* 13 (Fall/
    Summer): 260–284.
Joas, Hans. 1976. "Hannah Arendt 1906–1975." Obituary. *Social Research* 43 (Spring):
    3–5.
————. 1977. "Acting, Knowing, Thinking: Gleanings from Hannah Arendt's Philo-
    sophical Work." *Social Research* 44 (Spring): 25–43.
Kateb, George. 1984. *Hannah Arendt: Politics, Conscience, Evil*. Totowa: Rowman &
    Allanheld.
May, Derwent. 1986. *Hannah Arendt*. Harmondsworth: Penguin.
Moehle, Natalia. 1978. *The Dimensions of Evil and of Transcendence: A Sociological
    Perspective*. Washington, DC: University Press of America.
Nordquist, Joan. 1989. *Hannah Arendt*. Social Theory: A Bibliographic Series, No. 14.
    Santa Cruz, CA: Reference and Research Services.
O'Sullivan, N. K. 1973. "Politics, Totalitarianism, and Freedom: The Political Thought
    of Hannah Arendt." *Political Studies* 21 (June): 183–198.
Parekh, Bhikhu C. 1981. *Hannah Arendt and the Search for a New Political Philosophy*.
    London: Macmillan.
Tlaba, Gabriel Masooane. 1987. *Politics and Freedom: Human Will and Action in the
    Thought of Hannah Arendt*. Lanham: University Press of America.
Tolle, Gordon J. 1982. *Human Nature Under Fire: The Political Philosophy of Hannah
    Arendt*. Washington, DC: University Press of America.
Whitfield, Stephen J. 1980. *Into the Dark: Hannah Arendt and Totalitarianism*. Phila-
    delphia: Temple University Press.
Wolff, Kurt. 1961. "On the Significance of Hannah Arendt's 'The Human Condition'
    for Sociology." *Inquiry* 4 (Summer): 67–106.
Young-Bruehl, Elisabeth. 1982. *Hannah Arendt: For Love of the World*. New Haven,
    CT: Yale University Press.

Unpublished Material

Malhotra, Valerie, and Jeffrey Deneen. 1984. "Power Saturated vs. Appreciative Con-
    versations Between Adults and Children." Paper presented at the Eighth World
    Congress of Sociology, Mexico City.

VALERIE MALHOTRA BENTZ AND DEBRA WINEGARTEN

EMILY GREENE BALCH (1867–1961)

Emily Greene Balch is one of two American woman (Jane Addams* is the other) to be awarded the Nobel Peace Prize. Her intellectual work is of the first order: setting precedents in statistical studies of the United States, France, and Austria-Hungary; in the use of the concept of "role"; in comparative analyses of immigrant life in the "New" and "Old" worlds; in the study of the conceptual links between pacifism, feminism, and peaceful arbitration; and in the practical development of strategies for international cooperation.

BIOGRAPHY

Balch was born in Jamaica Plain, Massachusetts, January 8, 1867, into an established New England family. She was the daughter of Ellen Maria Noyes and Francis Vergnies Balch. Her early years were happy ones, although she soon learned that she was not considered physically attractive. This evaluation led to her determination at a very young age to be independent of traditional women's roles. A rather bookish young woman, she developed a close emotional and intellectual tie with her father that sustained her throughout her life.

She fortunately came of age when women were first allowed entry into higher education, and she flourished in this environment. She became a member of the first matriculated class at Bryn Mawr College, where she studied with the sociologist Franklin Giddings. He found her to be a brilliant student and became her mentor, encouraging her advanced education and writing. When she graduated in 1889, she was awarded the college's highest academic honor, the Bryn Mawr Fellowship for European Study.

She corresponded regularly with Giddings during her year in Paris. He supplied her with reading lists and followed her career closely for at least the next four years. Balch completed an original and important thesis for Emile Levasseur: *Public Assistance of the Poor in France*. It was published in 1893 by the American Economics Association when Giddings chaired the Publication Committee. In 1892 she participated in the Summer School of Applied Ethics at Plymouth, Massachusetts, again under Giddings's guidance. There she met Jane Addams, Julia Lathrop, Helena Dudley, and Vida Scudder, who became lifelong friends and colleagues.

In December 1892 Balch, Scudder, and Dudley cofounded a social settlement, Dennison House, in Boston. They quickly became involved in women's trade union activities, and the settlement became an organizing center for women laborers. Balch began teaching classes at the settlement, and continued her formal training in 1894 at Harvard Annex, now called Radcliffe College. During the summer of 1895 she studied at the University of Chicago under the tutelage of the sociologist Albion Small and renewed her ties with Hull-House. Next she traveled to Germany for a year's study with Adolf Wagner, Gustav Schmoller, and Georg Simmel. In July of 1896, on her way back to the United States, Balch attended the International Socialist Workers' Trade Union Congress. Here she made numerous socialist and Fabian alliances.

In 1896 Balch was offered a half-time position reading students' papers at Wellesley College. The next year, at the age of thirty, Balch held her first full-time job teaching socialism, statistics, sociology, and labor problems at this institution. From 1900 to 1919 Balch flourished in her position in sociology and economics at Wellesley College. She gained eminence and recognition in both the male and female networks of sociologists.

She was active in the America Sociological Society (later named the American Sociological Association), the National Women's Trade Union League, the College Settlement Association, the League of Nations (which was later reorganized as the United Nations), the American Civil Liberties Union, and the Women's International League of Peace and Freedom (WILPF). In the latter two groups, she was a founding member. She also was active in the research arm of the Progressive party in 1912. In this capacity, Balch, Edith Abbott, Jane Addams, Frances Kellor,* Mary McDowell, and Anna Garlin Spencer* united applied sociology with social research in a specific political platform. Balch also served on the Massachusetts State Commission on Industrial Education in 1908–1909, the Massachusetts State Commission on Immigration in 1913–1914, and the Boston City Planning Board from 1916 to 1919.

In 1915 Balch, Jane Addams, and Alice Hamilton, the first industrial physician in the United States, emerged as controversial leaders of the International Congress of Women at the Hague. Their joint publication of *The Women at the Hague* brought the meetings to worldwide attention and subsequently subjected these women to frequent personal ostracism and attack.

In 1916–1917 Balch took a sabbatical leave to devote her energies to the world peace movement. She spent eight months in Stockholm as a member of a neutral conference of experts searching for a peaceful resolution of the conflagration in

Europe. The next year she asked for another leave, embarrassed by the furor her work had evoked. For at this time and throughout the 1920s, Balch became the target of relentless and scurrilous red-baiting. This controversy was intolerable to the Board of Trustees of Wellesley College. In 1919 they refused to reappoint her, and her academic career ended.

Balch continued to work for peace the rest of her life. Her ability to withstand government investigations and public ostracism was remarkable. Although Balch and Jane Addams shared this opprobrium, the latter had significantly stronger institutional and friendship networks than the former. Although Addams was considered "the most dangerous woman in America," Balch often was ranked as the second most dangerous woman in America. Without Addams's charismatic personality and press, Balch bore her burden quietly and often alone.

Despite these painful criticisms, Balch held high positions of trust in the League of Nations and later in the United Nations. Her committee leadership of a group of experts who investigated Haiti's occupation by the United States led to massive policy changes and greater freedom for the Haitians. She became a backstage force in a variety of U.N. policies aimed at the peaceful arbitration of international disputes.

This outstanding work was recognized in 1946 with her being awarded the Nobel Peace Prize. She was astonished and pleased by the honor, and the general public was somewhat surprised to learn about this modest, worldwide leader who lived in a small cottage in Massachusetts. Balch lived a long and controversial life, and she died in a nursing home in Cambridge, Massachusetts, on January 9, 1961.

MAJOR THEMES

Like many of the women sociologists of her era, Balch combined cultural feminism with critical pragmatism. Unlike many of the women in her age cohort, however, she had extensive formal training in sociology as a profession. She set many sociological precedents that were well known at the time, but unrecognized in formal publications by male sociologists.

Balch, for example, used statistical data at a time when few male, American sociologists did so. Thus her study of *Public Assistance of the Poor in France* set a number of important historical precedents in her combination of theory and quantitative research. Here she documented the historical development of care for the poor and its relation to the bureaucracy administering these programs. The style of services offered, the disabilities covered, and the types of social problems found are discussed. Combining cost with statistical and demographic information, the thesis is one of the earliest sociological analyses of care for the indigent and disabled.

Balch's *Manual for Use in Cases of Juvenile Offenders and Other Minors in Massachusetts* is a practical document primarily of interest to historians of social welfare. Similarly, her 1903 publication, *A Study of Conditions of City Life*, is a bibliography on urban sociology remarkable for its outline of the discipline at that time. This extensive list of urban studies anticipated many of the concerns of the later, more legitimated "Chicago School" of sociology.

Our Slavic Fellow Citizens (1910) is her most important sociological book, again predating and in many ways complementing the more lauded volumes of *The Polish Peasant in Europe and America* (1918–1920), written by W. I. Thomas and Florian Znaniecki, Chicago sociologists. Balch spent most of 1905 in Austria-Hungary collecting observations, conducting interviews, and gathering quantitative data. She lived with Thomas Masaryk, Alice Masaryk,* and other family members during this year. She then spent another year visiting Slavic enclaves in the United States. She traveled from New York to Colorado, from the Upper Peninsula of Michigan to Galveston, Texas. She spent the fall of one year as a boarder in a working-class family living in New York City. Methodologically grounded, Balch's analysis is an in-depth study of Slovanians, Croatians, Austrian Poles, and Ruthenians in both the New and Old Worlds. It is a monumental, albeit unrecognized, classic statement.

Balch, in fact, critiqued the first two volumes of *The Polish Peasant in Europe and America* and found them of major scholarly interest. She had some reservations about using personal letters in such a format, however, calling it "spiritual vivisection in the name of science" (Balch 1918, 166).

Balch wrote more than a hundred articles on women, labor, and social settlements. In the writings published before 1920, she shared the interests of other Hull-House women, documenting the systematic inequality of women's lives and work in the United States.

The remainder of her writings revolve around international peace. Her work as a delegate to the International League Congress of Women at the Hague (this subsequently became the WILPF) in 1915 led to her coauthorship of a controversial report of the event and its plan to end world conflict. The conference wanted liberal peace terms, the establishment of a world court, no transfer of territory without the consent of the populace, and the representation of women in both international and national politics. (Anna Garlin Spencer also attend this conference.)

As a member of a peace envoy, Balch enacted these recommendations. She visited several heads of state to seek out ways of ending and limiting the fighting in Europe during 1915. This work brought her to public attention, resulting in scorn and social ostracism on a national level. Its effects on her sociological career were devastating, as noted earlier. Her ostracism by male sociologists was evident as early as 1915. At this time she was invited by the president of the American Sociological Society, E. A. Ross, to address the group on world peace. He found it nearly impossible to find male sociologists to discuss her work. (See discussion of this meeting below.)

Undaunted by this criticism, Balch continued to struggle for a peaceful settlement to World War I. In 1918 she edited a comprehensive volume, *Approaches to the Great Settlement*, that contained major statements by leaders and organizations on ways to end the war. As the international secretary-treasurer of the WILPF, led by Jane Addams as president, Balch wrote a number of reports and newsletter articles. In 1927, in conjunction with this work, Balch led a committee of the WILPF in an investigation of conditions in Haiti. Their compiled work, *Occupied Haiti*, was edited and largely written by Balch. Their recommendations for lessened U.S. governance and control over this country were subsequently adopted by President Herbert Hoover as national policy. Many of Balch's more obscure writings from these and later years were republished in *Beyond Nationalism* (Randall 1972).

All of her writings after 1915 echo the theme of world peace obtained through arbitration, investigation, public judgment, and international law. These ideas were implemented in powerful ways, leading in fact to the end of many injustices throughout the world. She worked tirelessly but modestly, more concerned with peace than with self-aggrandizement. Her Nobel Peace Prize attests to her influence and faith during long, hard years of struggle.

A collection of edited poems, *The Miracle of Living*, provides a glimpse into her philosophy and world view. The poems are simply written, complex in their context of international conflict and professional ostracism.

WRITINGS ABOUT EMILY GREENE BALCH

George E. Howard (see discussion of his mentoring of Hattie Plum Williams*) was one of the few male sociologists who was willing to critique (and support) Balch's controversial position on women as special proponents of peace in 1915. More than a dozen men were unwilling to do so at the annual meetings of the American Sociological Society (see Deegan 1981). (Other discussants were Anna Garlin Spencer; Lilian Wald, the noted social settlement leader; J. P. Lichtenberger; and Francis Tyson.)

One of the few sociologists to note and commend Balch's work was W.E.B. DuBois, the eminent black sociologist also shunned by his white male colleagues. DuBois found Balch's *Occupied Haiti* especially noteworthy (1927). Jane Addams coauthored a book and several articles with Balch, and their intellectual linkages are noted in passim in both women's writings (e.g., Addams's *Second Twenty Years at Hull-House*, 1930, 197–198).

The major biography of Balch was written by Mercedes Randall, a devoted friend of Balch. Randall had Balch's articles on peace—often published in obscure publications and newsletters—reprinted; she compiled and published Balch's poetry; she collected Balch's personal papers and donated them to the Swarthmore College Peace Collection; and finally, she wrote a personal, albeit uncritical, biography of Balch. Randall's work on behalf of her friend allows contemporary scholars to examine Balch's life more fully.

Balch's biography is most useful in its details on her friendships, reserved emotions, and chronological experiences. The book never probes Balch as a person, scholar, or leader. The reader is left wondering how such great accomplishments were enacted by this woman, given this superficial and protective portrait.

Allen F. Davis (1973) briefly discusses Balch in passim in his study of Jane Addams. Despite his cursory comments, he provides the best scholarly analysis of the context surrounding Balch's life from 1915 to 1930. Palmieri's (1980) excellent work on the women of Wellesley College similarly provides a thoughtful analysis of the women's lives and world that flourished during Balch's years there. These strong, women-centered community ties between women and for women help to explain how Balch could endure the years of opprobrium and hate. Catherine A. Faver is planning a book comparing the religious origins of female progressive thought in the writings of four women, and Emily Greene Balch is a major figure in this analysis. A preliminary paper on Balch's work was presented by Faver in 1986. David Adams (1987) has analyzed six steps that lead to the development of international consciousness that he found in the writings of Balch, Addams, DuBois, and others. Adams's psychological model is an excellent example of the type of innovative interpretation needed to bring Balch's work into the lives of contemporary pacifists in the nuclear age.

The only scholarly studies of Balch's sociology are mine. My institutional study of Wellesley College (1983) places Balch in a collegial network, an intellectual network, and a historical context directly tied to sociology as a discipline. My major points on Balch's work are echoed in this entry, while more information on her friends and life at Wellesley are provided. Similarly, my location of Balch in the golden era of women sociologists (1987, 1988) is covered here and in my introduction to this volume. The power of Balch's thought and activities have yet to be explicated: a notable project for future scholars.

BIBLIOGRAPHY

Selected Writings by Emily Greene Balch

1893. *Public Assistance of the Poor in France*. Baltimore: Guggenheimer, Weil.

1895. *Manual for Use in Cases of Juvenile Offenders and Other Minors in Massachusetts*. Boston: Conference of Child-Helping Societies. Rev. 1903, 1908.

1903. *A Study of Conditions of City Life: With Special Reference to Boston*. Boston: George H. Ellis.

1910. *Our Slavic Fellow Citizens*. New York: Charities Publication Committee.

1916. "The Effect of War and Militarism on the Status of Women." *Papers and Proceedings of the American Sociological Society* 10: 39–55.

1918. *Approaches to the Great Settlement*, introduction by Norman Angel (pseud.). New York: B. W. Huebsch.

1919. Balch, Emily Greene, ed. *Report of the International Congress of Women*. Zurich 1919. Geneva: Women's International League for Peace and Freedom.

1921. *Report of the Third International Congress of Women*. Third Congress of the Women's International League for Peace and Freedom, Vienna, 1921. Geneva: Women's International League for Peace and Freedom.

1927. *Occupied Haiti*. New York: Writers Publishing Co.

1941. *The Miracle of Living*. New York: Island Press.

1941, ed. 1972. *Beyond Nationalism: The Social Thought of Emily Green Balch*. New York: Twayne.

Coauthored Works

Addams, Jane, Emily Greene Balch, and Alice Hamilton. 1915. *Women at the Hague: The International Congress of Women and Its Results*. New York: Macmillan.

Balch, Emily Greene, and Mercedes M. Randall. 1945. "Appendix." In *Peace and Bread in Time of War*, by Jane Addams, pp. 253–267. New York: King's Crown Press of Columbia University Press.

Studies About Emily Greene Balch and Supplemental References

Adams, David. 1987. *Psychology for Peace Activists*. New Haven, CT: Advocate Press.

Addams, Jane. 1930. *The Second Twenty Years at Hull-House*. New York: Macmillan.

Davis, Allen F. 1973. *American Heroine*. New York: Oxford University Press.

Deegan, Mary Jo. 1979. "Emily Greene Balch." In *American Women Writers*, Vol. 1, edited by Lina Mainiero, pp. 97–98. New York: Ungar.

———. 1981. "Early Women Sociologists and the American Sociological Society: The Patterns of Exclusion and Participation." *American Sociologist* 16 (February): 14–24.

———. 1983. "Sociology at Wellesley College: 1900–1919." *Journal of the History of Sociology* 6 (December): 91–115.

———. 1987. "An American Dream: The Historical Connections Between Women, Humanism, and Sociology." *Humanity and Society* 11 (August): 353–365.

———. 1988. *Jane Addams and the Men of the Chicago School, 1892–1918*. New Brunswick, NJ: Transaction Books.

DuBois, W.E.B. 1927. "Review of *Occupied Haiti*." *Crisis* 34 (September): 227.

Howard, George E. 1916. "Discussion of 'The Effect of War and Militarism on the Status of Women.' " *Papers and Proceedings of the American Sociological Society* 10: 61–67.

Palmieri, Patricia. 1979. "Paths and Pitfalls: Illuminating Women's Educational History." *Harvard Educational Review* 49 (November): 534–541.

———. 1980. "Patterns of Achievement of Single Academic Women at Wellesley College, 1880–1920." *Frontiers* 5 (Spring): 63–67.

Randall, Mercedes M. 1964. *Improper Bostonian: Emily Greene Balch*. New York: Twayne.

Women's Trade Union League of Chicago. 1911. *Official Report of the Strike Committee*. Chicago: Women's Trade Union League of Chicago.

Unpublished Material

Faver, Catherine A. 1986. "Creative Apostle of Reconciliation: The Spirituality and Social Philosophy of Emily Greene Balch." Paper presented at the Society for the Scientific Study of Religion, Washington, DC.

Palmieri, Patricia. 1981. ''In Adamless Eden: A Social Portrait of the Academic Community at Wellesley College, 1880–1920.'' Ph.D. diss., Department of History,
Harvard University.

MARY JO DEEGAN

SIMONE DE BEAUVOIR (1908–1986)

Simone de Beauvoir created a powerful, internationally recognized literature on being a woman in modern society. Through fiction and nonfiction she explored the embodied dilemmas of being free and restricted. Her lifelong relationship with Jean-Paul Sartre profoundly influenced her thought and life, and placed her in an intellectual milieu that was the center of French thought. Despite her eminence as a scholar, sociologists tend to focus on her concept of women as "other," if they study her at all. Her ground-breaking analyses of mass media, modern society, aging, and autobiography have yet to be explored within the sociological vision.

BIOGRAPHY

Simone de Beauvoir incorporated autobiography in her theory, minutely examining her lived experience, embodiment, historical location, freedom, and philosophy, thereby creating a new way of being a woman. Thus her life story is intimately connected to her writings. She was born on January 9, 1908, as the first child of an aristocratic, yet middle-class Catholic family living in the Boulevard Raspail in Paris. Her examination of these religious and bourgeois roots literally fills volumes. Here I can present only the episodic facts of biography.

At the age of five de Beauvoir met one of her closest childhood friends, Zaza (Elizabeth Mabille), at their private, single-sex school. By the age of ten the precocious de Beauvoir "realises she is interested only in being a creative writer" (Okely 1986, xii). Shortly thereafter, in 1922, de Beauvoir made a radical break with her family's expectations by recognizing that she no longer believed in God. Her formal training proceeded apace with her completion in 1926 of her school examinations in philosophy and mathematics. She continued her studies first at the Institut Sainte-Marie in Neuilly and then at the Institut Catholique in Paris. At this time her family became agitated with de Beauvoir's decision to pursue more advanced training and judged her a failure because she wanted to study rather than marry. De Beauvoir faced their opposition, and enrolled in philosophy at the Sorbonne and continued on her own path. In 1927 she completed her degree in letters and philosophy, and the next year befriended two of her fellow teaching trainees, Claude Lévi-Strauss, who later became an eminent anthropologist, and Maurice Merleau-Ponty, who later became an eminent philosopher.

In 1929 de Beauvoir met Jean-Paul Sartre, and one of the greatest intellectual and passionate relationships of the twentieth century began. They were both students preparing for their examinations for the *agregation* in philosophy. Sartre placed first, in his second attempt to pass, and de Beauvoir, the youngest entrant, placed second out of seventy-six candidates. Two of the jury members recalled the difficulty in making this ranking: "If Sartre already showed great intelligence and a solid, if at times inexact, culture, everybody agreed that, of the two, she was the real philosopher" (Cohen-Solal 1987, 74).

Merleau-Ponty became deeply involved in the lives of de Beauvoir and Sartre at this point. Zaza, de Beauvoir's friend, wished to marry Merleau-Ponty, but after a family crisis disapproving of this marriage, she died. Several years later Merleau-Ponty and Sartre fundamentally differed on their philosophical viewpoints and irretrievably ended their relationship.

De Beauvoir and Sartre's "necessary" (sometimes translated "essential") relationship, with contingent lovers, deepened and evolved into an experiment in liberation and free choice. In 1931 and 1932 Sartre and de Beauvoir began a series of separations in their pursuit of truth, freedom, and commitment. In 1933 de Beauvoir, her former student Olga Kosakiewicz, and Sartre became a traumatic and tempestuous trio. Kosakiewicz and Sartre became lovers, and de Beauvoir experienced rejection, jealousy, and a heightened analytic consciousness. The volatile situation became the basis for de Beauvoir's first novel, *She Came to Stay* (begun in 1938 and published in 1943). De Beauvoir ironically, or perhaps humbly, dedicated the book to Kosakiewicz, acknowledging her key role in its plot and conundrums. This book is the first of many writings of de Beauvoir that are romans à clef.

These fictionalized accounts of de Beauvoir's life are not considered in this entry, which is written from a sociological perspective. This omission points to the huge gap within sociology to consider the whole range of fiction, from fictionalized accounts of reality to absurd accounts that are real only in the imagination. This dearth of sociological interpretations of literature, despite eminent exceptions, profoundly limits the disciplinary appreciation of many female sociologists (e.g., Harriet Martineau*and Charlotte Perkins Gilman*). Filling in this abyss of thought is beyond the scope of this entry or volume, which is both remarkably thorough and abjectly incomplete—a contradiction de Beauvoir would be able to encompass in her theory.

The complex intervening years between these beginnings as young professional and passionate writers and the worldwide acclaim that followed their prolific production of thought are summarized in dozens of volumes. The most shattering changes were precipitated by the Nazi invasion of Paris. This shocking brutality ended their politically naive years of concentrated intellectual work. The most important reflections on these times are provided by de Beauvoir in two of her stunning series of autobiographies (e.g., 1958 and 1972). Despite the assaults on their lives and times, everything that de Beauvoir published was first read by Sartre, and she, in turn, "read and reread, advised and supported the first writings of a man who was caving in under the weight of his depressions and philosophical systems that were far too heavy and awkward for fiction" (Cohen-Solal 1987, 283). She remained his major critic and intellectual inspiration throughout their long relationship (Cohen-Solal 1987, 378–379).

In 1949 de Beauvoir wrote the most important volume on women that was published during the dark years of women's intellectual labor in sociology, between 1920 and 1965. This tour de force, *The Second Sex,* reverberated in the lives of women from that year to the present. A mélange of scholarship, passion, and experience, *The Second Sex* was a feminist triumph written by a woman who sought individuality and shunned the women's movement she led for many years. (Later Merleau-Ponty severely criticized de Beauvoir's relationship with Sartre and its expression in *She Came to Stay*.) By 1973 *The Second Sex* had been translated into nineteen languages (Moritz 1973, 35). De Beauvoir's paradoxical role as a feminist leader was finally resolved with her emergence as a feminist in 1970.

In 1954 de Beauvoir became a fully recognized literary giant with the award of the Prix-Goncourt for *The Mandarins* (1954). This book chronicles the role of French existentialists in politics and social thought from the end of World War II until the late 1940s. It has been read as a fictionalized account of Sartre, Albert Camus, and other friends of de Beauvoir, although the line between fiction and fact has not been determined (Moritz 1973, 35). De Beauvoir's struggles for political freedom emerged during this era, including her support of Algerian liberation, the Russian experiment in communism, and the Vietnamese fight for independence.

These international conflicts are embedded in a series of romantic liaisons between de Beauvoir and Nelson Algren (1947–1951) and Claude Lanzmann (1952–1958) and between Sartre and a number of women. These affairs of the mind and emotions became one of many driving forces in de Beauvoir's struggle with being an individual, an intellectual, a woman, and a celebrity.

Finally, de Beauvoir and Sartre traveled throughout the world: observing, critiquing, and writing about the most mundane, outrageous, and horrifying events they witnessed. These journeys are chronicled and prismatically mirrored in the novel *The Mandarins* (1954) and in *The Long March* (1957). Her spirited reflections on America are found in *America Day by Day* (1948), a book overshadowed by the controversy sparked by *The Second Sex* (1949).

De Beauvoir's final days with Sartre are meticulously recorded in *Adieux* (1981). A series of interviews with Sartre are combined with de Beauvoir's reflections on his dying in a fascinating yet sometimes repulsive intensity. Still fighting and analyzing their lives, the couple "do not go gentle into that dark night." The years after Sartre's death in 1980 are filled with more writing, public interviews, and de Beauvoir's major struggles with freedom in the midst of absence. Her death in 1986 was mourned by feminists everywhere.

MAJOR THEMES

De Beauvoir has yet to be considered within the full range of her sociological import. She is, of course, an existentialist; a theorist who examines the very nature of being as problematic yet filled with choice. But she is much more than this, as well as being a unique voice within the existentialist movement. Her serious engagement with Georg Wilhelm Friedrich Hegel, Karl Marx, Martin Heidegger, Sigmund Freud, and Edmund Husserl, for example, appears largely unexplored. For English-speakers, like myself, the analytic study of her writings is severely limited by the translations from the French. Finally, de Beauvoir is the most important scholar of Jean-Paul Sartre, and her intellectual stature as an influence and critic has not been seriously considered in mainstream sociological scholarship. Her intellectual ties to Albert Camus, Claude Lévi-Strauss, and Maurice Merleau-Ponty also need thorough explication. She has chronicled aspects of their lives, but she also engaged in philosophical argument and debate as a member of a powerful generation of theorists that affect the very grounding of multidisciplinary thought.

The methodology underlying de Beauvoir's text is a blend of existential, phenomenological, autobiographical, and experiential techniques. Her work is fundamentally grounded in contradiction, history, biology, interaction, and human agency. This powerful focus of knowledge and being is applied to numerous areas of "specialization" within sociology (e.g., gender and age).

Her greatest book is *The Second Sex,* a towering intellectual portrait of woman as "the other." From birth to death, from ancient Christianity to the present, from the lover to the antagonist, "woman" is quintessentially less than the man, who is the standard, the basis of all admired action and judgment. De Beauvoir's masterpiece on women's existential alienation is the major analysis of women's lives during the dark era of sociology (1920–1965). It was written in 1949 and translated into English by H. M. Parshley in 1953. Despite serious criticisms of this translation, de Beauvoir's analysis inspired many women to reexamine their lives and ideas, moving them to choose greater freedom and responsibility. Feminist scholars, particularly in the humanities and women's studies, use de Beauvoir as the touchstone for their epistemology. Sociologists frequently acknowledge de Beauvoir's concept of "the other" (e.g., Virginia Olesen* and Alice Rossi*), but thorough explorations of the fundamental distance between social reality and women's reality are lacking.

Aging also is depicted in this holistic manner. The experience of aging (using the phenomenology of "being in the world") is ambiguous: Who am I as my body ages? Historical answers to this question are provided both for the society and for an individual. "Age changes our relationship with time: as the years go by our future shortens, while our past grows heavier" (de Beauvoir 1970, 536.) But the social definitions of future and past emerge from group contexts, including medicine, myth, and gender. This same encounter with time, gender, and human existence is examined in *Memoirs of a Dutiful Daughter* (c. 1958). De Beauvoir once more combines her autobiographical location with "public issues."

The international popularity of Brigitte Bardot is the subject of a sympathetic portrait by de Beauvoir. Bardot's embodiment of a depicted self that emerges from the combination of youthful innocence with sensuality unites complex paradoxes. Bardot is both accessible and inaccessible as a vulnerable ideal. The text is accompanied by numerous pictures of Bardot that interact with the subject as person, actress, and topic of abstract discussion.

De Beauvoir's corpus challenges the fundamental theoretical and methodological ways of doing sociology. Her thought is best accepted by feminist sociologists, including myself, who are moved, stimulated, and influenced by de Beauvoir but remain untrained and unsophisticated in their intellectual use of her work. The most important feminist analyses in English are done by scholars in other disciplines, particularly in women's studies and in English.

CRITIQUES OF SIMONE DE BEAUVOIR

The U.S. Library of Congress had seventeen books written in English on de Beauvoir in the fall of 1989; numerous untranslated French texts augment this list. This scholarly industry cannot be adequately summarized here. I have chosen instead to discuss a few of the writings that appear most relevant from a sociological perspective.

An exciting addition to the de Beauvoir literature is found in the 1987 publication of the intimate letters sent by Sartre to de Beauvoir. Although these letters still tell only part of their story, they support de Beauvoir's perception of their relationship and quell a number of critics who thought she exaggerated her importance to him.

Judith Okely has written a concise, sophisticated critique of de Beauvoir. A particularly interesting review of *The Second Sex* is contained here: a reflective section on its impact on Okely, a summary of its wider social influence, and an updated interpretation of its meaning in the 1980s. This book is a good introduction to de Beauvoir and her most important writing.

De Beauvoir's painfully detailed autobiographical style is taken to task by Mary Evans (1980) as "over-determined"; too rational; hostile to embodied existence; and pessimistic on physical, sexual relationships. Although Evans is too harsh in some of her interpretations, her analysis of de Beauvoir's autobiographical works as characterized by "ruthless, but somewhat incomplete, honesty of her relations with others" resonates with a chilling aftereffect I experience when reading de Beauvoir. Evans's later book (1986) has the same appreciative and critical tension found in this earlier article.

Margaret Walters (1976) similarly criticizes de Beauvoir for her abstraction of women's values and lived experience, and critiques the bourgeois foundation of her thought. This evaluation is based on Walters's perception of a flawed theoretical similarity between de Beauvoir, Mary Wollenstonecraft, and Harriet Martineau.* Walters views these three feminist theorists as tied to the male world view and capitalism: they are voices from the past and not the present or the future.

Any in-depth analysis of de Beauvoir's thought is intricately linked to that of Jean-Paul Sartre. Joint analyses of their prolific and profound thought are sorely lacking nonetheless. A notable exception is found in Axel Madsen's (1977) chronological analysis of their "common journey." Passing references to de Beauvoir are found throughout Annie Cohen-Solal's study of Sartre, providing a glimpse of the fruitful possibilities of a combined portrait. Cohen-Solal suggests that de Beauvoir's autobiographical writings were not reflected in Sartre's lived experience, and his silence on their shared life is both an intellectual and an existential puzzle (e.g., Cohen-Solal 1987, 74–76).

Josephine Donovan has written an important analysis of de Beauvoir as an existential feminist theorist (1985, 117–140). Donovan compares de Beauvoir with Mary Daly, a remarkable feminist philosopher who frequently uses de Beauvoir in her writings on metaethics. These comparisons are embedded in a larger text on feminist intellectual thought, including many of the female sociologists considered in this book.

Despite the wealth of interpretive material on de Beauvoir, her sociological vision is underexamined. For example, women's images in the mass media are the focus of considerable analysis in contemporary sociology, yet de Beauvoir's study of Brigitte Bardot is seldom cited in this body of thought. Expanding sociological critiques to de Beauvoir on aging, older women, the mass media, and social movements is an exciting prospect for future research.

BIBLIOGRAPHY

Please refer to Claude Francis and Fernande Gontier's *Les Ecrits de Simone de Beauvoir* (Paris: Gallimard, 1979) for a comprehensive bibliography that includes unpublished texts. I emphasize the nonfiction writings in de Beauvoir's corpus and used available English texts (and thus depended on predominantly male translators). Where known, initial copyright (c.) dates are provided.

Selected Writings by Simone de Beauvoir

c. 1943. *She Came to Stay,* translated by Yvonne Moyse and Roger Senhouse. London: Secker & Warburg, 1949.

c. 1947. *The Ethics of Ambiguity*, translated by Bernard Fretchman. Secaucus, NJ: Citadel, 1948.

c. 1948. *America Day by Day,* translated by Patrick Dudley. New York: Grove Press, 1953.

c. 1949. *The Second Sex,* translated and edited by H. M. Parshley. New York: Alfred A. Knopf, 1953.

c. 1954. *The Mandarins: A Novel,* translated by Leonard M. Friedman. Cleveland: World, 1956.

c. 1957. *The Long March,* translated by Austryn Wainhouse. Cleveland: World Publishers, 1958.

c. 1958. *Memoirs of a Dutiful Daughter,* translated by James Kirkup. New York: Harper & Row, 1974.

c. 1959. *Brigitte Bardot and the Lolita Syndrome,* translated by Bernard Fretchman. New York: Reynal, 1960.

c. 1960. The Prime of Life, Translated by Peter Green. Cleveland: World, 1962.

c. 1963. *Force of Circumstances*, translated by Richard Howard. New York: G. P. Putnam's Sons, 1965.

c. 1964. *A Very Easy Death*, translated by Patrick O'Brian. New York: Putnam's Sons, 1966.

c. 1970. *The Coming of Age*, translated by Patrick O'Brian. New York: Putnam, 1972.

c. 1972. *All Said and Done*, translated by Patrick O'Brian. New York: G. P. Putnam's Sons, 1974.

c. 1981. *Adieux: A Farewell to Sartre*, translated by Patrick O'Brian. New York: Pantheon, 1984.

Studies About Simone de Beauvoir and Supplemental References

Ascher, Carol. 1982. *Simone de Beauvoir: A Life of Freedom.* Boston: Beacon Press.

Barrett, Michelle. 1981. *Women's Oppression Today.* New York: Schocken Books.

Bieber, Konrad F. 1979. *Simone de Beauvoir.* Boston: Twayne.

Cohen-Solal, Annie. c. 1985. *Sartre: A Life*, translated by Anna Cancogni. New York: Pantheon, 1987.

Donovan, Josephine. 1985. *Feminist Theory: The Intellectual Traditions of American Feminism.* New York: Frederick Ungar.

Evans, Mary. 1980. "Views of Women and Men in the Work of Simone de Beauvoir." *Women's Studies International Quarterly* 3 (no. 4): 395–404.

———. 1986. *Simone de Beauvoir: A Feminist Mandarin.* New York: Methuen.

Madsen, Axel. 1977. *Hearts and Minds: The Common Journey of Simone de Beauvoir and Jean Paul Sartre.* New York: Morrow.

Marks, Elaine. 1973. *Simone de Beauvoir: Encounters with Death.* New Brunswick, NJ: Rutgers University Press.

————. 1987. *Critical Essays on Simone de Beauvoir*. Boston: Hall.

Moi, Toril. 1989. *Feminist Theory and Simone de Beauvoir*. Cambridge, MA: Blackwell.

Moritz, Charles, ed. 1973. "Beauvoir, Simone de." In *Current Biography*. New York: H. M. Wilson, pp. 33–36.

Okely, Judith. 1986. *Simone de Beauvoir*. New York: Virago/Pantheon Pioneers.

Patterson, Yolanda. 1989. *Simone de Beauvoir and the Demystification of Motherhood*. Ann Arbor, MI: UMI Research Press.

Sartre, Jean-Paul. 1987. *Thoughtful Passions: Jean-Paul Sartre's Intimate Letters to Simone de Beauvoir, 1926–1939*, translated by Matthew Ward with Irene Ilton and Marilyn Myatt. New York: Macmillan.

Schwarzer, Alice. 1984. *After the Second Sex: Conversations with Simone de Beauvoir*, translated by Marianne Howarth. New York: Pantheon.

Walters, Margaret. 1976. "The Rights and Wrongs of Women: Mary Wollenstonecraft, Harriet Martineau, Simone de Beauvoir." In *The Rights and Wrongs of Women*, edited by Juliet Mitchell and Anne Oakley, pp. 304–378. New York: Penguin Books.

Whitmarsh, Anne. 1981. *Simone de Beauvoir and the Limits of Commitment*. New York: Cambridge University Press.

MARY JO DEEGAN

JESSIE BERNARD (1903–   )

Jessie Bernard is a pioneer in several sociological specialties: marriage, the family, sex roles, the history of the discipline, race relations, social problems, community studies, public policy, and socioautobiography. Her long career encompasses major changes in ideas, the wider society, and professional practice. She has critically examined her life in a number of writings and helped to lead other women through the rapid changes initiated by the women's movement during the 1960s.

BIOGRAPHY

Jessie Bernard is a feminist who has generously reflected on her own growth as a mother and as a professional during her long adult life. She was born in the cold northern city of Minneapolis, Minnesota, on June 8, 1903, the daughter of David Solomon and Bessie Kanter Ravitch. Her maternal grandmother, Betsy Kanter, had immigrated to the United States in the late 1880s as a young Romanian Jew, and she became Jessie's role model for pioneering women. Kanter brought her young daughter Bessie, who would later become Jessie's mother, with her. Several years later they returned to Romania for an arranged marriage between Bessie and David Solomon Ravitch. The newly formed family unit returned to the United States where they settled in Minneapolis. Jessie became their third of four children, and, according to her, she was able to integrate the traditional Jewish culture of her grandmother with the secularized view of her older sister, Clara. Robert Bannister (in press), however, reveals a more conflicting and problematic picture of these relations and traditions.

Clara was instrumental in encouraging Jessie to enter the University of Minnesota in January 1920, when Jessie was only sixteen years old. By 1923 she had graduated from the University of Minnesota with a bachelor of arts degree, and earned a master's degree in 1924. During these college years she met the considerably older and charismatic sociologist L. L. (Luther Lee) Bernard. She was dazzled by his brilliance, and his early influence on her work and ideas was profound. Perceptively she noted:

The distance between a mentor-student relationship—flattering as it is on both sides—and bona fide courtship is not great. LLB, as he was known, read poetry and wrote sonnets to me. The sweep of his mind was breathtaking to an acolyte. And it was exciting to be part of the whole intellectual enterprise in which he was engaged and in which he encouraged me to participate. (1978, xix)

More than twenty-one years her senior and of a different religious faith, Bernard at first refused his proposal, but at age twenty-two, five years after meeting him, she accepted. Bannister examines the tumultuous development of this relationship with considerable detail.

Bernard's romanticized view of LLB contrasts markedly with that of Bannister (1987, in press), who depicts LLB as a womanizer and a manipulative person. This "backstage" view of LLB is not developed in Bernard's autobiographical accounts but it was done with her permission and knowledge.

Her naivete and traditional role as first a student and then a wife form a basis for her later radical transformation as a committed feminist scholar. One of the most fascinating aspects of her accounts is that in her autobiographical writings, she is creating a documented account of revolutionary change made by an innovative leader. Because we do not know how feminists can be nurtured and created in a patriarchal world, her autobiographical statements help us to examine the process in both its mundane and its dramatic phases.

Early in her career she worked at a series of jobs, often moving because of LLB's frequent job changes. In 1935 she completed her doctorate at Washington University, where her husband was on the faculty. Although Jessie Bernard was soon a recognized colleague of her more established and contentious husband, she wanted children and a greater sense of control over her life and ideas. The Bernards separated in 1936 over their differences, strongly disagreeing about the decision to have children. Later she reflected: "My flight from marriage constituted a kind of emancipation from his spell and having children became the price I put on my returning" (1978, xix). The newly independent Jessie traveled to Washington, D.C., where she worked for two years at the Bureau of Labor Statistics. LLB finally relented and agreed to her demands, and she returned to him. Their three children—Dorothy Lee, Charles, and David—were born over the next decade. Bernard has analyzed this traumatic period in her candid account of her life as a mother (Bernard 1978).

Like most parents, Bernard went through crises with each child. Her children were sometimes loving and sometimes hostile, but they were always a significant part of her life. What is important to those outside her family, however, is not that these things happened, but that she is willing to share them with us by mingling personal, philosophical, and sociological threads into her own tapestry of motherhood.

From 1940 to 1947 she was a professor of sociology at Lindenwood College in St. Charles, Missouri, while LLB taught at Washington University in St. Louis. In 1947 they moved to Pennsylvania State University, where she remained from 1947 to 1964. In 1951, when her last child was an infant, LLB was dying. She recounts the dramatic contrasts of comforting an elderly and feeble husband while running to meet the needs of a demanding and healthy newborn (Bernard 1978). During these busy years she wrote numerous articles and books, taught, mothered, and survived an era that was particularly hostile to women scholars. Some details of this hectic life are provided in her analysis and reflection on mothering (Bernard 1978), a generally optimistic book that does not dwell on barriers to women in sociology.

The 1950s were a tumultuous time for Bernard because of her interest in social problems and civil rights. She helped to found the Society for the Study of Social Problems in 1951, along with Elizabeth Briant Lee* and Al Lee. She served as president of the Eastern Sociological Society in 1953 and as president of the Society for the Study of Social Problems in 1963. The list of her professional activities, memberships, awards, and honors is lengthy, with the most memorable being the establishment in 1976 of the Jessie Bernard Award by the American Sociological Society. This national award is given to scholars who make outstanding contributions to the study of women, echoing the heritage of Bernard herself.

Her role as a national leader of feminists began innocently enough in 1968 when she was commissioned to write a book summarizing the literature on marriage. Bernard thought that this would be an easy task. "I felt that I could do it in a few months' time, leisurely, without too much effort. I had, after all, been myself in the mainstream of sociological research on marriage for over forty years" (Bernard, 1972, 291).

Meanwhile she was learning about the women's liberation movement and the underground press. This experience led her to question her way of presenting herself and, in turn, her professional knowledge and assumptions.

My first reaction was purely academic: I saw it primarily as something interesting to study, as something I had a professional obligation to observe. When, after considerable effort on my part, I received an invitation to a consciousness-raising session, one of the young women there said that I "threatened" her. Sitting quietly on the floor in their midst, showing, so far as I knew, no disapproval at all, my academic objectivity, my lack of involvement, my impersonality, was giving off bad vibrations. This incident gave me something to think about, including my stance vis-à-vis research and also my discipline. (Bernard, 1972, 292)

Thus Bernard began the long and difficult process of analyzing her professional life. As a skilled leader in sociology, she had little to gain from such a massive alteration in her perspective and much to lose: the respect of our cherished but patriarchal profession. It is difficult and courageous to have one's intellectual honesty take precedence over one's professional status.

Bernard's change in perceptions of "what society was" yielded a radical reinterpretation of the evidence on marital status. It allowed her to see that marriage was "bad for wives" (Bernard, 1972, 294). Her concepts of "his and her" marriages dramatically revealed the high cost of marriage for women and its numerous benefits for men. This massive compilation of evidence contradicted the popular patriarchal ideology that men are "trapped" in marriage, that it is an institution that primarily benefits women, and that wives lead a sheltered and protected existence while men give their health and peace of mind to support them.

Thus Bernard began a tradition of analyzing and publicly sharing her growth as a professional and as a person. In 1977 she continued this tradition when she published part of the log she kept while writing *Academic Women* sixteen years earlier. Although stating in that book that she was not writing a feminist critique, she privately was formulating feminist ideas that would subsequently become part of her book on *The Female World*.

Nov. 29, 1961   They [the data] show that women who receive Ph.D. degrees average considerably higher in testable intelligence than men. The reason is, of course, that they are a much more highly selected group; only a tenth of all doctor's degrees go to women and they are the very top of the bottle. But my problem is: why, if they have so much ability, do they achieve so much less? Many factors have been proposed and are relevant but the one that interests me most is what I call the "stag factor" or the exclusion of women from places where the best thinking is going on. Not by design or conspiracy, but just because men feel more free and comfortable without the presence of women when they are at work. That is my hypothesis. I also hypothesize that the quality of thinking is best in one-sex groups. (1977, 5)

This passage demonstrates that Bernard's development as a feminist sociologist did not spring full-blown in her "fourth" revolution. Quietly and carefully the groundwork for this change was occurring at least a decade earlier. In a characteristically frank passage, she notes that her own professional and personal commitments were partially begun fortuitously:

Jan. 31, 1962   I felt obliged to search my own career. I could not find the traces of discrimination there. It is, of course, impossible to document a vast amount of discrimination that is never publicized. How would people know how many times they had been blackballed, voted down, rejected for a job? My career had been unique. I had been "captured" in marriage before I had laid out any career plans. I had worked with and for my husband as I would have worked with him and for him if he had engaged me as an employee rather than married me. I had been "forced" to succeed, almost against my will. It was he who had insisted that I get a doctorate. No hurry. Take your time. But do not abandon the idea. (1977, 8)

Although each of these autobiographical statements is insightful, her most open and challenging self-statements are found in her self-portrait of her relationship with her children (1978). This compilation of letters exchanged between herself and her three children is a candid and sometimes painful book to read. She writes of her loves and doubts, her commitments to her family and her work, and the complexity of interaction that occurs in a living rather than a disembodied world.

Bernard's reflexiveness makes her an outstanding feminist and scholar. Her years of study and work in marriage and family emanate from her own understanding and confrontation with them. She was to many a superwoman, a sociologist, mother, wife, single parent, and widow who struggled through the years of oppression of female sociologists form 1930 to 1970. But through her candid autobiographical statements, she demythologizes the image of "super female sociologist." She made major life decisions for complex reasons. They were not always rational, and they are subject to critical analysis. Because I know of no other sociologist, living or dead, including reflexive or Marxist "superstars," who have been so open about their commitments and life-styles, Bernard is not only at the forefront of feminist sociology in this regard, but she also demonstrates to all sociologists how to intelligently reveal self-interests and the human being beneath the polished facade of publications.

This biographical/intellectual portrait can be contrasted to her formal work, which articulates this subjective openness and commitment in conjunction with massive statistical and empirical analysis. All of her writings are supported by extensive documentation. Each book is approached with a thorough literature review and integration of existing knowledge. Her early books are more formal, and identified with "professional" standards of an invisible author who writes with unquestioned knowledge. This style is partially due to the influence of LLB as well as to the professional, male training of sociology, but Bernard has transcended these limits, showing us how it can be done. Her growth as a feminist sociologist shows how each of us can grow until ultimately we work collectively as a liberated people.

MAJOR THEMES

No one can describe Jessie Bernard's feminist career better than she:

I am undoubtedly the only person, living or dead, who has participated in four revolutions in the American Sociological Association (ASA). The first in the 1920s, the second in the 1930s, the third in the 1950s, and the current, or fourth, in the 1970s. (Bernard 1973a, 11)

An empiricist (the first revolution), an independent thinker (part of the second revolution), a critic and generator of social policy (the third revolution), and a feminist (the fourth revolution), Bernard ranks as one of the outstanding scholars in sociology today. Because of her radical change in the 1970s, her books written since that period are already classic statements on women's world and life. Feminist sociologists turn to them for evidence of why women are angry, for documentation of women's oppressed status, and for recommendations for coping with this most unfair world.

The same problems she analyzed with depth and insight in the 1970s often were ignored or less penetratingly analyzed by her before that time. Ironically, it is Bernard's feminist analysis of the 1970s that forms part of the current knowledge base from which we critique her earlier work. All her works contain extensive and careful documentation of the issues they address. She provided perceptive leadership in the areas of discrimination and oppression, a concern with the community, and an emphasis on the role of meaning in everyday lives. Nonetheless, gendered inequality was not fully addressed by Bernard until the 1970s.

Bernard has studied the sociology of sociology in various formats. First, she is an expert on the history of the discipline. Her coauthored book on the history of sociology is a compendium of facts, institutions, names, and schools of thought that is without parallel. From a feminist perspective, however, its very power to define the past is problematic because the early history of women in sociology was systematically ignored. This glaring fault was dramatically addressed in Bernard's ground-breaking *Academic Women* (1964), which does address the formation of professional women in and through higher education. Here she looks at "the flowing and ebbing tides" of women in the academy, compares them with men's careers, and analyzes the way these patterns are reflected in subject matter, teaching, and research. Although she does not regard Edith Abbott,* Sophonisba Breckinridge,* and Marion Talbot* as sociologists, she does discuss and document their lives (pp. 242–250). She divides the eras shaping academic women into four periods: The late nineteenth century: On trial in the eyes of the world; 1900–1920: Reform in the elitist colleges, service in the land-grant colleges; 1920–1930: Surging flood of disillusion; and 1930–1960: The great withdrawal (Bernard 1964, 30–37). (I categorize these periods for women in sociology into the golden era from 1890 to 1920 and the dark era from 1920 to 1965, see Introduction here.) Bernard continues to study her sisters in the academy, pointing out the significance of feminist research in changing the very structure of knowledge (Bernard 1981).

Marriage and the family are major topics in Bernard's analysis. She analyzes the "two marriages" experienced by both sexes in her pathbreaking *The Future of Marriage* (1972). Here she systematically documents the differential expectations, experiences, and fates for both genders. Her concepts of "his and her" marriages are widely used by other scholars. She also analyzes the process of women seeking out male mates who are superior in intelligence, social class, and education. The resulting "marriage gradient" isolates and often frustrates high-status women. Her book on *Marriage and Family Among Negroes* (1966) is an important historical and demographic summary of Afro-Americans' family life. She dedicated it to "Negro women" years before the study of race, gender, and class became a "hot topic" in the 1980s (1966, x).

Women's active resistance to their limited opportunities is a continual theme. The social movement and individual struggle were organized in Bernard's analysis of *Women and the Public Interest*, in which she documents women's traditional functions, including "stroking" or supporting the male performer (1971, 88–102), and their conflicting expectations. She sees a resolution to these conflicts by changing the fundamental expectations about women's functions and a movement away from an overemphasis on employment issues.

Given the severe constraints of this entry, the more than a hundred articles and book chapters can only be noted. Codifying and connecting this continuing body of work are exciting tasks awaiting scholars.

CRITIQUES OF JESSIE BERNARD

Bernard's work is referred to in dozens of books and articles. Despite the immensity of the number of these references, there are few pieces that examine her body of work, all her intellectual concepts, and her general impact on the discipline. One of the best, concise overviews of Bernard's work is Jean Lipman-Blumen's (1979) entry in the *Encyclopedia of the Social Sciences* (see also Lipman-Blumen 1988). Muriel G. Cantor (1988) offers a biographical and personal overview of Bernard's life as well. Gwendolyn Styrvoky Safier (1972) provides a comprehensive overview of Bernard's work up to 1972. I read more than two dozen book reviews of her work, and found a gendered pattern of criticism, with male reviewers tending to be more unfavorable than female reviewers.

Gerald D. Lowe and Robert R. Smith retested Bernard's finding of "his and her" marriages in 1987. They found significant empirical support for her concepts, particularly for the idea that men benefit more from marriages than do women (1987, 306). "His and her" marriages also were empirically supported in the research of Arthur L. Greil, Thomas A. Leitko, and Karen L. Porter (1988). They interviewed twenty-two married infertile couples who evaluated and responded to infertility in dramatically different ways, with women experiencing "a cataclysmic role failure" and men seeing it "as a disconcerting event but not as a tragedy" (p. 172).

Robert Bannister has written a much-needed autobiography of Bernard. He has employed extensive archival data to support his interpretation of Bernard as more complex, conflicted, and contradictory than her autobiographical accounts present her (in press). His challenge to her perspective should initiate considerable scholarly debate. In addition, his book on sociology and scientism provides an interesting summary of LLB's role in leading the ASA in the 1930s (1987).

ACKNOWLEDGMENT

I interviewed Jessie Bernard on June 29, 1978 as part of a project documenting women's careers in sociology. We have met and corresponded several times a year since then. This dense background underlies my work here. Jean Lipman-Blumen briefly critiqued an earlier draft, and Robert Bannister provided both detailed comments and access to his unpublished papers.

BIBLIOGRAPHY

Selected Writings by Jessie Bernard

1942. *American Family Behavior*. New York: Harper & Brothers.

1949. *American Community Behavior*. New York: Holt, Rinehart and Winston. Rev. ed., 1962.

1953. "Review of Mirra Komarovsky *Women in the Modern World.*" *American Sociological Review* 18 (December): 709–710.

1956. *Remarriage, a Study of Marriage*. New York: Dryden Press. Reprinted 1971 in New York by Russell & Russell.

1964. *Academic Women*. University Park, PA: Pennsylvania State University Press.

1965. "Review of Mirra Komarovsky *Blue-Collar Marriage.*" *Journal of Marriage and the Family*. August 27: 425.

1966. *Marriage and Family Among Negroes*. Englewood Cliffs, NJ: Prentice-Hall.

1968. *The Sex Game*. Englewood Cliffs, NJ: Prentice-Hall.

1971. *Women and the Public Interest: An Essay on Policy and Protest*. Chicago: Aldine Publishing Co.

1972. *The Future of Marriage*. New York: World Publishers.

1973a. "My Four Revolutions: An Autobiographical History of the ASA." *American Journal of Sociology* 78 (January): 773–781.

1973b. *The Sociology of Community*. Glenview, IL: Scott Foresman.

1974. *The Future of Motherhood*. New York: Dial Press.

1975. *Women, Wives, Mothers: Values and Options*. Chicago: Aldine.

1977. "Log: Academic Women." *Sociologists for Women in Society Newsletter* 5, no. 2: 5+.

1978. *Self-Portrait of a Family: Letters by Jessie, Dorothy Lee, Claude and David Bernard*. Boston: Beacon Press.

1981. *The Female World*. New York: Free Press.

1987. *The Female World in a Global Perspective*. Bloomington: Indiana University Press.

Coauthored Works

Bernard, Jessie, and Carlfred Broderick. 1969. *The Individual, Sex and Society*. Baltimore: Johns Hopkins University Press.

Bernard, Jessie, Helen E. Buchanan, and William M. Smith, Jr. 1958. *Dating, Mating and Marriage: A Documentary Approach*. Cleveland: H. Allen.

Bernard, Jessie, and Lida Thompson. 1970. *Sociology: Nurses and Their Patients in a Modern Society*, 8th edition. St. Louis: Mosby.

Bernard, L. L., and Jessie Bernard. 1934. *Sociology and the Study of International Relations*. St. Louis: Washington University Press.
———. 1943. *Origins of American Sociology: The Social Science Movement in the United States*. New York: Crowell.
Lipman-Blumen, Jean, and Jessie Bernard, eds. 1979. *Sex Roles and Social Policy: A Complex Social Science Equation*. Beverly Hills, CA: Sage Publications.

Studies About Jessie Bernard and Supplemental References

Bannister, Robert. 1987. *Sociology and Scientism*. Chapel Hill, NC: University of North Carolina.
———. In press. *Jessie Bernard: The Making of a Feminist*. New Brunswick, NJ: Rutgers University Press.
Cavan, Ruth Shonle. 1983. "Review of *The Female World*." *American Journal of Sociology* 89 July: 260–261.
Cantor, Muriel G. 1988. "Jessie Bernard—An Appreciation." *Gender and Society* 2 (September): 264–270.
Deegan, Mary Jo. "Jessie Bernard: The Professional Growth of A Feminist Sociologist." *Midwest Feminist Papers*, Vol. 2. Pp. 17–22.
Greil, Arthur L., Thomas A. Leitko, and Karen L. Porter. 1988. "Infertility: His and Hers." *Gender and Society* 2 (June): 172–199.
Lipman-Blumen, Jean. 1979. "Bernard, Jessie." In *The Encyclopedia of the Social Sciences*, edited by David Sills, pp. 49–56. New York: Free Press.
———. 1988. "Jessie Bernard—A 'Reasonable Rebel' Speaks to the World." *Gender and Society* 2 (September): 271–273.
Lowe, Gerald D., and Robert R. Smith. 1987. "Gender, Marital Status, and Marital Well-Being: A Retest of Bernard's His and Her Marriages." *Sociological Spectrum* 8 no. 4: 301–307.

Unpublished Material

Bannister, Robert. 1987. "Sexism, Scientism, and American Sociology." Paper presented at the International American Studies Association, Finland.
Safier, Gwendolyn Styrvoky. 1972. "Jessie Bernard: Sociologist." Ph.D. diss., Department of Sociology, University of Kansas, Missouri.

MARY JO DEEGAN

SOPHONISBA BRECKINRIDGE
(1886–1948)

Sophonisba Preston Breckinridge was an early theorist in the sociology of law, combining a doctorate in law and another doctorate in political economy with practical knowledge as a lawyer and Hull-House resident. Her meticulous work on women spans numerous specialities: work, legal rights, housing, and voluntary organizations. She was embedded in a complex network of the Southern elite, community organizations, and professional women. Her major recognition is in social work instead of in the Chicago School of Sociology, or in home economics or university administration, fields she also helped to establish.

BIOGRAPHY

The Breckinridge family has a rich history of politicians, businessmen, journalists, and women leaders spanning two centuries in the American South (Klotter 1986). This highly respected and politically influential family encouraged young Sophonisba, who was born on April 1, 1866, in her pursuit of knowledge. Fortunately fragments of Breckinridge's autobiography exist, so that at least some of her childhood experiences and influence are recorded.

Her father, William Cambell Preston Breckinridge, was a noted orator, lawyer, and politician. She was extremely close to him, and this relationship echoes a pattern found in the lives of Jane Addams,* Florence Kelley,* and Edith Abbott.* Her mother, Issa Desha Breckinridge, was loved by her daughter, but the young "Nisba," as her friends called her, was devoted to her father. She had an older sister, Ella, two younger brothers, and a younger sister. Nisba took a radically different route from her patrician sisters and other Southern bourgeois women.

In 1884 Breckinridge entered Wellesley College in one of its first classes, where, despite her interest in law, she majored in Latin and mathematics. Here she met Marion Talbot* and possibly Mary Elizabeth Roberts Smith Coolidge,* who also was on this small faculty. Nisba became "fairly intoxicated with Calculus and Conic Sections" (Autobiography, "Coming to the University," p. 1), but this did not help her to develop her nebulous commitment to be trained in the law.

On graduation in 1888 she moved to Washington, D.C., under some tight financial constraints. Although she never planned to teach, she found herself nonetheless in the high school classroom teaching mathematics (Autobiography, "Coming to the University," p. 1). She continued this work until 1890, when her health failed and she returned to Kentucky. After a brief trip to Europe, Breckinridge returned to Kentucky and studied law in her father's office. In 1893 she became the first women admitted to the bar in that state.

Several problems faced the young woman. In 1892 her mother died, and an even greater blow followed in 1893. Her father was caught in a scandalous romance, and his political career was ruined. Finally, to her dismay, this pioneer female lawyer was unable to gain any clientele. Under these many harsh blows, Breckinridge experienced a deep depression. (This pattern is found in numerous entries, e.g., Beatrice Webb*.) Her father and her brother Desha became concerned about her health, and arranged for a college friend to invite her for a visit to Oak Park, a Chicago suburb. Responding to the new environment, Nisba flourished, renewing her ties with Marion Talbot, who was then at the University of Chicago.

Again encouraged by her father, Breckinridge visited the university and met several old friends from Wellesley. Breckinridge vaguely recalled this visit and the changes that ensued: "I don't know how it was managed but I moved over to a room on the fourth floor of Kelly Hall (a residence hall) and became a student in Political Science at the University. I was very poor, I had almost no clothes, and money that first year, I found no way of earning" (Autobiography, "My Arrival at the University," p. 2). Like many other women, Breckinridge had learned shorthand and typing while studying law. These secretarial skills were used in her first paying, albeit barely subsistence, job as an assistant dean of women (Autobiography, "Early Experiences at the University," p. 1). In addition to this heavy work load, Talbot arranged for Breckinridge to earn her bed and board by being an assistant in Green Hall (Autobiography, "Breckinridge Autobiography," p. 9).

Despite Breckinridge's low status and limited salary, she liked her work. Frequently the victim of sterile environments and unemployment, Breckinridge clung to this opportunity and was amply rewarded. In 1899 Talbot arranged for a separate Department of Household Administration, organized under the auspices of the Department of Sociology, and hired Breckinridge as a lecturer to teach five courses. Through these courses, Breckinridge came in contact with Edith Abbott and her sister Grace Abbott, as well as othei women who were later involved in the women's trade union movement.

Breckinridge's portrayal of herself as languorous and not in control of her fate during these years is somewhat misleading. She was an accomplished scholar, teacher, and administrator. Her work did lack direction, however, despite the fact that she was an ardent feminist. Meeting Edith Abbott helped her to find a sense of direction. Her first classroom encounter with Edith Abbott reveals both Nisba's humor and honesty as well as the great determination of her "student":

I shall never forget the fright she caused me when I said something about the way in which women had carried the work of the world while men were doing the fighting and hunting. "Do you mean to say?" she asked. "I thought I did," I replied. "I must look into that," she replied. And her "Looking into that" resulted in her first publication, *Women in Industry*. (Autobiography, "The Russell Sage Foundation," p. 13)

While teaching and being assistant dean of women, Breckinridge found time to complete a doctorate in political science in 1901. In 1904 she received a doctorate in law, being the first female graduate at the University of Chicago to complete this degree.

Although Breckinridge received some recognition of her early scholarly excellence, it was not until 1907 when she and Edith Abbott moved to Hull-House that her power as a social critic blossomed. A dramatic energy and enthusiasm that never failed her after this move became directed and organized. Breckinridge was by this time forty-one years of age, and almost half of her life had been spent being moved by others' drives and ambitions. Now she was inspired by the women at Hull-House and began a career devoted to the study of women, justice, and social change.

During these later years, her close relationship with Talbot continued and deepened. Not only were they academic colleagues, but they also coauthored a book (1912) and almost single-handedly taught a staggering course load in their separate Department of Household Administration. In Talbot's later years, in the 1920s and 1930s, they remained close friends, vacationing and living together.

Breckinridge was a leader in a wide variety of social movements. She served, for example, as the vice-president of the National American Woman's Suffrage Association (1911); secretary of the Immigrants Protective League (see their work discussed in Grace Abbott, 1917); a member of the Executive Committee of the American Sociological Association; general secretary of the Association of Collegiate Alumni (1908); and active officer and committee member of the National Conference of Social Work. She helped to draft many bills regulating women's wages and hours of employment, as well. She also was an active member of the National Women's Trade Union League, the Women's City Club of Chicago, and the Women's International League of Peace and Freedom.

As a pacifist, Breckinridge received some villification, but not as much as Jane Addams. Simultaneously her major work in these organizations often was behind the scenes. She was the person who took notes, drafted legislation, and sat on committees. The vast amount of information gathered in these settings helped her when she wrote on these topics. Her role in social work education, like Edith Abbott's, is central. Lifelong friends, their story is impossible to tell separately. Both Breckinridge and Abbott experienced deep hostility from male sociologists in the Department of Sociology. The complicated deprecation of their work by men of the Chicago School, and their dozens of influential students can only be hinted at in this short biography.

Breckinridge remained professionally active for years, although her peak academic productivity occurred between 1912 and 1936. She died in Chicago on July 3, 1948, well loved and respected by her remaining friends from her Hull-House days. Only six years younger than Jane Addams, Breckinridge was nonetheless a "second generation" at Hull-House. She lived, moreover, thirteen years longer than Addams. On Breckinridge's death, she had seen the establishment of the new profession of social work in an academic environment, and the school she cofounded had an outstanding reputation as a leader in the field. *Social Service Review*, the journal she cofounded with Edith Abbott, was preeminent in the field. Her active work in home economics also was firmly established. Deans of women were firmly established in institutions across the nation, but their historical connection to Breckinridge often was forgotten. In sociology, the power of the golden era, the sociological leadership of Jane Addams, and the strength of the women's movement were but memories. The "Chicago Women" had made their mark, but history was already rewriting their lives.

MAJOR THEMES

Breckinridge usually wrote on the problems of women: their difficulties in the economy, education, the home, and in public life. In many ways, Breckinridge was a clear and precise author, bridging the gap between Jane Addams's persuasive and eloquent writings and the unemotional, factual, and more cautious style of Edith Abbott. Breckinridge's first major book on women, *New Homes for Old* (1921), is a fascinating account of the difficulties facing immigrant women in American society. Chapters on altered family relationships, housecleaning, saving and spending money, and child care provide information on the dramatic changes in everyday life facing the foreign-born housewife in the United States. Organizations established to help mitigate the stress created by these situations were discussed, presenting a historical analysis of social welfare in this area.

Marion Talbot's influence on Breckinridge is clear in this book. Breckinridge, however, took the basic facts of housework and being a housewife and placed them in a larger framework than Talbot did. Breckinridge linked immigration to changing patterns in everyday life: she recorded the minute alterations that add up to large-scale displacements. Most poignantly she remarked on the new uselessness of the peasant women who used to control a small plot of land for their personal use or for financial remuneration. In American cities they became dependent on either exploitative labor in the marketplace or on their husbands' wage labor. This complicated loss was amplified by their divorce from extended kinship networks. Immigrant women became socially isolated within physically crowded living conditions. Thus anonymity and urban life surrounded women who had left rural areas for life in the slums.

Marriage and the Civic Rights of Women (1931) discusses the relation between marital status and citizenship, emphasizing the impact of the Cable Act of 1922. This law enabled American women to retain their citizenship after marrying a foreign national. The terseness and clarity of the text, the comprehensive work done by women internationally, and the case studies of foreign-born women in America make this an early classic on the legal status of women and the barriers they encountered in obtaining citizenship rights. Breckinridge powerfully combined her unique skills, training, and interests in this book. As a lawyer and social scientist, she analyzed the effect of legislation on women's rights, summarizing past, present, and recommended future policies. This book is a classic statement in the sociology of law.

Any student and scholar of women's role in society from 1890 to 1933 will find *Women in the Twentieth Century* (1933) mandatory reading. The growth of women's participation in life outside the home emerged from women's clubs, increased access to institutions of higher education, the suffrage movement, and political activities. Data were given on income and the distribution of women in various occupations, with a number of tables providing an invaluable baseline for assessing changes or stability in income, and distribution in occupations over time. Because this historical period was remarkable for its relatively high proportion of women professionals, the chapters that discuss their earnings and business careers provide us with a unique, comparative, historical base for analyzing the same issues today. Detailed accounts of early women politicians and women's voting behavior also are provided.

Women in the Twentieth Century focuses on three areas of women's participation in society: in the club movement and its antecedent voluntary organizations, in the labor market, and in the government. The book is somewhat optimistic about women's future participation in society as full members and citizens. Beneath this positive note, however, Breckinridge documented in various ways the declining organizational power of women; their low wages and increasingly low proportion of worker benefits, and their almost nonexistent role in government.

This book reflects the strengths and weaknesses of Breckinridge's views and knowledge. Comprehensive in her approach to club women and the changes they envisioned and instituted, she drily presented overwhelming evidence of women's restrictions in the marketplace. Similarly, the vision of the club women did not bear fruit in the political world, a fact that Breckinridge amply documents. Breckinridge's "objectivity," however, prevented her from stating obvious political facts: that the feminist movement was quiescent; that women had returned to a traditional niche, albeit one that allowed them the right to vote; that discrimination was structurally reinforced and unlikely to change without more overt and radical pressures from women; and that an era of women as professionals and national leaders was ending.

Edith Abbott and Breckinridge generated a remarkable series of books wherein they selected documents and case records to reveal the social construction of community issues. Each woman individually authored their books in the series, with each writing four, although their collaboration and intellectual stimulation runs throughout the set. These weighty tomes, ranging from 500 to 1,200 pages apiece, are recognized landmarks in social work. Their contribution to methodological innovations in sociology have remained completely hidden, however. Here I advance the argument that the "selected documents" concept was as methodologically innovative as W. I. Thomas and Florian Znaniecki's "life history" method (1918). The selected documents provide dense documentation of individual lives affected by social change, legislation, and public agencies.

In the same year that Edith Abbott began her work on the series, Breckinridge published *Family Welfare Work in a Metropolitan Community* (1924). Here she examined strains on the "modern" family: physical and mental illnesses, widowhood, the deserted family, unmarried mothers, industrial injuries, and care of family members who are very young or elderly. The critical pragmatism of Jane Addams clearly complements the topics Breckinridge selected. Legislation concerning the family was outlined, and the difficulty of enforcing it is a major focus for analysis. Case histories of families with multiple problems also are presented.

Breckinridge's next book in the series, *Public Welfare Administration of the United States* (1927), started with colonial legislation (in 1601) concerning institutions for the destitute and mentally ill. A hodgepodge of changes—the legacy behind today's welfare state—were traced through legal precedents and statements made by leading authorities of the day. In 1938 she revised the volume, and criticized the chaotic role of the government.

Social Work and the Courts (1934a) showed how law shapes and affects the definition of social problems and their resolution. This legislative focus was continued in the next volume, *The Family and the State*, also published in 1934. Rights concerning marriage and divorce, reciprocal responsibilities, property, and children were delineated. These two volumes were linked to family problems and state responses to them. The social worker acted as an intermediary between these two community forces.

Abbott and Breckinridge's eight books in this series constitute more than 5,000 pages, and are a dense analysis of significant social problems. The historical origin of community definitions of these problems was given an important role, and the legal system objectified these definitions. Community leaders helped to shape these definitions, clarifying them, or speaking for a distinct group's view. These books frequently were used as classroom textbooks in social work, thereby affecting the education of social workers for decades.

WRITINGS ABOUT SOPHONISBA BRECKINRIDGE

A thorough biography of Breckinridge has yet to be published. Hints of her life, however, are found in a series of articles and books. A special issue of *The Social Service Review* was devoted to Breckinridge in 1948 (see Abbott 1948 for issue information). Her life is further examined through the work of James C. Klotter (1986), who has written an outstanding family account of the Breckinridges. His complex analysis of this powerful family briefly considered Sophonisba (pp. 189–207) in her amazing family's context. Even briefer, formal accounts also are found in Lasch (1971) and in Deegan (1979). Ellen F. Fitz-patrick's book (1990) summarizes the work and influence of Edith Abbott, Sophonisba Breckinridge, Katharine Bement Davis,* and Frances Kellor.* This is an important addition to their combined biographies and their influence on their eras. This historical dissertation reviews important archival documents, but does not focus on the system of knowledge generated by them. Although I considered Breckinridge in passim in several articles (e.g., Deegan 1981) and my book on Jane Addams (1988), a serious sociological evaluation of her work is lacking.

Clues to her sociological influence are seen, nonetheless, in the *American Journal of Sociology*. Reviews of her books are found in this journal, leaving a record of their evaluation by her contemporaries. The imprint of the men of the Chicago School is large, both as a system of ideas and as the source of training or employment for most of the male reviewers. The men's critiques, in general, were more favorable to Breckinridge than similar reviews of Edith Abbott.

Thus Stuart Queen's review of *Public Welfare Administration of the United States* carries the clear imprint of the Chicago sociologist Robert E. Park. Queen begins the review by stating that Park classifies social problems "as those of (a) organization and administration, (b) policy and polity, (c) human nature" (1928, 657). Thus Breckinridge is immediately categorized into the first area. Queen continues that "students of social technology will find in it many interesting and significant documents made readily accessible." Queen compares the book with other sociological texts, and praises Breckinridge for her superior analysis of the ambiguity in the term "public welfare" (1928, 658). Queen (1935) also wrote a strong but brief review of *Social Work and the Courts*. Robert C. Angell, at one time a University of Chicago professor of philosophy and later the president of the University of Michigan, understood the context of *The Family and the State*, and noted its relation to other volumes in the series. Stressing that it is a work for social workers, Angell concluded that there is a "judicious selection of materials" and "careful introduction statements" (1934, 386).

George Elliott Howard, who was not aligned with the male Chicago School, wrote a glowing review of *Madeline McDowell Breckinridge*, calling it "a model of biographical writing" (1923, 48). Women reviewers praised Breckinridge's single-authored volumes (for reviews of her work with Edith Abbott and with Marion Talbot, see their respective entries). Grace Abbott (1922) wrote a com-

plex review of *New Homes for Old*. She shares Breckinridge's call for a recognition of "old values in the new world" instead of applying a simplistic
assimilation model to immigrants. Chase Going Woodhouse (1934) called Breckinridge's *Women in the Twentieth Century* "a masterly review of the activities
of women" (p. 268).

Breckinridge's contributions to social work are noted in various writings on
the foundations of that enterprise. A particularly noteworthy examination of her
scholarship in *The Social Service Review* is found in Diner (1977). A thorough
analysis and use of her concepts in sociology awaits development, however. For
example, although Breckinridge's work on the home usually is outdated for
analyses of modern life in the United States, many of these changes confront
rural women in developing countries today. Applying Breckinridge to analyses
done in these contexts could prove illuminating.

BIBLIOGRAPHY

Archive

University of Chicago, Regenstein Library, Department of Special Collections. Sophon-
    isba Preston Breckinridge Papers, "Breckinridge Autobiography."

Selected Writing by Sophonisba Breckinridge

1901. "Review of *Domestic Service.*" *American Journal of Sociology* 7 (September):
    282–283.
1903. *Legal Tender: A Study in English and American Monetary History.* Chicago:
    University of Chicago Press.
1905. "Two Decisions Relating to Organized Labor." *Journal of Political Economy* 13:
    593.
1906. "Legislative Control of Women's Work." *Journal of Political Economy* 14: 107–
    109.
1907. "Review of *Women's Work and Wages.*" *American Journal of Sociology* 13
    (November): 411–414.
1910. "Neglected Widowhood in the Juvenile Court." *American Journal of Sociology*
    16: 53–87.
1911a. "Beginnings of Child Labor Legislation." *Survey* 27 (October 21): 1044–1105.
1911b. "Review of *Half a Man.*" *American Journal of Sociology* 17 (November): 414–
    417.
1912. "Immigrant Lodger as a Factor in the Housing Problem." Proceedings. *Conference
    of Charities and Corrections* 39: 559.
1914. "The Family in the Community, but Not Yet of the Community." Proceedings.
    Conference of Charities and Corrections 41: 69.
1915. "A Recent English Case on Women and the Legal Profession." *Journal of Political
    Economy* 23: 64.
1921. *New Homes for Old.* New York: Harper & Brothers.

1923. "The Home Responsibilities of Women Workers and the 'Equal Wage.' " *Journal of Political Economy* 31: 521.

1924. *Family Welfare Work in a Metropolitan Community*. Chicago: University of Chicago Press.

1927. *Public Welfare Administration of the United States*. Chicago: University of Chicago Press. Rev. 1938.

1931. *Marriage and the Civic Rights of Women*. Chicago: University of Chicago Press.

1933. *Women in the Twentieth Century*. New York: McGraw-Hill.

1934a. *Social Work and the Courts*. Chicago: University of Chicago Press.

1934b. *The Family and the State*. Chicago: University of Chicago Press.

1934c. "Review of *An Introduction to Homemaking and Its Relation to the State*." *American Journal of Sociology* 40 (November): 387.

1939. *The Illinois Poor Law and Its Administration*. Chicago: University of Chicago Press.

Breckinridge, Sophonisba, ed., 1912. *The Child in the City*. Chicago: Hollister Press.

Coauthored Works

Breckinridge, Sophonisba, and Abbott, Edith. 1910. "Chicago Housing Problem." *American Journal of Sociology* 16: 289–308.

———. 1911a. "Housing Conditions in Chicago." *American Journal of Sociology* 17: 433–468.

———. 1911b. "Women in Industry: The Chicago Stockyards." *Journal of Political Economy* 19: 632.

———. 1912. *The Delinquent Child and the Home*. New York: Charities Publication Committee.

———. 1917. *Truancy and Non-Attendance in the Chicago Schools*. Chicago: University of Chicago Press. Rev. 1936.

———. 1936. *The Tenements of Chicago, 1908–1935*. Chicago: University of Chicago Press.

Talbot, Marion; and Sophonisba Breckinridge. 1913. *The Modern Household*. Boston: Whitcomb and Barrows.

Studies About Sophonisba Breckinridge and Supplemental References

Abbott, Edith. 1948. "Sophonisba P. Breckinridge: Over the Years." *Social Service Review* 22 (December): 417–423.

Abbott, Grace. 1917. *The Immigrant and the Community*. New York: Century.

———. 1922. "Review of *New Homes for Old*." *American Journal of Sociology* 27 (March): 666–668.

Angell, Robert C. 1934. "Review of *The Family and the State*." *American Journal of Sociology* 40 (November): 386.

Costin, Lela B. 1983. *Two Sisters for Social Justice: A Biography of Grace and Edith Abbott*. Urbana: University of Illinois Press.

Deegan, Mary Jo. 1979. "Sophonisba Preston Breckinridge." In *American Women Writers*, Vol. 1, pp. 219–223. New York: Ungar.

————. 1981. "Early Women Sociologists and the American Sociological Society." *American Sociologist* 17 (February): 14–24.

————. 1988. *Jane Addams and the Men of the Chicago School*. New Brunswick, NJ: Transaction Press.

Diner, Steven. 1977. "Scholarship in the Quest for Social Welfare: A Fifty-Year History of *The Social Service Review*." *Social Service Review* 51 (March): 1–66.

Fitzpatrick, Ellen. 1990. *Endless Crusade: Women Social Scientists and Progressive Reform*. New York: Oxford University Press.

Howard, George Elliott. 1923. "Review of *Madeline McDowell Breckinridge*." *American Journal of Sociology* 28 (January): 481–482.

Klotter, James C. 1986. *The Breckinridges of Kentucky: 1760–1981*. Lexington: University of Kentucky Press.

Lasch, Christopher. 1971. "Breckinridge, Sophonisba Preston." In *Notable American Women,* Vol. 1, edited by Edward T. James, Janet Wilson James, and Paul S. Boyer, pp. 233–236. Cambridge, MA: Harvard University Press, Belknap Press, 1971.

Queen, Stuart A. 1928. "Review of *Public Welfare Administration of the United States*." *American Journal of Sociology* 33 (January): 657–658.

————. 1935. "Review of *Social Work and the Courts*." *American Journal of Sociology* 41 (July): 138.

Thomas, W. I., and Florian Znaniecki. 1918. *The Polish Peasant*, Vol. 1. Chicago: University of Chicago Press.

Waller, Willard. 1931. "Review of *Marriage and the Civic Rights of Women*." *American Journal of Sociology* 37 (July): 147.

Woodhouse, Chase Going. 1934. "Review of *Women in the Twentieth Century*." *American Journal of Sociology* 40 (September): 268–669.

MARY JO DEEGAN

RUTH SHONLE CAVAN (1896–)

Ruth Shonle Cavan is one of the few women from her generation who has received national recognition for her achievements in sociology and criminology. Even though she had an extensive teaching career, which she continues today as an adjunct/emeritus professor, her major contribution is her many publications that span more than sixty years. She also was the first woman president of the Midwest Sociological Society. Although she defines herself as a "liberated woman" and not a feminist, her independent life-style as a young woman, her unending commitment to sociology, her enthusiasm for her work, and her intellectual imagination make this remarkable woman an inspiration to other women.

BIOGRAPHY

Cavan was born August 28, 1896, in Tuscola, a small town of 3,000 persons in central Illinois. She was the third child born to Annie and Charles Shonle. Charles Shonle owned his own tailor shop and was regarded as a skilled craftsman. Although Ruth grew up in a modest home, her family was highly respected in the community. Her intellectual curiosity manifested itself very early when she read and reread adventure books like *Treasure Island*, a children's series called *Elsie Dinsmoor*, and a set of histories. Her intellectual horizons were expanded on her twelfth birthday when she recalls "one of the big events was that my father took me to the library and signed for me. Thereafter, I could draw out books. . . . I read adult books. I read all the time. I spent Saturday afternoons in the library reading stacks of National Geographic Magazines" (Kuhn 1987, 3).

Cavan's love for writing also developed early in her childhood. She states:

"I just took naturally to reading and writing. . . . I can't really remember when I didn't love to write but my first clear memory of the joy of writing was when I was in the sixth grade in 1908" (1987, 1). Her teachers and her high school principal encouraged and supported her efforts. She completed high school in three years by taking extra courses, including a summer course between her junior and senior years. The latter course consisted of "my writing an essay each week for which I received credit for one semester in English. . . . I had a wonderful summer reading and writing these essays" (1987, 1). During Ruth's senior year the principal arranged for students to produce a small magazine in which Ruth wrote articles. At the principal's suggestion, she entered a competition for high school students sponsored by the Carnegie Foundation for Peace. She won third prize and $50 for an essay on international peace. She also received $3 for a one-paragraph piece that was published in a small magazine given to Sunday school pupils.

After high school graduation, Cavan moved to Decatur, Illinois, which had a population of 35,000. This was quite an independent step for a young woman who had seldom been out of her home town. She did clerical work for two years to earn enough money to attend Millikin University. She majored in English, and accumulated five semesters of credit before transferring to the University of Chicago. She states: "Eventually I seemed to outgrow both the small towns and the small university and focused my eye on Chicago—on the *city* of Chicago" (1972, 1). From this beginning she eventually emerged from the University of Chicago with a Ph.D. in sociology.

Cavan's first career goal was teaching

because this was the only profession for women that I had ever heard of or seen at close hand in our little town. I discarded this ambition about the time I moved to Chicago and replaced it by what had previously been a secondary interest—to become a free lance writer of current affairs and social problems. I made sure I would not weaken and teach by not taking education courses to qualify for a state certificate. Writing was my goal—not sociology. (1972, 1)

Cavan earned the first of her three University of Chicago degrees in 1921, a Ph.B. in English with a minor in economics. During those early years in Chicago, Cavan says that

officially I majored in English and soaked up lectures by some of the famous professors in the English Department. Unofficially I majored in concerts, theater, opera. . . . I graduated financially broke, and back I went to secretarial work with a serious attempt on the side at writing and getting articles published. I did not make much money but gained experience and enough small success to strengthen my determination to have a career in writing. (1972, 2)

While working full-time in Chicago, Cavan enrolled in graduate courses in sociology, taking a course each quarter.

My first motivation was simply to take promising courses and use them as background for a better understanding of the city and writing. As I became a familiar figure in the corridors and classrooms, Professor Ellsworth Faris said to me one day, "While you are getting this background, why don't you work for a Master's degree?" I forsook my job and a regular pay check and returned as a full-time, poverty stricken graduate student to the University. I received the degree in 1923. By that time I was "hooked" on sociology and without a break continued on to the Ph.D. which I received in the summer of 1926. (1972, 2)

As a student at the University of Chicago, Cavan studied with Albion Small, Robert E. Park, Ellsworth Faris, and Ernest Burgess. During graduate school she was an assistant to Faris and he was her dissertation adviser. In addition to her dissertation on suicide, which was published in 1928, Cavan had three research books published. She worked closely with Ernest Burgess on these research projects. Because no women were on the faculty, all her mentors were men.

As a graduate student, Cavan's goal shifted. She states: "I had begun to write and have some publications in sociology and my ambition was, first, to get into some kind of research and, second, teach sociology, with writing professionally in sociology with either" (1972, 2). Most of her early professional publications began as term papers for a specific class. For instance, her first professional paper was published in 1924 in the *Journal of Religion*, a University of Chicago publication. The second paper, which emerged from a term paper for anthropology, was published in 1925 in the *American Anthropologist*. After receiving her doctorate in 1926, Cavan worked for two years for the Religious Education Association and then was a research assistant/associate intermittently until the mid–1940s for several committees affiliated with the University of Chicago.

Ruth Shonle and Jordan True Cavan (1891–1971) met in 1926 at Jane Addams's* Hull-House, where they were both residents. Jordan was working on a doctorate at the University of Chicago and teaching full-time at Rockford College in Rockford, Illinois. They were married in June 1927 and lived at Hull-House for the first three months. Jordan then returned to Rockford while Ruth lived in Chicago, working at the university. Jordan traveled to Chicago on weekends for the first year. This is another indication of her independent life-style and her strong career commitment. Thereafter, she produced research and publications through intermittent employment with committees at the University of Chicago and taught courses intermittently at Rockford College (1935–1937). In the 1930s the Cavans had a daughter, Anna-Lee. During these years Rockford was the family residence, but Ruth lived part-time in Chicago. Cavan comments: "Somehow I managed to look after my family and carry on research part-time for the University of Chicago committees, chiefly on some phase of the family" (Moyer correspondence, March 1986). Finally, in 1947, she was hired as an assistant professor of sociology at Rockford College, where she retired in 1962 and was awarded emeritus status.

During the years at Rockford Cavan began writing textbooks on the family and then on criminology and juvenile delinquency. She simultaneously published in professional journals, including the *American Sociological Review* and *American Journal of Sociology*. In 1964 she began teaching in the sociology department at Northern Illinois University at DeKalb, where she taught full-time until 1971. Although she has retired from teaching, she remains an adjunct/emeritus professor at Northern Illinois University, where she has an office and has access to the library. Cavan's life can best be summarized in her own words: "My life has been a succession of changes with writing as the occupation that has given it continuity" (Moyer correspondence, March 20, 1986).

Throughout her lifetime Cavan has been recognized for her scholarship and service in the form of awards and honors by organizations and professional associations. She is nationally recognized as a Fellow of the American Sociological Association (1959) and of the American Society of Criminology (1965). She was honored with the Distinguished Scholar Award on October 15, 1987, by the National Historic Communal Societies Association.

She also has received numerous awards on the state and local level, including the following: Award for Distinguished Service, Illinois Academy of Criminology (1965); Certificate of Appreciation (1961) and Award of Appreciation (1967), John Howard Association; Award of Recognition and Appreciation, Illinois Sociological Association (1971); Appreciation of Outstanding Service (president 1964–1965), Illinois Council on Family Relations; and Award for Distinguished Service, Illinois Council on Family Relations (1973). In September 1976 the DeKalb Unitarian Fellowship named a room "the Cavan Meeting Room" and provided a plaque. The Gurler Heritage Association of DeKalb, Illinois, also honored Cavan with a statement of recognition on May 20, 1985, for her editorship of the *Gurler Chronicles*, a series of monographs on the history of DeKalb County.

Cavan was listed in *Leaders in Education* (1941), *Who's Who in Chicago and Illinois* (1950), *American Men of Science*, Vol. 3, *Social and Behavioral Sciences* (1953), and *Who's Who of American Women* (1958). Perhaps her highest and most enduring honor was christening the Ruth Shonle Cavan Auditorium at Northern Illinois University in 1974.

MAJOR THEMES

Ruth Shonle Cavan is a dedicated writer, as evidenced by her early interest and success in writing as a child, her professional publications in sociology and criminology, and the fact that she continues to write and publish in the 1990s. Cavan has published eighteen books and seventy-seven book chapters and professional articles. The books include her Ph.D. dissertation, *Suicide*, which was published by the University of Chicago Press in the prestigious Sociological Series in 1928 and reissued by Russell and Russell in 1965. Several of her books—*The Adolescent in the Family* (a research report prepared for the White House Conference on Child Health and Protection), *The Family and the Depres-*

sion, and *Personal Adjustment in Old Age*—were written when she was affiliated with the University of Chicago on special projects. Three other books, *Building a Girl's Personality, Delinquency and Crime: Cross-Cultural Perspectives*, and *Intermarriage in a Comparative Perspective*, were coauthored with her husband, Jordan T. Cavan.

She received the most recognition for her successful textbooks on the family, criminology, and juvenile delinquency. Cavan's anthology on the family and her textbooks on the family, juvenile delinquency, and criminology each had three revised editions. The third and fourth editions of her delinquency text were coauthored with Theodore Ferdinand while they were colleagues at Northern Illinois University. The second edition of the criminology text was selected for use by the U.S. Armed Forces Institute. Cavan comments:

The number of these books ordered by USAFI was fantastic, amounting to 34,000 during the five or six years when USAFI used it. I cannot believe that 34,000 men in service took USAFI's correspondence course in criminology. Sometimes I fantasize that on some remote island there is a thatched hut filled with lost paperbacked Criminologies. (Quote from correspondence, November 25, 1985)

Between 1924 and 1984 Cavan published an impressive number of articles in some of the most prestigious journals in the field of sociology and criminology. Seven articles were published in the *American Journal of Sociology*, five articles in *Marriage and Family Living*, three articles in the *Journal of Criminal Law, Criminology, and Police Science*, two articles in the *American Sociological Review*, two in *Social Forces*, and one each in *Sociological Quarterly* and *American Anthropologist*. These articles cover a wide variety of topics in criminology and sociology, including suicide, research methods, old age, world trends in criminology (based on her attendance at the U.N. Conference on Crime and Delinquency), the family, dating, marital relations of prisoners, the status of women, interreligious marriages, historical utopian societies, and the Chicago School.

Over the span of more than sixty years of writing, several themes frequently are found. For example, Cavan has demonstrated a sustained interest in historical utopian communes. The theme was introduced in her master's thesis, which analyzed isolated religious communities (Oneida and the Mormons). The topic is woven into many of her publications throughout the years. In "Underworld, Conventional and Ideological Crime" (1964) Cavan uses the criminal underworld as an example of extreme underconformity and the Mormons and their practice of polygamy as an example of extreme overconformity. Thus she returns to the theme of historical utopian communities to explain crime. Between 1977 and 1984 Cavan studied historical utopian societies, again publishing articles on the Anabaptists and the Amana, Oneida, and Amish communities. In these articles she also discusses the variations in family structures and the roles of women and the aged.

A survey of interreligious marriage produced a series of five articles in 1970 and 1971. Although Cavan's publications on religious communes and interreligious marriages suggest the theme of religion, Cavan explains that her study of religion was secondary to her interest in historical utopian communes and in the family.

Her interest in the family and criminology also appears in numerous publications, beginning in 1934 with a chapter on juvenile delinquency in *The Adolescent in the Family*. In a later chapter, "Emphasis for the Future: Social Absorption," Cavan suggests a policy to decrease incarceration and the length of sentences and to increase probation. She argues that prisons currently tend to cut off contact with the family. Her continuing work in this area is found in her study of marital relations among prisoners and published in two articles coauthored with Eugene Zemans in 1958. In these papers she argues that marital contacts may be a rehabilitative technique in a treatment program.

Another theme found throughout her publications is old age. Her first publication on this topic was in 1949, *Personal Adjustment in Old Age*, which she coauthored with E. W. Burgess, H. Goldhamer, and R. J. Havighurst. The study was based on her research for the Science Research Associates affiliated with the University of Chicago. She has developed this theme over the years with articles on issues of personal adjustment in old age and the role of the older person in the family. She currently is studying the elderly offender, a topic that combines her lifelong interest in criminology and in the older person.

A fourth theme is the study of women. Her first books on women were concerned with the interests and problems of business "girls" (1929) and the building of a girl's personality (1932). In the 1920s she also wrote several articles concerning lives and attitudes of business women. Cavan continued the traditions of Katharine Bement Davis* and Frances Kellor* when she wrote on women offenders and women's prisons in the second edition of her criminology text. Her original juvenile delinquency text included a chapter on delinquent girls. Because these texts were so successful, these chapters had the potential of introducing thousands of students to issues regarding women offenders. Of particular interest is her 1981 article on "The Contrasting Roles of Women at Oneida Community, the Midwestern Frontier, and the Urban East in the Mid-Nineteenth Century." Here Cavan points to the limits on women's lives in the Oneida community and the hardships on the Midwestern frontier, but she does not take this opportunity to point to the power differentials and inequalities between men and women.

Cavan's work is part of the Chicago School of sociology, although she is not limited to symbolic interaction and human ecology. In *Suicide*, for example, Cavan applies Burgess and Park's concentric zone theory to analyze trends in suicide rates in Chicago. She extended Chicago sociology by analyzing the suicidal process documented in diaries, coroner's records, and newspaper articles. Her presidential address for the Midwest Sociological Society, which was published in the *Sociological Quarterly*, however, was much more of a functionalist theory. In "The Concepts of Tolerance and Contraculture as Applied to Delinquency" Cavan "attempts to assign behavior to a place in the total social structure and to determine when misbehavior should be termed delinquency" (1961, 244). In this theoretical analysis Cavan declares that "even though we know behavior falls into a continuum, nevertheless we tend to think in terms of dichotomies of good or bad" (1961, 245). Behavior, according to Cavan (and the Chicago sociologist W. I. Thomas), can be represented on a continuum from extreme underconformity through various forms of tolerated deviance to extreme overconformity.

Cavan also used diverse methodologies. Although suicide is predominantly a qualitative study, she used quantitative survey data in her studies for the committees affiliated with the University of Chicago, interreligious marriage, and marital relations among prisoners. Finally, some of her publications, especially recent ones on historical utopian communes, were based on historical research. Cavan's intellectual imagination has provided a rich diversity to her work emerging from her innovative theoretical perspectives and range of research methodologies.

CRITIQUE OF RUTH SHONLE CAVAN

Cavan herself sees her greatest contribution to be her early research books and textbooks on the family, criminology, and delinquency. In Cavan's own words, "I found my niche in textbooks which I could write and which were widely used" (Kuhn 1987a).

A computer search for citations of Cavan's work in professional journals indicates that her textbooks have been widely recognized as a resource for other scholars. Among her other works, her research on old age (*Personal Adjustment in Old Age* [1949] and "Self and Role Adjustment During Old Age" [1962]) has frequently been cited, especially in gerontology journals in the 1980s. Her studies of *Suicide* (1928) and of *The Family and the Depression* (1938), which she coauthored with Katherine H. Ranck, have been widely cited in journals.

In an unpublished paper, "Dr. Ruth Shonle Cavan: A Sketch of Her Life in Research and Writing" (1987a), Terry Kuhn wrote an interesting biographical sketch of Cavan that concentrated heavily on her connections with Jane Addams and Hull-House. Theodore N. Ferdinand, who was coauthor of the third and fourth editions of Cavan's juvenile delinquency text, published an invited essay, "Ruth Shonle Cavan: An Intellectual Portrait," in *Sociological Inquiry* (1988). This tribute to Cavan presents an overview of her life and accomplishments in extending "the frontiers of knowledge" (p. 342).

Several papers on Ruth Shonle Cavan have been written by Imogene L. Moyer in recent years. In "The Life and Works of Ruth Shonle Cavan: Pioneer Woman in Criminology" (1989) Moyer has attempted to expand the appreciation of Cavan's scholarship. Although noting that Cavan has received recognition for her successful texts that have influenced thousands of students, Moyer expresses concern that

much of Cavan's important work in journals has been ignored by current scholars, especially criminologists. References to Cavan's theory on the continuum of behavior . . . are conspicuously absent in books and articles on criminological theory. . . . While Cavan incorporated this theory (originally published in *Sociological Quarterly* and the *Journal of Criminal Law, Criminology, and Police Science*) into her *Criminology* and *Juvenile Delinquency* texts, other criminologists have failed to acknowledge it. Again, while she receives some recognition for her research on suicide, most research studies in this area cite Durkheim but not Cavan. (1989, 196–197)

BIBLIOGRAPHY

Selected Writings by Ruth Shonle Cavan

1924. "The Christianizing Process Among Preliterate Peoples." *Journal of Religion* 4 (May): 261–280.

1925. "Peyote, The Giver of Visions." *American Anthropologist* 27 (January–March): 53–75.

1928. *Suicide*. The University of Chicago Sociology Series. Chicago: University of Chicago Press.

1929. *Business Girls: A Study of Their Interests and Problems*. Monograph No. 3. Chicago: Religious Education Association.

1942. *The Family*. New York: Thomas Y. Crowell.

1948a. "Family Life and Family Substitutes in Old Age." *American Sociological Review* 14 (February): 71–83.

1948b. *Criminology*. New York: Thomas Y. Crowell. 3rd ed. 1962.

1952. "Adjustment Problems of the Older Woman." *Marriage and Family Living* 14 (February): 16–18.

1953. *The American Family*. New York: Thomas Y. Crowell. 4th ed. 1969.

1956. "Family Tensions Between the Old and the Middle-Aged." *Marriage and Family Living* 18 (November): 323–327.

1959. *American Marriage*. New York: Thomas Y. Crowell.

1961. "The Concepts of Tolerance and Contraculture as Applied to Delinquency." *Sociological Quarterly* 2 (October): 243–258.

1962a. "Self and Role Adjustment During Old Age." In *Human Behavior and Social Process: An Interactionist Approach*, edited by Arnold Rose, pp. 526–536. Boston: Houghton Mifflin.

1962b. *Juvenile Delinquency: Development, Treatment, Control*. Philadelphia: J. B. Lippincott.

1964. "Underworld, Conventional and Ideological Crime." *Journal of Criminal Law, Criminology and Police Science* 55 (June): 235–240.

1970. "Concepts and Terminology in Interreligious Marriage." *Journal for the Scientific Study of Religion* 9 (Winter): 311–320.

1971a. "Interreligious Marriage: Official Religious Policies and Individual Mate Choice in the United States." *International Journal of Sociology of the Family* 1 (March): 83–93.

1971b. "Cultural Patterns, Functions, and Dysfunctions of Endogamy and Intermarriage." *International Journal of Sociology of the Family* 1 (May): 10–24.

1971c. "Jewish Student Attitudes Toward Interreligious and Intra-Jewish Marriage." *American Journal of Sociology* 76 (May): 1064–1071.

1971d. "A Dating-Marriage Scale of Religious Social Distance." *Journal for the Scientific Study of Religion* 10 (Summer): 93–100.

1977. "From Social Movement to Organized Society: The Case of the Anabaptists." *Journal of Voluntary Action Research* 6: 105–111.

1978a. "The Future of a Historic Commune: Amana." *International Review of Modern Sociology* 8 (January–June): 89–101.

1978b. "Roles of the Old in Personal and Impersonal Societies." *The Family Coordinator* 27 (October): 315–319.

1981. "The Contrasting Roles of Women at Oneida Community, the Midwestern Frontier, and the Urban East in the Mid-Nineteenth Century." *Communal Societies* 1: 67–88.

1984a. "Analysis of Health Practices Among the Amish with Reference to Boundary Maintenance." *Communal Societies* 4 (Fall): 67–73.

1984b. "Public and Private Areas and the Survival of Communal Subsocieties." *Journal of Voluntary Action Research* 13: 46–58.

Cavan, Ruth Shonle, ed. 1960. *Marriage and Family in the Modern World: A Book of Readings*. New York: Thomas Y. Crowell. 3rd 1969.

———. ed. 1964 *Readings in Juvenile Delinquency*. Philadelphia: J. B. Lippincott.

———, ed. 1976. "Communes: Historical and Contemporary." Special issue. *International Review of Modern Sociology* 6 (Spring): 1–226.

Coauthored Works

Cavan, Ruth Shonle, Ernest W. Burgess, H. Goldhamer, and R. J. Havighurst. 1949. *Personal Adjustment in Old Age*. Chicago: Science Research Associates. Reprinted, Ayer, 1979.

Cavan, Ruth Shonle, and Jordan T. Cavan. 1927. "The Attitude of Young Business Women Toward Home and Married Life." *Religious Education* 22 (October): 817–820.

———. 1955. "World Trends in Criminology." *Federal Probation* 19 (December): 42–47.

———. 1929. "Education and the Business Girl." *Journal of Educational Sociology* 3 (October): 83–93.

———. 1932. *Building a Girl's Personality: A Social Psychology of Later Girlhood*. New York: Abingdon Press.

———. 1968. *Delinquency and Crime: Cross-Cultural Perspectives*. Philadelphia: J. B. Lippincott.

———, eds. 1971. "Intermarriage in a Comparative Perspective." Special issue. *International Journal of Sociology of the Family* 1 (May): 1–165.

Cavan, Ruth Shonle, and Man Singh Das, eds. 1979. *Communes: Historical and Contemporary*. New Delhi: Vikas.

Cavan, Ruth Shonle, and Theodore Ferdinand. 1981. *Juvenile Delinquency*. Philadelphia: J. B. Lippincott.

Cavan, Ruth Shonle, and Katherine H. Ranck. 1938. *The Family and the Depression: A Study of One Hundred Chicago Families*. Social Science Studies, directed by the Social Science Research Committee of the University of Chicago, No. 35. Chicago: University of Chicago Press. Reprinted, Ayer, 1979.

Cavan, Ruth Shonle, and Eugene Zemans. 1958. "Marital Relationships of Prisoners in Twenty-eight Countries." *Journal of Criminal Law, Criminology, and Police Science* 49 (July–August): 133–139.

Levering, Johnson, Ruth Shonle Cavan, and Eugene S. Zemans. 1963. *Chicago Police Lockups: A History of Reform in Police Handling of Persons in Detention, 1947–1962*. Chicago: John Howard Association.

White House Conference on Child Health and Protection. 1934. *The Adolescent in the Family: A Study of Personality Development in the Home Environment*. Report of the Subcommittee on the Function of Home Activities in the Education of the Child, E. W. Burgess, chairman. Report prepared by Ruth Shonle Cavan. New York: Appleton-Century. Reprinted, Arno, 1972.

Zemans, Eugene, and Ruth Shonle Cavan. 1958. "Marital Relationships of Prisoners." *Journal of Criminal Law, Criminology, and Police Science* 49 (May–June): 50–57.

Unpublished Writings by Ruth Shonle Cavan

1923. "The Isolated Religious Sect." Master's thesis, Department of Sociology, University of Chicago.

1926. "Suicide: A Study of Personal Disorganization." Ph.D. diss., Department of Sociology, University of Chicago.

1972. "Chicago and I."

1987. "Experience in Writing, 1908–1987."

Studies About Ruth Shonle Cavan

Ferdinand, Theodore N. 1988. "Ruth Shonle Cavan: An Intellectual Portrait." *Sociological Inquiry* 58 (Fall): 337–343.

Moyer, Imogene L. 1989. "The Life and Works of Ruth Shonle Cavan: Pioneer Woman in Criminology." *Journal of Crime and Justice* 12, no. 2: 171–201.

Unpublished Material

Kuhn, Terry. 1987a. "Dr. Ruth Shonle Cavan: A Sketch of Her Life in Research and Writing."

———. 1987b. Interviews with Ruth Shonle Cavan.

Moyer, Imogene L. 1985. Interviews with Ruth Shonle Cavan.

———. 1980–1985. Informal conversations and correspondence with Ruth Shonle Cavan.

IMOGENE MOYER

MARY ELIZABETH BURROUGHS ROBERTS SMITH COOLIDGE (1860–1945)

Coolidge was a brilliant sociologist with a bewildering number of names. She pioneered a number of institutional roles for women and intellectual specialties. She was the first full-time female professor in sociology, briefly headed the South Park Social Settlement of San Francisco, and was a statistician on women's poverty. She also was an authority on social welfare, feminism, Chinese immigration to the United States, Victorian sexuality, and native Americans.

BIOGRAPHY

Mary Elizabeth Burroughs Roberts was born in Kingsbury, Indiana, on October 28, 1860, the daughter of Elizabeth Marr and Isaac Phillips Roberts. She had two brothers who are merely mentioned in her biographical literature, but she was deeply attached to her father, a professor and dean of agriculture who taught at Cornell University during most of his daughter's life. This academic heritage appealed deeply to Roberts, and she replicated these early years in her own life. In a brief autobiographical statement, Mary Roberts Coolidge reflected on her father's influence: "It was because of his generous attitude toward all women that I grew up without realizing the conventional limitations of girls in my day." She also praised her mother, who taught her traditional, womanly tasks. "I like it all," she wrote. "I still do—I really enjoy doing the more skillful parts of housekeeping like cooking and mending" ("How I Came to

Write 'Why Women Are So,' " p. 1, Coolidge Papers, Box 17, #5, Bancroft Library, University of California—Berkeley).

She first earned a bachelor's degree at Cornell in 1880, followed by a master's degree in 1882 (see also Florence Kelley* and Frances Kellor*). Roberts worked in a newspaper office in New York City from 1881 to 1882, which must have been an exciting job for the young woman. She taught high school from 1882 to 1884 in Washington, D.C., and then moved to a private school in Cincinnati, Ohio, for the next two years. After these adventures Smith returned to the East Coast, where she became an instructor in economics and history at Wellesley College from 1886 to 1890 (preceding Emily Greene Balch* in this department by nine years). During these years Roberts met a young mechanical engineer, Albert W. Smith, whom she married in 1890 when she adopted his patronym "Smith." Her new husband also was a professor, and after she—now named Smith—stayed home for a few years while he taught at Cornell and the University of Wisconsin, she followed him to the new Leland Stanford University in California.

As Mary Roberts Smith, the name she frequently used during the 1890s, she settled into her new home in California and began graduate work at Stanford in the daring new field of sociology. In 1896 she earned her doctorate there, and from 1894 to 1899 she was an assistant professor of social science; in 1899 she was promoted to an associate professor of sociology. During the 1890s some of her sociological colleagues were E. A. Ross, Amos G. Warner, H. H. Powers, Frank A. Fetter, and George E. Howard. She was the first woman to have a full-time academic position in sociology, and her department had a graduate program rivaling that of the University of Chicago and Columbia University. From 1894 to 1896 and again in 1899–1900 she taught a course on the sociology of the family, and from 1895 to 1898 she taught courses on "Principles of Household Management," "Crime and Penology," and "Charities and Corrections." In 1898 alone she taught courses on racial problems, statistics, poverty, criminology, and penology.

Smith had a lifelong friendship with one of her former students, the feminist scholar Clelia Duel Mosher. The latter earned a bachelor's degree at Wellesley College, a school she entered in 1888, when Smith was on the faculty. Mosher then attended Cornell—another tie between Smith and Mosher—and moved first to the University of Wisconsin and then to Stanford, where she taught in the latter academy from 1894 to 1930 (Coolidge 1932). Mosher's sexual surveys demonstrated that Victorian women had needs similar to those of their contemporary sisters, and this data created considerable controversy both then and in contemporary academic studies. Smith filled out Mosher's questionnaires and even administered them to a small Mothers' Club in Madison, Wisconsin, for her friend. She also helped Mosher with the statistical analysis.

Coolidge had another lifelong tie with a controversial woman: Anita Whitney. In 1925 Whitney, a noted suffragist and social worker, was convicted of criminal syndicalism and sentenced to prison. Coolidge and her husband raised funds, wrote letters, and helped to organize protests against this unjust conviction (see scattered references in Coolidge Papers, Boxes 13 and 15, Bancroft Library, University of California—Berkeley).

Smith worked at Stanford during the hotly contested firing of her colleague E. A. Ross and the dramatic resignations triggered by it in 1900 and 1901 (see Lucile Eaves* and Hattie Plum Williams*). Smith's husband urged her to stay despite the turmoil in the department and her own outrage at Stanford's treatment of her colleagues. Smith was temporarily appointed "major professor," but I am unclear about her permanent status as head of the department at this time. In addition to working in a badly unstaffed department in a university that many scholars condemned for limiting academic freedom, Smith had her own personal problems. Her increasingly unhappy marriage resulted in a painful divorce in 1903. She suffered a "mental collapse" after her divorce and resigned from Stanford for health reasons. She was acutely aware of her "shame" but did not regret her decision in later years.

By 1904 Smith had recovered her health, but Stanford would not rehire her. The new "Mary Elizabeth Burroughs Roberts Smith" accepted a position as the director of South Park Settlement in San Francisco in 1904 (after the resignation of Lucile Eaves). In 1906 an earthquake devastated San Francisco, leveling the settlement along with thousands of other buildings. The same year Roberts made a daring, romantic decision: to marry her somewhat eccentric former student Dane Coolidge. They moved to Berkeley and lived together in great happiness in a home called "Dwight Way End" until Coolidge's death in 1940.

Mary Roberts Coolidge strongly believed in her husband's ability, although his first book was not published until 1910. It was an immediate, if financially small, success. From that time until his death, Dane spent part of every year in the Southwest meticulously documenting the lives of the disappearing cowboys and native Americans. His photographs and detailed ethnography formed the basis for his thirty plus novels, including *Gunsmoke* and the "oldtimer" figure "Scotty," who later became widely known on the television show "Death Valley Days." This ethnographic information also became part of his nonfiction books, including the two books on native Americans that he coauthored with his wife.

Coolidge's sociological career continued in the applied realm outside the academy from 1903 to 1917, although she wanted to return to the academy. During these years she made a name for herself as a researcher, lecturer, city planner, and feminist. Thus her work for the Carnegie Institute resulted in her major study of *Chinese Immigration* (1909b). When she visited China many years later, she was highly regarded and honored as a respected scholar of China and of the Chinese people in America. Her thorough and systematic study of gender, *Why Women Are So* (1912), was a controversial analysis of the social origin of women's behavior. For many of these years she actively led San Francisco women in their struggle to obtain the franchise. In addition, she was a major figure in the women's work for the San Francisco Exhibition of 1915.

These were happy, lively years, although she was removed from the male main-stream in sociology and from graduate training.

In 1918 she finally found another academic position, at a private liberal arts school for women, Mills College. Although she had been hired as a temporary employee in the war effort, her "services were so valuable to the college and her associations so agreeable" (Owen 1945, 4), that her position became a full-time one. Here she established a department of sociology and was its first chair.

She retired from Mills College in 1926, and was given an honorary LL.D. degree from this institution the next year. After "retirement" Coolidge began a new career, as a scholar and author of works on Southwestern and Mexican native Americans. In this capacity she and her husband traveled widely over the sparsely populated lands, photographing a vanishing way of life and documenting the everyday patterns of an inundated people. Although this was physically hard work for a woman in her seventies, the Coolidges enjoyed it immensely. Dane died in 1940, and Mary died quietly on April 13, 1945, after a week's uncon-sciousness. Coolidge had a lively personality, a good singing voice, and a sociable manner. The scattered personal comments on this vivid woman provide a peek at a fascinating "human interest story" (Helen MacGill Hughes*) yet to be told.

MAJOR THEMES

Coolidge's life is marked by major changes, often accompanied by new in-stitutional affiliations and different names. As a result, she has been separately interpreted and noted in vastly different literatures. This is an example of "the social production of great women's obscurity" that emerges from their subor-dinate position in the intellectual enterprise and as wives whose professional lives are altered by their husband's careers, interests, mobility, and patrynomic names (Deegan, in preparation).

The first major theme revolves around the merging of critical pragmatism and cultural feminism, a pattern found in a number of women's writing from 1890 to 1915. Thus Coolidge believed that sociology would lead to reform and amel-ioration of social problems; women's lives were subject to gross inequities, and empirical, statistical documentation of these issues was vital. In the 1880s Cool-idge—then Roberts—was one of the earliest members of the American Collegiate Association (later named the American Association for University Women) along with the Chicago sociologist Marion Talbot.* Roberts and Talbot collaborated on an early study documenting that women could flourish in college instead of being incapacitated by such "unnatural brain work." Roberts continued to study education and women in a number of works (e.g., 1895b, 1898, and 1899a). She often was uneasy about the conflict between being "womanly" and liberated, and she increasingly became aligned with freedom instead of domesticity. Com-parison of her writings in 1899 with those after 1912 reveal this transition.

The second theme concerns her work for people in poverty, particularly women. Her analyses of poverty and old age, catastrophic disasters, and the criminal courts reveal a fundamental commitment to understanding and eliminating human suffering. Smith's dissertation on *Almshouse Women: A Study of Two Hundred and Twenty-Eight Women in the City and County Almshouse of San Francisco* (1896b) is a major document on women's poverty, aging, and relation to the state. It is an extension of her work and training under Warner that she applied to both sexes in her revisions of *American Charities* (1908, 1919). This latter book was one of the most important texts in applied sociology for four decades (see Deegan 1989). It is a compact, well-written analysis of changing social institutions defining deviance and providing welfare services. Coolidge's commitment to applied sociology is seen in her later review of the relief work after the San Francisco earthquake (1906, 1913). Her interest in reforming the night court system is another facet of these applied interests (1899b).

Coolidge's work to alleviate some of the sufferings of the San Francisco earthquake are recorded in a massive summary of social agencies' responses to the disaster. Her portion of the report was coordinated with a wider network of social workers and with another female sociologist, Jessica Peixotto (1913).

A third theme concerns the social construction of women as a distinct group. Coolidge was a major feminist theorist, and this is most visible in her insightful book on gender, *Why Women Are So* (1912). This text is based on her working hypothesis that "sex traditions rather than innate sex character have produced what is called 'feminine' as distinguished from womanly behavior" (p. v). This assumption reveals her "cultural feminism" rooted in the work of W. I. Thomas (see Jessie Taft*), Lester Ward (see Charlotte Perkins Gilman*), and H. G. Wells (see Jane Addams*). Coolidge believed that mothers made a major contribution to society, but this was not women's only contribution. Women, in general, were limited throughout their lives through dress, language, and the marketplace. Token women escaped some traditional female problems, but they experienced continuing problems in some aspects of their lives as well. She spent years arguing that women's suffrage did not alter the nature of politics, but was only a step toward increasing women's entry into that arena (e.g., 1914a, 1914b, and 1922). Coolidge used the argument that women must assume "wider citizenship" for economic and political and personal liberation.

A fourth theme revolves around the lives of minority people in the United States and in Mexico. Coolidge's first major study in this specialization was her study of *Chinese Immigration* (1909b). It is a meticulous classic statement on the issue. Here she combined a study of law and history to document the racial relations cycle between this exploited group and the white community. Her hard-hitting approach squarely puts the blame for Chinese social problems in the hands of the occidental majority. Her analysis of "Competition and assimilation" predated the more well-known work of Park and Burgess (1921) by more than two decades. Her work is much more sophisticated as well, for the men assume that a simplistic "free competition" occurs in all human society, whereas she reveals that competition was feared by the white community, who fought it with racist propaganda against the Chinese in America. Assimilation, to Coolidge, depended on the freedom to vote, speak, and work, and did not mean an erasure of culture and community. Coolidge's book is an overlooked gem of scholarship and theoretical power.

Coolidge specialized in a new area of minority studies after her "retirement" from Mills College: the study of native Americans. In 1929 she published her highly successful book on *The Rain-Makers: Indians of Arizona and New Mexico*. She cited and dedicated this book to the archaeologist Edgar Lee Hewitt, and used the materials of Elsie Clews Parsons,* but her relations with these anthropologists is unknown.

Dane Coolidge and Mary Roberts Coolidge joined forces in both *The Navajo Indians* (1930) and *The Last of the Seris* (1939). Although some academic critics find the Coolidges' books flawed by their popular language style—and everyone decries their occasionally condescending tone—the authors spent decades in academic training, ethnography, and work in the Southwest. Their meticulous documentation, photography, clear language, and theoretical clarity are a major contribution to our knowledge of a people oppressed by whites and Anglos.

CRITIQUES OF MARY E.B.R.S. COOLIDGE

I have studied Mary E.B.R.S. Coolidge for the past fifteen years—along with dozens of other early women sociologists—and can finally advance a few definite statements about her brilliance, life, and career. First, Coolidge was an outstanding and fearless leader in sociology who has been forgotten. Second, as a divorced and remarried woman with a doctorate and on the West Coast, she was outside the major female network in American sociology located in her era in Chicago. Third, Coolidge's wide-ranging changes in institutions, specializations, audiences for her writings, and names have created Balkanized critiques. Fourth, the death of her powerful mentor, Amos G. Warner, the disintegration of the sociology group at Stanford, her long and varied life, and her personal independence combined to make Coolidge a paradoxically powerful outsider in her own profession. These convoluted issues can only be hinted at here.

The major published study on "Smith" is on her "expertise on Victorian sexuality." Her work on behalf of Mosher led a subsequent biographer, Rosalind Rosenberg (1982), to mistakenly assume that sexuality was Smith's major specialization.

Frederick Dockstader's introduction to the 1971 reprint of *The Last of the Seris* is filled with similar types of problems. It contains a gold mine of information, embedded in considerable errors about the "amateur anthropologists" who wrote it. Ironically, better methodological information about the last stage of the Coolidges' lives is found in the University of Arizona Press's reprints of Dane Coolidge's ethnographies on cowboys (e.g., c. 1929; Ulph 1985).

[Smith] Coolidge's books were originally well received in professional journals. Gehlke's review (1919) of the third edition of *American Charities*, for
example, noted that the text "has remained the standard summary statement of
problems and methods in this field" (p. 720) for a quarter of a century. Hannah
B. Clark Powell found that *Why Women Are So* presented a convincing argument.
She ended her review by calling for a cessation of all limitations on women
(1913).

My own studies of Coolidge place her in the mainstream of sociological thought
and founding leaders. The first female sociologist in a graduate coeducational
institution, Coolidge is important for historical reasons alone. Her major revisions
of *American Charities* were significant contributions to course work in and
organization of the new field of applied sociology (Deegan 1989). Her complicated institutional and patrynomic name changes point to a major issue for
professional women: maintaining reputations with different married names over
time (Deegan, in preparation). Coolidge's exciting life and ideas have yet to be
adequately documented, and such work will enhance our understanding of wom-
en's contributions to sociology in a dramatic way. Coolidge is one of the most
important female sociologists who worked during the Golden Era of sociology.
I have started to fill in some of the gaps in the scholarship on her. Her central
role as the modest author who rewrote Warner's *American Charities* is partially
addressed in my introduction to the reprint of that work (Deegan 1989). The
"power of patrynomic naming" and the general, theoretical issues of naming
and women's dependence on men's mobility are discussed in my most recent
work (Deegan, in preparation). Extensive analysis of the biographical location
of this leading feminist sociologist remains to be done.

BIBLIOGRAPHY

Selected Writings by Mary E.B.R.S. Coolidge

Smith, Mary Roberts

1895a. "Almshouse Women." *Publications of the American Statistical Association* 4
       (September): 219–262.
1895b. "Recent Tendencies in the Education of Women." *Popular Science Monthly* 48
       (November): 27–33.
1896a. "Remarks on a Paper by Edward D. Jones, 'Round Numbers in Wages and
       Prices.' " *Publications of the American Statistical Association* 5 (September–
       December): 141.
1896b. *Almshouse Women: A Study of Two Hundred and Twenty-Eight Women in the
       City and County Almshouses of San Francisco*. Leland Stanford University Pub-
       lications. History and Economics, Vol. 3. Stanford, CA: Stanford University.
1898. "Education for Domestic Life." *Popular Science Monthly* 53 (August): 521–525.
1899a. "Domestic Services." *Forum* 27 (August): 678–689.

1899b. "Social Aspects of the New York Police Courts." *American Journal of Sociology* 5 (September): 145–154.

1900. "Statistics of College and Non-College Women." *Publications of the American Statistical Association* 7 (March–June): 1–26.

1901. "Bequest of Kamenamecha." *Charities* 13 (October): 12–16.

Coolidge, Mary Roberts

1906. "Relief Work in Its Social Bearings." *Charities* 16 (June 2): 308–311.

1909a. "Chinese Labor Competition on the Pacific Coast." *Annals of the American Academy of Political and Social Science* 34 (September): 340–350.

1909b. *Chinese Immigration.* New York: Henry Holt.

1912. *Why Women Are So.* New York: Henry Holt.

1913. "How Men Look to Women." *Harper's Weekly* 58 (August 23): 27–29.

1914a. "California Women and the Abatement Law." *Survey* 34 (March 14): 739–740.

1914b. "A Try-Out of Women Voters." *Harper's Weekly* 59 (October 10): 355–356.

1915. "Political Drama in San Francisco." *Harper's Weekly* 61 (November 27): 524.

1916. *What the Women of California Have Done with the Ballot.* San Francisco: California Civic League.

1929a. "The West—of One Woman." *Woman's Journal* 14 (January): 47.

1929b. "Hope Ahead for the Indians." *Woman's Journal* 14 (August): 5–7.

1929c. *The Rain-Makers: Indians of Arizona and New Mexico.* Boston: Houghton Mifflin.

1941. "Clelia Duel Mosher, the Scientific Feminist." *Research Quarterly of the American Physical Education Association* 12 (October): 633–645.

Coauthored Works

Coolidge, Dane, and Mary Roberts Coolidge. 1930. *The Navajo Indians.* Boston: Houghton Mifflin.

———.1939. *The Last of the Seris.* New York: E. P. Dutton. Reprinted, Rio Grande Press, 1971.

O'Connor, Charles J., Francis H. McLean, Helen Swett Artieda, James M. Motley, Jessica Peixotto, and Mary Roberts Coolidge. 1913. *The San Francisco Relief Survey: The Organization and Methods of Relief Used after the Earthquake and Fires of April 18, 1906.* New York: Survey Associates, Russell Sage Foundation.

Warner, Amos G. 1908. *American Charities,* revised by Mary Roberts Coolidge, with a biographical preface by George E. Howard. 2nd ed. New York: Thomas Y. Crowell. 3rd ed., 1919.

Unpublished Works by Mary E.B.R.S. Coolidge

Coolidge, Mary Roberts. "How I Came to Write *Why Women Are So*," October 1915? Coolidge Papers, Box 17, #5, Bancroft Library, University of California—Berkeley.

———. 1932. "Clelia Duel Mosher—the Questioner." Clelia Mosher Papers, SC 11, Cecil H. Green Library, Stanford University, University Archives.

Studies About Mary E.B.R.S. Coolidge and Supplemental References

Colcord, Joanna C. 1930. "From Charity to a Profession." *Survey* 65 (November 15): 231.

Coolidge, Coit. 1971. "Memoriam." In *The Last of the Seris,* by Dane Coolidge and Mary Roberts Coolidge. Glorieta, NM: Rio Grande Press.

Coolidge, Dane. 1929. *Texas Cowboys.* Reprint. Tucson: University of Arizona Press, 1985.

Dockstader, Frederick J. 1971. "Published Correspondence." In *The Last of the Seris,* by Dane Coolidge and Mary Roberts Coolidge. Glorieta, NM: Rio Grande Press.

Deegan, Mary Jo. 1987. "An American Dream: The Historical Connections Between Women, Humanism, and Sociology, 1890–1920." *Humanity and Society* 11 (August): 353–365.

———. 1988a. *Jane Addams and the Men of the Chicago School, 1892–1916.* New Brunswick, NJ: Transaction Books.

———. 1988b. "Transcending a Patriarchal Past: Teaching the History of Early Female Sociologists." *Teaching Sociology* 16 (April): 141–150.

———. 1989. "Introduction to the Transaction Edition: *American Charities* as the Herald to a New Age." In *American Charities: A Study in Philanthropy and Economics,* by Amos G. Warner, p. ix–xxviiii. New Brunswick, NJ: Transaction Books.

———. In preparation. "A Rose Is Not a Rosa, Is Not a Roseann: The Many Names of Mary Elizabeth Burroughs Roberts Smith Coolidge." In *Women's Narratives,* edited by Judith Long.

Degler, Carl N. 1980. "Introduction." In *The Mosher Survey: Sexual Attitudes of 45 Victorian Women,* by Clelia Duel Mosher, edited by James MaHood and Kristine Wenburg, p. xi–xix. New York: Arno Press.

Gehlke, C. E. 1919. "Review of *American Charities,* by Amos G. Warner, revised by Mary Roberts Coolidge." *American Journal of Sociology* 24 (May): 720–721.

Howard, George E. 1908. "Biographical Preface." In *American Charities,* by Amos G. Warner, revised by Mary Roberts Coolidge, p. v–xvii. 2nd ed. New York: Crowell.

———. 1919. "Biographical Preface." In *American Charities,* by Amos G. Warner, revised by Mary Roberts Coolidge, p. v–xv. 3rd ed. New York: Crowell.

Leonard, John William, ed. 1914. *Women's Who's Who in America.* New York: American Commonwealth.

McCoy, Robert B. 1971. "Publisher's Preface." In *The Last of the Seris,* by Dane Coolidge and Mary Roberts Coolidge. Glorieta, NM: Rio Grande Press.

MaHood, James. 1980. "Preface." In *The Mosher Survey: Sexual Attitudes of 45 Victorian Women,* by Clelia Duel Mosher, edited by James MaHood and Kristine Wenburg, p. v–ix. New York: Arno Press.

Owen, Elizabeth Kenyon. 1945. "Mary Roberts Coolidge, An Appreciation." *Mills Quarterly* 28 (May): 3–4.

Park, Robert E., and Ernest W. Burgess. 1921. *Introduction to the Science of Sociology.* Chicago: University of Chicago Press.

Powell, Hannah B. Clark. 1913. "Review of *Why Women Are So.*" *American Journal of Sociology* 18 (May): 825–827.

Rosenberg, Rosalind. 1982. *Beyond Separate Spheres*. New Haven, CT: Yale University Press.

Ulph, Owen. 1985. "Dane Coolidge: An Appreciation." In *Texas Cowboys*, by Dane Coolidge, p. 1–9. Tucson: University of Arizona Press.

Watson, Katherine C. 1916. "The Women's Civic League of California." *Survey* 36 (September 16): 601–605.

MARY JO DEEGAN

ROSE LAUB COSER (1916–   )

Rose Laub Coser is an international expert on women, work, and leadership. Her major theoretical emphases are the study of bureaucratic organizations, socialization, and social structure. Specifically, she has written about medical settings, especially hospitals, and about the family, focusing on the social roles of women at home and at work.

BIOGRAPHY

Rose Laub was born on May 4, 1916, in war-torn Berlin, Germany. Her parents were Elias and Rachel Lachowsky Laub. They were socialists associated with Rosa Luxemburg at the time of their daughter's birth, and they named their baby after this esteemed friend. Despondent after the shocking post–World War I events—from the murder of Luxemburg and Karl Liebknecht in 1919 to the early Hitler Putsch in 1923—and disillusioned with the politics of the radical parties, her parents moved the family at the beginning of 1924 to Antwerp, Belgium, where Rose spent most of her childhood and adolescence. She obtained a classical education and mastered four languages during these years. Young Rose was a foreigner, socialist, and Jew, but these outsider statuses were balanced by her multilingual talents and the socialist culture in which she matured. She notes: "My knowledge of languages early on also made me feel that, while I was lacking in many things, this was something that was special. I also believe now that I owe to my knowledge of languages (6, including Latin and Greek) my penchant for structural analysis" (Coser to author, p. 5, August 23, 1989).

The Laub family emigrated to the United States in 1939 after the 1938 invasion of Czechoslovakia (see Alice Masaryk*). In 1941 Rose met Lewis Coser, who later became an eminent conflict theorist. He, too, had been born in Berlin, and had studied in Paris at the Sorbonne from 1934 to 1938. He also shared her political commitment to socialism. He emigrated to the United States in 1941, where he met Rose, and in 1942 they married. Later both Cosers became naturalized citizens. Like so many other eminent women in sociology during this dark era, she developed a cooperative and collegial relationship with her husband, with the important distinction that his career took precedence over hers (e.g., Helen MacGill Hughes* and Caroline Baer Rose*). As Coser notes:

It was Lew who suggested I go to graduate school before he ever thought of going back himself. . . . At every step, even today, he pushes me on and on. And our daily tasks were very important to both our careers, especially during the early years. I want you to be aware of the fact that, while a woman stays somewhat behind because of household and child-care responsibilities, there is also a trade-off. If it hadn't been for Lew I would probably have followed the path of so many fifties women who didn't develop a career at all, and if they did, could not have learned as much. (Personal communication, Coser to author, August 23, 1989. p. 6)

Thus she provides us with a needed insight into the processes of history and circumstance surrounding many of the most eminent women trained during the dark era who almost always were able to survive through the support of a strong male ally in the profession.

The Cosers had two children, Ellen Coser Perrin and Steven, who were born in 1943 and 1953, respectively. Rose assumed the primary responsibility for their child care, while Lewis pursued his sociological career (see Rose Coser's theoretical discussion of this dual responsibility of women in 1981). Shortly after Ellen's birth, Rose continued her studies in philosophy at the Ecole Libre des Hautes Etudes, from 1943 to 1945. This institution had relocated from Nazi-occupied Paris to New York City during these years. It called itself a university in exile and operated as a branch of the New School for Social Research. In 1945 she was certified in philosophy from this school.

In 1947–1948, while a graduate student at Columbia University, Rose Coser was a research assistant to the psychoanalyst Rene Spitz in New York. Having fulfilled her graduate requirements, she accompanied her husband to the University of Chicago where he was to be an instructor in sociology. Rose was a research associate to David Riesman (see Virginia Olesen*) for the next two years. Rose and Lewis returned to New York for Lewis to complete his education. Rose also resumed her work with Rene Spitz from 1950 to 1951. Rose and Lewis both studied at Columbia University, where she was a student of Robert S. Lynd (see Helen Merrill Lynd*) and Robert Merton (see Mirra Komarovsky*). Lewis earned his doctorate there in 1954, and Rose earned her master's degree in 1951 and her doctorate in 1957.

Rose assumed her first full-time academic position in 1951, when she joined the faculty at Wellesley College. She left Wellesley as an assistant professor in 1959 to work in the psychiatry department at Harvard Medical School, where she remained for the next seven years. From 1959 to 1964 her work was funded by grants from the National Institute of Mental Health. She rose from assistant to associate in psychiatry during these years. From 1965 to 1968 she was an associate professor at Northeastern University in Boston, while she retained her position at Harvard from 1966 to 1968. In 1969 Coser and several colleagues prepared the posthumous publication of Anne Parsons's work in structural and psychological anthropology (Parsons 1969). Finally, in 1968, the Cosers both obtained positions as professors at a major graduate university, the State University of New York at Stony Brook (see her discussion of joint positions in Coser 1971). Rose currently is emerita professor there.

She is a member of numerous professional organizations, including the American Sociological Association (ASA) and the Society for the Study of Social Problems. She was president of the latter organization in 1973–1974, and in 1985–1986 she served as vice-president of the ASA, the year Matilda White Riley* was president, and as president of the Eastern Sociological Society. She also worked with Helen MacGill Hughes (1973) in the production of the report on *The Status of Women in Sociology, 1968–1972*.

Travel and research have been combined throughout Coser's life. She continues her active scholarship within this international framework. She currently is finishing a book on *The World of Our Mothers*.

MAJOR THEMES

Coser is an expert on labor in bureaucracies. She emphasizes how people learn certain behaviors and how social patterns shape our choices for action. Her application of these ideas occurs primarily in medical settings and in women's work.

Coser published a series of articles on hospitals (1956, 1958, 1960, 1961) that are major statements on the influence of bureaucracies and the organization of medical work on patients' care and recovery. For example, the arrangement and nature of surgery create a more authoritarian structure of labor and services compared with other types of medical services. The greater the observability of bureaucratic labor, the greater the conformity and adherence to professional standards. Portions of these articles were coordinated with new material in Coser's tightly written classic *Life in the Ward*, published in 1962. She convincingly argues here that the delivery of medical care is structured by the bureaucratic organization of work instead of by personalities or medical ideology alone. She adopted the perspective of the patient, using the role concepts of Talcott Parsons and Robert Merton to analyze the interaction between sickness, medical labor, and bureaucratic organization.

"Role" is a central concept in Coser's writings, elaborating on the work of Robert K. Merton. Her major reinterpretation of Erving Goffman's dramaturgical concept of "role distance" explains the separation of the self from expected norms and behaviors as a function of structured ambivalence in a social status

(1966). This socially patterned role is once more examined in her remarkable book *Training in Ambiguity* (1979). Here she studies the hazy boundaries between being an authority as a psychiatrist in a mental hospital, while learning how to become a psychiatrist. This patterned ambiguity affects other hospital staff and patients. When the structure of roles and contacts between patients and staffs breaks down, normlessness, or anomie, can appear and become visible through suicidal outbreaks among patients.

Social structure and its relation to the family are major themes in Coser's work. Her anthology on the family has a structural focus that is cross-cultural and cross-disciplinary (1964, 1974). This theme is reflected in a fascinating debate with Judith Lorber, Alice S. Rossi,* and Coser, in which they each critiqued the neo-Freudian view of mothering by Nancy Chodorow (Lorber, Coser, Rossi, and Chodorow 1981). Coser accepted some of Chodorow's argument but extended it to include more structural issues of the economy, and politics, and stressed a more social basis of parenting than Chodorow, a neo-Freudian, did.

Coser explains public resistance to busing children as a perceived threat of invasion into guarded territory. Geographical displacement, as she well understood from her own experience, is linked to social relations and change (1975a).

In her recent book on cross-national studies of women and elites (Epstein and Coser 1981), Coser showed how women consistently fill low-status, relatively powerless, and poorly paid occupations in the United States, Israel, and Russia. She uses Alice Rossi's concept of "diminishing flow" to explain this and the relation between the increasing presence of women in an occupation and its decreasing rewards (Epstein and Coser 1981, 17).

Very different styles of writing, theoretical approach, and authority are found in Coser's socialist work, especially that published in *Dissent*. In these articles Coser displays a penetrating political and feminist critique that is less evident in her more "objective" structural articles in her books and in mainstream sociology journals. For example, Alexandra (Aleksandra) Kollantai* is treated as an important feminist in Coser's review essay of *Bolshevik Feminist*, by B. E. Clements, and *Aleksandra Kollantai*, by B. Farnsworth (see bibliography of these books in Kollantai entry). But Coser casts serious doubts on Kollantai's integrity under the Stalin regime: "Yet in the end she capitulated completely, agreeing to make changes in her previous writings that would indict former colleagues, and acquiescing to everything demanded of her" (Coser 1982a, 235).

CRITIQUES OF ROSE LAUB COSER

Most of Coser's books have been widely reviewed and well received. *Life in the Ward* (1962) was particularly the focus of a number of critiques over a variety of disciplines. Rather than summarize this readily available body of critique, I summarize the scholarly work that extends or elaborates on her corpus.

The majority of Coser's critics and allies have emphasized her theme of the structural importance of roles. For example, Robert A. Stebbins (1967) critiqued Coser's structural analysis of role distance, presenting an interactionist counterpoint to her structural role analysis. Robert K. Merton, her mentor, colleague, and friend, is a strong advocate of Coser's work and, of course, an advocate of structural role analysis. His laudatory foreword (1979) to *Training in Ambiguity* compares Coser's work with classic monographs in organizational studies. A similar, empirical support for this position is found in a study by Judith Blau and Richard Alba. These authors examined six psychiatric facilities for children to discover patterns of participation by the patients and staff. Their "empowering nets of participation" show that complex organizational structure encourages democratic participation, whereas weaker bureaucratic structure discourages participation (1982). This organizational interpretation supports Coser's work on ambiguity in psychiatric settings.

Nancy Chodorow, the social objects feminist, represents a perspective that emphasizes the early years of socialization and women's mothering as a social construction. Coser's critique of Chodorow emphasizes the possibility of greater change for adult women than Chodorow's. The latter appears more pessimistic than Coser about movement from the society to the individual as a source of increased opportunities for women. Chodorow states that it is the "political organization that follows from women's mothering" (Lorber, Coser, Rossi, and Chodorow 1981, 509) to counter Coser's more logical argument that men control both political organization and the kinship structure.

Edward D. Boldt (1978) applied Coser's concept of "observability" in his study of Hutterite conformity. He contrasts her structural analysis of behavior to psychological and social psychological theories that stress internalization of norms and a dependence of approval to explain the community's limited patterns of deviance. This continues the debate reflected in Chodorow's reply.

In a series of studies, Mark LaGory is building a specialization in the sociology of space (e.g., 1982, 1988) that uses Coser's concepts of complexity of roles (Coser 1975b), cognitive structures, and their relation to social space (N.B. Coser 1986). LaGory finds that social groups develop patterns of thinking about space, reflected in conceptual and mapping skills, based on neighborhood and other urban experiences (1988).

Finally, and most recently, Coser's concept of a "seedbed of complexity" was supported by the research of Phyllis Moen, Robin W. Williams, Jr., and Donna Dempster-McCain (1989). They found that women's greater social integration with multiple roles was associated with greater longevity. Thus Coser's work is a source of both theoretical debate and empirical examination. Her socialist and feminist writings have room for considerable exploration, pointing to some new areas of critique and analysis.

ACKNOWLEDGMENT

My thanks to Rose Coser for her thoughtful and careful critique of an earlier draft of this entry. Her letters of August 23, 1989, March 14, 1990, March 21,

1990, and March 29, 1990, were extremely helpful. I assume responsibility for this final form, and appreciate the difficulty of reading about oneself and one's work in this introductory overview.

BIBLIOGRAPHY

Selected Writings of Rose Laub Coser

1951. "Political Involvement and Interpersonal Relations." *Psychiatry* 14 (May): 213–222.

1956. "A Home Away from Home." *Social Problems* 4 (July): 3–17.

1958. "Authority and Decision-Making in a Hospital: A Comparative Analysis." *American Sociological Review* 23 (February): 56–63.

1959. "Some Social Functions of Humor." *Human Relations* 12 (May): 171–182.

1960. "Laughter Among Colleagues: A Study of the Social Functions of Humor Among the Staff of a Mental Hospital." *Psychiatry* 23 (February): 81–95.

1961. "Insulation from Observability and Types of Conformity." *American Sociological Review* 26 (February): 28–39.

1962. *Life in the Ward*. East Lansing, MI: Michigan State University Press.

1963. "Alienation and the Social Structure." In *The Hospital in Modern Society*, edited by Eliot Freidson, pp. 231–265. New York: Free Press.

1966. "Role Distance, Sociological Ambivalence and Transitional Status Systems." *American Journal of Sociology* 72 (September): 173–187.

1967. "Evasiveness as a Response to Structural Ambivalence." *Social Science and Medicine* 6 (August): 203–218.

1971. "On Nepotism and Marginality." *American Sociologist* 6 (August): 259–260.

1975a. "Stay Home, Little Sheba: On Placement, Displacement and Social Change." *Social Problems* 22 (April): 470–480.

1975b. "The Complexity of Roles as a Seedbed of Individual Autonomy." In *The Idea of Social Structure: Papers in Honor of Robert K. Merton*, pp. 237–263. New York: Harcourt Brace Jovanovich.

1975c. "Affirmative Action: Letter to a Worried Colleague." *Dissent* 22 (Fall): 207–210.

1976a. "Das Mannereich Universitat: Diskriminierungen in den USA der in der Sowjetunion." *Geissener Universitatsblatter* 9 (December): 38–49.

1976b. "Suicide and the Relational System—A Case Study in a Mental Hospital." *Journal of Health and Social Behavior* 17 (December): 318–327.

1977. "Why Bother: Are Research Issues of Women's Health Worthwhile?" In *Women and Their Health: Research Implications for a New Era*, edited by Virginia Olesen, p. 3–9. Washington, DC: Department of Health, Education, and Welfare.

1978. "The Principle of Patriarchy: The Case of the Magic Flute."*Signs* 4 (Winter): 337–348.

1979. *Training in Ambiguity: Learning Through Doing in a Mental Hospital*, foreword by Robert K. Merton. New York: Free Press.

1981. "Where Have All the Women Gone? Like the Sediment of a Good Wine They Have Sunk to the Bottom." In *Access to Power: Cross-National Studies of Women and Elites*, edited by Cynthia Fuchs Epstein and Rose Laub Coser, p. 16–33. Boston: Free Press.

1982a. "Portrait of a Bolshevik Feminist." *Dissent* 29 (Spring): 235–239.

1982b. "The American Family: Changing Patterns of Social Control." In *Social Control: Views from the Social Sciences*, edited by Jack P. Gibbs, pp. 187–203. Beverly Hills, CA: Russell Sage Foundation.

1984. "The Greedy Nature of Gemeinschaft." In *Conflict and Consensus*, edited by Walter W. Powell and Richard Robbins, p. 221–240. New York: Free Press.

1986. "Cognitive Structure and the Use of Social Space." *Sociological Forum* 1 (Winter): 1–26.

1990. *In Defense of Modernity: Complexity of Social Roles and Individual Autonomy*. Palo Alto, CA: Stanford University Press.

In press. *The World of Our Mothers*. New York: Russell Sage Foundation.

Coser, Rose Laub, ed.

1964. *The Family, Its Structure and Its Functions*. New York: St. Martin's Press. 2nd ed., 1974.

1969. *Life Cycle and Achievement in America*. New York: Harper & Row.

Coauthored Works

Coser, Lewis A., and Rose Laub Coser. 1963. "Time Perspective and the Social Structure." In *Modern Sociology*, edited by Alvin M. Gouldner and Helen P. Goulder, pp. 251–265. New York: Harcourt Brace Jovanovich.

———. 1974. "The Housewife and Her Greedy Family." In *Greedy Institutions*, edited by Lewis Coser, pp. 89–100. New York: Free Press.

Coser, Rose Laub, and Lewis A. Coser. 1972. "The Principles of Legitimacy and Its Patterned Infringement." In *Cross-National Family Research*, edited by Mavin B. Sussman and Betty Cogswell, pp. 119–130. Leiden: E. J. Brill.

———. 1979. "Jonestown as Perverse Utopia." *Dissent* 26 (Spring): 158–263.

Coser, Rose, and Gerald Rokoff. 1971. "Women in the Occupational World: Social Disruption and Conflict." *Social Problems* 18 (Spring): 535–554.

Epstein, Cynthia Fuchs, and Rose Laub Coser, eds. 1981. *Access to Power: Cross-National Studies of Women and Elites*. Boston: Allen & Unwin.

Lorber, Judith, Rose Laub Coser, Alice S. Rossi, and Nancy Chodorow. 1981. "On *The Reproduction of Mothering*: A Methodological Debate." *Signs* 6 (Spring): 482–514.

Parsons, Anne. 1969. *Belief, Magic, and Anomie*, edited posthumously by Rose Laub Coser et al. New York: Free Press.

Tanur, Judith M., and Rose Laub Coser. 1978. "Pockets of 'Poverty' in the Salaries of Academic Women." *American Association of University Professors Bulletin* 64, no. 1: 26–30.

Studies About Rose Laub Coser and Supplementary References

Blau, Judith, and Richard Alba. 1982. "Empowering Nets of Participation." *Administrative Science Quarterly* 27 (September): 363–379.

Boldt, Edward D. 1978. "Structural Tightness, Autonomy, and Observability: An Analysis of Hutterite Conformity and Orderliness." *Canadian Journal of Sociology* 3, no. 3: 349–363.

Chodorow, Nancy. 1978. *The Reproduction of Mothering: Psychoanalysis and the Sociology of Gender*. Berkeley: University of California Press.

Hughes, Helen MacGill. 1973. *The Status of Women in Sociology, 1968–1972*. Washington, DC: American Sociological Association.

LaGory, Mark. 1982. "Toward a Sociology of Space: The Constrained Choice Model." *Symbolic Interaction* 5 (Spring): 65–78.

———. 1988. "The Organization of Space and the Character of the Urban Experience." *Publius: The Journal of Federalism* 18 (Fall): 71–89.

Moen, Phyllis, Robin W. Williams, Jr., and Donna Dempster-McCain. 1989. "Social Integration and Longevity: An Event History Analysis of Women's Roles and Resilience." *American Sociological Review* 54 (August): 635–647.

Stebbins, Robert A. 1967. "A Note on the Concept of Role Distance." *American Journal of Sociology* 73 (September): 247–250.

Warren, Donald I. 1968. "Power Visibility, and Conformity in Formal Organizations." *American Sociological Review* 26 (December): 951–970.

MARY JO DEEGAN

KATHARINE BEMENT DAVIS
(1860–1935)

Katharine Bement Davis was a feisty and popular sociologist and political figure. She held important positions in the women's reformatory movement, in municipal and state governments, and in politics. Her writings on women's sexuality and the early women's prison are classic and original statements.

BIOGRAPHY

Katharine Bement Davis was born in Buffalo, New York, on January 15, 1860, the eldest of three daughters. She also had two brothers. Her mother, Frances Bement, fought for antislavery, temperance, and women's rights. Katharine's father was Oscar Bill Davis, a successful businessman who suffered financial reverses in the late 1870s. Her family moved to Dunkirk, New York, when she was a toddler, and she attended grammar schools here. Despite the family's financial constraints, "lessons in music, dancing and 'art' " were added to the children's routine studies, and their childhood home "was always a center for neighborhood good times" (Davis 1933, 58).

In 1877 the family moved to Rochester, New York, where Davis graduated from the Rochester Free Academy in 1879. Because of family debts, she contributed to the family income by teaching chemistry and physics for a decade in the local high school in Dunkirk. This determined young woman continued her education by studying at night, which allowed her to enter Vassar College in 1890 as a junior, graduating with a bachelor's degree and Phi Beta Kappa in 1892. She then taught sciences at Brooklyn Heights Seminary in the morning and studied chemistry at Columbia University in the afternoon.

In 1893 she conducted an experiment on behalf of the New York State Commission for the World's Fair in Chicago. They built and furnished "A Workingman's Model Home" to illustrate life outside New York City on an annual income of $600. Davis installed a real family on the premises and demonstrated their daily life, including menus, to the interested public (Logan 1912). Jane Addams,* Anna Garlin Spencer,* Edith Abbott,* Marion Talbot,* and other daring female social scientists also visited this international centerpiece that flourished a few blocks away from the new University of Chicago.

In the fall of 1893 Davis assumed the head worker position at the College Settlement of Philadelphia, cofounded by socially committed young women who had completed their college education but lacked vocational opportunities. Davis worked there for four years, but found the work stressful and unsatisfactory. In 1897 she returned to school, this time attending that daring pioneer experiment in higher education, the University of Chicago. There she studied with Thorstein Veblen, W. I. Thomas, Marion Talbot, George Vincent (who later became President of the Rockefeller Foundation), Albion Small, and Charles Henderson (Davis 1933, 61). In 1898–1899 she was awarded a European Fellowship from the New England Women's Educational Association, and she studied in Berlin and Vienna, as her male mentors in Chicago had done. In 1900 she earned her doctorate in political economy and sociology (Logan 1912: 538). During these years Davis collected statistical data on the housing conditions of Bohemian immigrants in Chicago for a committee headed by Jane Addams (Report by the Investigating Committee of the City Homes Association 1901, 3). Davis also met a lifelong colleague and friend, Mary B. Harris (Davis 1933: 61; Harris 1934), while she was studying in Chicago.

Davis was recruited by Josephine Shaw Lowell through the latter's ties with Marion Talbot to become the first superintendent of the New York State Reformatory for Women at Bedford Hills. She worked here for thirteen years, recruiting in her turn a group of able female investigators from the University of Chicago to conduct research on women criminals (see Jessie Taft*). Her numerous innovations in female penology are considered in depth in Estelle Freedman's excellent book (1981) on this topic.

In the middle of her tenure as superintendent at Bedford Hills, in 1909, Davis was traveling in Europe when a severe earthquake devastated Medina, Sicily. Davis instantly began organizing emergency relief, workshops, clothing distribution, and financial aid through the American Red Cross (Davis 1909b). For her amazing and indefatigable work, Davis was awarded medals from the Red Cross and King Victor Emmanuel of Italy and a commendation from the pope.

Davis experienced a rapid growth in power and national visibility after 1912. In this year John D. Rockefeller funded a major experimental and research project on female criminals, led by Davis and called the Laboratory for Social Hygiene. Through this position and later ones, Davis played a pivotal role in placing female sociologists trained at the University of Chicago in Eastern, particularly New York City, networks (see Jessie Taft and Frances Kellor*). She also worked closely with one of her Chicago mentors, Charles Henderson, in a variety of national and international prison reform issues. Finally, she helped to establish the Bureau of Social Hygiene, and was an active contributor to its journal, *Social Hygiene*. Her writings on women's sexuality made her a controversial author and public figure (Fitzpatrick 1990).

Several honorary degrees were bestowed on Davis, acknowledging her public and academic leadership—a doctor of laws degree from Mount Holyoke College in 1912, an honorary degree from Western Reserve in 1914, and a master's degree from Yale University in 1915. She also became a trustee of her alma mater, Vassar College. In 1916 she took part in the Republican party's presidential campaign. In this role she stomped across the United States giving speeches and meeting voters, often from a railcar platform (Davis 1916b).

Davis's pivotal place in the female network of sociologists, progressives, and suffragists was recognized in the list of sponsors of her testimonial dinner on her retirement in 1928. Here we find Grace Abbott, Sophonisba Breckinridge*; the suffragist Carrie Chapman Catt; Mary Drier of the Women's Trade Union League; the noted investigator of medical schools and social hygienist Abraham Flexner; the progressive minister John Haynes Holmes; Paul Kellogg, editor of *The Survey*; Mary Simkovitch; Anna Garlin Spencer; Mary van Kleeck*; Lilian Wald, head of Henry Street Settlement; and Mary E. Wooley, president of Mount Holyoke College and suffragist ("Katharine Bement Davis, Testimonial Dinner," 1928). Davis tried in vain to have her autobiography published during the Great Depression. A short, spirited account of her life was published in 1933 in which she warned her readers not to "look for 'glamorous' affairs" (1933, 58). Her friend Mary B. Harris fills in some information on Davis's professional life (Harris 1934), and Ellen Fitzpatrick provides a more in-depth analysis of the arduous path that Davis walked.

MAJOR THEMES

Davis wrote three dry and precise pieces on traditional political economy issues: the price of farm products, published in 1898; a statistical error in Austrian wage figures, published in 1899; and wages of Bohemian laborers, published in 1900. In between these correct analyses, Davis wrote a strong review of W.E.B DuBois and Isabel Eaton and their project, *The Philadelphia Negro* (1900). After writing her conservative analyses for the University of Chicago's major journal in political economy, Davis turned her back on this approach and never did it again.

Davis soon found her life's work in the Bedford Hills State Reformatory for Women. Here she led a national intellectual and pragmatic plan for women criminals. In 1909 she advocated "Outdoor Work for Women Prisoners" (1909a), and in 1910 she argued for "Modern Methods of Dealing with Offenders" in the *Annals of the American Academy of Political and Social Science* (1910a) and at "The International Prison Congress at Washington" (1910b).

(At the international congress she also spoke on behalf of children.) The prisoners' problems at the New York State Reformatory for Women became the topic of numerous studies (e.g. 1911, 1913a, 1913b, 1915a), especially on the problems of venereal disease (e.g., 1918a, 1918b), and women's unpaid work and connection to prostitution (e.g., 1913b). These latter two problems became specialized, lifelong interests. Davis often took a narrow view of women's "promiscuity," particularly with men, but her objective reporting of women's sexual habits was both radical and informative (Davis 1929). Her work on "normal married women" set a baseline of information that has been frequently ignored in the intervening years. Her interest in unmarried women complemented this earlier research (1928).

Davis was part of a movement to promote indeterminative sentencing. This type of sentencing was intended to keep criminals incarcerated until they were "reformed." The perniciousness of this power was offset by her hard work for parole and leniency when such a stance was warranted by "good" behavior (e.g., Davis 1915a).

CRITIQUES OF KATHARINE BEMENT DAVIS

There are fragments of interesting biographical information about Davis in reference books, and in the writings of Mary B. Harris (1934) and Rosalind Rosenberg (1982), and I (Deegan 1986) briefly consider her within a network of women scholars. Ellen Fitzpatrick's analysis of Davis's career (1990) broadens our understanding of her graduate years, her work in criminology, and her years of triumphs and ultimate dismissal from the Bureau of Social Hygiene.

The best scholarship on Davis has been done by the women's studies scholar Estelle Freedman (1981). Freedman has written a major interpretation of Kellor's historical and intellectual role in women's prison reform (see Frances Kellor). Her work powerfully explains the intersection of ideas and history surrounding the work of Kellor and Katharine Bement Davis. She has laid a vital foundation for reexamining Davis's sociology. This information is extended by Ellen Frances Fitzpatrick, a women's studies scholar and historian, who provides a biographical and historical analysis of Davis and her cohort at Chicago.

John D'Emilio and Estelle B. Freedman (1981) have examined Davis's study of women's sexuality in their book on *Intimate Matters: A History of Sexuality in America* (1981). This book is one of the few to examine the importance of Davis's work, and its weaknesses and strengths within its historical milieu. As excellent as these resources are, Davis's role as a sociologist has yet to be fully examined and awaits further research and discovery.

BIBLIOGRAPHY

Selected Writings by Katharine Bement Davis

1896. "Civic Efforts of Social Settlements." *Proceedings of the National Conference of Charities* 23: 131–137.

1898. "Tables Relating to the Price of Wheat and Other Farm Products Since 1890." *Journal of Political Economy* 6 (June): 403–410.

1899. "An Error in Austrian Wage Statistics." *Journal of Political Economy* 8 (December): 102–106.

1900a. "Review of *The Philadelphia Negro* by W.E.B. DuBois." *Journal of Political Economy* 8 (March): 248–263.

1900b. "The Modern Conditions of Agricultural Labor in Bohemia." *Journal of Political Economy* 8 (September): 491–523.

1909a. "Outdoor Work for Women Prisoners." *Proceedings of the Conference of Charities and Corrections* 36: 290–294.

1909b. "Relief Work for the Messina Refugees in Syracuse." *Survey* 22 (April): 37–47.

1910a. "Reformation of Women—Modern Methods of Dealing with Offenders." *Annals of the American Academy of Political and Social Science* 36 (July): 37–42.

1910b. "The International Prison Congress at Washington. IV. Section on Children." *Survey* 25 (November 5): 222–224.

1911. "The New York State Reformatory for Women." *Survey* 25 (February 18): 851–854.

1913a. "A Plan of Rational Treatment for Women Offenders." *Journal of the American Institute of Criminal Law and Criminology* 4 (September): 402–408.

1913b. "A Study of Prostitutes Committed from New York City to the State Reformatory for Women at Bedford Hills." In *Commercialized Prostitution in New York City*, edited by George J. Kneeland, p. 163–252. New York: Century.

1915a. "Report of Committee on Probation and Parole." In *Proceedings of the Annual Congress of the American Prison Association*, pp. 389–397. Indianapolis: William B. Burford.

1915b. "The Department of Corrections." *Proceedings of the Academy of Political Science* 5 (April): 564–575.

1916a. "Delinquency and Mental Defect." *Addresses and Proceedings of the National Education Association* 54: 815–817.

1916b. "Women in the Presidential Campaign." *Woman Voter* 7 (December): 8–10.

1918a. "Women's Education in Social Hygiene." *Annals of the American Academy of Political and Social Science* 79 (September): 167–177.

1918b. "Social Hygiene and the War." II. Women's Part in the Campaign. *Social Hygiene* 4 (October): 515–560.

1919. "Some Institutional Problems in Dealing with Psychopathic Delinquents." *Journal of the American Institute of Criminal Law and Criminology* 10 (November): 385–408.

1922–1923. "Study of the Sex Life of the Normal Married Woman." *Journal of Social Hygiene* 8 (April [1922]): 173–189; 9 (January [1923]): 1–26; 9 (March [1923]): 129–146.

1924–1925. "A Study of Certain Auto-Erotic Practices Based on the Replies of 2,255 Women." *Mental Hygiene* 8 (July [1924]): 668–723; 9 (January [1925]): 28–59.

1928. "Why They Failed to Marry." *Harper's Magazine* 156 (March): 460–469.

1929. *Factors in the Sex Life of Twenty-Two Hundred Women*. New York: Harper & Brothers.

1933. "Three Score Years and Ten." *University of Chicago Magazine* 26 (December): 58–62.

Katharine Bement Davis, director. 1922. *Housing Conditions of Employed Women in the Borough of Manhattan.* New York: Bureau of Social Hygiene.

Unpublished Material

Survey Papers, Social Welfare History Archives Collection, "Katharine Bement Davis: Testimonial Dinner," SWAI, Folder 462.

Studies About Katharine Bement Davis and Supplemental References

"Davis, Katharine Bement." 1930. In *National Cyclopaedia of American Biography*, Vol. A, pp. 262–263. New York: James T. White.

"Katharine Bement Davis, Testimonial Dinner." New York: privately printed and distributed pamphlet, 1928.

Deegan, Mary Jo. 1986. "The Clinical Sociology of Jessie Taft." *Clinical Sociology Review* 4: 30–45.

D'Emilio, John, and Estelle B. Freedman. 1981. *Intimate Matters: A History of Sexuality in America.* New York: Harper & Row.

Eichel, Mabel Jacques. 1930. "Dr. Davis." *Survey* 63 (January 15): 488.

Fitzpatrick, Ellen. 1990. *Endless Crusade: Women Social Scientists and Progressive Reform.* New York: Oxford University Press.

Freedman, Estelle. 1981. *Their Sisters' Keepers: Women's Prison Reform in America, 1830–1930.* Ann Arbor: University of Michigan Press.

Harris, Mary B. 1934. "A Re-Educational Institution." *University of Chicago Magazine* 26 (April): 207–210.

Hunt, Sara L. Hart. 1947. *The Pleasure is Mine.* Chicago: Valentine-Newman.

"Katharine Bement Davis Retires." 1928. *Journal of Social Hygiene* 14 (January): 48–51.

Leonard, John William, ed. 1914. "Davis, Katharine Bement." In *Women's Who's Who of America*, p. 30, 233. New York: American Commonwealth Company.

Lewis, W. David. 1971. "Davis, Katharine Bement." In *Notable American Women*, Vol. 1, ed. by Edward T. James, p. 439–441. Cambridge, MA: Harvard University Press, Belknap Press.

Logan, Mary S. 1912. "Katharine Bement Davis." In *The Part Taken by Women in American History*, p. 538. Wilmington, DE: Perry-Nalle.

Potter, Frank Hunter. 1910. "A Reformatory Which Reforms." *Outlook* 94 (February 5): 303–307.

Report by the Investigating Committee of the City Homes Association. 1901. Text by Robert Hunter. *Tenement Conditions in Chicago.* Chicago: City Homes Association,

Rosenberg, Rosalind. 1982. *Beyond Separate Spheres.* New Haven, CT: Yale University Press.

MARY JO DEEGAN

(ELLEN) IRENE DIGGS (1906–   )

Irene Diggs is an outstanding scholar of the worldwide black experience. Her sociological career flourished with her work as assistant to W.E.B. DuBois from 1932 to 1943. She continued her academic training with Fernando Ortiz in Cuba and began a series of studies in the sociology of the African diaspora in Latin America. Through extensive international research and travel, she studied patterns of inequality, race, class, cultural generation, the sociology of art, and charismatic leadership.

BIOGRAPHY

Ellen Irene Diggs was born in Monmouth, Illinois, on April 13, 1906. One of several children, she was raised by an industrious working-class family in an agricultural region. Her parents were Alice Scott and Charles Henry Diggs, and they encouraged her educational aspirations throughout her life. As a child, she loved to read and wanted to travel throughout the world. These early habits became the foundation for a life of international scholarship and cosmopolitan influence.

Diggs attended Monmouth College in Monmouth, Illinois, in 1923–1924 after being awarded a tuition scholarship. She wanted a broader range of courses, however, and transferred to the University of Minnesota, where she earned a bachelor of arts degree in 1928. She was a student of Pitirim Sorokin, and maintained a friendship with him for several years after leaving Minnesota. She experienced her first blatant racism at this institution, causing her to analyze her own roots and need for black role models.

Pursuing this ambition, Diggs entered Atlanta University, where she studied with the eminent sociologist W.E.B. DuBois. In 1933 she earned a master of arts degree from Atlanta University under his tutelage. A remarkable period of personal and intellectual growth ensued, from 1932 to 1943, when Diggs became DuBois's assistant. During these years she helped him research and produce several major works (discussed more fully below) and cofounded *Phylon: A Journal of Race and Culture*. She worked with the complete support of DuBois, who gave her few guidelines or restrictions, allowing her to follow her own scholarly inclinations in the course of this work.

By the early 1940s Diggs pursued an independent career and followed her early dreams of travel. After vacationing in Cuba in 1941, she returned the next summer and learned Spanish at the Universidad de la Habana. She continued to work in Cuba under the auspices of a Roosevelt Fellowship in the Institute for International Education to the Universidad de la Habana, where she completed her doctorate in 1945. Here she was mentored by Fernando Ortiz, the internationally known ethnographer whose work complemented that of DuBois in its emphasis on the black experience and the sociology of art. Ortiz also studied deviance, archaeology, folklore, and criminology. In Cuba, Diggs was trained in field work, where she was "collecting folklore, recording music, photographing festivals and observing rituals and dance" (Bolles 1988).

After the end of World War II, Diggs traveled extensively throughout Central and South America. In 1946 she was an exchange scholar in Montevideo, Uruguay, where she engaged in both ethnographic studies and archival research. By 1947 she had completed a 21,000-mile trek through these vast lands, where she often was interviewed by the press and addressed the public. Her research then and later included work in Puerto Rico, Jamaica, Argentina, Haiti, Chile, Peru, Panama, Guatemala, and Mexico.

In addition to this international scholarship, Diggs conducted research in Israel, Egypt, and the U.S.S.R. She also has traveled to England, France, Holland, Belgium, and Germany. For many years Diggs wrote newspaper columns on her travels and ideas that were syndicated by the Associated Negro Press.

Diggs worked from 1947 until her retirement in 1976 at Morgan State University as a professor of anthropology and sociology. Although she had a very high teaching load—often offering six courses a semester—she loved to teach and enjoyed its opportunities for learning and human growth. She requested a varied teaching load, with its many course preparations, to prevent her own boredom, and often designed new courses, such as one comparing the Israeli and black experiences. Her dedication to black students generated thousands of well-trained and articulate members of the community. She also served as a guest professor at a number of schools, including Barnard College, Harvard Summer School of Arts and Sciences, and the University of Maryland.

Diggs has filled many honored roles in professional organizations. She currently is a fellow in the American Association of Applied Anthropology, the American Physical Anthropologists, and the American Association for the Advancement of Science, and has been a member of the American Sociological Society, the Eastern Sociological Society, the American Association of University Women, the American Association of University Professors, the International African Institute, and the New York Academy of Science. Diggs has served on several committees and boards of art museums, including the Baltimore Museum of Art and the Women's Board of the Peabody Institute.

Politically, Diggs has served on a number of commissions investigating social issues. She was an adviser to the Maryland Association for Mental Health and the Governor's Task Force on Corrections, Probation, and Parole; she chaired the latter's Committee on Correctional Decision Making, Training, and Research in 1968.

In 1964 Diggs received the Distinguished Alumni Award from Monmouth College, and in 1976 she returned to Havana as a U.N. special visitor and scholar. The Association of Black Anthropologists honored Diggs in 1978 for her distinguished research, scholarship, and struggles on behalf of the black community for more than fifty years. In 1990 the Black Sociologists Association recognized her outstanding contributions as well.

Diggs continues to actively write and conduct research as an emeritus professor of the University of Maryland.

MAJOR THEMES

Diggs is the preeminent scholar who both analyzes DuBois and engages in DuBoisian analysis. Although W.E.B. DuBois is recognized as a major black sociologist in dozens of books and articles, few scholars extend and replicate his work. Diggs has spent her life amassing and completing such scholarship. Her Duboisian analyses fall into several categories or stages.

First, Diggs directly influenced and participated in the production of several of DuBois's books while she was his research assistant. These books include *Black Reconstruction* (1935), *Black Folk Then and Now* (1939), the revision of *The Negro* (1915), and *Dusk of Dawn* (1940). The latter book was reprinted with an introduction by Diggs in 1984, which is part of the fifth category of her DuBoisian scholarship discussed below. DuBois, who studied under the well-known sociologist Max Weber, brought a Weberian, interpretive emphasis to his work that is reflected in Diggs' subsequent work.

Second, Diggs researches the black American experience, documenting its historical foundation (1980), structural impact, organizational struggle as a civil rights and collective movement (1958, 1973b), and its basis in race (1954a) and class relations (1954a, 1959). This work clearly follows the agenda for research and study established by DuBois.

Third, Diggs has emphasized the African diaspora experience and the international force of black people. One of her major contributions to this literature is her documentation of the worldwide influence of black people in *Black Chronology*. This encyclopedic reference book traces the people, events, and struggles of black people from 4000 B.C. to the abolition of the slave trade. Similarly, her coediting of the preparatory volume of *The Encyclopedia of the Negro* (1945) with DuBois, among others, places her in a pivotal role in a vast network of scholars documenting the black experience and community. Her analysis of race is multidimensional, intersecting with the economic, political, social, and cultural definitions of the situation.

Fourth, Diggs has particularly emphasized the study of the African diaspora in the Caribbean and Latin America. This reflects her combination of the work of Ortiz and DuBois. Her analysis of the *quilombos*, or cooperative communities of fugitive slaves, in Brazil points to the courage and resistance of the first Africans exploited there (e.g., 1953b, 1953a). Her celebration of Chilean leadership by Zambo-Peluca (1952a) echoes DuBois's concern with the talented tenth who could provide new visions and models for the disenfranchised community. Her studies of charismatic leadership are part of a humanistic scholarship celebrating the black community and its formation.

Fifth, Diggs documents the thought and scholarship of DuBois. Her exquisite study of DuBois's analysis of children as central to life and hope (1976) draws together a major theme in his work that is not emphasized elsewhere. His persistent documentation of children's suffering by the personal and structural viciousness of racism is moving and inspiring. She also places his work within the democratic struggle found in critical pragmatism and the work of Jane Addams,* Florence Kelley,* and Frances Kellor.* Diggs' analysis of DuBois's writings on women is an outstanding example of her thorough scholarship and comprehensive grasp of his vast, often uncharted corpus. Her documentation of DuBois's work in the Afro-American Amenia conferences (1973b), the Pan-African Congresses (1972), and autobiography (1983) not only contribute to the literature on DuBois's work, but also focus on aspects that only she could know as his colleague and student (see 1965a, 1972, and 1974).

Finally, in both her personal and her professional life, Diggs has emphasized the sociology of art, again echoing the interests of her mentors and an understudied aspect of DuBois's sociology. Her studies of Afro-Cuban music (1951) and dance (1951b) demonstrate this aspect of her thought.

Diggs is at the forefront of comparative historical sociology, a field that is currently experiencing a revitalization. Her comparisons of Latin American with North American race relations extend our knowledge of the intersection of class and race in colonial contexts. Her multiple racial and class model is historically documented through archival analysis of the centuries of legal and social classifications that fortunately yielded a morass of politically unworkable categories of race in colonial Spanish America (1953f).

The variations in the definition of race in different countries, eras, and political contexts reflect its social construction. This aspect of Diggs' thought reveals an affinity to symbolic interactionism, also found in DuBois and his work with William James at Harvard in the 1890s. In this way the circle through the critical pragmatism of early women sociologists is completed.

CRITIQUES OF (ELLEN) IRENE DIGGS

Lynn Bolles has written two outstanding analyses of Diggs' work and contributions (1988, forthcoming), emphasizing the anthropological aspects of the latter's thought. Bolles has connected the work of Diggs to contemporary scholarship on black Americans, the African diaspora, and anthropological thought. In many ways Bolles continues Diggs' legacy of celebrating charismatic leadership and documenting the black experience and community in a historical context.

Despite the massive amount of literature on DuBois, Diggs' central role in his research and her extension of his thought has been understudied. The reasons for her neglect are many, including the definition of comparative sociology as anthropology, her work in an undergraduate institution that trained few advanced scholars, racism and sexism within the discipline, and a historical myopia toward early contributors to the profession. It is hoped that such shortsightedness will not continue, and that her outstanding scholarship and stature will be recognized more thoroughly in sociological thought.

ACKNOWLEDGMENTS

My thanks to Wilbur Watson who first told me about Irene Diggs, to Lynn Bolles who generously shared her work on Irene Diggs, and to Florence Bonner who organized the honorary award and presentation to Irene Diggs by the Black Sociologists Association. Dr. Diggs responded to numerous telephone interviews and a lengthy face-to-face interview throughout 1987–1990.

BIBLIOGRAPHY

Selected Writings by (Ellen) Irene Diggs

1947a. "Amalgamation and Race Relations." *America* 77 (April 5): 14–16.
1947b. "How South America Thinks About Race." *Black World* 5 (August 10): 52–56.
1947c. *El Negro en los Ustados Unidos*. Bibleoteca Artigas-Washington (Montevideo) 3, #1 (1947)
1950. "O Aleijadinho." *Americas* 2 (September): 24–27, 44.
1951a. "Afro-Cuban Folk Crisis." *Crisis* 58 (June–July): 390–393.
1951b. "Singing and Dancing in Afro-Cuba." *Crisis* 58 (December): 661–664, 696.
1951c. "The Negro in the Viceroyalty of Rio de la Plata." *Journal of Negro History* 36 (July): 281–301.
1952a. "Zambo-Peluca." *Phylon* 13, no. 1: 43–47.
1952b. "Negro Painters in Uruguay." *Crisis* 59 (May): 299–301.
1952c. "Arabs in Israel." *Crisis* 59 (November): 580–581.
1952d. "Across Minority Lines." *World Affairs* 115 (Winter): 105–106.
1953a. "Argentine Diptych: Meliton and Schimu." *Crisis* 60 (June–July): 352–354.
1953b. "Zumbi and the Republic of Os Palmares." *Phylon* 14, no. 1: 62–70.

1953c. "Brindis de Salas: King of the Octaves." *Crisis* 60 (November): 537–541.

1953d. "Crafty Slave." *Crisis* 59 (January): 21–22.

1953e. "Israel." *Phylon* 14, no. 4: 422–427.

1953f. "Color in Colonial Spanish America." *Journal of Negro History* 38 (October): 403–427.

1954a. "The Sociologist Looks at the Negro in the United States." *Zaire, Revue Congolaise* (Brussels) 8 (May).

1954b. "A Note on Fernando Ortiz and Afro-Cuban Music." *Zaire, Revue Congolaise* (Brussels) 8 (March).

1955a. "Economic Status of the Negro in the United States." *Zaire, Revue Congolaise* (Brussels) 9 (January).

1955b. "Sayago the Burglar." *Crisis* 62 (October): 471–472.

1956a. "The Indian in East Africa." *Crisis* 63 (April): 215–217, 254.

1957. "Lysistrata à l'Africaine." *Crisis* 64 (June–July): 345–348, 383.

1958. "Desegregation and Integration in the United States." (33rd International Congress of Americanists). In *Actas del XXXIII Congreso Internasional de Americanistas*, Tomo 2, p. 673–691. San Jose de Costa Rica.

1959. "Skin Color and Social Class." In *Plantation Systems of the New World*, pp. 164–179. Seminar on Plantation Systems of the New World, San Juan, P.R. 1957. Social Science Monographs, No. 7. Washington, DC: Pan American Union.

1961. "Reviewer's Reply to Author's Reply About the Book *New Nigerian Elite*." *Crisis* 68 (March): 187–188.

1964. "The Negro and the African." In *The Spiritual Personality of Emergent Africa*. Washington, DC: Catholic Commission on Intellectual and Cultural Affairs.

1965a. "A Tribute to William Edward Burghardt DuBois." *Freedomways* 5 (Winter): 18–19.

1965b. "Contemporary Definitions of Race." *Crisis* 72 (May): 282–286, 325.

1970. *Chronology of Notable Events and Dates in the History of the African and His Descendants During the Period of Slavery and the Slave Trade*. Washington, DC: The Association for the Study of Negro Life and History.

1971a. "DuBois, Revolutionary Journalist Then and Now, Part I." *A Current Bibliography on African Affairs* 4 (Ser. 2, March): 95–117.

1971b. "Attitudes Toward Color in South America." *Negro History Bulletin* 34 (May): 107–108.

1972. "DuBois and the Pan African Congresses." *A Current Bibliography on African Affairs* 5 (Ser. 2, March): 123–184.

1973a. "DuBois and Marcus Garvey." *A Current Bibliography on African Affairs* 6 (Spring): 140–182.

1973b. "The Amenia Conferences: A Neglected Aspect of the Afro-American Struggle." *Freedomways* 13, no. 2: 117–134.

1974. "DuBois and Women." *A Current Bibliography on African Affairs* 7 (Summer): 260–303.

1975. *Black Innovators*. Chicago: Institute of Positive Education.

1976. "DuBois and Children." *Phylon* 37 (December): 370–399.

1980. "The Biological and Cultural Impact of Blacks on the United States." *Phylon* 51, no. 2: 153–166.

1983. *Black Chronology: From 4000 B.C. to the Abolition of the Slave Trade*. Boston: G. K. Hall.

1984. "Introduction." In *Dusk of Dawn*, by W.E.B. DuBois, pp. vii–xxvi. New Brunswick, NJ: Transaction Books, 1984.

Contributions by (Ellen) Irene Diggs

DuBois, W.E.B., and Guy B. Johnson, with the cooperation of E. Irene Diggs, Agnes C. L. Donohugh, Guion Johnson, Rayford W. Logan, and L. D. Ruddick. 1946. *Encyclopedia of the Negro: Preparatory Volume with Reference Lists and Reports*. Rev. and enlarged ed. New York: Phelps-Stokes Fund.

Unpublished Writings by (Ellen) Irene Diggs

1933. "A Study of Fifty Delinquent Negro Girls in the City of Atlanta." Master's thesis, Atlanta University.

1945. "La Vida y la Obra de Fernando Ortiz." Ph.D. diss., Universidad de Habana, Habana, Cuba.

Studies About (Ellen) Irene Diggs and Supplemental References

Bolles, A. Lynn. 1981. "Irene Diggs: Coming of Age in Atlanta, Havana and Baltimore." Paper presented at the Annual meeting of the American Anthropological Association, Los Angeles.

———. 1983. "Irene Diggs: A Biographical Sketch." *Outreach* (Morgan State University and the Middle Atlantic Writers Association) 5: 1–2.

———. 1988. "Diggs, Ellen Irene (1906–)." In *Women Anthropologists: A Biographical Dictionary*, edited by Ute Gacs, Aisha Khan, Jerrie McIntyre, and Ruth Weinberg, pp. 59–64. Westport, CT: Greenwood Press.

———Forthcoming. ["Irene Diggs"]. In [*Black Pioneers in Anthropology*], edited by Ira Harrison, St. Clair Drake, and Glenn Jordan. Urbana: University of Illinois Press.

"Diggs, Ellen Irene." 1948. In *Who's Who in Colored America*, edited by Thomas Yenser, p. 154. New York: Thomas Yenser.

"Diggs, Irene." 1985. In *Who's Who Among Black Americans*, p. 225. Lake Forest, IL: Educational Communications.

MARY JO DEEGAN

FRANCES R. DONOVAN (1880–1965)

Frances R. Donovan's monographs are representative of the urban behavior research at the University of Chicago during its Golden Age (1918–1940). She remains nonetheless a sociological outsider whose contributions to the sociology of work and occupations and whose depictions of the social worlds of women in three traditional occupations are largely unacknowledged. Using the participant observation and life history techniques, Donovan's strengths lie in her seeing the world through the eyes of her research subjects and in her incisive perceptions of women as a devalued group.

BIOGRAPHY

Cora Frances Robertson was the oldest of five children born to Frank and Eva Bissell Robertson on April 6, 1880, in St. Clair, Michigan, where her parents owned a small business and enjoyed a comfortable life-style. Although her childhood was happy and secure, after high school graduation she spurned the life of a debutante and decided to become a teacher. Rather than wait until a suitable husband came along (as was apparently her father's wish), she chose one of the few occupations open to women at the time.

This period of Donovan's life is recorded in one chapter of *The Schoolma'am*. Her persona, Ellen Macmillan, is actually the name of a beloved aunt who went west on a wagon train in the early nineteenth century. Because Donovan's father refused to send her to the university, she procured a rural teaching certificate and taught at an ungraded school during 1898–1899. The next year she attended Ypsilanti (Michigan) Normal College with tuition paid by her grandfather. After receiving her diploma in 1901, she taught for several years before taking a position in Great Falls, Montana, at nearly twice her previous salary.

Donovan's social life in Great Falls centered around the Episcopal church, where she met William Donovan—"Billy" as she called him—a Chicago-trained architect who was ten years her senior. They married in December 1907. Donovan resigned her teaching position and spent the next seven years socializing with the local intellectuals in the Woman's Club and the Literary Society. She attended "pink teas" and bridge parties that represented to her the wasteful leisure of some upper-middle-class women. Although undated, three short stories found in her papers represent "clear retrospectives on her years as a socialite" in which she seemed to be "working through some of the feelings she had about women of privilege" (Kurent 1982).

Her life of leisure ended abruptly after war was declared in Europe in August 1914, and Great Falls suffered a financial crisis as the copper smelting plant and the banks closed. Bill Donovan quickly found work with a Chicago architectural firm, and the couple moved to Chicago's South Side, near the University of Chicago, where Donovan enrolled to enhance her teaching credentials and, possibly, fill the intellectual void experienced at the teachers' college. Bill Donovan soon became ill with a terminal disease that would leave him an invalid for four years. By 1916, when it was obvious that Donovan would soon be alone and self-supporting, she took her first sociology courses. Unlike most male Chicago researchers of this period, Donovan focused on urban women in three traditional occupations. She took a class in occupational survey, with her first laboratory exercise in a restaurant. This experience culminated in *The Woman Who Waits* (1920).

In 1918 Donovan earned an undergraduate degree in English from the University of Chicago, the same year her husband died. While writing *The Woman Who Waits*, Donovan managed a teachers' agency and began substitute teaching, where she met Letitia Parry James Owen, who became a lifelong friend. Owen's daughter, Elizabeth Borst, clearly remembers the day her mother came home and declared that she had just met "an extraordinary and brilliant woman." Donovan became a fixture in the Owen home, even though one woman was the antithesis of the other: Donovan, the strong, authoritative intellectual; Owen, a petite, volatile, nonintellectual. It was there Donovan met Bob Hughes, who owned the Chicago Temple Book Shop, which she managed from 1921 to 1923. In 1924, however, she took a permanent position at Calumet High School in Chicago. Except for a stint as saleswoman for two summers, Donovan never again held a position outside of teaching.

As a woman and as a part-time student in the 1920s, Donovan occupied a marginal position in the sociology department at the University of Chicago. References to her are fragmentary and scattered. Robert Faris, in his history of Chicago sociology, discusses the proposed research of a graduate student, Norman Hayner, on hotel life, and indicates that Hayner met with (Robert) Park, (Ernest) Burgess, and a Mrs. Donovan, who was acquainted with people in some of Chicago's leading hotels and promised to distribute a questionnaire for him (1967, 81). When Faris was questioned about Donovan in 1981, he noted that although graduate students read her books, he could not recall anyone speaking of her as a friend (cited in Kurent 1982, 91). The latter point was corroborated by other graduate students from the 1920s. In his sample of this group, James Carey noted that although *all* knew Donovan's name (and many read her books in class), *no one* listed her as a friend (cited in Kurent 1982, 50). Nels Anderson (1980) referred to her as a "sad woman in the confines of a teacher's job."

She apparently had some friends, however. Zorbaugh, in his acknowledgments in *The Gold Coast and the Slum*, thanked his many friends and fellow students (including Donovan) who had generously shared their research. Although Helen MacGill Hughes* (1980–1981, 39) did not know Donovan well, she referred to her as a lone self-starter sociologist who produced a small classic, *The Schoolma'am*, without a grant or a research team. Her equipment was a note pad and pencil; her method, the face-to-face interview. Additionally, Donovan attended some evening meetings of the Society for Social Research in the 1920s and possibly the 1930s.

In 1945 Donovan retired to Eureka Springs, Arkansas, where old friends had gone. The urban environment she had described so enthusiastically years before had become her prison; city noises distracted her. Although her decision to strike out for new territory after retirement took a great deal of courage, she quickly was identified as a pioneer. In 1953 she began what was to be a fourth book, a community study of Eureka Springs titled *I Have Found It: A Social Study of a Small Town*. She wrote to the University of Chicago Press, asking if anyone might suggest recent community studies as a model for her own. Perhaps the press viewed her ambitious project as an unrealistic endeavor by an amateur, an elderly woman. At any rate her manuscript was ultimately rejected. In a proud and indignant response, she contended that she was not the nobody the respondent assumed, mentioned her publications, and suggested that someone more qualified—perhaps a sociologist—should read the manuscript. Although one might see this last scholarly project as spunky and ambitious, the incident also underscores Donovan's marginal status at the University of Chicago. Because of massive health problems, she entered a newly opened nursing home near Eureka Springs in July 1963 and died there on November 2, 1965.

MAJOR THEMES

Donovan remains one of many women whose contributions to the founding years of sociology in the United States have until recently been largely ignored. Her three monographs are part of the Chicago School of Sociology, an unusually fruitful time from 1918 to 1940 for urban behavior research at the university. Labeled the Golden Age, this research tradition did not involve a monolithic orientation, but reflected the attitudes and perspectives—a particular world view—of those who identified with it. Several research techniques were used: case studies (life histories) of individuals or communities; statistics; human ecology, which focused on the interaction between urban dwellers and their environment; and observation, which grew out of Park's dictum to students to explore the city of Chicago, the human laboratory, to observe life as it unfolded. Donovan used life histories and participant observation to look at the social worlds of women in traditional occupations.

Donovan's three books, *The Woman Who Waits*, *The Saleslady*, and *The Schoolma'am*, were written during and after a period of far-reaching changes that affected women's lives: suffrage had been won, a professional class had emerged as a result of women's increasing presence at universities and in the work force, and new groups of white-collar workers (as saleswomen) were emerging. Donovan was aware of these changes and attempted to address these issues in her writings. "There is now no talk of back to the home. The war [World War I] has made conclusive a revolution . . . already begun" (1920, 14). Until Donovan's monographs, the Chicago studies failed to focus on women in the urban scene.

Donovan's contributions to the sociology of work and occupations are her insightful depiction of the social worlds of three groups of women whose lives, except for the schoolteacher, were very different from her own. One of the strengths of her work lies in her seeing the world through the eyes of these women themselves; thus she assigned major importance to people's interpretations of their own experiences and explanations for their behavior. She started in commonplace and familiar situations and, in the case of the teacher, took advantage of her own special expertise. Donovan's monographs are essential pieces of the mosaic that made up the city of Chicago itself.

The Woman Who Waits (1920), the most descriptive, realistically portrays the work environment of the waitress who has no security in a dead-end, low-status job representing one kind of dirty work. Often the waitress is ashamed of what she does and tries to conceal her occupation from friends. Whatever her age, she is a "girl" called by her Christian name. Her humble status is further reflected in various indignities to which she is subjected—dirty kitchens and washrooms and sexual advances by customers and/or the boss.

To gather her data, Donovan worked for nine months in numerous kinds of restaurants, from hash houses in the Chicago Loop to more fashionable places in other parts of the city. In this role she moved far from her own WASP world to cross social class and ethnic lines. In the individualistic world of the waitress, teamwork is unknown; yet the camaraderie, sociability, and group life make waitressing far preferable to housework. She made many friends and felt a sense of disloyalty in writing their intimate life stories (a theme often echoed in other participant observation research).

Donovan recognized that the problems of waitresses must be resolved from within by organizing and, when necessary, from without by legislation. She writes of the Waitresses' Alliance, established in Chicago in 1915, which provided a common meeting place for waitresses and worked to improve working conditions. The Alliance was of inestimable value, serving as a support group that helped to win the eight-hour working day and higher wages for waitresses.

Data for *The Saleslady* (1929), part of the University of Chicago Sociological Series, were gathered during the summers of 1924 and 1925 when Donovan played the role of saleswoman at two New York department stores, presumably Saks Fifth Avenue and Macy's. Park's introduction notes that this volume contributes to knowledge about changes in the "life and character" of women as a result of their entrance into broader fields of economic life. *The Saleslady* is more analytical than *The Woman Who Waits* but less analytical than *The Schoolma'am*. Also, the socialization process, although more complex and lengthier for the saleswoman than for the waitress (one takes physical and mental tests as well as daily classes in sales procedures), is less arduous than for the schoolteacher. Further, although the saleswoman plays a more prestigious role than the waitress, both are more or less at the mercy of their employers and customers. These are service occupations of sorts—the customer is always right—and yet the waitress and the saleswoman can establish control (involving impression management) in situations that seem, on the surface, only to involve interaction between those not equal.

Donovan perceptively notes subtle distinctions and hierarchies within the saleswoman's role. When she was no longer a neophyte, she found a camaraderie among her fellow employees: "like soldiers in trenches, they are buddies" (1929, 189). Using the dramaturgical model, Donovan depicts the store as theater with front and back regions, the customers as the audience, the selling force as the actors, and the nonselling force and managers as the stagehands. Although few people get behind the scenes, these "unseen springs" are most intriguing. Backstage, saleswomen hone their selling skills by engaging in role playing, pretending to be the customer during slack times. Serving to bind together the employees of the store (which is like a small town) is the house organ (*Sparks* at Macy's), which is similar to a country newspaper and filled with items of interest to employees. Donovan's analysis ends with the "Songs of the Saleslady," published in various editions of *Sparks*, including "The Merry Hatters" and "The Buyer's Song." As Park indicates and Donovan elaborates, the little shopgirl, whose fortunes were touchingly described by O. Henry, has largely been superseded; the saleswoman is likely to be older, may be married or widowed, but lives an independent existence.

The Schoolma'am (1938), Donovan's longest and most analytical work, reflects her years as a teacher, and is supplemented by information obtained as the department manager of a large teachers' agency. Although many of the last century saw teaching as ideal preparation for women for marriage and motherhood, data from teachers themselves substantiate that women entered teaching—as did Donovan—because they needed the work. The curious position of the occupation as "honored but disdained, praised as dedicated service, but lampooned as easy work" (Lortie 1975, 10) points up the ambivalence felt toward teachers in American society and is a theme reiterated by Donovan. Further, although teaching involves a long, expensive socialization process, the pay is not commensurate. Presumably this situation exists largely because teaching has been seen as women's work. Donovan's comments that men usually are considered more valuable in dollars and cents than women, no matter what the occupation, and that most teachers are women and most administrators and policymakers are men lend credence to this point.

This thorough, far-ranging work discusses all facets of the teacher's role, including pupils' expectations, discriminatory practices toward married teachers in the 1930s, teachers' organizations, and the denigrating and inferior economic position of being "just a teacher." After detailing various stereotypes of teachers, including the insulting epithet of the "old maid," Donovan draws a typology of nine types, ranging from the creative teacher to the paycheck teacher who hates her job and is one of the "unwilling permanents."

Donovan alludes to the situation in the Chicago public schools in the 1930s in which teachers who had never been politically active were radicalized. For several years teachers' paychecks were late, or they were given scrip, or nothing at all. Independent activist groups such as the Volunteer Emergency Committee, led by John Fewkes and three other high school teachers, surfaced. Quite possibly Donovan was one of the three, as she apparently worked closely with Fewkes to organize the teachers' strikes. On two occasions 8,000 teachers marched down Michigan Boulevard to a bank where they demanded cash for their scrip. These marches expressed the participants' anger and served as a uniting function out of which a sense of power from working with others arose.

Donovan's works contain explicit and implicit observations about the position of women in American society during the first third of the twentieth century. Although she points to the costs of independence for women, the emancipation of a group always involves a breakdown of social order on the part of the individual and society. Donovan herself, however, held traditional ideas about marriage and motherhood (as did even some feminists), and her comments regarding the waitress reflect ethnocentrism toward another social class. These biases are offset, however, by trenchant, shrewd comments such as these:

Only the exceptional man . . . is willing to risk the rivalry of marriage with a woman as intelligent in mind and as independent in attitude as many a teacher. Men . . . do not marry either their feminine equals or superiors. . . . Some even insist upon gentle, appealing little girls like Copperfield's Dora who can't add up the grocery bills . . . women teachers are often not cut to this pattern. (1938, 65–66)

CRITIQUES OF FRANCES R. DONOVAN

Book reviews, including one in *The American Journal of Sociology*, then the official organ of the discipline, note the lively, readable style that, alongside the scientific worth of the material, present the humanistic point of view to contribute to the "new sociology." Donovan was urged to study other occupational groups of women, using a representative sample, so that generalizations could be made.

Kurent's dissertation (to which I am greatly indebted) thoroughly discusses Donovan's place in the Chicago School. As a social investigator following her mentor Park's urging, she linked private experiences with social knowledge. She was the only Chicagoan to explore the connections between personality, culture, and a specific occupation; the sexual dynamics of the workplace; and the city as a female frontier in which women were not simply creatures of oppression, but creatures of great potential as well. Kurent draws an illuminating parallel between Donovan and the anthropologist Ruth Benedict. Both, in exhibiting independence and maverick spirits, lived in two mutually exclusive worlds (Donovan as student, author, and high school teacher) but did not share the other life with either group. Donovan's works are a unique reminder of an exciting period in the social sciences.

Donovan's memberships in the Society of Midland Authors, League of American Penwomen, and the American Sociological Society reflect her self-identity as a writer and as a sociologist. Park's sponsorship dramatically legitimated her sociological work. Her books were read and discussed in classes and at meetings of the Society for Social Research. *The Woman Who Waits* gave her an authority with other students; Cressey (1932), for example, notes the exploitation and the "sex game" in the taxi-dancer research. The fact that such a major recognized author integral to the Chicago School has been forgotten lends strong support to the patriarchal nature of sociology in which women as researchers and as subjects are not deemed worthy of attention. A trickle of references to her work continues to mount in what one hopes may become a stream. Goffman (1959, 171) acknowledges the saleswoman's role taking as a technique for "derogating the absent audience." Ryan (1975) briefly includes the books in a social history of women, and Tentler (1979) makes fleeting reference to waitresses as a work community of women.

Park's characterization of the *Sales Lady* as "impressionistic and descriptive rather than systematic and formal" points up the tension that exists between what has come to be labeled the quantitative/qualitative dichotomy or, in Park's day, statistics versus description. Further, a recently emerging research model, expounded by feminist scholars among others, has reexamined the notion that knowledge consists of a tidy bundle of objective facts and that science is a value-free enterprise. Rather, an ideology of some sort—with particular values, beliefs, and assumptions—underlies *all* knowledge and scientific research. Research is not a set of techniques carried out by "non-people" in "non-places" (Bell and Encel 1978, 5), but represents a social and political activity that is an extension of the self. Thus it is a learning experience in which we change in the process. This emerging research model seems to be the most useful and fitting context to evaluate Frances R. Donovan and her significant contributions as a sociologist of the Chicago School.

BIBLIOGRAPHY

Selected Writings by Frances R. Donovan

1920. *The Woman Who Waits*. Boston: Gorham Press.
1929. *The Saleslady*. Chicago: University of Chicago Press.
1938. *The Schoolma'am*. New York: Frederick A. Stokes.

Studies About Frances R. Donovan

Cressey, Paul G. 1932. *The Taxi-Dance Hall*. Montclair, NJ: Patterson Smith.
Fish, Virginia Kemp. 1977. "The Chicago School Revisited: Whatever Happened to Annie Marion MacLean and Frances R. Donovan?" Paper presented at the Annual Meeting of the Midwest Sociological Society, Minneapolis, April.
———. 1979. "Frances R. Donovan." *American Women Writers*, Vol. 1, pp. 519–521. New York: Frederick Ungar.
Goffman, Erving. 1959. *The Presentation of Self in Everyday Life*. Garden City, NY: Doubleday Anchor.
Howes, Durward. ed. 1935–1940. "Donovan, Frances R. (Mrs. William E. Donovan)." *American Women 1935–1940: A Composite Biographical Dictionary*, Vol. 1. Los Angeles: American Publication. (Reprint, Detroit, MI: Gale Research, 1981, p. 239).
Hughes, Helen MacGill. 1980–1981. "On Becoming a Sociologist." *The Journal of the History of Sociology: An International Review* 3 (Fall–Winter): 27–39.
Kurent, Heather Paul. 1982. "Frances R. Donovan and the Chicago School of Sociology: A Case Study in Marginality." Ph.D. diss., University of Maryland.
Ryan, Mary P. 1975. *Womanhood in America: From Colonial Times to the Present*. New York: New View Points.
Tentler, Leslie Woodcock. 1979. *Wage Earning Women*. New York: Oxford University Press.

Book Reviews

Amidon, Beulah. 1929. "The Girl in the Shop." *The Nation* 129 (October 23): 470–471.
Anderson, Nels. 1929. "Salesladies." *The Survey* 63 (November 15): 230.
Blanchard, Phyllis. 1921. Book Review of *The Woman Who Waits*. *American Journal of Sociology* 26 (March): 640.
———. 1929. Book Review of *The Saleslady*. *The Bookman* 70: 10.
Cavan, Ruth Shonle. 1930. Book Review of *The Saleslady*. *The American Journal of Sociology* 35 (January): 676.
"Life, Character, and Work of the Saleslady." 1929. *New York Times Book Review* (November 3): 3, Cols. 2–4.
New Books. 1938. A Reader's List. Book Review of *The Schoolma'am*. *New Republic* 96 (September 21): 195.

Schwartz, Nellie. 1921. Book Review of *The Woman Who Waits*. *The Survey* 45 (February 5): 675–676.
"The Woman Teacher and Her Profession." 1938. *New York Times* (August 21): 4.

Unpublished Material

Anderson, Nels. 1980. Personal communication. Undated letter of February.
Hughes, Everett C. 1977, 1979. Personal communication. Letters of January 20, February 28, and April 25, 1977; October 12, 1979.

Other Works

Bell, Colin, and Sol Encel. 1978. *Inside the Whale*. Rushcutters Bay, Australia: Pergamon.
Faris, Robert E. L. 1967. *Chicago Sociology 1920–1932*. Chicago: University of Chicago Press.
Lortie, Dan C. 1975. *School Teacher: A Sociological Study*. Chicago: University of Chicago Press.
Park, Robert E. 1915. "The City: Suggestions for the Investigation of Human Behavior in the Urban Environment." *The American Journal of Sociology* 20 (March): 577–612.
Zorbaugh, Harvey Warren. 1929. *The Gold Coast and the Slum: A Sociological Study of Chicago's Near North Side*. Chicago: University of Chicago Press. Midway reprint 1983.

VIRGINIA KEMP FISH

LUCILE EAVES (1869–1953)

Lucile Eaves was a research and applied sociologist, a professor, and an activist. She was fired by a desire to change women's status and that of laborers, anticipating the contemporary concern with the structural ties between class and sex. She worked in the South Park Social Settlement of San Francisco, and as a faculty member at Stanford University, the University of Nebraska, and Simmons College. Her work for the Women's Educational and Industrial Union generated numerous quantitative studies of women's lives in a variety of contexts. She is one of the first sociologists to study medical sociology, especially women with physical disabilities.

BIOGRAPHY

Eaves was born in the Midwest, in Leavenworth, Kansas, on January 9, 1869. She was the daughter of David William and Anna Cowman Weir Eaves. Like many other female sociologists of her day (e. g., Edith Abbott* and Sophonisba Breckinridge*), her father was a lawyer. She had at least one sister, Ruth, who lived with Lucile most of her life. She graduated from the Peoria (Illinois) High School, and then taught elementary school in that city for one year. She followed this work with three years of teaching in an industrial school for the Nez Percé Indians at Lapwai, Idaho. Next she taught in the public schools of Portland, Oregon, for a year. In 1892, when Leland Stanford, Jr., University opened its doors to women, she rushed to obtain more advanced education.

As an early feminist, Eaves entered the first class of Leland Stanford, Jr., University and graduated with a bachelor's degree in 1894. For the next four years Eaves headed the history department at San Diego (California) High School. She studied at the University of Chicago during 1898–1899, where she was a lecturer in university extension. (Sophonisba Breckinridge, Katharine Bement Davis,* Frances Kellor,* and Marion Talbot* also were there during this year.) In 1899 she returned to Stanford, where she was hired as a history instructor. During the summers of 1899 and 1900 she continued her studies in sociology, economics, and philosophy at the University of Chicago. As a student and later a faculty member at Stanford, she worked closely with sociologists E. A. Ross and George E. Howard (both men later became presidents of the American Sociological Society) and Mary Elizabeth Burroughs Roberts Smith Coolidge.* Eaves held this position until 1901 when she lost her position due to her public support of her mentor, E. A. Ross who was fired. After her resignation from Stanford, Eaves was offered a summer position at the South Park Social Settlement in San Francisco. She was partially forced to accept the position out of financial need, but she soon developed a strong commitment to this work.

Eaves first achieved public attention through her role as head resident at the South Park Settlement in San Francisco, but these were lonely times for her. She wanted to continue in academic life, but believed that it was impossible to do so at this time. Ross (and later Howard, who resigned in protest over his colleague's dismissal) was hired by the University of Nebraska, whereas Eaves had to start her professional life anew. The settlement kept her busy, however, serving 700 to 800 persons each week. Although she preferred academic work, she wryly noted that "the problem of popular education is after all a most important one" (Eaves to Ross, November 25, 1901, p. 4, Ross Papers). Following Jane Addams's* model of the ideal women sociologist and her agenda for social change, Eaves was closely integrated into "women's work in sociology." In her work at the social settlement, Eaves actively investigated child labor and campaigned for a better state law, which was passed in 1905. As a result of this work, Eaves became a special agent of the State Labor Bureau and appeared at hearings in Sacramento in behalf of the bill.

Despite her active life, Eaves believed that she was getting "provincial," and wanted a doctorate in applied sociology. She intended, however, to return to the settlement and provide greater leadership to it as a result. She turned to Ross for recommendations to enter Columbia University and study with Franklin Giddings (mentor of Elsie Clews Parsons* and Anna Garlin Spencer*). She also was offered a scholarship at the University of Chicago at this time but she preferred studying in New York. She turned her position at South Park over to Mary Elizabeth Burroughs Roberts Smith Coolidge, who had fallen into financial difficulties as a newly divorced woman.

After the devastating San Francisco fire in 1906, Eaves returned to California to assist in the relief work (Eaves 1906). A year later she had completed the text for her book on California labor legislation after obtaining a fellowship from the University of California and working for the Carnegie Institution.

In 1909 she received good news from her mentor Howard, who had not forgotten her. He hired her at the University of Nebraska as an associate professor of practical sociology. The next year she completed her Ph.D. degree in applied sociology at Columbia University. Eaves worked successfully at Nebraska for several years. During the ensuing years she wanted, but did not get, more money and a promotion from the University of Nebraska (Deegan 1981). This discrimination structurally limited her professional opportunities. In 1913 she took a sabbatical from Nebraska and assumed a lectureship in economics at the University of California. She returned to Nebraska despite her dissatisfaction with her position there. For example, Eaves ruefully declined an offer from Ross to participate in a scholarly conference at Princeton University. "You know this university pays me a very modest stipend and I have a sister and a farm to support" (November 12, 1914, 1). In 1915 she regretfully resigned from the University of Nebraska because of financial pressures.

Eaves immediately found employment as a lecturer and as the director of research at Simmons College in Boston. In 1921 she was promoted to associate professor, and in 1925 promoted to full professor. The graduate program at Simmons was operated through the Women's Educational and Industrial Union (WEIU), in which she trained more than sixty students and continued the traditions established by Annie Marion MacLean,* Amy Hewes,* and Susan Kingsbury.* (See Eaves' brief description of the WEIU, 1924b.) Eaves' students became affiliated with social work rather than sociology, however. Eaves continued her Nebraska connections throughout her career at the WEIU, jointly addressing meetings of the American Sociological Society with her former colleagues (e.g. 1917) or having her work critiqued by them (see section on critiques).

Eaves was an active member of the American Sociological Society and an elected member of its executive committee from 1924 to 1926. From 1917 to 1924 she worked on the Committee to Standardize Research in an effort to make annual, national, cooperative studies part of the sociological enterprise. She also held memberships in the American Economics Association, the Royal Economic Society, the American Association for University Women, the American Association for Social Workers, the American Association of University Professors, and Phi Beta Kappa. She served as an associate editor of *The Journal of Applied Sociology* from 1923 to 1929.

After her retirement from Simmons and the WEIU, Eaves became the director of the North End Union, a philanthropic organization operated by the Unitarians. She died in Brookline, Massachusetts, on January 20, 1953, after an extremely active life.

MAJOR THEMES

Cooperative research was a major goal for early women sociologists. They believed that the self was personally and professionally embedded in larger social entities, and sociologists were a particular group dedicated to improving the lot of people in everyday life. Eaves articulated these general ideas in specific research, organized under the auspices of the American Sociological Society.

Eaves worked on a committee to conduct such work in 1917, and in 1919 she investigated women's old-age support. This plan was published in the *American Journal of Sociology* in 1920, and the study was completed in 1922. She continued this style of research over a series of studies (e.g., 1923, 1927, and 1929), but not under the sponsorship of the American Sociological Society, which became increasingly conservative in the 1920s, especially in their collegial relations with women scholars.

A good example of Eaves' early role in the women's network of the American Sociological Society is her participation at the 1918 meetings, where she and Marion Talbot critiqued the work of Anna Garlin Spencer. Here they supported the "Ideals and Methods in the Social Education of Women" articulated by Spencer. In 1917 Eaves participated in the meetings of the same group as a discussant of the work of Kelsey on social control and war. She argued for cooperative research and reviewed her research studies and their alliance with that of Sophonisba Breckinridge and British sociologists.

This role as a person who conceptualized female sociologists' practices is seen in several articles. Thus in 1923 she wrote on the relation between applied sociology and social work, and in that same year she reported on "Women in Conference on Industrial Problems," where Mary van Kleeck,* Florence Kelley,* and Sophonisba Breckinridge were major speakers. This conference was plagued by anti-Communists, who saw these women as threats to capitalism.

The statistical studies conducted by Eaves complement the work of her female cohort (e.g., Edith Abbott, Amy Hewes, and Mary van Kleeck). Eaves examines the limited income, housing, family obligations (e.g., 1921, 1921c; 1925), and even the budgetary constraints on nutritious food for working women (1917).

The life cycle was a major theme in Eaves' writings, echoed in many contemporary writings (e.g., Alice S. Rossi* and Matilda White Riley*). Her cooperative, statistical studies of *Aged Clients of Boston Social Agencies* (1925), *Children in Need of Special Care; Studies Based on Two Thousand Case Records of Social Agencies* (1923c), and *Old Age Support of Women Teachers* (1921c) reveal a complex pattern of disadvantage related to both youth and old age. This pattern is exacerbated for women with physical disabilities, who are limited in employment opportunities, pay, and physical endurance. Eaves' *Gainful Employment for Handicapped Women* (1921b) documents the meager lives of this still underresearched population. Her pathbreaking work on women with physical disabilities is the earliest sociological analysis on this population.

This massive survey research work is a marked contrast to her early studies on labor history and legislation. Her major writing is *A History of California Labor Legislation* (this book is dedicated to Howard "by his pupil and coworker," 1910). The first chapter, on the "San Francisco Labor Movement," was her doctoral dissertation, written under Giddings's guidance at Columbia University. It examines the geographical location of the city, its concentrated population, racial composition, and historical development of trade unions. Eaves presents a sympathetic interpretation of workers' rights to organize, and documents in particular the racism of anti-Chinese organizations. Eaves herself supported the exclusion of Chinese labor, a racist stance, arguing from the populist, white working-class perspective. This was a "radical" perspective, a major cause of Ross being fired at Stanford, since it supported unionizing the poor and laborers. It also was a "conservative" perspective in its protectionist and racist application. (Eaves used the same argument in her 1918 discussion of Kelsey's work.) In this way she followed the more racially bigoted writings of E. A. Ross and Franklin Giddings than the more egalitarian work of Mary Elizabeth Burroughs Roberts Smith Coolidge. Despite this *major* flaw in Eaves' thought, she wrote a complex study of the interaction of class, race, and history in a "democratic," populist context. Her scholarship here remains a classic statement on this often forgotten struggle for workers' rights in a pioneer era marked by tumultuous racial conflict within and across all classes.

Eaves used her expertise on the sociological and historical development of California to critique the work of Katherine Coman (1913a) in *The American Journal of Sociology*. The former's review of the latter's two volumes on *Economic Beginnings of the Far West* lauded their painstaking research, comprehensiveness, and interdisciplinary strengths. She used her knowledge of women's work in the marketplace to critique and support Mary van Kleeck's work in *Women in the Bookbinding Trade* (Eaves 1913b).

The problems of health for the poor (1929a, 1929b, and 1929c), people with cancer (1927b), and children victimized by industrial accidents (1921a) are examined in a series of informative articles. The Flynn physical exercise system (1911), the study of women with disabilities (1921b), and the analysis of food (1917) point to Eaves' focus on the relation of the body to social functioning. This work comprises some of the earliest studies in medical sociology.

CRITIQUES OF LUCILE EAVES

Lucile Eaves was connected to several networks in sociology, through Stanford University, the University of Nebraska, the Women's Educational and Industrial Union, and social settlements. Her books were widely reviewed and well received within this complex professional network.

George E. Howard and E. A. Ross reflected both her Stanford and Nebraska ties. Howard (1922) actively supported Eaves' intellectual project in his positive critique of her cooperative research. He cited her years of preparing and organizing such innovative work, her skill in producing it, and her leading role in sociology. E. A. Ross also wrote a glowing review of *Old Age Support of Women Teachers* for the *American Journal of Sociology* in 1922. He wrote, "If this is not material for sociology, nothing is" (p. 241), making a significant attempt to keep her work defined as sociology instead of as social work.

Chase G. Woodhouse, active in the women's network in sociology, reviewed *A Legacy to Wage-Earning Women* (1926). Woodhouse found the work "prepared with the same care as have earlier ones in the series" (p. 651), referring to work by Amy Hewes, Susan Kingsbury, and Annie Marion MacLean at the Women's Educational and Industrial Union. Lillian Brandt, active in social work circles, positively reviewed *A History of California Legislation*, but also, unfortunately, supported the exclusion of Chinese and convict laborers that Eaves advocated. Unionization is defined, according to Brandt, as a democratic rather than revolutionary process. This book was one of Eaves' most important writings, but it received only a paragraph note in *The American Journal of Sociology* (review of *A History of California Legislation* [1910]).

A brief description of South Park Settlement was written by Katherine Coman in 1903. Another brief entry on its work is found in Robert A. Woods and Albert J. Kennedy (1922, 20–22). Mary Elizabeth Burroughs Roberts Smith Coolidge also provides information about the settlement and the Stanford network in which Eaves worked.

Unfortunately few contemporary scholars use the writings of Lucile Eaves. Leslie Woodcock Tentler, however, has used Eaves' studies on working women's budgets and food to document the frugality and loneliness of their lives (1979, 124–128). Eaves' relation to the American Sociological Society is briefly considered in an article on the early sexual division of labor in that organization (Deegan 1981). In general, Eaves' work, writings, and biography have been overlooked in scholarly annals.

BIBLIOGRAPHY

Selected Writings by Lucile Eaves

1906. "Where San Francisco Was Sorest Stricken." *Charities and the Commons* 16 (May): 161–163.

1910. *A History of California Labor Legislation.* Berkeley: University of California Press. Ph.D. diss., Columbia University, 1910, included as one chapter.

1913a. "Review of *Economic Beginnings of the Far West.*" *American Journal of Sociology* 18 (May): 819–821.

1913b. "Review of *Women in the Bookbinding Trade.*" *American Journal of Sociology* 19 (September): 247–249.

1914. "Social Policy in California." *American Economic Review* 4 (June): 450–454.

1917. *The Food of Working Women in Boston.* Boston: Women's Educational and Industrial Union.

1918. "Discussion of a Paper by Carl Kelsey, 'War as a Crisis in Social Control.' " *Papers and Proceedings of the American Sociological Society* 12: 34–38.

1919a. "Training Children for Work After the War." *American Labor Legislation Review* 9 (March): 59–61.

1919b. "Discussion of a paper by Anna Garlin Spencer, 'Ideals and Methods in the Social Education of Women.' " *Papers and Proceedings of the American Sociological Society* 13: 28–33.

1920a. "Plans for Co-operative Research." *American Journal of Sociology* 25 (March): 568–571.

1920b. *Training for Store Service: The Vocational Experiences and Training of Juvenile Employees of Retail Department, Dry Goods and Clothing Stores in Boston.* Boston: Women's Educational and Industrial Union.

1921a. "The Child and the Machine." *Survey* 45 (January 8): 536–537.

1921b. *Gainful Employment for Handicapped Women.* Boston: Women's Educational and Industrial Union.

1921c. *Old Age Support of Women Teachers; Provision for Old Age Made by Women Teachers in the Public Schools of Massachusetts.* A study by the Department of Research of the Women's Educational and Industrial Union. Boston: Spartan.

1923a. "Women in Conference on Industrial Problems." *Journal of Applied Sociology* 7 (March–April): 201–206.

1923b. "Applied Sociology in Relation to Social Work." *Journal of Applied Sociology* 8 (September): 26–30.

1923c. *Children in Need of Special Care; Studies Based on Two Thousand Case Records of Social Agencies.* Boston: Women's Educational and Industrial Union.

1924a. "The Social Workers' Clients." *Social Forces* 2 (May): 497–501.

1924b. "The Women's Educational and Industrial Union of Boston." *Social Forces* 2 (May): 574.

1925. *Aged Clients of Boston Social Agencies.* Boston: Women's Educational and Industrial Union.

1927a. "Social Sciences in the Sixth International Congress of Philosophy." *Social Forces* 5 (March): 407–413.

1927b. "Massachusetts' Cancer Hospital." *Survey* 59 (October 15): 79–80.

1928. "Pensions or Poorhouses?" *Survey* 59 (February 15): 613–615.

1929a. "Almshouse Care for Chronic Patients." *Survey* 61 (March 15): 807–808.

1929b. "Children Who Are Chronically Sick." *Survey* 62 (May 15): 241–243.

1929c. "When Chronic Illness Hits the Wage-Earner." *Survey* 62 (July 15): 448–450.

1929d. "Studies of Breakdowns in Family Income." *Family* 10 (December): 227–236.

Coauthored Works

Eaves, Lucile, and associates. 1925. *A Legacy to Wage-Earning Women.* Introduction by Richards M. Bradley. Studies in Economic Relations of Women, Vol. 12. Boston: Women's Educational and Industrial Union.

Flynn, W. Earl, and Lucile Eaves. 1911. *The Flynn System of Health Culture.* Lincoln: Woodruff.

Studies About Lucile Eaves and Supplemental References

Brandt, Lillian. 1910. "Books for Social Workers." *Survey* 25 (December 17): 479–481.

Coman, Katherine. 1903. "The South Park Settlement, San Francisco." *Commons* 8 (August): 7–10.

Davis, Allen F. 1967. *Spearheads for Reform.* New York: Oxford University Press.

Deegan, Mary Jo. 1981. "Early Women Sociologists and the American Sociological Society: Their Patterns of Exclusion and Inclusion." *American Sociologist* 16 (February): 14–24.

"Eaves, Lucile." 1956. In *The National Cyclopaedia of American Biography*, Vol. 41, p. 67–68. New York: James T. White.

Hertzler, Joyce O. 1979. "A History of Sociology at the University of Nebraska," edited and introduced by Mary Jo Deegan. *Journal of the History of Sociology* 1 (Spring): 40–62.

Howard, George E. 1922. "An Experiment in Co-operative Social Research." *Journal of Applied Sociology* 6 (February): 21–25.

———. 1988. "Sociology in the University of Nebraska, 1898–1927," edited by Michael R. Hill. *Mid-American Review of Sociology* 13 (Winter): 3–19.

"Review of *A History of California Legislation*." 1910. *The American Journal of Sociology* 14: 852.

Ross, Edward A. 1922. "Review of *Old Age Support of Women Teachers*." *American Journal of Sociology* 28 (September): 240–241.

———. 1936. *Seventy Years of It*. New York: D. Appleton.

Rossiter, Margaret. 1982. *Women Scientists in American*. Baltimore: Johns Hopkins University Press.

Tentler, Leslie Woodcock. 1979. *Wage-Earning Women*. New York: Oxford University Press.

Woodhouse, Chase G. 1926. "Review of *A Legacy to Wage-Earning Women*." *Social Forces* 4 (March): 650–652.

Woods, Robert A., and Albert J. Kennedy. 1922. *The Settlement Horizon*. New York: Russell Sage Foundation.

Unpublished Material

Deegan, Mary Jo. 1985. "Nebraska Women and the Golden Era of Women Sociologists: 1892–1924." Unpublished paper, Department of Sociology, University of Nebraska-Lincoln.

Wisconsin State Historical Society, Madison, Wisconsin. Ross Papers.

MARY JO DEEGAN AND MICHAEL R. HILL

CHARLOTTE PERKINS GILMAN
(1860–1935)

Charlotte Perkins Gilman was a prolific writer who produced a plethora of written work across several disciplines. She published approximately 2,173 written works (Scharnhorst 1985b), covering the areas of sociology, political science, economics, literature, and womens' studies. She was a major contributor to the emerging discipline of sociology, influenced by and expanding on the works of such notable sociologists as Lester Ward, Jane Addams,* Edward Ross, and Edward Bellamy. As a sociologist, Gilman helped to transform perceptions of cultural feminism and social reform.

BIOGRAPHY

Charlotte Perkins Gilman was born July 3, 1860, in Hartford, Connecticut, to Mary Westcott and Frederic Beecher Perkins. She was descended from a long line of prominent Beechers, including her great aunt, Harriet Beecher Stowe, author of *Uncle Tom's Cabin*. Her father worked as a librarian and as an assistant editor of various newspapers and magazines. After her parent's divorce in 1869, she was raised under the stout Christian tutelage of her mother. Despite this traditional female upbringing, Gilman attended the public schools of Providence, Rhode Island, and later the Design College of Providence (Gilman 1935).

In May 1884 Gilman married Charles Walter Stetson, an aspiring Providence artist. She became increasingly despondent in this relationship, and after the birth of their daughter, Katharine Beecher Stetson, in 1885, she had a severe nervous breakdown. This experience was the foundation for her semiautobiographical account of a woman's descent into madness in "The Yellow Wallpaper" (1892). She attributed this breakdown to the repressive mores of marriage

(Gilman 1935). Gilman separated from Stetson in 1885, moved to Pasadena, California, and was granted a divorce in 1894.

Between 1890 and 1895 Gilman supported herself as a writer and popular lecturer. In 1894 Gilman coedited with Helen Campbell *The Impress*, the official journal of the Pacific Coast Woman's Press Association. She became actively involved in the Women's Congress both in 1894 and again in 1895. During the latter Congress she met Jane Addams and accepted an invitation to visit Hull-House in Chicago, where she lived from 1895 to 1896. In 1896 she was a delegate to the International Socialist and Labor Congress in London, where she met Beatrice Webb* and George Bernard Shaw, and became interested in Fabian sociology. She was an active member of the American Sociological Society from its formation in 1905 until her death in 1935. She presented papers at the sociological conferences of 1907 and 1908, and her works were published in both the *American Journal of Sociology* and the *Publications of the American Sociological Society*, the forerunner of the *American Sociological Review*.

In 1900 Gilman married her cousin, George Houghton Gilman, a nephew of Daniel Coit Gilman, the first president of Johns Hopkins University. They moved to New York City, where she continued to actively pursue her work. Between 1900 and 1934 Gilman published several books and hundreds of articles. In 1909 Gilman founded a monthly magazine titled *The Forerunner*, in which she wrote and edited nearly all the copy. This brilliant enterprise was never a financial success, and the magazine folded in 1916. During her seven years as editor, Gilman estimated that her writing would have filled twenty-eight books of 36,000 words apiece (Gilman 1935, 304). In 1913 Gilman spoke at the International Suffrage Convention in Budapest, and in 1915 she helped to found, with Jane Addams and others, the Women's Peace party. When the feminist movement lost some of its momentum in the 1920s, Gilman lectured less frequently but continued to actively publish.

During 1932 Gilman was diagnosed as having breast cancer. Her illness was contained until 1934. After her husband's death in May, Gilman moved to Pasadena to live with her daughter's family. Preferring quick death to the long and painful one brought on by cancer, she chose to end her life on August 17, 1935. She was cremated and her ashes were scattered.

MAJOR THEMES

Many scholars during the last quarter of the nineteenth century focused on social reform, and Gilman was captivated by their discussions. Edward Bellamy (*Looking Backward*, 1888), Henry George (*Progress and Poverty*, 1879), and Helen Campbell (*Problems of the Poor*, 1882) were particularly strong influences. Drawing on their writings, Gilman focused on women's suffrage and the social status of women in the industrial age. She combined the utopianism of Edward Bellamy with the refined evolutionary thought of Lester Frank Ward

(*Dynamic Sociology*, 1883) to effectively address the relation of women to an industrial society.

Her early sociological work examined the culturally repressed status of women and their barriers to full intellectual development. This work, as suggested by Terry (1983), is analogous to Harriet Martineau's* earlier observations on the perpetuation of "female enslavement." A reflection on her own life, "The Yellow Wall-paper" (1892) is a phenomenological analysis of the dependent position of women on men in society and her personal experiences of mental breakdown encountered in a society that represses the opportunities of women. Another work, "Similar Cases" (1890), gained national recognition as a satirical poem challenging the natural order of society, especially men's and women's roles in society. She emerged from these works as a radical feminist, with an underlying theme of women and industry. This orientation gained international recognition in the field of sociology during the first quarter of the twentieth century, being especially prominent among women sociologists Susan Kingsbury,* Florence Kelly,* Mary Van Kleeck,* and Jane Addams.

Elaborating on Ward's gynecocentric theory, Gilman addressed women's productive labor as a factor of social evolution in *Women and Economics* (1898). Like Ward, Gilman opposed Herbert Spencer's theory of social determinism. She supported Ward's contention that humans are dynamic agents who, instead of being determined by inherited traits and ruthless competition, are able to plan and direct their destiny. Through her widespread lectures, Gilman helped to give international impetus to Ward's gynecocentric theory, which proposed that women are the original and dominant form of the species, while men serve only as assistants in the fertilization process. This theory of a female-dominated culture was superseded in sociology by the androcentric theory of male domination.

Gilman argued that the androcentric orientation deprives society of its full potential because women are socially created to depend on men for all their needs. For this reason, she rejected the basic tenets of Marxism as a "class struggle" (Gilman 1935, 131). As Hobbs (1987, 157) notes, Gilman believed that the underlying social demarcations in society were based on sex, not class, differences. In *Human Work* (1904c) Gilman viewed work as the greatest expression of personal fulfillment and accomplishment. Attacking the basic social institutions, she contended that women's social repression into the singular role of motherhood minimizes female creativity and expression. As described by Gilman in *The Man-Made World* (1911a) and "Are Women Human Beings" (1912), society ultimately suffers because men are allowed both parenthood and productive work, whereas as women are forced to choose between them. The domination of a patriarchal order impedes social and human development through the elimination of "women's qualities" of cooperation and peacefulness. These and other works, including "Social Ethics" (1914), *Herland* (1915), and *With Her in Ourland* (1916), represent both satirical and serious attempts to document the discrimination of women that is intricately imbedded within our social order (see e.g., Sachs, Maggard, and Randolph, 1981).

Although traditional social roles encouraged women to become mothers, Gilman believed that the role of motherhood could negatively impact both women and children. Children, she argued, should not be raised in a milieu of strict obedience because this retards, rather than expands, their minds (Gilman 1900). The welfare of children would be promoted, Gilman pointed out, by entrusting them to child-care specialists trained to expand young minds. Because most mothers are mere amateurs, with little training or experience in the art of child care, they, too, would benefit from child specialists through the uninterrupted pursuit of their professional careers. In *The Home: It's Work and Influences* (1903) Gilman contended that the home and its duties oppress women through domestic chores and child care. To concentrate on the home, women must ignore their civic duties ("Kitchen Dirt and Civic Health," 1904), which has negative consequences for women, children, and society.

Gilman's association with Fabian sociology and her interest in social reforms were directed at the inefficiency, waste, and exploitation of labor, in both the household and the wider society. Her article on "How Home Conditions React upon the Family" (1909a) addressed how women's economic dependence impedes marital relations, motherhood, and child care. In "The Waste of Private Housekeeping" (1913) Gilman contended that private housekeeping is an inefficient use of domestic resources, such as kitchens and household experience, that produces an overall disregard for human life. This waste is the result of a domestic economy in which women are expected to labor, independently from one another, in their husbands' homes as private domestic servants (Gilman 1904a). Duties performed by the housekeeper generate greater levels of waste for individual households and the nation alike. Although theoretically more complex than Gilman acknowledged in "The Housekeeper and the Food Problem" (1917), she suggested that the household and the economy would be more productive and efficient if all women were employed in the labor force and if cooperative kitchens that resembled food laboratories were established to mass-produce food in the place of female housekeepers. Food preparation, Gilman believed, is no more a domestic requirement today than making clothing.

Unfortunately Gilman's attack against the oppression of women in society was not oriented toward a pragmatic solution of these problems. Like Jane Addams, Gilman utilized democratic principles and education as tools to improve social awareness, but Gilman also condoned more authoritarian and eugenic methods. She argued that men were instilled with masculine characteristics of desire, combat, and self-expression, which manifested themselves in the continuation of violence and war (e.g., Gilman 1911a, 208–226). Only through the beneficent leadership of women, who display qualities of compassion, love, and patience, can society be improved. Gilman even implied in "Herland" (1915) that society could never fully progress until men, and their biological traits, were eliminated.

In searching for a perfect society, Gilman believed that strong state agencies were necessary to maintain a homogeneous population that epitomized her ideals.

In "Moving the Mountain" (1911b) Gilman wrote of her "humane" society, a society that enforces "compulsory socialization" of all immigrants, permits childbirth only to those people judged to be physically, morally, and mentally capable, and either resolves problems of deviants or kills them. Moreover, in addressing the problems associated with human races, Gilman deviates from her insistence on egalitarian social positions in society when she assumed that the Negro race is inferior rather than equal to the white race. In "A Suggestion of the Negro Problem" (1908c) and "Race Improvement" (1909b) Gilman calls for a state-organized compulsory enlistment of the "nonproductive" Negro population to produce a homogeneous "American" population through enforcement by state agencies.

Although Gilman was a pacifist (Hobbs 1987, 159), her utopian dream justified violence when security was threatened. Murder was permissible as a moral act of self-defense, whether to cast off the oppressive chains of bondage (*Herland*) or to chastise the aggressive threat of a wayward nation. As Hobbs (1987, 164) concludes, Gilman "developed a sympathetic, yet still often critical, understanding of women and their oppression, and placed her hope for the future of humanity largely in women's hands."

CRITIQUES OF CHARLOTTE PERKINS GILMAN

The massive body of work that Gilman produced has been extensively critiqued by sociologists and others. In a selected bibliography, Scharnhorst lists more than 200 such references (1985b, 194–213). The sociologist Lester F. Ward was so impressed by her work that he initiated a personal correspondence that lasted for many years (Scharnhorst, 1985b, 201, 232). Ward refered to Gilman as a "cosmic thinker" and noted that her "Similar Cases," although "read by nearly everyone in the country . . . [was] the most telling answer that has ever been made [to social evolutionists]" (Hill 1980, 265). Similarly, the Progressive sociologist Edward Ross wrote that she was "the most brilliant woman I have known" (Ross 1936, 60).

Gilman was seriously addressed by early women sociologists. On the one hand, Anna Garlin Spencer* and Jessie Taft* found Gilman's analyses of traditional families and home life to be too extreme. On the other hand, Jane Addams and Florence Kelley* were extremely supportive of Gilman's ideas in *Women and Economics*. (See their respective entries for fuller presentations on these scholars' views on the family.) Nancy Cott's analysis of the feminist context of ideas, especially during the first twenty years of this century (1987), is helpful in interpreting this intellectual network.

Gilman scholarship is flourishing in women's studies today. Two major biographies, by Mary Hill (1980) and Ann J. Lane (1990), greatly expand our knowledge of Gilman's life. Hill presents a detailed analysis of Gilman's early life and career, whereas Lane looks at the influence of significant people in Gilman's life. Both biographies are informative, but they do not examine Gilman's sociological work in depth. A fascinating account of Gilman's ideas about space and women's work in the home is found in Polly Wynn Allen (1988). This book, although not sociological in its interpretive framework, is a major examination of Gilman's intellectual work on the home and the needed transformation of space to liberate women in their everyday lives. An outstanding collection of articles, written primarily from a literary perspective, is found in Sheryl L. Meyering (1989). The major statements in several distinct subjects, such as "The Yellow Wallpaper" and Gilman's utopian visions, are found here. Lois N. Magner (1978) compared the influence of scientific language and concepts on the work of several feminists, including Gilman. Josephine Donovan (1988) also considers Gilman as both a theorist and in a comparative context.

Several major scholars have written important introductions to Gilman's reprinted books (see bibliography). In addition to these writings, these scholars often incorporate Gilman in their other writings. Thus William O'Neill (1967) has analyzed Gilman's role in changing ideas about divorce, the family, and the home. His book also considers the work of several male sociologists who influenced Gilman, as well as the work of Elsie Clews Parsons.* Carl N. Degler is widely recognized for his work on Gilman as well (e.g., 1966; see also Meyering 1989, 11–29).

Gilman is being rediscovered in sociology, too, through readings integrated into the classroom. Thus three articles in *Teaching Sociology*, by James L. Terry (1983), Mary Jo Deegan (1988), and Susan Gotsch-Thomson (1990), examine how to integrate Gilman's ideas into sociological training. Deegan (in progress) is systematically examining Gilman's satirical critique of male sociologists in the latter's utopian novels on "Herland" and "Ourland." The text is doubly viewed as a comment on patriarchal practice and on Gilman's social thought. Margaret Hobbs (1987) analyzed Gilman's pacifism, thereby being one of the first scholars to examine this important element in her epistemology. Alice S. Rossi* (1973), in a brief but important introductory statement, calls Gilman "The Militant Madonna," evoking the powerful but conflicting themes in the latter's thought. Despite this rich scholarship on Gilman, her genius and influence in sociology are barely tapped. A full appreciation of her work would place her within the circle of major founding scholars.

ACKNOWLEDGMENT

Thanks to Helena Franklin, editor at Pantheon Press, for providing a copy of Ann J. Lane's *To Herland and Beyond: The Life and Work of Charlotte Perkins Gilman* to include in this entry.

BIBLIOGRAPHY

Selected Writings by Charlotte Perkins Gilman

1890. "Similar Cases." *New England Magazine* 3 (September): 134–135.
1892. "The Yellow Wall-paper." *New England Magazine* 5 (January): 647–656. Re-

printed, *The Yellow Wallpaper*. Boston: Small, Maynard, 1899; with an afterword by Elaine Hedges. Old Westbury, NY: Feminist Press, 1973.

1893. *In This Our World*. Oakland, CA: McCombs and Vaughan.

1898. *Women and Economics: A Study of the Economic Relation Between Men and Women as a Factor in Social Evolution*. Boston: Small, Maynard. Reprinted, with an introduction by Carl N. Degler. New York: Harper & Row, 1970.

1900. *Concerning Children*. Boston: Small and Maynard.

1903. *The Home: Its Work and Influences*. New York: McClure and Phillips. Reprinted, with an introduction by William O'Neill. Urbana: University of Illinois Press, 1972.

1904a. "Domestic Economy." *Independent* 56 (June): 1359–1363.

1904b. "Kitchen Dirt and Civic Health." *Independent* 57 (December): 1296–1299.

1904c. *Human Work*. New York: McClure & Phillips.

1907. Comment on "Social Darwinism," by D. Colins Wells, and on "Social Consciousness," by Charles Horton Cooley. *American Journal of Sociology* 12 (March): 713–14, 690–691.

1908a. Comment on "The Basis of Social Conflict," by T. N. Carver. *American Journal of Sociology* 13 (March): 644–645.

1908b. Comment on "Class Conflict in America," by John R. Commons. *American Journal of Sociology* 13 (May): 781.

1908c. "A Suggestion of the Negro Problem." *American Journal of Sociology* 14 (July): 78–85.

1909a. "How Home Conditions React upon the Family." *American Journal of Sociology* 14 (March): 592–605.

1909b. "Race Improvement." *Independent* 66 (March): 629–632.

1909–1916. *The Forerunner*, Vols. 1–7. New York: Charlotte Perkins Gilman. Reprinted Westport, CT: Greenwood Press, 1968.

1911a. *The Man-Made World*. London: T. Fisher Unwin.

1911b. *Moving the Mountain*. New York: Charlton.

1912. "Are Women Human Beings?" *Harper's Weekly* 56 (May): 11.

1913. "The Waste of Private Housekeeping." *Annals of the American Academy of Political and Social Science* 48 (July): 91–95.

1914. "Social Ethics." *Forerunner* 5 (January): 20–25; (February): 48–53; (March): 76–82; (April): 102–108; (May): 130–136; (June): 160–166; (July): 187–193; (August): 216–222; (September): 244–249; (October): 271–277; (November): 300–305; (December): 327–332.

1915. *Herland*, with an introduction by Ann J. Lane. Reprinted New York: Pantheon, 1980.

1916. *With Her in Ourland*. Reprinted with an introduction by Mary Jo Deegan with the assistance of Michael R. Hill. Westport, CT: Greenwood Press, in progress.

1917. "The Housekeeper and the Food Problem." *Annals of the American Academy of Political and Social Science* 74 (November): 123–130.

1923. *His Religion and Hers: A Study of the Faith of Our Fathers and the Work of Our Mothers*. New York: Century. Reprinted, Westport, CT: Hyperion Press, 1976.

1935. *The Living of Charlotte Perkins Gilman: An Autobiography*, with foreword by Zona Gale. New York: Appleton-Century.

1980. *The Charlotte Perkins Gilman Reader*, edited by Ann J. Lane. New York: Pantheon.

Studies About Charlotte Perkins Gilman and Supplementary References

Allen, Polly Wynn. 1988. *Building Domestic Liberty: Charlotte Perkins Gilman's Architectural Feminism*. Amherst: University of Massachusetts Press.

Cott, Nancy F. 1987. *The Grounding of Modern Feminism*. New Haven, CT: Yale University Press.

Deegan, Mary Jo. 1988. "Transcending a Patriarchal Past." *Teaching Sociology* 16 (April): 141–159.

Deegan, Mary Jo, with the assistance of Michael R. Hill, In Progress. "The Journey from Herland to Ourland." Introduction to *With Her in Ourland*. Westport, CT: Greenwood Press.

Degler, Carl N. 1966. "Introduction to *Women and Economics*." New York: Harper & Row.

———. 1973. "Charlotte Perkins Gilman." In *Notable American Women*, edited by Edward T. James, pp. 39–43. Cambridge, MA: Harvard University Press.

Dell, Floyd. 1913. *Women as World Builders: Studies in Modern Feminism*. New York: Forbes.

Donovan, Josephine. 1985. *Feminist Theory*. New York: Frederick Ungar.

Gale, Zona. 1935. Foreword in *The Living of Charlotte Perkins Gilman: An Autobiography*, by Charlotte Perkins Gilman. New York: Appleton-Century. Reprinted, Salem, NH: Arno, 1972.

Giddings, Franklin H. 1908. "Are Contradictions of Ideas and Beliefs Likely to Play an Important Group-Making Role in the Future?" *American Journal of Sociology* 13 (May): 784–810.

Gotsch-Thomson, Susan. 1990. "The Integration of Gender into the Teaching of Classical Social Theory." *Teaching Sociology* 18 (January): 69–73.

Hill, Mary. 1980. *Charlotte Perkins Gilman: The Making of a Radical Feminist, 1860–1896*. Philadelphia: Temple University Press.

Hobbs, Margaret. 1987. "The Perils of Unbridled Masculinity: Pacifist Elements in the Feminist and Socialist Thought of Charlotte Perkins Gilman." In *Women and Peace: Theoretical, Historical and Practical Perspectives*, edited by Ruth Roach Pierson, with the assistance of Joanne Thompson, Soner Brodribb, and Paula Bournes, pp. 149–169. New York: Croom Helm.

Lane, Ann J. 1990. *To Herland and Beyond: The Life and Work of Charlotte Perkins Gilman*. New York: Pantheon.

Lasch, Christopher. 1965. *The New Radicalism in American, 1889–1963*. New York: Alfred A. Knopf.

Magner, Lois N. 1978. "Women and the Scientific Idiom: Textual Episodes from Wollstonecraft, Fuller, Gilman, and Firestone." *Signs* 4 (Autumn): 61–80.

Meyering, Sheryl L., ed. 1989. *Charlotte Perkins Gilman: The Woman and Her Work*. Foreword by Cathy M. Davidson. Ann Arbor: UMI Research Press.

O'Neill, William. 1967. *Divorce in the Progressive Era*. New York: New Viewpoints.

Park, Clara Cahill. 1936. "Review of *The Living of Charlotte Perkins Gilman*." *American Journal of Sociology* 41 (May): 701–702.

Pearson, Carol. 1981. "Coming Home: Four Feminist Utopias and Patriarchal Experience." In *Future Females: A Critical Anthology*, edited by Marlene S. Barr, pp. 63–70. Bowling Green, OH: Bowling Green State University Popular Press.

Rawls, M. 1986. "Herland and Out of the Silent Planet—A Comparison of a Feminist Utopia and a Male-Characterized Fantasy." *Mythlore* 48: 51–54.

Rossi, Alice S. 1973. "The Militant Madonna: Charlotte Perkins Gilman." In *The Feminist Papers*, edited by Alice S. Rossi, pp. 566–572. New York: Columbia University Press.

Ross, Edward A. 1936. *Seventy Years of It*. New York: Century.

Rubinow, I. M. 1909. "Women and Economic Dependence." *American Journal of Sociology* 14 (March): 618.

Scharnhorst, Gary. 1985a. *Charlotte Perkins Gilman*. Boston: Twayne.

———. 1985b. *Charlotte Perkins Gilman: A Bibliography*. Metuchen, NJ: Scarecrow.

Taft, Jessie. 1915. *The Woman Movement from the Point of View of Social Consciousness*. Chicago: University of Chicago Press.

Terry, James L. 1983. "Bringing Women . . . In: A Modest Proposal." *Teaching Sociology* 10 (January): 251–261.

Ward, Lester F. 1906. "The Past and Future of the Sexes." *Independent* 8 (March): 541.

BRUCE KEITH

MARGARET JARMAN HAGOOD
(1907–1963)

Margaret Jarman Hagood takes her place as a pioneer in statistics and demography, both of which were to become central to the study of sociology in the late twentieth century. Equally important is her contribution to qualitative sociology and to advocating by example a sociological methodology that combined the quantitative with the qualitative.

BIOGRAPHY

Hagood was born October 26, 1907, in Newton County, Georgia, the second child of four daughters and two sons of Lewis and Laura Harris Jarman. Her Scotch-Irish and English parents were strict Presbyterians. Lewis Jarman, a mathematician by training, farmed and taught school. He actively encouraged his daughters' education. Both Margaret and one of her sisters in fact earned doctorates.

Margaret, a precocious youngster, organized a Sunday school class for local mill children when she was thirteen and gave violin lessons at an early age. She attended a preparatory high school, Emory-at-Oxford, in Covington, California. Afterward she attended Scott College in Atlanta but left college in 1926 to marry a childhood sweetheart, Middleton Howard Hagood. In 1927 she gave birth to her only child, also named Margaret.

Meantime Hagood's father had become president of Queens College in Charlotte, North Carolina. Margaret resumed her college education there, graduating in 1929. In 1930 Hagood completed a master's of arts degree in mathematics at Emory University in Atlanta, where her husband was studying dentistry. Subsequently she taught for four years at the National Park Seminary in College Park, Maryland.

In 1935 Howard Odum, a family friend from Newton County and at that time head of the Institute for Research in Social Science at the University of North Carolina, Chapel Hill, offered Hagood a graduate fellowship in sociology. She joined a group of young scholars mentored by Odum—Rupert Vance, Katharine Jocher, and Guy and Guion Johnson. Hagood soon became a key figure in this group, noted for her intensity of purpose and capacity to become immersed in her work. Her strong background in mathematics had prepared her for work in two rapidly developing, related sociological areas: statistics and demography.

Among Hagood's friends at this time were some of the Chapel Hill radicals of the 1930s. In fact, that brought her an encounter with McCarthyism twenty years later, when she was prevented by the Federal Bureau of Investigation from attending an international conference in Rome because of her alleged communist sympathies.

In 1936 Margaret Hagood and her husband divorced. A year later she finished her dissertation, a pioneering statistical analysis of the fertility patterns of white women in the rural southeast, then the region of highest population growth in the nation.

Hagood received her Ph.D. from the University of North Carolina, Chapel Hill, in 1937. Subsequently she was appointed to the department of sociology in the same university and became a research associate in the Institute for Research in Social Science there. Soon thereafter Hagood began to examine the same population she had analyzed in her dissertation but from a different perspective. Traveling through several southern states, she interviewed farm tenant wives at length and wrote a careful and well-received qualitative study of tenant life. Published in 1939 as *Mothers of the South*, this work is a sensitive document of a vanishing way of life and considered one of the best records available of the daily experience of white Southern farmers in the midst of the Depression. Hagood's work was sponsored by the Subregional Laboratory for Social Research and Planning under the auspices of the Institute for Research in Social Science at the University of North Carolina.

Hagood then began another project that also belongs with the documentary expression of the thirties. With a fellow sociologist, Harriet Herring, and two photographers from the staff of the Farm Security Administration, Marion Post and Dorothea Lange, she compiled a detailed photographic record of the patterns of agriculture and farm life in the Southeast. This study formed the basis for an exhibit at the University of North Carolina in 1940 and, but for the disruption of World War II, would doubtless have been made into a book.

Hagood continued to refine and expand her interest and work in statistics and demography. At this time the social sciences were becoming increasingly quantitative, relying on emerging complex statistical methods. Hagood wrote *Statistics for Sociologists*, published in 1941 and in several later editions. The popular text influenced two generations of social science students.

Hagood left Chapel Hill in 1942 with the onset of U.S. involvement in World War II. She worked at the U.S. Department of Agriculture in the Bureau of

Agricultural Economics and in the Farm Population and Rural Life Branch of the Agricultural Marketing Service from 1942 to 1962. After 1952 she headed the Population and Rural Life Branch.

In 1947 Hagood was made an honorary member of the International Population Union. She was consultant on the Manpower Panel of the Research and Development Board, National Military Establishment, from 1948 to 1953. In 1949 Hagood participated in the World Statistical Conference, and in 1955–1956 she traveled as population expert and consultant with the U.N. Technical Assistance Mission to Barbados, West Indies. Hagood was a member of the Technical Advisory Committee on Population for the 1950 and 1960 censuses and participated in the World Population Conference in 1954.

Hagood is noted for her active participation in scientific and professional associations. In 1954 she served as president of the Population Association of America. In 1955 she served as a Fellow and member of the Board of Directors of the American Statistical Association and on the Executive Committee of the Council of the American Sociological Society. She was president of the Rural Sociological Society in 1956.

During 1951 Hagood was a visiting professor at the University of Wisconsin. She received the honorary degree of doctor of science from Queens College in 1955.

By the mid–1950s Hagood had developed a rheumatic heart condition; the sturdy young woman who had climbed Mount Mitchell three times gradually became frail and lost her capacity for hard work and research. She retired in 1962, and died of a heart attack in 1963 in San Diego, California, the home of one of her brothers.

MAJOR THEMES

Hagood demonstrated expertise in both quantitative and qualitative sociology and combined the two methodologies in her work with population and demography in the rural South. *Mothers of the South* (1939), written in the documentary expression characteristic of the 1930s, was an effort to get at the daily reality behind the statistics of the Depression. The combination of statistical, case, and survey methods is admirably adapted to the material. The cases studied were checked by various indices of mobility, education, age, age at marriage, number of years exposed to pregnancy, fertility, and occupation to show the extent to which they could be considered representative of the region from which they were selected.

For sixteen months Hagood traveled from tenant house to tenant house until she had visited 254 homes in the Carolina piedmont and in Georgia and Alabama, some of them several times. Her subjects found her ''not too far from former country ways to be able to understand.'' Consequently the reader gains some sense of the variety of individual personalities subsumed under the general term ''tenant wives.''

The book has three major divisions: Part I, "Farms"; Part II, "Mothers"; and Part III, "Meanings." Part I is a discussion of the general characteristics of the cultural pattern of Southern farming. Part II records the findings from detailed interviews with tenant women on issues that are of fundamental importance to women—field work, housekeeping, childbearing, child-"raising," wifehood, and community participation. Seven-eighths of the women interviewed preferred field work to housework and were more proud of their talents and accomplishments in the field and tobacco shed than they were of their talents and accomplishments in the kitchen. There seemed to be no complaint about a division of labor that put women in the field while discouraging men from taking part in housework or child care.

Hagood found the women and families she studied to have inadequate diet, housing, medical treatment, education, social life, and recreation. She found that "the burden of involuntary and over frequent childbearing" (1939: 243) often endangered the health and welfare of both mothers and children. After analyzing her data, Hagood concluded the following: "The account which we have presented of these disadvantaging conditions and their effects shows that the basic fact of high reproductivity under such conditions is socially undesirable for strictly sociological reasons" (1939: 244). As possible remedial measures, Hagood discusses regional planning, state contraception programs, evaluation and change of the single-crop system, and stronger national interest in the South's problems.

Hagood might be classified as a "socialist feminist." There are hints of Marxist theoretical perspective in *Mothers of the South*. It is the economy of the South that causes misery for not only mothers, but also for fathers and children. The oppressor is a "system" that oppresses low-status males and all females.

Soon after *Mothers of the South* went to press, Hagood, Harriet Herring, Dorothea Lange, and Marion Post created a comprehensive visual study of thirteen piedmont North Carolina counties. Together these women photographed sharecroppers, houses, fields, churches, county courthouses, tobacco barns, tobacco auctions, eroded land, growing crops, and landlords. In so doing they developed a visual image of the society and the economy of the region. Lange and Post took most of the pictures, while Hagood and Herring wrote the accompanying text. Hagood, the versatile methodologist, anticipated what has recently become known as "visual sociology" when she wrote to Roy Stryker of the Farm Security Administration: "I consider it an opportunity for us to demonstrate to ourselves and others some of the potentialities of Photography as a tool for social research."

But Hagood was both a qualitative and a quantitative sociologist. Her *Statistics for Sociologists*, first published in 1941 and revised in 1952 with Daniel O. Price, was a standard introductory text with emphasis on the correct application of statistical methods to sociological data and the careful interpretation of results. Moreover, while with the U.S. Department of Agriculture and particularly as head of the Farm Population and Rural Life Branch of the Agricultural Marketing

Service, Hagood created a "level-of-living index" for each county in the United States—an index that could be modified after each successive census and that enabled policymakers to make useful comparisons among counties.

CRITIQUES OF MARGARET JARMAN HAGOOD

Anne Firor Scott classifies *Mothers of the South* with *Middletown*, among others, as a significant record of an era that is rapidly being lost to living memory and one of the best nonfiction documentaries of its time. Accordingly, Scott effected the publication of a 1977 edition of the book. In Scott's words,

Hagood was too good a social scientist to draw more from her data than was justified and too sensitive a human being to turn her subjects into abstractions. She did not force her material into some a priori pattern of what was typical, not mistake the unusual for the norm. Her prose was plain and forceful, and she wrote with the mixture of detachment and involvement which is the hallmark of good social reporting. (1977: V)

Leonard W. Doob, reviewing *Mothers of the South*, called for more thorough interviews and a set of psychological theories that could have guided the interviews. Doob acknowledges, however, that "in terms of its expressed purpose this is an excellent book."

Reviewer Carl O. Taylor (1940) concluded "that the research method utilized is sound in making typological studies, and that the interpretations of the facts constitute valid sociological research materials." Reviewer William E. Cole (1940) saw the work as "adding new material and a new incentive to the all-important task of Southern development." According to Margaret Warnken Ryan (1940), "the major contribution of this book lies in the skill with which the author has used the methods and techniques of the case study to present a clear and unemotional picture of the white tenant farm woman."

Reviewing the first edition of *Statistics for Sociologists*, William M. Fuson (1942) found Hagood's "unique contribution" in "the simplicity and clarity of her description of the complicated settings in which statistical methods are or can be useful to the sociologist." Reviewer C. Horace Hamilton called *Statistics for Sociologists* an "up-to-date, comprehensive, and well-written text" (1942: 113).

The revised (1952) edition also was favorably received. Some critics argued that the text was improved by its revision. But at least two reviewers called for greater emphasis on the place of statistics in sociological methodology. According to Fred L. Strodtbeck,

statistics must be taught to our students in such a way that the substantive concerns of sociology and the logic of inquiry are more closely related. . . . Neither the book under review nor any other text known to the writer satisfies these criteria. (Strodtbeck 1953, 624)

Reviewer Frederick F. Stephan agreed: "The reviewer would prefer to slight some of the techniques in order to develop explicitly, and with well-chosen examples, the function that statistical analyses play in the larger context of research methodology" (1953: 367).

Asked to describe Hagood, her friends and colleagues typically related how hard she worked. She has been remembered not only for her intelligence, but also for her physical vigor, intensity of purpose, and single-minded dedication. She is pictured in some recollections as a person so caught up in her work that she might forget to comb her hair or eat regularly. Hagood's life illustrates the compromises traditionally required of women by marriage. The young woman dropped out of college to be married. She received her master's degree from the school that her husband had chosen to attend. After her divorce Hagood increasingly set her own professional direction.

BIBLIOGRAPHY

Selected Writings by Margaret Jarman Hagood

1939. *Mothers of the South: Portraiture of the White Tenant Farm Woman*. Chapel Hill: University of North Carolina Press.
1941. *Statistics for Sociologists*. New York: Reynal and Hitchcock. 2nd ed., New York: Holt, 1947.
1945. "Statistical Methods for Delineation of Regions Applied to Data on Agriculture and Population." *Social Forces* 11 (March): 287–297.
1948. "Changing Fertility Differentials Among Farm-Operator Families in Relation to Economic Size of the Farm." *Rural Sociology* 13 (December): 373–393.
1951. *Rural-Urban Migration in Wisconsin, 1940–1950*. Madison: Wisconsin Experiment Station.
1952. *Farm-Operator Family Level-of-Living for Counties of the United States; 1930, 1940, 1945, and 1950*. Washington, DC: U.S. Bureau of Agricultural Economics.

Coauthored Works

Bogue, Donald J., and Margaret J. Hagood, assisted by Gladys K. Bowle, Ruth W. Smith, and Elizabeth J. Bogue. 1953. *Subregional Migration in the United States*. Vol. 2. *Differential Migration in the Corn and Cotton Belts*. Oxford, OH: Miami University, Scripps Foundation.
Ducoff, Louis J., and Margaret J. Hagood. 1947. *Labor Force Definition and Measurement: Recent Experience in the United States*. New York: Subcommittee on Labor Force Statistics of the Committee on Labor Market Research.
———. 1952. *Differentials in Productivity and in Income by Size of Enterprise and by Regions*. Washington, DC: U.S. Bureau of Agricultural Economics.
Hagood, Margaret J., and Daniel Price. 1952. *Statistics for Sociologists*, rev. ed. New York: Holt.
Hagood, Margaret J., and Emmit F. Sharp. 1951. *Rural-Urban Migration in Wisconsin, 1940–1950*. Madison: University of Wisconsin Press.

Hagood, Margaret J., and Jacob S. Siegel. 1951. *Projections of the Regional Distribution of the Population of the United States*. Washington, DC: U.S. Department of Agriculture, Bureau of Agricultural Economics.

Studies About Margaret Jarman Hagood and Supplementary References

Cole, William E. 1940. "Review of *Mothers of the South*." *Social Forces* 18: 450–451.

Doob, Leonard W. 1940. "Review of *Mothers of the South*." *American Journal of Sociology* 46 (November): 408–409.

Eldridge, Hope. 1964. "Margaret Jarman Hagood, 1907–1963." *Population Index* 30 (January): 30–32.

Fuson, William N. 1942. "Review of *Statistics for Sociologists*." *American Sociological Review* 7 (June): 440–441.

Hamilton, C. Horace. 1942. "Review of *Statistics for Sociologists*." *Rural Sociology* 7 (March): 112–114.

———. 1953. "Review of *Statistics for Sociologists*, Revised Edition." *Rural Sociology* 18 (September): 275–277.

Ryan, Margaret Warnken. 1940. "Review of *Mothers of the South*." *Rural Sociology* 5 (June): 271.

Scott, Anne Firor. 1977. "Introduction to the Norton Library Edition." In *Mothers of the South*, by Margaret J. Hagood, p. iii–x. New York: W. W. Norton.

———. 1980. "Hagood, Margaret Loyd Jarman." In *Notable American Women: The Modern Period*, p. 297–298. Cambridge, MA: Harvard University Press, Belknap Press.

Stephan, Frederick F. 1953. "Review of *Statistics for Sociologists*, Revised Edition." *Social Forces* 31: 367.

Strodtbeck, Fred L. 1953. "Review of *Statistics for Sociologists*, Revised Edition." *American Journal of Sociology* 58 (May): 623–624.

Taeuber, Conrad. 1963. "Margaret Jarman Hagood, 1908–1963." *American Statistician* 17 (October): 37.

Taylor, Carl C. 1940. "Review of *Mothers of the South*." *American Sociological Review* 5 (October): 787–789.

———. 1964. "Margaret J. Hagood, (1907–1963)." *Rural Sociology* 29 (March): 97–98.

Tibbitts, Clark. 1942. "Review of *Statistics for Sociologists*." *American Journal of Sociology* 48 (September): 263–665.

AGNES RIEDMANN

AMY HEWES (1877–1970)

Amy Hewes was an outstanding early graduate and practitioner of the Chicago school of sociology. Unlike many of her male cohort in this school of thought, Hewes innovatively changed their apolitical interpretations by focusing on issues of labor, social policy, and women in the public sphere. She combined her scholarship on democracy and education with socialism, unionization, and labor movements in other countries.

BIOGRAPHY

Amy Hewes was born in Baltimore, Maryland, on September 8, 1877, the daughter of Edwin and Martha Gardner (Gover) Hewes. Details of her childhood and youth remain unknown. She must have been a bit of a rebel, for she was part of the earliest cohort of women to obtain higher education. She earned a bachelor of arts degree from Goucher College in 1897 and received some graduate training at the University of Berlin (Office of Press Relations, p. 1, Mount Holyoke College, Hewes Papers, Mount Holyoke Library, College Archives, hereafter referred to as "Hewes Papers"). This Germanic background gave her a career pattern similar to that of young male sociologists of her day.

Hewes decided to enter the new discipline of sociology, and matriculated at the new and leading department at the University of Chicago. Her brilliance as a scholar was soon apparent, and she became a "fellow" in the sociology department from 1898 to 1899. She was the only woman given such recognition from 1892 to 1920, although there were three to five such scholarships available per year (*University of Chicago Annual Register*, 1897–1898, p. 203). In 1903 she finished her doctoral dissertation at Chicago, *The Part of Invention in the Social Process*.

From 1903 to 1905 Hewes was unable to find employment as an academic. A brief correspondence between Hewes and Albion Small, the chair of the department at Chicago, poignantly reveals her struggle to find an academic placement. These letters are remarkable documents because they show her personal fight for a place in the academy, and they reveal the public barriers facing female sociologists who wanted to enter the academy as professors.

The first letter is written by Hewes to Small on June 11, 1904, a year after she completed her doctorate (Hewes to Small, Small Papers, Box 1, Folder 6, University of Chicago, Regenstein Library, Department of Special Collections, hereafter referred to as "Small Papers"). It is typed on letterhead from "the Educational Department of Underwood and Underwood, Publishers in New York City." She starts by politely declining an offer for employment, arranged by Small, to teach German. She notes:

I want very much to teach. I know that unless I do it next year, the chances are I never will, for I must settle down to something permanent.

In political science—civics, constitutional and diplomatic history, elementary economics and sociology—or something within hailing distance of these I should not hesitate—but German is a sight too wide of the mark.

Another obstacle is the salary since for the present there are demands which make that a question I cannot neglect. The compensation here is $1200, which would probably be $1500 next year, though the expenses of New York of course make this only the equivalent of a less sum elsewhere. . . . If there is a chance for any real teaching I should be very glad indeed to know more of the position. There is no future here for me at any rate so that I am determined upon some change.

After writing this letter, Hewes wrote Small again, urging his support in her quest for an academic position, and fearful that her refusing the position in "German" would be interpreted as "ungrateful." "I trust you did not regard me concerning the Florida position as indifferent. On the contrary, while as it stood, it was not what one might wish, I hoped some rearrangement of the proposition might be made, which would be acceptable" (Hewes to Small, June 28, 1904, Small Papers).

After two years of struggle, Hewes finally won a niche in a female academy as an instructor in economics and politics at Mount Holyoke. Although this institution was a well-known college for women, her position as instructor and the departmental work were not commensurate with her skills and training.

Hewes rapidly became recognized as a scholar, however, and by 1909 she had reached the rank of professor and was appointed chair of the department of economics and sociology. She held this position from that time until her retirement in 1943. She was an emeritus professor from 1943 until her death in 1970. Clearly, Hewes retained her identification with sociology; this is reflected in the title of the department she chaired. Professional recognition by sociologists, however, was limited. She was widely honored in the discipline of economics but not of sociology.

Despite Hewes' achievement of eminent credentials from the University of Chicago as a sociologist, her life's work was rooted in the female division of labor in the discipline. Her interest in a female Chicago school of women's paid labor (evident in the work of Edith Abbott,* Sophonisba Breckinridge,* and Annie Marion MacLean,* among others) and in social reform activities sponsored by women of the Chicago school is evident. From 1913 to 1915 she served on the first Massachusetts Minimum Wage Commission after the first such law was passed in the United States in 1912. The Minimum Wage Law was actively promoted by Jane Addams,* Edith Abbott, Emily Greene Balch,* and Florence Kelley,* among others. Similarly, Hewes, like Annie Marion MacLean, Lucile Eaves,* and Susan Kingsbury,* served as supervisor of research for the Women's Educational and Industrial Union in Boston. She also worked as the executive secretary of the Committee on Women in Industry, Council of National Defense, along with Mary Van Kleeck* from 1917 to 1919.

Hewes' numerous other activities for social change, especially improved labor conditions for women, are summarized in the following statement:

During her career, Miss Hewes also served [as] . . . supervisor of Industrial Service Section, Ordinance Department, United States Army; . . . member of the Advisory Council of State Employment Offices and members of the executive committees; member of the Advisory Board of Massachusetts Consumers League; member of the U.S. State Department Sub-Committee on labor standards and social security; member of the U.S. Department of Labor Advisory technical committee on standard adequate budgets; member of the Women in Industries Committee of the Massachusetts State Federation of Women's Clubs, member of a special commission to investigate operation of the Massachusetts Minimum Wage Law; and member of the Advisory Council of the Massachusetts Unemployment Compensation Commission. (Office of Press Relations, pp. 1–2, Hewes Papers)

In these committees she worked closely with other critical pragmatists, especially with Mary van Kleeck and the women who staffed the Women's Bureau in Washington, D.C.

Hewes also participated in the exciting workers' educational experiment at the Bryn Mawr Summer School for Women Workers (discussed more fully in the entry on Susan Kingsbury). A humorous account of Hewes is briefly related in the film *The Women of Summer,* in which the former students recall at a reunion in the 1970s that "Miss Hewes" would carry water to them during their softball games. She would run and shout that they were bourgeoise, whereas she was a mere proletariat at their beck and call.

Hewes retired from Mount Holyoke College in 1943 after a lengthy and eminent career dedicated to women and their right to work in the marketplace. The Department of Economics and Sociology flourished under her guidance. Many of the graduates went on to graduate training, particularly in social work.

She continued an active political and scholarly life for the next two decades. On March 16, 1962, she received a citation from the Secretary of Labor, Arthur J. Goldberg, "in recognition of her significant and outstanding contribution toward furthering the work of the Department of Labor'' to foster, promote, and develop the welfare of the wage earners of the United States. By 1969 her companion Madeline Grant noted that Hewes had become senile, and they were searching for a nursing home that would accept both of them. Hewes, nonetheless, continued to maintain a spunky spirit despite her degeneration. For example, when Grant asked her how she felt, Hewes replied: ''I have no brain, but I look out upon the world pleasantly'' (Madeline Grant to ''Mary,'' June 15, 1969, p. 1, Hewes Papers). Hewes died on March 25, 1970 after a full and productive life, filled with many friends and accomplishments.

MAJOR THEMES

Hewes dedicated her life to greater equality for laborers, particularly female laborers. She headed cooperative research teams of working-class women studying at the Bryn Mawr Summer School for many years (e.g., in 1923, 1925, 1926, 1934). Hewes incorporated systematic analysis *by workers* of their lives into their formal education. She worked to empower them, partly by making their lives visible to others. The workers' studies reveal the harsh employment conditions they experienced and their exploitation even under the National Recovery Act of 1934. Hewes' commitment to worker and vocational education while she labored in an elite, private women's college must have been a striking paradox in her everyday life.

Hewes firmly believed in the collection of quantitative data as a means of education, sociological methodology, and social change. This system of belief is now considered ''mainstream'' sociology, but in her training it was considered technical and relatively trivial ''women's work.'' She continued her pattern of doing collective research at Mount Holyoke, too. In this way she established the model later formalized by Lucile Eaves in her work on cooperative research.

Her book on *Women as Munition Makers* (1917a) examined the rise of the armament industry in Bridgeport, Connecticut, immediately prior to the United States entry into World War I. Hewes documented the dangerous and hard work of predominantly local women who needed money. This study would allow an interesting comparison with the women munition workers of World War II who were subjected to the government propaganda on ''Rosie the Riveter.'' Hewes did, in fact, publish her work in conjunction with a similar study by Henriette R. Walter on *Munition Workers in England and France*. (This study was even bound in the same volume I read.) Women in all three countries engaged in this gendered war work with similar financial needs and domestic circumstances.

The status of women in the marketplace is a key theme in all Hewes' writings. Her work augments that of her female colleagues, particularly the women who worked and studied at the University of Chicago. She was particularly close to the work of Edith Abbott, including the study of early women's history (Hewes 1928a) and the work on the Wickersham Commission (see discussion of Hewes in Hill 1989). She also shared the interests of Susan Kingsbury in studying the

U.S.S.R. (Hewes 1920c, 1922a, 1922b, 1923a, 1923c). Hewes and Kingsbury shared a mutual interest in the Bryn Mawr Summer School (Hewes 1925b), cofounded by Kingsbury, while Jessie Taft* also worked there. Women's education was another theme in Hewes' work, shared with her sister students, and reflecting the influence of Marion Talbot* (Hewes 1911). Hewes focused on issues of labor, social policy, and women in the public sphere. This was combined with her scholarship on socialism, unionization, and labor movements in other countries. In the latter areas she overlapped with the interests of Beatrice Webb* and other fabian socialists (e.g., Hewes 1920a, 1922c, 1926a, 1928c,).

Like these other Chicago sociologists, Hewes was increasingly aligned with social work. Her study of *The Contributions of Economics to Social Work* (1930b) is a sociological analysis of social work as an occupation, shaped and interacting with material resources. It is a sophisticated analysis of liberal economic theory, political constraints, and the formation of social welfare as work. Hewes worked here within a liberal framework questioning the limits on the occupation in the United States.

WRITINGS ON AMY HEWES

Three of Hewes' books were reviewed in *The American Journal of Sociology*, reflecting the gendered division of labor in sociology. Edith Abbott positively reviewed *Women as Munition Makers*, particularly praising her analyses of processes of work and the impact of nighttime labor on women (Abbott 1918). Ordway Tead, then Secretary of the Massachusetts Commission on Unemployment, found *Industrial Home Work in Massachusetts* (1915) confusing. Tead's bias against paying women a living wage and argument for greater power in the hands of government administrators blatantly disqualified him as an objective judge of Hewes (Tead 1916). Finally, J. F. Steiner (1931) criticized her book on *The Contribution of Economics to Social Work* by claiming that "economists" should be more interdisciplinary than Hewes. The social workers did not like this book either, as shown in Helen R. Wright's analysis in *Social Service Review*. Wright found the book confusing in its intent and in its "voice" to an audience (1931).

Hewes is basically forgotten in the annals of the discipline today. To obtain background information on her life and work, I used the archives of Mount Holyoke with the help of the very supportive archivists there. Despite this neglect, Hewes was a major figure in the Chicago women's development of sociology. As a colleague, author, professor, and researcher, she elaborated on other women's studies of women's work in everyday life, in women's colleges, and in women's sociological institutions located in Boston and in Bryn Mawr. As a doctoral graduate from the University of Chicago, Hewes anticipated a full academic career in mainstream sociology. She was thwarted in this ambition but survived and flourished in her adaptation to the women's world in sociology.

BIBLIOGRAPHY

Archives

Amy Hewes Papers. Mt. Holyoke College, Library, College Archives.

Albion Small Papers. University of Chicago, Regenstein Library, Department of Special Collections. Box 1, Folder 6.

Selected Writings by Amy Hewes

1899. "Seminar Notes: Social Interest and the Riemann Surface." *American Journal of Sociology* 5 (November): 392–403.

1903. "The Part of Invention in the Social Process." Ph.D. diss., Department of Sociology, University of Chicago.

1911. "Marital and Occupational Statistics of Graduates of Mount Holyoke." *American Statistical Association Publications* 12 (December): 771–797.

1915. *Industrial Home Work in Massachusetts*. Prepared under the joint direction of the Massachusetts Bureau of Statistics and Amy Hewes, Supervisor of the Department of Research. Boston: Women's Educational and Industrial Union.

1916. "Bridgeport on the Rebound." *Survey* 37 (October 14): 49–51.

1917. "Women as Munition Makers." *Survey* 37 (January 6): 379–385.

1917b. *Women as Munition Makers*. New York: Russell Sage Foundation.

1919. "Dependents of College Teachers." *Publications of the American Statistical Association* 16 (December): 502–511.

1920a. "Rent Restrictions in England." *Survey* 44 (September 1): 687–688.

1920b. "The H. C. of L. in England." *Survey* 44 (September 15): 701–702.

1920c. "Labor Conditions in Soviet Russia." *Journal of Political Economy* 28 (November): 774–783.

1921. "New Wine in Old Bottles." *Survey* 47 (December 3): 372–373.

1922a. "Russian Wage System under Communism." *Journal of Political Economy* 30 (April): 274–278.

1922b. "The Attitude of the Soviet Government Toward Cooperation." *Journal of Political Economy* 30 (June): 412–416.

1922c. "Guild Socialism: A Two Years' Test." *American Economic Review* 12 (June): 209–237.

1922d. "Standardization of the Whipple Healy Tapping Test." *Journal of Applied Psychology* 6 (June): 113–119.

1923a. "The Russian Labor Code of 1922." *Current History* 18 (June): 456–460.

1923b. "Note on the Racial and Educational Factors in the Declining Birth-Rate." *American Journal of Sociology* 29 (September): 178–187.

1923c. "Trade Union Development in Soviet Russia." *American Economic Review* 13 (December): 618–637.

1924. "The International Labor Conference." *Review of Reviews* 70 (November): 511–515.

1925a. *Women Workers and Family Support*. Bull. No. 49. Women's Bureau, U.S. Department of Labor.

1925b. "Bryn Mawr Summer School." *American Federationist* 32 (August): 654–658.

1926a. "England's Unemployed." *Review of Reviews* 73 (January): 61–64.

1926b. "The 'Aged Citizens' of Massachusetts." *Survey* 55 (February 15): 554–556.

1926c. "Kettles and Shiners." *Survey* 56 (September 15): 637.

1926d. *Changing Jobs*. Bull. No. 54. Women's Bureau, U.S. Department of Labor.

1927a. "The Savings of Women Workers." *American Federationist* 34 (January): 72–77.

1927b. "Education for Everybody." *Survey* 57 (February 15): 653–654.

1927c. "The Economic and Social Status of the Injured Workman Under the New York Compensation Law." *Social Service Review* 1 (December): 606–620.

1928a. "Early Eighteenth Century Women (1689–1750)." In *The Commonwealth History of Massachusetts*, Vol. 2, edited by Albert B. Hart, p. 355–385. New York: States History Co.

1928b. "Further Adventures in Learning." *Goucher Alumnae Quarterly* 7 (April): 3–7.

1928c. "Functional Representation in the International Labor Organization." *American Political Science Review* 22 (May): 324–338.

1929. "Municipal Spending." *Social Forces* 8 (December): 274–283.

1930a. "Clerical Occupations." In *Encyclopaedia of the Social Sciences*, Vol. 3, edited by E.R.A. Seligman and Alvin S. Johnson, p. 550–554. New York: Macmillan.

1930b. *The Contributions of Economics to Social Work*. New York: Columbia University Press.

1930c. "Economic Myths." *Social Service Review* 4 (March): 23–30.

1930d. "Scribes and Scriveners." *Goucher Alumnae Quarterly* 9 (November): 11–16.

1930e. "Use of Electrical Appliances in the Home." *Social Forces* 9 (December): 235–242.

1941. "Lyman Terrace: A Small Housing Project." *Social Service Review* 16 (March): 86–102.

1957. "Workers' Education in the United States." *International Labour Review* 76 (November): 1–23.

Coauthored Works

Hewes, Amy, Charlotte Arnold, Edith Buck, Katharine Merriam, and Julia Stockover. 1925. "A Study of Delinquent Girls at Sleighton Farm." *Journal of the American Institute of Criminal Law and Criminology* 15 (February): 598–619.

Hewes, Amy, director, with Mildred Holt, Sophie Meranski, and Julia Snell. 1924. "Mental Age and School Attainment of 1007 Retarded Children in Massachusetts." *Journal of Educational Psychology* 15 (April): 297–301.

————, director with Nine Students at Mount Holyoke College. 1930. "Municipal Revenue in Massachusetts." *Bulletin of the National Tax Association* 16 (November): 45–50.

Studies About Amy Hewes and Supplementary References

Abbott, Edith. 1918. "Review of *Women as Munition Makers*." *American Journal of Sociology* 23 (January): 551–552.

Dietrich, Ethel Barbara. 1937. "Origin and History of the Department." In *Centennial Bulletin of the Department of Economics and Sociology*, p. 4–8. South Hadley, MA: Mount Holyoke College.

"Hewes, Amy." 1973. In *Who Was Who in America*, Vol. 5, p. 330. Chicago: Marquis.

Steiner, J. F. 1931. "Review of *The Contribution of Economics to Social Work.*" *American Journal of Sociology* 36 (March): 844–845.

Tead, Ordway. 1916. "Review of *Industrial Home Work in Massachusetts.*" *American Journal of Sociology* 21 (May): 701–702.

University of Chicago Annual Register, 1897–1898. 1898. Chicago: University of Chicago Press.

Walter, Henriette R. 1917. *Munition Workers in England and France.* New York: Russell Sage Foundation.

Wright, Helen R. 1931. "Review of *The Contribution of Economics to Social Work.*" *Social Service Review* 5 (March): 141–142.

Film with Mention of Amy Hewes

The Women of Summer. c. 1986. A film by Suzanne Bauman and Rita Heller. Distributed by Filmmakers Library, New York.

Unpublished Material

Hill, Michael. 1989. "Roscoe Pound and American Sociology: A Study in Archival Frame Analysis, Sociobiography, and Sociological Jurisprudence." Ph.D. diss., Department of Sociology, University of Nebraska–Lincoln.

MARY JO DEEGAN

LETA STETTER HOLLINGWORTH (1886–1939)

Leta Anna Stetter Hollingworth is noted for her scientific scholarship in psychology, education, and feminist issues. Her research, advocacy, and administrative work in the areas of the social psychology of the intellectually gifted and of adolescents gained her an international reputation. Hollingworth's recognition as a sociologist is overdue. In fact, she began her professional career as a sociologist but left the field when she shifted to a "women's department," the Teachers College at Columbia University.

BIOGRAPHY

Hollingworth was born May 25, 1886, on a homestead near Chadron, Nebraska. She was the oldest of three daughters of John G. and Margaret Elinor Danley Stetter. Her father was a second-generation German immigrant. Her mother, devoted and well educated, died in 1890. Seventeen years later, in one of her many personal letters, Leta wrote: "Nobody knows how I have longed for her to be alive." For eight years after their mother's death, the daughters were reared by their maternal grandparents, to whom Leta later dedicated one of her books, *Gifted Children* (1926). At age twelve Leta and her sisters went to live with their father, by then remarried, in Valentine, Nebraska. Family life in Valentine was apparently unhappy for Leta, who later described these years as a "fiery furnace."

After attending Valentine High School, Hollingworth entered the University of Nebraska in 1902 at age sixteen. There she qualified for a teaching certificate and also specialized in creative writing, being selected class poet. With her future husband she received her bachelor's degree from the University of Nebraska in 1906, graduating with Phi Beta Kappa honors.

On graduation Hollingworth taught in Nebraska high schools until she married Harry Levi Hollingworth on New Year's Eve, 1908, and moved to New York City in 1909. Harry, a graduate student at Columbia University, subsequently became professor of psychology there. But the intervening five years were difficult financially.

During much of that time Leta was intellectually frustrated and occasionally discouraged and depressed. As a married woman, she found herself ineligible to teach in New York's public schools. She continued to write and took graduate courses in literature but was unable to market her work. She applied for various scholarships and fellowships but was unsuccessful in that area as well.

Three years after her marriage, the couple's finances improving, Leta returned to academic work. She specialized in sociology and education. In June 1913 she received both the master of arts degree and the master's diploma in education from Columbia University. Her professors at Columbia included educational psychologist Edward L. Thorndike and sociologist Franklin Giddings.

Her master's diploma in education qualified Hollingworth for temporary part-time work administering the recently developed Binet, Goddard, and Terman mental tests at the New York City Clearing-House for Mental Defectives. In 1914 psychologists administering such tests were put under New York City's civil service supervision, and Hollingworth became one of the first such psychologists appointed. Transferred the next year, 1915, to the psychopathic service of Bellevue Hospital, Hollingworth worked in the emerging field of clinical psychology and helped to found the American Association of Clinical Psychology. In 1916 Hollingworth completed her doctorate in sociology and education at Columbia University, with Professor Henry Suzzallo, an educational sociologist, as a member of her doctoral committee. By this time she was author of one book and nine scientific papers, all concerned with the social psychology of women.

When Professor Naomi Norsworthy died in 1916, Hollingworth was asked to fill her position at Teachers College, Columbia University. In accepting the position, Hollingworth moved into a "women's department" where, among others, Elsie Clews Parsons,* and Anna Garlin Spencer* also found employment. Here she joined other female sociologists who were making similar necessary adaptive transitions—away from male-dominated sociology and into the more accessible "women's professions," such as teaching and social work. Among these were Julia Lathrop, Jessie Taft,* and Ethel Sturgess Dummer. Hollingworth remained at Columbia for the rest of her life, becoming a full professor of education in 1929.

While at Columbia Hollingworth served as adviser to the department of ungraded classes in the New York City school system and to other administrators who were originating special education programs nationally and internationally. In 1920 she published *The Psychology of Subnormal Children*, largely responsible for the establishment of what are now called special education classes. Also interested in the psychology of adolescence, Hollingworth published *The Psy-*

chology of the Adolescent in 1928, a text that became the field standard and gained international acclaim. Meanwhile Hollingworth became professionally interested in the intellectually gifted, or "favorable deviates," as she termed them. Her volume *Gifted Children* (1926) gained international attention. By 1936 an "experimental" school for gifted children, the Speyer School (P.S. 500), opened in New York City with Hollingworth in charge of research programs. Conducted in cooperation with Columbia University, the Speyer project was to continue for five years. Hollingworth's death in 1939 prevented her from seeing the project to its finish.

Hollingworth was an active member of the Woman's Suffrage party and, with her husband, a frequent suffrage marcher. Her early work on the social psychology of women established her as a scientific spokesperson for the women's movement. With colleagues Elsie Clews Parsons and Charlotte Perkins Gilman,* Hollingworth was a member of and frequent speaker before a luncheon club of New York City feminists known as Heterodoxy.

Hollingworth was a member of Chi Omega, Kappa Delta Phi, the American Psychological Association, and the National Education Association. She received a number of formal honors during her lifetime, including biographical sketches in *American Men of Science, Who's Who in Literature*, and *Who's Who in the East*. On June 6, 1938, Leta S. Hollingworth received the honorary degree of doctor of laws from the University of Nebraska. Eighteen months later, November 27, 1939, at age fifty-three, Leta Stetter Hollingworth died in the Columbia-Presbyterian Medical Center in New York City of abdominal cancer. She is buried in Wyuka Cemetery, Lincoln, Nebraska.

MAJOR THEMES

Hollingworth's work in psychology and education is documented elsewhere (Rosenberg 1984; Shields 1975). This section addresses Hollingworth's contributions to sociology. A sociological imagination permeated virtually every scientific piece Hollingworth wrote, and she should be considered one of the early theorists in what is today called "sociology of knowledge." Consistently interested in separating scientific fact from myth, Hollingworth demonstrated not only that much of what passed as science was unfounded in research, but also how scientific mythology ("armchair dogma") works as a device for social control.

Hollingworth's first major sociological work was *Functional Periodicity: An Experimental Study of the Mental and Motor Abilities of Women During Menstruation* (1914a). Her research, she explained, was "an effort to treat objectively this phenomenon concerning which such a remarkable variety of folk-lore and superstition has survived." She tested twenty-three women and two men, the latter used as controls, over a period of three months in various perceptual, motor, and mental tasks. She found no differences in performance associated with any phase of the menstrual cycle. Hollingworth took the occasion to point out that despite a dearth of experimental research, "scientific opinion has expressed itself frequently and freely." The unfounded "dogma" of menstrual mystery, "once formulated has been quoted on authority from author to author until the present day." Hollingworth pointed out that the myth served to legitimate institutional barriers to women. For example, authorities used the dogma to support opposition to medical education and public administration careers for women.

A second "scientific fiction" (cf. Larry T. Reynolds, "A Note on the Perpetuation of a 'Scientific Fiction,' " Sociometry 29 [1966]) debunked by Hollingworth was the popular variability hypothesis. (Interestingly, Professor Edward Thorndike, who had supervised Hollingworth's research on functional periodicity, was a staunch proponent of the variability hypothesis.)

The variability hypothesis held that women, as a category, were less variable intellectually than men. After a thorough literature review and a pioneering series of experimental research projects conducted in part at the Clearing House, Hollingworth concluded that "the theory exists, but the evidence does not." She pointed to what sociologists would later term the "social construction of reality" and to the function of that reality in sexism:

About a century ago the anatomist Meckel . . . concluded . . . that the human female was more variable than the human male; and he thought that, "since woman is the inferior animal, and variation a sign of inferiority, the conclusion is justified." Later, when variability came to be regarded as a sign of superiority and as a trait affording the greatest hope for progress, anatomists and naturalists arrived at the conclusion that the male is more variable. Men of science . . . declared women's failure in intellectual achievement to be due to this fact. . . . It scarcely seems likely that much trustworthy information will be accessible on this subject till women have prosecuted their own researches into it. (Lowie and Hollingworth 1916, 283–284)

In designing her own variability research, Hollingworth was unquestionably sociological. For example, in one project she chose to compare anatomical measurements from newborn males and females rather than from adults. Newborns, she reasoned, would be free of divergent socialization and institutional effects. Women's and men's lives, she argued, "are lived under conditions so different as to constitute practically different environments." Because men, but not women, "are free to follow a great variety" of professions, "we should expect to find adult males more variable." More than likely the cause for sex differences in achievement or "eminence" is that women have been relegated to housekeeping, "a field where eminence is not possible."

If eminence is not possible in housekeeping—nor in childbearing and child rearing—how is it, Hollingworth asked, that women so predictably follow this life course? Her answer, in "Social Devices for Impelling Women to Bear and Rear Children" (1916a), lays the theoretical groundwork for subsequent work in the social construction of pronatalism. Socially constructed "types," such as the "womanly woman," institutionalized by the medical profession, media, law, education, and art, effect "a continuous social effort to insure" reproduction. Moreover, that social control is primarily in the hands of relatively powerful men, the "social guardians." In using the concept "social guardians," Hollingworth anticipates Howard Becker's better known concept "morals entrepreneurs" in *Outsiders* (1963).

The greater share of Hollingworth's work in the sociology of knowledge concerns the status of women. A "cultural feminist," Hollingworth believed in the power of methodologically rigorous scientific inquiry to promote gender equality. Only when "the literature of opinion" finally gave way to "the literature of fact," Hollingworth believed, could women's status improve.

For Hollingworth, the "woman question" was how to reproduce the species and at the same time realize work's full reward in accordance with one's individual ability. The eventual solution proceeded from the perspective of reality construction. Not only would "folk-psychological prejudices" against women be scientifically debunked, but also individual women, by choosing to lead a myriad of "experimental lives," would challenge and change institutionally reified and repressive beliefs, values, and norms.

SURVEY OF CRITICISM

Hollingworth's death was noted in the *New York Times*, in a Report of the President of the Carnegie Corporation, in the *American Journal of Psychology*, and in *Science*. A. T. Poffenberger, in the *American Journal of Psychology*, reviewed her writings and other professional activities and argued that these placed her "among the eminent psychologists of her time." Arthur I. Gates, in *Science*, wrote that Hollingworth's

intense interest in and devotion to the living individual, undistorted by sentimentality, and coupled with the clear-eyed vision of the scientist, of whose tools she was a master, account for the unique scientific validity and practical value of Professor Hollingworth's work. (1940: 11)

Harry L. Hollingworth (1943) wrote a biography of his wife in which he examined her childhood and college years, along with her professional work. He also wrote a brief introduction to his wife's *Children Above 180 I.Q.* (1942), published posthumously. Therein he briefly described his wife's work on the book before her death and her aborted plans for its completion.

Shields (1975) examined Hollingworth's work in the psychology of women. She suggests that Hollingworth's early frustration as a full-time housewife in New York City helped to motivate her to research women's issues. Rosalind Rosenberg (1984) reviews Hollingworth's early contributions to the psychology of women. Rosenberg argues that Hollingworth might never have studied sex differences at Columbia University had she not been married to Professor Harry Hollingworth, who, in contrast to many of his Columbia colleagues, was an outspoken defender of feminism. Ludy T. Benjamin, Jr., reviewed Hollingworth as "psychologist, educator, feminist" for a June 1984 special issue on women in Nebraska history. Rheta Childe Dorr (1924) and Judith Schwartz (1982) discuss Hollingworth's participation in Heterodoxy as a valued member and speaker on the social psychology of women.

Hollingworth's career is one marked by the sort of compromise exacted of women but not of men. She sought to combine intellectual stimulation with marriage and, although successful, encountered difficulty. Although she was fortunate to have a supportive husband, even he allowed the couple to choose to further only his career early in the marriage when money was tight. Despite her later success in the "woman's field" of education—and despite her recognition, primarily among women, as an important early scientist in the psychology of women—Hollingworth's is a poignant picture of absent institutionalized support. In the words of her husband:

For her actual work, at any designated responsibility, she was always rewarded with promotion and due compensation. But she was never successful, as many appear easily enough to be, in enlisting the aid of any of the social agencies, foundations, or institutions in any original enterprise of hers, however significant.

No one will ever know what she might have accomplished for human welfare, always her dominant motive, if some of the sponsorship freely poured out on many a scholarly dullard had been made available for her own projects. (1943, 99)

CRITIQUES OF LETA STETTER HOLLINGWORTH

The best biography on Leta Stetter Hollingworth is her husband's fond and personal account (1943). He also was integral to the production of two outstanding special issues of *Teachers College Record*. The first issue, on "Education and the Individual," summarizes her life; contains a thorough bibliography and list of her doctoral students' dissertations; and summarizes her work in six areas of specialization (1940). The second issue is devoted to the "Education for the Gifted" (1941), providing a broad overview of her foundational role and influence in this area.

Ludy T. Benjamin, Jr., (1984) and Stephanie A. Shields (1975, 1982, Benjamin and Shields, 1990) have written a series of informative biographical and analytical articles on Hollingworth. Both stress her work as a psychologist, with Benjamin having slightly more emphasis on Hollingworth's early roots in Nebraska and Shields placing more of a focus on Hollingworth's role as a woman and as a scholar on women. Shields carefully explicates the role of Hollingworth in debunking the "variability hypothesis" that men were biologically both more capable and more evil than women. Rosalind Rosenberg also examines Hollingworth's contributions within the history of ideas and, in particular, psychology.

Additional background information on Hollingworth is found in Rheta Childe

Dorr's autobiography (1924), which includes reflections on Dorr's early years in Nebraska and her membership in Heterodoxy, the iconoclastic New York club for feminists. These reminiscences reflect much of Hollingworth's milieu and influences during this era. Judith Schwartz (1982) provides even fuller details on Heterodoxy and its often flamboyant members.

BIBLIOGRAPHY

Selected Writings by Leta Stetter Hollingworth

1913. "The Frequency of Amentia as Related to Sex." *Medical Record* 84 (October 25): 753–756.

1914a. *Functional Periodicity: An Experimental Study of the Mental and Motor Abilities of Women During Menstruation.* New York: Teachers College, Columbia University.

1914b. "Variability as Related to Sex Differences in Achievement." *American Journal of Sociology* 19 (January): 510–530.

1915. "The Medically Defective as Cases in the Courts of New York City." *Medical Record* 87 (February 27): 337–341.

1916a. "Social Devices for Impelling Women to Bear and Rear Children." *American Journal of Sociology* 22 (July): 19–29.

1916b. "Phi Beta Kappa and Women Students." *School and Society* 4 (December): 932–933.

1920. *The Psychology of Subnormal Children.* New York: Macmillan.

1922. "Differential Action upon the Sexes of Forces Which Tend to Segregate the Feeble-Minded." *Journal of Abnormal and Social Psychology* 17 (April–June): 35–37.

1923a. *Special Talents and Defects: Their Significance for Education.* New York: Macmillan.

1923b. "The Vocational Aptitudes of Women." In *Vocational Psychology: Its Problems and Methods,* H. L. Hollingworth, pp. 222–244. New York: D. Appleton.

1926. *Gifted Children: Their Nature and Nurture.* New York: Macmillan.

1927. "The New Woman in the Making." *Current History* 27 (October): 15–20.

1928. *The Psychology of the Adolescent.* New York: Appleton, 1928.

1930a. "The Child of Very Superior Intelligence as a Special Problem in Social Adjustment." *Mental Hygiene* 15 (January): 3–16.

1930b. "The Systematic Error of Herring-Binet in Rating Gifted Children." *Journal of Educational Psychology* 21 (January): 1–11.

1931. "The Achievements of Gifted Children Enrolled and Not Enrolled in Special Opportunity Classes." *Journal of Educational Research* 24 (November):1–7.

1939. "Problems of Relationship Between Elementary and Secondary Schools in the Case of Highly Intelligent Students." *Journal of Educational Sociology* 13 (October): 90–102.

1940a. *Prairie Years: A Collection of Verse, with Photograph and Brief Autobiography.* New York: Columbia University Press.

1940b. *Public Addresses.* Lancaster, PA: Science Press.

1942. *Children Above 180 I.Q.* Yonkers, NY: World Book.

Coauthored Works

Hollingworth, Leta S., and Max G. Schlapp. 1914. "An Economic and Social Study of Feeble-minded Women." *Medical Record* 85 (June 6): 1025–1028.

Lowie, Robert H., and Leta S. Hollingworth. 1916. "Science and Feminism." *Scientific Monthly* 4 (September): 277–284.

Montague, Helen, and Leta S. Hollingworth. 1914. "The Comparative Variability of the Sexes at Birth." *American Journal of Sociology* 20 (January): 335–370.

Studies of Leta Stetter Hollingworth and Supplementary References

Becker, Howard S. 1963. *Outsiders: Studies in the Sociology of Deviance*. London: Free Press of Glencoe.

Benjamin, Ludy T., Jr. 1984. "Leta Stetter Hollingworth: Psychologist, Educator, Feminist." In *Perspectives: Women in Nebraska History*, edited by Susan Pierce, p. 16–28. Nebraska Department of Education and the Nebraska State Council for the Social Studies, June, Special Issue.

Benjamin, Ludy T., Jr., and Stephanie A. Shields. 1990. "Leta Stetter Hollingworth (1886–1939)." In *Women in Psychology*, edited by A. N. O'Connell and N. F. Russo. Westport, CT: Greenwood Press.

Dorr, Rheta Childe. 1924. *A Woman of Fifty*. New York: Funk & Wagnalls.

"Education for the Gifted." 1941. Special Issue on Leta S. Hollingworth. *Teachers College Record* 42 (February): 375–460.

"Education and the Individual." 1940. Memorial Issue for Leta S. Hollingworth. *Teachers College Record* 42 (December): 183–264.

Gates, A. L. 1940. "Leta S. Hollingworth: Obituary." *Science* 91 (January 5): 9–11.

Hollingworth, H. L. 1943. *Leta Stetter Hollingworth: A Biography*. Lincoln: University of Nebraska Press.

Poffenberger, A. T. 1940. "Leta Stetter Hollingworth: 1886–1939." *American Journal of Psychology* 50 (April): 299–301.

Roemele, Victoria S. 1971. "Hollingworth, Leta Anna Stetter." In *Notable American Women, 1607–1950: A Biographical Dictionary*, vol. 2, edited by Edward T. James et al., p. 206–208. Cambridge, MA: Harvard University Press, Belknap Press.

Rosenberg, Rosalind. 1984. "Leta Hollingworth: Toward a Sexless Intelligence." *In the Shadows of the Past: Psychology Portrays the Sexes*, edited by Miriam Lewin, pp. 77–96. New York: Columbia University Press.

Shields, Stephanie A. 1975. "'Ms. Pilgrim's Progress: The Contributions of Leta Stetter Hollingworth to the Psychology of Women." *American Psychologist* 30 (August): 852–857.

———. 1982. "The Variability Hypothesis: The History of a Biological Model of Sex Differences in Intelligence." *Signs* 7 (Summer): 769–797.

Shields, Stephanie A., and Mary E. Mallory. 1987. "Leta Stetter Hollingworth Speaks on 'Columbia's Legacy.' " *Psychology of Women Quarterly* 11 (September): 285–300.

Schwartz, Judith. 1982. *The Radical Feminists of Heterodoxy*. Lebanon, NH: New Victoria Publishers.

AGNES RIEDMANN

JOAN HUBER (1925–   )

Joan Huber, 1989 president of the American Sociological Association, is part of a generation of women sociologists who made their mark at a time when the feminist movement (and related social change) shaped politics and the profession. Huber's interest in social stratification, initially directed toward class and American politics, found expression in her pioneering work on gender stratification. Huber has combined research, teaching, professional leadership, and academic administration into a remarkable, coherent career. Her recent work develops macrosocial and microsocial theory linkage change in men's and women's employment and family roles to technology and economic production.

BIOGRAPHY

Joan Huber's life history is easy to recover because she has made frequent use of biography to further sociological insight. She was born in 1925 in Bluffton, Ohio. Her parents lived in Wooster, where her father was an entomologist with the Agricultural Experiment Station. Expecting twins, her mother had gone to Bluffton to be with her mother for the birth. All four grandparents, of Scotch, German, and Swiss descent, had grown up on farms in the area. By the time her parents were adolescents, her mother's family lived in town, while her father was sent to board in town for high school. Her parents' education was much enhanced by the presence of a liberal arts college in Bluffton, and her father went on to earn a Ph.D.

Attending high school in Wooster, Joan benefited from a high school challenged by proximity to one of Ohio's strong liberal arts colleges. She was captain of the debate team and editor of the school paper. As a sophomore, she placed first in the state world history examination, a success she modestly attributes "to having a really brilliant teacher supply me with the right books and to having acquired a bad case of flu three weeks before the exam so that I had plenty of time to study" (Huber 1988c).

Huber majored in German as an undergraduate at Pennsylvania State University, despite a formal introduction to sociology through George Simpson's introductory course and some informal socialization as the Simpson family baby-sitter. She graduated in two years (1945), and was admitted to graduate work in history at Radcliffe College. She remained in Pennsylvania, however, and married Tony Rytina the next year. (They were divorced some years later.) Barely into her twenties, she was hired as an instructor in the Pennsylvania State University German department, and when returning GIs poured into the university, she learned "in the process that I did not want to spend the rest of my life teaching the German subjunctive. It changes, but not so fast that you notice it in your own lifetime" (Huber 1988c).

Another year of employment as a "gal Friday" in New York, and Joan, by now the mother of two, became a full-time housewife (and volunteer) until she returned to college in the early sixties. (Both children also have earned Ph.D.s in sociology: Nancy Rytina from Duke University and Steve Rytina from the University of Michigan.)

Reflection on her personal life is a significant part of Huber's sociological writing. In addition to offering an existential grasp of categorical disadvantage, the everyday life of the household provided her with a handy set of metaphors to illuminate sociological concepts: "If she flutes the mushrooms to make *boeuf bourguignon*, her status is higher than if she peels carrots to make beef stew, but the job operations are about the same" (Huber and Form 1973, 5). This homely observation initiates a sharp critique of the literature on alienation and anomie, which had ignored sex stratification.

Huber's experience of striking academic achievement followed by domesticity was typical of postwar women of the college-educated stratum. Women such as Huber went against the grain in aspiring to professional careers. But Huber and some other women sociologists of her generation differ from later professional cohorts in their history of involvement in conventional domesticity while they deferred careers or pursued them part-time. What is unusual about Huber is the degree to which she has put this experience to good advantage in sociological analysis. Her usage becomes a statement about the interdependence of public and private spheres in stratification systems.

Huber returned to school to earn a master's degree (Western Michigan University, 1963) and a Ph.D. (Michigan State University, 1967) degree in sociology. She had considered other fields of study, retaining a love for history and possessing a deep interest in philosophy. However, "its labor market combined with [her] sex made it hopeless as an occupation. Sociology seemed to combine everything [she] liked best" (Huber 1988c). At Michigan State, Bill Form described Huber as "the brightest student I ever had" (D'Antonio 1988b). Her determination matched her ability, for she traveled 100,000 miles to obtain her degrees and then commuted one hundred miles to a part-time teaching position at the University of Notre Dame (1967–1969), where she taught for another two years as a full-time assistant professor. During this period of establishing her career as a sociologist, she published three books! In 1971 Huber and William Form married and took positions at the University of Illinois, where Huber served as department chair (1979–1983) and director of the women's studies program (1978–1980). In 1984 Huber and Form were on the staff of Ohio State University.

Huber has received many awards, including the Jessie Bernard Award of the American Sociological Association (1985). She frequently has been elected to office in professional organizations, serving as president of the American Sociological Association (1989), the Midwest Sociological Society (1979–1980), and Sociologists for Women in Society (1972–1974). She has served on numerous editorial boards.

Two organizational commitments are worth highlighting because they indicate that Huber's intellectual concern with stratification and inequality carries over into a commitment to work toward equality in the profession. Huber was one of the founders of Sociologists for Women in Society, which began in 1969 as a Women's Caucus of the American Sociological Association. The group was formally organized in 1971, and Huber followed Alice Rossi* as president. They and other early leaders of the organization pushed hard for the inclusion of women in the governing structure of professional organizations and on editorial boards. Egalitarianism was internal as well as external, with attention to the needs and problems of graduate students a priority. Nationally recognized as a feminist leader (see "Interviews," *U.S. News and World Report* 1976), Huber has striven as an administrator to put objective review standards in place to minimize informal discrimination against women and other minorities.

One of those minorities is homosexuals, and Huber chaired an American Sociological Association Task Force on Homosexuality. This group conducted a survey to document and make recommendations regarding treatment of homosexual students and faculty and of homosexual issues in the classroom, in university departments, and in materials on homosexuals in sociology courses (Huber et al. 1982).

In teaching, Huber has primarily addressed stratification and inequality, although she also is well liked as a teacher of massive sections of introductory sociology. At the University of Notre Dame she offered one of the first sociology courses on poverty—twenty years later the course is still being taught. Huber is known as a stimulating teacher, informal in manner, thorough in preparation, and an inspiration to students to meet her high expectations of them. She has had strong professional relations. She has regularly collaborated with faculty and student colleagues (see bibliography). She takes a keen interest in students, devoting considerable energy and thought to advising them on intellectual projects and careers.

Huber enjoys administration, which she is inclined to view in down-to-earth human terms: "Being a Dean is a lot like being the mother of a houseful of preschoolers; someone always needs a bandaid or an expensive new toy'' (Huber 1988c). This quotation epitomizes the way in which Huber's personality and biography infuse her professional work, yet in no way threaten accomplishment. In fact, Huber's publication record is so extensive that a review of her work must be limited to primary themes and major works.

MAJOR THEMES

Huber's characteristic approach is to cast empirical data into a broad historical and theoretical framework to explore politically important questions concerning the stratification of society by race, class, and gender.

Income and Ideology (Huber and Form 1973), an empirical study of political beliefs, reveals the containment of popular dissatisfaction through an ideology of individualism that legitimates inequality. Having access to power, the rich are the most likely to see the American political system as pluralistic and least resistant to the domination of decision making by the powerful. Huber and Form's exploration of their data yields a detailed understanding of the American polity and a challenge to the supposed authoritarianism of lower-income groups. Her other books on stratification and theory published in the early seventies are *Marxist Theory and Indian Communism* (Loomis and Huber 1970) and *The Sociology of American Poverty* (Huber and Chalfant 1974).

A broad interdisciplinary approach to sociology and stratification has been a consistent theme in Huber's career. In ''Comparative Poverty Programs in Industrialized Countries'' (1978a), for example, Huber argues the necessity of an interdisciplinary approach to ''interstitial'' problems, located at the boundaries of economics, history, sociology, and political science. Well prepared by a broad education, Huber has drawn on anthropology, demography, and social history as well as sociology to develop a comprehensive theory of sex stratification.

For, as the women's movement developed, Huber's sociological attention turned to gender. She edited one of the earliest such volumes on the sociology of women (Huber, ed. 1973). A personal account (Huber 1973a) makes the now obvious, but then novel, point that gender is a major axis of stratification in society, hence an essential component of stratification systems.

Huber shaped the study of gender by placing it in a macrosocial framework. Gender research that initially was concentrated in medical and family sociology ''gave a social psychological and nonquantitative stamp to much of the sex roles research produced by women'' (Huber 1986: 479; see also Huber 1978). Huber has consistently challenged sociology to maintain a structural perspective. She argued that connecting research on gender to stratification theory that directs attention to women's participation in labor markets is essential to channel the sociologist toward the historical and comparative data necessary to develop and test gender theory.

In addition to articles on the women's movement and the Equal Rights Amendment (Huber 1976c, 1978; Huber, Rexroat, and Spitze, 1978); sex bias in the workplace and educational evaluation (Ferber and Huber 1975; Ferber, Huber, and Spitze 1979); reviews of research on women and sex stratification (Huber 1976a, 1976b, 1986); Huber and Glenna Spitze published a major theoretical and empirical study of *Sex Stratification* (1983; also Spitze and Huber 1981, Huber and Spitze 1980).

Huber and Spitze use data from a national sample survey to test an evolutionary theory of sex stratification that draws on Lenski's work (1966; Lenski and Lenski 1982), among others, connecting subsistence economy to gender roles and family form. Examining the industrial era, she looks back to the nineteenth century to identify a "men's movement," the labor movement arising out of changes in men's economic roles and directed toward equity. The later, but parallel, women's movement is a consequence of women's massive entry into the labor force in the twentieth century. The division of household labor, a new variable in gender stratification after 1950, is analogous to the division of labor important in nineteenth-century stratification theory (see Huber 1986).

In this perspective, the women's movement becomes part of the transformation of stratification from status to contract rather than amorphous collective behavior. Major historical transformations in which peasants became urban laborers and housewives became workers were followed by changes in the household division of labor and in attitudes toward gender roles (Huber and Spitze 1983).

One component of Huber's metatheory is a macrotheory of change in women's roles attributed to declining mortality and rising education. This leads to increased labor force participation because of the need for service and clerical workers and because of the declining rewards of children (Huber 1980) permitted by such technological developments as baby bottles and reliable contraceptives.

The macro factor of increased labor force participation, the variable demonstrating the most recent change, is used as the independent variable in tests of a variety of microtheories relating to family, sex roles, divorce, and fertility. Huber and Spitze compare their theory to Gary Becker's (1976, 1981) "new home economics," which explains family and gender roles primarily by changes in the husband-wife wage ratio, treating "taste for children" as a constant. Predictions from each theory are tested against the survey data, with Huber and Spitze's formulations receiving more support. Huber and Spitze anticipate that these long-term trends in labor force participation and fertility will continue to force change toward greater gender equality in the household and the workplace.

From this survey data a body of work on gender roles and depression was developed by University of Illinois colleagues Catherine Ross and John Mirowsky in collaboration with Huber (e.g., Ross and Huber 1985; Ross, Morowsky, and Huber). Material conditions are the point of departure for an exploration of variation in this psychological phenomenon.

Huber's analysis of gender roles in the family has developed into a comprehensive theory of the family (Huber 1988b; Huber and Spitze 1980, 1983). Subsistence technology and its compatibility with women's procreative tasks determines the division of labor and, in turn, gender stratification. This theory expands the parameters of family sociology considerably. "Family sociologists . . . tended to ignore both men's and women's work. Instead, they focused primarily on personal interaction, assuming that the major contribution of the modern family was to its members' happiness" (Huber and Spitze 1983, 2). However, "the study of personality and sexual adjustment may provide useful information for therapists, but it cannot explain long-term shifts in marriage patterns" (Huber and Spitze 1983, 107). "In preindustrial societies marriage was situated in a web of economic reciprocities. Tearing that web decreased the durability of marriages, not because modern husbands and wives get along less well, but because they have other options if they grow to dislike one another" (Huber and Spitze 1980, 88).

Huber is eclectic in her use of theoretical paradigms; her gender stratification/ family theory uses Marxist, exchange, and evolutionary perspectives. Her work is Marxist only in the broad sense of assigning subsistence technology and economic production a central role. Huber uses the terms "materialist" and "ecological" to communicate this principle; she is not a self-identified Marxist. Nor does she otherwise make use of Marxist concepts. In fact, she has been quite ready to point out Marxism's methodological pitfalls (Huber and Loomis 1970) and shortcomings as a theory of gender stratification (Huber and Spitze, 1983).

Huber explicitly refers to exchange theory, particularly to Gary Becker's "new home economics" microanalysis involving the changing utilities of traditional and egalitarian forms of the division of household labor (Becker, 1976; 1981). She differs from Becker in treating "taste for children" as a variable, not a given. At the macro level, Huber's perspective on the family is evolutionary (although not linear) and comparative, examining the family in hoe, plow, herding, and industrial societies.

CRITIQUES OF JOAN HUBER

Huber's elaboration of a comprehensive family theory is too recent to have been fully examined by critics. The selection of Huber (and frequent collaborator Spitze) to write the review of family sociology for the *Handbook of Sociology* marks a respect for her perspective and expertise.

Sex Stratification was appreciated for its scope, as a major and comprehensive theory of gender stratification. Judith Treas (1984) commented that it "injects a healthy dose of sociological thinking into an area recently dominated by microeconomic calculus" (p. 277), while Thomas Kando (1985) lauded the sociologists' interest in comparative study of large-scale social change, ground usually given to anthropologists.

Sex Stratification has frequently been cited in the years since it appeared, and has stimulated further research. Its careful creation of a theoretical context for an empirical study and its testing of competing hypotheses are exemplary (Kando 1985).

Some reviewers criticized the data analysis (Marini 1984; see also Hiller 1984), whereas others spoke of "methodological sophistication" (Treas 1984, 277) and "impressive" research design and execution (Kando 1985, 877). Some critics faulted the links between theory and data and/or between macro and micro levels of the theory (Marini 1984; Hiller 1984). One took issue with the feminist and materialist perspectives grounding the work (Kando 1985). All found the theory interesting and challenging.

Huber's most provocative work was her 1973 critique of symbolic interactionism (Huber 1973b; Huber and Loomis 1970). Questioning the validity of the methodology proposed by Herbert Blumer (1969) to construct "emergent theory," Huber argued that this atheoretical approach results in the shaping of problem and theory by the political status quo. Replies were posted with dispatch by such eminent symbolic interactionists as Blumer (1973) and Gregory Stone (Stone et al. 1974). The resulting debate (Huber 1974) turned on differing definitions of theory; the appropriate use of concepts to order sense data; lack of consensus on an adequate standard of validity; arguments about relative bias in conventional quantitative methodology compared with participant observation/ grounded theory; the adequacy of the corrective provided by "triangulation"; whether symbolic interactionism excluded the powerful from its scrutiny; and the correct explication of Hegel's dialectic.

Although the debate was seen by both sides to concern the Chicago school more than the Iowa school, Sheldon Stryker attributes a general decline in the vigor of symbolic interactionism in the 1960s and early 1970s in part to political criticism from the left, in which category he places Huber's article (Stryker 1987). "Left" is, of course, a relative term. Although dedicated to the discovery and eradication of social inequality, Huber could be more appropriately described as a liberal feminist (and would probably prefer to remain unlabeled). Her criticism of symbolic interactionism is concerned with issues of validity and inequality.

In summing up Joan Huber's place in sociology, her work in gender stratification is most important. It rests on a broad concern with the nature of social inquiry and the need for primary attention to social structure. Huber's writings on gender stratification and the family have become more comprehensive and well integrated over the years. Recent formulations represent a major theoretical statement connecting gender stratification and family roles to social and economic change.

Of a piece with her intellectual work is Huber's leadership in professional organizations and universities and her professional relations as colleague, teacher, and mentor. An early leader in the second wave of feminism, she has advanced the equality of women in society and in the profession.

ACKNOWLEDGMENT

My thanks to Joan Huber for her careful reading and comment on this entry, particularly in 1988. William V. D'Antonio also provided information useful in completing this project. Final responsibility, of course, resides with the author.

BIBLIOGRAPHY

Selected Works by Joan Huber

1970. "What Marx Really Meant: Reply to Elling, Eckstein, and Petras." *American Sociological Review* 35 (October): 915–916.

1973a. "From Sugar and Spice to Professor: Ambiguities in Identity Transformation." In *Academic Women on the Move*, edited by Alice S. Rossi and Ann Calderwood, pp. 125–135. New York: Russell Sage Foundation.

1973b. "Symbolic Interaction as a Pragmatic Perspective" *American Sociological Review* 38 (April): 274–284.

1973c. "But Who Will Scrutinize the Scrutinizers? Reply to Blumer." *American Sociological Review* 38 (December): 798–800.

1974. "The Emergency of Emergent Theory: Reply to Schmitt, Stone, Maines, Farberman, Stone, and Denzin." *American Sociological Review* 39 (June): 463–467.

1976a. "Introduction: Recent Studies in Sex Stratification." Special issue. *Social Science Quarterly* 56 (March): 547–552.

1976b. "Sociology Review: Research on Women, 1973–1975." *Signs* 1 (Spring): 685–697.

1976c. "Toward a Sociotechnological Theory of the Women's Movement." *Social Problems* 23 (April): 371–388.

1978a. "Comparative Poverty Programs in Industrialized Countries." In *Problems and Prospects in Sociology*, edited by Milton Yinger and Stephen Outler. New York: Free Press. Pp. 109–125.

1978b. "Looking Back, Looking Ahead: Generational Views of the Women's Movement." In *Women in the U.S. Labor Force*, edited by Ann Cahn, pp. xiv–xxxii. New York: Praeger.

1980. "Will U.S. Fertility Decline Toward Zero?" *Sociological Quarterly* 21 (Autumn): 481–492.

1986. "Trends in Gender Stratification 1970–1985." *Sociological Forum* 1 (?): 476–495.

1988a. "Trends in Family Sociology." In *Handbook of Sociology*, edited by Neil Smelser, pp. 425–448. Newbury Park, CA: Sage.

1988b. "A Theory of Family, Economy, and Gender." *Journal of Family Issues* 9 (March): 9–26.

1988c. Interview and conversation with Mary Ann Lamanna.

1973. Huber, Joan, ed. *Changing Women in a Changing Society*. Chicago: University of Chicago Press.

Coauthored Works

Ferber, Marianne, and Joan Huber. 1975. "Sex of Student and Instructor: A Study of Student Bias." *American Journal of Sociology* 80 (January): 949–963.

———. 1979. "Husbands, Wives, and Careers." *Journal of Marriage and the Family* 41 (May): 315–325.

Ferber, Marianne, Joan Huber, and Glenna Spitze. 1979. "Preference for Men as Bosses and Professionals." *Social Forces* 58 (December): 466–476.

————. 1980. "Will U.S. Fertility Decline Toward Zero?" *Sociological Quarterly* 21 (Autumn): 481–492.

Form, William, and Joan Huber [Rytina]. 1968. "Sociology Reference Periodicals." *Sociology and Social Research* 53 (October): 95–98.

————. 1969. "Ideology and the Distribution of Power in the United States." *American Sociological Review* 34 (February): 19–31.

Honigsheim, Paul. 1968. *On Max Weber*, translated by Joan Huber [Rytina]. New York: The Free Press.

Huber, Joan, and Paul Chalfant, eds. 1974. *The Sociology of American Poverty: A Text-Reader*. Boston: Schenkman.

Huber, Joan, and William Form. 1973. *Income and Ideology: An Analysis of the American Political Formula*. New York: The Free Press.

Huber [Rytina], Joan, William Form, and John Pease. 1970. "Income and Stratification Ideology: Beliefs About the American Opportunity Structure." *American Journal of Sociology* 75 (January): 703–716.

Huber, Joan, John Gagnon, Suzanne Keller, Ronald Lawson, Patricia Miller, and William Miller. 1982. "Report of the American Sociological Association's Task Group on Homosexuality." *The American Sociologist* 17: 164–180.

Huber [Rytina], Joan, and Charles P. Loomis. 1970. "Marxist Dialectic and Pragmatism." *American Sociological Review* 35 (April): 308–318.

————. 1971. "Income, Race, and the Ideology of Political Efficacy." *Journal of Politics* 33 (August): 659–688.

Huber, Joan, Cynthia Rexroat, and Glenna Spitze. 1978. "ERA in Illinois: A Crucible of Opinion on Women's Status." *Social Forces* 57 (December): 549–565.

Huber, Joan, and Glenna Spitze. 1980. "Considering Divorce: An Expansion of Becker's Theory of Marital Instability." *American Journal of Sociology* 86 (July): 75–89.

————. 1983. *Sex Stratification, Children, Housework, and Jobs*. New York: Academic Press.

Loomis, Charles, and Joan Huber [Rytina]. 1970. *Marxist Theory and Indian Communism*. East Lansing: Michigan State University Press.

Ross, Catherine, and Joan Huber. 1985. "Hardship and Depression." *Journal of Health and Social Behavior* 26 (December): 312–327.

Ross, Catherine, John Mirowsky, and Joan Huber. 1983. "Dividing Work, Sharing Work, and In-between: Marriage Patterns and Depression." *American Sociological Review* 48 (December): 809–823.

Spitze, Glenna, and Joan Huber. 1981. "Wives' Employment, Household Behaviors, and Sex-Role Attitudes." *Social Forces* 60 (September): 150–169.

Ulbrich, Patricia, and Joan Huber. 1981. "The Effect of Observing Parental Violence on Sex-Role Attitudes." *Journal of Marriage and the Family* 43 (August): 623–631.

————. 1982. "Effects of Anticipated Consequences on ERA Opinion." *Social Science Quarterly* 63 (June): 323–332.

————. 1983. *Sex Stratification: Children, Housework, and Jobs*. New York: Academic Press.

Studies About Joan Huber and Supplemental References

Becker, Gary 1976. *The Economic Approach to Human Behavior*. Chicago: University of Chicago Press.

————. 1981. *A Treatise on the Family*. Cambridge, MA: Harvard University Press.
Blumer, Herbert. 1969. *Symbolic Interactionism: Perspective and Method*. Englewood Cliffs, NJ: Prentice-Hall.
————. 1973. "A Note on Symbolic Interactionism." *American Sociological Review* 38 (December): 797–798.
d'Antonio, William. 1988. Personal communication with Mary Ann Lamanna.
Eckstein, Paul. 1970. "Comment on Marxism and Social Control." *American Sociological Review* 35 (October): 912–913.
Elling, Ray H. 1970. "Comment on Power and Knowledge." *American Sociological Review* 35 (October): 912.
Hiller, Dana V. 1984. "Review of *Sex Stratification*." *Journal of Marriage and the Family* 46 (February): 251–252.
"Interview with Joan Huber, Professor of Sociology." 1976. *U.S. News and World Report* (June 7): 46, 48.
Kando, Thomas. 1985. "Review of *Sex Stratification*." *Social Forces* 63 (March): 877–878.
Lenski, Gerhard. 1966. *Power and Privilege*. New York: McGraw-Hill.
Lenski, Gerhard, and Jean Lenski. 1982. *Human Societies*. 4th ed. New York: McGraw-Hill.
Marini, Margaret Mooney. 1984. "Review of *Sex Stratification*." *Contemporary Sociology* 13 (September): 562–564.
Rhodes, Robert I. 1970. "Comment on Marx's Epistemology." *American Sociological Review* 35 (October): 913–915.
Stone, Gregory, David R. Maines, Harvey A. Farberman, Gladys I. Stone, and Norman K. Denzin. 1974. "On Methodology and Craftsmanship in the Criticism of Sociological Perspectives." *American Sociological Review* 39 (June): 456–462.
Stryker, Sheldon. 1987. "The Vitalization of Symbolic Interactionism." *Social Psychology Quarterly* 50 (March): 83–94.
Treas, Judith. 1984. "Review of *Sex Stratification*." *Sociology and Social Research* 68 (January): 276–277.

MARY ANN LAMANNA

HELEN MACGILL HUGHES (1903–   )

Helen MacGill Hughes wrote several classic statements on news, deviance, the city, and ethnic relations in her active years. She also was a powerful organizer who has helped to form the ideas of the profession in several key roles. For seventeen years she took a strong behind-the-scenes role as managing editor of *The American Journal of Sociology*; she influenced her more visible husband/ sociologist Everett C. Hughes; she helped to ease women into the mainstream of professional roles in the early 1970s, especially in the American Sociological Association; and she is one of the few ''inside'' women from her era to legitimate the claims of women as second-class citizens in the discipline. Hughes has played a major role in a massive project to bring high-quality scholarship to a high school audience.

BIOGRAPHY

Helen MacGill Hughes was born in the Victorian era, in 1903, in Vancouver, British Columbia, Canada, and now leads other professional women in the neo-modern age. Her transition from a traditional past to a modern present was foreseen in the life of her remarkable mother, Helen Gregory MacGill. As a young woman, Helen Gregory had earned a bachelor's degree in 1886 and a master's degree in 1889(?), and a doctor of laws degree in 1938 from Trinity University in Toronto. Helen Gregory had been part of the generation of Jane Addams* and Charlotte Perkins Gilman.* In fact, she knew both of these women. Helen MacGill's father, James Henry MacGill, was a pioneer lawyer. Helen writes: ''I was grown up before I realized an intriguing affinity in my parents' avocations: each was fascinated by a particular interest in the expansion of democracy'' (1977, 73). Thus Helen was brought up believing in the work and ideals of the pioneer generation of female sociologists, although she was not taught that this was specifically sociology: This was the ideal way of life and meaning. Both her parents were "newspaper people" who kindled an early interest in their daughter for the mass media as well (Hughes 1940, "Acknowledgement," n.p.)

Helen's childhood was idyllic. She played in beautiful woods with her brothers and sisters and lived in a comfortable and politically active home, surrounded by family and friends. She attended the University of British Columbia with a brief foray to Saint Hilda's, the Anglican College for Women at the University of Toronto, during her third year. She returned to the University of British Columbia and graduated with a bachelor's degree in 1925. She discovered W. I. Thomas's *The Unadjusted Girl* (1923) at the library, and it captivated her imagination. (This book draws heavily on the work of juvenile courts and the work of early women sociologists, e.g., Jessie Taft.*) Because Helen's mother was a juvenile court judge, Helen was drawn to this intriguing field of study. She applied to the Carole Woershofer School of Economics at Bryn Mawr College, directed by Susan Kingsbury,* and was awarded a fellowship.

But her graduating essay from the University of British Columbia had been on the anti-Oriental immigration legislation of British Columbia (echoing the interests of Mary Elizabeth Burroughs Roberts Smith Coolidge*), and Hughes was on her way to doing "women's work" in sociology. Robert E. Park's research assistant, Winifred Raushenbush, lectured on Chinatown to Helen's senior class. "We never supposed sociology could be so good!" wrote the still ebullient Hughes more than fifty years later (1977, 75). Park visited the class later, and persuaded Helen to go to the University of Chicago instead of Bryn Mawr College.

At the University of Chicago, in 1925, she was the only woman fellow in sociology among six or seven men. Here she was thrown into the vibrant environment of a powerful institution. "Each of us fellows worked up the basic facts of a community, and our reports were eventually published in the *Local Community Fact Book of Chicago*" (Hughes 1977, 75). Her master's thesis, "Land Values as an Ecological Factor in the Community of South Chicago," used the human ecology model in which urban patterns are compared with biological models of growth and distribution of resources. The thesis was completed in 1926. At the end of the summer of the same year, the very busy Helen married a fellow graduate student, Everett C. Hughes. From this point her career became a patchwork of personal independence and dependence on her husband's career.

Her new husband took his first academic appointment at McGill University in the fall, and she followed him. She continued her graduate studies as well, and in 1927 began filling the residency requirements for her doctorate in Chicago. In 1932 she went to Europe with Everett while he was on sabbatical, and in 1937 she completed her doctorate. Three years later her dissertation on human interest stories was published. She and Everett also worked on *French Canada in Transition* during these years. In 1938 Everett was invited to join the faculty at their alma mater, the University of Chicago. From 1938 to 1969 Helen MacGill Hughes became "The Maid of All Work or Departmental Sister-in-Law" (Hughes 1973a) as a faculty wife employed on the academic campus of her husband. During these same years Helen bore two daughters, Helen MacGill Cherrington Brock and Elizabeth Gregory Cherrington Schneewind, who, respectively, became scholars in the classics and philosophy.

For seventeen years Helen worked on *The American Journal of Sociology.* This work "was rewarding in everything but salary" (Hughes 1977, 76). Hughes edited all the papers, doing the backstage work of making others' writings presentable to a public audience. She expanded her meager job into real intellectual labor. She heavily edited the manuscripts and made numerous suggestions for improvement, generating a high quality of readability to the journal as a whole. She had this major role in shaping the journal partially because three of the journal's editors (Herbert Blumer, Everett Hughes, and Louis Wirth) had been joint fellows in sociology in 1925 when she was one of their cohort. She had been a student of Ernest Burgess, another editor she worked under, and the wife of Everett as well. Although her sex remained her barrier to full membership to this eminent, privileged circle, she continually pushed its boundaries. She also filled various other positions, too numerous to mention here. One of the more fascinating ones was her work from 1944 to 1948 as a part-time correspondent for *Time*, reporting research in science, medicine, and education.

In 1961 Everett moved to Boston, and Helen once more followed. She again created a part-time niche at the Joint Center for Urban Studies of Harvard University and the Massachusetts Institute of Technology. From 1963 to 1970 she was a faculty research associate at the Florence Heller School of Advanced Studies in Social Welfare at Brandeis University. From 1966 to 1972 she held a major position as an editor of six textbooks for the massive secondary-school project, the Sociological Resources for Social Studies project sponsored by the American Sociological Association.

In 1969, moreover, Hughes dramatically reversed her earlier pattern of helpmate. She joined and helped lead the women's caucus, which later evolved into Sociologists for Women in Society. Helen MacGill Hughes was a stately, yet outspoken figure in the early 1970s. She became an outstanding leader for women's new demands for equality in the profession. I first became aware of her in this role, fired by her documentation of structural inequality toward women in sociology (1973b) and by her honest account of her second-class status at the University of Chicago as a managing editor (1973a). She also assumed highly visible roles in the American Sociological Association, serving on the Public Information Committee (1972–1977), chairing the Teaching of Sociology and Social Studies in Secondary Schools Committee (1973), and serving on the Nominations Committee (1973–1975) and as its vice-president (1980). In 1980 she also was president of the Eastern Sociological Society.

I have been an awed acquaintance of Helen MacGill Hughes since 1976. We met occasionally at professional meetings and corresponded on various professional issues in the intervening years. Although I do not share her high regard for Robert E. Park and other notable men of the Chicago school, our joint interest in reclaiming women's heritage in sociology enlivened our interactions. She was feeling too ill to write an entry for this volume in 1986, although she was highly supportive of this project. In 1987 she entered a nursing home.

MAJOR THEMES

Helen MacGill Hughes' career has distinct stages. The first part is close to the human ecology, ethnographic emphasis of the Chicago school developed by her mentor Robert E. Park, among others (Hughes 1980). Although this stage flourished from 1927 until 1944, intellectual interests that emerged during her early professional years continued throughout her life (Hughes 1968, 1980). The second stage was dominated by her invisible, backstage work for the *American Journal of Sociology* from 1944 to 1961. This period was marked by few publications and undocumented years of professional influence. Her last stage of work emphasized women's work, especially as sociologists. Her life backstage was brought to the front of sociological controversy and respect. Only a woman like Hughes with such strong credentials and hidden power could have made claims about the "dark era" for professional women in the hostile context of patriarchal sociology and been believed. Each of these stages is analyzed here.

The Chicago school interests in urban life, personal documents, and human experience are reflected in Hughes' master's and doctoral work. Her doctoral dissertation on newspapers emerged directly from Park's interests as a former journalist (1940). She added a historical dimension by her analysis of the origins of newspapers, as well as the social constructions of "newsworthy" accounts. She also emphasized the political nature of news and the media, adding a dimension often lacking in the work of her male cohort.

Human interest stories vary by culture (1936), historical situation (1937a), and form of government (1937b). They can reveal structural processes in an interesting, captivating format (1975b). This concept of human interest stories spanned several decades of work, and is grounded to the study of popular culture and mass communication.

Another Chicago school emphasis was race relations, a specialty of Park as well as of Everett C. Hughes. Helen and Everett successfully collaborated in this area. Their book *Where Peoples Meet* (1952) is a clearly written, liberal interpretation of intergroup relations. It was a popular textbook because of its arguments and simplicity of style. Helen also participated in the collection of data for Everett's well-received *French Canada in Transition* (1943), although the degree and amount of influence she had in forming the text is not documented at this time. Helen also worked with a former student, Lewis G. Watts, to analyze the process of neighborhood integration by "new men," Afro-Americans living in previously all-white communities (Hughes and Watts, 1964).

Everett and Helen shared another Chicago school interest, the sociology of occupations. In this area they collaborated with Irwin Deutscher in a major study of nurses, their changing professional definitions, medical training, and research skills (1958).

The second stage of Hughes' work, dominated by her editorial work for *The American Journal of Sociology*, is documented primarily in her autobiography written in 1973 (1973a). To appreciate her backstage work, interviews, altered manuscripts, and correspondence are needed to fill in the large gap in our information about the nature and range of her influence in the discipline.

In the third stage Hughes continued her Chicago interests in her collaborative work with Howard S. Becker in 1961. Here they followed the work of earlier Chicago sociologists who had used "life history documents" and "autobiographies" to generate the sense of self and social world of a member of a minority or "deviant" group. Their replication of a young woman's account of drug addiction greatly expanded the male-dominated sociological literature on this subject. This early classic on women and drugs is severely underrated.

Hughes also began a series of studies on women's work in sociology. Her two papers on Caroline Baer Rose* (1913–1975) pointed out the lived experience of being a second-class citizen in sociology, particularly when a supportive husband/sociologist was present. This situation was echoed in her life and in that of other eminent women in her cohort, such as Alice S. Rossi* and Rose Laub Coser.* This was an important occupational pattern: they began with weaker sponsorship, moved with their husbands, helped in their husbands' work and career, and worked part-time. "They are found on the margins, both as to institutional structure and as to category of student. They start lower down and do not catch up" (Hughes 1975b, 217–218). They hold fewer full-time positions, at less prestigious schools, and with lower salaries (Hughes 1973b).

Hughes began editing a series of fascinating anthologies, published in 1970, during this third stage. These books were intended for a high school program, but they are highly readable and quality statements. I read them in fact in my graduate training in 1971. One book is on life in families (with two selections by Mirra Komarovsky*), stressing the changing nature and structure of family life in the United States and worldwide (1970c). Another book is an overview on delinquents and criminals from a Chicago perspective. Her former classmate Ruth Shonle Cavan* has an entry defining delinquency, and other Chicago scholars describe the class structure of criminality, its social construction, and wide range of inclusive actions (1970b). A volume on city life pulls together a major statement on urban sociology from a Chicago school perspective (1970a). This high-quality series was sponsored by the American Sociological Association and partially funded by the National Science Foundation. Six volumes were published between 1970 and 1971.

In 1956 Hughes worked with Roy R. Grinker, a physician, to edit a collection of papers presented at a series of conferences. This high-power "invisible college" applied systems theory, with three selections by Talcott Parsons, to generate a unified theory of human behavior (Grinker, with the assistance of Helen MacGill Hughes 1956). This was the frontline of sociological and interdisciplinary theory in 1956 but far from Hughes' interests in "symbolic interaction." Perhaps this was part of a "good job" for a "part-time" backstage scholar.

CRITIQUES OF HELEN MACGILL HUGHES

News and the Human Interest Story (1940) has become a classic statement in sociology. It was widely and positively reviewed when it appeared, and it, or chapters from it, have been widely reprinted. Malcolm M. Willey, for example wrote that her "analysis is shrewd and lively . . . (with) more insight . . . than is found in any other single volume devoted to the contemporary newspaper" (1940, 242). Forty years later Arlene Kaplan Daniels (1981) noted its continuing influence as a classic analysis.

James F. Short, Jr., included part of Hughes' work on human interest stories and political news in his anthology on Chicago sociology (1971). Summarizing her work in three sentences, Short does not significantly evaluate it, but he does recognize her part in a major school of sociology. This type of casual inclusion of Hughes in the Chicago school of sociology is found in various writings. Even more distressing, Everett Hughes is seriously considered as a major figure in the Chicago schools of race relations and occupations, whereas Helen's work is virtually invisible. Their book *Where Peoples Meet* (1952) was given a perfunctory review by Leonard Broom. He praised their clarity of writing but criticized their "unexceptional" analysis (1953).

Marlene Shore's outstanding analysis of the Chicago school's influence on Canadian sociology provides an interesting addition to our knowledge of Helen MacGill Hughes (see especially 1987, 254–266). Although the discussion centers on Everett, his work and its context at McGill University were key factors in shaping Helen's life and work too.

The Fantastic Lodge (1961) also has become a classic statement, reprinted at least five times and translated into French. It received scant academic notice when it was published, however. Kenneth Polk gave it one paragraph in its only professional review. He treats it as an invaluable, if sordid, book (1962, 879), in other words, as a type of tintillating human interest story.

A major biography on Hughes is needed to document her leadership of women during a time of transition. Much of her influence is known only through unpublished information, and scholarly critiques of her writings are scarce. Her outstanding work formulating a basic introduction to six major specialties in sociology is the type of irreplaceable work that is seldom honored in a patriarchal discipline. Her backstage power is an untold "human interest story."

BIBLIOGRAPHY

Selected Writings by Helen MacGill Hughes

1936. "The Lindbergh Case: Of Human Interest Stories and Politics." *The American Journal of Sociology* 42 (July): 32–54.

1937a. "A Geneology of Human Interest Stories." *Journalism Quarterly* 14 (March): 1–6.

1937b. "Human Interest Stories and Democracy." *Public Opinion Quarterly* 1 (April): 73–84.

1940. *News and the Human Interest Story*. University of Chicago Sociological Series. Chicago: University of Chicago Press.

1942. "The Social Interpretation of News." *The Annals of the American Academy of Political and Social Science* 219 (January): 11–17.

1945. "Newspapers and the Moral World." *The Canadian Journal of Economics* 11 (May): 177–188.

1947. "The Compleat Antivivisectionist." *The Scientific Monthly* 65 (December): 503–507.

1959. "William Fielding Ogburn—1886–1959." *Social Forces* 38 (October): 1–2.

1968. "Robert Ezra Park." In *The International Encyclopedia of the Social Sciences*, vol. 11, ed. by David L. Sills, pp. 416–419. New York: Macmillan and Free Press.

1973a. "The Maid of All Work or Departmental Sister-in-Law?: The Faculty Wife Employed on Campus." *The American Journal of Sociology* 78 (January): 5–10.

1975a. "Caroline Baer Rose, 1913–1975." *Social Problems* 22 (April): 469–470.

1975b. "Women in Academic Sociology, 1925–1975." *Sociological Focus* 3 (August): 215–222.

1977. "Wasp/Woman/Sociologist." *Society* 14 (July–August): 69–80.

1980. "Robert Ezra Park: The Philosopher-Newspaperman-Sociologist." In *Sociological Traditions from Generation to Generation*, edited by Robert K. Merton and Matilda White Riley, pp. 67–79. Norwood, NJ: Ablex.

1980–1991. "On Becoming a Sociologist." *Journal of the History of Sociology* 3 (Fall–Winter): 27–39.

1961. Hughes, Helen MacGill, ed. *The Fantastic Lodge: The Autobiography of a Girl Drug Addict*. Boston: Houghton Mifflin. ("The recordings on which this book is based were made by Howard S. Becker in the course of his work as a research sociologist in a comprehensive study of drug addiction among young people," p. vi).

1970a. *Cities and City Life*. Readings in Sociology Series. Foreword by Robert C. Angell. Boston: Allyn & Bacon.

1970b. *Delinquents and Criminals: Their Social World*. Readings in Sociology Series. Foreword by Robert C. Angell. Boston: Allyn & Bacon.

1970c. *Life in Families*. Readings in Sociology Series. Foreword by Robert C. Angell. Boston: Allyn & Bacon.

1970d. *Racial and Ethnic Relations*. Readings in Sociology Series. Foreword by Robert C. Angell. Boston: Allyn & Bacon.

1971a. *Social Organizations*. Readings in Sociology Series. Foreword by Robert C. Angell. Boston: Allyn & Bacon.

1971b. *Population Growth and the Complex Society*. Readings in Sociology Series. Foreword by Robert C. Angell. Boston: Allyn & Bacon.

1971c. *Crowd and Mass Behavior*. Readings in Sociology Series. Foreword by Robert C. Angell. Boston: Allyn & Bacon.

1973. *The Status of Women in Sociology, 1968–1972: Report to the American Sociological Association of the Ad Hoc Committee on the Status of Women in the Profession*, Washington, DC: American Sociological Association.

Unpublished Writings of Helen MacGill Hughes

Hughes, Helen MacGill [Helen Elizabeth Gregory MacGill]. 1927. "Land Values as an Ecological Factor in the Community of South Chicago." Master's thesis, Sociology and Anthropology, University of Chicago.

Coauthored Works

Grinker, Roy R., with the assistance of Helen MacGill Hughes. 1956. *Toward a Unified Theory of Human Behavior*. New York: Basic Books.

Hughes, Everett C., with partial data collection by Helen MacGill Hughes. 1943. *French Canada in Transition*. Chicago: University of Chicago.

Hughes, Everett C., and Helen MacGill Hughes. 1952. *Where Peoples Meet: Racial and Ethnic Frontiers*. Glencoe, IL: Free Press.

Hughes, Everett C., Helen MacGill Hughes, and Irwin Deutscher. 1958. *Twenty Thousand Nurses Tell Their Story*. Philadelphia: J. B. Lippincott.

Hughes, Helen MacGill, and Lewis G. Watts. 1964. "Portrait of the Self-Integrator." *Journal of Social Issues* 20 (April): 103–115.

Simmons, Ozzie G., with the collaboration of Helen MacGill Hughes. 1965. *Work and Mental Illness: Eight Case Studies*. New York: John Wiley & Sons.

Star, Shirley A., and Helen MacGill Hughes. 1950. "Report on an Educational Campaign for the United Nations." *American Journal of Sociology* 60 (January): 389–400.

Studies About Helen MacGill Hughes and Supplementary References

Broom, Leonard. 1953. "Review of *Where Peoples Meet*." *American Sociological Review* 18 (June): 343.

Daniels, Arlene Kaplan. 1981. "Introduction to the Transaction Edition." *News and the Human Interest Story*. New Brunswick, NJ: Transaction.

Polk, Kenneth. 1962. "Review of *The Fantastic Lodge*." *American Sociological Review* 27: 879–880.

Reissman, Leonard. 1959. "Review of *Twenty Thousand Nurses Tell Their Story*." *American Journal of Sociology* 64 (March): 531–532.

Shore, Marlene. 1987. *The Science of Social Redemption: McGill, the Chicago School, and the Origins of Social Research in Canada*. Toronto: University of Toronto Press.

Short, James F. Jr., ed. 1971. *The Sociology Fabric of the Metropolis: Contributions of the Chicago Sociology of Urban Sociology*. Chicago: University of Chicago Press.

Willey, Malcolm M. 1940. "Review of *News and the Human Interest Story*." *The Annals of the American Academy of Political and Social Science* 211 (September): 242.

MARY JO DEEGAN

FLORENCE KELLEY (1859–1932)

Florence Kelley was a militant feminist, socialist, activist, and theorist who established the foundations for major legislative changes for women and children in the United States. Her work for international pacifism and socialism made her a target of attack by the U.S. government for several decades. Her brilliant and successful career, particularly through her work as general secretary for the National Consumers' League, brought her many honors, usually outside the male academic network in sociology.

BIOGRAPHY

Life was never dull around Florence Kelley, a large, vibrant woman with strong opinions, great intellect, and massive energy. She was the daughter of William Darrah Kelley and his second wife, Caroline Bartram Bonsall Kelley. Her father was a self-educated lawyer, judge, and a member of the U.S. House of Representatives for almost thirty years. He was nicknamed "Pig-Iron Kelley" as "the determined champion and fighter for a high tariff for basic American Industries" (Goldmark 1953, 6). His daughter would later oppose his position on tariffs, but she learned from him to love justice and the law. Her mother and her mother's adopted family influenced Florence deeply as well. Five of Florence's seven siblings died in infancy, dramatically enacting the plight of mothers and children for young Florence. The Quaker background of her mother provided the hot-tempered Florence with a hard-won sense of serenity.

An avid student plagued by illnesses, Florence read major portions of her father's library, where she was tutored by people who were "not college-bred. My college preparation," wrote Kelley, "was in fact pure sham" (1927a, 557). Despite her weak training, Kelley yearned to attend college. Thus, at age sixteen and with the full support of her father, Kelley entered Cornell University in 1876: "an almost sacramental experience" (Kelley 1927a, 557). (See also Mary Elizabeth Burroughs Roberts Smith Coolidge.*)

As a freshman, Kelley met an exciting senior, M. Carey Thomas, who later became the president of Bryn Mawr College (see Susan Kingsbury*) and a lifelong friend. Although Kelley reveled in college life, she frequently was ill and her attendance at Cornell University was sporadic. Thus she did not graduate until 1882, when she completed a legal thesis, "On Some Changes in the Legal Status of the Child Since Blackstone." This subject proved to be a lifelong interest and kindled her desire to become a lawyer, like her father.

Kelley applied to the University of Pennsylvania to study law with anticipation, but to her deep shock and anger, she was denied admittance because of her sex. The next year, in 1883, Kelley toured Europe where she met M. Carey Thomas on a chance encounter. The feisty Thomas related similar tales of discrimination. Thomas had studied a year at Leipzig, but on completion of her work, she was denied a degree. After this debilitating experience, Thomas studied at and graduated from the University of Zurich. Kelley soon enrolled there, too, and was immediately swept into the "new wildfire of socialism" (Goldmark 1953, 16; see also Alexandra Kollontai*). She translated Engels' *The Condition of the Working Class in England in 1844* into English and began an important scholarly relationship with him that lasted for more than a decade.

The upheaval in Kelley's politics was matched by an emotional one. A romantic, young medical student, Lazare Wishniewski, entered Kelley's life. As a Polish Jew and a socialist, Wishniewski shared Kelley's foreign status in Zurich; their union with international workers must have pointed to a radically different future. In June 1884 they married. A young son, Nicholas, was born the next year, and in 1886 the Wishniewskis embarked for New York. At first Florence was welcomed into the network of New York socialists, but a year later she was expelled from the party.

Initially Friedrich Engels was supportive of Kelley's work as his English translator and as a leading American socialist. She worked ardently on his behalf and believed in his commitment to women's rights. When Engels came to New York in 1888, however, he flagrantly ignored Kelley. His conspicuous sexism in visiting only the men in the American socialist organizations left Kelley first stunned and then outraged. This event was crucial in Kelley's reevaluation of socialism and feminism. Although she remained both a socialist and a feminist throughout her life, Kelley placed female workers' interests at the forefront of her intellectual and political interests, and was skeptical of men's commitments to women's rights.

The young wife and mother continued to write, but her husband was financially unsuccessful. Two more children, Margaret (1886) and John Bertram (1888), arrived while the bills went unpaid. The couple suffered from mounting debts, anger, and disappointment. In 1891 the now estranged couple divorced. Florence resumed her maiden name and took her children to Chicago. She moved into

Hull-House, found a temporary home for her children with the social reformer Henry Demarest Lloyd, and began a life as a theorist and an activist.

Kelley arrived at Hull-House in a horse-drawn carriage on a bitter, wintry day in December 1891. For the next eight years she lived there, with her three children sharing her life and living with Kelley's mother in a nearby apartment during a portion of these years. Nicholas Kelley (1954) fondly remembered these Hull-House years as happy and formative, affectionately recalling as well his "adopted home" with Henry Demarest Lloyd.

In addition to Kelley's busy new life as census taker, author, speaker, and Hull-House resident, she managed to study law at nearby Northwestern University, where she completed her law degree in 1894. Although Kelley never practiced law, she helped to write many influential briefs, including the *Oregon vs. Mueller* brief, which established legal precedent on the use of sociological evidence to develop her argument on the minimum wage. She combined legal and social scientific knowledge to argue on behalf of workers' rights for the rest of her life. Her influential legal allies included Louis Brandeis, later the chief justice of the Supreme Court, and Felix Frankfurter, Harvard Law professor and later a member of the Supreme Court.

Kelley was actively involved in the child labor and sweatshop struggles in Chicago, and many of her colleagues in these battles were men from the powerful department of sociology at the University of Chicago. "In large part because of Florence Kelley's influence, the Illinois legislature in 1893 passed a factory act limiting hours of work for women, prohibiting child labor, and controlling tenement sweatshops" (Wade 1977, 317). As a result of this work, Kelley was appointed a factory inspector and wrote several exposés of abuses she discovered. This courageous work documenting the exploitative practices of manufacturers led, on one occasion, to a gunman shooting at her. Fortunately Kelley escaped from this encounter unharmed.

In the spring of 1893 *A Special Investigation of the Slums of Great Cities* was undertaken by the U.S. Department of Labor; Kelley headed the Chicago investigation. These census data became the foundation for the maps used in *Hull-House Maps and Papers*, one of the most important sociological texts written in the 1890s and integral to the development of the Chicago school of sociology (Deegan 1988a).

In 1899 Kelley accepted the position of general secretary of the National Consumers' League. With deep regret at leaving Hull-House, but with high expectations for her new job and home with Lillian Wald at Henry Street Settlement, Kelley returned with her children to New York. This remained her home and work for the rest of her busy life. In her highly visible role, Kelley stomped across the country, speaking to large and small audiences, in factories and in academies, to the rich and the poor, and to professional and working-class audiences. In 1905 Kelley's daughter died shortly after entering Smith College as an undergraduate. Julia Lathrop sympathetically recalled the last time she had seen Kelley's daughter: "so beautiful, so charmingly maternal and whimsical with the little Greek baby at Hull-House, so proud of you and with such a gay independence at the same time'' (Lathrop quoted in Addams 1935, 127). Kelley bore this sorrow, like so many others in her life, with fortitude. After Kelley's death, Lathrop (1932) recalled that Kelley spoke ''in that flute-like voice as if she was delighted to have the privilege, praising and stimulating others, asking nothing of herself.'' She effectively helped to train Mary van Kleeck* and Frances Perkins, the first woman to hold a Cabinet-level post in the U.S. government (Perkins 1954).

She was active in numerous professional organizations as well, including the National Child Labor Committee, the National Conference of Social Workers, the American Social Science Association, the American Sociological Society, and the National American Woman Suffrage Association. She, along with many other female sociologists (e.g., Jane Addams*, Ida B. Wells-Barnett*, and Anna Garlin Spencer*), was a cofounder of the National Association for the Advancement of Colored People.

The Red Scare of 1919 and the witch hunting that ensued surrounded Kelley throughout the 1920s. Unlike many of her sister sociologists in the Golden Era, Kelley was a neo-Marxist, confrontive and interpersonally aggressive.

She was much influenced by Marx and did not hesitate to show her feeling that employers were enemies who could be constrained to a minimum of decency only by legislation, nor did she fear to state openly that the goal for which she worked could never be achieved while production was carried on for profit. (Wright 1932, 555)

Kelley also was the center of a deeply divisive feminist issue: to support the Equal Rights Amendment and oppose protective legislation for working-class women and/or to support protective legislation and oppose the Equal Rights Amendment. Kelley chose the latter course and became a persona non grata among feminist activists and scholars during the 1960s, the 1970s, and most of the 1980s. Ironically the radical socialist feminist who worked with working-class women became a symbol of the ineffectual, bourgeoise reformer for many years.

Kelley remained an adamant fighter with a take-charge personality despite her attacks from the political right, left, and center. Her many friends mourned her death in 1932, when many of them were aged and ailing too. Her close friend Julia Lathrop died shortly after Kelley, and Jane Addams had cancer by this time. Kelley left a profound legacy of scholarship, activism, and an undefeated, fighting spirit.

MAJOR THEMES

Marxist thought informed all Kelley's scholarship, beginning with her English translation of Engels's work in 1887. She also translated Karl Marx's *Free Trade* (the text of a speech given in 1848) in 1902. Her correspondence with Engels

(Blumberg 1964; Trachtenberg 1953) provides an important link for understanding his relations to women and to Americans. The intellectual thought, ideological commitments, and practice of Jane Addams were equally important to Kelley's sociology, however. This Marxian and Addamsian influence is clear in Addams's and Kelley's first joint writing venture, the coediting of *Hull-House Maps and Papers*. This sociological classic established the major substantive issues examined by Chicago sociologists for many years. These topics include the study of the city, immigration, and juvenile delinquency. Kelley's central role in writing, editing, and producing *Hull-House Maps and Papers* is documented in my work on Jane Addams (Deegan 1988a, 55–69). *Hull-House Maps and Papers* was used as a model for W.E.B. DuBois's groundbreaking sociological work in *The Philadelphia Negro* (Deegan 1988b) and other major writings that need further analysis in light of this tradition of Hull-House sociology.

Another example of Kelley's and Addams's mutual intellectual development is found in their simultaneous teaching of two similarly titled courses offered under the auspices of the University of Chicago's Extension Program. Addams's course was "Survivals and Intimation [?] in Social Ethics"; Kelley's course was "Ethical Gains Through Legislation." Both sociologists later published books on related topics, Addams's *Democracy and Social Ethics* (1902) and Kelley's *Some Ethical Gains Through Legislation* (1905a) (printed syllabi in Ely Papers, classes scheduled during July and August, "ca 1900," State Historical Society of Wisconsin, Madison).

Kelley brilliantly discussed the cause of poverty as "the regular by-product of certain industries without standards, of certain sub-normal industries" in her article on "Minimum-Wage Boards" (1911, 303). The policy of profit making at the expense of workers, their families, and the community reveals Kelley's sophisticated epistemology combining themes from Marx, Addams, and American applied sociology, enacted through legislative change and social movements.

The elimination of child labor was a major issue to Kelley and to the men from the Chicago school of Sociology. Their joint sociological focus is reflected in Kelley's articles in *The American Journal of Sociology*, the house organ for these men. Her three articles on this topic, published between 1896 and 1904 in that journal, discuss the theoretical issues surrounding children's rights to education and to play. They also document the centrality of this knowledge in applied sociology at that time. Her work on the eight-hour day (1898), minimum wages (1911), and the consumers' league (1899) use both a theory of sociological jurisprudence and an enactment of it through legislation.

Kelley also wrote a series of book reviews for *The American Journal of Sociology*. This body of critique is significant because she often analyzed books and projects of her female colleagues and developed a public forum for their joint enterprise. Thus she reviewed two volumes (7 and 8) of the massive eighteen-volume *Report on the Condition of Women and Child Wage-Earners in the United States* (1912a), initiated by Edith Abbott* and Mary McDowell among others, and Jane Addams's *A New Conscience and an Ancient Evil* (1912c), and supported the pacifism of another (1912b; see also 1915, 1916). She compared Robert Hunter's *Poverty* (1905b) with the groundbreaking work of Engels, although Hunter's work is now largely forgotten while Engels's is not. I emphasize her publications in *The American Journal of Sociology* because this was the most important journal in the discipline and because many of her articles and book reviews were overlooked in the compiled indexes of these journals.

Kelley also wrote dozens and dozens of short articles on social reform issues, especially in *Charities, The Survey, The Journal of Political Economy, The Annals of the American Academy of Political and Social Science, Arena, The Independent, Outlook,* and *The Century.* A complete analysis of these writings would enhance our understanding of her intellectual and activist heritage. Charlotte Perkins Gilman,* for example, republished a short leaflet by Kelley and Mary Beard on the need for a federal amendment to obtain women's suffrage (Gilman 1916). (An extensive bibliography is available in Mattson [1956].) Even a cursory examination, nonetheless, reveals that these works are filled with details on specific social issues accompanied by pragmatic plans for ameliorative action. A complete scholarly analysis of this corpus from a sociological perspective is beyond the scope and intent of this entry. Her specific proposals need to be evaluated in light of contemporary values as well.

CRITIQUES OF FLORENCE KELLEY

Rich biographical material on Florence Kelley is available. Jane Addams (1935, 116–131) warmly recalls Kelley's friendship and work with Julia Lathrop. This book analyzes Hull-House during the years Kelley lived there, and places Kelley in a context of shared interests and practices. In addition, most biographies on Addams provide at least some information on Kelley as well (see Jane Addams's entry). Kelley's lifelong friend Josephine Goldmark wrote a popular account of Kelley's vivid life (1953). More scholarly analyses are provided by Dorothy Rose Blumberg (1964, 1966) and Kathryn Kish Sklar (1986). Sklar, furthermore, is preparing a book on Kelley's life and thought. A superb, detailed analysis of Kelley's several dozen speeches on child labor is found in Ramona Tomlin Mattson's dissertation (1956).

Jill Conway (1971) wrote an influential article comparing Jane Addams and Florence Kelley. Conway depicted these two sociologists as ideal types exemplifying either "Victorian sages" (Addams's type) or "professional experts" (Kelley's type).

The first is a borrowing from European culture, the type of the sage or prophetess who claimed access to hidden wisdom by virtue of feminine insights. The second is the type of the professional expert or the scientist, a social identity highly esteemed in American culture but sexually neutral. (p. 167)

My discussion of Conway's work emphasizes the commonality between Kelley and Addams as professional sociologists (Deegan 1987).

Kelley's work is briefly considered in the writings of Edith Abbott and So-
phonisba Breckinridge.* For example, a discussion of the influence of the National Consumers' League is found in Sophonisba Breckinridge's *Women in the
Twentieth Century* (1933). Abbott and Breckinridge also cited Kelley's work on
behalf of child labor in their study of truancy of school children (1917). Edith
Abbott wrote a detailed critique of the early history of child labor legislation in
America in which she unequivocally states that Kelley's analysis in *Some Ethical
Gains in Legislation* is lacking in historical depth (Abbott 1908, 36). Another
early female sociologist, Elsie Clews Parsons,* had a brief debate with Kelley
over the nature of social change and the value of social settlements (see Elsie
Clews Parsons).

Charles R. Henderson wrote a glowing review of *Some Ethical Gains Through
Legislation* (1906), and A. B. Wolfe wrote a favorable, but more critical review
of *Modern Industry in Relation to the Family, Health, Education, and Morality*
(1917) for *The American Journal of Sociology*. Generally well received, both
books were reviewed by major scholarly journals outside sociology as well.

Louis Athey's article on Kelley's work with the National Association for the
Advancement of Colored People and with W.E.B. DuBois is an outstanding,
carefully documented account. Her feisty and honorable stands on racial issues
endured during some of the most racist years experienced under the tyranny of
Jim Crow society. DuBois's obituary on Kelley is a tribute to their friendship
and to her moral courage.

Despite the array of scholarship on Kelley, her outstanding social thought
remains largely undiscovered in sociology. It can be unearthed through an epistemological analysis of her roots in both Marxian and Addamsian thought. Her
critical praxis as a sociologist and as a lawyer also awaits a thorough critique.

BIBLIOGRAPHY

Selected Writings by Florence Kelley

1895. "The Sweating System" and "Wage-Earning Children" (second author, Alzina
      P. Stevens). In *Hull-House Maps and Papers, by Residents of Hull-House, a
      Social Settlement, a Presentation of Nationalities and Wages in a Congested
      District of Chicago, Together with Comments and Essays on Problems Growing
      Out of the Social Conditions*, pp. 27–45, 48–88. New York: Crowell.
1896. "The Working Boy." *American Journal of Sociology* 2 (November): 358–368.
1898a. "The Illinois Child-Labor Law." *American Journal of Sociology* 3 (January):
      490–501.
1898b. "The United States Supreme Court and the Eight Hour Law." *American Journal
      of Sociology* 4 (July): 21–34.
1899. "Aims and Principles of the Consumers' League." *American Journal of Sociology*
      5 (November): 289–304.
1904. "Has Illinois the Laws for Protection of Children in Illinois?" *American Journal
      of Sociology* 10 (November): 299–314.

1905a. *Some Ethical Gains Through Legislation*. New York: Macmillan.
1905b. "Review of *Poverty*." *American Journal of Sociology* 10 (January): 555–556.
1911. "Minimum-Wage Boards." *American Journal of Sociology* 17 (November): 303–314.
1912a. "Review of *The Report on the Condition of Women and Child Wage-Earners in the United States (Vols. 7 and 8)*." *American Journal of Sociology* 17 (January): 550–552.
1912b. "Review of *Beyond War. A Chapter in the Natural History of Man*." *American Journal of Sociology* 18 (July): 270–272.
1912c. "Review of *A New Conscience and an Ancient Evil*." *American Journal of Sociology* 18 (September): 271–272.
1914. *Modern Industry in Relation to the Family, Health, Education, and Morality*. New York: Longmans, Green.
1915. "Review of *The Modern Factory*." *American Journal of Sociology* 20 (March): 711–712.
1916. "Review of *Wage-Earning Pittsburgh*." *American Journal of Sociology* 21 (January): 557–559.
1926. "My Philadelphia." *Survey* 57 (October 1): 7–11, 50–61.
1927a. "When Co-education Was Young." *Survey* 57 (February 1): 557–561, 600–602.
1927b. "My Novitiate." *Survey* 58 (April 1): 31–35.
1986. *Notes of Sixty Years: The Autobiography of Florence Kelley, with an Early Essay by the Author on the Need for Theoretical Preparation for Philanthropic Work*, ed. and intro. by K.K. Sklar. Chicago: Charles H. Kerr, Illinois Labor History Society.
Kelley, Florence, ed. 1910. *Twentieth Century Socialism: What It Is Not; How It May Come*, by Edmond Kelly, introductions by Franklin H. Giddings and Rufus W. Weeks. New York: Longmans, Green.
Kelley, Florence, trans. 1887. *The Lage der Arbitenden Klasse in England in 1844*, by Friedrich Engels. New York: L. Weiss. New ed., London, 1892, with a special preface by Friedrich Engels.
c. 1902. *Free Trade: An Address Delivered Before the Democratic Association of Brussels, Belgium, January 9, 1848*, by Karl Marx, preface by Frederick Engels. New York: New York Labor News.

Published Correspondence of Florence Kelley

Blumberg, Dorothy Rose, ed. 1964. " 'Dear Mr. Engels,' Unpublished Letters, 1884–1894 of Florence Kelley (-Wischnewsky) to Friedrich Engels." *Labor History* 5 (Spring): 103–133.
Trachtenberg, Alexander, ed. 1953. *Letters to Americans, 1848–1895: A Selection*, by Karl Marx and Friedrich Engels. New York: International Publishers, 1953.

Coauthored Work

Beard, Mary, and Florence Kelley. 1916. "Amending State Constitutions." *The Forerunner* 7 (August): 216.

Studies About Florence Kelley and Supplementary References

Abbott Edith. 1908. "A Study of the Early History of Child Labor Legislation in America." *American Journal of Sociology* 14 (July): 15–37.

Abbott Edith, and Sophonisba Breckinridge. 1917. *Truancy and Non-Attendance in the Chicago Schools*. Chicago: University of Chicago Press.

Addams, Jane. 1935. *My Friend, Julia Lathrop*. New York: Macmillan.

Athey, Louis L. 1971. "Florence Kelley and the Quest for Negro Equality." *The Journal of Negro History* 56 (October): 249–261.

Blumberg, Dorothy Rose. 1966. *Florence Kelley: The Making of a Social Pioneer*. Fairfield, NJ: Augustus M. Kelley.

Breckinridge, Sophonisba. 1933. *Women in the Twentieth Century*. New York: McGraw-Hill.

Conway, Jill. 1971. "Women Reformers and American Culture: 1870–1930." *Journal of Social History* 5 (Winter): 164–182.

Deegan, Mary Jo. 1987. "An American Dream: The Historical Connections Between Women, Humanism, and Sociology." *Humanity and Society* 11 (August): 553–565.

———. 1988a. *Jane Addams and the Men of the Chicago School, 1892–1918*. New Brunswick, NJ: Transaction Press.

———. 1988b. "W.E.B. DuBois and the Women of Hull-House, 1898–1899." *American Sociologist* 19 (Winter): 301–311.

DuBois, W.E.B. 1932. "Postscript." *Crisis* 39 (April): 131.

———. 1973. *The Correspondence of W.E.B. DuBois, Vol. 1, 1877–1934*, edited by Herbert Aptheier. Amherst: University of Massachusetts. 1916.

Gilman, Charlotte Perkins. 1916. "Obstacles to Suffrage by States." *The Forerunner* 7 (August): 215–216.

Goldmark, Josephine. 1953. *Impatient Crusader: Florence Kelley's Life Story*. Urbana: University of Illinois Press.

Henderson, Charles R. 1906. "Review of *Some Ethical Gains Through Legislation*." *American Journal of Sociology* 11 (May): 846–848.

Kelley, Nicholas. 1954. "Early Days at Hull House." *Social Service Review* 28 (December): 424–429.

Lathrop, Julia. 1932. "Florence Kelley—1859–1932." *Survey* 67 (March 15): 677.

Perkins, Frances. 1954. "My Recollections of Florence Kelley." *Social Service Review* 28 (March): 12–19.

Sklar, Kathryn Kish. 1986. "Introduction." In *Notes of Sixty Years: The Autobiography of Florence Kelley, with an Early Essay by the Author on the Need for Theoretical Preparation for Philanthropic Work*, edited and introduced by K. K. Sklar., pp. 5–19. Chicago: Charles H. Kerr, for the Illinois Labor History Society.

Wade, Louise C. 1977. "Florence Kelley." In *Notable American Women*, vol. 2, edited by Edward T. James, Janet Wilson James, and Paul S. Boyer. Cambridge, MA: Belknap Press of Harvard University Press, pp. 316–319.

Wolfe, A. B. 1917. "Review of *Modern Industry in Relation to the Family, Health, Education, and Morality*." *American Journal of Sociology* 22 (March): 694–697.

Wright, Helen R. 1932. "Kelley, Florence." In *Encyclopedia of the Social Sciences*, vol. 7, edited by Edwin A. Seligman and Alvin Johnson, pp. 555. New York: Macmillan.

Unpublished Material

Ely Papers, State Historical Society of Wisconsin, Madison.
Mattson, Ramona Tomlin. 1956. "A Critical Evaluation of Florence Kelley's Speaking on the Child Labor Issue." Ph.D. diss., Department of Speech, University of Iowa.

MARY JO DEEGAN

FRANCES A. KELLOR (1873–1952)

Frances Kellor was a major figure in New York's intellectual life and national politics. As the research director of the Progressive party in 1912, she raised women, social science, and policy planning to new heights. Her work with Afro-American women, especially domestic workers, ultimately led to her major role in founding the National Urban League. Kellor's studies of blacks, women laborers, immigrants, criminals, arbitration, and unemployment laid the foundation for present-day analyses.

BIOGRAPHY

Kellor was born in Columbus, Ohio, on October 20, 1872, the second daughter of Daniel and Mary Sprau Kellor. Her early childhood was financially difficult after her father abandoned his family and her mother assumed financial responsibility. The latter worked as a laundress after she brought her children to Coldwater, Michigan. Her adolescent daughter, Frances, did the same work to help support herself in high school. In 1890, after two years of high school, she dropped out of school and became a local newspaper reporter for *The Coldwater Republican*. In 1891 she joined the First Presbyterian Church, where she was influenced by its pastor, Henry P. Collin, to study social problems. In 1894–1895 she lived with Mary A. and Frances E. Eddy, two sisters who later financially helped her to attend Cornell University (O'Connell 1980, 393).

Admitted to Cornell University by examination, Frances Kellor worked her way through college and graduated in 1897 with a law degree from Cornell Law School. She was a graduate student in sociology from 1898 to 1900 at the University of Chicago, where she studied with W. I. Thomas, Albion W. Small, and Charles R. Henderson. Simultaneously, she lived at Hull-House in Chicago until she moved to the Rivington Street College Settlement in New York. Although Henderson was her major adviser during her sociological training, Kellor's writings shared and predated many assumptions found in the more recognized writings of Thomas, particularly on race and immigrants. In 1900 the Chicago Women's Club sponsored Kellor's research on Afro-Americans and crime in the South, during an era of rampant Jim Crow laws and biological racism. In a series of popular articles (1900a, 1900b, 1901), Kellor reported on her observations and data, dispelling many of the major racist myths and advocating change through the application of various educational and democratic techniques: more vocational education, employment bureaus, labor organizations, and community organizing.

Kellor studied at the New York Summer School of Philanthropy in 1901, and became a fellow of the College Settlement Association in 1902. She intermittently lived at Hull-House from 1901 until 1905, when she permanently moved to New York City.

Kellor actively worked for black civil rights, especially black women's rights, through associations for the protection of black women who traveled North to find work. Kellor served as vice-president of both the New York and the Philadelphia Association of the League for the Protection of Colored Women between their respective founding in 1905 and 1907. In addition, she was employed as the general director of Inter-Municipal Household Research, an organization that documented the exploitation of Afro-American women in the North. These groups were modeled after the more well documented Immigrants' Protective Leagues found in most large, Northern American cities. (Grace Abbott, for example, was the director of the Immigrants' Protective League in Chicago from 1909 until 1919.) Kellor's efforts resulted in legislation that remedied the most outrageous violations of workers' rights. In 1906 she founded the National League for the Protection of Colored Women, one of three organizations that consolidated in 1911 to form the National Urban League.

In 1908 Charles E. Hughes, New York's governor, appointed Kellor to the State Commission of Immigration. In 1910 she became the first woman to head the New York Bureau of Industries and Immigration; this office evolved into the Division of Industrial Relations. Kellor developed classes in English as a second language and foreign language pamphlets about life in the United States, and she promoted industrial safety. Kellor's key role as an immigrant advocate cannot be overstressed. "In 1910 five hundred and eighty thousand five hundred and seventeen were landed at Ellis Island" (Bennet 1915, 171), the gateway for three-quarters of all immigrants for that year. Kellor's job was to help protect them from exploitative white slave traffickers and hustlers. She published public announcements in many languages, in various newspapers, and in handbills concerning exploitative practices directed toward immigrants. She also established grievance procedures to handle the immigrants' complaints, helped to reorganize the railway handling of baggage and ticketing and its ties to illicit lodgings, eliminated "phony" banks that were fleecing the illiterate, and mediated legal complaints (Bennett 1915).

Kellor became a popular and controversial public figure in New York City, and was a close friend of Theodore Roosevelt. When the latter became the presidential candidate for the newly formed Progressive party in 1912, Kellor was in a strong position to influence the Progressive party, despite women's lack of suffrage. In fact, she chaired the Progressive party's National Service in 1912 and actively campaigned for women's suffrage in this position. Under her leadership, Edith Abbott,* Jane Addams,* Emily Green Balch,* and Mary McDowell worked on various committees for legislation, immigration, and suffrage.

In 1914 she worked on the Committee for Immigrants in America, and she directed the National Americanization Committee in 1916. She worked for an understanding of immigrants' lives and cultures in the "Old World," but many of her coworkers in these groups did not. During World War I Kellor began to fear that dissatisfied immigrants posed a national threat, resulting in her adopting a more conservative immigration stance. From 1915–1916 Kellor edited *The Immigrants in America Review*, a journal she cofounded.

Kellor also was active in many academic associations, particularly the American Sociological Society and the Association of Collegiate Alumni. Her ties to academic sociology weakened through time, and by the end of World War I she worked primarily as a lawyer and international arbitrator. Her major role from 1926 until her death in 1952 was as the vice-president and chief administrator of the American Arbitration Association. This group worked to settle industrial disputes and organized for workers' rights throughout the world. Her work here was more progressive and compatible with the cooperative model and critical organizing she had enacted before World War I than her ideological positions during and immediately after the war. She was active in the League of Nations, like Emily Greene Balch and Edith Abbott, and a member of the executive board of the Pan American Union. In the latter position she helped to promote arbitration and improved economic relations between North and South America.

Lucille O'Connell (1980, 395) described Kellor as "brusque and businesslike . . . though not unfriendly, (she) discouraged closeness." Kellor's close friend Celia Parker Wooley, however, portrays Kellor as an enthusiastic modern woman with "an unconquerable purpose . . . joy in her chosen work (and permeated by) the sense of growth" (1903, 89). Many of Kellor's closest colleagues and friends were women, including her frequent coauthor Antonia Hatvany. Further research into Kellor's life, supportive of the women-identified life, will show that Kellor was warm, determined, and vibrant. She died in New York City in 1952 at the age of seventy-eight.

MAJOR THEMES

Kellor was part of a female Chicago school of race relations that has remained hidden in the annals of sociology (other members include Edith Abbott, Jane

Addams, Katharine Bement Davis,* Florence Kelley,* Ida B. Wells-Barnett,* Annie Marion MacLean,* Mary McDowell, and Mary White Ovington. Kellor wrote on crime and employment and their relation to gender. A series of articles in a widely distributed magazine, *The Arena* (1900–1901), examined blacks and criminology. Here she dismissed most of the major theories and stereotypes about black criminals, particularly those that concerned black female criminals. Kellor did exhibit, however, a strong antagonism to black churches and religion, and blamed these institutions as well as white people for many problems that beset the black community.

Another series of articles (1905–1908) examined employment opportunities for black women in the North. The problems of unscrupulous employment bureaus were especially stressed, and the selling of women into houses of prostitution and near-slave work contracts were documented. Contrary to the rosy promises of employment recruiters who sought out young black women, the major category of "honest" work available to black women was hard and unglamourous domestic work. Northern cities also were inundated with immigrants who competed for unskilled, poorly paid, back-breaking labor.

Women criminals were widely studied by another neglected group in which Kellor participated: the female Chicago school of criminology (most of the women noted above were in this network). Kellor's early work on Lombroso's criminal "nature versus nurture" argument documented that women in jail did not exhibit any measurable physiological difference from other women. The incarcerated women, moreover, exhibited traits usually associated with "masculine" behavior, which Kellor thought emerged from the harsh lives they experienced. These two articles were published in *The American Journal of Sociology* (see 1900c) and were probably part of her intended, but never completed, dissertation on the topic.

In 1901 Kellor published *Experimental Sociology* with a comprehensive critique of methodology and empirical data on criminal behavior. Undergraduate teaching in methodology was outlined, and her program for graduate study was adopted almost a quarter of a century later in the mapping and other empirical work conducted by students at the University of Chicago. The child study laboratory of Dorothy Swaine Thomas* also adopted many of Kellor's suggestions. Criticisms of the existing penal system and jurisprudence were raised in this seminal book as well.

Kellor shared the interests of many other female sociologists when she and Gertrude Dudley examined women in sports in 1909 (e.g., Lucile Eaves*). Her athletic handbook is largely a technical book on games with occasional excursions into the value of cooperation, team participation, and the need for a strong body.

Between 1920 and 1924 Kellor traveled extensively throughout Europe, "making a special study of port and transit conditions and of the treaty foundations of peace; visiting twenty-one countries; crossing seven seas; and being on the scene of action during many of the controversies herein narrated" (Publisher's Note, in Kellor and Hatvany, 1924, I, v). This immense investigation, with

Hatvany as collaborator, resulted in two volumes called *Security Against War*. The first volume recounts the circumstances and responses to ten international controversies brought before the then-new League of Nations. The second volume provides more analysis of these conflicts, arguing for the "outlawry of war." Kellor persuasively argued that the League of Nations emerged from epistemological assumptions that war was inevitable, legal, and manageable. This world view supported and created wars instead of eliminating them, which was the original goal of the founders. This radical and detailed set of books was not well received by American male sociologists, who considered the existence of the League of Nations a radical step toward peace (e.g., Todd 1926).

After 1924 Kellor wrote several complex law books on arbitration. Although a sociological viewpoint underlies this work, it is more jurisprudence than sociology. *Arbitration in Action* became a standard text on the legal resolution of conflicts, and it is commonly found today in law libraries. "As a member of the editorial board of *Arbitration Journal*, she prepared a code of ethics for arbitration that remained in effect for many years" (O'Connell 1980, 395). Her books on the history of management of the League of Nations are less well known (e.g., Kellor and Hatvany 1924, 1925), partially because they are increasingly dated.

CRITIQUES OF FRANCES KELLOR

Kellor's seminal work in sociology received mixed reviews in sociology journals. It was generally highly praised before World War I and then increasingly criticized after that time. For example, her book *Out of Work* received a glowing review in *The American Journal of Sociology* in 1905 from her mentor, Charles R. Henderson. When this book was reprinted in 1915, Ordway Tead, a Massachusetts state official whose type of work was criticized in the text, gave it mixed reviews in this journal. Thus the reviews were very different in their acceptance of this type of work within a short period of time.

Like that of many other female sociologists, Kellor's work was largely neglected in formal, intellectual accounts. Persons casually notes her work (1987, 17–18), but he does place her within the bounds of the Chicago school of ethnic studies. Generally, sociological critiques on women criminals, domestic workers, race relations, and immigrants fail to even mention Kellor's writings. Feminist sociologists are studying the lives of black women and women criminals more frequently today than in the past, but these new scholars seldom acknowledge or analyze Kellor's ideas.

Estelle Freedman (1981), a women's studies scholar, has written a major interpretation of Kellor's historical and intellectual role in women's prison reform. Praising Kellor for her critiques of Lombroso's biological criminology and careful data collection, Freedman also criticizes Kellor for her individualistic environmentalism—her overdependence on social forces to explain criminal behavior. Freedman's work powerfully explains the intersection of ideas and history surrounding the work of Kellor and Katharine Bement Davis. Freedman has laid a vital foundation for reexamining Kellor's sociology. This information is extended by the work of Allen F. Davis (1967), a historian, who provides details on some of Kellor's political activities.

Gilbert Osofsky (1964), another historian, beautifully documents and summarizes the unique contributions of Kellor and Mary White Ovington. Osofsky shows why their work was central to the study of race relations and to the establishment of organizations to fight against Jim Crow laws. Kellor's work for the National Urban League also is briefly mentioned in Arvah Strickland's study of the Chicago Urban League (1966).

Kellor's biography and some of her ideas and professional networks are discussed in the dissertations of William Joseph Maxwell (1968) and in the master's thesis of Phyllis Palmer (1967). Ellen Fitzpatrick has expanded our knowledge of Kellor's biography and political career (1990). Fitzpatrick emphasizes Kellor's role in progressive politics and examines her life in the context of other female sociologists (i.e., Edith Abbott,* Sophonisba Breckinridge,* and Katharine Bement Davis*). A thorough sociological analysis of Kellor's theory and praxis has not been done, however. Given the vibrancy of her life and times, Kellor's role in social thought is central to our understanding of the practice of sociology.

BIBLIOGRAPHY

Selected Writings by Frances A. Kellor

1899. "Criminal Anthropology in Its Relation to Criminal Jurisprudence." *American Journal of Sociology* 4 (January): 515–630; (March): 630–648.

1900a. "Criminal Sociology: The American vs. the Latin School." *Arena* 23 (March): 301–307.

1900b. "Criminality Among Women." (May): 516–524.

1900c. "Psychological and Environmental Study of Women Criminals." *American Journal of Sociology* 5 (January): 527–543; (March): 671–682.

1901a. *Experimental Sociology*. New York: Macmillan.

1901b. "The Criminal Negro." *Arena* 25 (January): 59–68; (February): 190–197; (March): 308–316; (April): 419–428.

1904. *Out of Work*. New York: G. P. Putnam's Sons. (Revised, 1915; New York: Putnam.)

1905a. "Southern Colored Girls in the North." *Charities* 13 (March 11): 584–585.

1905b. "Assisted Emigration from the South: The Women." *Charities* 15 (October 7): 13–14.

1905c. "Associations for Protection of Colored Women." *Colored American Magazine* 9 (December): 695–699.

1916a. *A Call to National Service*. New York: Macmillan.

1916b. *Straight America*. New York: Macmillan.

1920. *Immigration and the Future*. New York: Macmillan.

1923. *The United States of America in Relation to the Permanent Court of International*

Justice of the League of Nations and in Relation to the Hague Tribunal. New York: n.p.

1934. *Arbitration in the New Industrial Society*. New York: McGraw-Hill.

1941. *Arbitration in Action: A Code for Civil, Commercial and Industrial Arbitration*. New York: Harper and Brothers.

1948. *American Arbitration: Its History, Functions and Achievements*. New York: Harper & Brothers.

Coauthored Works

Dudley, Gertrude, and Frances Kellor. 1909. *Athletic Games in the Education of Women*. New York: Henry Holt.

Kellor, Frances, and Antonia Hatvany. 1924. *Security Against War*. 2 vols. Vol. I: *International Controversies*. Vol. II: *Arbitration, Disarmament, Outlawry of War*. New York: Macmillan.

———. 1925. *The United States Senate and the International Court*. New York: Thomas Seltzer.

———. 1944. *Arbitration in International Controversy*. New York: N.Y. Commission to Study the Organization of Peace and the American Arbitration Association.

Studies About Frances A. Kellor and Supplementary References

Bennett, Helen Christine. 1915. "Frances A. Kellor." In *American Women in Civic Work*, pp. 161–179. New York: Dodd, Mead.

Davis, Allen F. 1967. *Spearheads for Reform: The Social Settlements and the Progressive Movement*. New York: Oxford University Press.

Fitzpatrick, Ellen Frances. 1990. *Endless Crusade: Women Social Scientists and Progressive Reform*. New York: Oxford University Press.

Freedman, Estelle. 1981. *Their Sisters' Keepers: Women's Prison Reform in America, 1830–1930*. Ann Arbor: University of Michigan Press.

Goldmark, Josephine. 1953. *Impatient Crusader: Florence Kelley's Life Story*. Urbana: University of Illinois Press.

"Kellor [name misspelled "Kellar"], Frances Alice." 1916. In *National Cyclopaedia of American Biography*, Vol. 15, p. 249. New York: James T. White.

Leonard, John William, ed. 1914. "Kellor, Frances." In *Women's Who's Who of America*, p. 450. New York: American Commonwealth Co.

O'Connell, Lucille. 1980. "Kellor, Francis." In *Notable American Women: The Modern Period*, edited by Barbara Sicherman and Carol Hurd Green, pps. 395–397. Cambridge, MA: Harvard University Press, Belknap Press.

Osofsky, Gilbert. 1964. "Progressivism and the Negro: New York, 1900–1915." *American Quarterly* 16 (Summer): 153–168.

Persons, Stow. 1987. *Ethnic Studies at Chicago, 1905–45*. Urbana: University of Illinois Press.

Rosenberg, Rosalind. 1982. *Beyond Separate Spheres*. New Haven, CT: Yale University Press.

Shields, Stephanie A. 1982. "The Variability Hypothesis: The History of a Biological Model of Sex Differences in Intelligence." *Signs* 7 (Summer): 769–797.

Strickland, Arvah E. 1966. *History of the Chicago Urban League*. Urbana: University of Illinois Press.
Wooley, Celia Parker. 1903. *The Western Slope*. Evanston, IL: William S. Lord.

Unpublished Material

Maxwell, William Joseph. 1968. "Frances Kellor in the Progressive Era: A Case Study in the Professionalization of Reform." Ph.D. diss., Teachers College, Columbia University.
Palmer, Phyllis. 1967. "Two Friends of the Immigrant." Master's thesis, Ohio State University.
Todd, Arthur J. 1926. "Review of *Security Against War*." *American Journal of Sociology* 31 (January): 548–549.

MARY JO DEEGAN

SUSAN KINGSBURY (1870–1949)

Susan Kingsbury's life was as diverse as her academic interests. She began her academic career as a student of history but emerged as a prominent sociologist. Although her work covered an array of different areas, the underlying theme of her career centered on the labor force participation of women. This work established her as a pioneer in empirical research, methodology, and sociology.

BIOGRAPHY

Susan Kingsbury was born on October 18, 1870, in San Pablo, California, the daughter of Willard Belmount and Helen Shuler Kingsbury. Her father, a physician, traveled to California from Michigan after his discharge from the Union Army at the end of the Civil War. He died when Susan was six, leaving his wife, Helen, to support Susan and her sister, Mary Kingsbury Simkhovitch (later to found the social settlement Greenwich House in New York City). Susan's mother supported the family through her position as dean of women at the College of the Pacific in Stockton, California. Here Susan was educated, receiving a bachelor's of arts in history and graduating with honors in 1890.

Between 1892 and 1899 Kingsbury taught history at a local boys school, cared for her ailing mother, and pursued a master's degree in history at Stanford University. Under the tutelage of the sociologist George R. Howard, she was awarded the degree in 1899, and after the death of her mother in 1900, she went east to study sociology at Columbia University. She earned a doctorate in 1905, after spending a year in England on scholarship as a fellow of the Women's Educational Association of Boston (1903–1904) and a year as an instructor at Vassar College (1904–1905).

While in England, Kingsbury became acquainted with the studies of women done by Beatrice Webb* and the cost-of-living analyses conducted by Seebohm Rowntree. This work turned her attention toward an analysis of the home and factory conditions of employed women and children in the United States. After receiving her doctorate, Kingsbury became chief investigator for the Massachusetts Commission on Industrial and Technical Education. The study, which focused on the relation of women and children to industry, made Kingsbury a pioneer in the area of social research.

Between 1906 and 1915 Kingsbury was employed at Simmons College in Boston, where she became a professor of social economics. She continued her social research, becoming in 1907 the director of research with the Women's Educational and Industrial Union. She also participated in several professional associations during this period. Among these were memberships on the Board of Directors of the North Bennet Street Industrial School of Boston; the Labor Committee of the Twentieth Century Club; the Executive Committee of the Massachusetts Labor Legislation Association; the Boston Social Research Council; and the Boston Branch Association of Collegiate Alumnae. During this period Kingsbury also served as president of the New England History Teachers Association and joined the Boston Equal Suffrage Association, the American Historical Association, and the American Economic Association.

Kingsbury's presentation to the Association of Collegiate Alumnae in 1912 on the conditions of women workers in Massachusetts was received favorably by M. Carey Thomas, president of Bryn Mawr College. Within two years of the meeting, Thomas invited Kingsbury to join the faculty at Bryn Mawr College. In 1915 Kingsbury accepted the appointment as professor of social economy and the first director of the Carola Woerishoffer graduate department of social economy and social research. Under her leadership, Bryn Mawr became the first school in the United States to offer advanced courses in social research as an integral part of the graduate curriculum. Here she trained a number of doctoral students, including sociologists Belle Boone Beard and Mabel Elliot. She remained at Bryn Mawr until her retirement from academia in 1936.

In 1921 Kingsbury and Thomas established the Bryn Mawr Summer School for Women Workers in Industry. The school's objective was to provide additional educational opportunities to women who were manual factory workers. The school was formally created January 1, 1921, and opened its doors that summer. Nine women from various industries were invited to attend the school. The students discussed ways to expand the influence of women in the factory with the intention of giving impetus to women's suffrage and providing an egalitarian milieu for women workers.

Kingsbury's work on women and industry was clearly recognized by several disciplines. In 1919 she was elected vice-president of the American Economic Association. Later that year she helped to establish the American Association of Schools of Social Work. She joined the American Sociological Society in 1917 and was elected by her colleagues to serve on the Executive Committee of that organization in 1920. She remained an active member of the American Sociological Society for the next two decades.

In her international effort to examine the working conditions of women and children, Kingsbury traveled extensively, attending conferences and collecting numerous observations on the economic conditions of women. During 1921 and 1922 she toured China and India. Then in 1929, 1930, 1932, and 1936 Kingsbury and her research associate, Dr. Mildred Fairchild, traveled to the Soviet Union to observe the living and working conditions of women.

From 1933 until 1942 Kingsbury was chair of the American Association of University Women Committee on Economic and Legislative Status of Women (later renamed the Status of Women Committee). In this capacity she sought to improve the economic and legal status of women throughout the United States. From 1936 to 1940 Kingsbury served as president of the Women's University Club, the Philadelphia branch of the American Association of University Women. After her retirement in 1936 Kingsbury continued to maintain an active role in the women's suffrage movement until her death on November 29, 1949.

MAJOR THEMES

Susan Kingsbury began her academic career with a focus on institutional history. Her dissertation led to the publication of the records of the Virginia Company, an English trading company of the sixteenth and seventeenth centuries (Kingsbury 1906a). This work established Kingsbury's scholarly reputation.

Yet it was sociology, and not history, that was to become the prominent theme throughout much of Kingsbury's academic work. Her early collaboration with Beatrice Webb in London sparked an interest in the study of stratification within the work force and a concern with the employment conditions of women and children in industry. This theme emerged both in her participation in various associations and in her numerous studies on the labor force.

Her early studies examined the historical evolvement of labor legislation and its subsequent impact on educational attainment and occupational mobility. Through a historical examination of labor legislation in Massachusetts between 1835 and 1910, Kingsbury traced the development of the state process that established legislative regulations to protect educational opportunities for the worker and decrease the exploitation of women and children (Kingsbury 1911).

As director of the Massachusetts Commission on Industrial and Technical Education, Kingsbury examined variations in the level of educational attainment between skilled and unskilled workers (Kingsbury 1906b). This study reported that adolescents who obtain skilled jobs previously completed an educational program, whereas the early dropouts remained unskilled laborers. She concluded that there was a need for stronger educational programs.

Between 1906 and 1925 Kingsbury's scholarly interests focused on the living standards of women. Several studies (Kingsbury 1910a, 1911, 1921a) centered on the minimum income levels necessary for the sustenance of self-dependent and married women workers. Kingsbury and her associates found that although most college-educated women were largely self-supporting, they earned less than a minimum standard of living (Kingsbury 1911). Moreover, the findings from a subsequent Bryn Mawr survey of 11,073 families found that 89 percent of all mothers who entered industry did so because the wages of the husband were inadequate to meet the needs of the family, with a 54 percent of all families dependent on the financial support of the woman (Kingsbury 1920). Of all working mothers interviewed, 73.4 percent had sole responsibility for all household chores, resulting in a double workday for women.

The findings of these studies indicate that the lives of many working women are enormously overburdened by excessive social and familial responsibilities. Kingsbury argued that a transition away from the home and into the industrial market was inevitable. As such, she called for a stronger educational program for youth, an equal wage for equal time and service, and a welfare insurance program that would eliminate or reduce the travesties beset by broken families and aging parents (Kingsbury 1921a).

During the late 1920s Kingsbury turned her attention toward a comparative analysis of living standards and working conditions between the Soviet Union and the United States. From her travels throughout the Soviet Union, she observed that an attempt had been made to liberate women and produce equality between the sexes in the industrial sector (Kingsbury 1931). A demographic analysis of the economic system of the Soviet Union between 1913 and 1930 revealed that a transition to the socialist economy had produced a leveling effect in regard to the distribution of economic resources, thereby increasing the overall standard of living, wages, and productivity (Kingsbury and Fairchild 1931).

Kingsbury described the Soviet Union in 1929 as a progressive country, alleviating the persistent social inequities that once stratified that society. The increase in basic equalities between the sexes in regard to rights, educational privileges, and wages was noted as being a consequence of the political and economic system (Kingsbury 1932). Women are encouraged to enter industry (Kingsbury 1933) and are retained after marriage or the birth of a child, providing them with an economic sense of worth and accomplishment (Kingsbury and Fairchild 1935).

During the 1930s Kingsbury directed her attention toward the ethical and unethical standards of the newspapers. Utilizing a content analysis of forty-four national newspapers, Kingsbury and her associates identified the degree of journalistic bias on issues concerning sensationalism, political controversies, headlines, and consumer reports (Kingsbury et al. 1937). By developing an index that ranged from $+41$ (for business reports) to -53 (for sensationalized money-sex reports), the authors were able to document the relative degree of bias to which each newspaper showed partisanship when compared with the median score of the complete list of papers. These findings were replicated more than fifty years later, and the results showed conclusive validity for Kingsbury's analysis (Mozer 1989).

CRITIQUES OF SUSAN KINGSBURY

Kingsbury's work was reviewed by a diverse audience of readers. In 1914 Kingsbury received a citation in *Womens' Who's Who of America*. Her life's work was summarized in *Who Was Who in America* (1963) and *Notable American Women*. On her death, Kingsbury's lifetime accomplishments were noted in several obituaries. *The Social Service Review* briefly summarized her life work in which Edith Abbott, as editor, acknowledged her academic work and active participation in several associations. The *New York Times* referred to her as a "champion of equal economic and political rights for women." *The American Association of University Women* documented her association with that organization, and *School and Society* discussed her work in the area of education.

The *Report of the Massachusetts Commission on Industrial and Technical Training* was praised by C. R. Richards in *Charities and the Commons* (1906). He credited Kingsbury with "the most original and valuable contribution of the report" in identifying the serious educational deficiencies with which children entering industry are confronted (p. 335). In addition, her books were reviewed in the *American Journal of Sociology* (see Todd 1933) and the *American Sociological Review* (see Harris 1938).

After her presentation of the "Relation of Women to Industry" at the 1920 Conference of the American Sociological Society, Kingsbury received rather staunch criticism from Helen Glenn Tyson of the University of Pittsburgh, who argued that the paper produced nothing more than "another analysis of the encroachment of machine industry and urbanization on traditional home life" (1921, p. 158). Yet Tyson appeared to miss the point of Kingsbury's argument when she turned her attention toward the apparent trend of some companies to hire married women part-time instead of addressing the issue of equal pay for equal service as Kingsbury had done.

Mary van Kleeck,* as chair of the Program Committee for the 1931 World Social Economic Congress, praised Kingsbury and Fairchild for their demographic analysis of the Soviet Union in the preface of the book (see Kingsbury and Fairchild 1931), noting that they were the first to accomplish this task. Moreover, in 1935 their text *Factory, Family, and Women in the Soviet Union* was referred to as the "finest book in its field" by the editors of *Scribners' Magazine*.

Kingsbury's sharpest scholarly criticism came from the publication of *Newspapers and the News*. Lawrence Murphy of the University of Illinois was highly critical of the methodology used in the analysis. He argued that the book failed to establish a reference as to what ethical journalism should be, and selected an unrepresentative sample of newspapers for analysis.

Despite these critiques and her longstanding membership in the American Sociological Society, Kingsbury's work has been neglected by contemporary sociologists. Her extensive and scholarly research in the areas of stratification, labor force participation, and women and society fail to be cited in contemporary research. Her work, which paved the way for subsequent research, has been neglected in favor of others' works, largely those of male sociologists.

BIBLIOGRAPHY

Selected Works of Susan Kingsbury

1906a. *The Records of the Virginia Company of London*. Vol. 1. Washington, DC: Library of Congress.
1906b. "Report of the Sub-committee on the Relation of Children to Industries." *Massachusetts Commission on Industrial and Technical Education Report*.
1907. "What Is Ahead for the Untrained Child in Industry?" *Charities and the Commons* 19 (October): 808–819.
1910a. *The Economic Position of Women*. New York: Academy of Political Science.
1910b. "The Economic Efficiency of College Women." *Magazine of the Association of Collegiate Alumnae* 3 (February): 1–20.
1910c. "College Courses in Economics Applied to the School of Household Economics." *Journal of Home Economics* 2 (October): 248–250.
1911. "Standards of Living and the Self-Dependent Woman." *Proceedings of the Academy of Political Science*, Vol. 1, pp. 72–80.
1913. "Research Related to Household Economics." *Journal of Home Economics* 5 (April): 109–116.
1921a. "Relation of Women to Industry." *Papers and Proceedings of the Fifteenth Annual Meeting of the American Sociological Society*, Vol. 15, pp. 141–158.
1921b. "Women Workers of the World." *The Survey* 47 (December): 376.
1925. "The Worker at School." *The Survey* 53 (February): 600–603.
1930. "News and the Newspaper." *New Republic* 64 (October): 201–204.
1931. "Everyday Russia." *Woman's Journal* 16 (January): 8–10, 46.
1932. "Social Process in Russia." In *Social Problems and Social Processes*, edited by Emory S. Bogardus, pp. 33–48. New York: Books for Libraries Press.
1933. "Social Welfare." In *The New Russia*, edited by Jerome Davis, pp. 196–218. New York: John Day Co.
Kingsbury, Susan, ed. 1911. *Labor Laws and Their Enforcement*. New York: Longmans.

Coauthored Works

Kingsbury, Susan, and Mildred Fairchild. 1931. *Employment and Unemployment in Pre-War and Soviet Russia*. Report submitted to the World Social Economic Congress in Amsterdam. Hague: International Industrial Relations Association.
————. 1935. *Factory, Family, and Women in the Soviet Union*. New York: G. P. Putnam.
Kingsbury, Susan, Hornell Hart, and associates. 1937. *Newspapers and the News*. New York: G. P. Putnam.

Kingsbury, Susan, and Mabelle Moses. 1915. *Licensed Workers in Industrial Homework in Massachusetts*. Boston: Wright & Potter.

McBride, Christine, and Susan Kingsbury. 1917a. "Social Welfare in Time of War and Disaster: A Bibliography 1." *The Survey* 39 (October): 94–96, 100.

———. 1917b. "Social Welfare in Time of War and Disaster: A Bibliography 2." *The Survey* 39 (December): 287–289, 301.

———. 1918a. "Social Welfare in Time of War and Disaster: A Bibliography 3." *The Survey* 39 (January): 441–443.

———. 1918b. "Social Welfare in Time of War and Disaster: A Bibliography 4." *The Survey* 39 (February): 570–572.

———. 1918c. "Social Welfare in Time of War and Disaster: A Bibliography 5." *The Survey* 39 (March): 682–684.

Studies About Susan Kingsbury and Supplemental References

"Book Review of *Factory, Family, and Women in the Soviet Union*." 1935. *Scribner's Magazine* 98 (May): 7.

Harris, Frank. 1938. "Book Review of *Newspapers and the News*." *American Sociological Review* 3 (February): 120–121.

"Kingsbury, Susan Myra." 1914. In *Women's Who's Who of America*, edited by John Leonard, p. 459. New York: American Commonwealth.

Meigs, C. 1956. *What Makes a College: A History of Bryn Mawr*. New York: Macmillan.

Merwin, Fred. E. 1937. "Book Review of Newspapers and the News." *Journalism Quarterly* 14 (September): 280.

Murphy, Lawrence W. 1937. "Notes on the Kingsbury-Hart Study." *Journalism Quarterly* 14 (September): 382–391.

Obituary. 1949a. "Susan Kingsbury, Feminist, 78, Dies." *New York Times* (November 29): 30.

Obituary. 1949b. "Susan Myra Kingsbury." *School and Society* 70 (December): 382.

Obituary. 1950a. "Susan M. Kingsbury." *American Association of University Women* 43 (January): 97.

Obituary. 1950b. "Notes and Comment by the Editor." *The Social Service Review* 24 (March): 107.

Richards, C. R. 1906. "The Report of the Massachusetts Commission on Industrial and Technical Education." *Charities and the Commons* 16 (June): 334–339.

Todd, Arthur. 1933. "Book Review of *Employment and Unemployment in Pre-War and Soviet Russia*." *American Journal of Sociology* 39 (July): 151.

Tyson, Helen Glenn. 1921. "Discussion of Susan Kingsbury's Report on the Relation of Women to Industry." *Papers and Proceedings of the Fifteenth Annual Meeting of the American Sociological Society* 15: 158–159.

van Kleeck, Mary. 1931. "Preface." *Employment and Unemployment in Pre-war Soviet Russia*. The Hague: International Industrial Relations Association.

Watson, Frank D. 1921. "Discussion of Susan Kingsbury's Report on the Relation of Women to Industry." *Papers and Preceedings of the Fifteenth Annual Meeting of the American Sociological Society*. 15: 160–162.

Woodbury, Mildred Fairchild. 1971. "Susan Myra Kingsbury." In *Notable American*

Women, 1607–1950, edited by Edward T. James, Janet James, and Paul Boyer, pp. 335–336. Cambridge, MA: Harvard University Press.

Unpublished Material

Mozer, Mindy. 1989. "Susan Myra Kingsbury in 1929 and 1989: A Role Model Then and Now." Unpublished manuscript, Department of Sociology, University of Nebraska-Lincoln.

BRUCE KEITH

VIOLA KLEIN (1908–1973)

Viola Klein is best known for her penetrating analysis of "scientific" views of women's character. She was the first sociologist to propose and demonstrate that even "objective" views of women's nature and attributes are socially constructed. Klein was an Austrian refugee scholar who settled in Britain at the beginning of World War II. She subsequently entered the field of sociology, becoming a student and protégé of Karl Mannheim at the London School of Economics.

After the war Klein turned her attention away from the analysis of feminine nature to focus on the study of women's roles and work. She was one of the first social investigators to document the large-scale movement of married women into the paid labor force. Her research contributed to the recognition of women's changing family and occupational roles in postwar Western industrial societies.

BIOGRAPHY

Little is known about the life of Viola Klein before she arrived in Great Britain as a refugee in March of 1939. She was born on August 20, 1908, and presumably was raised in Vienna, Austria. Her early family life and education were disrupted by the rise of Hitler and the spread of fascist ideology and Nazi troops across central Europe. On the day she entered Vienna University, for example, fighting between fascist and socialist students resulted in the closing of the university for the term. After her family moved from Austria and resettled in Czechoslovakia, Klein continued her education at the University of Prague. Concentrating on the study of modern languages and social philosophy, she ultimately earned the degree of doctor of philosophy.

Klein had completed her studies and was teaching languages and managing an independent political review when the Germans invaded and annexed western Czechoslovakia in 1938. Klein fled from the Nazi-occupied zone and succeeded in gaining asylum in England the next spring. Tragically, she left behind both of her parents, who were arrested and sent to concentration camps, where they died.

Like many other educated refugees arriving in Britain, Viola Klein initially found employment as a domestic servant. After several years, with the assistance of a scholarship from the Czech government in exile, she was able to enter the London School of Economics. In 1944 she earned her second doctorate, a Ph.D. in sociology. One of her faculty tutors, and the adviser for her doctoral dissertation, was the distinguished social theorist Karl Mannheim. Mannheim served as a mentor, actively supporting Klein's research and its publication. According to Klein, Mannheim took a genuine interest in her thesis from its inception to completion. With his endorsement, the dissertation was selected to be one of the first volumes issued by the International Library of Sociology and Social Reconstruction. *The Feminine Character: History of an Ideology*, with a foreword by Karl Mannheim, was published in 1946.

MAJOR THEMES

The cornerstone of Klein's doctoral study was a groundbreaking analysis of established views of feminine character. Her dissertation included an original and informative historical analysis of women's place in British society.

Klein was one of the first sociologists to undertake a research project based on the sociology of knowledge. Furthermore, she was the first to apply the theory to the topic of women. Her study was innovative not only in its theoretical framework and subject matter, but also in its approach. Utilizing an integrative, interdisciplinary method, Klein critically examined and compared views of femininity held by experts in the fields of biology, philosophy, psychoanalysis, experimental psychology, psychometric testing, history, anthropology, and sociology.

She discovered that there was little consensus about the nature of women among those considered to be authorities on the subject. Adopting the position that knowledge is socially constructed, Klein concluded that scholars' views of women are shaped by their disciplines and by the social context in which they work and live. Even scientific observers, Klein argued, "are intellectually dependent on the social, cultural and historic climate of their time" (1972, xv).

After completing her graduate education, Klein retained an intermittent affiliation with the London School of Economics until the early 1960s. Immediately after the war, Klein worked at the British Foreign Service Office translating and editing captured German documents. She subsequently returned to the school as a staff member and research officer in the Department of Social Science and Administration. In the early 1950s, according to a former colleague (Smith 1979, 434), this department was "mainly staffed and managed by women." In this context, Klein became increasingly productive and visible professionally, presenting papers at professional meetings and publishing articles based on her research on women's roles. Especially noteworthy were several lengthy articles on married women workers that she was invited to prepare for a series of occasional papers published by the Institute of Personnel Management.

Although Klein was not yet an established member of the academy, she was associated with a number of very able women scholars working at the London University in the 1950s and early 1960s (Smith 1988). During this era Viola Klein agreed to collaborate with Swedish sociologist Alva Myrdal* on a study of women's changing roles in four Western countries. In the course of their collaboration, the two women agreeably discovered that they were "in basic agreement on all of the major issues" involved in the project. Although the coauthors were geographically separated from each other, and both had other full-time occupational responsibilities, their joint monograph, *Women's Two Roles: Home and Work*, was completed and published in 1956. According to Myrdal, the volume was the product of their "harmonious co-operation" (1968, xiii).

After an absence of more than twenty years, Klein finally returned to Europe in 1960, embarking on a lecture tour to Vienna and Prague. Thereafter she became increasingly involved in international research activities and organizations, including the International Sociological Association. She was, for example, a participant at the Association's International Seminar on Family Relations in Yugoslavia in 1961. She was a member of the Board of Editors of the *International Journal of Comparative Sociology*. Under the auspices of the multinational Organization for Economic Cooperation and Development, she also directed a study of women workers in twenty-one countries. A volume based on this survey, titled *Women Workers: Working Hours and Services*, was published in 1965.

Despite Klein's growing international reputation and body of scholarly work, she was professionally active for two full decades before she acquired an official academic post. In 1964 Viola Klein was first appointed lecturer in sociology at Reading University. She subsequently was promoted to senior lecturer in 1967 and reader in 1971. She retired from the university in 1973 but remained actively engaged in her work. Unfortunately, only a few months after her retirement, on October 17, 1973, Viola Klein suddenly died.

During her years at Reading, Klein continued her research and writing on women's roles and work. A monograph titled *Britain's Married Women Workers* was published in 1965. A revised edition of the volume *Women's Two Roles: Home and Work* was printed in 1968. *The Feminine Character* was reissued in 1971 and an American edition published in 1972.

CRITIQUES OF VIOLA KLEIN

Klein's analysis and explanation of established theories of feminine nature were undoubtedly her most original and lasting contributions. The significance of this work, unfortunately, was not fully appreciated at the time of its initial publication. Faulting Klein for merely examining experts' views of feminine character, some early critics clearly misunderstood the analytical nature and purpose of her study. It is gratifying to note, however, that as time has passed, most reviewers of *The Feminine Character* have become much more astute and positive in their judgments.

Klein's study of conceptions of femininity was a highly ambitious and original undertaking. She not only collected and analyzed the ideas of leading scholars writing about women, but she also attempted to integrate and explain their theories. According to one assessment, written twenty-five years after the volume's initial publication, "the most surprising thing about this book is that it could have been originally published in 1946. . . . Klein manages to combine a good deal of scholarly research with a very provocative feminist analysis" (Jo Freeman, backcover notes, *The Feminine Character*, 1972).

Intellectually, Klein undoubtedly was a feminist. She consistently argued that so-called "feminine traits," like ideas about women, "are sociologically rather than biologically determined." Although she rejected the label of militant feminist, she publicly acknowledged that she was "an accidental—or even incidental—one" ("A Woman's Woman" 1960). Klein was an advocate for women, but she was not a social or political activist. First, last, and foremost Viola Klein was an intellectual: a social theorist, social investigator, and analyst.

Although her early theoretical work is better known, for most of her professional career Klein was actively engaged in quantitative research that focused on patterns of women's employment. For example, Klein was among the first to document and analyze the movement of married women into the postwar labor force. Among her most noteworthy research publications was the volume, based on a comparative study of women in four nations, that she coauthored with Alva Myrdal. When the monograph was issued in 1956, *The Times Literary Supplement* described it as "the most realistic, responsible and stimulating discussion of the 'woman's place' problem yet written."

Two other studies, carried out in cooperation with Mass Observation, Ltd., exemplify Klein's widely circulated and respected research on British women workers. Lengthy reports, titled *Working Wives* and *Employing Married Women*, were initially released and distributed by the Institute of Personnel Management. These reports were later incorporated into the volume *Britain's Married Women Workers*, and published with an introductory essay and a forward-looking concluding chapter.

Viola Klein's research frequently focused on conflicts arising from married women's dual family and occupational roles. Like many other professional women of her generation, Klein never married. Although she publicly stated that she preferred her independence, Klein was not a solitary person. She had an active social life and a wide range of professional contacts. The strongest commitment in Klein's adult life, nevertheless, appears to have been her commitment to her work and occupation.

Viola Klein was a pioneer in the sociology of gender and in women's studies. Despite a marginal, personal employment history, Klein had a productive professional career. Her contributions to sociology are important and multidimensional. Klein's research on concepts of feminine character not only contributed significantly to social theory and the sociology of knowledge, but also led to the development of the sociology of sex roles. Her innovative empirical research on women also helped to build a body of sociological knowledge that challenged myths about women's family and occupational roles in postwar Western industrialized societies.

BIBLIOGRAPHY

Selected Works by Viola Klein

1946. *The Feminine Character: History of an Ideology.* London: Kegan Paul. (2nd ed., University of Illinois Press, 1971).

1950. "The Stereotype of Femininity." *Journal of Social Issues* 6, no. 3: 3–12.

1960a. "Married Women in Employment." *International Journal of Comparative Sociology* 1 (September): 254–261.

1960b. *Working Wives.* Occasional Papers, No. 15. London: Institute of Personnel Management.

1961. *Employing Married Women.* Occasional Papers, No. 17. London: Institute of Personnel Management.

1963–1964. "Industrialization and the Changing Role of Women." *Current Sociology* 12, no. 1: 24–34.

1965a. *Britain's Married Women Workers.* London: Routledge & Kegan Paul.

1965b. *Women Workers: Working Hours and Services, A Survey of 21 Countries.* Paris: Organization for Economic Cooperation and Development.

1966. "The Demand for Professional Womanpower." *British Journal of Sociology* 17 (June): 183–197.

1984. "The Historical Background." In *Women: A Feminist Perspective*, 3rd ed., edited by Jo Freeman, pp. 519–532. Palo Alto, CA: Mayfield.

Coauthored Work

Myrdal, Alva, and Viola Klein. 1956. *Women's Two Roles: Home and Work.* London: Routledge & Kegan Paul. 2nd ed., 1968.

Studies About Viola Klein and Supplemental References

"Dr. Viola Klein." 1973. Obituary. *The Times* (October 18): 20.

Farganis, Sondra. 1986. *The Social Construction of the Feminine Character.* Totowa, NJ: Rothman & Littlefield.

Giele, Janet Zollinger. 1971. "New Developments in Research on Women." In *The Feminine Character: History of an Ideology*, by Viola Klein, pp. xix–lvi. Urbana: University of Illinois Press.

Mannheim, Karl. 1946. "Foreword." In *The Feminine Character*, by Viola Klein, pp. vii–xiv. London: Kegan Paul.

Smith, John H. 1979. "The Human Factor in Social Administration." *Journal of Social Policy* 8, Part 4 (October): 433–447.

Spender, Dale. 1983. "On Whose Authority? Viola Klein (?–1973)." In *Women of Ideas and What Men Have Done to Them*, by Dale Spender, pp. 698–704. London: Ark.

"Tandem Toilers." 1965. Review of *Britain's Married Women Workers*. *The Times Literary Supplement* (December 2): 1107.

"A Woman's Woman." 1960. *The Times* (January 11): 15.

Unpublished Material

Smith, John H. 1988. Personal correspondence, October 18 and 26.

KAY RICHARDS BROSCHART

ALEXANDRA KOLLONTAI
(1872–1952)

Alexandra Kollontai (Aleksandra Kollontay) was a towering intellectual who developed feminist Marxism in the historical context of revolutionary Russia. She was a leader in both the Russian and the international Marxist women's movement, particularly between 1908 and 1922. She critiqued and documented women's struggles within Marxist thought and praxis during these years. Her feminist praxis included the analysis of sexuality and the Bolshevik mandate. Her full appreciation by English readers awaits the wider dissemination and translation of her corpus.

BIOGRAPHY

Alexandra Domontovich, an international leader of women and the proletariat, was a member of the Russian aristocracy. She was born in St. Petersburg on March 19, 1872, to Mikhail and Alexandra Domontovich. She was the first child of their marriage, although her mother had two daughters and a son from a previous marriage. Her father was a titled landowner and general who helped to draft the First Constitution of Bulgaria. His liberal politics (de Palencia 1947) led to a short period of tension in 1878 that the family spent in Sofia. Alexandra was educated at home with a highly skilled, feminist governess, Maria Strakhova, but the young girl longed for more advanced classroom training. During her early adolescence, her sister, Jenny, was an opera singer who traveled widely and broadened Alexandra's dreams and ambitions.

At sixteen she wanted to enter the university, but her parents would not allow it. Under protest, she continued her education under Strakhova, who trained her in the writings of Mary Wollstonecraft, Charles Darwin, and John Stuart Mill, among others. In 1888 Kollontai was granted a teaching diploma, and two years later she met and fell in love with Vladimir Kollontai, her second cousin. Her parents did not approve of her marrying him, and in 1892 they took her to Berlin and Paris to dissuade her from this romance. They failed in their efforts, and in 1893 the Kollontais married.

In 1894 Alexandra Kollontai bore a son, Misha, but she was desperately unhappy with her restrictions as a wife. In retrospect she wrote: "I still loved my husband, but the happy life of a housewife and spouse became for me a 'cage' " (1971, 11). She taught evening classes to workers at the Mobile Museum of Teaching Aids after her marriage, and in 1896 she distributed leaflets in a textile workers' strike and helped to raise funds for the workers. She started writing about children's education, like Jane Addams* and Florence Kelley,* during this time as well.

In 1898 she went to Zurich to study, having decided to divorce Vladimir. She remained in Zurich for three years, studying with Professor H. Herkner, a Marxist with a less revolutionary focus than that of Kollontai. In an attempt to persuade her closer to his position, he advised her to visit England to study the British labor movement. So in 1899 she went "armed with letters for Sidney and Beatrice Webb,* . . . but [she] was soon reaffirmed in her convictions and not . . . attracted by the Webbs' theories" (dePalencia 1947, 37). One sign of her renewed militance is that Kollontai began underground revolutionary work after a brief visit to St. Petersburg before she returned to Zurich. Kollontai and Herkner increasingly disagreed about Marxism, and in 1901 she left Zurich before she completed her doctorate. On her return to Russia, her divorce was finalized, and she joined a revolutionary Marxist group. She left Russia once more to study and travel. In Zurich she met Rosa Luxembourg, in Paris she met Paul and Laura Lafargue, and in Geneva she met Karl Kautsky and Georgi Plekhanov. In 1901–1902 her first writings on Finland appeared.

From 1905 to 1908 Kollontai becomes more and more noted as a feminist, author, and speaker. For example, in April 1905 she addressed the first women's meeting in St. Petersburg, opting for women's revolutionary socialism instead of the bourgeois women's movement. In September 1906 she attended the congress of the German Social Democratic party, where she met with August Bebel and Clara Zetkin, among others. In the spring and summer of 1908 she helped to organize the first All-Russia Women's Congress and worked on *The Social Basis of the Women's Question*. By September state proceedings were initiated against her revolutionary activities and writings, and she went underground. She attended the congress, but was forced to flee to Berlin to avoid arrest.

A decade of chaotic, revolutionary, and intellectually exciting work ensued. Kollontai traveled all over the world, addressing congresses of women and of workers. She initially was in opposition to World War I, and she lived a hunted existence traveling across Europe and speaking against the bitter conflagration. For example, on August 1, 1914, she arrived in Berlin on the day war was declared and was immediately arrested. Three days later she was released and meeting with Rosa Luxembourg and Clara Zetkin. She then traveled to Denmark, and was soon sought by the authorities there. In 1915, at Lenin's request, she wrote the pamphlet *Who Needs the War?* and it was soon translated into several languages and distributed "in millions of copies" (phrase from her autobiography, deleted under Stalin's censorship, 1971, 26) worldwide. The same year she undertook a five-month tour in the United States, where she spoke in eighty-one cities and lectured in German, French, and Russian.

In March 1917, after the czar had been deposed, Kollontai returned to Russia where she was greeted as a comrade. Four months later, in the beginning of July 1917, she was arrested by the provisional Kerensky government. Ironically, the secretary of Kerensky was the young sociologist Pitirim Sorokin, who became an eminent theorist later in the United States. He was bitterly and violently opposed to Kollontai's sociological thought and practice (Sorokin 1924). Kollontai was released under house arrest almost two months later. Meanwhile the fiery revolution in Russia began in earnest, and she ultimately took an active role on behalf of women and served as a liaison between the Bolsheviks and other nations.

From 1919 to 1922 Kollontai participated in the new Russian committees and governing bodies. The toll of her stressful life is reflected in her heart attack on January 1, 1919. The same year Kollontai suffered from typhus and became delirious for a period (Porter 1981, 26). In 1920, still reeling from the problems of illness and lack of nutrition, she was appointed director of *Zhenotel*, the women's bureau, in the government. Her positions on women, sexuality, marriage, the family, and workers' control of government, however, were increasingly problematic to the governing men of the U.S.S.R. In March 1921 her ideas were denounced by all party leaders. Kollontai recanted her positions, and her future leadership was severely constrained. The next year Lenin had a stroke, and a new Stalin regime began.

During her entire adult life, Kollontai struggled for the right to choose her lovers, life-style, career, and comrades. Her integrity and courage in speaking on behalf of women, passion, and workers until 1922 are inspiring and impressive. Her repeated disillusionment with men who wanted to control her is an important part of her autobiography, theory, and practice. It led to her being misunderstood and misinterpreted as a philanderer. "According to the most famous legend, Alexander Kollontai is supposed to have declared that sexual contacts were matters as simple and as unproblematic as drinking a glass of water" (Fetscher 1971, 111). This gross misinterpretation of "new women's" right to choose sexual partners can only be attributed to the patriarchal biases of Kollontai's opponents, many of whom were Marxists.

In addition to these misunderstandings, Kollontai's behavior during the Stalin regime remains shrouded in questions. Coser* (1982), for example, has raised serious, unanswered questions about Kollontai's integrity and courage under the murderous Stalin tyranny.

From 1922 until her death thirty years later Kollontai played several roles as an ambassador for Russia. Although these were fruitful years, she had defied Lenin, and the subsequent Stalin years were violent and unstable. She was only marginally tolerated, and this limited her ability to speak and act freely. It is ironic that while women in the United States were suffering from being called Communists (e.g., Jane Addams and Emily Greene Balch*), Kollontai was suffering in a communist state from being considered not communist enough.

In 1922 Kollontai was the U.S.S.R. plenipotentiary representative in Norway, and visited the International Peace Congress convened by the Amsterdam International Federation of Trade Unionists. From 1922 to 1926 she worked successfully on improving relations between Norway and the Soviet Union. In 1926 she worked for the U.S.S.R. in Mexico, and after a brief illness returned in 1927 to Norway. From 1930 to 1935 she served as the Russian ambassador to Sweden. In 1935 she was appointed to the Soviet delegation at the League of Nations, a post she held until 1937. During this latter work she met a number of women leaders, including Grace Abbott (Abbott* 1939; de Palencia 1947; 193–195), whom she befriended.

Kollantai received many honors during these years: the Order of Lenin (1933), the Order of the Red Banner of Labour (1942 and 1945), and the rank of Ambassador Extraordinary and Plenipotentiary (1943). In 1945 she was nominated for the Nobel Peace prize. From 1946 to 1952 Kollontai served as an adviser to the U.S.S.R. Ministry for Foreign Affairs. On March 9, 1952, she died of a heart attack. Her death and old age were hidden in obscurity, with no indication that her ideas would be rediscovered by future generations.

MAJOR THEMES

Kollontai shared numerous themes with her sister sociologists from the Golden Era. Many of Kollontai's analyses of other issues are markedly different, however. The common themes include women and paid labor, the women's movement, feminism, motherhood, protective legislation, suffrage, and autobiography. Her different themes include her Marxist, Soviet epistemology; her analyses of the Russian and international Marxist women's movement; and her explication of women's right to control their sexuality.

These themes frequently are intertwined in her thought. Kollontai's autobiographical writings, for example, document the Russian and international Marxist women's movement and women's right to control their own sexuality. Her opposition to "bourgeois feminism" arose from an attempt to align working women with bourgeois women *without changing class relations*. Thus feminists who struggled for improved opportunities for working women—such as protective legislation for mothers, including limits on physical endurance and hours of labor—were not bourgeois feminists.

Kollontai's massive work on *Society and Motherhood* is not available in

English. The preface is translated (1984, 97–112), however, giving English readers a hint of its contents. A footnote to this translation summarizes its contents: The first section deals with the reasons for state maternity insurance, the causes of the falling birthrate, and the effect of living conditions and female labor on infant mortality. A voluminous appendix provides statistics on maternity insurance laws in fourteen countries and a bibliography in six European languages (1984, ft. 37, p. 193). Clearly, this volume was a major statement on women, mothers, and the state.

Between March and August 1914 three groups of women in Paris, Cracow, and St. Petersburg managed to produce a newspaper, *The Woman Worker*. Kollontai and Armand Krpskya worked together in Poland on this project, which was halted by the beginning of World War I (Porter 1981, 21–22).

War and peace were passionate issues to Kollontai. Her powerful and intellectually violent pamphlet *Who Needs the War?* (1915; 1984, 75–91) exhorted workers to fight capitalists everywhere, and to refuse to kill their fellow and sister workers on the battlefield: "My enemy is in my own country, and this enemy is the same for all workers of the world. This enemy is *capitalism*. This enemy is the *rapacious, corrupt class government*. This enemy is *the lack of rights suffered by the working class*" (1984, 90).

This pamphlet was popular throughout the world, and translated into numerous languages. Although Lenin had initially supported it, he changed his position to an interpretation of war as an opportunity for civil revolt. Kollontai's popular opposition then became problematic to both Lenin and Kollontai. She publicly supported his position by stopping her open opposition to World War I. She was committed to peaceful relations between the poor of all countries, nonetheless, especially the body of soldiers who were serving in combat. In this context, her many years spent on negotiating peaceful relations between the U.S.S.R. and the international community become understandable.

Kollontai's writings on sexuality are an original contribution to Marxist praxis. She argued for women's rights to control their bodies and their choice of lovers independent of their economic life, and to divorce. Her autobiography explores these themes in her own life and is an important document. In addition, many of her ideas about her role in the revolution, her criticisms about the Soviet government, and her ideas about sexuality were deleted in the first printings of her autobiography. The 1971 edition of her autobiography italicizes the deleted sections, providing an important document of ideas considered "inappropriate" and "too radical" during the Stalin era.

Sexuality and relationships are explored in Kollontai's fiction. Two of these novels, *Red Love* and *A Great Love*, are translated into English. Porter (1981) argues that the latter book is about the impassioned affair between Lenin and Armand Krupskaya, a relationship denied by Lenin followers for many decades. It appears that these novels are neither great literature nor great sociology. They lack the clarity and power of Kollontai's other, nonfictional analyses.

CRITIQUES OF ALEXANDRA KOLLONTAI

Kollontai's stature as a theorist and leader is increasingly recognized in the West. Isabel de Palencia's biography (1947) is filled with information and background on Kollontai, including letters and documents first published here. It is a laudatory narrative with little critique.

Sheila Rowbotham was instrumental in bringing Kollontai's life and ideas on sexual freedom to the attention of English-speaking feminists in the 1970s (e.g., 1972, esp. 134–160). Germaine Greer (1971) served a similar role and function, introducing Kollontai's fascinating autobiography on sexual freedom to many readers. This unedited edition of Kollontai's autobiography shows the effect of censorship on her ideas and freedom of expression. Iring Fetscher's afterword in this edition (1971) is filled with important biographical and intellectual information as well.

I. M. Dazhina has published sections of Kollontai's diaries in Russian, and these should be interesting reading. Her introduction to Kollontai's selected readings (1984) is mundane, however, and covers up the tumultuous relationship between Kollontai and the Soviet government.

More complex critiques are now available in Bernice Glatzer Rosenthal (1977) and in Richard Stites (1978). Their analyses help to explain the complex history of women's struggles in the U.S.S.R. and their interaction with revolutionary battles and state repression.

The only reference to Kollontai by a male sociologist that I found reveals deep patriarchal hostility. Pitirim Sorokin, a Russian émigré to the United States, wrote a distorted view of Kollontai in his diary, which was later published.

It is plain. . . . that her revolutionary enthusiasm is nothing but gratification of her sexual satyriasis. In spite of her numerous "husbands," Kollontai, first the wife of a general, later the mistress of a dozen men, is not yet satiated. She seeks new forms of sexual sadism. I wish she would come under the observation of Freud and other psychiatrists. (Sorokin 1924, 59)

As the editor of this volume, I had commissioned two female, American sociologists to write an entry on Kollontai. Both of them failed to do so, resulting in my assumption of the task. My inability to read Russian and my dependence on English translations was frustrating as a scholar and author of this entry. The translations now available, nonetheless, reveal Kollontai to be a major intellectual with complex similarities to and differences from her sister sociologists in the West. There are intriguing similarities between the work and interests of Kollontai and Florence Kelley on the topics of children, motherhood, laborers, and the role of government from a feminist, Marxist perspective in two very different nations in the same era. I am similarly fascinated by the comparison of Kollontai's theories of sexuality with Elsie Clews Parsons's* ideas on parenting, social conventions, and marriage. Finally, I envision that contemporary feminist Marxists could dramatically strengthen their arguments, historical understanding, and relations to the international women's movement by analyzing Kollontai in depth.

BIBLIOGRAPHY

Selected Writings by Alexandra Kollontai (emphasizing English Translations)

A list of Kollontai's major publications in the Russian language is found in Alix Holt (1978).

1903. *The Life of Finnish Workers (Zhizn' Finliandskikh Rabochikh)*.

1909. *The Social Foundations of the Women's Question (Sotsial'nye Osnovy Zhenskogo Voprosa)*.

1913. *Society and Maternity (Obshchestvo i Maternstvo)*.

1920a. *The New Morality and the Working Class (Die neue Moral and die Arbeiterklasse)*. Berlin.

1920b. *Communism and the Family*, New York: Contemporary Publishing Association.

1921a. *The Workers' Opposition in Russia (Die Arbeiter-Opposition in Russland)*, with critical notes by R. Korpelanski, member of the Revolutionary Workers Opposition (KAP) of Russia, Berlin, O/J. Reprinted according to the text of the Russian original (*Rabochaia Oppozitsia*, Moscow, 1921) in *Arbeiterdemokratie oder Parteidiktatur*, edited by Frits Kool and E. Oberlander, Olten u. Freiburg i. Br. 1967, pp. 182–240.

1921b. *The Workers' Opposition in Russia*. Chicago: Industrial Workers of the World.

1925. *Wege der Liebe*. Berlin: Malik Verlag.

1927. *Red Love*. Reprinted, Westport, CT: Hyperion, 1973.

1932. *Free Love*, translated by C. J. Hogarth. London.

1971. *The Autobiography of a Sexually Emancipated Communist Woman*, edited with an afterword by Iring Fetscher, translated by Salvador Attanasio, and foreword by Germaine Greer. New York: Herder & Herder.

1972. *Sexual Relations and Class Struggle*. Translated and introduced by Alix Holt. Bristol, England: Falling Water Press.

1978a. *Alexandra Kollontai: Selected Writings*, edited and translated by Alix Holt. Chicago: Chicago Review.

1978b. *Love of Worker Bees*, translated by Cathy Porter. Chicago: Academy Chicago Publishers.

1981. *A Great Love*, translated and introduced by Cathy Porter. London: Virago.

1984. *Alexandra Kollontai: Selected Articles and Speeches*, compiled by I. M. Dazhina, M. M. Mukhamedzhanov, and R. Y. Tsivlina; translated by Cynthia Carlile. New York: International Publishers.

Studies About Alexandra Kollontai and Supplemental References

Abbott, Edith. 1939. "Grace Abbott: A Sister's Memories." *Social Service Review* 13 (September): 351–408.

Clements, Barbara Evans. 1979. *Bolshevik Feminist*. Bloomington: Indiana University Press.

Coser, Rose Laub. 1982. "Portrait of a Bolshevik Feminist." *Dissent* 29 (Spring): 235–239.

Dazhina, I. M. 1984. "An Impassioned Opponent of War and Champion of Peace and Female Emancipation." In *Alexandra Kollontai: Selected Articles and Speeches*, compiled by I. M. Dazhina, M. M. Mukhamedzhanov, and R. Y. Tsivlina; translated by Cynthia Carlile, pp. 5–15. New York: International Publishers.

Farnsworth, Beatrice. 1980. *Alexandra Kollontai: Socialism, Feminism, and the Bolshevik Revolution*. Stanford, CA: Stanford University Press.

Fetscher, Iring. 1971. "Afterword." In *The Autobiography of a Sexually Emancipated Communist Woman*, by Alexandra Kollontai; edited with an afterword by Iring Fetscher; translated by Salvador Attanasio; and foreword by Germaine Greer, pp. 105–135. New York: Herder & Herder.

Greer, Germaine. 1971. "Foreword." In *The Autobiography of a Sexually Emancipatea Communist Woman*, by Alexandra Kollontai; edited with an afterword by Iring Fetscher; translated by Salvador Attanasio; and foreword by Germaine Greer, pp. vii–xvi. New York: Herder & Herder.

Holt, Alix. 1978. "Introduction, Translator's Note, and Commentaries." In *Alexandra Kollontai: Selected Writings*, edited and translated by Alix Holt, pp. 13–27, 7, in passim. Chicago: Chicago Review.

de Palencia, Isabel. 1947. *Alexandra Kollontai: Ambassadress from Russia*. New York: Longmans, Green.

Porter, Cathy. 1980. *Alexandra Kollontai: The Lonely Struggle of the Woman Who Defied Lenin*. New York: Dial.

———. 1981. "Introduction." In *A Great Love*, translated and introduced by Cathy Porter, pp. 7–29. London: Virago.

Rosenthal, Bernice Glatzer. 1977. "Love on the Tractor: Women in the Russian Revolution and After." In *Becoming Visible: Women in European History*, edited by Renate Bridenthal and Claudia Koonz, pp. 370–399. Boston: Houghton Mifflin.

Rowbotham, Sheila. 1970. "Alexandra Kollontai: Women's Liberation and Revolutionary Love." *The Spokesman* 4 (June): 27–31. 5 (Summer): 15–18, 31–32.

———. 1972. *Women, Resistance and Revolution*. New York: Penguin.

Sorokin, Pitirim. 1924. *Leaves from a Russian Diary*. New York: E. P. Dutton.

Stites, Richard. 1978. *The Women's Liberation Movement in Russia: Feminism, Nihilism, and Bolshevism*. Princeton, NJ: Princeton University Press.

MARY JO DEEGAN

MIRRA KOMAROVSKY (1905–   )

Mirra Komarovsky (Mrs. Marcus A. Heyman)—researcher, teacher, and feminist—also is well known for her writings on the theory, method, and discipline of sociology. Only the second woman to be elected president of the American Sociological Association (1972–1973) since its founding in 1905, she has spent most of her career on the faculty of Barnard College. Her advocacy on behalf of women puts her in the long tradition of female sociologists, starting with Harriet Martineau,* who devoted much of their work to improving women's lives (Reinharz 1989). Komarovsky's empirical research is concerned with changing roles and attitudes, particularly insofar as they produce conflict within the individual and society. Her work has always been rewarded, whether through grants and awards, extensive citation and reprinting of her books, acceptance of her articles in esteemed journals, ascent in professional societies, or enthusiastic reviews. Yet, for many years, she thought that her abilities were not fully realized. Once she obtained the needed personal and institutional support, her work flourished, as it now does in her productive "retirement."

BIOGRAPHY

Born in the Caucasus Mountains in 1905 to Manuel Komarovsky and Anna Steinberg, Mirra was taught privately in small groups of girls from Russian Jewish professional homes. In 1922 her family emigrated to the United States. Her solid education enabled her, shortly after her arrival in Wichita, Kansas, to move to New York City and start her lifelong association with Barnard College, at that time the premier institution for undergraduate training in the social sciences (Rosenberg 1982, 213). There Mirra studied with anthropologists Franz Boas and Ruth Benedict, economists Emilie Hutchinson and Elizabeth Baker, and sociologist William Ogburn, among others. Recognized as the member of her graduating class with the greatest academic potential, she won the Caroline Durer Fellowship for a year of graduate study. Nevertheless, Komarovsky was puzzled by Barnard for extolling intellectual excellence while discouraging women from pursuing careers. The placement office and some faculty even reinforced social discrimination against students with professional aspirations, particularly those who were Jewish or foreign-born. Institutional contradictions such as these were to become a focal theme in Mirra's subsequent research.

In 1926, after three and a half years of college, Mirra graduated Phi Beta Kappa and married. Two years later, at the onset of the Great Depression, she left her job as instructor at Skidmore College, summoned the courage to divorce her unsuitable husband, and took a position as research assistant at the Yale Institute for Human Relations. In 1933 she became a naturalized citizen, left New Haven, and returned to New York City to work as research associate with George Lundberg, director of the Westchester Leisure Project at the Columbia Council for Research in the Social Sciences. The next year she published her first book, *Leisure, A Suburban Study*, in collaboration with Lundberg and Mary Alice McInerny.

Mirra then began graduate studies at Columbia University while working as a research associate at the International Institute for Social Research. Her study of the effect of the male breadwinner's unemployment on his authority in the family was a continuation of the *Studien uber Autoritat and Familie* published by Max Horkheimer in 1936. This initial study of men as a social group would become her dissertation, published in 1940 as *The Unemployed Man and His Family*. One of its findings was that female-headed households fared better than male-headed households during the Depression. Mirra's Columbia training gave her access to some of the best-known sociologists of the day—for example, William Ogburn, who supervised her master's thesis ("Invention: A Step in a Process"); Paul Lazarsfeld, who supervised her doctoral dissertation; Robert MacIver, whose official obituary she was to write for *The American Sociologist*; and Willard Waller, with whom she coauthored her first article. In addition, Robert K. Merton became a valued colleague to whom she could always turn for intellectual and editorial help.

While pursuing her graduate degrees, Mirra began teaching in Barnard's sociology department, first as a part-time and then as a full-time instructor, a rank she held until the end of World War II. Despite her accomplishments, she felt blocked during most of this period, perhaps because many of the undergraduates were xenophobic and challenged the ideas of "foreign" teachers. At Columbia, women were welcome as graduate students, but not as faculty. And her research focus on cultural contradictions was not well received at first by the sociological community. "The men were not especially interested and the women were not especially involved" (telephone conversation, July 1987). Into the 1940s and beyond "the choice of women's issues as a research specialty exacted a price. . . . The area lacked academic chic and was not likely to advance her career as some other specialty might" (1982a, 10). Even Barnard students complained that too much time in her course on the family was devoted to women's issues. Nevertheless, Mirra remained committed to marriage, family, and gender studies precisely because of the "stress and ambivalences [she] was experiencing as a professional woman" (1982a, 10).

Komarovsky's ability to reach her potential increased significantly when in 1940, at the age of thirty-five, she earned her doctorate, published *The Unemployed Man and His Family*, and married Marcus A. Heyman, a temperamentally congenial businessman who "made life easy for [her] by valuing what [she] was doing, who wanted the kind of life [she] wanted, and who gave [her] space for [her]self" (telephone conversation, July 1987). Her satisfying marriage became a model of egalitarian relations between the sexes she thought was needed "to replace the traditional ones so deeply etched in social consciousness" (1976, 249). At the same time she knew women's fulfillment would require the reorganization of institutions, not only satisfying personal relations.

Komarovsky received some criticism for *The Unemployed Man* because its sample was small and her interviews were not recorded (Bain 1941). Most reviews, however, were enthusiastic. Robert Angell labeled her study "a model of sociological research . . . the greatest step forward in the personal document method since *The Polish Peasant*" (1945, 220). Given this endorsement and her happy personal life, Komarovsky began a steady stream of publications, including articles reviewing family research and analyzing the voluntary associations of urban dwellers. In 1946 "Cultural Contradictions and Sex Roles" appeared, which described the "incompatible sex roles imposed by our society upon the college woman" (p. 184). Komarovsky drew attention to the practice of "playing dumb" as one unfortunate consequence of women's role conflicts. Fifty thousand copies of this article were eventually sold in the Bobbs-Merrill reprint series in addition to its being reprinted in many anthologies.

Komarovsky remained an assistant professor until the age of forty-two, when Millicent McIntosh became president of Barnard and gave her institutional support. At a time when the rest of the country, in its postwar transition, emphasized the virtues of mothering and homemaking, McIntosh strove to enhance women's intellectual opportunities. Exuberant, self-confident, a democratic administrator, and a powerful role model, McIntosh had Komarovsky promoted first to associate (1948–1953) and then to full professor (1954–1970). In addition, she hired Gladys Meyer, who had earned her doctorate at Columbia one year after Mirra and was an expert in social welfare. Until her retirement in 1974 and death in 1986, Meyer was a close colleague and friend of Mirra.

Shortly after receiving tenure, Mirra was appointed chair of the department, a position she retained nearly until her retirement in 1970, aside from a short interruption as the Buell G. Gallagher professor of sociology at City College, City University of New York. With another long-term department member, Bernard Barber, Komarovsky set the tone of sociology at Barnard for decades. As chair, she added Renee Fox and Roberta Simmons to the department, strengthening the presence of female sociologists and providing role models for students. Following on the heels of tenure, she was elected vice-president in 1949, and president in 1955, of the Eastern Sociological Association. Shortly thereafter she became associate editor of *The American Sociological Review* and a few years later, chair of the Section on the Family of the American Sociological Association. Immediately thereafter she served on the Council of the American Sociological Association (1966–1969). From the late 1950s on she was always able to obtain research funds from highly regarded external agencies in addition to sources available within Columbia and Barnard.

As a teacher, Komarovsky was particularly concerned, at first, not to indoctrinate students, as Max Weber had urged. As the institution in which she worked became less ambivalent, her guard relaxed. By 1951 she was confident enough in her role as teacher to publish a set of recommendations that parallel C. Wright Mill's "sociological imagination." Komarovsky particularly wanted her students to learn how to convert experience into ideas, linking them in ways that make life material for the intellect. Similarly, she converted their experience into her research material. For example, data for "Cultural Contradictions and Sex Roles" (1946a) and "Functional Analysis of Sex Roles" (1950), containing one of the earliest uses of the term "sex roles," were drawn from student essays. Even though she now sees this research as methodologically unsophisticated in comparison with her recent studies, it reflects her desire to understand her students' lives. For nearly four decades she has repeatedly studied entering freshmen at "an elite women's college" to ascertain changing values over time (1982b).

Between 1940 and 1965 Komarovsky lectured on problems that women face, particularly their conflict-ridden roles. She made television appearances (e.g., participation in Eleanor Roosevelt's "Prospects of Mankind") and published polemical articles in the popular press (e.g., *Harper's*, *New York Times*). In these she challenged biological and psychological arguments, such as Freud's notion that "anatomy is destiny" and Helene Deutsch's that "female achievers are pathological." Today perceived as "somewhat to the right of the present mainstream of feminist thought . . . for a decade or two, [she] was a left deviationist" (1982a, 10). Contributing "at the point of her pen" became her form of feminist activism, "a supplement to affirmative action, ERA and the other political movements for sex equality" (1982a, 9). Mirra continues to advocate for women's equal access to the public domain and for men's equal responsibility in child rearing and homemaking. In 1953, fed up with what she called neoantifeminism, she published *Women in the Modern World*. Although acknowledging the existence of sex differences, in this book she stressed that the overlap of scores testing men's and women's traits points to great similarities and the need for social change to release human potential. The book failed to ignite the women's movement perhaps because "it was written in tones of sweet reasonableness and was friendly to men" (1982a, 9) or perhaps because she was "a prophet in the wilderness" (Huber 1985).

Komarovsky went on to publish one major research monograph per decade.

In addition to articles in the major sociology journals, she edited two collections and an article concerning the discipline itself. The first collection (1957) deals with the relation between sociology, economics, and history; the second (1975) deals with sociology's contribution to public policy, focusing on an analysis of presidential commissions; and the article deals with "interdisciplinary polemics." Only one of her books (*Leisure*) is out of print. *Blue-Collar Marriage* (1964) is the only book Komarovsky wrote with a collaborator (anthropologist Jane H. Philips). It has sold 70,000 copies to date, and was reissued in 1987 by Yale University Press with larger type, a new preface, and revised concluding chapters. *Dilemmas of Masculinity* (1976) has been translated into Japanese. In addition, she has published chapters in some sixty readers and symposia.

Komarovsky retired from Barnard, according to mandatory procedures, in 1970 but was allowed to teach for another two years. The year she retired she became vice-president, and two years later president, of the American Sociological Association. In her role as president, she arranged for officers to discuss problems of the discipline at a time other than the annual meeting so as to increase opportunities for interaction between officers and members. After serving as president, Mirra once again joined the Council of the American Sociological Association (1973–74).

After her official retirement from Barnard, Mirra was special lecturer at the School of General Studies, Columbia University (1974–1977) and visiting professor on the graduate faculty of the New School for Social Research (1975–1978). During the period 1976–1980 she served as associate editor of the *Journal of Marriage and the Family* and received Barnard's Distinguished Alumna award (1976). The next year she received three major awards: the American Sociological Association's Jessie Bernard Award for research on the family and sex roles; the Eastern Sociological Society's Merit Award for "contribution to the development of sociology"; and Barnard College's Emily Gregory Award for "excellence in teaching." In 1978, eight years after "retiring," she returned to Barnard to chair the women's studies program. She has been professor emerita and special lecturer at Barnard since 1979, where each year she teaches the course Gender and Society. In 1979 she earned an honorary doctorate from Columbia University, in 1983 Barnard's Medal of Distinction, and in 1986 the National Council on Family Relation's Burgess Award. She was honored with the Commonwealth Award in 1990. Since "retirement" Komarovsky has published two books, edited a third, and published numerous articles. Her spectacular achievements at this point in her career illustrate the importance of not imposing retirement on productive, active scholars.

MAJOR THEMES

In 1950 Komarovsky summarized her three central scientific objectives as "(1) revealing the functional significance of sex roles, (2) locating cultural contradictions, and (3) assessing possibilities for change" (1950, 509). Most of her work fulfilled these objectives, and was guided by Merton's variety of role theory combined with Ogburn's social lag theory. Inconsistencies within social roles and how these inconsistencies change reflect her concern with change rather than order, and her goal of challenging social stereotypes. Thus Komarovsky's role theory incorporates the criticisms made of it: neglect of individuality and of social change. In particular she has been interested in the problems that arise as unintended consequences of values, and in changes that arise within integrated systems, the subject of her presidential address to the American Sociological Association (1973b).

Her sociology of conflict draws on concepts such as institutional malfunctioning, contradictions, inconsistencies, maladaptation, and strain. Her attention to dissensus led her to a view of the family that contrasted with Talcott Parson's stress on the utility of a sex-based division of expressive and instrumental functions. Komarovsky described conflicts within the family and between the family and society. Her view ultimately had greater explanatory power, given its ability to predict dissatisfaction with familial roles and the reemergence of the women's movement. Many of Komarovsky's explanations of social conflict stem from time lag and changing norms concerning roles. Although she sees conflict as the product of both impersonal "system malfunctioning" and interpersonal politics, she writes about malfunctioning and slippage, not oppression and patriarchy.

Komarovsky's work is as much about class as about gender. Her studies of the unemployed and of blue-collar families were intended to compensate for sociology's tendency not to study non–middle-class groups, to apply to the lower classes generalizations derived from the study of the middle and upper classes (1946b, 687), and to overlook *stable* working-class families. At the same time, her two books on college students delve into the contradictions faced by men and women of the more privileged classes.

Komarovsky firmly believes that "general formulations [can be] redefined into propositions which [are] actually potentially testable by empirical techniques" (1950, 509). At the same time, her empirical work has always been inspired by theory, which in turn is refined by data, and data are meaningful only when placed in the context of theory. Komarovsky's goal of increasingly refining and differentiating among concepts (see Komarovsky and Mayer 1984) has led her to introduce many changes in her methods. Overall, she considers herself to be a qualitative researcher both by preference and by default, and most of her studies are based on an intensive analysis of a small number of cases. For example, her influential "Functional Analysis of Sex Roles" was based on "twenty intensive case histories of middle class urban married women, in the summer of 1949" (1950, 508). *The Unemployed Man* was based on interviews of at least three members of fifty-nine families on relief, and *Blue-Collar Marriage* was based on an intensive examination of the interviews of fifty-eight couples. Yet her 1946 article about voluntary associations is based on 2,223 questionnaires, and some of her latest studies rely heavily on statistical analyses of questionnaires, scales, and psychological tests, in addition to interviews (see

1982, 1985; Komarovsky and Mayer 1984). Her 1985 book, *Women in College*, used a random sample, stratified by race and religion, of "241 students who each received a set of questionnaires, scales, and tests, from which a 96 percent response rate yielded a sample of 232 students" (p. 7).

Unlike many sociologists, Komarovsky has stressed the importance of adding a psychological dimension to sociological research, particularly personality variables that contribute to the differences found in social patterns. Beginning with her study of contradictions in male roles, she has used psychological instruments, such as projective tests, the California Personality Interview, the Gough Adjective Check List, and Sidney Jourard's self-disclosure questionnaire, and has employed clinical psychologists to analyze scored tests and prepare psychological profiles.

Mirra has carried out her research with teams of associates and assistants, rather than with coinvestigators, an autonomous style that may reflect her college, rather than her university or research institute, appointment. Only two of her major articles— her first, reviewing studies of the family between 1900 and 1945, and her latest, a study of female gender attitudes—were coauthored. Her research teams have been interdisciplinary groups of sociologists, anthropologists, statisticians, and psychologists, all of whom are generously praised in her publications. As a member of her teams, she has always done a considerable number of interviews herself.

Mirra's interviews contain both structured questions and probes so as "to test causal relations in a single case by probing the facts and relations set forth by those interviewed" (Angell 1941, 494). Because she recognizes that attitudes and behavior frequently are discrepant, and that the latter is more telling (1950, 514), she tries to ascertain values and behavior and instructs her interviewers in ways of checking accounts of behavior. In addition to gathering new data, Komarovsky has used other researchers' data to test her hypotheses. When data are lacking, she has written articles formulating hypotheses in need of testing. When the data then became available, she has published additional articles evaluating her former hypotheses (1956).

CRITIQUES OF MIRRA KOMAROVSKY

Numerous researchers have replicated or built on Komarovsky's work (see Wallin 1950), among them feminist sociologists Nancy Seifer, Kathleen McCourt, and Lillian Rubin. Ann Oakley contrasted *Blue-Collar Marriage* with Lee Rainwater, Richard Coleman, and Gerald Handel's *Workingman's Wife* to make an important distinction between role and task. Komarovsky urges women to study men, not just women (see her 1973a article and *Dilemmas of Masculinity* [1976]). Her study of men suggests not only that women are like men in their abilities, but also that men are like women in their dilemmas. Her call for the feminist study of men has been taken up by people ranging from psychologist Joseph Pleck to sexologist Shere Hite, yet it is not widely practiced. Many scholars have noted Komarovsky's ability to extract complex findings from qualitative techniques and to "tease out the real significance of her findings" (Bernard 1965, 425). So, too, her methodological advance of interviewing both husbands and wives in the study of marriages has been lauded. Finally, Komarovsky believes that sociologists should study both inequities and successful social inventions that have alleviated them. Society's responsibility, in turn, is to allocate resources needed for such studies.

BIBLIOGRAPHY

Claiming to be bored with the past and to live for the future, Komarovsky has established no archives and has declined publishers' requests to write an autobiography. The single autobiographical article to which I had access is her "Women Then and Now: A Journey of Detachment and Engagement," *Barnard Alumnae* (Winter 9) 1982:7–11. For the preparation of this chapter, I met with Professor Komarovsky once in New York City, and conducted a telephone interview in July 1987, neither of which was recorded. We also have corresponded about this entry, a longer version of which is titled "Finding a Sociological Voice: The Work of Mirra Komarovsky" (1989).

Selected Writings by Mirra Komarovsky

1940. *The Unemployed Man and His Family: The Effect of Unemployment upon the Status of the Man in Fifty-nine Families*. New York: Dryden Press. Ph.D. diss., Columbia University, 1940.

1946a. "Cultural Contradictions and Sex Roles." *American Journal of Sociology* 51 (November): 184–189.

1946b. "Voluntary Associations of Urban Dwellers." *American Sociological Review* 11 (December): 686–698.

1950. "Functional Analysis of Sex Roles." *American Sociological Review* 15 (August): 508–516.

1951. "Teaching College Sociology." *Social Forces* 30 (December): 252–256.

1953. *Women in the Modern World: Their Education and Their Dilemmas*. Boston: Little, Brown.

1956. "Continuities in Family Research: A Case Study." *American Journal of Sociology* 62 (July): 42–47.

1973a. "Cultural Contradictions and Sex Roles: The Masculine Case." *American Journal of Sociology* 78 (January): 873–884.

1973b. "Presidential Address: Some Problems in Role Analysis." *American Sociological Review* 38 (December): 649–652.

1974. "Patterns of Self-disclosure of Male Undergraduates." *Journal of Marriage and the Family* 36 (November): 299–314.

1976. *Dilemmas of Masculinity: A Study of College Youth*. New York: W. W. Norton.

1982b. "Female Freshmen View Their Future: Career Salience and Its Correlates." *Sex Roles* 8 (March): 299–314.

1985. *Women in College: Shaping New Feminine Identities*. New York: Basic Books.

1987. "Some Recurrent Issues in Interdisciplinary Polemics." *Sociological Forum* 2: 556–563.

1988. "The New Feminist Scholarship: Some Precursors and Polemics." *Journal of Marriage and the Family* 50 (August): 585–594.

Forthcoming. Prefatory chapter. *Annual Review of Sociology* 15.

1957. Komarovsky, Mirra, ed. *Common Frontiers of the Social Sciences*. Glencoe, IL: Free Press.

1975. *Sociology and Public Policy: The Case of Presidential Commissions*. New York: Elsevier.

Coauthored Works

Komarovsky, Mirra, and Ellen Mayer. 1984. "Consistency of Female Gender Attitudes: A Research Note." *Social Forces* 62 (June): 1020–1025.

Komarovsky, Mirra, with the collaboration of Jane H. Philips. 1964. *Blue-Collar Marriage*. New York: Random House. 2nd ed., Yale University Press, 1987.

Komarovsky, Mirra, and Willard Waller. 1945. "Studies of the Family," 1900–1945. *American Journal of Sociology* 50 (May): 443–451.

Lundberg, George, Mirra Komarovsky, and Mary Alice McInerny. 1934. *Leisure: A Suburban Study*. New York: Columbia University Press.

Studies About Mirra Komarovsky and Supplemental References

Angell, Robert. 1941. "Review of *The Unemployed Man*." American Journal of Sociology 47 (November): 493–495.

———. 1945. "A Critical Review of the Development of the Personal Document Method in Sociology." In *The Use of Personal Documents in History, Anthropology, and Sociology*, by Louis Gottschalk, Clyde Kluckholm, and Robert Angell, pp. 177–232. Bull. No. 53. New York: Social Science Research Council Bulletin.

Bain, Read. 1941. "Review of *The Unemployed Man*." *American Sociological Review* 6 (June): 432–435.

Bernard, Jessie. 1965. "Review of *Blue-Collar Marriage*." *Journal of Marriage and the Family* 27 (August): 425.

Huber, Joan. 1985. Book flap of *Women in College*, by Mirra Komarovsky. New York: Basic Books.

"Komarovsky, Mirra." 1978. In *American Men and Women of Science: Social and Behavioral Sciences*, 13th ed., edited by Jaques Cattell Press, p. 671. New York: R. R. Bowker.

Oakley, Ann. 1975. *The Sociology of Housework*. New York: Pantheon.

Rainwater, Lee, Richard Coleman, and Gerald Handel. 1959. *Workingman's Wife*. New York: Oceana.

Reinharz, Shulamit. 1989. "Teaching the History of Women in Sociology: Or Dorothy Swaine Thomas, Wasn't She the Woman Married to William I?" *The American Sociologist* 20 (Spring): 87–94.

———. 1989. "Finding a Sociological Voice: The Work of Mirra Komarovsky." *Sociological Inquiry* 59 (Fall): 374–395.

Rosenberg, Rosalind. 1982. *Beyond Separate Spheres*. New Haven, CT: Yale University Press.

Wallin, Paul. 1950. "Cultural Contradictions and Sex Roles: A Repeat Study." *American Sociological Review* 15 (April): 288–293.

SHULAMIT REINHARZ

ELIZABETH BRIANT LEE (1908–)

Elizabeth Briant Lee is known for her research on eminent American women. She also is recognized for her role in establishing progressive sociology associations, her tireless efforts in support of those organizations, and her personal and professional commitment to a more just and humane society.

BIOGRAPHY

Elizabeth Briant Lee was born in Pittsburgh on September 9, 1908, to William W. Briant and Adah Crane Riley Briant. Elizabeth grew up with two older brothers—William W. Briant, Jr. (1903–1988) and Richard Crane Briant (1905–1974). By her fifth birthday Elizabeth and her family had experienced a great deal of sadness. Her third brother, Lloyd, born in 1911, lived only a few months and died in a nursing home, while her mother, stricken with tuberculosis, spent a year and a half in a sanitarium.

Elizabeth's parents were married in their hometown of Parkersburg, West Virginia, on July 19, 1901. Elizabeth's mother, Adah, a strict Republican with a middle-class background, was an independent woman and an activist. She was president of a women's club and cofounder, along with her husband, of a Baptist church. Over the years she worked as a homemaker, store clerk, and secretary to the head of a congress of women's clubs.

Elizabeth's father, William, also was a Republican—until his life changed substantially during the Great Depression. After losing his personnel job in a factory, he found himself down to his last $37. Rather than lose their house, the family rented it and moved to a farm where William raised chickens and sold eggs. To William's dismay, none of his church friends or fellow Masons helped him while he was unemployed for a year and a half. He stopped attending church and became a socialist.

Elizabeth's parents put a high priority on education. Both her mother, who earned a high school degree, and her father, who deeply regretted that he left college after the first year, wanted to make sure that all of their children got a college education. The children did just that. William became a physician, Richard was a dentist, and Elizabeth studied sociology.

Elizabeth was an exceptional high school student, and entered the University of Pittsburgh in 1925. After arriving, she decided to continue studying diligently, but also to have some fun. Elizabeth was a bright, cute, lively redhead who liked to date (on Saturdays). She was elected secretary of the first-year women's class and joined a social sorority, Kappa Kappa Gamma.

During her first year at the university, Elizabeth met Alfred McClung Lee on a blind date. He was a tall, dark, handsome member of the Sigma Chi fraternity. Because he had been editor of the yearbook, Elizabeth thought Al had to be intelligent. She took one look at Al and decided that this was the man she wanted to marry—even though they had not yet spoken a word.

They were wed in the Episcopal cathedral in Pittsburgh on February 15, 1927. Before that winter ended, Elizabeth dropped out of school—as married women were supposed to do in those days. But Elizabeth was ''bored stiff'' at home and returned shortly. She finished her degree in 1930—three years after Al completed his bachelor's degree and had started working, first as an editor of a night school bulletin and then as a traveling salesman for a chemicals company.

In 1931 Elizabeth and Al completed their work for a master's degree in sociology at the University of Pittsburgh and enrolled in the doctorate program at Yale University. Al completed his doctorate in sociology in 1933, but Elizabeth did not receive her degree until 1937. Elizabeth's work had been slower in part because she temporarily dropped out of the program to type her husband's dissertation and then gave birth to their first son, Alfred McClung Lee III, in 1934. She also followed her husband to his first teaching job at the University of Kansas.

In 1937 Elizabeth and Al returned to Yale when he began a one-year research position in the Institute of Human Relations. The Lee family expanded to four in New Haven when Elizabeth gave birth to her second son, Briant Hamor Lee, on May 6, 1938.

Meanwhile Elizabeth was looking for the right job. But the only position the faculty at Yale suggested for her was at a small college in Pennsylvania where she would be head of the sociology department, dean of women, and coach of the women's basketball team. She passed up that opportunity.

Elizabeth's teaching positions (e.g., at Brooklyn College, Hartford Theological Seminary, and Wayne State University) were always temporary and usually part-time. She encountered resistance from people who thought that a married woman holding a job was depriving some man from working and/or that she was overeducated. She also experienced the covert or overt discrimination that has surrounded the possible hiring of a spouse.

Even when Al retired and was offered a visiting scholar position at Drew University, the university was slow to offer Elizabeth a similar appointment. In fact, the position might not have been offered at all if a group of women on the faculty had not helped to arrange the appointment. Even then it was in anthropology, not sociology.

Despite all the obstacles, Elizabeth compiled an impressive record. She has been a visiting lecturer in universities and research institutions in twelve countries. She was a co-organizer of the Society for the Study of Social Problems, the Association for Humanist Sociology, and the Sociological Practice Association (formerly the Clinical Sociology Association). She has been president of the Association for Humanist Sociology, vice-president of the Society for the Study of Social Problems, and twice secretary-treasurer of the Eastern Sociological Society. She also accepted many committee assignments in sociology organizations and never hesitated to do all the unheralded kind of work that keeps organizations in existence.

Al has been Elizabeth's best friend, coauthor, and husband for more than sixty years, and together they have been honored with numerous professional awards. For example, the Society for the Study of Social Problems established its Founders Award in their name. Elizabeth also has received the Eastern Sociological Society's first Merit Award, the Distinguished Career Award of the Clinical Sociology Association, and, in 1986, a Certificate of Recognition from the Sociological Practice Association. Both Lees were awarded the 1990 American Sociological Association Practice Distinguished Career Award for the Practice of Sociology.

Elizabeth has described herself, on different occasions, as a theoretical socialist, a humanist existentialist, a registered Democrat, and an agnostic member of a local Quaker meeting. She also says that she is an activist who gets impatient with people who do not get things done.

Elizabeth Briant Lee has spent her life as an active member of organizations that focus on the potential of people and on the development of supportive social structures. She fervently wants sociologists to recognize the importance of these goals and not to lose the field's basic mission—contributing to the resolution of pressing social problems.

Elizabeth lives with her husband in a well-kept, comfortable, eight-room house in a small college town in New Jersey. She is surrounded by their books and papers, photos of their children and grandchildren, and her own paintings of landscapes and flowers.

MAJOR THEMES

Manuel Elmer, head of the sociology department at the University of Pittsburgh, suggested the topic of Elizabeth Briant Lee's 1931 master's thesis. Elmer asked Lee to study community agencies and determine whether they would like to have social workers who have had graduate training. Lee surveyed seventy-three agencies belonging to the Pittsburgh Federation of Social Agencies. Her thesis demonstrated the need and directly contributed to the founding of the university's School of Social Work.

Lee's dissertation topic, eminent American women, has been her consuming interest for more than fifty years. Beginning in 1932 Lee reviewed all the biographies of women, starting with Emma Abbott and ending with Fannie Bloomfield Zeisler, in the twenty volumes (1928–1936) of *The Dictionary of American Biography* (DAB).

After completing her dissertation at Yale University in 1937, under the direction of Albert Keller and Maurice Davie, Lee continued to review the biographies of women that appeared in the first six DAB supplements. Lee conducted this sociohistorical review until 1960 for three reasons: (1) to keep a record of the large number of women (949) who had accomplished a great deal, (2) to determine what motivated these women, and (3) to understand the conditions under which they succeeded.

Lee has written eight cards for each of the women, and each card contains information about one of these factors: birth/death information, characteristics of the family of origin, and information about their youth, religion, education, marriage, career, and residence during the time of eminence.

Lee's office at home, with its sign "Women in Particular" on the door, contains boxes filled with 7,592 cards. She has, over the years, continued to spend some time analyzing the information on the cards but is only now beginning to really work on the book-length manuscript she had hoped to complete many years ago.

Lee's work on eminent women is known because she has given numerous talks to women's groups in many countries and at professional meetings in the United States. She also has written several short papers based on her data (e.g., "American Women" [1984b].)

Lee's major publications have not been on eminent women but rather on topics of interest to her and her husband. These jointly authored publications include a 1939 study of propaganda that has been reprinted, in part, in more than fifteen textbooks in sociology, rhetoric, semantics, philosophy, mass communications, and language.

Other coauthored projects include a social problems text, a marriage and family text, articles on the Society for the Study of Social Problems, and an article on teaching humanist sociology. The following quotes from the latter article directly show the values held by Elizabeth Briant Lee and Alfred McClung Lee (1987):

We believe that scientists cannot and should not be value free and that the values they hold should be ones appropriate to those dedicated to human service. . . . We attempt to express our findings in language that is understandable to many people. . . . We have tried to portray in sociology three particular challenges: the frontier, humanitarianism and emancipation. . . . We look for challenging and important social problems.

Elizabeth Briant Lee, by herself and with her husband, has written reviews and letters that have appeared in a number of popular progressive publications (e.g., *The Churchman, In These Times,* and *Friends Journal*). She also has assisted him with many of the books and articles that he has written. In describing her role in their jointly authored work, she has said that she doesn't write much of the initial material. Her major contributions are in reworking the drafts, editing, and proofing.

Elizabeth Briant Lee's most recent work—for example, her article on Mary Ellen Richmond, her reviews of books about women, and her developing manuscript on eminent American women— represent a new phase. Her written work will now be not only those important pieces that she has coauthored with her husband, but also her independent work. She says that she always had put aside her independent work because, at the time, she believed that the other projects and persons—particularly aging parents—had to be completed first.

CRITIQUES OF ELIZABETH BRIANT LEE

There are few critiques of Elizabeth Briant Lee's independent work. Although Beth Hess, in a speech in 1987, identified Lee as a "founding figure" in the "quiet revolution taking place in contemporary sociology due to the impact of the New Feminist Movement," Lee's independent work mainly consists of presentations and articles—the kind of work that often is not reviewed in writing.

The books that Lee has coauthored with her husband have been given a good deal of attention. Reviewers described the marriage text as "excellent," "very clear," and "encyclopedic" (see Bowerman 1962). The social problems text, a book of readings, was called "fascinating," and the authors were said to have done their job "thoughtfully, carefully and completely." Merrill (1950, 248) commented that "they have done [their job] so well that nobody else needs to do it."

Probably the best testimony to their writing is the coverage given their groundbreaking book on propaganda analysis. This work, reviewed favorably in more than fifty newspapers, magazines, and journals, has been cited in textbooks in many fields because of the simplicity, clarity, and importance of the analysis.

BIBLIOGRAPHY

Selected Writings by Elizabeth Briant Lee

1957. "Editorial and Publications Committee." Report of the Committee Chair, Society for the Study of Social Problems. *Social Problems* 4 (January): 277.
1959. "As the Twig Is Bent." *Fellowship* 25 (March 1): 21–24.

1979. "Working Proposals." Report of the Chair of the Committee on Internal Structures. *Newsletter of the Association for Humanist Sociology* 4 (September 7): 5–7.

1980. "A History of Women's Participation in the Eastern Sociological Society." *SWS Network* 10 (July): 5–6.

1981. "Thoughts About Present-Day American Middle-Class Marriage and Family Living." *Humanist Sociologist* 6 (September): 13–14.

1982. "Revisions for Ethics Code." Report of the Chair of the Clinical Sociology Association Ethics Committee. *Clinical Sociology Newsletter* 5 (Spring): 10.

1985. "Early Famous American Women: All Born in Ireland." In *Irish Heritage Week: 1985*, ed. by Elizabeth Logue, pp. 16–18. Clifton, NJ: Irish American Unity Conference, New Jersey Branch.

1986. "Coughlin and Propaganda Analysis." *Humanity and Society* 10 (February): 25–35.

1988. "Mary Ellen Richmond (1861–1928)." *Humanity and Society* 12 (May): 160–165.

1989. "How Some Women Became Eminent Social Scientists." Presidential address, Association for Humanist Sociology, 1978. *Humanity and Society* 13 (February): 16–28.

Unpublished Writings by Elizabeth Briant Lee

1931. "Personnel Aspects of Social Work in Pittsburgh." Master's thesis, Department of Sociology, University of Pittsburgh.

1937. "Eminent Women: A Cultural Study." Ph.D. diss., Department of Sociology, Yale University.

1981. "Liberated Women and Liberating Education." Paper presented at the Conference on the Mission of Higher Education, State University of New York at New Paltz, January 30.

1984a. "Women Humanist Sociologists in the Service of Social Change." Paper presented at the annual meeting of the Society for the Study of Social Problems, August.

1984b. "American Women: Changing Relations Between Sex and Eminence Before 1960." Paper presented at the Second Annual New Jersey Research Conference on Women, May 22.

Coauthored Works

Lee, Alfred McClung, and Elizabeth Briant Lee. 1939. *The Fine Art of Propaganda: A Study of Father Coughlin's Speeches*. New York: Institute for Propaganda Analysis and Harcourt Brace. Reprinted. New York: Octagon Books, 1972.

———, eds. 1949. *Social Problems in America: A Source Book*. Revised ed. by E. B. Lee and A. M. Lee, 1955. New York: Henry Holt.

———. 1961. *Marriage and the Family*. New York: Barnes and Noble, rev. ed. 1967.

Lee, Elizabeth Briant, and Alfred McClung Lee. 1974. "The Society for the Study of Social Problems: Visions of Its Founders." *SSSP Newsletter* 5 (Fall): 2–5.

———. 1976. "The Society for the Study of Social Problems: Parental Recollections and Hopes." *Social Problems* 24 (October): 4–14.

———. 1979. "The Fine Art of Propaganda Analysis—Then and Now." *ETC: A Review of General Semantics* 36 (Summer): 117–127.

―――. 1981. "Two Clinicians Tandem in Social Action." *Clinical Sociology Newsletter* 4 (Fall): 3–4.

―――. 1984. "Clarence Marsh Case (1874–1946)." *The Humanist Sociologist* 9 (January): 7–8.

―――. 1985. "Some Thoughts on SSSP's Mission." *SSSP Newsletter* 17 (Fall): 9–12.

―――. 1986. "Propaganda Analysis in 1937–42—and Now?" *Quarterly Review of Doublespeak* 12 (January): 2–4.

―――. 1987. "Teaching Humanist Sociology: An Introduction." In *The Humanist Sociology Resource Book*, edited by Martin D. Schwartz, pp. 1–4. Washington, DC: American Sociological Association.

―――. 1988. "The Continuing Values of SSSP." *SSSP Newsletter* 19 (Winter): 4–5.

Pfautz, Harold W., Ray H. Abrams, Elizabeth B. Lee, and S. M. Miller. 1956. "The Climate of Opinion and the State of Academic Freedom." *American Sociological Review* 21 (June): 353–357.

Rose, Arnold, ed. and committee chair, with Mabel Elliott, Hornell Hart, Jerome Himelhoch, et al. 1955. *Mental Health and Mental Disorder*. Samuel Koenig, Elizabeth Briant Lee, New York: W. W. Norton.

Studies About Elizabeth Briant Lee and Supplemental References

Bowerman, Charles E. 1962. "Review of *Marriage and the Family*." *American Sociological Review* 27 (April): 274..

House, Floyd N. 1949. "Review of *Social Problems in America: A Source Book*." *American Journal of Sociology* 55 (September): 233–235.

Kirkpatrick, Clifford. 1962. "Review of *Marriage and the Family*." *American Journal of Sociology* 67 (May): 718–719.

"Lee, Elizabeth Briant." 1978. In *American Men and Women of Science: Social and Behavioral Sciences*, 13th ed., edited by Jacques Cattell Press, p. 707. New York: R. R. Bowker.

Merrill, Francis E. 1950. "Review of *Social Problems in America*." *International Journal of Opinion and Attitude Research* 4 (April): 246–248.

Young, Kimball. 1941. "Review of *The Fine Art of Propaganda*." *American Sociological Review* 6 (February): 118–119.

JAN MARIE FRITZ

ROSE HUM LEE (1904–1964)

Rose Hum Lee is noted for her studies of the Chinese in the United States. As an American-born daughter of Chinese immigrants, Lee gave an "insider's" view of the social structure and assimilation patterns of the American-Chinese. As a professor at Roosevelt University in Chicago, she became chairperson of the sociology department, the first American of Chinese descent to do so. Strongly committed to integration, Rose Lee was active in the community as well as in academia.

BIOGRAPHY

Rose Hum Lee was born in Butte, Montana, on August 20, 1904. Her father, Hum Wah-Lung, had left his homeland of China to start anew in the United States, or the "Gold Mountain," as it was referred to by the Chinese. Her mother, Hum Lin Fong, also migrated to America to begin a new life, as a mail order bride. Hum Wah-Lung had various jobs as a ranch hand, a miner, and a laundry worker before starting his own business and marrying Hum Lin Fong, many years his junior. Rose Hum Lee was the second of seven children (four girls and three boys).

After her father's death, Lee's mother took over the business despite her illiteracy, and encouraged her children to go to school rather than work in the family trade. Rose Lee graduated from Butte High School and began working as a secretary. She married Ku Young Lee, a Chinese student studying in Philadelphia, and returned to China with him in the late 1920s. Unlike many Chinese at this time, Rose Lee's marriage was for love and met with family disapproval, and assumed community disapproval as well. Lee lived in China for about ten years, working various jobs as a secretary or saleswoman for government agencies and private corporations. When the Japanese invaded China, Rose Hum Lee assisted the Chinese government by organizing emergency relief services for refugees and orphaned children.

Her interest in social welfare and human relations continued when she returned without her husband to the United States along with her adopted daughter, a war orphan. Lee was determined to continue her education, and she supported herself and her daughter by free-lance writing and lecturing. She lectured independently as well as for several organizations, including the Adult Education Council. Her writing during this time included two children's plays: "Little Lee Bo-Bo" (which was produced by the Goodman Theatre in Chicago) and "Shoes for Shoe Street." Again Lee's mother encouraged her to continue her education, despite considerable opposition from her more traditional relatives. She received her bachelor's degree in social work from Carnegie Institute of Technology in 1942, her master's degree in sociology from the University of Chicago in 1943, and her doctorate in sociology, also from the University of Chicago, in 1947, at the age of forty-three.

Rose Hum Lee began teaching at Roosevelt University in Chicago in 1945 and remained there until 1961. She was named chairperson of the sociology department in 1956, a first for a woman of Chinese ancestry at an American university. Active as a sociologist, Lee was a member of the Chinese Sociology Club, the American Sociological Society, the American Academy of Political and Social Science, the American Association of University Women, the Society for the Study of Social Problems, the Midwest Sociological Society, Phi Delta Alpha, and Phi Delta Gamma, and contributing editor of the *Journal of Human Relations*. She wrote numerous articles on the assimilation patterns and social institutions of the American-Chinese (Lee preferred the term "American-Chinese" to "Chinese-American," so her usage is adopted here), as well as a book, *The Chinese in the United States of America* (1960). Lee also published an urban sociology text, *The City: Urbanism and Urbanization in Major World Regions* (1955).

Along with her academic work, Lee was active in the community, continually working to improve racial and human communication. She served on the education committee of the Chicago Commission on Human Relations, was active in the National Conference of Christians and Jews, and was a board member of the Hyde Park–Kenwood Community Conference. In 1959 she received the Woman of Achievement Award of B'nai B'rith.

In 1951 Lee married Glenn Ginn, an American-Chinese lawyer from Phoenix, Arizona who specialized in immigration cases. Like Lee, Ginn was involved in helping Chinese immigrants in their struggle with the American way of life. During the 1950s Lee traveled to Europe and Asia, giving her future work an international flavor and advancing cross-cultural knowledge and understanding.

On March 25, 1964, Rose Hum Lee died of a stroke in Phoenix, Arizona, at the age of fifty-nine. Although her years as a sociologist were relatively few, her achievements were many. Lee's legacy to the study of the Chinese in America is very much alive today, as she is widely cited in others' work. At the time of her death Lee was writing a book about her father and his life as an immigrant, as well as studying local problems of social welfare.

MAJOR THEMES

Lee's work follows the theoretical approach of Robert E. Park and his colleagues from the Chicago school of sociology. She followed Park's advice and ventured out to explore urban life. Not unlike numerous other ''natural histories'' resulting from the studies of the city of Chicago, many of Lee's essays on the Chinese in America describe Chinatowns and the social worlds therein. In Rose Lee's urban sociology textbook, *The City: Urbanism and Urbanization in Major World Regions* (1955), she emphasizes worldwide urbanization, but the framework uses a demographic and ecological model from the Chicago school (complete with an acknowledgment to Louis Wirth for his guidance and advice).

Beginning with her master's thesis on welfare services in Canton, China (1943), Lee's work has been almost exclusively based on the Chinese. Her doctoral dissertation, ''The Growth and Decline of Chinese Communities in the Rocky Mountain Region'' (1947), explored the social institutions of Chinatowns and factors affecting their growth, development, and decline. Her research in this vein continued with her essay ''Social Institutions of a Rocky Mountain Chinatown'' (1948), which was a study of her birthplace, Butte, Montana. In this essay Lee discusses which social institutions the Chinese attempt to preserve when separated from their homeland and living in a new land. ''The Decline of Chinatowns in the United States'' (1949a) is considered Lee's most famous essay, and has been reprinted in many books on race and the minority experience in America. Again, Lee was attempting to discover why Chinatowns have developed, flourished, and declined over the years.

With a grant from the Social Science Research Council in 1949, Rose Lee began to study recent Chinese immigrant families in the San Francisco–Oakland area. She published several articles from this research comparing established Chinese families with recent immigrant families, and comparing ''native-born'' with ''China-born'' on various issues. Other essays were written on the history of Chinese and American relations, the Chinese abroad, Chinese population changes, and the ''stranded'' Chinese in the United States. In a more sociopsychological vein, Lee wrote about the types of marginality and the conditions that created them.

In 1960 Rose Hum Lee published *The Chinese in the United States of America*, a comprehensive look at almost all aspects of Chinese immigration. The book begins with an overview of American-Chinese relations and demographic trends. Chinatowns are discussed as well as the subgroups of the Chinese population. Social organizations, family patterns, political institutions, religion, social class, health, delinquency, old age, and many other issues also are discussed. The concluding chapters deal with American attitudes toward the Chinese, Chinese attitudes toward themselves, a look at the past, and predictions for the future.

In an effort to illustrate that the Chinese are by no means homogeneous, but rather a group with many cleavages, Lee divided the Chinese population into three distinct subgroups: the "sojourners," the "intellectuals," including students, and the "American-Chinese." Because of the different reasons for each group being in America, their assimilation patterns and life-styles differ greatly. "Sojourners" are those Chinese who intend to return to China after improving their economic status; they are oriented toward China. Although the "students and intellectuals" also may intend to return to China (but may be stranded in America because of political reasons), they usually are of a higher social class and live outside Chinatowns. The "American-Chinese" are citizens of the United States either by birth or by fulfilling the legal residence requirements. This group considers the United States their home and wants to be part of the larger culture. According to Lee, because of the diversity of the Chinese in America, the assimilation process is impeded. Other factors that hinder total integration are the existence of Chinatown ghettos, a lack of American-oriented leadership, and a high number of Chinese who are not American citizens.

Lee forcefully argues for use of the term "American-Chinese" rather than "Chinese-Americans," believing that the latter "carries the connotation of the descendants of a racial and cultural group against whom prejudicial and discriminatory acts have been directed." According to Lee, the expression implies that they are Chinese before they are American and therefore second-class citizens.

Lee's belief in assimilation is clear throughout her work. Although there is a conflict between the sojourners (who are opposed to assimilation and want to retain their Chinese customs) and the American-Chinese (who want to be accepted), Rose Lee pleads that total integration is necessary: "The American-born, especially, must resist the pressure of the older Chinese who try to impose Chinese norms, values and attitudes on them or woo their loyalty by exhortations to 'save the face of the Chinese.' " According to Lee, assimilation is a two-way process, and the Chinese need to do their part to find their place in American society. Americans, on the other hand, need to be less concerned about racial ancestry.

Rose Hum Lee's work covers the gamut of Chinese life in America. Reading her studies gives one an "insider's" view, as well as a rich history of Chinese culture. Although nowhere does Lee define herself as a feminist, her writing clearly does. Many times, she identifies the sexual double standard in discussing Chinese culture, and concerns herself with the effects immigration has had on women. Although some of her work is demographic, the majority is rich with meaning as well as statistics.

CRITIQUES OF ROSE HUM LEE

Rose Hum Lee's work is still widely recognized in academia today. Citations of her work can be found in journals ranging from psychiatry to economics. Because of the wide range of issues Lee addressed in her research on the Chinese, her work has been of interest not only to sociologists, but also to historians, anthropologists, psychologists, economists, social workers, educators, gerontologists, psychiatrists, and political scientists.

Both of Rose Hum Lee's books were reviewed in *The American Sociological Review*. John H. Burma (1961) found *The Chinese in the United States of America* to be a much needed scholarly, descriptive, and analytical work dealing with the Chinese in America. Ira de A. Reid (1955), in reviewing *The City: Urbanism and Urbanization in Major World Regions*, finds the emphasis on worldwide urbanization "not without merit," although this emphasis should have been continued throughout the text. Also Reid suggests that Lee may have omitted some important works by utilizing only the Chicago school of thought.

Roger Daniels (1974), a professor of history, criticized Lee's work in the *Pacific Historical Review*, stating that *"The Chinese in the United States of America* is a treatment by a sociologist and badly flawed by a lack of historical understanding and factual errors." But by failing to cite any examples of alleged imperfections, one is left to wonder what they are, or if Professor Daniels is assuming that sociologists may not know their history very well (a stereotype that, unfortunately, often is true).

Other criticisms of Rose Hum Lee's work are minor in comparison. Ivan Light (1974) criticized Rose Lee and others for assuming that the decline of disorder (i.e., drugs and prostitution) in American Chinatowns was caused by the normalization of the sex ratio. According to Light, this explanation has a number of empirical difficulties, and needs supplementation. Yawsoon Sim (1975) disagrees with several of Lee's predictions for the future of Chinatowns and Chinese assimilation. Unlike Lee, Sim does not see American-Chinese becoming totally assimilated, nor does he see Chinatowns vanishing.

Although the more current literature does not criticize Rose Hum Lee personally for her ideas of total assimilation, there is most definitely a new era of ethnic consciousness of which Lee is not a part. For example, both Albert H. Yee (1973) and Stanley L. M. Fong (1973) cite Rose Lee's work on numerous issues in their research, but neither share her views on assimilation, and instead embrace a more pluralistic stance. These researchers and others have found that many American-Chinese youths are showing signs of greater ethnic consciousness, and interest in their community and its problems. They are asking themselves who they are and whether it is necessary to reject their Chinese heritage. Sim suggests that changes that occurred in the mid-sixties, such as liberalization of immigration laws and the passage of the civil rights act, changed the atmosphere of the nation, making it more relaxed for all ethnic groups.

Lee was aware of the merits of cultural pluralism (see Lee 1960, 131), but she still believed that the loss of Chinese characteristics would be beneficial to the American-Chinese in the long run. By losing their cultural characteristics they become part of the mainstream, and therefore not discriminated against.

The importance of Rose Hum Lee's work is exemplified in the number of scholars who have cited her research, not only in sociology, but in many other disciplines as well. Researchers continue to follow her lead, and take on the challenging history of ethnic relations in hopes of improving our understanding of society.

BIBLIOGRAPHY

Selected Writings by Rose Hum Lee

1946. "Chinese Population Trends in the United States." *South-Western Journal* 2 (Spring): 97–104.

1948. "Social Institutions of a Rocky Mountain Chinatown." *Social Forces* 27 (October): 1–11.

1949a. "The Decline of Chinatowns in the United States." *American Journal of Sociology* 54 (March): 422–432.

1949b. "Chinese Dilemma." *Phylon* 10 (Second Quarter): 137–140.

1949c. "Research on the Chinese Family." *American Journal of Sociology* 54 (May): 497–504.

1949d. "Occupational Invasion, Succession, and Accommodation of the Chinese of Butte, Montana." *American Journal of Sociology* 55 (July): 50–58.

1950. "A Century of Chinese and American Relations." *Phylon* 11 (Third Quarter): 240–245.

1952a. "Delinquent, Neglected, and Dependent Chinese Boys and Girls of the San Francisco Bay Region." *Journal of Social Psychology* 36 (August): 15–34.

1952b. "Chinese Americans." In *One America*, edited by F. S. Brown and J. S. Roucek, pp. 309–319. New York: Prentice-Hall.

1955. *The City: Urbanism and Urbanization in Major World Regions*. Philadelphia: J. B. Lippincott.

1956a. "The Recent Immigrant Chinese Families of the San Francisco–Oakland Area." *Marriage and Family Living* 18 (February): 14–24.

1956b. "The Marginal Man: A Re-Evaluation and Indices of Marginality." *Journal of Human Relations* 4 (Spring): 27–39.

1956c. "The Chinese Abroad." *Phylon* 17 (September): 257–270.

1957a. "Chinese Immigration and Population Changes Since 1940." *Sociology and Social Research* 41 (January–February): 195–202.

1957b. "The Established Chinese Families of the San Francisco Bay Area." *Midwest Sociologist* 20 (December): 19–26.

1958. "The Stranded Chinese in the United States." *Phylon* 19 (July): 180–198.

1960. *The Chinese in the United States of America*. New York: Oxford University Press.

Unpublished Writings by Rose Hum Lee

1943. "Maternal and Child Health and Welfare Services in Canton, China." Master's thesis, Social Service Administration, University of Chicago.

1947. "The Growth and Decline of Chinese Communities in the Rocky Mountain Region." Ph.D. diss., Department of Sociology, University of Chicago.

Studies About Rose Hum Lee and Supplemental References

Burma, John H. 1961. "Review of *The Chinese in the United States of America.*" *American Sociological Review* 26 (February): 147–148.

Burr, William. 1980. "Lee, Rose Hum." In *Notable American Women: The Modern Period*, edited by Barbara Sicherman and C. H. Green, pp. 414–415. Cambridge, MA: Harvard University Press, Belknap Press.

Daniels, Roger. 1974. "American Historians and East Asian Immigrants." *Pacific Historical Review* 43 (November): 449–472.

Fong, Stanley L.M. 1973. "Assimilation and Changing Social Roles of Chinese Americans." *Journal of Social Issues* 29, no. 2: 115–127.

"Lee, Rose Hum." 1968. In *Who Was Who in America*, Vol. 4, pp. 565. Chicago: Marquis-Who's Who.

Light, Ivan. 1974. "From Vice District to Tourist Attraction: The Moral Career of American Chinatowns, 1880–1940." *Pacific Historical Review* 43 (November): 367–394.

Reid, Ira de A. 1955. "Review of *The City: Urbanism and Urbanization.*" *American Sociological Review* 20 (June): 495–496.

"Rose Hum Lee, 1904–1964." 1965 Obituary. *American Sociological Review* 30 (February): 127–128.

Sim, Yawsoon. 1975. "Chinese-Americans and Bananas: An Analysis of Their Identity Crisis and Militancy." *International Review of History and Political Science* 12 (February): 17–48.

Yee, Albert H. 1973. "Myopic Perceptions and Textbooks: Chinese Americans' Search for Identity." *Journal of Social Issues* 29, no. 2: 99–113.

TERRI PHILLIPS

HELENA ZNANIECKA LOPATA
(1925–   )

Helena Znaniecka Lopata was the first woman in her family to raise her own children and be a full-time homemaker. After ten years of this life in the United States, she visited her Polish homeland and was inspired to rekindle her scholarly ambition. She chose women's social roles of homemaker, mother, worker, and widow as major areas of her research agenda. Since that time she has amassed an astounding record: author or coauthor of ten books, series editor for *Research on the Interweave of Social Roles* and for *Current Research on Occupations and Professions*, thirty-five journal articles, contributor to twenty-eight book chapters, and leadership positions in more than ten professional organizations. A full professor and director of the Center for the Comparative Study of Social Roles at Loyola University in Chicago, Lopata finds that she can now write much faster because she is more confident of her abilities.

BIOGRAPHY

Born October 1, 1925, in Poznan, Poland, Helena Znaniecka Lopata was the only child of Florian and Eileen Markley Znaniecki. Her father was born in 1882 into the landed gentry that was part of the Polish intelligentsia. He studied at the University of Geneva and the Sorbonne, earning his doctorate in philosophy from the University of Crakow. Znaniecki quickly published two books, but was unable to obtain a chair at a university for political reasons, mainly his previous involvement in student protest activities (Bierstadt 1969). He took a position at the Emigrant Protective Society, and it was because of this work that William I. Thomas (husband of Dorothy Swaine Thomas*) invited him to the United States to work on a project about Polish immigrants.

While in Chicago, Znaniecki's first wife died suddenly. Shortly after that he met Eileen Markley, who became his second wife and Helena's mother. A remarkable person in her own right, Markley had received a bachelor's degree in English Literature from Smith College, a master's degree in history from Columbia University, and a law degree from the University of Chicago, even though, as a woman, she had to sit in the hall outside the classroom for many of her classes. On her marriage, she quit her job with the Legal Aid Society and worked with her husband on the writing of *The Polish Peasant in Europe and America* (Thomas and Znaniecki, 1918–1920).

After W. I. Thomas left the University of Chicago, the Znanieckis returned to Poland, where Florian Znaniecki was appointed the first chair of sociology in Poland. Five years later Helena was born.

In 1939 Znaniecki gave a series of lectures at Columbia University. The German invasion prevented him from returning to Poland; however, if he had made it home, the family would have perished because his name was on both the Communists' and the Nazis' black list. Because Helena and her mother were members of the intelligentsia, the Nazis placed them in a concentration camp for later deportation to an extermination camp. On the day the cattle cars arrived, her mother lied to the Nazis about her current citizenship status, informing the commander of the camp that she was an American citizen with important political connections. She demanded, and was granted, release for herself and her "orphaned niece." Barely escaping almost certain death, even years later Helena feels "some sense of guilt over having deserted my country in her hour of need" (Lopata 1975, 70).

Her father had accepted an academic position at the University of Illinois, where Helena and her mother joined him. Because Helena looked and spoke differently than the other girls, she felt foreign in her new environment. After high school she began college at the University of Illinois, and much to her surprise, her humanist father advised her to join a sorority. She soon discovered the value of being a sorority member: this was how she became "Americanized." Helena had a wonderful time at the university, where she met her future husband, whom she describes as one of the last of the "Renaissance men" (Lopata 1975, 71). In 1946 she got her degree, became an American citizen, and married Richard (Dick) Lopata, a second-generation Polish-American fresh out of the Marine Corps. They were both twenty years old.

Although her parents were not happy about her marrying so young, they offered the couple meals and lodging for $25 a month on the stipulation that they leave the house in the morning and not return until dinner. During this period Dick completed his bachelor's degree and Helena earned her master's degree. In 1949 she entered graduate school at the University of Chicago "with all those fantastic faculty and students."

This was the period of expanding university enrollments because of veterans' benefits. There were 200 students in her department, many of whom are now famous sociologists (e.g., Joseph Gusfield, Howard Becker, Erving Goffman,

Rhoda [Goldstein] Blumberg, Gladys Lang, and Kurt Lang). The faculty also were notable. Her committee consisted of Everett Hughes, Louis Wirth, and Herbert Blumer; others in the department included William Ogburn, Ernest Burgess, Peter Blau, Anselm Strauss, Morris Janowitz, and Harvey Smith.

It was at the University of Chicago that Helena was fully confronted with the consequences of carrying a famous name. Married, she could have avoided living under the shadow of her father's legacy, but she chose to use both Znaniecka and Lopata. This decision was both a boon and a bust to her own developing career. Although her father's name gained her respect and opened some doors, it also limited her exploration of new areas of study. Even her dissertation topic was constrained by her committee's expectations of Znaniecki's daughter. She originally wanted to do a theoretical piece, but her professors told her to "go back and find out why your Father predicted the Polish community in America would die, and it hasn't." She reluctantly did what they expected, writing a dissertation on "The Functions of Voluntary Association in an Ethnic Community: Polonia" (1954), a topic that became a major research interest for her in future years.

The other way her father's name affected her was more serious. Because her father's work was highly valued, and because people identified her through him, she doubted her own abilities. For instance, she earned her doctorate in 1954 with honors in social psychology, but she thought that they had given her the degree out of respect for her father. Lacking self-confidence, she immersed herself in family life, caring for her home and raising her two children, Theodora, born in 1951, and Stefan, born in 1955, one year after she received her doctorate. She was by this time thoroughly Americanized; she had become a "housewife."

In her homemaker role, Helena lost contact with other sociologists. She was too embarrassed to go to meetings when she was not publishing. She taught evening courses part-time at DePaul University from 1956 to 1960 and at Roosevelt University from 1960 to 1964. When students at Roosevelt signed a petition to get her a full-time position, she became an assistant professor. But she did not become active in research until she returned from a trip to Poland in 1966. She recalls the impact of this trip on the development of her sense of noblesse oblige:

I felt guilty because my life had been saved and here I had this fantastic background and I wasn't doing anything with it. So many of the people in Poland had been killed and people felt an obligation to help rebuild the world—that came right back to me on that visit to Poland. I felt I had to do something to contribute. (Interview, February 19, 1988)

This period of her life, from the time of earning her doctorate until her commitment to pursuing an academic career, is one Lopata describes as a cross section of cultural adaptations.

Becoming an American in this ideologically open and democratic country converted me, at least for a while, not only from being a Pole but also from being a sociologist, because of my identity as a woman. Reidentification with basically sexist Poland, on the other hand, moved me back into scientific life. (1975, 74)

MAJOR THEMES

Lopata's initial research project was on the role she had been experiencing for the past twelve years: the social role of homemaker in suburbia. In her first book, *Occupation: Housewife* (1971), she defined housewife as an occupation that contained four phases over the life course. Lopata's next major project logically followed the last stage of the housewife role. She studied widows because she wanted to analyze the changed social role of housewife after the wife's role is modified by the death of the husband. In 1968 she developed a typology of widows based on the degree of social relationship involvement in this role (Lopata 1973).

When the Social Security Administration funded her to do comparative work on widows, she found that the social role theme did not work well because of subcultural differences. She modified the social role framework by breaking the role into "couplets" based on the fact that support is a duty and a right between a person and a member of the social circle. From this perspective she was able to do comparative work on the support system of widows.

After publishing *Women as Widows: Support Systems* (1979) Lopata continued this work on a worldwide scale, and in 1988 edited a two-volume book on widowhood in a variety of countries (1987). In doing this project Lopata became interested in further study in India. She traveled to India in late 1987 to facilitate work on the life-style and support systems of diverse Indian widows. Although emersed in widowhood studies since the mid–1970s, Lopata began a major research project on city women and their occupational involvement. This study on the interweave of women's family and work roles resulted in a two-volume work (Lopata et al. 1984, 1985).

Lopata's research led her to a critique of social policy. She discovered the strongest support for widows was their own resources, family, and friends, although social security was important because it allowed widows to live independently. Community services and social agencies provided little, if any, support for her subjects. For women working outside the home, she found a societal failure to create a work environment that considers the multidimensional aspect of their lives. Because of the disjunction between the inflexibility of work and other aspects of women's experience, including changes that occur over the life course, Lopata called for a restructure of work patterns and the "rhythm of careers" (Lopata 1978, 417). More recently she has critically examined the effects of inadequate and unequal social security programs that contribute to societal arrangements, causing women to be in a dependent status position (Lopata and Brehm 1986).

Lopata identifies herself as a symbolic interactionist who uses the humanist coefficient, that is, the "definition of the situation," since "that is what symbolic interaction is.'' She considers herself "basically a social interactionist who works with social role, which is in-between social interaction and more formal sociology" (Lopata interview, February 19, 1988). Her symbolic interactionist perspective is seen most clearly in her work on the process of identity construction, beginning in her early work. In *Occupation: Housewife* (1971) she discusses the process of "becoming" and then "being" a housewife when a woman becomes a different person viewing the world through a changed framework symbolized by a new residence and name. In *Widowhood in an American City* (1973) she studied how widows thought that their identities had changed and what identity reconstructions they underwent to adjust to the loss of their husbands. Over time Lopata's interest in identity became even stronger. Recent examples of her focus on identity are a paper she gave in Wales on "The Self-concept, Identities and Traumatic Events: The Death of a Husband," which was later published as "Becoming and Being a Widow: Reconstruction of the Self and Support Systems" (1986a), and her article "Time in Anticipated Future and Events in Memory" (1986b).

Lopata's work became more feminist oriented. She examined the meaning of the terms "sex roles" and "gender" (Lopata and Thorne 1978), focused on how women are constrained by a strong gender stratification system, and began using the term "male dominance" (see Lopata 1987c). In the last decade she has taken the position that there is no such thing as a sex role based on biological sex identification (Lopata 1976a). Rather than a sex or a gender role, people develop gender identities that are fundamental elements of social roles and social stratification. It is not role restrictions, but gender identification that "pushes, pulls, encourages, or discourages entrance into functionally organized social roles" (Lopata and Thorne 1978, 720).

Lopata argues that there is no more a sex-gender role than there is a race role or a class role. But because sexism has not been taken as seriously as race and class inequality, sex-gender role terminology has focused on individuals and socialization instead of on social strata. Thus relations of power and inequality have been masked (Lopata and Thorne 1978).

If being a woman or a man had *ever* been a separate social role rather than a more or less pervasive identity, it would have had to be a status role, that is a social role whose only function was the preservation of status distinctions. (Lopata 1980, ix)

INTELLECTUAL INFLUENCES

Lopata's father was her "strongest and most lasting influence, both on the personal and professional level." Indeed, her father's work had become her work when, after his death, she prepared his unfinished book *Social Relations and Social Roles* (1965) for publication. Influential teachers and colleagues include Herbert Blumer, E. T. Hiller, Everett Hughes, Louis Wirth, Joseph Gusfield, Howard Becker, Rhoda Blumberg, and David Maines. When she began her reentry into academia, her former, now distinguished, classmates provided her with valuable assistance. For example, Erving Goffman advised her to turn her work on her father's book into articles (Lopata 1964, 1966). When her first book turned out to be 800 pages long, Howard Becker advised her how to shorten it and then recommended it for publication.

Lopata attributes this nearly all-male list of early influences to the lack of women in the university in her graduate student days. During the 1970s, after the founding of Sociologists for Women in Society, she became involved in this organization that provided an important resource for women in the discipline. And, over the years, she has come to know many notable women sociologists. For instance, she is a friend of Helen MacGill Hughes,* whom she met while at the University of Chicago. Caroline Rose* she knew well when Rose was one of the key people with the Midwest Council for Social Research on Aging. Ethel Shanas* is a longtime colleague whom Lopata still sees regularly. Also, she knew professionally and/or personally Joan Huber,* Mirra Komarovsky,* Alice Rossi,* Ruth Shonle Cavan,* Rosalie Wax,* Rose Laub Coser,* Jessie Bernard,* and Matilda White Riley.*

Lopata's mother was a strong influence in her life. Although her mother had exceptional abilities, she created a role model of a totally devoted wife who accepted a secondary position. Striking out in a scholarly direction while being a wife and a mother was difficult for Helena. She considers that to be a result of American culture, but her mother's example contributed to her conflict on this issue.

Feminism became an important influence in her career development and research agenda. Lopata's early work reflects a feminist influence, although at this time it was more reactive than consciously feminist. An unsettling experience led her to develop a deeper feminist analysis. This was the outcome of a think-tank meeting when Nona Glazer suggested she rethink her conception of housewives. Her first reaction was embarrassment and confusion; she thought, "Oh my God, I'm a feminist—what is she talking about?" Nonetheless, she did exactly what Glazer suggested: rethink. Lopata realized that she had an unreflective perception about married women and economic "parasitic" dependency. She reevaluated her assumptions and realized that she had failed to give credit to women's work at home. The widowhood study and the ways widows' lives are limited also deepened her awareness about women's position in society.

A final influence on her development, also connected to her growing feminist awareness, was her recognition of the fact that even though her male colleagues had influenced her, she had not influenced them. They were not interested in the work she was doing, since "after all, who considers housewives important?" She identifies her work as the study of social phenomena, which can be done by studying juvenile delinquents or politicians or any other group. But because she studied women, she believes that much of her work has been discounted in the discipline. Thus, for the most part, her work has been influential only to those other sociologists interested in the study of women's everyday lives.

CRITIQUES OF HELENA ZNANIECKA LOPATA

Over the years reviews of Lopata's work have overwhelmingly been favorable (Boles 1981; Price-Bonham 1976) or at least mixed (Galaskiewicz 1977; Lasswell 1979; Miller 1984). An early critique centered on methodological issues (Oppenheimer 1973), with other critics occasionally faulting her for conceptual inadequacies and integrative insufficiency (Papanek 1982). For instance, Farber's review of *Widowhood in an American City* questioned her failure to show how widows differ from widowers, or divorced men and women (1974), and Matthews commented that her book on *Widows and Dependent Wives* covered much territory but failed "to bound it" (1987, 732).

Despite some negative comments, the overall evaluative view of Lopata's research is positive. Jacobs (1981) defines her work on widows as a valuable breakthrough for other researchers; Wartenberg calls her research path-breaking and a major contribution to theories of modernization that show that "social changes affect women—who have been left out of these theories—differently than men" (1988, 832); and Hertz (1987) considers her work on city women to have been an important service to the academic and professional community. *Polish Americans* was reviewed positively (Roysdon 1976), with Galaskiewicz finding "our understanding of ethnic Americans is greatly enhanced by Lopata's new book" (1977, 270). The Association of College and Research Libraries has consistently provided favorable reviews of her work. For instance, *Women as Widows* was called "a gold mine of information for sociologists and academics" (1979:1095), and *Polish Americans* was praised for its extensive bibliography and for effectively assailing "several myths regarding immigrant ethnic groups in the U.S." (1976, 1058).

Her work has stood the test of time. Lopata's publications have been cited in countless studies, her support systems typology for widows has been replicated in such diverse countries as Korea, Iran, and Australia, and, after more than twenty-five years, her four-stage analysis of the homemaker role continues to be used by others in their research. For example, Imamura (1987) recently used it for her work on urban housewives in Japan.

Helena Znaniecka Lopata was able, eventually, to resolve the same conflict of competing social roles that were present in many of her subjects' lives. Once she integrated her personal and professional lives, she succeeded in building an impressive list of achievements. In addition to the body of research previously discussed, Lopata's organizational record shows that she has been president and/or vice-president of the Society for the Study of Social Problems, Midwest Sociological Society, Illinois Sociological Association, the Midwest Council for Social Research on Aging, and Polish Academy of Arts and Science in America. Further, she has served as section or committee chair for numerous organizations, including the Committee on Professions and four sections for the American Sociological Association. She also has been active in the Gerontological Society of America, Sociologists for Women in Society, International Sociological Association, and International Gerontological Association.

Lopata's accomplishments reveal a consistency in her interest areas over time. On her return to academic life, she went back to the Polish-American community and developed a new theoretical framework to study this ethnic group, publishing a book on this work (Lopata 1976b). She is in her second decade of studying widows and is currently restudying suburban women. Through interviews with women occupying the same homes that were involved in her original study, she is looking for levels of social involvement and attachment to community life today.

Lopata's career shows that she has followed in her father's footsteps in two important ways. First, she has done so in terms of methodology. In *Cultural Reality* he argued for an empirical experiential methodology of social research (Znaniecki 1919). An examination of her publications finds that women's life experiences, including those closely connected to her own, are imprinted in her work. Second, she has continued her father's analysis of social roles, deepening it by her own contributions. For even though she maintains that her interest has been on social roles, role clusters, and support systems—not housewives, widows, or work and family integration—she has consistently made women the subject of her research. Not only has she made a career out of studying women, but she has done so with an increasing feminist analysis. Thus she has carried on the legacy of Florian Znaniecki's work by expanding it to include the specific nature of women's roles in patriarchal society.

ACKNOWLEDGMENTS

Major sources of biographical data were an interview with Helena Znaniecka Lopata on February 19, 1988; an interview by David Maines (1983); and "A Life Record of an Immigrant" (Lopata 1975). Unless otherwise noted, direct quotes in the text are from the February 19 interview.

BIBLIOGRAPHY

Selected Writings by Helena Znaniecka Lopata

1964. "A Restatement of the Relation Between Role and Status." *Sociology and Social Research* 40 (October): 58–68.
1966. "The Life Cycle of the Social Role of Housewife." *Sociology and Social Research* 51 (October): 5–22.
1971. *Occupation: Housewife.* New York: Oxford University Press.
1973. *Widowhood in an American City.* Cambridge, MA: Schenkman.
1975. "A Life Record of an Immigrant." *Transaction/Society* 13 (November–December): 64–74.
1976a. "Sociology." *Signs* 2 (Autumn): 165–176.

1976b. *Polish Americans: Status Competition in an Ethnic Community.* Englewood Cliffs, NJ: Prentice-Hall.

1978. "Work and Social Policy." Guest Commentary. *Alternative Lifestyles* 1 (November): 417.

1979. *Women as Widows: Support Systems.* New York: Elsevier–North Holland.

1980. "Preface" and "Introduction." *Research in the Interweave of Social Roles: Women and Men* 1: vii–ix, xi–xix.

1986a. "Becoming and Being a Widow: Reconstruction of the Self and Support Systems." *Journal of Geriatric Psychiatry* 19, no. 2: 203–214.

1986b. "Time in Anticipated Future and Events in Memory." *American Behavioral Scientist* 29 (July–August): 695–709.

Lopata, Helena Znaniecka, ed. 1978. *Family Factbook.* Chicago: Marquis Academic Media.

1987. *Widows: Volume I: The Middle East, Asia, and the Pacific. Vol. II: North America.* San Francisco: Duke.

Coauthored Works

Lopata, Helena Znaniecka, Debra Barnewolt, and Cheryl Allyn Miller. 1985. *City Women: Work, Jobs, Occupations, Careers.* Vol. 2. *Chicago.* New York: Praeger.

Lopata, Helena Znaniecka, and Henry P. Brehm. 1986. *Widows and Dependent Wives: From Social Problem to Federal Program.* New York: Praeger.

Lopata, Helena Znaniecka, with Cheryl Allyn Miller and Debra Barnewolt. 1984. *City Women: Work, Jobs, Occupations, Careers.* Vol. 1. *America.* New York: Praeger.

Lopata, Helena Znaniecka, and Barrie Thorne. 1978. "On the Term Sex Roles." *Signs* 3 (Spring): 718–721.

Unpublished Material by Helena Znaniecka Lopata

Lopata, Helena Znaniecka. 1954. "The Functions of Voluntary Association in an Ethnic Community." Unpublished diss., Department of Sociology, University of Chicago.

———. 1988. Interview, February 19.

Studies About Helena Znaniecka Lopata and Supplemental References

Bierstadt, Robert. 1969. Introduction. In *On Humanistic Sociology: Selected Papers*, by Florian Znaniecki, edited by Robert Bierstadt. Chicago: University of Chicago Press.

Boles, Jacqueline. 1981. "Review of *Women as Widows*." *Social Forces* 59 (March): 874–875.

Farber, Bernard. 1974. "Review of *Widowhood in an American City*." *American Journal of Sociology* 80 (July): 269–271.

Galaskiewicz, Joseph. 1977. "Review of *Polish Americans*." *American Journal of Sociology* 83 (July): 270–272.

Hertz, Rosanna. 1987. "Review of *City Women: Work, Jobs, Occupations, Careers*,

Vol. I: *America*; Vol. II: *Chicago.*" *Contemporary Sociology* 16 (March): 152–154.

Imamura, Anne E. 1987. *Urban Japanese Housewives: At Home and in the Community.* Honolulu: University of Hawaii Press.

Jacobs, Ruth Harriet. 1981. "Review of *Women as Widows.*" *Contemporary Sociology* 10 (January): 143–144.

Lasswell, Marcia E. 1979. "Review of *Family Factbook.*" *Contemporary Sociology* 8 (July): 583.

Maines, David R. 1983. "Coming to Grips: Aspects of the Life History of Helena Z. Lopata." *Midwest Feminist Papers* 4: 112–124.

Matthews, Sarah H. 1987. "Review of *Widows and Dependent Wives.*" *Contemporary Sociology* 16 (September): 732–733.

Miller, Karen A. 1984. "Review of *Research in the Interweave of Social Roles: Families and Jobs*, Vol. III." *Contemporary Sociology* 13 (July): 487–488.

Oppenheimer, Valerie Kincade. 1973. "Review of *Occupation: Housewife.*" *Social Forces* 52 (September): 133–134.

Papanek, Hanna. 1982. "Review of *Research in the Interweave of Social Roles: Women and Men*, Vol. I." *Contemporary Sociology* 11 (May): 292–295.

Price-Bonham, Sharon. 1976. "Review of *Widowhood in an American City.*" *Contemporary Sociology* 5 (January): 29.

"Review of *Polish Americans.*" *Choice* 13 (October): 1058.

"Review of *Women as Widows.*" *Choice* 16 (October): 1095.

Roysdon, C. M. 1976. "Review of *Polish Americans.*" *Library Journal* 101 (June): 1442.

Thomas, William I., and Florian Znaniecki. 1918–1920. *The Polish Peasant in Europe and America.* 5 vols. Chicago: University of Chicago Press. 2nd ed., 2 vols. New York: Alfred A. Knopf, 1927.

Wartenberg, Hannah. 1988. "Review of *Widows*, Vols. I and II." *Contemporary Sociology* 17 (November): 831–833.

Znaniecki, Florian. 1919. *Cultural Reality.* Chicago: University of Chicago Press. Reprinted Houston: Cap and Gown, 1983.

———. 1965. *Social Relations and Social Roles: The Unfinished Systematic Sociology.* San Francisco: Chandler.

———. 1969. *On Humanistic Sociology: Selected Papers*, edited and with an introduction by Robert Bierstadt. Chicago: University of Chicago Press.

BARBARA RYAN

HELEN MERRELL LYND (1896–1982)

Helen Merrell Lynd was a wide-ranging, interdisciplinary theorist and ethnographer. Her most famous books on life in a small Midwestern town, coauthored with her husband, Robert S. Lynd, establish her as a powerful interpreter of American community and meaning. In addition, she was a dedicated teacher and pedagogist, historian, and social psychologist. She actively fought for greater equality and tried to articulate the possibility for social roots in modern society.

BIOGRAPHY

Helen Merrell Lynd was born on March 17, 1986, in La Grange, Illinois, the heart of the Midwest, which she later studied intensely. She was one of three daughters of Edward Tracy and Mabel Waite Merrell. They were both devoted Congregationalists, and their vision of humanity embraced all people, regardless of race, sect, or nationality. Her father edited a Congregationalist magazine, *The Advance*, and her mother attended Mount Holyoke College for two years, providing their daughter with an interest in writing and learning. This heritage was augmented by other relatives. Her paternal grandfather helped to found Ripon College in Wisconsin, and some of his children later founded Whitman College in Walla Walla, Washington (Rothman 1985, 2).

Helen attended primary and secondary school in La Grange, where she excelled. When her father was offered a job in Framingham, Massachusetts, Helen was able to attend nearby Wellesley College. She was an active figure there, enjoying the intellectual life and professors. She became particularly attracted to philosophy and began studying with Mary S. Case, who became a lifelong influence and mentor. Helen was well trained in Hegelian dialectics here, providing a bridge between her early religious training and her later interest in economic democracy. She graduated Phi Betta Kappa in 1919, the year that Emily Greene Balch* was fired from that institution.

Merrell taught secondary school for a year at the Ossining School for Girls in Ossining, New York, followed by a year at Miss Master's School in Dobbs Ferry, New York. She met Robert S. Lynd in 1919 while they were each hiking on Mount Washington. Two years later, in 1921, they married and moved to New York City. Here they moved in with his parents while she earned a master's degree in history from Columbia University.

In 1924 the Institute for Social and Religious Research of the Rockefeller Foundation hired Bob to study the religious life of a small town. The Lynds became involved with the entire community process and spent the next two years living in Middletown (Muncie, Indiana). The original committee that funded the study was displeased "with the voluminous final manuscript, calling it a savage satire on religion, and refused to publish it" (Rothman 1985, 5). From 1926 to 1929 the Lynds polished their work. Although it was coauthored by both, Robert needed it for his doctoral dissertation, so they tried "the fake process" of removing Helen's work to meet the bureaucratic demands of the university (Lynd 1983, 38). They finally obtained permission from the funding committee, to publish the study, and Harcourt, Brace accepted it for publication after an intensive search for new sponsors.

The Lynds had two children: Staughton, born in 1929, immediately after the first Middletown study was published, and Andrea Merrell (Mrs. Joseph Nold), born in 1934, shortly before the second Middletown study was published,

Helen Merrell Lynd's academic career centered around Sarah Lawrence College, where she taught from 1929 to 1964. (Before settling at this college, she had briefly lectured at Vassar College.) Her years at Sarah Lawrence were fruitful. She enjoyed teaching at the progressive liberal arts college, where she could have close contacts and a flexible format in the classroom. Many of her assumptions about teaching are found in her books *Field Work in College Education* (1945) and *Toward Discovery* (1965).

Robert S. Lynd was more accepted in the powerful male academy and discipline than his wife, echoing the lives of Dorothy Swaine Thomas* and W. I. Thomas, Arnold Rose and Caroline Rose*, Helen MacGill Hughes* and Everett C. Hughes, and Elizabeth Bryant Lee* and Al Lee. Thus Helen Merrell Lynd earned her doctorate in 1944 from Columbia University, many years after her professional career was established, and many years after her husband had completed his degree there and joined the faculty. Despite the extreme patriarchal bias of the profession and the academy, the Lynds had a rich, full life together, including a highly successful professional life.

An activist, Lynd's commitment to democracy and social equality led to major roles in the American Federation of Teachers and the American Civil Liberties Union (the latter organization was cofounded by Jane Addams* and Emily Greene Balch). Because of these activities and the ideas supporting them, Lynd was called before the Jenner Committee in the early 1950s. This red-scare harassment, echoed in the lives of Jane Addams and Emily Greene Balch, followed Lynd's public support of three professors who were fired from the University of Washington during the late 1940s. A public debate with Sidney Hook led to national attention with both attacks and support for her stance. "Letters of approval and thanks poured in from other professors who were thinking the same thing but were too cowardly or endangered to write themselves" (Rothman 1985, 11).

Despite this witch-hunting and a lack of full recognition within the sociological community, Lynd led a full and often recognized role in the academic world. Thus, in 1962, she was awarded an honorary doctor of letters degree from Ripon College. She also continued to teach a reduced load at Sarah Lawrence after her "official" retirement in 1964 until just before her death in 1982.

MAJOR THEMES

Lynd's commitment to democracy and education for social equality mark her as a critical pragmatist. Although she wrote and studied years—if not decades—after Jane Addams and her cohort, Lynd has a significant intellectual tie with them.

Her most important books were coauthored with her husband, Robert S. Lynd. The first volume, *Middletown: A Study in Contemporary American Culture*, was published in 1929, just before the start of the Great Depression. Their second, longitudinal study, *Middletown in Transition: A Study in Cultural Conflicts*, was published in 1935 in the midst of that devastating economic age. Each volume is comprehensive, accurate, and well documented, and could stand alone as a major analysis of community life in a small Midwestern city. Together, they form a formidable intellectual statement.

In 1924 and 1925 the Lynds and their research staff lived in this community and collected information from a variety of sources, in a manner analogous to anthropologists studying a foreign culture. The major activities for community survival structure their analysis. These include earning a living, making a home, training the young, engaging in religious practices, and participating in community activities. Although the Lynds end this volume with a cautious note that rapid social change can quickly alter such communities, the overall prosperity and optimism are evident.

Their caveat was well placed, for the Great Depression made earning a living, staying healthy, and general survival vastly different enterprises in 1935 when the Lynds returned to Middletown. The city's ability to recover and retain its optimism is striking, however, even with the financial collapse of the national economy. Class privileges and strains are more apparent in the second study, yet a sense of workers' solidarity is lacking. Radical changes in social class did not emerge from the radical change in the marketplace. Instead, the community adhered to "the American way," hoping for a better future.

These remarkable community studies provide a systematic view of an American city in times of stability and change. They also set a high standard of sociological expertise, making them landmark studies of community development. From the time of their first publication until the present the Middletown studies were benchmarks for similar work. Helen Merrell Lynd did not continue working in this area of research, however. She increasingly emphasized historical analysis, teaching, and the links between the individual and the larger social canvass.

In *Field Work in College Education* (1945) Lynd studied student–teacher interaction and the application of social science principles to everyday life. Here, too, she was on the forefront of sociological issues with contemporary significance. Advocating an active collaboration between social science and the community, she provides concrete examples of student projects and ways to make sociology a living science for young college students.

England in the Eighteen Eighties: Toward a Social Basis for Freedom (1944) is a scholarly, beautifully written analysis of personality and social structure as it emerges from an era of social ferment. This period in England's history established a new social philosophy that enhanced individual freedom as well as articulated the community's responsibility to its members. The inequalities spawned by economic liberalism became more apparent at this time, and increasing demands were made for social planning and welfare services. Although the revolutionary momentum of organized labor was blunted, the Fabians were able to capture the public's support for specific, democratic alteration in government roles and services. This book is a sweeping and powerful study of the interaction between ideas, material changes, and social movements. It helps to establish the basis for critical pragmatism in sociology, although Lynd did not overtly link it to the profession in her text. (See Beatrice Webb.*)

A more modern treatment of the interface between the person and society is presented in *On Shame and the Search for Identity* (1958). This book critiques the work of the psychoanalyst Sigmund Freud, and Lynd's contemporary sociologist Talcott Parsons. She finds that both men lack an understanding of historical bases for belonging to a social group and neglect the role of social values in shaping the self. Lynd depicts contemporary men and women as vulnerable to the rapid social change characteristic of modern life. There are myriad opportunities for social recognition as well as social loss and degradation. "Shame," the failure to reach one's self-ideal and to suffer disgrace in the eyes of others, points not only to a painful exposure of the self, but also to the human striving for a sense of achievement and meaningful action. Lynd believed that each person had a moral obligation to extend his or her experience and communicate these events to others. The need to transcend prescribed codes and the limits of one's given society was necessary to creatively act in everyday life. Lynd was clearly expressing her own lived philosophy as well as articulating a scholarly vision here.

Toward Discovery (1965) is a compilation of Lynd's writings, making some of her more obscure publications easily accessible and combining these with major themes from her books. Her editor, Loewenberg, notes that the theme of "discovery" underlies Lynd's diverse interests. The history of ideas, education, the effect of specific events and cultures, and their interaction with specific people are linked through Lynd's search for meaning and "facts." By seeing commonalities where others see differences, Lynd overcame the divisions and specializations that divide people and issues.

CRITIQUES OF HELEN MERRELL LYND

The major critiques of Lynd's work revolve around the Middletown studies. These books tower over the intellectual landscape in sociology analyzing the Great Depression. The Lynds' data and interpretations are a baseline analysis of a particular community undergoing change in two specific historical contexts. This base has become the resource for hundreds of other studies, reports, and filmed documentaries. An insightful and critical analysis of the Middletown studies is found in Maurice R. Stein's critique of their intellectual depth amid beguiling descriptive detail (1960, 47–69). In addition, all the major American sociology journals, including *The American Journal of Sociology*, *The American Sociological Review, Social forces*, and *Sociology and Social Research*, reviewed one or both books.

The original Middletown studies are being replicated today. These contemporary studies (e.g., Caplow, Bahr, Chadick, Hill, and Williamson 1982) find great continuity in Middletown life, despite the popular image of constant and revolutionary change in America. The structural changes of the past half century also can be determined and documented. With new census data on the era from 1850 to 1880, some of the Lynds' findings can be corrected (Bahr and Bracken 1983) and integrated into mainstream, contemporary work. Middletown has become a permanently studied center of American life. (See the extensive bibliography of these several dozen studies in Caplow et al. 1982, 411–422.) Unfortunately there is a strong trend to analyze this work as that of Robert S. Lynd (see the special issue on his work published by *The Journal of the History of Sociology*, 1979) instead of analyzing it as the joint project of two scholars.

Bert James Loewenberg tried to pull together Lynd's corpus by analyzing them as a set of writings united by the search for innovation, or discovery. He clearly analyzes her wholistic approach to knowledge but fails to capture the structure of her thought and its significance as an intellectual enterprise.

Andrew Weigert, J. Smith Teitge, and Dennis W. Teitge briefly note Lynd's creative work on identity: "Her book (1958) serves as an important transition piece from psychoanalytic writings to work more central to sociological psychology" (1986, 10). They locate her ideas in a chain of scholarship leading to contemporary symbolic interactionist perspectives on identity (1986, 14). This sociological critique is important, since her book won widespread critical acclaim by psychiatrists (Horowitz 1979, 475) but significantly less notice within sociological circles.

Except for the Middletown books, Lynd's social thought has received little systematic study in sociology. A notable exception to this neglect is Irving Louis Horowitz's systematic, albeit brief, study of her work (1979). This general neglect arises partially because her other books do not have the legitimation of the Middletown studies, partially because she increasingly specialized in history instead of sociology, and partially because of her gender. The combination of these reasons has generated the anomalous situation in which her work in one area is lauded as remarkable and ground-breaking, whereas her major work in other areas remains hidden and underanalyzed. Reviewing her work as a whole, she is clearly a major theorist in sociology who blended traditional women's work in the discipline with a lifelong dedication to the investigation of human meaning and action.

BIBLIOGRAPHY

Selected Works by Helen Merrell Lynd

1944. *England in the Eighteen Eighties: Toward a Social Basis for Freedom*. New York: Columbia University Press.

1945. *Field Work in College Education*. New York: Columbia University Press.

1949a. "Must Psychology Aid Reaction?" *Nation* 168 (January 15): 5–6.

1949b. "Truth at the University of Washington." *American Scholar* 18 (July): 346–353.

1951. "Love and Reason." *Nation* 173 (September 22): 240–241.

1952a. "Realism and the Intellectual in a Time of Crisis." *American Scholar* 21 (January) : 21–32.

1952b. "Undiscovered Language." *Nation* 174 (May 31): 527–529.

1958. *On Shame and the Search for Identity*. New York: Harcourt, Brace.

1965. *Toward Discovery*, edited by Bert James Loewenberg. New York: Hobbs, Dorman.

1983. *Possibilities*. Ohio: Ink Well Press.

Coauthored Works

Lynd, Robert S., and Helen Merrell Lynd. 1929. *Middletown: A Study in Contemporary American Culture*. New York: Harcourt, Brace.

————. 1935 *Middletown in Transition: A Study in Cultural Conflicts*. New York: Harcourt, Brace.

Studies About Helen Merrell Lynd and Supplemental References

Bahr, Howard M., and Alexander Bracken. 1983. "The Middletown of Yore: Population Persistence, Migration, and Stratification, 1850–1880." *Rural Sociology* 48 (Spring): 120–132.

Caplow, Theodore, Howard M. Bahr, Bruce A. Chadick, Rueben Hill, and Margaret Holmes Williamson. 1982. *Middletown Families: Fifty Years of Change and Continuity*. Minneapolis: University of Minnesota Press.

Deegan, Mary Jo. 1981. "Helen Merrell Lynd." In *American Women Writers*, vol. 3, edited by Lina Mainiero, pp. 59–60. New York: Ungar.

Horowitz, Irving Louis. 1979. "Lynd, Robert S. and Helen Merrill." In *International Encyclopedia of the Social Sciences: Biographical Supplement*, vol. 18, edited by David L. Sills, pp. 471–477. New York: Free Press.

Jacobs, Glenn., ed. 1979–1980. "Robert S. Lynd." Special issue on the work of Robert S. Lynd. *Journal of the History of Sociology* 2 (Fall-Winter): 1–131.

"Lynd, Helen Merrell." 1967. In *Who's Who of American Women*. 5th ed. p. 745. Chicago: A. N. Marquis.

Stein, Maurice R. 1960. *The Eclipse of Community: An Interpretation of American Studies*. Princeton, NJ: Princeton University Press.

Weigert, Andrew J., J. Smith Teitge, and Dennis W. Teitge. 1986. *Society and Identity: Toward a Sociological Psychology*. Arnold and Caroline Rose Monograph Series of the American Sociological Association. New York: Cambridge University Press.

Unpublished Material

Bracken, Alexander. 1978. "Middletown as a Pioneer Community." Ph.D. diss., Ball State University.

Rothman, Ronni H. 1985. "Beyond Middletown: The Life Work of Helen Merrell Lynd." Paper submitted for course (conducted by Shulamit Reinharz) on "Women's Intellectual Work," Brandeis University.

MARY JO DEEGAN

ANNIE MARION MACLEAN
(1870?–1934)

Annie Marion MacLean was one of the first women to embark on a professional career as a sociologist. She analyzed immigration, women's work, teaching by correspondence, and the experience of illness. She fit the expectations of religious, never-married women that early male sociologists thought ideal, but her mind and ambitions exceeded the confines of her "proper place."

BIOGRAPHY

Annie Marion MacLean was a pioneering woman with close ties to her family and the land of her birth. Born at St. Peter's Bay, on Prince Edward Island, Canada, and raised in Nova Scotia, she was the daughter of the Reverend John and Christina MacDonald MacLean. She was, like many of her male peers and mentors, the child of a clergyman, and this background influenced her life and writings. Her family ties appear in the dedications of three of her books. *Our Neighbors* (MacLean 1922a) opened with a statement to "my beloved brother M. Haddon MacLean"; *Some Problems of Reconstruction* (MacLean 1921) is "dedicated to my sister, Mildred MacLean, whose clear vision has helped to focus my attention on the need for a reconstructed world"; and *Women Workers and Society* (MacLean 1916a) began with a note to Haddon and Pearl Harris MacLean, probably her nephew and his wife. Her commitment to Canada is reflected in several studies, including her dissertation, and her focus on the problems of immigration per se.

The details of MacLean's early life are not well known. Limited biographical materials are found in "Death Takes Educator" (1934), "Annie Marion MacLean" (1934), and Fish (1981a, 1981b). MacLean's birth date is extrapolated from her later educational activities. I assume that she was born circa 1870, since she earned a bachelor's degree (or an N.S. degree, according to one source) from Nova Scotia's Acadia College in 1893 and a master's degree in 1894 with "honors in philosophy and modern languages" (Leonard 1914).

Three years after earning her Canadian degrees, MacLean immigrated to the United States to study. She became the first woman to earn a master's degree in sociology at the University of Chicago (Faris 1967, 141), and in 1900 was the second woman to earn a doctorate there, writing a dissertation on "The Acadian Element in Nova Scotia's Population." Before completing her doctorate, she had published three papers in the *American Journal of Sociology* (MacLean 1897, 1899a, 1899b).

MacLean was profoundly influenced by three professors at the University of Chicago: Albion W. Small, Charles R. Henderson, and George Herbert Mead. Small, the first chair of the department of sociology at Chicago, was trained in the ministry and in history. He was an ardent social reformer and a deeply religious man. Henderson, an applied sociologist, also was clerically trained and often supported women's rights. Mead was a key founder of "symbolic inter-actionism," and played a central role in training several women scholars (for example, see the entries on Jessie Taft,* Edith Abbott,* and Katherine Bement Davis*).

Albion Small and MacLean held similar views on religion and women. Small believed in the "doctrine of the separate spheres"; that is, he trained religious women to ameliorate social problems outside the academy. MacLean embodied his expectations, and she dedicated herself to applied sociology. She was con-cerned about people's lives, worked in subsidiary roles in universities, and held leadership roles in "women's organizations."

Small served on both MacLean's doctoral and master's committees at Chicago. MacLean (1926, 47) characterized him as "a teacher and scholar [who] was encouraging, inspiring, stimulating; as a superior departmental officer, the soul of liberality." As a friend, he was "loyal, sympathetic, appreciative, full of remembrance."

MacLean also developed a strong professional and interpersonal bond with Charles Henderson. For example, when MacLean (1910) conducted a major study of women workers, Henderson served on her advisory board, and she dedicated the book to him. MacLean (1904) also contributed a chapter on the relief system in France to Henderson's book on *Modern Methods of Charity*.

Significantly, Mead served on MacLean's master's committee (*University Record* 1897–1898; 103). His attitudes toward women professionals were even more open and liberated than those of MacLean's other male mentors. Mead's relationships were more egalitarian and less "religiously" oriented (Deegan 1988).

All three men—Small, Henderson, and Mead—were actively associated with social settlements, then the major source of employment for female sociologists. Substantively, the men were concerned with topics central to MacLean's inter-ests: economic issues, immigration, urban life, and social change. Nonetheless, MacLean was primarily active in a series of groups organized by women, and had only a marginal role in the men's professional organizations, such as the American Sociological Society (Deegan 1981). Women, not men, were her most important colleagues during her later professional life.

MacLean was an outstanding sociology student, and far surpassed the productivity of her male peers, three of whom (W. I. Thomas, George E. Vincent, and Ira Howerth Woods) were later hired by the Chicago department. Because of sexism, MacLean was never hired as a full faculty member, despite her qualifications. Instead, from 1903 until her death in 1934 she was a sociologist in the "Extension Department" at the University of Chicago.

In her part-time position as an extension instructor, MacLean taught sociology through the mail by correspondence (''Annie Marion MacLean'' 1934). She was a passionate teacher, a fact documented in two of her articles (MacLean 1923b, 1927). Partially as a result of illness, her correspondence work and writing books were her major employment for nearly two decades. By 1927 her extension teaching flourished: "The number in my courses seldom falls below 125 and, on account of the nature of the subject, the students are more or less mature" (MacLean 1927, 104).

Teaching involved MacLean's entire life. She often graded reports while on vacation and invited students to visit her home. She seldom had the opportunity to teach sociology majors or graduate students (MacLean 1923, 464), but she introduced hard-working adults to the new topic of sociology. The author of her obituary in the *American Journal of Sociology* noted:

> Dr. MacLean had the practice of writing personal letters to the students and extended her interest in them beyond the more formal academic aspects of her courses. Thousands of students in all parts of the world have had reason to be grateful to her for personal assistance in their more intimate problems. ("Annie Marion MacLean" 1934, 104)

She was a humane teacher with a sense of humor.

MacLean kept a record of her students' foibles and entertaining excuses for delayed lessons. The latter included a potential marital engagement, bronco-busting, teething babies, and sick puppies. One student pounced on her while she was recovering from anesthesia. Asked whether humans had descended from monkeys, MacLean (1923, 470) answered with etherized abandon, "Yes, yes, men *are* monkeys." Another student, who cried "half the night over an indecipherable grade," quickly received MacLean's reassurance by special delivery (MacLean 1923, 471).

By 1923 MacLean's instructional repertoire included six correspondence courses: Introduction to Sociology, Social Technology, Rural Life, Problems of Industry, Modern Immigration, and History of the Social Reform Movement (MacLean 1923, 462). Through her courses MacLean contributed to the traditions of Chicago's women sociologists.

MacLean held various academic positions in addition to her correspondence work, including appointments at Royal Victoria, John B. Stenson, and Adelphi

Colleges. She became professor of sociology in 1906 at Adelphi, a post she held for ten years. MacLean also held several jobs typical of "women's work" in sociology, including a brief stint at the Women's Educational and Industrial Union of Boston (see also the entries on Susan Kingsbury* and Lucile Eaves*). MacLean was professor of sociology at the National Training School of the Young Women's Christian Association from 1903 to 1916. Low pay coupled with high ambition accounts in part for her often heavy workload.

MacLean's classroom duties ended in 1916 because of illness, probably arthritis (MacLean [1913] wrote a satire about a professional woman's search for an arthritis cure). From 1916 until her death eighteen years later scholarly writing and correspondence work at the University of Chicago occupied her time. Without a full-time professorial job, her professional interactions were curtailed, but her publication output after 1916 (four books and numerous articles) was nevertheless impressive.

MacLean's strong qualifications for teaching are reflected in her ability to laugh at herself, her involvement in the lives of her correspondence students, and her dedication to their work. An honorary doctor of letters degree was bestowed by Acadia College in 1923. Regrettably her talents were marginalized at the University of Chicago, where she taught many students but few with graduate training or advanced sociological interests. MacLean died in Pasadena, California, in May 1934.

MAJOR THEMES

The study of women's status in the marketplace is a central feature of MacLean's work. She began with a thesis on "Factory Legislation for Women in the United States" (MacLean 1897) and wrote several articles on women in various occupations. MacLean's analyses were based on quantitative and qualitative data. As a participant observer, she slept in the cold (MacLean 1909b), worked late hours (MacLean 1899a), and sewed piecework in Chicago's volatile garment industry (MacLean 1903). MacLean systematically documented that working women engaged in menial labor with low pay and minimal workers' consciousness. She explicated the human context of women's labor and portrayed her subjects' human dimensions: friendly and greedy, disorganized yet persevering, victimized and self-willed. In her writings MacLean emphasized the everyday lives of the women she studied and keyed her findings to general audiences and popular magazines (a technique used by both the women and the men of the Chicago school of sociology).

MacLean's (1910) greatest intellectual achievement, *Wage-Earning Women*, drew on her participatory background and the massive inquiries of a team of investigators. Her study surveyed 13,500 women laborers employed in 400 institutions in more than twenty cities. MacLean used the women's sociology network to hire a staff that included twenty-nine women. Chicago-trained women who made major contributions to the study included Amy Tanner, a philosophy graduate, and sociologist Amy Hewes.*

Methodologically, the investigations for *Wage-Earning Women* used four survey schedules (a fifth was added in the Pennsylvania coal-mining region). In each region surveyed, local demographic data were collected, as were data on housing, cooperative clubs for working women, ethnicity, and the number and types of job positions available. MacLean found that women workers commonly faced problems of low income and poor housing. Many women workers augmented their incomes by renting space in their homes to other workers, thus culturally and economically reinforcing the development of ghettos.

One of the most detailed sections of *Wage-Earning Women* focused on the Pennsylvania coal region. It was accomplished in part because of the work and expertise of Amy Tanner. When MacLean (1908) published an article on the Pennsylvania studies in the *American Journal of Sociology*, Tanner (1909) accused MacLean of plagiarism. MacLean (1909a) replied that Tanner and others were hired only for the purpose of collecting data and had no claims to the data. Ethically, I believe that MacLean should have shared her authorship. In failing to do so, she reflected an unethical and alienating practice that is all too common in sociology today.

Citing Edith Abbott's (1910) work, MacLean (1910) documented the discriminatory treatment of women by employers. Taken together, Abbott and MacLean provide a detailed picture of working-class women before 1910. Both scholars relied heavily on statistical data. Both advocated labor organizations, but noted that women joined such groups reluctantly. MacLean, however, gave more emphasis to social betterment work and devoted two chapters to the subject. The major findings of both books are the same: women work because they need the income and are poorly compensated for their labor. Both books are classics. Together, they provide a comprehensive analysis of factory legislation, wages, housing, organization, and employment for women in the United States during the early years of the twentieth century.

MacLean's major work was supplemented by *Women Workers and Society* (MacLean 1916a). This book was oriented to more general audiences, including classroom use. It was part of the National Social Science Series to which Charles Henderson, one of MacLean's mentors, also contributed (and he may have facilitated the inclusion of MacLean's manuscript in the series).

MacLean (1916a) organized her new book by topic rather than by geographical region, making it more readable. Scholarly trappings were curtailed; the bibliography was but a single page (one that nevertheless featured references to Edith Abbott and Charles Henderson). *Women Workers and Society* was favorably and properly reviewed as a popular book intended to disseminate sociological information to the general public (Bernard 1917).

In *Women Workers and Society* MacLean was a strong advocate for working-class women, but she did not adopt a Marxist position. She was optimistic about workers' ability to organize and change the current economic system to respond to their needs. She articulated the problems of working-class women, including overwork and underpayment. MacLean supported labor unions at a time when such advocacy was considered radical. Because of the failure of capitalists to pay adequate wages to labor, MacLean (1916a, 62) believed that democracy was failing. Democracy was a major theme addressed by all Chicago sociologists, and MacLean was one of the first to sharply criticize its effectiveness.

MacLean's concern with labor also was a constant thread in her books on immigration, her other major area of study. Two books, *Modern Immigration* (MacLean 1925) and *Our Neighbors* (MacLean 1922a), were for popular audiences (popular writing was her main source of income at this time). *Modern Immigration*, modeled after the scholarly documents series compiled by Edith Abbott and Sophonisba Breckinridge,* was published in Lippincott's popular Sociological Series. A fund of information, the book described the status quo but offered little discussion. MacLean glossed over the inequity of social and economic restrictions based on race and nationality. She adopted the "Americanization" or assimilation perspective but was weak on theory. She did, however, touch critically on the low status of women in some cultures (MacLean 1925, 49) and the dignity of life in different cultures. MacLean studied immigrant groups from the British Empire and South America, whereas male Chicago sociologists primarily studied Eastern Europeans. Her documentation of these less studied groups is the significant feature of the book.

Our Neighbors (MacLean 1922a) is an even more folksy book on immigration. MacLean again emphasized the cooperative aspects of democracy. Despite her simplification of democratic principles, the book reveals the humanity often hidden by abstract statistics. Eliot's (1925) positive review of the book observed that MacLean showed that unemployment is experienced by laborers as "a human terror," a reality too often forgotten when aggregate unemployment data are presented as abstracted facts. On balance, MacLean's works on wage-earning women are stronger and more original than her contributions on immigration.

MacLean's (1921) *Some Problems of Reconstruction* dealt with the aftermath of World War I. Significantly, she published this work after a period of bitter political unrest in the United States, including a "red scare" that vilified Jane Addams* and many other female sociologists. MacLean stressed the right of labor to unionize and to retain social welfare programs enacted during the war. MacLean's contributions to the sociology of reconstruction were not central to her main lines of inquiry, and her views on reconstruction did not represent the many controversial female sociologists who were pacifists during the war.

CRITIQUES OF ANNIE MARION MACLEAN

Virginia Kemp Fish (1981a, 1981b) is the only sociologist who has analyzed MacLean's work and contributions. Many of the points noted above are supported by Fish's interpretation. Building on Fish's work, I emphasize MacLean's links to other Chicago sociologists, especially the women. The few reviews in sociological journals of MacLean's writings are typically favorable. In general, however, MacLean was not strongly tied to either the male or the female networks in sociology. She was one of the few women who endeavored to fit the male sociologists' ideal conception of a female sociologist. MacLean was, nonetheless, a pioneer scholar on the subject of working women. Although her statistics are rudimentary by today's standards, she comprehensively documented working women's lives from approximately 1897 to 1916. This was a formidable accomplishment.

MacLean carved her own niche as a textbook writer. Her writing style compared favorably and often was superior to that found in many early textbooks. Nonetheless, her texts had less impact and less legitimation in the classroom than those written by white males. MacLean lacked the institutional ties and support from the male sociology network necessary to develop a more profitable and influential textbook market. Without access to graduate students, without a full-time position at a major university, and without participation in the major professional associations (all activities barred to her because of her sex), she was unable to shape the discipline through the classroom, despite her well-written textbooks and her correspondence courses.

Barred from the classroom by sex discrimination and later by illness and disability, MacLean transcended her limitations. Compared with the male sociologists of her era, MacLean was methodologically more advanced. She used statistics as well as participant observation. Within the limits imposed by institutionalized sexism, MacLean accomplished significant research and was part of the early Chicago sociology tradition. Her spirit, insight, and stamina should be celebrated, as well as her overt scholarly accomplishments.

BIBLIOGRAPHY

Selected Writings by Annie Marion MacLean

1897. "Factory Legislation for Women in the United States." *American Journal of Sociology* 3 (September): 183–205. Master's thesis, University of Chicago, Department of Sociology.

1899a. "Two Weeks in Department Stores." *American Journal of Sociology* 4 (May): 721–741.

1899b. "Factory Legislation for Women in Canada." *American Journal of Sociology* 5 (September): 172–181.

1900. "The Acadian Element in the Population of Nova Scotia." Ph.D. diss., Department of Sociology, University of Chicago.

1903. "The Sweat-Shop in the Summer." *American Journal of Sociology* 9 (November): 289–309.

1904. "France." In *Modern Methods of Charity*, by Charles R. Henderson, pp. 512–555. New York: Macmillan.

1905. "Significance of the Canadian Migration." *American Journal of Sociology* 10 (May): 814–823.

1908. "Life in the Pennsylvania Coal Fields, with Particular Reference to Women." *American Journal of Sociology* 14 (November): 329–351.

1909a. "A Question of Literary Property." Letter to the Editor. *Nation* 88 (February 25): 193.

1909b. "With Oregon Hop Pickers." *American Journal of Sociology* 15 (July): 83–95.

1910. *Wage-Earning Women*. New York: Macmillan.

1913. *Mary Ann's Malady*. New York: Broadway.

1915a. "Trade Unionism Versus Welfare Work for Women." *Popular Science Monthly* 87 (July): 50–55.

1915b. "The Plight of the Rich Man in a Democracy." *American Journal of Sociology* 21 (November): 339–344.

1915c. "Discussion of James B. Reynolds, 'Reasonable Restrictions upon Freedom of Speech.'" *Papers and Proceedings of the American Sociological Society* 9: 59–62.

1916a. *Women Workers and Society*. Chicago: A. C. McClurg.

1916b. "Fifty Years of the Y.W.C.A." *Survey* 35 (January 22): 481–484.

1918. *Cheero!* New York: Womans Press.

1921. *Some Problems of Reconstruction*. Chicago: A. C. McClurg.

1922a. *Our Neighbors*. New York: Macmillan.

1922b. "Where Color Lines Are Drawn." *Survey* 48 (July 1): 453–454.

1923a. *This Way Lies Happiness*. New York: Womans Press.

1923b. "Twenty Years of Sociology by Correspondence." *American Journal of Sociology* 28 (February): 461–472.

1925. *Modern Immigration*. Philadelphia. J. B. Lippincott.

1926. "Albion Woodbury Small: An Appreciation." *American Journal of Sociology* 32 (July): 45–48.

1927. "College by Correspondence." *Scribner's Magazine* 81 (May): 476–478.

1932. "I Become American." *Sociology and Social Research* 16 (May–June): 427–433.

Studies About Annie Marion MacLean and Supplemental References

Abbott, Edith. 1910. *Women in Industry: A Study in American Economic History*. New York: D. Appleton.

"Annie Marion MacLean." 1934. Obituary. *American Journal of Sociology* 40 (July): 104.

Bernard, Francis Fenton. 1917. "Review of *Women Workers and Society*." *American Journal of Sociology* 22: 850.

"Death Takes Educator." 1934. *Pasadena Star News* (May 2): 13, 20.

Deegan, Mary Jo. 1981. "Early Women Sociologists and the American Sociological Society." *American Sociologist* 16 (February): 14–24.

———. 1988. *Jane Addams and the Men of the Chicago School, 1892–1918*. New Brunswick, NJ: Transaction Books.

Eliot, S. W. 1925. "Review of *Our Neighbors*." *American Journal of Sociology* 30 (May): 727–728.

Faris, Robert E. L. 1967. *Chicago Sociology: 1920–1932*. Chicago: University of Chicago Press.

Fish, Virginia Kemp. 1981a. "Annie Marion MacLean: A Neglected Part of the Chicago School." *Journal of the History of Sociology* 3 (Spring): 43–62.

———. 1981b. "Annie Marion MacLean." In *American Women Writers*, vol. 3, edited by Lina Mainiero, pp. 102–104. New York: Ungar.

Kellogg, Paul U. 1915. "The Old Freedoms Discussed by Twentieth Century Sociologists." *The Survey* 33 (January 9): 406–412a.

Leonard, John William, ed. 1914. In *Woman's Who's Who of America*, p. 527. New York: American Commonwealth.

Tanner, Amy E. 1909. "A Question of Literary Property." Letter to the Editor. *Nation* 88 (February 25): 193.

MARY JO DEEGAN

HARRIET MARTINEAU (1802–1876)

Harriet Martineau authored the first systematic methodological treatise in sociology, conducted extended international comparative studies of social institutions, and translated Auguste Comte's *Cours de philosophie positive* into English, thus structurally facilitating the introduction of sociology and positivism into the United States. In her youth she was a professional writer who captured the popular English mind by wrapping social scientific instruction in a series of widely read short novels. In her maturity she was an astute sociological theorist, methodologist, and analyst of the first order. To the extent that any complex institutional phenomenon such as sociology can have identifiable founders, Alice Rossi* (1973, 118–124) justly celebrates Harriet Martineau as "the first woman sociologist."

BIOGRAPHY

The major data source on Martineau's life is her *Autobiography*, written in 1855, but published posthumously in 1877 together with Maria Chapman's biographically important *Memorials of Harriet Martineau*. Martineau (1877; 1985, 35–49) also prepared her own obituary notice, and it contains a self-estimate of her work. Martineau's personal experiences are reflected in her *Household Education* (1849), *Life in the Sick-Room* (1844), and "Berkeley the Banker," one of the didactic novels in her *Illustrations of Political Economy* (1832–1834). A selection of her private correspondence is also available (Martineau 1983). Martineau's modern biographers typically emphasize themes of particular interest to students of English literature rather than sociology. Several such accounts (e.g., Pichanick 1980) are found in most university libraries.

Harriet Martineau, born 1802, was the sixth of eight children in a middle-class English family. Her younger brother, James, was a well-known cleric (Jackson 1901). Her father's occupation as a manufacturer placed Harriet in comfortable surroundings. Her childhood was marred, however, by strong feelings of fearfulness and self-doubt. She was nonetheless intellectually industrious, and applied herself to both secular and religious studies. She was educated largely at home, with the exception of two years in private, coeducational classes and a year in a boarding school for girls. Through self-study she rigorously augmented her early exposure to subjects routinely taught only to males. University study was barred to women, but Martineau maintained a regimen of intense, self-directed investigation throughout her life. Troubled by increasing deafness as a child, Martineau required an ear trumpet during adulthood.

The Martineau family suffered severe economic losses in the 1820s, when Harriet's father died. Harriet was left to her own resources. While Harriet faced the exigencies of earning her living in a patriarchal society, she wrote: "I began to feel the blessing of a wholly new freedom" (Martineau 1877, I: 108). Martineau escaped the confines of middle-class Victorian marriage when her fiancé unexpectedly died. She remained happily single and independent for the rest of her life. She successfully supported herself as an author in various forms, including essays, tracts, reviews, novels, travelogues, biographies, how-to manuals, journal articles, newspaper columns, histories, children's stories, and sociologically informed nonfiction.

Martineau's life is a chronicle of intellectual maturation and deepening sociological insight. Raised as a devout Unitarian, Martineau's first literary efforts were fervently religious. Adoption of "Necessarianism" provided her with an intellectual bridge to a social scientific perspective, and the *Illustrations of Political Economy* (1832–1834) signaled her departure from ecclesiastical dogma. In the *Illustrations* she used fiction to explicate the principles of the new science of political economy, and the results met with popular success. She lived in London during this period, and her intellectual circle came to include Charles Babbage, Thomas Carlyle, George Eliot, Florence Nightingale, Charles Dickens, Thomas Malthus, William Wordsworth, Charlotte Bronte, Charles Lyell, and Charles Darwin. The *Illustrations* marked her entry into English literary society and set her on the road to financial independence.

In 1834 Martineau began a two-year study tour of the United States. She reported her observations in *Society in America* (1837) and *Retrospect of Western Travel* (1838a). These empirical studies emerged hand in hand with her foundational treatise on sociological data collection. *How to Observe Morals and Manners* (1838b) insightfully articulated the principles and methods of empirical social research. This period marked Martineau's achievement of a mature and incisive sociological imagination.

In subsequent years Martineau refined her metatheoretical orientation and moved even farther from her Unitarian upbringing. After a trip to the Middle East, reported in *Eastern Life, Present and Past* (1848), she openly embraced atheism (cf., Atkinson and Martineau 1851). In 1851 she began an English translation/condensation of Auguste Comte's *Cours de philosophie positive*. The introduction of positivist sociological ideas into the United States was greatly facilitated by Martineau's momentous rendition of Comte's (1853) most influential sociological work.

By choice, Martineau's later years unfolded not in London, but in the Lake District, where she built a house at Ambleside. She paid off her mortgage with royalties from her controversial *Letters on the Laws of Man's Nature and Development* (Atkinson and Martineau 1851). The beauty and peacefulness of the Lake District stand in strong contrast to the years of personal trial, illness, exhaustion, deafness, and social and literary controversy that confronted Martineau throughout most of her life.

For Martineau, her profession was a Weberian calling:

> Authorship has never been for me a matter of choice. I have not done it for amusement, or for money, or for fame, or for any reason but because I could not help it. Things were pressing to be said; and there was more or less evidence that I was the person to say them. (Martineau 1877, I: 143)

Martineau, like all significant sociological theorists, gave life and direction to vital intellectual questions with insight, originality, and a deep sense of personal and social mission. Harriet Martineau died at seventy-four years of age, in 1876.

MAJOR THEMES

Compiling a list of the topics to which Martineau turned her prolific pen is no small task. Joseph Rivlin's (1947) comprehensive bibliography lists dozens of separately published books. The 3,479 pages of the *Illustrations of Political Economy* alone were originally published in twenty-five installments. There is no thorough bibliography of Martineau's reviews and journal articles (several early articles are reprinted in her *Miscellanies* [1836] and a selection of later articles appears in her *Health, Husbandry, and Handicraft* [1861]). As a journalist, Martineau wrote more than 1,500 newspaper columns (Webb 1959). Martineau's written corpus is a massive reservoir awaiting modern sociological critique.

Martineau undertook pioneering studies—substantive, theoretical, and methodological studies—in what is now called sociology. She was an ardent Unitarian, abolitionist, critic, feminist, social scientist, and avowed atheist. Her writing topics included biography, disability, education, history, husbandry, legislation, manufacturing, mesmerism, occupational health, philosophy, political economy, religion, research techniques, slavery, sociology, travel, and women's rights.

Of Martineau's numerous works, *Society in America* (1837) is the most widely known to sociologists in the United States. Her methodological strategy confronted the problem of ethnocentrism. Rather than compare the United States with England, she identified the moral principles to which Americans claimed allegiance, and compared them with observable social patterns—a methodologically insightful distinction between rhetoric and reality. Martineau documented a wide chasm between extant institutional patterns and the values of democracy, justice, equality, and freedom that Americans claimed to cherish. Beyond *Society in America*, Martineau's other economic, political, and historical studies remain largely uncited by sociologists. Her systematic observations of society are directly relevant to historical and comparative sociologists who would unravel the complexities of Victorian England and nineteenth-century life generally.

In *How to Observe Morals and Manners* (1838b) Martineau provided the first-known systematic methodological treatise in sociology. It is a theoretically sophisticated, yet practical guide to sociological observation. Metatheoretically, she offered the classic positivist solution to the correspondence problem between intersubjectively verifiable observables and unobservable theoretical entities. Confronting the problem of studying a society as a whole, she creatively attacked problems of bias, generalization, samples, reactivity, interviews, corroboration, and data-recording techniques. She outlined studies of the major social institutions, including religion, education, family, arts and popular culture, markets and economy, prisons, government, and philanthropy. *How to Observe* also is a precedent-setting work of theory. Before Karl Marx, and decades before Émile Durkheim and Max Weber, Martineau sociologically examined social class, forms of religion, types of suicide, national character, domestic relations and the status of women, delinquency and criminology, and the intricate interrelations between repressive social institutions and the individual (Hill 1989).

Thematic study of Martineau's extensive corpus provides a wealth of untapped opportunities for modern sociologists. For example, it is well known that Martineau translated Comte's (1853) major sociological treatise, but the metasociology of Martineau's condensation still awaits modern analysis. Her contributions to feminist thought (Martineau 1985) deserve sociological review. Martineau's *England and Her Soldiers* (1859) is an uncited tour de force on occupational health, and she provides detailed portraits of nineteenth-century industrial and agricultural practices in *Health, Husbandry, and Handicraft* (1861). Her *Illustrations of Political Economy* and other didactic tales are untapped models of literature *as sociology* (cf., Bonser 1929; Hill 1987). Thematically, Martineau's sociological imagination was unbounded; it reached from micro to macro, from theory to observation, from objective description to informed critique.

CRITIQUES OF HARRIET MARTINEAU

The early precedence of Martineau's work has long been ignored by the patriarchal historians of sociology. In a survey of the "continuities among women as subjects and objects of intellectual work," Shulamit Reinharz (1989, 92) notes:

There were the continuities of not being remembered—e.g., the fame of de Tocqueville vis a vis Harriet Martineau, although both wrote at the same time about the same topic; and the fame of Durkheim's treatise on method as compared to Martineau's although hers predates his by sixty years and is nearly analogous.

Martineau was forgotten, not only in sociology, but also, to large extent, in the disciplines of literature, history, and journalism. Spender (1982) critically addresses this issue, and correctly faults the male academic establishment for the patriarchal exclusion of Martineau's work from sociology.

Paul Riedesel's (1981) apologetic exemplifies the patriarchal bias. He seriously discounted Martineau even while calling attention to her work. He claimed that Martineau "left no corpus of theory" but failed to cite Martineau's sophisticated methodological classic *How to Observe Morals and Manners* (Riedesel 1981, 77). At best, such essays damn with faint praise.

Seymour Martin Lipset (1962, 39), who otherwise admired Martineau's sociological skills, suggested that "to those who wonder why such a sophisticated analyst has been allowed to linger for so long in the obscurity of nineteenth-century editions, the answer must be that the blame rests with Harriet Martineau herself." Lipset implied that Martineau was overlooked only because she wrote lengthy works that are "tedious to some readers." Thus liberal patriarchs defend the male academy for dismissing the reality, rigor, and precedence of Martineau's accomplishments.

The patriarchal negation of Martineau's foundational work is crosscut by disciplinary complexities and exceptions. For example, it was a male literary critic, Thomas Gillian (1985, 33), who said of Martineau's *How to Observe Morals and Manners*: "Written in an atypically verbose style, it is not much more than a lengthy essay that anticipates many of the observations she would make about American institutions and social mores." Similarly, it was a female literary critic, Valerie Pichanick (1980, 75), who also vastly underrated Martineau's scientific acumen when she credited Martineau with having outlined nothing more than a "primitive" sociological methodology.

On the other hand, it was a male sociologist, Seymour Martin Lipset (1962, 37), who concluded that *How to Observe Morals and Manners* "testifies to the considerable sophistication" that Martineau brought to methodological issues. A male literary historian, Robert K. Webb, wrote critically of Martineau's literary style (Webb 1960), but nonetheless laboriously compiled the virtually irreplaceable index to Martineau's hundreds of newspaper articles (Webb 1959). And to Joseph Rivlin (1947) all scholars are indebted for his meticulous bibliographic description of Martineau's separately published books. If most males have erased Martineau from the received canon, there are other scholars—men and women—who help keep her name alive.

James Terry (1983, 253) argues that Martineau and Charlotte Perkins Gilman* are "two women who have been excluded from the sociological canon whom I consider on a par with the traditional masters." He concludes that Martineau's "writings in political economy and scientific methods, her comparative study of American and European societies, and her insights into the subordination of women in American society in the 1830s deserve recognition and study in their own right" (Terry 1983, 253–254). Terry recommends inclusion of Martineau's work in the basic sociology curriculum.

Seymour Martin Lipset (1962) astutely summarized the major theses and arguments in *Society in America*. He pointed out that "in emphasizing the value system as a causal agent, Martineau was an early precursor of one of the major sociological orientations, an approach that attempts to analyze the effect of values on structure and change" (Lipset 1962, 10). On the publication of Lipset's abridged edition of Martineau's *Society in America*, John Cawelti (1963, 208) characterized Martineau as a Victorian combination of Margaret Mead and Hannah Arendt.* Comparing her work with de Tocqueville's well-known studies of the same era, Cawelti credited Martineau with providing a viable alternative analysis of "the pressure toward conformity" in American society. Her analysis, he concluded, suggests further "avenues of approach to the problem that are surely worthy of investigation by historians and sociologists" (Cawelti 1963, 213).

Edith Abbott* (1906, 615) attributed "the most convenient and definite statement regarding the early employment of women" in the United States to Martineau (cf., 1837, II: 131–151). Mary van Kleeck* (1913, 18) cited Martineau's data on women bookbinders in van Kleeck's landmark study of the bookbinding industry. Abbott, however, faulted Martineau's accounting of the occupations open to women, and argued that Martineau's underreporting of occupational possibilities for women lent unintended support to "comforting generalizations regarding the multiplication of industrial openings for women" in the decades subsequent to Martineau's report (Abbott 1906, 616). Nonetheless, Abbott appreciatively noted Martineau's perceptive and critical conclusion that "it is difficult . . . for women to earn their bread." Abbott wrote that "one could not go far wrong in saying that the lot of the poor woman is still sad. Opportunity of employment is scarce now as it was then" (Abbott 1906, 626).

Finally, it must be remembered that Auguste Comte was extremely pleased with Martineau's translation/abridgment of his foundational *Cours de philosophie positive*. He wrote to her:

And looking at it from the point of view of future generations, I feel sure that your name will be linked with mine, for you have executed the only one of those works that will survive amongst all those which my fundamental treatise has called forth. (Comte, quoted in Harrison 1913, xvii–xviii)

In the hands of subsequent male sociologists, Comte's prophesy of Martineau's fame went unfulfilled. As a result, the available major interpretations of Martineau have been authored primarily by scholars in disciplines other than sociology (recent examples include Deirdre David [1987] and Linda Peterson [1986]).

These interesting, but asociological works pose a challenge to modern sociologists. Whatever the value of Martineau's work to literature, history, journalism, women's studies, and other disciplines, the evaluation of her original contributions *to sociology* requires sustained, intelligent critique by sociologically sensitive scholars. To this end, Abbott (1906), Bonser (1929), Cawelti (1963), Hill (1987, 1989), Lipset (1962), Rossi (1973), Spender (1982), and Terry (1983) provide points of departure for more thorough explications of Martineau's metasociological framework, sociological theories, methodologies, and empirical findings, analyses, and social critiques.

BIBLIOGRAPHY

Selected Writings by Harriet Martineau

1832–1834. *Illustrations of Political Economy*. 25 nos. in 6 vols. London: Charles Fox.
1836. *Miscellanies*. 2 vols. Boston: Hilliard, Gray.
1837. *Society in America*. 3 vols. London: Saunders & Otley. Abridged edition, by Seymour Martin Lipset, Anchor Books, 1962; reprinted, New Brunswick, NJ: Transaction Books, 1981.
1838a. *Retrospect of Western Travel*. 2 vols. London: Saunders & Otley.
1838b. *How to Observe Morals and Manners*. Philadelphia: Lea & Blanchard. Sesquicentennial edition, with introduction, appendices, and analytical index by Michael R. Hill. New Brunswick, NJ: Transaction Books, 1989.
1844. *Life in the Sick-Room*. Boston: Bowles & Crosby.
1848. *Eastern Life, Present and Past*. Philadelphia: Lea & Blanchard.
1849. *Household Education*. Philadelphia: Lea & Blanchard.
1859. *England and Her Soldiers*. London: Smith, Elder.
1861. *Health, Husbandry, and Handicraft*. London: Bradbury.
1877. *Harriet Martineau's Autobiography*, edited by Maria Weston Chapman. 2 vols. Includes *Memorials of Harriet Martineau*, by M. W. Chapman. Boston: James R. Osgood.
1983. *Harriet Martineau's Letters to Fanny Wedgewood*, edited by Elisabeth S. Arbuckle. Stanford, CA: Stanford University Press.
1985. *Harriet Martineau on Women*, edited by Gayle G. Yates. New Brunswick, NJ: Rutgers University Press.

Coauthored Works

Atkinson, Henry George, and Harriet Martineau. 1851. *Letters on the Laws of Man's Nature and Development*. Boston: Mendum.
Comte, Auguste. *The Positive Philosophy of Auguste Comte*, translated and condensed by Harriet Martineau. 1853, Reprinted New York: William Gowans, 1868 (New York: AMS Press, 1974).

Studies About Harriet Martineau and Supplemental References

Abbott, Edith. 1906 "Harriet Martineau and the Employment of Women in 1836." *Journal of Political Economy* 14 (December): 614–626.

Bonser, Helen A. 1929. *"Illustrations of Political Economy*: An Early Example of the Case Method." *Social Service Review* 3 (June): 243–251.

Cawelti, John G. 1963. "Conformity and Democracy in America: Some Reflections Occasioned by the Republication of Martineau's *Society in America.*" *Ethics* 73 (April): 208–213.

David, Deirdre. 1987. *Intellectual Women and Victorian Patriarchy: Harriet Martineau, Elizabeth Barrett Browning, George Eliot.* New York: Cornell University Press.

Gillian, Thomas. 1985. *Harriet Martineau.* Boston: Twayne.

Harrison, Frederic. 1913. "Introduction." In The *Positive Philosophy of Auguste Comte*, vol. 1, by A. Comte, translated by Harriet Martineau, pp. v–xix. London: G. Bell.

Hill, Michael R. 1989. "Empiricism and Reason in Harriet Martineau's Sociology." In *How to Observe Morals and Manners*, by H. Martineau, pp. xv–lx. Sesquicentennial edition. New Brunswick, NJ: Transaction Books.

Jackson, A. W. 1901. *James Martineau.* Boston: Little, Brown.

Lipset, Seymour Martin. 1962. "Harriet Martineau's America." In *Society in America*, by Harriet Martineau, abridged and edited by S. M. Lipset, pp. 5–42. New York: Doubleday. Reprinted, New Brunswick, NJ: Transaction Books, 1981.

Peterson, Linda H. 1986. "Martineau's *Autobiography*: The Feminine Debate over Self-interpretation." In *Victorian Autobiography: The Tradition of Self-Interpretation*, by L. H. Peterson, pp. 120–155. New Haven, CT: Yale University Press.

Pichanick, Valerie K. 1980. *Harriet Martineau: The Woman and Her Work, 1802–76.* Ann Arbor: University of Michigan Press.

Reinharz, Shulamit. 1989. "Teaching the History of Women in Sociology: Or Dorothy Swaine Thomas, Wasn't She the Woman Married to William I.?" *The American Sociologist* 20 (Spring): 87–94.

Riedesel, Paul L. 1981. "Who *Was* Harriet Martineau?" *Journal of the History of Sociology* 3 (Spring–Summer): 63–80.

Rivlin, Joseph B. 1947. *Harriet Martineau: A Bibliography of Her Separately Published Books.* New York: New York Public Library.

Rossi, Alice. 1973. *The Feminist Papers.* New York: Bantam Books.

Spender, Dale. 1982. "Harriet Martineau." In *Women of Ideas and What Men Have Done to Them*, by Dale Spender, pp. 125–135. London: Routledge & Kegan Paul.

Terry, James L. 1983. "Bringing Women . . . In: A Modest Proposal." *Teaching Sociology* 10 (January): 251–261.

van Kleeck, Mary. 1913. *Women in the Bookbinding Trade.* New York: Survey Associates.

Webb, Robert K. 1960. *Harriet Martineau: A Radical Victorian.* New York: Columbia University Press.

Unpublished Material

Hill, Michael R. 1987. "Harriet Martineau's Novels and the Sociology of Class, Race, and Gender." Paper presented at the meetings of the Association for Humanist Sociology.

Webb, Robert K. 1959. "A Handlist of Contributions to the *Daily News* by Harriet Martineau, 1852–1866." Copy on deposit in Widener Library, Harvard University.

MICHAEL R. HILL

ALICE MASARYK (1879–1966)

Alice Masaryk (Masarykova) is an eminent Czechoslovakian sociologist. As an applied sociologist, she was actively engaged in social organization and the abolition of social injustices. As a humanitarian, Masaryk was a staunch defender of human rights, an active feminist, and an organizer of social work. As a political activist she sought to integrate humanitarian concerns with an applied study of the social order in an attempt to alleviate the inequalities brought on by war and social organization.

BIOGRAPHY

Alice Masaryk was born May 3, 1879, in Vienna, Austria, the eldest child of Thomas Garrigue Masaryk of Czechoslovakia and Charlotte Garrigue Masaryk of Brooklyn, New York. Her father, born of peasant serfs, became a distinguished professor of philosophy, a noted sociologist, and the first president of the Czechoslovakian Republic. Her mother came from a prosperous New York family, receiving a professional education at the Conservatory of Music in Leipzig, Germany. In 1881, when Alice was three, her father accepted an appointment at the University of Prague after the publication of his prominent book *Suicide as a Social Mass Phenomenon*.

Alice began her studies in 1886 with both a formal education at the church school St. Egidius in Prague and private tutorial lessons in music, Russian, and French. She then advanced to the city middle school but left in 1891 to attend Minerva, the newly founded women's gymnasium in Prague (the equivalent of an American high school). On the passage of her formal examination, Masaryk began to study medicine at Charles University. Although successful during her first year, she believed that the application of medicine did not fully coincide with her interests in social organization. Subsequently she left the field of medicine to study philosophy at Charles University. Masaryk studied at the University of Berlin during 1901–1902, traveling several times to England to gather data on her doctoral dissertation, "The Magna Charta of Freedom of King John Lockland, 1215." She was awarded a doctorate in philosophy from Charles University on June 23, 1903.

In 1904 Alice received an invitation from Mary McDowell, director of the University of Chicago Social Settlement (UCSS), to work in residence at the settlement. She accepted, and arrived in Chicago during February 1904, where she stayed until 1905. Her initial contact with McDowell had been through her father, Thomas Masaryk, who had been invited by Charles R. Crane and William R. Harper to present the first summer lecture series at the University of Chicago in 1901. It was here, in Chicago, that she became acquainted with many prominent Americans, including Mary McDowell and Jane Addams.*

During her stay Alice Masaryk witnessed firsthand the social conditions that plagued the immigrants who worked as a source of cheap labor in the sweatshops and stockyards of Chicago. At the UCSS she witnessed the complete breakdown of social order with the onset of the Chicago stockyard strike of 1904. Her residence at the UCSS brought her into contact with Upton Sinclair, also a settlement resident, who was collecting data for his book *The Jungle*, and Jane Addams* of Hull-House, of whom she was a guest for two weeks.

After her return to Czechoslovakia in 1905, Masaryk accepted a position as an instructor of history and geography at the Girls' Lycee in České Budějovice, a town seventy-five miles south of Prague. In 1910 a new lycee was founded in Prague, where Masaryk accepted a position to teach. During 1911, in collaboration with the Czech Student Union at the University of Prague, Masaryk founded the Sociological Section of the university. This centered on a lecture series made up of distinguished people who were invited to discuss the pathologies of various social conditions. Topics included in these discussions were the reality of poverty, the working and living conditions of the industrial workers of Prague, neglected children and the family, alcoholism, venereal disease, nutrition, and social hygiene. As noted by her friend Anna Berkovcova, in her biography of Alice Masaryk, Masaryk chose sociology as a career because she believed that all people, students and laypeople alike, should be aware of the social pathologies surrounding their lives. Her objective in establishing the sociology section at the university was to enlighten students on the pathologies embedded within the social structure.

During the height of World War I in Europe, on October 28, 1915, Alice Masaryk was arrested on suspicion of having hidden the political works of her father, who had been forced into exile after being accused of treason against the Austrian Empire. She was jailed for eight months, with discussion of her possible execution, until pressure to release her was placed on the Austrian government by the U.S. State Department. A letter from Thomas Masaryk to Mary McDowell in April of 1916 informed her of Alice's predicament. From April until her release in July public sentiment was stirred in the United States. Several small articles were printed in the *Chicago Herald*, one of which was a petition signed by 40,000 persons and sent to the Austrian government asking for Masaryk's release. Among the prominent people involved in this petition drive were Jane Addams, Mary McDowell, Lillian Wald, and Florence Kelly.* An additional article was carried in the *New York Times* on April 30, 1916. This article noted the active involvement of Julia Lathrop, then the highest ranking woman in the federal government as chief of the Children's Bureau in the Department of Labor. Lathrop petitioned the U.S. State Department to intervene on behalf of Alice Masaryk. The State Department did intervene, and Alice Masaryk was released on July 3, 1916.

After her release from prison, Masaryk was not permitted to resume her teaching position at the lycee. Disappointed, she turned her attention toward applied sociology. Because the sociological section of the university had been disbanded during the war, Masaryk privately conducted lectures in sociology from her home on a tutorial basis. Here she discussed the principles of sociology and the methods of investigation. These lectures and the interest of her students led her to establish, with the help of Anna Berkovcova, the first Czechoslovakian School of Social Work during the fall of 1918. The objective of the school was to provide a pragmatic application of workable social hypotheses that would attempt to alleviate identifiable social pathologies. This sociology was similar to that developed by Jane Addams and George Herbert Mead at the University of Chicago and applied at Hull-House and the UCSS.

On October 28, 1918, the Czechoslovakian Republic was established, with Thomas Masaryk as the first president of the republic. Because of the illness of her mother, who later died on April 30, 1923, Alice acted as the official hostess, essentially becoming the First Lady of Czechoslovakia. In addition, she was appointed, in February 1919, as the first president of the Czechoslovakian Red Cross. In this capacity she was responsible not only for the wounded during and after the war, but also for the development of objectives to renovate the decaying Austrian welfare system. To accomplish this momentous task, Masaryk requested that Mary McDowell of UCSS organize a small American task force to aid her in the creation and distribution of a social survey of the health, educational, recreational, and welfare systems. The task force, which arrived in Czechoslovakia in 1919, acted promptly, completing the survey within a year and publishing the results shortly thereafter.

Throughout the next twenty years Masaryk remained active in the Czechoslovakian and International Red Cross. From 1919 to 1939 Masaryk served as the president of the Czechoslovakian Red Cross. During 1928 she served as the president of the first International Conference of Social Work in Paris, and in 1930 she was elected to the Executive Committee of the International Red Cross. In this capacity Masaryk directed the Red Cross to act as a national peacetime welfare agency, one that would integrate the organization and application of public health services. She outlined the responsibility of the Red Cross as being that of a methodological agency oriented toward the implementation of humanitarian ideals within the operation of social institutions such as schools and welfare agencies.

On the death of her father on September 30, 1937, and the election of a new president of Czechoslovakia, Masaryk left her residence at the Presidential Palace in Prague. She continued her role as president of the Red Cross until the German invasion of Czechoslovakia in February 1939. After the invasion she was invited to stay at the UCSS by its president, Dr. Walter Palmer.

En route to Chicago, Masaryk was awarded an honorary doctorate at the University of Pittsburgh for her critical pragmatism and national service in the Republic of Czechoslovakia. On September 1, 1939, she began a lecture tour in the United States to replace her brother, Jan, who had been scheduled to speak but was unable to do so. The tour, focusing on the social conditions of Czechoslovakia, was not well received by her audiences, and this led to the cancellation of the tour during January 1940. After a short rest with friends, Masaryk returned to the UCSS during April but soon became dissatisfied with the simple chores assigned to her. The numerous traumatic incidents led her to become increasingly depressed and, as a result, she was moved to the Mitchell Sanatorium on July 4, 1940. In November of 1941 she was transferred to a hospital in White Plains, New York, so that Jan would be able to visit her more frequently. She remained at this hospital until the surrender of the Germans in 1945.

After the end of the war in 1945, Masaryk returned to Czechoslovakia. Yet, soon after her return, Czechoslovakia was once again under siege, this time by the Soviet Union. She remained there, trying to locate friends and papers until Jan, then the prime minister of Czechoslovakia, was found dead on March 10, 1948, on the pavement below his apartment. Initially ruled a suicide, the death was later documented as an assassination as a means of removing all obstacles to the Soviet overthrow of the Czech government. This finding caused great social unrest, and is said to be a factor in the 1968 uprising in Czechoslovakia. The Soviet takeover forced Masaryk into exile again; this time she found a permanent haven in the United States.

She continued to be politically active, even in light of her declining health. From 1950 to 1954 Masaryk frequently spoke on Radio Free Europe, encouraging those remaining in Czechoslovakia to remain steadfast in their struggle for democracy. From 1954 through 1960 she began to write her memoirs. Then, in 1960, she established the Masaryk Publications Trust with the intention of publishing, in English, many of the known works of the Masaryk family. Her last few years were spent in Miami, Florida, and later in Chicago, where she died on November 29, 1966.

MAJOR THEMES

Like other prominent women in sociology, such as Susan Kingsbury,* Alice Masaryk began her academic studies in philosophy and history. Yet her attention turned to sociology as a resident at the UCSS, when, in her mid-twenties, she witnessed firsthand the social injustices brought on by the emergence of a stratified industrial empire. This permanently impacted her later work, in which she became active in shaping a democratic and socially just society in her native country of Czechoslovakia.

During most of her life Masaryk was actively involved in the political and social reorganization of Czechoslovakia. Although she published few formal works on her sociological orientation toward critical pragmatism, her greatest contribution as a sociologist rests in her application of pragmatic idealism to the liberation and reorganization of Czechoslovakia. The theme throughout most of her work can be found in her numerous unpublished manuscripts, personal letters, and professional presentations, in which she clearly outlined her theoretical and methodological approach of practical idealism toward social organization. Pragmatism, as developed by George Herbert Mead, Jane Addams, and Edith Abbott,* among others, is centered on the identification of concrete solutions to existing social problems and the continual development of working hypotheses that will alleviate social injustices in a dynamic society. During her residence at the UCSS this methodological approach became an essential component of her political and social legacy.

Her early academic work was largely descriptive in nature, but the focus of this work gives some insight into her later interest in social organization. While she was a resident of UCSS, Masaryk published a descriptive analysis of the Bohemian population in Chicago. She noted that all but 1.2 percent of this group were literate, with 30 percent being skilled employees. Within this work, Masaryk described the religious and political affiliations of the Bohemians, as well as their educational orientation and cultural heritage.

In contrast, her later published work revealed a specific orientation toward the pragmatic expression of humanitarian goals. During a presentation at the National Conference of Social Work in 1939, Masaryk spoke of a "world crisis . . . a world torn into fragments by hostility." She spoke of the need for each country to pursue "liberty, equality, and fraternity" as a means of producing a democratic unity of all people, a unity that would humanely sanctify the uniqueness of all individuals while subsequently protecting their social development. She stressed that a democracy truly concerned about the welfare of all people would be economically stabler and politically more humane. Moreover, she argued that the unbridled expansion of capitalism for the pursuit of profit was a dangerous consequence of the industrial age. Masaryk contended that the advances of science should be put to use to increase the mental and physical development of all people, through a fair and equal wage, shorter workdays, and a discretion in the pursuit of profit and production. Progressive advances in society do not, Masaryk argued, come from the technological advances of production at the expense of the worker. Rather, "the critical question of today's world crisis," she argued, "is how to combine personal freedom with social justice" in a manner that leads society forward instead of a "step backward toward primitivism.'' The answer, she contended, is to be found in the work of sociology.

Masaryk's pragmatism was enacted in her survey of Prague's social institutions. With the data, Masaryk hoped to identify ways in which the population of Czechoslovakia could best be served in education, health, recreation, and welfare. Her persistent speeches and active participation in numerous organizations was an attempt to create a truly democratic society with the interests of each individual citizen considered. Were it not for the short duration of the Czechoslovakian Republic, the application of her sociological ideals may have become a reality. The legacy she left behind serves as an example of the impact that a pragmatic approach to sociology can have in the interests of the humanitarian organization of a social order.

CRITIQUES OF ALICE MASARYK

Alice Masaryk's work, largely unpublished, is found in a few archives throughout the United States and Czechoslovakia. The largest collections are found at Indiana University and the University of Pittsburgh. As a result, there are few published critiques of her work, and these typically focus on her life as a political activist.

The most informative critique is the unevenly written biography of Masaryk edited by Ruth Mitchell (1980), an American assistant on the early survey of Prague. Through Masaryk's personal correspondence and her own association with Masaryk, Mitchell reconstructs the major themes and emotional debacles of Masaryk's life. Highly praiseworthy of Masaryk's dedication to Czechoslovakia and her humanitarian concerns, Mitchell portrays her as an ardent supporter of human rights. A lifelong social worker, Mitchell often confuses Masaryk's sociological perspective on social organization and stratification with the individual attention associated with social work. Masaryk, it may be said, was a social worker intermittently throughout her life, particularly the years after World War I. But she was predominantly a social organizer, a person who keenly examined society and the world surrounding her to discover pragmatic solutions for the pathologies imbedded in the structure of the society.

Many of her critiques came from the women with whom she worked closely throughout her life. These women, many of whom were sociologists in their own right but ostracized from the male-dominated discipline circa 1920, developed networks through which they critiqued the work and accomplishments of one another. The concern of women within this network was most evident when Masaryk was arrested during 1915–1916. The *Chicago Herald* on April 19, 1916, and again on April 25, 1916, published articles on her captivity and the widespread concern over her safety through informants familiar with this network. It was noted that a petition calling for her release was signed by 40,000 Americans, all of them known by women in this network. Other articles regarding her imprisonment were found in the *London Times* on June 9, 1916, and in the *New York Times* on April 30, 1916, and August 20, 1916.

Another such critique came from Mary McDowell (1930), the founder of the UCSS. In this article on Masaryk, McDowell emphasized the connection between her early residence at UCSS and her lifelong involvement with the reorganization of social institutions. She praised Masaryk's dedication to her work from her early years at the settlement to her later years at president of the Czechoslovakian Red Cross.

The survey of Prague was hailed by Bruno Lasker as a "method of international cross-fertilization of social ideas," one in which several nations could participate in an examination of the pathologies of social institutions. He praised Masaryk's pragmatic approach to the examination of social problems through the keen observations of the task force in identifying the weaknesses of Czechoslovakia's institutions.

BIBLIOGRAPHY

Selected Works by Alice Masaryk

1904. "The Bohemians in Chicago." *Charities and the Commons* 13 (December): 206–210.
1920a. "Foreword." In Mary E. Hurlbutt's *Social Survey of Prague.* Vol. 3, pp. 7–8. Prague: Ministry of Social Welfare.
1920b. "From an Austrian Prison." *The Atlantic Monthly* 126 (November): 577–587.
1920c. "The Prison House." *The Atlantic Monthly* 126 (December): 770–779.
1921a. "A Message from Alice Masaryk." *The Survey* 46 (June): 333.
1921b. "The Program of the Czechoslovak Red Cross After 18 Months." *Revue Internationale de la Croix-Rouge* (July 15): 736–739.
1921c. "Help for Russia." *Revue Internationale de la Croix-Rouge* (August 15): 863–864.
1939. "The Bond Between Us." *Proceedings of the National Conference of Social Work.* New York: Columbia University Press, pp. 69–74.

Studies About Alice Masaryk and Supplemental References

Bydzovska-Kominkova, Marie, ed. 1949. *Alice G. Masaryk in Life and Work: A Collection of Memories on the Occasion of Her 70th Birthday.* Prague: Private ed.
Crawford, Ruth. 1921. "Pathfinding in Prague." *The Survey* 46 (June): 330.
Hurlbutt, Mary. 1920. *Social Care for the Individual: The Prague Social Survey.* Vol. 3. Prague: Czechoslovak Ministry of Social Welfare.
Laskar, Bruno. 1921. "Pragues Window to the West: The Survey of Greater Prague." *The Survey* 46 (June): 337–345.
McDowell, Mary. 1930. "Alice Masarykova." *The Survey* 63 (March): 633–635.
Mitchell, Ruth Crawford. 1980. *Alice Garrigue Masaryk.* Pittsburgh: University of Pittsburgh Press.

Platt, Phillip. 1920a. *Directory of Social Agencies in Prague: The Prague Social Survey.* Vol. 1. Prague: Czechoslovak Ministry of Social Welfare. 1920b.

————. 1920b. Public Health: The Prague Social Survey. Vol. 2. Prague: Czechoslovak Ministry of Social Welfare.

Smith, Anne Rylance. 1920. *Recreation: The Prague Social Survey.* Vol. 4. Prague: Czechoslovak Ministry of Social Welfare.

BRUCE KEITH

ALVA MYRDAL (1902–1986)

In 1975, International Women's Year, the Women's International League for Peace and Freedom awarded Alva Myrdal the Peace and Freedom Award. The award was presented to Alva Myrdal "in recognition of her outstanding leadership towards the new world women want." Alva Myrdal, a sociologist, noted author, diplomat, and Nobel Peace Prize winner, died on February 1, 1986, at the age of eighty-four, after two years of illness in Stockholm. She is best remembered for her deep commitment to nuclear disarmament and world peace. Her genuine concern for a humane society surfaced early in her career with a focus on the issues of families, women, and population. Data for this biographical account were gathered in the fall of 1987. Information was collected from the Archives of the Labour Movement located in Stockholm.

BIOGRAPHY

Alva Reimer was born in Uppsala, Sweden, on January 31, 1902. She was the oldest in a family of five children. According to the *Women's Book of World Records and Achievements*, Alva recognized at an early age that her mother was decidedly unhappy with such a large family, and she was determined to avoid such a situation. Her father and grandfather were both dedicated Social Democrats and maintained an active interest in issues of societal concern. Alva met Gunnar Myrdal, noted economist and author, when she was seventeen, and they later married. Alva did her undergraduate work at Stockholm University and completed some graduate work in social psychology in New York as well as at Uppsala University in Sweden.

Alva and Gunnar had three children, two girls, Kaj and Sissela, and one boy, Jan. Kaj, now Kaj Folster, lives in Göttingen, West Germany. Sissela, now

Sissela Bok, lives in Cambridge, Massachusetts, and has gained extensive recognition as a philosopher. She is married to Derek Bok, president of Harvard
University. Jan Myrdal has pursued a career as a writer and reporter. He is
recognized as an authority on Chinese affairs after having spent a number of
years in China. He also has written several plays, novels, and historical works,
and is married to photographer-artist Gun Kessle.

In 1929 and 1930 Alva studied social and child psychology in the United
States and Geneva. In 1932, at age thirty, she published her first article (Myrdal
1932) about the conditions of service flats in Sweden. She continued to publish
books and articles on important human issues throughout her lifetime. During
the 1930s Alva addressed social issues related to family life, such as the need
for greater access to education, support for families, and improved working
conditions for parents. In 1936 she established the Swedish Training College
for Preschool Teachers, and remained its director from 1936 until 1948. Also
in the 1930s she became concerned with the falling birthrate in Sweden, and in
1934 she, along with Gunnar, published *The Population Problem in Crisis* (*Kris
i belfolkningsfragan*).

From 1938 until 1940 Alva and Gunnar lived in the United States. They
returned to Sweden and published *Contact with America* (*Kontakt med Amerika*),
which is an account of their experiences in the United States, focusing on the
similarities between Sweden and the United States. Between 1940 and 1942 they
again returned to the United States. After returning to Sweden, Alva pursued
an interest in the refugee question and postwar planning. Throughout her life
she served on and chaired numerous committees and commissions related to her
interests. For example, from 1943 until 1944 she was on the postwar commission
of the labor movement. In 1947 they moved to Geneva, and in 1949 she was
appointed director of the U.N. Department of Social Affairs, which necessitated
a return to New York to start her duties at the United Nations. In 1951 she
moved back to Europe when she was made director of the UNESCO Department
of Social Sciences in Paris. She remained in Paris until 1955, when she left the
U.N. service to accept a Swedish offer to be the first woman appointed as
ambassador to India, Ceylon, Burma, and Nepal. In 1961 she returned to Sweden
and served as Swedish ambassador at large.

Since 1961 most of Alva Myrdal's attention was given to the promotion of
peace and disarmament among nations. In 1962 she was elected to the Swedish
parliament, and from 1962 until 1973 she was head of the Swedish delegation
to the committee on disarmament in Geneva. Her list of awards is impressive,
including the West German Peace Prize in 1970, the Wateler Peace Prize in
1973, the Royal Institute of Technology Award in 1975, the Albert Einstein
Peace Award in 1980, the Peoples Peace Prize in 1982, and the co-winner of
the Nobel Peace Prize in 1982. She was the founder and first chairperson of the
Stockholm International Peace Research Institute. Throughout her life she dedicated herself to the study and elimination of social and economic problems.
During the late 1970s and early 1980s Alva Myrdal extended her work on nuclear

disarmament and war to the general issue of societal violence, specifically the connection between wars, weapons, and violence. She donated her Nobel Peace Prize funds to the Myrdal Foundation for two particular projects. The first was a scientific study of the naval arms race, which resulted in the book *The Denuclearisation of the Oceans* (Byers 1986). The second project focused on the ethical aspects of the present cult of violence, including the arms race. She was an adviser to the program "Education for Peace." This program is designed to educate children about the issues of peace and the consequences of violence. It is a joint project between the Alva and Gunnar Myrdal Foundation, the Swedish Red Cross, and the Swedish UN-Association, and is administrated by the Myrdal Foundation.

MAJOR THEMES

Although Alva Myrdal's writings cover a wide range of topics, it is possible to identify some recurrent themes throughout her works. These include a commitment to population planning, an early commitment to the "resistance movement," a belief in the power of social science, and a connection between intrasocietal violence and war.

In the 1930s and early 1940s Alva's work focused on the issues important to the institution of the family and the institution of education. She wrote on such topics as working hours for parents, a woman's right to work, equality, and the problems of single motherhood (Terling 1987). In the early 1940s the Carnegie Corporation invited Alva and Gunnar Myrdal to the United States to research two areas of social policy: race relations and population control. For Gunnar Myrdal and his associates, this was the beginning of his studies on the position of blacks in the United States, and in 1944 he published *An American Dilemma*. Alva's focus was on population policy, and in 1941 she published *Nation and Family*. Contemporary researchers have criticized this work because of statements that involve eugenics; however, the main themes of *Nation and Family* are themes that Alva continued to support throughout her lifetime. They include, first, the need for population planning, not allowing populations to increase or decrease by random chance; second, that families should be paid when they have children, with either cash or services in kind such as dental care or day care; and third, that children should not be born without being planned (Myrdal 1941).

From 1961 until her death Alva was committed to working for world peace. She was appointed minister without portfolio in charge of disarmament and church affairs for the Swedish government, and represented Sweden in the Geneva Disarmament Committee in 1962 (Myrdal 1980). She was critical of the popular usage of "peace movement" when it lacked substance and became simply a cliche. "My use of the term 'resistance movement' is intentional as, in my opinion, it describes the acute situation of today much more adequately than does the vaguer term 'peace movement,' while peace, of course, remains the ultimate goal" (Myrdal 1983–1984, 44).

In her speech when receiving the Einstein Peace Prize, Alva presented a three-tiered pattern to promote world peace. First, she made a call for resistance at the grass-roots level. We "must create a resistance movement of public opinion against the war propaganda—the whole ongoing militarization of our culture" (Myrdal 1980, 49). Second, she made a call for a refocus on education and peace research specifically to find the institutions and publications working on peace-related issues. She called these institutions "truth centres" and called for the social sciences to have more influence on social policy. Alva Myrdal believed that the physical sciences had too often been turned toward the goals of military research while social science research was ignored and trivialized. "And so, my final conclusion is this: what our world needs today is a large scale transfer of intellectual talent from military research to research for peace and development" (Myrdal 1982, 55). Third, she called for establishing some nonofficial but powerful forum for international precrisis management (Myrdal 1980).

Throughout her work Myrdal showed a clear commitment to an empirical social science. As mentioned in her earlier speech, she called institutions carrying out social science research "truth centres" (Myrdal 1980). To stop societal violence, we must understand the society and the cultures from which it arises; this is the arena of the social scientist.

The final theme in Alva Myrdal's work is the connection she drew between war, weapons, and violence. It was Alva's belief that violence is something supported by our cultures and societies; therefore, before we can have a peaceful society, the issue of violence must be addressed within all aspects of societal culture. The purpose of the Education for Peace (Skola för Fred) program is to promote peace in all societal levels and in all age-groups.

CRITIQUES OF ALVA MYRDAL

Alva Myrdal's works were and are widely read by both academics and the general population. She has an audience among various disciplines, including sociologists, economists, and political scientists.

Nation and Family, which was first published in 1941, was a description of the social planning in Sweden designed to deal with the problems of the family and population growth. Because both she and Gunnar Myrdal were active proponents of changing public policy and public opinion concerning population problems in Sweden at the time, the book was a well-thought-out commentary on the problem. It was highly praised by reviewers to such a point as one reviewer commenting that "the high quality of this book makes it almost impregnable to adverse criticism" (Kirkpatrick 1942, 270).

Alva Myrdal's work coauthored with Viola Klein,* *Women's Two Roles: Home and Work*, was published in 1956, and argued that women should direct their energies toward full-time employment after their children were old enough. Although this argument certainly does not seem so radical in today's time, it created a small amount of controversy in 1956. Evelyn Ellis Elmer in her review called the proposals of Myrdal and Klein unrealistic and inapplicable to American women. She claimed that the book was a "well-intentioned but naive effort to solve the much-discussed 'dilemma' of modern women" (Elmer 1957, 250). Elmer went on to claim that the conflict between housewife and employment in America was a problem for only a small number of women who were well-educated, intelligent, and highly motivated (Elmer 1957). However, there was not a consensus of opinion on this work. Mirra Komarovsky* wrote that it was a "well-reasoned, direct, and unequivocal argument in favor of one particular solution . . . that of gainful employment of married women during the major part of their lives" (Komarovsky 1957, 336). In fact, Komarovsky commented on the book's "realism" and how applicable it was to women in the United States.

   The Game of Disarmament is perhaps the most controversial book written by Alva Myrdal. It explains why the superpowers have failed to achieve nuclear disarmament. She shows that the United States and the Soviet Union have been serving their own interests in maintaining an arms race often at the expense of other nations' independence (Myrdal 1976). The comments on this book range from glowing support to nasty put-downs. The *Economist* wrote that Alva Myrdal simply attempts to oversimplify a complex issue and that she has a "blithe way of ignoring things that don't fit" (*Economist*, 1977). The primary outcome of this book, however, has been an increase in the awareness of the issues involved in nuclear disarmament. Emma Rothschild wrote for the *New York Times* that "her words—and her experience as Sweden's Minister of Disarmament, acting with moral courage in the real world of disarmament negotiations—break the set of preconceptions that surround U.S. arms policy" (Rothschild 1977, 124). The test of time has shown the work to be indeed an important contribution. As Alva Myrdal concludes in her 1982 preface to *The Game of Disarmament*, "An American Update—1982, So Much Worse": "The ruin of the planet is there for all to contemplate. But so, too, is its potential richness if we learn to cooperate. We still have a choice. But we must act now as never before" (Myrdal 1982, xxiv).

ACKNOWLEDGMENT

   I am grateful to Lars Wessman, director of the Arbetarrorelsens Arkiv, for his invaluable assistance as well as to the members of the Alva och Gunnar Myrdals Stiftelse for taking the time to talk with me about Alva Myrdal's life.

BIBLIOGRAPHY

Selected Writings by Alva Myrdal

1932. "Kollektiv bostadsform I." *Tiden* 14: 10, S.601–608.
1935. *Stadsbarn: en bok om deras fostran i storbarnkammare*. Stockholm: Kooperativa forbundet.

1941. *Nation and Family: The Swedish Experiment in Democratic Family and Population Policy.* New York: Harper & Brothers.

1944a. *Efterkrigsplanering.* (*Postwar Planning.*) Stockholm: Informationsbyran Mellan folkligt samarbete for fred och Varldssamling for fred, Svenska kommitten.

1944b. *Kommentarer.* Stockholm: Bonnier.

1963. "The Status of the Nuclear Test Ban Negotiations." In *Disarmament Is Possible: A World Veterans Federation Report,* pp. 43–50. Copenhagen: 1963.

1965. "The Dag Hammarskjold Foundation" and "Disarmament and the United Nations." In *The Quest for Peace: The Dag Hammarskjold Memorial Lectures,* edited by Andrew W. Cordier and Wilder Foote, pp. vii–xi, 149–165. New York: Columbia University Press.

1966. "Neglected Needs of the Generation of the Future." *American Journal of Public Health and the Nation's Health* 56 (May): 712–719.

1968. "Political Problems of Peace." *Internationale Spectator: Tijdschrift voor Internationale Politiek* 12 (May): 653–673.

1971. "The Cultural Bonds with Europe." In *Sweden in Europe,* by Royal Ministry for Foreign Affairs. Stockholm: The Swedish Institute.

1975. *The Right to Conduct Nuclear Explosions: Political Aspects and Policy Proposals.* Stockholm: Stockholm International Peace Research Institute.

1976. *The Game of Disarmament: How the United States and Russia Run the Arms Race.* New York: Pantheon. New ed., 1978; revised and updated ed., 1982.

1980. "Statement by Alva Myrdal upon Receiving the International Award from the Albert Einstein Peace Prize Foundation, 29 May 1980." *Disarmament: A Periodic Review by the United Nations* 3 (November): 45–51.

1981. "Dynamics of European Nuclear Disarmament." In *The Dynamics of Nuclear Disarmament,* by Rudolf Bahro, K. Coates, J. Galtung, et al., pp. 209–276. Nottingham: Spokesman for European Nuclear Disarmament and the Bertrand Russell Peace Foundation.

1982. *The Game of Disarmament.* Rev. and updated. New York: Pantheon.

1983. "Nobel Lecture." *Scandinavian Review* 71: 6–16.

1983–1984. "The New Resistance Movement." *Spokesman* 44, End papers 6 (Winter).

1984. "The New Resistance Movement." *End Papers* 6: 3–5.

Coauthored Works

Myrdal, Alva, and Viola Klein. 1956. *Women's Two Roles: Home and Work.* London: Routledge & Kegan Paul. (2nd ed. 1968).

Myrdal, Alva, and Gunnar Myrdal. 1934. *Kris i befolkningsfragan.* (*The Population Problem in Crisis*). Stockholm: A. Bonnier.

———. 1941. *Kontakt med Amerika.* Stockholm: A. Bonnier.

Myrdal, Alva, and Paul Vincent. 1949. *Are We Too Many*? London: Bureau of Current Affairs.

Studies About Alva Myrdal and Supplemental References

Bok, Sissela. 1987. *Alva: Ett Kvinnoliv.* Stockholm: A. Bonnier.

Byers, R. B. 1986. *The Denuclearisation of the Oceans.* Foreword by Arvid Pardo. New York: St. Martin's Press.

Elmer, Evelyn Ellis. 1957. "Review of *Women's Two Roles*." *American Sociological Review* 22 (April): 250–251.

Kirkpatrick, Clifford. 1942. "Review of *Nation and Family*." *Annals of the American Academy of Political and Social Science* 220 (March): 270–271.

Komarovsky, Mirra. 1957. "Review of *Women's Two Roles*." *American Journal of Sociology* 63 (November): 336–337.

Lindskog, Lars G. 1981. *Alva Myrdal*. Kristianstad: Sveriges Radio Forlag.

"Review of *The Game of Disarmament*." *Economist* 264 (August 13): 95.

Rothschild, Emma. 1977. "Review of *The Game of Disarmament*." *New York Review of Books* 23 (January 20): 24.

Skaug, Arne. 1943. "Review of *Nation and Family*." *American Sociological Review* 8 (April): 234–235.

Terling, Barbro. 1987. *Alva Myrdal: kommenterad bibliografi, 1932–1961*. Stockholm: Alva och Gunnar Myrdals Stiftelse. Includes comprehensive list of Alva Myrdal's publications up to 1961.

Unpublished Material

Archival papers at Arbetarrorelsens Arkiv och bibliotek, Upplandsgatan 5, Box 1124; 111 81, Stockholm, Sweden.

Carlson, Allan C. 1978. "The Roles of Alva and Gunnar Myrdal in the Development of a Social Democratic Response to Europe's 'Population Crisis,' 1929–1938." Ph.D. diss., Ohio University.

JANE C. OLLENBURGER

VIRGINIA OLESEN (1925–   )

Virginia Olesen is a leading authority on women's health, socialization in health care occupations, and qualitative methods. She uses a feminist perspective in a symbolic interactionist and phenomenological framework, thereby creating a humanistic, yet rigorous analysis of both everyday life and the structural constructions of reality. She has extended the connection between the self, health, and illness, and the larger social structures such as the workplace, gender, class, and race.

BIOGRAPHY

Virginia Lee Olesen was born on July 21, 1925, in the then small desert town of Lovelock, Nevada. She is the daughter of Ole H. and Leora Noel Olesen and the sister of Barbara Olesen.

Olesen completed her bachelor's degree at the University of Nevada in 1947, and worked for the next seven years as an editor in the U.S. Civil Service. In 1954 she began work in the interdisciplinary mass communication program at the University of Chicago, where she studied with David Riesman, Anselm Strauss, and Everett Hughes. After completing her master's degree in 1956 she commenced doctoral study at Stanford University. In 1957 she became a research assistant at the Stanford Research Institute where she worked for the next two years. In 1961 she completed her doctorate at Stanford University under the guidance of Edmund Volkart, a founder of medical sociology.

After she finished her doctorate, David Riesman put her in contact with Anselm Strauss and Fred Davis who had also studied at Chicago. This began her long association with them and the University of California School of Nursing, where she has taught and done research with graduate students in sociology and in nursing. Starting as an assistant research sociologist in 1960, she moved to the tenure track in 1966, and was promoted to associate professor in 1967. In 1973, she was advanced to full professor, the position she now holds. She was the first chair of the University of California–San Francisco (UCSF) Department of Social and Behavioral Sciences (1972–1975).

Olesen was among the first medical sociologists to recognize the critical research and policy issues inherent in the sociology and social psychology of women's health. In 1973 she and a colleague in anthropology (Lucile Newman, now of Brown University) organized the first academic course in the United States in the sociology and anthropology of women's health. In 1975 she organized and implemented the first national research conference in women's health, and in 1983, with Sheryl Ruzek and Ellen Lewin, she organized the Women, Health and Healing Program, which she now codirects with Adele Clarke. This program trains doctoral candidates in the research on and teaching of multiple aspects of women's health as a domain imbedded in race, class, and gender issues.

With aid from the Fund for the Improvement of Post-Secondary Education, she, Ruzek, Lewin, and Clarke trained national and international scholars in the new women's health literature. I have participated in two of these Women, Health, and Healing Program Institutes, and can attest to their powerful reorientation of knowledge and networking of scholars studying women's health from many aspects.

She has lived and worked in Egypt, where she was a distinguished visiting professor at the American University in Cairo in the winter and spring of 1976, and in Great Britain, where she was a visiting research lecturer in 1987. She has twice delivered the plenary address for the Annual British Medical Sociology Conference (1980, 1990). Among her other honors is the 1988 Leo G. Reeder Distinguished Medical Sociologist Award from the Medical Sociology Section of the American Sociological Association. She chaired this section in 1978–1979.

Her intellectual ties have remained consistently strong with qualitative or interpretive sociologists in the United States and Britain, with medical and feminist anthropologists, as well as with nurse scholars in these arenas.

Olesen currently holds membership in the American Anthropological Association, the Society for Medical Anthropology, the American Sociological Association, the Medical Sociology Group of the British Sociological Association, the International Sociological Association, the Society for the Study of Symbolic Interaction, the Midwest Sociological Association, the Pacific Sociological Association, Sociologists for Women in Society, and the Older Women's League.

She currently is working on projects that continue her longstanding interests and open new topics for feminist analysis. With Anne Davis she is looking at socialization of baccalaureate student nurses in China, and she is attempting new interpretations of women's lives with data from the women whom the UCSF team studied in the early 1960s (Olesen forthcoming). Her work on self-care of mundane ailments has led to new thinking "on the problematic body" (Olesen et al. forthcoming), an issue of growing interest to feminists. She also has been working on constructions of and meanings for peace in women's popular magazines and the diffusion of new knowledge about women's health from the Women, Health, and Healing Summer Institutes. She currently is collaborating with scholars concerned about the health of women of color to produce videotapes on that topic. In her teaching she continues to integrate, apply, and generate feminist theory, including postmodern thought, to better understand the pressing issues she sees in women's health.

MAJOR THEMES

Olesen is a feminist scholar whose work has always concerned the topic of women, but her awareness of the political dimensions of our lives has increased over the past three decades of her work and writings. Her feminism is grounded in a scholarly analysis of data interpreted through a framework of human possibility and liberation. As she so ably expressed it: "Rage is not enough" (1977). We need reflective theories and humane praxis. Her other major foci have been the social psychology of health and illness, especially women's socialization into health care occupations, and qualitative methods. Each theme is addressed here.

The intellectual ground of feminist thought is examined by Olesen in a series of writings. Each explores taken-for-granted views of the everyday world as constructed by patriarchy and by feminists. Her coauthored article on "equality" (Nelson and Olesen 1977a) examines the hierarchical nature of society and the ethnocentric assumptions of Western feminists. The "veil of illusion" of liberal thought pronounces equality as both given and good without reflecting on the nature of difference.

What is missing from the radical feminists' critique, and from that of the liberals for that matter, is any *systematic linking* between subjective affective factors and objective conditions or any understanding of how these subjective-affective themes are linked to the economic structures of society. (p. 19)

In her research on work she uses Dorothy E. Smith's* epistemological theory, arguing for the liberation of women in the workplace, but emphasizing women as actively creating meaningful action for themselves rather than viewing them as passive, cultural victims.

Women's health is analyzed in three anthologies (Lewin and Olesen 1985a; Olesen 1977a; Olesen and Woods 1986). These collections of articles have expanded our understanding of women's health in various illnesses, childbearing, life cycle stages, and work settings, leading, as in the Olesen–Woods collection, to definitions of new areas of analysis, or in her policy paper on the toxic shock issue (Olesen 1986) to consciousness of how health issues emerge for women.

Professional and adult socialization are other themes in Olesen's work. This is seen most clearly in her work with Elvi Whittaker (e.g., 1966, 1968). Their book *The Silent Dialogue* (1968) is both a qualitative and a quantitative analysis of a group of student nurses. Despite the comprehensiveness of their sample and six-year commitment to collecting data on student nurses, the emphasis on lived experience, ambiguity, and the formation of a new self and identity is clear. The processes of legitimating a new persona in a gendered occupation are examined as they are embodied in time and generations.

A perceptive article, written with Fred Davis in 1965, on the contradictory expectations of women's conflicts between the home and marketplace and their embeddedness in institutions such as social class and nursing training remains exciting today. They weave together the work of Simone de Beauvoir,* Viola Klein,* Mirra Komarovsky,* Alva Myrdal,* and Alice Rossi* to show how social change for women is problematic. Her work on women's innovative definitions of work and success is discussed in her article with Ellen Lewin on "lateralness" (1980). Here they criticize the theme that women "fear success" and show that personal satisfaction, new organizational challenges, and work interactions are defined as "success" by the women studied, both those on the career ladder and those moving laterally. Long interested in women in non-elite occupations, Olesen also found in studying temporary clerical workers that they exercise more control and creativity than the occupational theories, oriented to female passivity, would predict (Olesen and Kathsuranis 1977).

"Caregiving" as a hidden dimension of health services is another form of emotional and instrumental labor, affecting both sexes. Olesen sees this as an area of study that is an increasing challenge to medical sociologists (1989). Increased analysis of the interaction between gender, race, and class also needs to be included in the study of health, the self, and the workplace.

Although Olesen uses both quantitative and qualitative methods, her early work emphasizes the Chicago school program of ethnography and knowledge mutually constructed by research and participants (Olesen 1990; Olesen and Whittaker 1967). She has also analyzed the epistemology of qualitative research and analysis with an exploration of fieldwork contexts (1990) and is currently reviewing the tensions between issues of validity and the new interests in text, voice, and narrative in sociological ethnography.

CRITIQUES OF VIRGINIA OLESEN

Olesen and Whittaker's socialization model, especially in *The Silent Dialogue* (1968), was widely viewed as having extended theoretical issues in professional socialization by demonstrating how to analyze the interplay of self, role, and situation (Mizrehi 1986). Some believed that Olesen and Whittaker had modified the theory of role socialization with their emphasis on negotiated roles involving new perspectives on the self, while accepting role as a structural concept (Light 1979). Her ethnographic work also is cited as a model of providing description of research rationale, evolving design, and research role management strategies within research design (Marshall and Rossman 1989). Ellen Lewin has extended Olesen's work on nurses and on feminism to an analysis of the role of feminism in nursing (1977). Lewin discovered that workplace structures were a major factor in the development of autonomy and changing sex roles, rather than the socialization of nurses in training.

Olesen and Whittaker's socialization model (1968) also is examined by Ida Harper Simpson and her colleagues in their study of nurses (Simpson et al. 1979). Simpson compares what she calls Olesen's "reactive model" with the "deductive model" of nursing. In other words, do nursing students enter a profession with an established standard of practice, or do they enter a complex working environment that assumes precedence over formal professional structure and ideals? Simpson finds that the reality of the workplace, like Olesen suggests, is more powerful in shaping nurses and that increasing college training does not result in a more firmly established career commitment.

Olesen's work on women's health and health care is widely recognized. Her exquisite, feminist theory, however, has been underappreciated. Her understanding of equalitarian, emergent relations between sociologist and actor, the complexities of being in a "woman's occupation" such as nursing, and the sociological emergence of the self in context are major elaborations of feminist theory. Much of this work was done before "feminist sociology" appeared as a specialty, and is published in the specialization of "medical sociology," so it has yet to be integrated into the theoretical ideas of contemporary feminism.

ACKNOWLEDGMENT

My thanks to Virginia Olesen for her thoughtful comments on this entry, particularly her correspondence of April 10, 1990. My complex debts to her ideas are difficult to date and document. Final responsibility for this entry resides with me.

BIBLIOGRAPHY

Selected Writings by Virginia Olesen

1971. "Context and Posture: Notes on Socio-Cultural Aspects of Women's Roles and Family Policy in Contemporary Cuba." *Journal of Marriage and the Family* 33 (August): 548–560.

1973. "What Happens After Schooling: Notes on Post-Institutional Socialization in the Health Professions." *Social Science and Medicine* 7 (January): 61–75.

1975. "Convergences and Divergences: Anthropology and Sociology in Health Care." *Social Science and Medicine* 9 (August–September): 421–425.

1977. "Rage Is Not Enough." In *Women and Their Health: Research Implications for a New Era*, edited by Virginia Olesen, pp. 1–2. Washington, DC: National Center for Health Services Research, Health Resources Administration, U.S. Public Health Service, HEW.

1982. "Ethical Issues in Estrogen Replacement Therapy." In *Changing Perspectives on Menopause*, edited by Ann Voda et al., pp. 346–360. Austin: University of Texas Press.

1986. "Research Issues in Analyzing Emergent Issues in Women's Health: The Case of Toxic Shock." In *Cultural Aspects in Menstrual Cycle Research*, edited by Virginia Olesen and Nancy Fugate Woods, pp. 51–62. Cambridge, MA: Hemisphere.

1989a. "Caregiving, Ethical and Informal: Emergent Challenges in the Sociology of Health and Illness." *Journal of Health and Social Behavior* 30 (March): 1–10.

Forthcoming. "Self-assessment and Change in One's Profession: Notes on the Phenomenology of Aging Among Mid-Life Women." *Journal of Women and Aging*.

Forthcoming "Immersed, Amorphous and Episodic Field Work: Theory and Policy in Three Contrasting Contexts." In *Field Work Issues*, edited by Robert Burgess. Greenwich, CT: JAI.

1977. Olesen, Virginia, ed. *Women and Their Health: Research Implications for a New Era*. Washington, DC: National Center for Health Service Research, Health Resources Administration, U.S. Public Health Service, HEW.

Coauthored Works

Davis, Fred, and Virginia Olesen. 1965. "The Career Outlook of Professionally Educated Women." *Psychiatry* 28 (November): 334–345.

Lewin, Ellen, and Virginia Olesen. 1980. "Lateralness in Women's Work: New Views on Success." *Sex Roles* 6 (August): 619–629.

———. 1985a. "Occupational Health and Women: The Case of Clerical Work." In *Women, Health and Healing: Toward a New Perspective*, edited by Ellen Lewin and Virginia Olesen, pp. 53–85. New York: Tavistock-Methuen.

———. eds. 1985b. *Women, Health and Healing: Toward a New Perspective*. New York: Tavistock-Methuen.

Nelson, Cynthia, and Virginia Olesen. 1977a. "Veil of Illusion: Some Critical Notes on the Assumption of Equality in Feminist Thought." *Catalyst* 10/11 (Summer): 8–36.

———, eds. 1977b. "Feminist Thought." Special issue. *Catalyst* 10/11 (Summer).

Olesen, Virginia, and Frances Kathsuranis. 1977. "Urban Nomads: A Study of Temporary Clerical Employees." In *Women and Work*, edited by Shirley Harkness and Ann Yates, pp. 316–338. Belmont, CA: Mayfield.

Olesen, Virginia, and Elvi Whittaker. 1966. "Adjudication of Student Awareness in Professional Socialization: The Language of Laughter and Silence." *Sociological Quarterly* 7 (Summer): 381–396.

———. 1967. "Role-Making in Participant Observation." *Human Organization* 26 (Winter): 273–281.

———. 1968. *The Silent Dialogue*. San Francisco: Jossey-Bass.

Olesen, Virginia, Leonard Schatzman, Nellie Droes, Diane Hatton, and Nan Chico. Forthcoming. "The Mundane Ailment and the Physical Self: An Area for Analysis in the Social Psychology of Health and Illness." *Social Science and Medicine*.

Olesen, Virginia, and Nancy Fugate Woods, eds. 1986. *Cultural Aspects in Menstrual Cycle Research*. Cambridge, MA: Hemisphere.

Studies About Virginia Olesen and Supplemental References

Lewin, Ellen. 1977. ''Feminist Ideology and the Meaning of Work: The Case of Nursing.'' *Catalyst* 10/11 (Summer): 78–103.

Light, Donald. 1979. *Becoming Psychiatrists*. New York: W. W. Norton.

Marshall, Catherine, and Gretchen B. Rossman. 1989. *Designing Qualitative Research*. Beverly Hills, CA: Sage.

Mizrahi, Terry. 1986. *Getting Rid of Patients*. New Brunswick, NJ: Rutgers University Press.

Simpson, Ida Harper, with Kurt W. Back, Thelma Ingeles, Alan C. Kerckhoff, and John C. McKinney. 1979. *From Student to Nurse: A Longitudinal Study of Socialization of Nurses*. New York: Cambridge University Press.

MARY JO DEEGAN

ELSIE CLEWS PARSONS (1874–1941)

Elsie Clews Parsons is a noted anthropologist, although she was trained and worked in sociology for many years before she changed her professional identification. A recognized feminist theorist, Parsons focused on the study of the family, education, religion, and social relations during these early years. The intersection of human ties and social freedom was a continuous theme. Later she did extensive ethnographic study and participant observation of native Americans in the southwestern United States, including the Pueblo Indians, the Hopi, and the Zuni.

BIOGRAPHY

Parsons was born into a wealthy and socially prominent New York family. This background gave her the financial freedom to combine an academic life with marriage and a family, although she had to rebel against the role of the young debutante to do so. Despite her family's opposition, she enrolled in Barnard College, where she earned her bachelor's degree in 1896 and began a lifetime of scholarly work. Her master's degree was completed at Columbia University under the guidance of the sociologist Franklin Giddings, and her doctorate was completed under Nicholas Murray Butler of the philosophy department. On her graduation in 1899, Giddings hired her as an assistant in his sociology course, while she simultaneously was a fellow at Hartley House, a New York social settlement. She continued in this instructor position until 1905, when she finally was promoted to the low rank of lecturer in sociology. (See Giddings' early role in the career of Emily Greene Balch.*) Parsons translated *The Laws of Imitation*, by Gabriel Tarde, in 1903. Tarde was at that time a leading sociologist, but he was soon to lose his battle over the definition of sociological work with the then young professor Émile Durkheim. Parsons's role as translator, therefore, was tied to the fate of a "former star" of sociology.

In 1900 she married Herbert Parsons, a lawyer who was an active reform politician. In 1901 Elsie had her first child, Elise (Lissa), and in 1903 her son John Edward was born. Both Herbert and Elsie were active in social reform in New York during these years. In 1904 Herbert supported Theodore Roosevelt for president. With the latter's successful campaign, Herbert Parsons's political career was greatly enhanced. In 1905 he was elected to Congress, and his wife left her teaching job to accompany him to Washington.

During the course of her marriage, Elsie Clews Parsons bore six children, four of whom survived into childhood. Two of these children were born while she was teaching at Barnard, and the remaining ones were born while she lived in Washington. She lived in Washington until 1911, far from the academic life she enjoyed. Her last surviving child, Henry McIlvaine, was born in 1911, as well. These years were frustrating until she began observing the activities and people around her as a social scientist, instead of as an unreflexive and bored participant. This ethnographic work was closer to the interests of Franz Boas than Franklin Giddings (although the Chicago school of sociology was developing along similar lines to Boas's work at this time), so Parsons developed a greater collegial tie with Boas. In addition, Parsons was never fully supported as an equal faculty member in sociology at Columbia and wanted more recognition and freedom.

Her transition from sociology to anthropology occurred gradually from approximately 1913 to 1920. (Peter Hare [1985, 20], among others, marks the transitional year as 1915, but Parsons's pacifism during World War I was intellectually tied to the female sociologists' agenda, and she continued to publish sociologically oriented work until 1919.) During these years she increasingly identified herself interpersonally with anthropologists, but she continued to be active in the American Sociological Society, reviewed in its journal, and published there.

These were important years for Parsons's public role as a social commentator. During these years she was a member of Heterodoxy, a lively, irreverent group of women who supported one another's challenges to social restrictions. She wrote popular articles widely read and discussed in New York's intellectual circles, and even helped to found *The New Republic*. These years were spent increasingly outside of sociological networks, although Parsons continued to publish numerous professional books and essays.

Parsons's much more powerful role in anthropology than in sociology is briefly summarized here. She worked for the newly established New School for Social Research in New York, and recruited a remarkable woman to anthropology there: Ruth Benedict. She served as the treasurer (1916–1922) and president (1923–1925) of the American Ethnological Society, and as vice-president of the American Folklore Society (1932–1934). She also was the associate editor of the *Journal of American Folklore* from 1918 until her death in 1941. She contributed more than $30,000 to the journal, and donated significant sums to further students' careers, support fieldwork, and subsidize publications (Friedlander 1988, 288).

Parsons was the first woman to be elected as president of the American Anthropological Association. She was to preside over the 1941 meetings when she became ill in December 1941. She died soon after of complications resulting from an appendectomy. According to her wishes and reflecting her alienation from social conventions, she was cremated with "no funeral, and no religious services whatsoever" (Hare 1985, 167).

MAJOR THEMES

From 1899 until 1907 Parsons was a pragmatist, often writing on women's work, the academic development of sociology, and the nature of specific concepts. With the publication of *The Family* in 1906, Parsons was thrust into the national limelight with her brief recommendation of contractual marriages. It was so controversial that she even sent Theodore Roosevelt, then president of the United States, a copy of her book to judge for himself its lawlessness and evil intention. He did not find it egregious, but the political impact on the career of Parsons's husband led her to publish her next book, on religious chastity, under the pseudonym of "John Main" in 1913.

The same year Parsons published a major book on women across eras and cultures (1913a). This was part of her series of works on feminism, the right of women for greater sexual and social freedoms, and the need to question the institution of motherhood. Parsons questioned the cultural feminism popular in the writings of many female sociologists of her era, and later argued that women should be assured the rights and freedoms experienced by men. Parsons's ideas are highly compatible with those of Leta Stetter Hollingworth.* Both women worked in New York in the same era, studied at Columbia University at different times, focused on the problems of motherhood, and were members of a radical intellectual club, Heterodoxy. They also were members of a group called the "Heretics" from about 1914 to 1916. If they were mutually influenced, friends, or even more than vaguely familiar with each other is undocumented at this time. Common patterns of life experiences and interests are found in their work and biographies, nonetheless.

Parsons wrote a large number of articles on women's rights, particularly the distinctions between being a wife and a mother (e.g., 1916c, 1916d, 1916e, 1916f). Here, and in other popular articles not included in this selected bibliography, Parsons argues for the distinction between consenting adults with a wide range of human choices and parents who filled a major social obligation. Parsons's views on parenting were quite conservative, stressing social class and kinship obligations that are a major contrast to her general arguments against social conventions (e.g., 1915d, 1916g).

Antimilitarism informed Parsons's writings during World War I. Unlike many female sociologists of her era (e.g., Jane Addams*), Parsons did not base her argument on women's distinct, cooperative culture. In 1915 (1915d) she argued that men opposed women's entry into combat because they opposed women's admission to most aspects of public life. The next year (1916g) she argued that war emerged from fear, similar to other fears of the unknown, of God and of death. Finally, in 1917, Parsons saw war as part of a larger, American world view. Business advantages, catchwords, and social class favored the continuance of international violence. Parsons's controversial stance against World War I drew her closer to people outside the mainstream culture in the United States and helped her to separate even more from the male mainstream views in sociology. Her antimilitarism resolves some of the conflicts between cultural feminism and critical pragmatism, however, that were unresolved by most female sociologists of her day (see discussion in Jane Addams).

A major methodological technique adroitly used by Parsons combined a comparative, historical, and classificatory framework. She combined this in her anthropological studies with fieldwork, or, as sociologists often call it, "participant observation." Parsons actively collected information, stories, artifacts, and information on rituals. Hare suggests that part of Parsons's motivations and actions were self-glorifying and manipulative in the field (1985), but such criticisms were difficult for me to assess, given the relatively small amount of serious study on Parsons at this time. Parsons also innovated a now popular technique for studying oppressed people, examining the social construction of everyday life instead of only the lives of the elite or the unusual (1923; see Dorothy E. Smith).

Whatever Parsons's motives were, she clearly studied native Americans during an era when most American sociologists were ignoring them. This "push" away from sociological definitions and toward anthropological ones is echoed in the lives of other female sociologists (e.g., Mary Elizabeth Burroughs Roberts Smith Coolidge,* Rosalie Wax,* and Irene Diggs*). I have not ventured too far into an analysis of her anthropological work—its distinctions from and continuities with sociology. Her early career, from 1899 to 1920, echoes the lives and struggles of her sister sociologists, and during these years she made major contributions to the discipline of sociology. The complete analysis of her biography, career, ideas, and intellectual impact awaits future scholarship.

CRITIQUES OF ELSIE CLEWS PARSONS

Like many other early women sociologists, Parsons was critiqued as a full, albeit generally misunderstood, colleague during the first two decades of this century. Thus two of her books, *Religious Chastity* and *The Old-Fashioned Woman*, were reviewed in the *American Journal of Sociology*. F. Stuart Chapin (1914) found the former book filled with ethnological data but lacking in generalizations and theory. He appears to have missed Parsons's major point that evolutionary progress was not as documented as men assumed it was. Frances

Fenton Bernard (1913) reviewed the second book, and found it a powerful statement on the factual nature of women's lives. Many reviews of Parsons's work in sociological journals are critical when the reviewers were sociologists. Reviews by anthropologists writing in sociological journals were the opposite. These latter colleagues, including Robert Redfield (1937) and A. I. Hallowell, (1939), praise Parsons for her ethnographic detail, breadth of analysis, and innovativeness.

Anna Garlin Spencer* (1923), a cultural feminist and minister, found Parsons's views on marriage a threat to the traditional, viable family. Jessie Taft* (1916) shared these criticisms. Florence Kelley* found Parsons liable to speaking harshly about social settlements without a knowledgeable basis for her critique. Thus many of the most active and powerful women in sociology were not supportive of Parsons's ideas.

Parsons led a remarkably varied and rich life and had a charismatic personality. Peter H. Hare's (1985) biography draws on her private correspondence and reveals her experimentation with new social and intimate relations. He discusses her frustrations with upper-class conventions for women, the expectations of politicians' wives, and the lack of personal freedom for women. She clearly anticipated many of the struggles facing contemporary female professionals and strived to balance a moral world with adventure and excitement. The biographer has provided us with access to an intimate view of this inspiring and major theorist, but the account is not sensitive to the complexity of her struggles and world view.

Rosalind Rosenberg's study of the intellectual roots of modern feminism (1983) examines Parsons's early years as a feminist theorist. Rosenberg stresses the continuity in Parsons's work as an anthropologist, despite the fact that Parsons was primarily active as a sociologist during the era studied. Rosenberg's analysis, nonetheless, places Parsons in an important intellectual context, supplying more in-depth information on Parsons's thought, network, and life than that provided here.

The only sociological study of Parsons was completed by Barbara Keating (1978). Further scholarly resources are found in the January–March 1943 issue of the *Journal of American Folklore* dedicated to Elsie Clews Parsons. The memorial article by Reichard (1943) includes a comprehensive bibliography of Parsons's work (Reichard 1943, 48–56). Desley Deacon (1989) is preparing a book manuscript emphasizing the early years of Parsons's career and her sociological legacy, and there are rumors of several other biographies in preparation. Given the rich life and thought of Parsons, this scholarship promises a rich harvest for sociological thought.

ACKNOWLEDGMENT

My thanks to Desley Deacon for her comments on Parsons's ideas and biography.

BIBLIOGRAPHY

Selected Writings by Elsie Clews Parsons

1899. *Educational Legislation and Administration of the Colonial Governments*. Columbia University Contributions to Philosophy, Psychology, and Education. New York: Macmillan.

1900. "Field Work in Teaching Sociology." *Educational Review* 20 (September): 159–169.

1906a. "The Religious Dedication of Women." *American Journal of Sociology* 11 (March): 610–622.

1906b. *The Family: An Ethnological and Historical Outline, with Descriptive Notes*. New York: G. P. Putnam's Sons.

1909. "Higher Education of Women and the Family." *American Journal of Sociology* 14 (May): 758–763.

1913a. *The Old-Fashioned Woman: Primitive Fancies About the Sex*. New York: G. P. Putnam's Sons.

1913b. [John Main] *Religious Chastity: An Ethnological Study*. New York: Macaulay.

1914a. "Avoidance." *American Journal of Sociology* 19 (January): 480–484

1914b. "Teknonymy." *American Journal of Sociology* 19 (March): 649–650.

1914c. *Fear and Conventionality*. New York: G. P. Putnam's Sons.

1915a. *Social Freedom: A Study of the Conflicts Between Social Classifications and Personality*. New York: G. P. Putnam's Sons.

1915b. "Aversions to Anomalies." *Journal of Philosophy, Psychology, and Scientific Methods* 12 (April): 212–219.

1915c. "Circumventing Darwinism." *Journal of Philosophy, Psychology, and Scientific Methods* 12 (October): 610–612.

1915d. "Anti-suffragists and War." *Scientific Monthly* 1 (October): 44–45.

1916a. *Social Rule: A Study of the Will to Power*. New York: G. P. Putnam's Sons.

1916b. "Seniority in the Nursery." *School and Society* 3 (January): 14–17.

1916c. "When Mating and Parenthood Are Theoretically Distinguished." *International Journal of Ethics* 26 (January): 207–216.

1916d. "Wives and Birth Control." *New Republic* 6 (March): 187–189.

1916e. "Feminism and Sex Ethics." *International Journal of Ethics* 26 (July): 462–465.

1916f. "Marriage and Parenthood—A Distinction." *International Journal of Ethics* 25 (July): 514–517.

1916g. "Mysticism in War." *Scientific Monthly* 3 (September): 258–288.

1917. "Patterns for Peace or War." *Scientific Monthly* 5 (September): 229–238.

1933. *Hopi and Zuni Ceremonialism*. Menasha, WI: American Anthropological Association.

1936a. *Mitla, Town of the Souls: And Other Zapoteco-speaking Pueblos of Oaxaca, Mexico*. Chicago: University of Chicago Press.

1936b. *Peguche: A Study of Andean Indians*. Chicago: University of Chicago Press.

1939. *Pueblo Indian Religion*. 2 vols. Chicago: University of Chicago Press.

Parsons, Elsie Clews, ed. 1922. *American Indian Life*. Lincoln: University of Nebraska Press.

Parsons, Elsie Clews, trans. 1903. *The Laws of Imitation*, by Gabriel Tarde, translated from the 2nd French ed. Introduction by Franklin H. Giddings. New York: Henry Holt.

Studies About Elsie Clews Parsons and Supplemental References

Bernard, Frances Fenton. 1913. "Review of *The Old-Fashioned Woman*." *American Journal of Sociology* 19 (November): 414–417.

Bernard, L. L. 1916. "Review of *Social Freedom*." *American Journal of Sociology* 22 (November): 402–403.

Boyer, Paul. 1971. "Elsie Clews Parsons." In *Notable American Women*, edited by Edward T. James, et al. pp. 20–23. Cambridge, MA: Harvard University Press, Belknap Press.

Chapin, F. Stuart. 1914. "Review of *Religious Chastity*." *American Journal of Sociology* 19 (March): 693–695.

Friedlander, Judith. 1988. "Elsie Clews Parsons." In *Women Anthropologists: A Biographical Dictionary*, edited by Ute Gacs, Aisha Khan, Jerrie McIntyre, and Ruth Weinberg, pp. 282–290. Westport, CT: Greenwood Press.

Hallowell, A. I. 1939. "Review of *Pueblo Indian Religion*." *American Sociological Review* 4 (December): 881–883.

Hare, Peter H. 1985. *A Woman's Quest for Science: Portrait of Anthropologist Elsie Clews Parsons*. New York: Prometheus Books.

Keating, Barbara. 1978. "Elsie Clews Parsons: Her Work and Influence in Sociology." *Journal of the History of Sociology* 1 (Fall): 1–10.

Kelley, Florence. 1905. "Letter." *Charities* 13 (October 14):104–105.

Kroeber, Alfred L. 1943. "Elsie Clews Parsons, Part II." *American Anthropologist* 45 (April–June): 252–255.

Lurie, Nancy Oestrich. 1968. "Parsons, Elsie Clews." In *International Encyclopedia of the Social Sciences*, Vol. 11, edited by David. L. Sills, pp. 426–428. New York: Macmillan and the Free Press.

Redfield, Robert. 1937. "Review of *Mitla, Town of the Souls*." *American Journal of Sociology* 42 (January): 601–602.

Reichard, Gladys E. 1943. "Elsie Clews Parsons." *Journal of American Folklore* 56: 45–56.

Rosenberg, Rosalind. 1983. *Beyond Separate Spheres*. New Haven, CT: Yale University Press.

Spier, Leslie. 1943. "Elsie Clews Parsons, Part I." *American Anthropologist* 45 (April–June): 244–251.

Spencer, Anna Garlin. 1923. *The Family and Its Members*. Philadelphia: J. B. Lippincott.

Taft, Jessie. 1916. *The Woman Movement from the Point of View of Social Consciousness*. Chicago: University of Chicago Press.

Unpublished Material

Deacon, Desley. 1989. "Is Elsie Clews Parsons Good Enough to Teach?" Paper presented at the American Sociological Association Meetings, August.

MARY JO DEEGAN

MATILDA WHITE RILEY (1911–   )

Matilda White Riley is a leading expert on aging and its interaction with history and social structure. She has also specialized in developing sociological models for data collection and analysis, and in the measurement of the sociology of communications. She has recently examined the relation between biography and history in the lives of sociologists.

BIOGRAPHY

Matilda White was born in Boston, on April 19, 1911, into an affluent and well-established American family. Her ancestors arrived on the *Mayflower*, and they were largely writers, historians, and ministers. Matilda was the eldest daughter of four children born to Percival and Mary Cliff White. Her father founded the field of market research and directed a a powerful organization in this field, Market Research Company of America, where Matilda worked during the summer while in college. He also wrote numerous books on various marketing commodities, such as food and clothing, and on money-making processes. His work and ideas had a major influence on his daughter and her subsequent career. The family was involved in many outdoor activities, as well, including gliding (White and Riley 1931) and sailing.

For a brief period, in 1927–1928, Matilda White studied at Simmons College and then transferred to Radcliffe College because she wanted a "more intellec-tual" environment. In 1931 she completed her bachelor's degree and on June 19 of that year married a first-year graduate student in the new Department of Sociology at Harvard University, John (Jack) W. Riley, Jr. In the early 1930s, when the noted sociologist Paul Lazarsfeld visited the United States to study social survey methods, he called on Percival White. The latter was about to leave on an extended business trip, however, and he recommended that Lazarsfeld talk to his daughter. The young Matilda thereby began a long, productive relationship with the then-young Viennese scholar, and this led to her studying at the University of Vienna in 1935.

During the Depression years Jack and Matilda were in graduate school together at Harvard. She became the first research assistant in the new department, having been turned down for a fellowship because "she was a woman" (Riley 11 June 1990). Jack completed his master's degree in 1933 and his doctorate in 1936, and Matilda completed her M.A. in 1937. She did not complete a Ph.D., however, because she chose to devote more time to raising her family. Talcott Parsons once advised her on this issue: "Matilda, you have already earned more than two degrees. Why bother [with getting a Ph.D.]? I got along very well without one" (cited by Riley June 11, 1990). And so did Matilda.

The Rileys have built a flourishing personal and public life. They are the parents of two children: John W. Riley III, now a physician, and Lucy Ellen Sallick, now an artist. The Rileys have eight grandchildren and have coauthored many works, beginning with articles on contraceptive behavior in the early 1940s and continuing with a shared interest in the life course and socialization.

In 1938, she became the vice-president and research director of her father's and stepmother's business, Market Research Company of America. She held these positions from 1938 to 1949. She also served during World War II, from 1942 to 1944, as the chief consulting economist for the U.S. War Production Board. From 1949 to 1960 she was the first person to fill the position of executive officer of the American Sociological Association (ASA), while Jack served as the ASA secretary. This job brought her into contact with professional sociologists and involved her in social issues.

During the years that Riley worked for the ASA she held various part-time positions in the academy: such as visiting professor in the Graduate School at New York University from 1954 to 1961, and as a lecturer in sociology at Harvard University in the summer of 1955. She held a series of positions at Rutgers University from 1950 to 1973 where she is now an emerita university professor. During these years at Rutgers, Riley was able to change their nepotism rules and opened new avenues and opportunities for other female graduate students. She also taught for five years (1973–1978) at Bowdoin College where she was the Daniel B. Fayerweather professor of political economy and sociology, a position she also holds emerita. Bowdoin College awarded her an honorary doctor of science degree in 1972, and Rutgers University awarded her an honorary doctor of humane letters degree in 1983.

She has been active in community associations (the Association for the Aid of Crippled Children, 1964–1966, now the Foundation for Child Development). She has been a consultant to numerous groups, such as the U.S. Air Force, Human Resources Branch; the Salk Institute; the National Council on Aging; the World Health Organization, and the Russell Sage Foundation. Her committee work on panels and boards has been similarly extensive, including the National

Institute of Child Health and Human Development; the National Institutes of
Health; Aspen Seminars on Life-Course Transitions, the Institute of Medicine;
the Committee on International Exchange of Persons (Fulbright); the Society for
the Study of Social Biology; the Harvard Board of Overseers Visiting Committee
(sociology); and the Carnegie Commission on College Retirement.

Many awards and honors have been bestowed upon her work including the
Lindback Award for distinguished research on aging and society (Rutgers, 1970);
the Social Science Award, Andrus Gerontology Center (University of Southern
California, 1974); the Radcliffe Distinguished Alumnae Award, for pioneering
the sociology of aging (1982); the Distinguished Research Award, American
Association for Public Opinion Research (1983); the First Section Award for
Sociological Practice, ASA (1983); and the Distinguished Scholar Award, Section on Aging, ASA (1988). In 1977 the Matilda White Riley Award in Sociological Methodology was established at Rutgers, and in 1987 an undergraduate
prize for research was established at Bowdoin College. She has held many
lectureships as well (e.g., the Winkelman Lectureship [Michigan, 1983], and
the Selo Lectureship [University of North Carolina, 1987]).

She was president of the ASA in 1986, and co-president (with Jack) of the
District of Columbia Sociological Society in 1987. She has been a fellow of the
Center for Advanced Study in the Behavioral Sciences, and has held a number
of professional offices, including president of the Eastern Sociological Society;
chair of the Research Committee of the Gerontological Society, of the Social
and Economic Sciences Section of the American Association for the Advancement of Science, and of the Committee on Life-Course Perspectives of the Social
Science Research Council. She is a senior member of the Institute of Medicine
(National Academy of Sciences), a member of the American Academy of Arts
and Sciences, and was presented with the Common Wealth Award in Sociology
in 1984.

Currently, Matilda White Riley is an associate director for Behavioral and
Social Research of the National Institute on Aging, National Institutes of Health.
She is actively engaged in a series of projects on aging and is involved in a wide
range of personal activities. Her longtime associate Anne Foner noted that Riley
"is a skier, back-backer, mountain-climber, hiker, (and) camper" (Foner 1985:
14), as well as being the author of two books on "soaring and gliding" (e.g.,
White and Riley 1931).

MAJOR THEMES

Like most women in sociology trained during that era, Riley has had a varied
career. She explains this pattern as a product of taking "advantage of the professional opportunities as they came along" (Riley 11 June 1990). Thus, she has
contributed to the sociology of age, to research methods, communications research, and intergenerational relation. The sociology of age is unquestionably
her most important area of specialization. Her major books here are *Aging and*

Society, 3 volumes (*Volume 1. An Inventory of Research Findings*, Riley, Foner, Moore, Hess, and Roth 1968; Volume 2. *Aging and the Professions*, Riley, J. W. Riley, Jr., and Johnson 1969; Volume 3. *A Sociology of Age Stratification: Of Aging and Society*, Riley, Johnson, and Foner 1972). This series set out the accepted propositions that aging is a life-long process, that it is not biologically determined, that aging processes are influenced by social change, and that varying patterns of aging, in turn, bring about changes in society.

This influential series was quickly followed by other edited books on aging. This time the topic was analyzed through the collected studies of others' research in the two volumes of *Aging in Society* (Volume 1: *Selected Reviews of Recent Research*, edited by Riley, Hess, and Bond 1983); *Aging from Birth to Death* (Volume 1. *Interdisciplinary Perspectives*, edited by Riley 1979); (Volume 2. *Sociotemporal Perspectives*, edited by Riley, Abeles, and Teitelbaum 1982); *Perspectives in Behavioral Medicine: The Aging Dimension* by Riley, Baum, and Matarazzo 1987; and *Social Change and the Life Course*, two volumes (Volume 1. *Social Structures and Human Lives*; Volume 2. *Sociological Lives*, 1988). These books combine to make a major contribution to the study of age stratification, the interaction between the person and history, and the current trends in life expectancy.

Riley's multidimensional approach not only extends traditional boundaries in sociology but also links sociology to other disciplines, such as medicine (Riley and Bond 1983), anthropology, gerontology, and gereconomics. Her leadership has led to her writing numerous chapters and articles on the state of the field (1981, 1987, 1988).

The rapid increases in longevity that have occurred during this century have involved changes in sex roles, family structure, occupations, age of retirement, and the appearance of new cross-generational and intergenerational issues. This broad structural alteration is linked to wider social changes in knowledge, especially in medicine and technology. The emergence of the sociology of age as an increasingly powerful academic and applied specialization is a product of all these changes. "The oldest old" (Suzman and Riley 1985) were the topics of one of the special issues she edited that illustrated the new types of services and expectations created by a growing number of people in their 80s and older (See related issues in Riley and Jack W. Riley, Jr. 1986).

Occupations and their interaction with age is also a theme in several works (Riley, J. W. Riley, Jr., and Johnson 1969). Riley has specialized in studying professions, especially sociologists. She has pointed to changing roles for "retired" professors (1986), and has remembered old friends and mentors such as Samuel Andrew Stouffer (1961) and Talcott Parsons (1979). Her coedited volume, *Sociological Traditions form Generation to Generation: Glimpses of the American Experience* (Merton and Riley; 1988), is a scholarly and biographical statement on the rich heritage of sociological leaders.

Riley shares the concerns of Alice Rossi* on the interaction between gender, professional women, and aging (e.g., Abeles and Riley 1977, Riley 1985). Their joint emphasis on the "life course" is part of a new literature examining inter-personal relations and changes in institutional structures. Changes in life ex-pectancy affect more than the later years. The entire pattern of one's life is systematically altered including new definitions of youth, middle age, and career commitments. History and generations are thereby redefined, as well. As early as 1940 Riley was documenting the use of contraceptives (J. W. Riley, Jr. and Riley 1940, 1941).

The knowledge base that Riley employs is built upon firm procedures for data collection and rigorous research designs. Her methodological writings have, therefore, often emphasized conceptual clarification and quantitative techniques, such as the use of scaling (Riley and Toby 1952; Riley and J. W. Riley, Jr., and Toby 1954), questionnaire design and applicability (Riley, J. W. Riley, Jr., and Toby 1954), and the problems of measuring such concepts as consensus (Riley, Riley, and Toby 1952). Her two volumes on *Sociological Research* (Riley, J. W. Riley, Jr., Cohn, Moore, Johnson, Boocock, and Foner 1963) organized methodological information and generated a coherent case approach and workbook for student use. It was widely adopted for two decades. In 1974 she extended her methodological work to include qualitative methods in her book on *Sociological Observation: A Strategy for New Social Knowledge* (Riley and Nelson), although she occasionally had analyzed qualitative techniques earlier as well. Throughout her methodological work, Riley has emphasized the group as a unit of analysis and the social system as the essential conceptual frame for study.

Riley's early work on communications is worthy of brief comment. Here, too, the social system is the key. Both communication and audience are embedded in social structure which influence what is said and received. From 1951 to 1959 Riley studied mass communications from both a macrostructural (Riley, and J. W. Riley, Jr. 1959) and a microstructural level (Riley and Cohen 1958; Riley, and Flowerman 1951). An indication of the continuing importance of this com-ponent in her work is the fact the she and her husband were given the Distin-guished Research Award from the American Association for Public Opinion Research in 1983.

CRITIQUES OF MATILDA WHITE RILEY

Riley has defined major issues, both conceptual and methodological, in the sociology of age. Scholars in this area often use her work as a starting point for their own research. She has coauthored extensively with other women sociolo-gists, including such former, now eminent, students: Anne Foner, Beth B. Hess, Joan Waring, and Marilyn Johnson. They have continued to work on the topic of aging, amplifying and extending the work of their mentor. For the past decade, Riley has exerted a broad influence on social and behavioral research on human development and the life course through her position in the National Institutes on Aging.

ACKNOWLEDGMENTS

I thank Matilda White Riley for her help in preparing this chapter, especially her correspondence of February 11, 1989, May 17, 1990, and June 11, 1990. Beth Hess also provided extremely helpful advice. Final responsibility resides with me.

BIBLIOGRAPHY

Selected Writings by Matilda White Riley

1960. "Membership of the American Sociological Association, 1950–1959." In association with Mary E. Moore, Arthur Liebman, Nellie Keshisman, and other members of the staffs of the Executive Office and the Rutgers Research Group. *American Sociological Review* 25 (December): 914–926.

1961. "Samuel Andrew Stouffer." Obituary. *Social Forces* 39 (March): 284.

1964. "Sources and Types of Sociological Data." In *Handbook of Modern Sociology*, edited by Robert E. L. Faris, pp. 978–1026. Chicago: Rand McNally.

1978. "Aging, Social Change, and the Power of Ideas." *Daedalus* 104 (Fall): 39–52.

1979. "Tribute to Talcott Parsons, 1902–1979: Organization Man." *ASA Footnotes* (August): 7–8.

1980. "Age and Aging: From Theory Generation to Theory Testing." In *Sociological Theory and Research: A Critical Appraisal*, edited by Hubert Blaclock, Jr., pp. 339–348. New York: The Free Press.

1985. "Women, Men, and the Lengthening Life Course." In *Gender and the Lifecourse*, edited by Alice S. Rossi, pp. 333–347. ASA Presidential Volume. New York: Aldine.

1986a. "The Dynamisms of Life Stages: Roles, People, and Age." *Human Development* 29 (May–June): 150–156.

1986b. "On Future Demands for Older Professors." *Academe* 72 (July–August): 14–16.

1987. "On the Significance of Age in Sociology." *American Sociological Review* 52 (February): 1–14.

1979. *Aging from Birth to Death*. Vol. 1. *Interdisciplinary Perspectives*. AAAS Selected Symposium, No. 30. Boulder, CO: Westview Press.

1988. *Sociological Lives*. Vol. 2. *Social Change and the Life Course*. ASA Presidential Series. Newbury Park, CA: Sage.

In press. "The Influence of Sociological Lives: Personal Reflections." *Annual Review of Sociology*.

Coauthored Works

Abeles, Ronald P., and Matilda White Riley. 1977. "A Life-Course Perspective on the Later Years of Life: Some Implications for Research." In *Social Science Research Council Annual Report*, pp. 1–16. New York: Social Science Research Council.

Merton, Robert K., and Matilda White Riley, eds. 1980. *Sociological Traditions from Generation to Generation: Glimpses of the American Experience*. Norwood, NJ: Ablex. Chinese ed., 1988.

Riley, John W., and Matilda White Riley. 1940. "The Uses of Various Methods of Contraception." *American Sociological Review* 5 (December): 89–903.

Riley, John Winchell, and Matilda White Riley. 1941. "Actual and Preferred Sources of Contraceptive Information." *American Sociological Review* 6 (February): 33–36.

Riley, Matilda White, Ronald P. Abeles, and Michael S. Teitelbaum, eds. 1982. *Aging from Birth to Death*. Vol. 2. *Sociotemporal Perspectives*. AAAS Selected Symposium, No. 79. Boulder, CO: Westview Press.

Riley, Matilda White, and Kathleen Bond. 1983. "Beyond Ageism: Postponing the Onset of Disability." In *Aging in Society: Selected Review of Recent Research*, edited by Matilda White Riley, Beth B. Hess, and Kathleen Bond, pp. 243–252. Hillsdale, NJ: Lawrence Erlbaum Associates.

Riley, Matilda White, and Richard Cohn. 1958. "Control Networks in Informal Groups." *Sociometry* 21 (March): 30–49.

Riley, Matilda White, and Samuel H. Flowerman. 1951. "Group Relations as a Variable in Communications Research." *American Sociological Review* 16 (April): 174–180.

Riley, Matilda White, and Anne Foner. 1978. "Old Age: Social Aspects of." In *The New Encyclopaedia Britannica*, Vol. 13, 15th ed., pp. 546–552. Chicago: Encyclopaedia Britannica.

Riley, Matilda White, and Anne Foner, in association with Mary E. Moore, Beth Hess, and Barbara K. Roth. 1968. *Aging and Society*. Vol. 1. *An Inventory of Research Findings*. New York: Russell Sage Foundation.

Riley, Matilda White, Beth B. Hess, and Kathleen Bond, eds. 1983. *Aging in Society: Selected Reviews of Recent Research*. Hillsdale, NJ: Lawrence Erlbaum Associates.

Riley, Matilda White, in association with Bettina J. Huber and Beth B. Hess, eds. 1988. *Social Structures and Human Lives*. Social Change and the Life Course, Vol. 1. ASA Presidential Series. Newbury Park, CA: Sage.

Riley, Matilda White, Marilyn Johnson, and Anne Foner. 1972. *Aging and Society*, Vol. 3. *A Sociology of Age Stratification*. New York: Russell Sage Foundation.

Riley, Matilda White, and Edward E. Nelson, eds. 1974. *Sociological Observation: A Strategy for New Social Knowledge*. New York: Basic Books.

Riley, Matilda White, and John W. Riley, Jr. 1951. "A Sociological Approach to Communications Research." *Public Opinion Quarterly* 15 (Fall): 445–460.

———. 1986. "Longevity and Social Structure: The Added Years." *Daedalus* 115 (Winter): 51–75.

Riley, Matilda White, in association with J. W. Riley, Jr., R. M. Cohn, M. E. Moore, M. E. Johnson, S. S. Boocock, and A. Foner, under the general editorship of Robert K. Merton. 1963. *Sociological Research*. 2 vols. New York: Harcourt, Brace & World.

Riley, Matilda White, John W. Riley, Jr., and Marilyn Johnson. 1969. *Aging and Society*, Vol. 2. *Aging and the Professions*. New York: Russell Sage Foundation.

Riley, Matilda White, John W. Riley, Jr., and Jackson Toby, eds., in association with Marcia L. Toby, Richard Cohn, Harry C. Bredemeir, Mary Moore, and Paul Fine. 1954. *Sociological Studies in Scale Analysis*. New Brunswick, NJ: Rutgers University Press.

Riley, Matilda White, John W. Riley, Jr., and Marcia L. Toby. 1952. "The Measurement of Consensus." *Social Forces* 31 (December): 97–106.

Riley, Matilda White, and Clarice S. Stoll. 1968. "Content Analysis." In *International Encyclopedia of the Social Sciences*, Vol. 3, edited by David L. Sills, pp. 371–377. New York: Macmillan and the Free Press, 1968.

Riley, Matilda White, and Jackson Toby. 1952. "Subject and Object Scales: A Sociological Application." *American Sociological Review* 17 (June): 287–296.

Suzman, Richard, and Matilda White Riley, guest eds. 1985. "The Oldest Old." Special issue, editors' introduction by Suzman and Riley, pp. 177–186. *Milbank Memorial Fund Quarterly* 63 (Spring): 174–454.

White, Percival, and Mat[ilda] White [Riley]. 1931. *Gliding and Soaring: An Introduction to Motorless Flight*. New York: McGraw-Hill.

Studies About Matilda White Riley and Supplemental References

Foner, Anne. 1985. "Matilda White Riley: Of Her Times and Ahead of Her Time." *Footnotes* 13 (August): 11, 14.

Rossi, Alice. 1983. *Seasons of a Woman's Life*. Amherst, MA: Hamilton I. Newell.

MARY JO DEEGAN

CAROLINE BAER ROSE (1913–1975)

Caroline Baer Rose was a first-rate sociologist who spent her career around the margins of the profession. Married to a prominent sociologist, Arnold Rose, and faced with nepotism rules, she pieced together a career of collaborative research and writing. Her professional accomplishments include being a model at mentoring and teaching undergraduate and graduate students.

BIOGRAPHY

Caroline was born in 1913 and became a young sociologist with a bachelor's degree from West Virginia University in 1935. In a state that then and now is deeply cut by unemployment and economic depression, Caroline became involved in the labor movement, teaching education classes for the Steelworkers' Organizing Committee. Later she worked for the state's employment office and a local Works Progress Administration program. She would never forget the structural factors that contribute to personal hardship, nor the tragedies in the lives of the people with whom she worked. As a budding "applied" sociologist, Caroline had been bit with the sociological imagination. Throughout her life she would watch for structured inequality and work to change it.

In 1942 Caroline enrolled in the graduate program at the University of Chicago, where she met Arnold Rose, four years her junior. They were married that year. She completed her master's thesis on workers' education in the United States, 1920 to 1940, based on her experiences in West Virginia. During World War II she interrupted her graduate work to go to Washington, D.C., as an assistant economist in the Statistical Research Section of the War Labor Board.

In 1943 the newlywed Roses were hard at work on the research for *An American Dilemma*. Arnold Rose was given more and more responsibility for the project over time, ultimately being in charge of the final draft. The more backstage work of Caroline Baer Rose on this project is echoed in the life of Dorothy Swaine Thomas* and Alva Myrdal*. The work was controversial before it was published, and with Caroline as his silent partner (collaborator and editor), he was under considerable professional pressure and scrutiny (see Southern 1987, 47). The Roses were committed to a strongly worded version of the research, and like many Jews in these decades, they were personally aware of the parallels between the Jewish and black experiences of prejudice. Both were active in civil rights activities throughout their lives.

The Roses came to the University of Minnesota in 1952, where he was an associate professor, and she taught in all the nooks and crannies of a university: night school, extension, correspondence courses, branch campuses, and even an innovative introductory sociology course by telephone. Although Caroline did not choose to be out of the center ring of sociology, she was surprised that her "side shows" lasted as long as they did. She never finished her doctorate work, feeling that one doctorate was "sufficient for the two" (Aldous, 1975, 21). Nonetheless, Caroline made a mission of her work with teaching undergraduate, returning students, and working in remedial programs.

In the early years in Minnesota, Caroline and Arnold had three children (Richard, Ruth, and Dorothy), and her investment shifted to her children and their activities, volunteer work, and editing Arnold's writing. They edited several books together, and he continually acknowledged her help in his solo works. "It is appropriate, therefore, that the Arnold and Caroline B. Rose Monograph Series [administered through the American Sociological Association] bears both their names. The two of them created a shared existence. . . . Caroline once remarked that she had never found anyone else with whom she so enjoyed discussing sociology, the arts, politics, and the myriad other concerns that made their lives so full" (Aldous 1975, 21).

Caroline continued her own academic life as associate professor of sociology and chair at Federal City College from 1968 to 1970.

Helen MacGill Hughes* uses the careers of Caroline and Arnold Rose as a case study of women in academic sociology from 1925 to 1975 in her Golden Anniversary Lecture to the North Central Sociological Association (Hughes 1975b). She traces the chronology of each spouse's academic career, noting Arnold's linear climb in the profession in contrast to Caroline's lateral movement. In an obituary for Caroline, Hughes describes the pattern this way:

Her professional career took the old pattern characteristic of women in academic life. She held temporary appointments in several institutions; she lectured to soldiers at an air base; she worked on high school curricula in the Department of Education. She gave correspondence courses in sociology through the Department of Independent Study; she held night sessions in the Extension Division. And she wrote books, co-authored books, and produced articles and book reviews.

Now all these undertakings are indispensable functions of the academic world. Typically, women perform them. Whether as graduate students or as faculty wives—often as the campus relics, survivors of dispersed families or of marriages broken by discord or death—they are the availables, willingly carrying water to the elephants, year in and year out; on rarer occasions, basking in the applause and sparkle of the Big Top. Caroline served in all these capacities; she taught at the University of Minnesota for 23 years. (Hughes 1975a, 469)

Only after Arnold's death, and thus freedom from nepotism rules, was she able to serve in the department of sociology as a regular faculty member. Even without the doctorate, she was given the rank of full professor. Some faculty in the department could not tolerate the dissonance between her skills and service versus the minimal institutional recognition and rewards she had received. Being brought into the center ring did not change what Caroline did, however. She still taught the large sections of introductory sociology, served on the less prestigious committees, and had an office in the quadrant where the graduate students were located.

Hughes's metaphor of the Big Top is well chosen. People who knew her could easily imagine her short, stocky build in a circus costume; graduate students joked that she and Margaret Mead used the same clothing designer. We can imagine her "act"—keeping the plates spinning on the sticks. She runs briskly from one stick to another, saving a teetering plate from falling. She is not in the center ring, but off to the side, carrying out this remarkable trick without much applause. Caroline's career is made "cultivating the margins" (Hughes 1975b, 217).

Caroline understood exactly what she was doing with her career. Although we cannot underestimate the structural factors in academic life that limited her full participation, neither can we see her as victim. She had all those spinning plates—all those commitments. She was active in the lives of her three children, in Minnesota's Democratic-Farmer-Labor party politics, in the Girl Scouts, in the American Civil Liberties Union, and in other civic work. On campus she cofounded the Council for University Women's Progress, an organization that included faculty, staff, and students. It is consistent with Caroline's approach that she would be part of an organization that was inclusive instead of elitist in its emphasis on women's common concerns and need for support rather than status distinctions.

Vitas are scholars' representations of themselves. Looking over Caroline's short, two-page vita tells us a lot about her presentation of self. She has researched and written on many topics, she has published in a range of outlets from community newsletters to scholarly journals, she worked as a team member even though individual work is rewarded by the profession. Some of her publications are coauthored with Arnold, but several book chapters, a textbook, and an influential article in the *American Journal of Sociology* (1950) are her own.

Caroline Rose, more so than her husband, gave her spouse explicit professional credit for his help to her. Thus, in her introduction to sociology (1965) as a profession, she lists him as a consultant, a role she often provided to him as well. The second edition of *Minority Problems* (1972) was edited by Caroline several years after Arnold's death in 1968, and two-thirds of the readings were new. She kept his name as coeditor, nonetheless. This pattern of uneven attribution of credit was common for many academic couples in these times, a gendered practice where women's contributions were much less visible than their husbands'.

Under the heading "Education," she lists her doctoral work at the University of Chicago, adding: "I have never completed a dissertation, and do not hold the Ph.D." Concerning her University committee work, her vita states:"I must admit that I'm not sure what most of these committees do or what I'm doing on them, so maybe it's a waste of time instead of service to the University" (Aldous 1975, 21). This characteristic forthrightness is a pleasant change from academic vita padding.

MAJOR THEMES

Caroline had a continuing commitment to equality across racial, class, gender, and religious lines and would not tolerate unearned privilege. Her work with Arnold Rose and Gunnar Myrdal on *An American Dilemma* and her master's thesis on "Worker Education in the United States" were sociologically sound but ideologically committed products. She led a campaign to integrate a St. Louis hotel that barred blacks, but was slated as the site for the Midwest Sociological Society meeting. She would later become that society's first woman president in 1973. The society would later (1976) name its annual student paper award competition in her honor.

Within the department of sociology at the University of Minnesota, Caroline was a voice of conscience. She spoke out against sexual harassment when others were silent.

Sociologists know the importance of the mentoring process and how women, as a minority group within many professions, often are without mentors. Caroline was a vital force in helping the few women students in the early 1970s who were enrolled in graduate work. She wasn't a role model, for the students were sufficiently well socialized to know that she was not in the center ring. But she was not to be ignored. In a luncheon gathering on women and careers she bluntly stated: "You know, it's impossible to be a career sociologist by the male model and be a good mother, too."

Caroline was particularly influential in the lives of undergraduates, both men and women. She was an extremely approachable faculty member, and could resonate with the contingencies that made up the life of a returning woman student, a veteran, a full-time worker, a political activist, a religious convert, and every other variety of student that a large, heterogeneous university setting presents. After she died of cancer, a memorial fund was established as a source of loan money for returning women students who may need baby-sitting, books, or other resources to get their education. Tangible help from an exceptional mentor.

In her writing Caroline jumped from the macro to the micro and back again. Her early work on structured social inequality was not abandoned as she and Arnold became key spokespeople for the symbolic interaction perspective. She continued to work on symbolic interaction after his death, although she did not publish formal papers. Caroline was a person of intellectual breadth, a teacher, a transmitter of knowledge. Whereas Arnold pursued a more traditional and specialized form of scholarship, she continued to spin all the plates in the discipline. This eclecticism is best evident in her love for teaching introductory sociology.

Caroline brought all the spinning plates, of sociology and of personal life, into one arena in the classroom. She often said that sociology can provide a lifelong window on social processes, inform us about social change, and allow us to take the self as "other." She came as close as anyone to actually imparting the sociological imagination to the neophyte.

For example, she talked about the Girl Scouts as a formal organization, with all the elements of a Weberian bureaucracy. Thousands of students can never buy a box of cookies without thinking of the transaction as more than a one-on-one act of philanthropy.

As she lay dying at home, aware of the few visitors she had, she talked about the discomfort that others feel when confronted with a terminally ill person. She was not only sensitive to others, but also was constantly "taking the role of the other" in her daily life.

The professional contributions of Caroline Rose resemble the unsung work of the housewife: invisible and essential work that largely goes without tangible rewards. The life of Caroline Rose is measured in thousands of undergraduates who were well educated in their introduction to sociology, in acknowledgments in books and dissertations, in women who stayed in graduate school with her support, in committee work that was accomplished well and that resulted in positive changes, and in unethical or cowardly behavior that got "called on the carpet." Like many career women in the decades 1950 to 1970, Caroline Rose had a life that resembled a three-ring circus. She danced, juggled, tumbled, and bounced through her various roles. In one of her articles with Arnold, Caroline, then unaffiliated, listed herself as "Caroline Rose, Sociologist." I like thinking of Caroline Rose (and her lingering spirit) as a sociologist at large, someone who served the discipline and pursued a life path worthy of our applause.

CRITIQUES OF CAROLINE BAER ROSE

Rose's life is important for documenting the "backstage" work of women in the dark era. Most of the sociological labor produced by women during these decades remains shrouded in supposition. Hughes (1975a, 1975b), in particular, helped to keep Rose's contributions in a more prominent position. My work

(Howery 1983) provides more information, particularly on teaching style, on this remarkable woman.

America Divided (1948) and *Minority Problems* (1965) received favorable reviews in the *American Sociological Review* (see Koenig 1949; Yamamura 1966) and in the *American Journal of Sociology* (see Manheim 1950). The second edition of *Minority Problems* (1972), basically a new edition and edited by Caroline alone, was not reviewed. Of course, a second edition is less desirable to review than a first edition, but a professional opinion on Caroline's work here is lacking.

BIBLIOGRAPHY

Selected Writings by Caroline Baer Rose

1950. "Morale in a Trade Union." *American Journal of Sociology* 56 (September): 167–174.
1965. *The Study of Sociology*. Consultant, Arnold M. Rose. Columbus, OH: Charles E. Merrill.

Unpublished Writings by Caroline Baer Rose

Rose, Caroline Baer. 1943. "Worker Education in the United States." Master's thesis, University of Chicago.

Coauthored Works

Rose, Arnold M., and Caroline Baer Rose. 1948. *America Divided: Minority Group Relations in the United States*. New York: Alfred A. Knopf.
————, eds. 1965. *Minority Problems: A Textbook of Readings in Intergroup Relations*. New York: Harper & Row. 2nd. ed., New York: Harper & Row, 1972.

Studies About Caroline Baer Rose and Supplemental References

Aldous, Joan. 1975. "Caroline B. Rose." Obituary. *ASA Footnotes* (August): 21.
Howery, Carla B. 1983. "The Life Path of Caroline Baer Rose— 1913–1975." *Midwest Feminist Papers* 2: 36–41.
Hughes, Helen MacGill. 1975a. "Caroline Baer Rose, 1913–1975." *Social Problems* 22 (April): 469–470.
————. 1975b. "Women in Academic Sociology, 1925–1975." *Sociological Focus* 3 (August): 215–222.
Koenig, Samuel. 1949. "Review of *America Divided*." *American Sociological Review* 14 (June): 435–437.
Manheim, Ernest. 1950. "Review of *America Divided*." *American Journal of Sociology* 55 (January): 423–424.

Myrdal, Gunnar; with the assistance of Richard Sterner and Arnold Rose. 1944. *An American Dilemma*. New York: Harper & Brothers.

Yamamura, Douglas S. 1966. "Review of *Minority Problems: A Textbook of Readings in Intergroup Relations*." *American Sociological Review* 31 (October): 742.

CARLA B. HOWERY

ALICE S. ROSSI (1922–   )

Alice S. Rossi is a Renaissance scholar. She is a leader in several specialties within sociology and between sociology and other disciplines. Her studies of women, occupations, the family, the life course, sociobiography, and socialization bring together work and ideas from sociology, biology, history, psychology, and anthropology. Her far-ranging academic interests are matched by her influence in the wider society and within professional circles.

BIOGRAPHY

Brooklyn, New York, was a vital immigrant area when Alice Schaerr was born there on September 24, 1922. She was born and raised in a brownstone townhouse with three generations of her maternal family: "a German-Lutheran immigrant grandfather and one aunt on the street floor; two unmarried aunts on the second floor; (and) my parents and me and an unmarried uncle on the third floor" (Rossi 1983, 3). They shared their evening meals together in a communal kitchen and dining room located on the basement floor. Her mother was "shy and yielding . . . the hub of my world . . . in perpetual fear of displeasing either her father or her husband" (Rossi 1983, 5). With her daughter, however, she shared warmth and interests in food, fabric, and flowers.

Her grandfather was a socialist and carpenter who combined his political and religious ideals in his work on an Episcopal church in Manhattan. Her three aunts were lively women who shared their world with her. Her father was an experimental machinist who created machinery for scientists at the Rockefeller Institute. He was quiet but supportive of his young daughter's dreams.

This idyllic, albeit traditionally gendered, world abruptly ended with the Great Depression. The family slipped into hard times; her father began drinking more, while her mother did janitorial labor. Young Alice began scrubbing clothes and floors, escaping this dreary round of daily struggle through reading her weekly ration of five library books. A tall adolescent, she was more at home in high school than in junior high school. In high school she "edited the newspaper, served in the student senate, was president of the Poetry Club, and dared to dream of college" (Rossi 1983, 8). She did enter Brooklyn College, where she met Louis Schneider, who inspired her to switch from a major in literature to sociology.

At nineteen, a few weeks after Pearl Harbor was bombed, Alice Schaerr married a former economics teacher who was twelve years her senior. By the spring of 1942 she was an army wife, and moved between various towns in the South throughout the war years. She worked in a variety of settings, ranging from a day-care center to a prisoner-of-war camp. She "even delivered a black baby in South Carolina, when [she] volunteered to find out why [her] landlady's 'girl' did not show up for work, and found her alone in advanced labor" (Rossi 1983, 9).

After the war ended she returned to college and earned her bachelor's degree in 1947, and entered Columbia University for graduate work in sociology. After a difficult decision to divorce and "several foolish affairs" (Rossi 1983, 10), she married Peter Rossi at the age of twenty-nine. "This has been a lasting love, with sparks in the mind, shared tastes of palate and politics, a spicy difference in intellectual flair, a mutual love of hard physical work—a heady brew still potent after thirty years" (Rossi 1983, 10).

Alice Rossi worked briefly for Alex Inkeles at the Russian Research Center at Harvard, and then with Peter Rossi in a community research project at the Graduate School of Education at Harvard. Then Peter Rossi accepted a job at the University of Chicago, when Alice Rossi was pregnant with their first child. She quickly bore three children in four years in her middle and late thirties. Applying superwoman standards in her public and private life, she found herself with insomnia and neuritis misdiagnosed as arthritis. They were living in a gracious Victorian home in Chicago, but it was more picturesque than the lives of this growing family. Rossi has described this stressful time in detail (Rossi 1983, 10–11; 1973, 43—46, 72–75) elsewhere, but succinctly she resented giving up her professional work, her own income, and staying home; she became engrossed in having and being with her children, and felt socially and professionally isolated. After being fired by an anthropologist at the University of Chicago who wanted to claim her ideas and work as his own, Rossi intimately understood the problems of sex discrimination on the job.

This experience was the impetus "to rethink the functionalist sociology I had swallowed whole from Columbia" (Rossi to author, March 7, 1990). Her first feminist publication that resulted from this reanalysis of sociology was her classic article, "Equality Between the Sexes: An Immodest Proposal." She also fought back against this oppression through her work for the reform of abortion laws in Illinois (e.g., Rossi 1966), cofounding the National Organization for Women in 1966 and Sociologists for Women in Society (SWS) in 1970. Meanwhile her productivity as a scholar dramatically increased along with her national visibility. She was elected president of SWS in 1971, president of the Eastern Sociological Society in 1974, and both vice-president and president of the American Sociological Association in 1974 and 1978, respectively. In 1989 Rossi was awarded the Common Wealth Award in Sociology (Peter Rossi was similarly honored in 1985). In addition, she has received honorary degrees from Towson State College, Rutgers University, Simmons College, Goucher College, and Northwestern University.

Harriet Martineau's* foundational role in sociology was heralded by Rossi in her outstanding anthology *The Feminist Papers* (1973). When Rossi was honored with a named chair at the University of Massachusetts—Amherst, she chose, as the first occupant, to name the position the "Harriet Martineau Professor of Sociology."

In her sixties today, Rossi is planning new adventures and a return to old childhood dreams. "And so, at sixty, I feel closer to the Alice of thirteen than to the Alice of twenty or thirty. I like this new-old Alice better, too. Does anyone know of a play calling for a woman character with a purple cape and a walking cane? I feel old enough and young enough, to finally take center-stage" (Rossi 1983, 28).

MAJOR THEMES

Rossi's early work encompassed voting behavior (e.g., Rossi and Gleicher 1950), intergroup relations, the sociology of occupations, and the Soviet social system. These early writings, published primarily in the 1950s until the early 1960s, are individually of high quality, yet as a set of writings they do not carve out a special area in which Rossi was the leading intellectual. In contrast, her writings on women, parenting, the life course, and the feminist movement have been path-breaking, and they are the focus of interest here.

A major segment of Rossi's writings emerge from a blend of feminism, biography (sometimes autobiography, noted above, e.g., 1964, 1983), history, life course, and intellectual critique. This innovative approach was evident in her rediscovery of Harriet Taylor and her influence on John S. Mill (Rossi 1970b). This scholarship was brought to a new height and development in her classic anthology *The Feminist Papers: From Adams to de Beauvoir* (1973). This book presents an account of political action that combines a sociological and feminist perspective with major intellectual statements written primarily by women. Rossi's sociological text on women's theory crossed academic and popular boundaries as well as disciplinary lines in scholarship.

The linkage between the individuals and life cycle changes is increasingly a focus of Rossi's writings. Rossi integrates four bodies of thought, from distinct disciplines, in her study of adulthood: "life-span developmental psychology, sociology of age and the life course, sociology of the family, and biosocial science'' (Cheryl Ann Miller 1981, 87).

The biological basis of parenting is a controversial and compelling feature of Rossi's work over the past decade. Her ''biosocial perspective on parenting'' (Rossi 1977) emphasizes the role of endocrinology (hormones) in parenting. She italicized the following point in her argument: *''A biosocial perspective does not argue that there is a genetic determination of what men can do compared to women; rather, it suggests that the biological contributions shape what is learned, and that there are differences in the ease with which the sexes can learn certain things''* (Rossi 1977, 4). This italicized thesis and data on endocrinology, aging, and comparative parenting are examined in other writings as well (e.g., Rossi 1980b, 1983, 1984). This theme is reflected in a fascinating debate with Judith Lorber and Rose Laub Coser* in which they each critiqued the neo-Freudian view of mothering by Nancy Chodorow (Lorber, Coser, Rossi, and Chodorow 1981). Rossi stressed a more biological basis of parenting than Chodorow, a neo-Freudian, does.

In 1983, Rossi chose the theme, gender, and life course for the annual American Sociological Association meetings. She stimulated scholarship on this topic, as well as coordinated sessions and papers that resulted in an anthology (Rossi 1985). She boldly rejected all existing sociological theories on gender and parenthood as inadequate if they did not integrate biological and social constructs (Rossi 1985, 6; see also Rossi 1984). Here, as elsewhere, she supported the work of Matilda White Riley* (1985, 333–347).

Women's paid labor is analyzed by Rossi in a variety of occupations. Professional work, especially within the academy, is a hallmark of her emphasis on socialization, gender, and historical opportunities in contemporary contexts (e.g., Rossi and Calderwood 1973).

Rossi's early work on politics emerged again in her panel study of women: *Feminists in Politics: A Panel Analysis of the First National Women's Conference* (1982).

CRITIQUES OF ALICE S. ROSSI

Alice Rossi is part of a rich network of scholarship. Many authors cite her works as starting points for their own statements. A number of authors in the anthology by Martha T. Schuch Mednick, Sandra Schwartz Tabgri, and Lois Wladis Hoffman (1975), for example, cite Rossi's work on women in the professions and women as achievers. A similar pattern is found in other anthologies published on women in the past fifteen years. This pattern points to the wide scholarly audience inspired by Rossi's work, but this is different from more complex analyses of her ideas.

This more thorough extension of Rossi's work is found in that of her eminent female colleagues. For example, Matilda White Riley (e.g., 1989) and Alice Rossi (e.g., Rossi 1985) publish each other's works, sometimes share comments before publication, and apply their common ideas to the topic of aging and the life course (Rossi frequently uses Riley's ideas, noted above). Rose Laub Coser has a similar pattern (e.g., Coser 1985). Of course Rossi's comments on the work of Nancy Chodorow also fit this pattern (1981). Chodorow (Lorber et al. 1981, 5–6, 507, 511–513), however, found Rossi too biological in her interpretation of parenting, an interesting comment for a psychoanalytic sociologist.

A major interpretation of Rossi's work was done in 1981 by a group of scholars working collectively. Kathlelen S. Crittenden began the analysis explaining Rossi's biographical location and significance in sociology: Rossi's blend of "politics, passion, and personal experience." (1981, 74). Carla Howery positively examined Rossi's activism, including her writing as a form of practice. Howery notes: "Rossi's strength as an activist comes from her position on the margin" (1981, 94). This outsider status is embedded in Rossi's positions of privilege as well as her continual questioning of such power. Martha E. Thompson (1981) examined how this activism is specifically located in Rossi's feminism. Cheryl Ann Miller (1981) examined "Rossi and Adult Development," elaborating on the complexity of Rossi's thought, interdisciplinary skill, and innovativeness.

Rossi's most controversial analysis is her interpretation of biology and parenting. Martha McClintock criticized Rossi's biosocial perspective on parenting (1979; Rossi's reply, 1979), and McClintock's concerns are echoed by many other scholars (e.g., Chodorow 1981; Miller 1981).

In what may fairly be called a controversial critique, Mildred Kerlin Verhein (1981) noted that the strength of Rossi's *Feminist Papers* was the intellectual and situational blending of women's ideas. Verhein found Rossi ambivalent about "the impact of a woman's intimate relationships upon the direction, scope, and intensity of her feminist productivity. . . . Even the possibility of lesbianism mutes Rossi's insight, as does the suggestion of intimacy among the sibling set" (p. 77). Rossi's inability to link feminism, women's lives, and passion is a fatal flaw, according to Verhein.

Dale Spender draws on Rossi's historical and biographical work to generate a complex rebuilding of women's intellectual and theoretical contributions (1985, 107—118, 219–223). Spender assesses Rossi's writings on Harriet Taylor and John Stuart Mill as "a revision of history which took women's experience as its starting point" (1985, 112). Spender was inspired by Rossi's *Feminist Papers* to write *Women of Ideas—And What Men Have Done to Them* (1982; role of Rossi noted in 1985, 230). Deegan, as the editor of this volume, and Hill, as the biographer of Harriet Martineau,* frequently drew on Rossi's sociobiographies. The introductory essay in *Feminist Papers* was particularly helpful in thinking through the process of writing the introduction to this volume.

ACKNOWLEDGMENT

My thanks to Alice S. Rossi for her thoughtful and careful critique of an earlier draft of this entry. Her letter of March 7, 1990, was particularly helpful.

I assume responsibility for this final form and appreciate the entrant's difficulty in reading about herself and her summarized in an overview.

BIBLIOGRAPHY

Selected Writings by Alice S. Rossi

1964a. "Equality Between the Sexes: An Immodest Proposal." *Daedalus* 93 (Spring): 607–652.

1964b. "A Good Woman Is Hard to Find." *Trans-Action* 2 (November–December): 20–23.

1965. "Barriers to Career Choice of Engineering, Medicine, or Science Among American Women." In *Women and the Scientific Professions*, edited by A. Mattfeld and R. C. G. Van Aken, pp. 51–127. Boston: MIT Press.

1965b. "Naming Children in Middle Class Families." *American Sociological Review* 30 (August): 499–513.

1966. "Abortion Laws and Their Victims." *Trans-Action* 3 (September–October): 7–11.

1968. "Transition to Parenthood." *Journal of Marriage and the Family* 30 (February): 26–39.

1969. "Abortion and Social Change." *Dissent* 16 (July-August): 338–346.

1970a. "Sentiment and Intellect: The Story of John Stuart Mill and Harriet Taylor Mill." In *Essays on Sex Equality*, by John Stuart Mill and Harriet Taylor Mill, edited by Alice S. Rossi, pp. 11–63. Chicago: University of Chicago Press.

1970b. "Status of Women in Graduate Sociology Departments: 1958–1969." *American Sociologist* 5 (February): 1–12.

1972a. "Maternalism, Sexuality, and the New Feminism." In *Contemporary Sexual Behavior: Critical Issues in the 1970s*, edited by Joseph Zubin and John Money. pp. 145–274. Baltimore: Johns Hopkins University Press.

1972b. "Roots of Ambivalence in American Women." In *Readings on the Psychology of Women*, edited by Judith Bardwick, pp. 125–128. New York: Harper & Row.

1972c. "Family Development in a Changing World." *American Journal of Psychiatry* 128 (March): 1057–1066.

1977. "A Biosocial Perspective on Parenting." *Daedalus* 106 (Spring): 1–31.

1979. "Reply by Alice Rossi to 'Considering' A Biosocial Perspective on Parenting." *Signs* 4 (Summer): 712–713.

1980a. "Aging and Parenthood in the Middle Years." In *Life Span Development and Behavior*, vol. 3, edited by P. B. Bates and Orville G. Brim, Jr., pp. 137–205. New York: Academic Press.

1980b. "Life Span Theories and Women's Lives." *Signs* 6 (Autumn): 4–32.

1982. *Feminists in Politics: A Panel Analysis of the First National Women's Conference.* New York: Academic Press.

1983. *Seasons of a Woman's Life.* Amherst, MA: Hamilton Newell.

1984. "Gender and Parenthood." *American Sociological Review* 49 (February): 499–513.

1988. "Growing Up and Older in Sociology, 1940–1990." In *Social Change and the Life Course*, edited by Matilda White Riley, pp. 43–64. Newbury Park, CA: Sage.

1973. *The Feminist Papers: From Adams to de Beauvoir.* New York: Columbia University

Press. Reprinted, New York: Bantam Books, 1974; republished, Boston: Northeastern University Press, 1988.

1985. *Gender and the Life Course*. An American Sociological Association Presidential Volume. New York: Aldine.

Coauthored Works

Lorber, Judith, Rose Laub Coser, Alice S. Rossi, and Nancy Chodorow. 1981. "On *The Reproduction of Mothering*: A Methodological Debate." *Signs* 6 (Spring): 482–514.

Rossi, Alice S., and Ann Calderwood, eds. 1973. *Academic Women on the Move*. New York: Russell Sage Foundation.

Rossi, Alice S. ("Kitt"), and David Gleicher. 1950. "Determinants of Voting Behavior." *Public Opinion Quarterly* 14 (Fall): 395–412.

Rossi, Alice S., Jerome Kagan, and Tamara K. Hareven, eds. 1978. *The Family*. New York: W. W. Norton.

Rossi, Alice S., and Robert K. Merton. 1950. "Contributions to the Theory of Reference Group Behavior." In *Continuities in Social Research*, edited by Robert K. Merton and Paul F. Lazarsfeld, pp. 40–105. Glencoe, IL: The Free Press.

Rossi, Peter E., and Alice S. Rossi. 1977. "Body Time and Social Time: Mood Patterns by Menstrual Cycle Phase and Day of Week." *Social Science Research* 6 (December): 273–308.

Rossi, Peter H., and Alice S. Rossi. 1957. "Background and Consequences of Parochial School Education." *Harvard Educational Review* (Summer 1957):

Studies About Alice S. Rossi and Supplemental References

Bermant, Gordon, 1972. "Sisterhood Is Beautiful." *Psychology Today* 6 (August): 40–46, 72, 74–75.

Chodorow, Nancy. 1978. *The Reproduction of Mothering: Psychoanalysis and the Sociology of Gender*. Berkeley: University of California Press.

Crittenden, Kathlelen S. 1981. "Why Alice Rossi?" In *Midwest Feminist Papers, No. 2*, edited by Martha E. Thompson and Mary Jo Deegan, pp. 73–77. Chicago: Northeastern Illinois University Printing Office.

Howery, Carla. 1981. "Alice Rossi as an Activist Group of One." In *Midwest Feminist Papers, No. 2*, edited by Martha E. Thompson and Mary Jo Deegan, pp. 92–96. Chicago: Northeastern Illinois University Printing Office.

Mednick, Martha T. Schuch, Sandra Schwartz Tabgri, and Lois Wladis Hoffman, eds. 1975. *Women and Achievement: Social and Motivational Analyses*. Washington, D.C.: Hemisphere.

McClintock, Martha. 1979. "Considering 'A Biosocial Perspective on Parenting.' " *Signs* 4 (Summer): 703–710.

Miller, Baila. 1981. "Bringing Baby Back In: Where Do We Put the Body?" In *Midwest Feminist Papers, No. 2*, edited by Martha E. Thompson and Mary Jo Deegan, pp. 84–87. Chicago: Northeastern Illinois University Printing Office.

Miller, Cheryl Ann. 1981. "Rossi and Adult Development." In *Midwest Feminist Papers, No. 2*, edited by Martha E. Thompson and Mary Jo Deegan, pp. 87–91. Chicago: Northeastern Illinois University Printing Office.

Spender, Dale. 1982. *Women of Ideas—And What Men Have Done to Them*. London: Routledge & Kegan Paul,

————. 1985. "Can Men Qualify? Alice Rossi's Political Is Personal." In *For the Record: The Making and Meaning of Feminist Knowledge*, by D. Spender, pp. 107–118. London: The Women's Press.

Thompson Martha E. 1981. "Wrestling with Feminism." In *Midwest Feminist Papers, No. 2*, edited by Martha E. Thompson and Mary Jo Deegan, pp. 79–83. Chicago: Northeastern Illinois University Printing Office.

Verhein, Mildred Kerlin. 1981. "The Feminist Papers : An Interpretive Note." In *Midwest Feminist Papers, No. 2.*, edited by Martha E. Thompson and Mary Jo Deegan, pp. 77–79. Chicago: Northeastern Illinois University Printing Office.

MARY JO DEEGAN AND MICHAEL R. HILL

ETHEL SHANAS (1914–   )

Ethel Shanas is noted for her studies in gerontology, the sociology of aging, and the sociology of health care. She has conducted a variety of research projects in these fields, and in related areas: family sociology, intergenerational relations, retirement, and demography. After a long period of service at the University of Chicago, she was appointed a full professor in 1965 at the University of Illinois at Chicago, where she held appointments in the department of sociology and in the School of Public Health at the University of Illinois Medical Center. She became professor emerita in 1982 and continues to write and consult in her specialty areas.

BIOGRAPHY

Ethel Shanas was born in Chicago on September 6, 1914. She was the daughter of Alex Shanas and Rebecca Rich, who had three sons and two daughters; her parents also raised two foster children. Ethel attended the public schools in Chicago, and because of her scholastic achievements, her parents and teachers encouraged her to continue her education. She attended a local junior college, and in her junior year she transferred to the University of Chicago, which awarded her three degrees: bachelor's, 1935; master's, 1937; and a doctorate, 1949. When she entered the University of Chicago, she aspired to a career as a social worker because she thought it was a way to earn a living during the depths of the world economic depression. Her undergraduate adviser incorrectly told her that there was no undergraduate major in social work and suggested that she major in sociology. Shanas followed the adviser's suggestion and enrolled for her first course in sociology, taught by Herbert Blumer, one of the most stimulating scholars of the era. Blumer's intellectual appeal stemmed from his primary interest in social psychology, which also was Shanas's initial interest. He quickly recognized Shanas's intellectual qualities, and they became close friends and colleagues for more than half a century.

Ethel Shanas was elected to Phi Beta Kappa with an almost straight A average. One exception was a course in economics, in which she was disappointed to receive a B. (The only student in the class to receive an A was Paul A. Samuelson, who, in 1970, received the second Nobel Prize in Economic Science.)

Shanas's academic achievements and her deep interest in sociology stimulated her to continue her education in sociology at the University of Chicago. She applied for a graduate fellowship and was interviewed by the chairman of the department, Ellsworth Faris. She tried to explain her reasons for continuing her education. Faris ended the interview by saying, "Little girl, why don't you go home and get married!" Despite this rebuff, she went on to become one of the department's outstanding graduate students.

Shanas did not regard women's choices as either getting an education or getting married, for she intended to succeed in both roles. On May 17, 1940, she married a young chemist, Lester J. Perlman (called Steve by family and friends). They have one child, Michael Stephen, born in 1945. Ethel Shanas and her husband had an informal understanding that he would provide the support for her to obtain her graduate education in sociology, and then he would return to continue his graduate work in chemistry and she would provide economic support. The Perlman educational plan was changed, however, because of World War II. Her husband became a navy officer, and their son was born in Annapolis. After the war Steve took a position with a small company as a chemist. In time the small company became part of a large company, and he ultimately became an executive and never returned to graduate work.

During her undergraduate days Ethel Shanas's research and writing talents were recognized early, and she became a research assistant on various projects. She continued this pattern of working on various research studies with her former teachers, who soon became her colleagues. During the years 1943–1944 she was chief, Research and Statistics, Venereal Disease Control Project, Health Department of the city of Chicago. From 1947 through 1952 she was research associate and instructor for the Committee on Human Development at the University of Chicago. During these years she began her research in the sociology of aging, and published several articles with Robert J. Havighurst. She published her first article on the personal adjustment of people on old-age assistance in Volume 5 of the *Journal of Gerontology*.

Shanas's career illustrates the difficulty experienced by women in securing a tenured position at the University of Chicago. After five years as an instructor she worked for the city of Chicago from 1952 to 1953 as senior analyst, Office of the Housing and Redevelopment Coordinator. From 1954 to 1956 she was a lecturer in social science at the University of Illinois at Chicago. She returned to the University of Chicago, and from 1956 to 1961 she was a senior study director, National Opinion Research Center, and research associate (associate professor), department of sociology. Then from 1961 to 1965 she held the position of research associate (associate professor) in both the department of sociology and the Committee on Human Development. The University of Chicago used the parenthetical title of (associate professor) to indicate that a person had a title but not a tenured budgetary position. After many years of outstanding service at the University of Chicago, where she worked closely with a number of senior professors, Shanas left her alma mater and moved across town to the University of Illinois at Chicago and immediately was appointed full professor in 1965. Shanas's experience at the University of Chicago was rather common for other women sociologists. In 1987 there was only one tenured woman in the sociology department and two female assistant professors among twenty-three faculty members.

The list of her professional activities for more than a quarter of a century covers three pages of single-spaced type. Here I can offer only a sample of her many important positions in national and international professional and policy-shaping organizations. Shanas was elected president of the Gerontological Society of America in 1974, and from 1963 to 1969 she was its secretary. She also served on a number of committees. From 1965 to 1972 she was a member of the Executive Committee of the International Association of Gerontology. She also held the office of vice-president of the Research Committee on Aging of the International Sociological Association from 1975 to 1981, and was chair of the section on aging of the American Sociological Association in 1986. Her service to various government agencies is long and illustrious: the United Nations, World Health Organization, International Center of Social Gerontology (Paris), U.S. National Committee on Vital and Health Statistics, National Center for Health Statistics, National Heart-Lung Institute, National Institute on Aging, National Institute of Child Health and Human Development, Social Security Administration, U.S. Department of Labor, U.S. Senate and House of Representatives as an expert witness, and the White House Conference on Aging (1961, 1971, 1981).

She was elected to the presidency of the Illinois Sociological Society and also the Midwest Sociological Society. Shanas has served on many boards and committees for the city of Chicago and for various health and public service organizations in the Midwest and abroad. She has been an editor or advisory editor to such professional journals as *Sociological Quarterly*, *The Gerontologist*, *Journal of Health and Social Behavior*, and *The Journal of Gerontology*.

Shanas is a fellow of the American Sociological Association and of the Gerontological Society of America. Her honors include the Keston Memorial Lectureship, University of Southern California (1972); the Kleemeier Award, Gerontological Society of America (1977); the Burgess Award, National Council on Family Relations (1978); the Brookdale Award, Gerontological Society of America (1981); and the Distinguished Scholar Award, Section on Aging, American Sociological Association (1987). She was awarded an honorary doctor of humane letters degree by Hunter College, City University of New York, in 1985, and her major honor was election to the Institute of Medicine, National Academy of Science, 1979. Shanas has been an invited lecturer at more than thirty universities in the United States and in a number of foreign countries.

In summary, the professional activities, awards, and honors mark a most distinguished lifetime of professional achievement in sociology and gerontology and in the related academic, public service, and policy fields.

MAJOR THEMES

The continuity and longevity of Shanas's academic, professional, and public services parallel her many publications. She is the author, coauthor, or editor of eight books, four monographs, and dozens of articles in refereed journals and chapters in books. The sheer number of publications is matched by the diversity and breadth of her intellectual interests.

Ethel Shanas is a prototype of the twentieth-century social scientist, for her career is marked by a high degree of team work. Her early research was collaborative with her teachers and mentors at the University of Chicago, and through the years a high degree of collaboration has marked her research activities and publications. The years of apprenticeship served Shanas and others very well, and created a cadre of sociologists who were trained in empirical research in both qualitative (ethnographic) and quantitative sociological methods.

After she earned her bachelor's degree, Ethel Shanas spent most of the next thirty years at the University of Chicago. Her career reflects three characteristics of the university: (1) a broad educational tradition, represented by the scope and diversity of her professional interests; (2) a strong commitment to sociology as a social science and to the employment of empirical research methods; and (3) a dual emphasis on investigating social problems informed by the theoretical perspectives of sociology. The scope of her work is shown by the fact that her first book in 1942 was a study of recreation and delinquency. In the same year she wrote an important critique of Dodd's *Dimensions of Society*, a book that was one of the first attempts to create a mathematical approach to the study of society.

Perhaps Shanas's most important research project is the unique cross-national study of the elderly in Britain, Denmark, and the United States. The resulting book, *Old People in Three Industrial Societies* (1968) has six coauthors. Shanas was the major coordinator of the three research teams that carried out comparable studies of the living conditions and behavior of elderly people. Conducting a national sample survey of approximately 2,500 persons in one country is a complex undertaking, but organizing a team of researchers in three countries is much more difficult. They used the same sampling procedures, an interview guide that is strictly comparative, and also used the same analytical techniques on three complex data sets. To coordinate such a huge undertaking requires a rare combination of talents: diplomacy, tact, firmness, and persistence to guide the work to completion.

Old People in Three Industrial Societies has a theoretical framework developed by the several authors that focuses on one persistent and important question: "Are old people integrated into society or are they separated from it?" (p. 3). This broad question of integration and segregation can take three forms: (1) historical changes in the attitudes, roles, and relations of the elderly; (2) individual aging through the life span involving engagement and disengagement; (3) the relation between the generations—young and old, particularly within the family.

The broad results are somewhat surprising: people over age sixty-five in industrial societies are integrated more strongly into their society than usually is assumed both by the general public and by many of the aged. The authors state this clearly and succinctly: "Most old people are fairly securely knotted into the social structure. Physical activity is largely self-sustaining. Integration with the family and local community is maintained by the network of personal or 'privatized' relationships, based on reciprocity, common interest, inculcated loyalties, and affection" (p. 425). The authors add, however, that there are major problems to be observed among some elderly; such as poverty, isolation, and lack of adequate care.

Another important multidisciplinary enterprise in which Shanas played a major role was as coeditor of the 1976 and 1985 editions of the *Handbook of Aging and the Social Sciences*. In both *Handbooks* Shanas and Maddox coauthored the chapters on health, health resources, and the utilization of care. They demonstrated that health is the major variable in the subjective well-being of older adults. Furthermore, the differentials in morbidity and mortality over the life course are related to age, gender, ethnicity, and, significantly, socioeconomic status. Still individual differences in health behavior and in morbidity and mortality rates exist. Shanas's longtime interest in health and related behaviors and social characteristics needs to be stressed.

The most recent publication in which she had a role is the important monograph *The Aging Population in the Twenty-first Century: Statistics for Health Policy* (edited by Gilford 1988). It provides a broad and detailed review of the social, economic, and demographic changes among the elderly and summarizes valuable statistical data, sources, and limitations on such topics as health transitions, health promotion, the compression of mortality, long-term care, and health services utilization.

One of Shanas's major contributions to sociology is her linking of traditional areas of study. For example, her early paper "Family Responsibility and the Health of Older People" (1960) showed how families are involved in the health situation of their members. Other linkages are shown in her paper on "Living Arrangements of Older People in the United States" (1961) and in "Family Help Patterns and Social Class in Three Countries" (1967).

Shanas's interest in work and retirement is noted in the three-country study for which she wrote the chapter on the meaning of work. Her paper "Health and Adjustment in Retirement" (1970) links together her research on health and its importance to adjustment to retirement. A stimulating paper focusing on retirement as a social process is in the book edited by Frances Carp (1972), in which Shanas stresses retirement as a social process consisting of substitution and accommodation. Shanas sees the individual adjustment to retirement "as dependent on the individual's accommodation to these life changes" (p. 235).

Shanas served the feminist cause by being a role model to women through her many accomplishments in a largely male world. She was trained in a typical sexist department of sociology at a time when it was considered "natural" for women to use their intellectual talents as research associates. She recognized that there was discrimination against women and knew that she had to work harder and perhaps be better than most men in the field to succeed.

Shanas readily acknowledges that she never could have reached her high level of accomplishment without the total support of her husband of almost fifty years. Although he was a busy corporation executive himself, he was able to manage the household responsibilities during her frequent trips to Washington and to countries throughout the world for research collaboration or conferences. He was proud of her accomplishments, and she, in turn, was fully supportive of his demanding schedule and success in corporate America.

CRITIQUES OF ETHEL SHANAS

Formal criticisms of her writings are limited. There is wide recognition of Shanas's work, as demonstrated by the many awards she has received. *Old People in Three Industrial Societies* (Shanas, Townsend, Wedderburn, et al. 1968) is a landmark in its field. When Margret Dieck (1984), a German social scientist, reviewed and evaluated thirty cross-national studies, she concluded that the Shanas et al. book was still the outstanding study of cross-national aging because of its rigor and strict research comparability.

Shanas's achievements and her world recognition as an outstanding sociologist and gerontologist occurred in a climate less supportive to women scholars than exists today. But her quiet dedication, talents, focus, and perseverance enabled her to combine career, marriage, and motherhood in ways that are a model for women of any generation.

BIBLIOGRAPHY

Selected Writings by Ethel Shanas

1942a. *Recreation and Delinquency: A Study of Five Selected Chicago Communities.* Chicago: Chicago Recreation Commission.

1942b. "A Critique of Dodd's *Dimensions of Society.*" *American Journal of Sociology* 48 (September): 214–230.

1945. "The *American Journal of Sociology* Through Fifty Years." *American Journal of Sociology* 50 (May): 522–533.

1958. "Facts Versus Stereotypes: The Cornell Study of Occupational Retirement." *Journal of Social Issues* 14, no. 2: 61–62.

1960a. "How Sick Are Older People?" *Journal of the American Medical Association* 172 (January 9): 169–170.

1960b. "Family Responsibility and the Health of Older People." *Journal of Gerontology* 15 (October): 408–411.

1961. "Living Arrangements of Older People in the United States." *The Gerontologist* 1 (March): 27–29.

1962. *The Health of Older People: A Social Survey*. Cambridge, MA: Harvard University Press.

1963. "National Surveys of Older People in the United States." In *Processes of Aging: Social and Psychological Perspectives*, vol. 2, edited by Richard H. Williams, C. Tibbitts, and W. Donahue, pp. 9–24. New York: Atherton.

1965. "Health Care and Health Services for the Aged." *The Gerontologist* 5 (December): 240, 276.

1967a. "Family Help Patterns and Social Class in Three Countries." *Journal of Marriage and the Family* 29 (May): 257–266.

1967b. "Old People and Illness: Will Medicare Make a Difference?" *New York State Journal of Medicine* 67 (December 15): 3205–3208.

1968. "A Note on Restriction of Life Space: Attitudes of Age Cohorts." *Journal of Health and Social Behavior* 9 (March): 86–90.

1969. "Sociological Factors in Aging Significant to the Clinician." *Journal of the American Geriatrics Society* 17 (March): 284–288. Discussion: 289–291.

1970a. "Health and Adjustment in Retirement." *The Gerontologist* 10 (Spring, Pt 2): 19–21.

1970b. "Aging and Life Space in Poland and the United States." *Journal of Health and Social Behavior* 11 (September): 183–190.

1971a. "Measuring the Home Health Needs of the Aged in Five Countries." *Journal of Gerontology* 26 (January): 37–40.

1971b. "Sociology of Aging and the Aged." *Sociological Quarterly* 12 (Spring): 159–176.

1972. "Adjustment to Retirement: Substitution or Accommodation?" In *Retirement*, edited by Frances M. Carp, pp. 219–243. New York: Behavioral Publications.

1973. "Family-Kin Networks and Aging in Cross-Cultural Perspectives." *Journal of Marriage and the Family* 35 (August): 505–511.

1974. "Health Status of Older People: Cross-National Implications." *American Journal of Public Health* 64 (March): 261–264.

1977. "Living Arrangements and Housing of Older People." In *Behavior Adaptation in Late Life*, edited by Ewald W. Busse and E. Pfeiffer, pp. 111–129. 2nd ed. Boston: Little, Brown.

1979a. "Social Myth as Hypothesis: The Case of the Family Relations of Old People." *The Gerontologist* 19, no 1: 3–9.

1979b. "The Family as a Social Support System in Old Age." *The Gerontologist* 19, no. 2: 169–174.

1980. "Old People and Their Families: The New Pioneers." *Journal of Marriage and the Family* 42 (February): 9–15.

1981. "Social Research on Aging and the Aged: Where Are We Now?" *Mount Sinai Journal of Medicine* 48 (November–December): 552–556.

1984. "Old Parents and Middle-aged Children: The Four- and Five-Generation Family." *Journal of Geriatric Psychiatry* 17, no. 1: 7–19.

1984. "Cooperative Socio-Medical Studies of the Elderly." *American Journal of Public Health* 74 (November): 1196–1197.

Unpublished Writings by Ethel Shanas

1937. "The Nature and Manipulation of Crowds." Master's thesis, Department of Sociology, University of Chicago.
1949. "The Personal Adjustment of Recipients of Old Age Assistance: With Special Consideration of the Methodology of Questionnaire Studies of Older People." Ph.D. diss., Department of Sociology, University of Chicago.
1978. "Final Report. National Survey of the Aged." A report to the Administration on Aging. Typescript.

Coauthored Works

Binstock, Robert H., and Ethel Shanas., eds. 1976. *Handbook of Aging and the Social Sciences*. New York: Van Nostrand Reinhold. 2nd ed., 1985.
Fogel, Robert W., Elaine Hatfield, Sara B. Kiesler, and Ethel Shanas, eds. 1981. *Aging: Stability and Change in the Family*. New York: Academic Press.
Havighurst, Robert J., and Ethel Shanas. 1953. "Retirement and the Professional Worker." *Journal of Gerontology* 8 (January): 81–85.
Jaffe, A. J., and Ethel Shanas. 1939. "Economic Differentials in the Probability of Insanity." *American Journal of Sociology* 44 (January): 534–539.
Shanas, Ethel, and Phillip M. Hauser. 1974. "Zero Population Growth and the Family Life of Old People." *Journal of Social Issues* 30, no. 4: 79–92.
Shanas, Ethel, and George L. Maddox. 1976. "Aging and the Organization of Health Resources." In *Handbook of Aging and the Social Sciences*, edited by Robert H. Binstock and Ethel Shanas, pp. 592–618. New York: Van Nostrand Reinhold.
———. 1985. "Health, Health Resources, and the Utilization of Care." In *Handbook of Aging and the Social Sciences*, edited by Robert H. Binstock and Ethel Shanas, pp. 697–726. 2nd ed. New York: Van Nostrand Reinhold.
Shanas, Ethel, and John Madge, eds. 1968. *Methodological Problems in Cross-National Studies in Aging*. Interdisciplinary Topics in Gerontology, Vol. 2. Basel: Karger.
Shanas, Ethel, and Gordon F. Streib, eds. 1965. *Social Structure and the Family: Generational Relations*. Englewood Cliffs, NJ: Prentice-Hall.
Shanas, Ethel, and Marvin B. Sussman, eds. 1977. *Family, Bureaucracy, and the Elderly*. Durham, NC: Duke University Press.
———. 1981. "The Family in Later Life: Social Structure and Social Policy." In *Aging, Stability and Change in the Family*, edited by Robert W. Fogel, E. Hatfield, S. B. Kiesler, and Ethel Shanas, pp. 211–231. New York: Academic Press.
Shanas, Ethel, Peter Townsend, D. Wedderburn, H. Friis, P. Milhoj, and J. Stehouwer. 1968. *Old People in Three Industrial Societies*. New York: Atherton.

Studies About Ethel Shanas and Supplemental References

Dieck, M. 1984. *Cross-National Research and Intergenerational Comparative Research in Gerontology: A Preliminary Inventory*. Berlin: Deutsches Zentrum fur Altersfragen.

Gilford, Dorothy M., ed. 1988. *The Aging Population in the Twenty-First Century: Statistics for Health Policy*. Washington, DC: National Academy Press.

Unpublished Material

Streib, Gordon F. Conversations with Ethel Shanas, extending over a period of several years.
———. 1988. Interview with Ethel Shanas.

GORDON STREIB

DOROTHY E. SMITH (1926–   )

Dorothy E. Smith is the most widely recognized feminist theorist in sociology today. Her meticulous arguments emerge from a blend of theoretical roots and the practices performed by feminists in everyday life. Smith's focus on the everyday world and women's lived experience in an economic and politically disadvantaged status links micro and macro levels of social thought and action. The "personal is political" throughout her analyses.

BIOGRAPHY

"Dorothy E. Smith presents a fascinating study for the biographer: a sociologist who insists on the social locatedness of knowledge, she is remarkably indirect in reference to her own personal life" (Lengermann and Niebbrugge-Brantley, 1988, 308). Given this meager information, only a sketch of her biographical data is available. She was born in Great Britain in 1926. She attended the London School of Economics, and in 1955 she earned her bachelor's degree in sociology with a major specialization in social anthropology (1st Class Honours) from the University of London. In 1963 she earned her doctorate in sociology from the University of California at Berkeley. During these years her life was filled with major life changes, and sometimes chaos: when she married, immigrated to Canada, bore children, divorced, and filled the best jobs she could find (Smith 1979, 151).

Her employment in sociology began with a research position at Berkeley, followed by a lectureship at Berkeley, another lectureship at the University of Essex, Colchester, England, and then a position as associate to full professor in sociology at the University of British Columbia. Since 1977 she has been professor of sociology in education at the Ontario Institute for Studies in Education in Toronto, Canada (Lengermann and Niebbrugge-Brantley 1988, 308). In 1983 she was the Kreeger-Wolf Professor at Northwestern University, where, she writes, her longtime friend Arlene Kaplan Daniels "sustained me in more ways than one" (Smith 1987, 11).

She has been active in the Canadian Sociology and Anthropology Association, the Canadian Sociology Association, and on editorial boards for scholarly journals. She also has served as a member of the advisory committee of *Ms*. magazine.

The feminist movement is incorporated in her everyday life, her professional writings, and pedagogy. This enterprise is fraught with problems that she discusses as "the problem of institutional capture." To avoid such an institutional pattern, she worked with other women to establish an independent research center for women. A number of women-organized projects ensued, including workshops, broadsheets, a conference, and locally conceptualized and controlled research. "But a research center organized in such a way could not get funding" (Smith 1987, 216). Smith and other women worked in Toronto to build a Wollstonecraft Research Group for studies for women in education. This project also foundered for lack of money. The increasingly subtle ways to prevent government sponsorship of such community-organized work used bureaucratization, class fragmentation, and ideological domination to subvert women-controlled research.

Despite institutional constraints, Smith has worked to train a feminist cohort of scholars who are beginning to complete their doctoral training.

MAJOR THEMES

Feminist theory is the mainspring of Smith's corpus. It crosses many boundaries established in patriarchal theories. Marxism, feminism, and phenomenology inform her thought instead of being interpreted as separate, if not antagonistic, schools. Smith's work transcends the limits of patriarchal sociology by beginning with critiques of sexist categories of thought, practice, and performance in the discipline (e.g., 1974a, 1974b, 1977a). Her earliest work begins with the dual focus on the social construction of social theories and a call for an analysis of women's everyday life, free of the encumbering biases of everyday and professional constructs.

She writes about what she calls an "insider's sociology," which describes the standpoint of women in the actualities of their everyday lives. In a series of papers collected and extended in her *The Everyday World as Problematic* (1987) she pursues a line of inquiry raising critical issues for sociology from women's standpoint, as she defines it. From this standpoint, things are always seen in perspective: there is not an archimedian point from which society can be objectively examined. Rather than treating this as invalidating any claim to objective knowledge, Smith argues that the standpoint of women shows the way of doing sociology that explores society as it looks from where women are. In other research she looks at objective knowledge from women's standpoint, showing how it comes into view as socially organized practices integral to patriarchal relations of ruling.

Her study of the sociology of knowledge also is applied to psychological and psychiatric labels. Her first book (Smith and David 1975) juxtaposed women's experience of mental illness with powers and practices of psychiatry. Thus the overwhelmingly accepted "facts" that women are twice as likely as men to be labeled mentally ill, hospitalized, and medicated for mental disturbance are traceable to the definitions of mental illness. Because these studies of "nonorganic" mental illness define the categories used to determine statistical patterns, men's most common mental illness, organic degeneration caused by severe alcoholism, is omitted from analysis (Smith 1975a). Later she subjects the social construction of self-killing as "suicide" to textual analysis, and explores "the encoding process" and psychiatric "interpretive schema" involved in the making of psychiatric case histories. The female subject's meaning and experience are transformed in the objectification of self-killing as a "social fact." Smith analyzes the distancing and distorting practices involved in such objectification in an analysis of a narrative of Virginia Woolf's last months of life before her suicide in 1941 (Smith 1983). Her feminist analysis and studies of the practices of objectification are brought together in her works on *The Conceptual Practices of Power: A Feminist Sociology of Knowledge* (1990a) and *Texts, Facts, and Femininity: Exploring the Relations of Ruling* (1990b).

She has written a series of Marxist-feminist analyses, beginning with her paper on "Women, the Family, and Corporate Capitalism" (1975d). Her insight into the work of self-presentation that is done by mothers and wives in the interests of corporate capitalism is an innovative combination of everyday life and its intersection with international financial and political structures. The clearest articulation of her position is her small pamphlet on the subject, published in 1977(b). In a preliminary exploration of the method she later developed in *The Everyday World as Problematic* (1987), she showed how the lives of Canadian farm wives could be understood in the context of the changing political economy of the Canadian farm (1977). These women were potentially both more restricted as drudges and exhausted childbearers and less restricted as self-employed workers of the land than either the male working class or the male farmer. Later she extended traditional Marxist analysis in a study of the relations of women, class, and family and explored the significance of masculinist ideology for sustaining the apparatus of ruling in contemporary capitalism (1988). More recently she has written critically of the masculinist presuppositions built into contemporary political economy (1989).

CRITIQUES OF DOROTHY E. SMITH

Sylvia M. Hale (1988) has written a stunning analysis of male knowledge about Indian women in purdah and paid employment. Using Smith's perspective on patriarchal research methods and "commodity fetishism" of concepts, Hale sweepingly shows how male-based knowledge was absolutely inaccurate in predicting the behavior of women purdah. For example, the sociological ideology predicted that these women would be unwilling to work in the marketplace because of sexual innuendo, harassment, and gossip. Such barriers did exist to a considerably smaller degree than expected, but they were counteracted by even stronger support and understanding for such work and its generation of income. Hale also analyzes feminist sociology, including Smith's, in her analysis of controversies in sociology (1990).

Smith's centrality in sociological theory is discussed by Patricia Madoo Lengermann and Jill Niebbrugge-Brantley in their chapter on "Contemporary Feminist Theory" in George Ritzer's textbook on contemporary theory (1988). Lengermann and Niebbrugge-Brantley evaluate Smith's theory as the most important one for fundamentally reorienting and reconceptualizing sociology and its practice. Sandra Harding discusses Smith as one of "the standpoint theorists" in her *The Science Question in Feminism* (1986). Alison Jagger's *Feminist Politics and Human Nature* (1983) similarly contains useful references to Smith and her relation to other feminist scholars.

Marxist scholars have critiqued Smith's stand on the relation between materialism and idealism. Thus Veronica Schild, in her master's thesis "The Eclipse of Criticalness in Marxist Social Science: Habermas's and Smith's Analysis" (1982), places these two theorists in a broader context of Marxist criticism. Pradeep Bandyopadhyay (1974) also critiqued Smith's "The Ideological Practice of Sociology" from a Marxist perspective. Bandyopadhyay sees a contradiction in Smith's work: if the objective methodology of sociology is rejected, then the possibility of achieving consensus is undermined. Smith's emphasis on the sociology of knowledge is counter to Marx's materialist basis for behavior and meaning, thereby invalidating the use of his concepts in an analysis of the power of words.

A number of feminist scholars have completed their doctoral training under Smith's guidance, and they are applying her perspective to a range of issues on the cutting edge of feminist epistemology. Adele Mueller (1987) has explored the conceptual practices structuring professional perspectives on Third World women. Gillian Walker (in press) has traced the evolution and significance of state control for the concept of family violence. Marie Campbell has examined the "document-based" management of nursing as a form of administrative control over nurses (1984). Ann Manicom (1988) has analyzed the class relations underlying the organization of teachers' labor. Finally, Marilee Reimer (1988) has shown how job descriptions and evaluations fashion gender hierarchies in public administration. This body of work greatly expands the parameters of Smith's epistemology and empirical basis.

Smith's integral role in feminist theory is seen in half the articles published in a special issue of *The American Sociologist* on "Feminist Scholarship in Sociology" (1989). A beginning critique of Smith also is visible in Joey

Sprague's (1989) review of *The Everyday World as Problematic* (Smith 1987). Sprague criticizes some of Smith's jargon and discussion of old issues. Overall, however, Sprague found that Smith had "significantly advanced the conversation about . . . feminist methodology" (p. 645). My own work is imbued with the framework developed by Smith. An example of this practice is given in the introduction to this biobibliography.

Dorothy Smith's influence permeates a wide range of topics with rapidly expanding alterations of the thought and practice of the sociological enterprise.

ACKNOWLEDGMENT

My thanks to Dorothy E. Smith for her clarification of issues relevant to her work in both a telephone conversation in February 1990 and a detailed letter in March 1990.

BIBLIOGRAPHY

Selected Writings by Dorothy E. Smith

1974a. "Women's Perspective as a Radical Critique of Sociology." *Sociological Inquiry* 44, no. 1: 7–13.

1974b. "The Ideological Practice of Sociology." *Catalyst* 8 (Winter): 39–54.

1974c. "The Social Construction of Documentary Reality." *Social Inquiry* 44, no. 4: 257–268.

1975a. "The Statistics on Mental Illness: What They Will Not Tell Us About Women and Why." In *Women Look at Psychiatry*, edited by Dorothy E. Smith and Sarah J. David, pp. 73–119. Vancouver: Press Gang.

1975b. "Women and Psychiatry." In *Women Look at Psychiatry*, edited by Dorothy E. Smith and Sarah J. David, pp. 1–19. Vancouver: Press Gang.

1975c. "An Analysis of Ideological Structures and How Women Are Excluded." *Canadian Review of Sociology and Anthropology* 12 (November): 353–369.

1975d. "Women, the Family, and Corporate Capitalism." *Berkeley Journal of Sociology* 20: 55–90.

1975e. "What It Might Mean to Do a Canadian Sociology: The Everyday World as Problematic." *Canadian Journal of Sociology* 1, no. 3: 363–376.

1977a. "Some Implications for a Sociology of Women." In *Woman in a Man-made World*, edited by Nona Glazer and Helen Y. Waehrer, pp. 15–39. Chicago: McNally.

1977b. *Feminism and Marxism—A Place to Begin, A Way to Go.* Vancouver: New Star Books.

1978. "A Peculiar Eclipsing: Women's Exclusion from Man's Culture." *Women's Studies International Quarterly* 1, no. 4: 281–296.

1979. "A Sociology for Women." In *The Prism of Sex: Essays in the Sociology of Knowledge*, edited by Julia A. Sherman and Evelyn Torton Beck, pp. 135–87. Madison: University of Wisconsin Press.

1981. "On Sociological Description: A Method from Marx." *Human Studies* 4 (October–December): 313–337.

1983. "No One Commits Suicide: Textual Analyses of Ideological Practices." *Human Studies* 6 (October–December): 309–359.

1984. "Textually Mediated Social Organization." *International Social Science Journal* 36 (Fall): 59–75.

1987. *The Everyday World As Problematic: A Feminist Sociology*. Boston: Northeastern University Press.

1988. "The Deep Structure of Gender Antithesis: Another View of Capitalism and Patriarchy." In *A Feminist Ethic for Social Science Research*, edited by the Nebraska Sociological Feminist Collective, pp. 23–36. Lewiston, NY: Edwin Mellen.

1989. "Feminist Reflections on Political Economy." *Studies in Political Economy* 30 (Autumn): 37–59.

1990a. *The Conceptual Practices of Power: A Feminist Sociology of Knowledge*. Boston: Northeastern University Press.

1990b. *Texts, Facts, and Femininity: Exploring the Relations of Ruling*. London: Routledge.

Coauthored Works

Hacker, Sally. 1990. *Doing It the Hard Way: Essays in Gender and Technology*, edited by Dorothy E. Smith. Boston: Unwin & Hyman.

Sealander, Judith, and Dorothy E. Smith. 1986. "The Rise and Fall of Feminist Organizations in the 1970s" *Feminist Studies* 12 (Summer): 321–342.

Smith, Dorothy E., and Sarah J. David, eds. *Women Look at Psychiatry*. Vancouver: Press Gang.

Studies About Dorothy E. Smith and Supplemental References

Bandyopadhyay, Pradeep. 1974. "A Critical Comment on Smith." *Catalyst* 8: 55–61.

Godard, Barbara. 1985. "Redrawing the Circle: Power, Poetics, Language." *Canadian Journal of Political and Social Theory* 9 (Winter–Spring): 1–2.

Hale, Sylvia M. 1987. "The Documentary Construction of Female Mismanagement." *Review of Canadian Sociology and Anthropology* 24 (November): 489–513.

———. 1989. *Controversies in Sociology*. Canada: Copp Clark Pitman.

———. 1990. "Male Culture and Purdah for Women: The Social Construction of What Women Think Women Think." *Review of Canadian Sociology and Anthropology* 25 (May): 276–298.

Harding, Sandra. 1986. *The Science Question in Feminism*. Ithaca, NY: Cornell University Press.

Jagger, Alison. 1983. *Feminist Politics and Human Nature*. Totowa, NJ: Rowman & Allanheld.

Lengermann, Patricia Madoo, and Jill Niebbrugge-Brantley. 1988. "Contemporary Feminist Theory." In *Contemporary Sociological Theory*, edited by George Ritzer, pp. 282–325. 2nd ed. New York: Alfred A. Knopf.

Mueller, Adele Dorraine. 1980. "Linking Capitalism and Patriarchy: Issues in Marxist Feminism." *Harvard Educational Review* 50 (February): 71–79.

Neitz, Mary Jo, ed. "Feminist Scholarship in Sociology." Special Issue. *The American Sociologist* (Spring).

Ng, Roxanna. 1988. *The Political Economy of Community Organization*. Toronto: Garamond.

Sprague, Joey. 1989. "Book Review of *The Everyday World As Problematic.*" *Contemporary Sociology* 18 (July): 644–645.

Walker, Gillian. In press. *Conceptual Practices and the Political Process: Family Violence as Ideology*. Toronto: University of Toronto.

Unpublished Material

Campbell, Marie. 1984. "Information Systems and Management of Hospital Nursing: A Study in the Social Organization of Knowledge." Ph.D. diss., University of Toronto.

Manicom, Ann. 1988. "Constituting Class Relations: The Social Organization of Teachers' Work." Ph.D. diss., University of Toronto.

Mueller, Adele Dorraine. 1987. "Peasants and Professionals: The Social Organization of Women in Development." Ph.D. diss., University of Toronto.

Reimer, Marilee. 1988. "The Social Organization of the Labour Process: A Case Study of the Documentary Management of Clerical Labour in the Public Service." Ph.D. diss., University of Toronto.

Schild, Veronica. 1982. "The Eclipse of Criticalness in Marxist Social Science: Habermas's and Smith's Analysis." Master's thesis, University of Toronto.

MARY JO DEEGAN

ANNA GARLIN SPENCER (1851–1932)

Anna Garlin Spencer is noted for her pacifism, study of the family, founding work in sociology and social hygiene, and religious leadership as a Unitarian minister. She was a leader in feminist thought first in New England, then in the Midwest, and finally in New York. One of the first American women to be recognized as a sociologist, Spencer basically severed her ties to sociology after she was fired from the Meadville Theological Seminary in 1918.

BIOGRAPHY

Spencer was born in Attleboro, Massachusetts, April 17, 1851. She was the third daughter and youngest of four children of Nancy Mason and Francis Warren Garlin. Both parents came from established New England families. Her father died while serving in the navy during the Civil War, and her mother was a staunch abolitionist. Anna Garlin Spencer attended public schools and arranged for ''private collegiate work.'' By 1869 she had embarked on a career in journalism, working for the Providence, Rhode Island, *Journal* from 1869 to 1878. In the latter year she married the Reverend William H. Spencer. They had two children, Fletcher Carpenter, who died as an infant, and Lucy. Spencer joined her husband in his ministry in Haverhill and Florence, Massachusetts, and Troy, New York.

In 1891 she was formally ordained and became the minister for the Bell Street Chapel in Providence. She was the first woman minister in the state, and her ordination generated considerable debate and controversy. During these early years she attained notice as a lecturer on social problems and the gospel. Her husband retired from the ministry in 1893, and he actively supported her interests until his death, after a decade of invalidism, in 1923. She is the only pioneer female sociologist who was a minister, although this was a common background for many male sociologists of her day.

In 1893 she took an active role in the sociology session at the Parliament of Religions held in Chicago (Mercer 1893, 263), along with Chicago sociologists such as Albion Small and Charles Henderson (Mercer 1893, 261–282). She also presided at the session of the International Conference of Charities and Corrections held at the Chicago Columbian Exposition (Spencer and Birtwell 1893), and participated in the Congress of Women (Spencer 1894).

In 1903 she left her parish to become the associated leader of the New York Society for Ethical Culture. She held this position until 1909, along with several others. Thus she was associate director and staff lecturer of the New York School of Civics and Philanthropy from 1903 to 1913, and a special lecturer on social services and social aspects of education at the University of Wisconsin from 1908 to 1911. While at Wisconsin she frequently worked as a colleague to the noted sociologist E. A. Ross. She directed the Institute of Municipal and Social Service in Milwaukee, Wisconsin, in 1910 and 1911 and the Summer School of Ethics for the American Ethical Union from 1908 to 1911. From 1913 to 1918 she was the Hackley Professor of sociology and ethics at the Theological School, Meadville, Pennsylvania (later renamed Meadville Theological Seminary). In the summer of 1918 she lectured at the University of Chicago. From 1918 to her death in 1931 she was a lecturer at Teachers College, Columbia University, and director of the Division of Family Relations of the American Social Hygiene Association.

Spencer was a national leader for suffrage and women's rights. Thus she served as secretary and vice-president of the New England Suffrage Association, and was an active member of the Women's Christian Temperance Union, the National League of Women Voters, the National American Women's Suffrage Association, and the Women's International League of Peace and Freedom. In addition, Spencer was involved in an array of professional organizations, particularly the American Sociological Society and the American Social Hygiene Association, where she worked with a number of male sociologists, especially Franklin Giddings, E. A. Ross, and Charles R. Henderson. She was most connected, however, with the vast network of women sociologists. She was a close friend and colleague of Jane Addams,* and worked with many Hull-House colleagues, especially Mary McDowell, Sophonisba Breckinridge,* and Emily Greene Balch.* Her work was critiqued by Lucile Eaves* and Marion Talbot* as well. Spencer also was strongly rooted in the New England feminist network, which included Susan B. Anthony, Carrie Chapman Catt, Lucretia Mott, and Mrs. Cheney of the New England Hospital for Women. Finally, she was tied to an international network of feminists who fought for world peace and the end of the white slave trade.

Spencer was a member of the platform committee of the Women's Peace party (WPP), and arranged for the opening of their first conference in 1915. Both

Addams and Carrie Chapman Catt also were on this committee. Spencer wrote the preamble to the platform, which included the following statements:

We, Women of the United States . . . demand that war be abolished. . . . As women, we feel a peculiar moral passion of revolt against both the cruelty and the waste of war. . . . We are especially the custodian of life of the ages. . . . We are particularly charged with the future of childhood and with the care of the helpless and the unfortunate. . . . We have built by the patient drudgery of the past the basic foundation of the home and of peaceful industry. . . . We are called upon to start each generation onward toward a better humanity. . . . We demand that our right to be consulted in the settlement of questions concerning not alone the life of individuals but of nations be recognized and respected. (Spencer cited in Degen 1939, 40–41)

As a member of the Executive Board of the WPP, Spencer was a leader in the organization from its inception. She, unlike Addams, refused to participate in Henry Ford's Peace Ship. Arguing that unless she were assured that "at least ten men known and deservedly trusted as peace advocates of experience and good judgment for the leadership of the expedition were also undertaking the journey," she would not participate. Her leadership influenced other women to refuse to attend the proposed conference, which became a fiasco in the peace movement. (See her letter in "Ford Hopes Troops Will Start a Strike" 1915.)

Her most powerful and visible work in sociology occurred during her years at Meadville. There she organized the students into social service and sponsored annual lectures with the most noted thinkers of the day. She was so successful, in fact, that the more conservative faculty and administration increasingly opposed her work and influence. In 1914 she proposed abolishing the undergraduate program and moving the entire institution to Chicago to coordinate the seminary's work with that done at the University of Chicago. As Leaming pithily notes: "Her plan worked so well that by March of 1917 the trustees decided that a full time professor of social ethics was no longer needed" (1951, 89). Clearly there is more to the story, probably rooted in her successful reorganization of the institution, her charismatic effect on the students there, and her notoriety as a pacifist during wartime.

After her brief stint at the University of Chicago in 1918, Spencer permanently relocated in New York City. There she joined a "women's department," the Teachers College of Columbia University, where Leta Stetter Hollingworth* and Elsie Clews Parsons* also found employment. She also engaged in the social hygiene movement, making a transition toward social work and away from sociology. Here, too, she joined other women sociologists making similar transitions, for example Julia Lathrop, Jessie Taft,* and Ethel Sturgess Dummer.

Spencer labored to abolish prostitution, venereal disease, and the distinction between "good and bad" women. She promoted sex education in the schools following this set of values. Active to the end of her very long life, she died at home on February 12, 1931.

MAJOR THEMES

Spencer believed that women were the most original and fundamental group in society. She thought that their values were superior to those of men and was, therefore, a "cultural feminist." She closely followed the ideas of Franklin Giddings and Otis Tufts Mason. In fact, Mason's book *Women's Share in Primitive Culture* provided the model for her book *Women's Share in Social Culture* (1913b). Here she tried to show how then modern women continued to provide the foundation of society through their traditional values and concerns centering around the home and family.

Her book is filled with pithy insight, connected to feminist thought, emerging out of the historical context of women in the United States, and plans for greater social equality. Calling for women to be democratized so that democracy could be socialized, she linked the themes of social action, government and the home into one unit. Noting women's roles as consumers, she preceded the work of many later theorists on this subject by many years. She decried the lack of "teamwork" and "sex solidarity" among women, leading her to support the women's trade union movement and the development of mentoring among women professionals. She advocated job sharing and the infusion of humane values into the marketplace.

Feminist theorists and sociologists were critiqued here and in her other writings. She found Charlotte Perkins Gilman's* work too extreme, and Ellen Key's to limiting of the role of fathers. She praised the work of Josephine Butler, here and in a number of other places. Kropotkin's view of labor and pacifism was adopted by her, as it was by Jane Addams. Spencer's book was first published in 1913, when it was serialized in the popular periodical *The Forum*. It was revised in 1925.

Her major book on the family, *The Family and Its Members* (1923), reads more like a contemporary feminist book on the family than the very conservative texts that dominated the sociological literature written after Spencer. She advocated a radical increase in men's involvement in housework and child rearing. She wanted to bring the marketplace and home into greater alignment, and including men in the home was one way of doing this.

She advocated similar education for both sexes in grammar school, although she saw distinct training for the sexes as justifiable in their later training. Women's unity as a group was a priority, and acting across class lines was a major way to build this shared vision. She lauded the work of unmarried women of her era, "the age of the spinster." She saw this as a temporary step, however, needed to close the deep gulf between women's ideals and their reality.

A major sociological statement is found in her "Social Education of

Women,'' presented to the American Sociological Society in 1918. Here she again critiqued the feminist theorists noted above, as well as Elsie Clews Parsons and Lucy Salmon. She found Parsons too extreme in wanting to separate, instead of unite, mating and parenting, while Salmon's views complemented Spencer's.

Like Addams, Spencer emphasized social reform to mitigate, if not eliminate, social inequality. Spencer's critical pragmatism, or belief in democracy and education to eliminate social injustice, was more dependent on the women's philanthropy network and world view than that of Addams. Spencer's religious ties were woven into her thought, making the Social Gospel and New England liberal thought explicit components.

In 1893 Spencer played a major role in the National Conference on Charities and Corrections held at the Chicago World's Fair. Probably she established her strong ties to sociologists from Chicago at this time. Even at this early stage she was advocating state, not private, intervention to ease the lives of the poor and disenfranchised. Her definition of religion was grounded in a humanistic understanding of power and force that was not specifically gendered or rooted in denominational doctrine. In fact, her writings during the 1920s sound more moralistic than many of her writings in the 1890s.

Her firm antiwar stance and theory emerged from both her cultural feminism and her critical pragmatism. Thus Spencer believed that women's values supported cooperation; that war not only destroyed life and property, but also specifically undermined the family as well as women's roles as mothers and caretakers, and that women needed to organize and act on this knowledge.

Spencer's arguments against war were well thought out and innovative. Starting, in ''Women and War'' (1915), with Gidding's idea of insiders/kin and outsiders/enemy, Spencer stated that women were just beginning to enter politics with an international perspective of all humans as ''kin.'' This recent start was cut off by the emergence of national conflict. Female pacifists, moreover, had unique reasons for their opposition to war, distinct from those of male pacifists. First, women were the most punished prey of the enemy, the most victimized, physically abused, and raped. Second, women's status was a marginal one, dependent on the generation of the law to protect their hardearned status. With the restoration of social order, women were relegated again to domestic bondage. Third, women were given the work of caring for the weak, the handicapped, the frail. These populations were greatly increased by war and became lifelong burdens for women. Fourth, men contracted social diseases, which made them unfit spouses and caused physical and mental handicaps, once again borne by women caretakers. Fifth, the remaking of the social order called for drudgery and sacrifice; hard physical labor reduced by technology was again reinstated while women labored under limited finances and resources. Sixth, women were urged to bear children, to become ''breeders'' to replace the men lost in war. Men were encouraged to marry before leaving for war, leaving fatherless children and widows behind. These arguments, stressing women's exploitations and bearing on the final costs of war without the pomp of male rhetoric, are hard-hitting and unromantic. They are found in various forms in her writings on peace.

Spencer was an outspoken defender of the feminine world view and possibility. She linked suffrage, state welfare, the family, religion, pacifism, sociology, and social action into one world view. Her role as a major theorist and practitioner has never been fully recognized, which is briefly documented below.

CRITIQUES OF ANNA GARLIN SPENCER

Spencer's work was widely recognized in sociology during its founding years from 1892 until 1930. Thus she was the only woman sociologist included in the *International Encyclopedia of the Social Sciences*, and her death was noted in the *American Journal of Sociology*. The *Journal of Social Hygiene* published obituaries and one article summarizing her life work immediately after her death in 1931. Benjamin Andrews (1932) notes her seminal leadership in the study of the family and her organizational acumen. Keyes (1931), however, wrote a maudlin obituary, showing how women's work is trivialized by making it the embodiment of angels.

Lucile Eaves (1919) and Marion Talbot (1919) both discussed Spencer's "The Social Education of Women." Eaves missed the point of Spencer's argument, lamenting the killing of men during the war instead of critiquing the latter's view on unmarried women or needed new training for women. Talbot criticized Spencer's stand on these issues, citing Spencer's own ideas on "vestigal functions of the families" to criticize family life in America. A third discussant, Thomas Eliot, entirely missed the point of Spencer's paper, providing a document on how her ideas were specifically ignored by men even in formal settings. Charles Zeublin, a sociologist forced to resign from his sociological position at the University of Chicago in 1908, reviewed *Woman's Share in Social Culture* (1913) as "overwhelmingly" documenting the "absurd prejudices against women." After 1931, however, Spencer was largely ignored in the writings of all sociologists.

Scholarship in women's studies has documented, often briefly, her role as a feminist and pacifist, but she has not been linked to the discipline of sociology in this literature. Earlier work on women's suffrage, by Kraditor (1968), among others, only briefly mentions Spencer's role as a speaker. A more interesting portrait of her work is offered in Howard B. Radest's analysis of the ethical culture movement (1969). Spencer's continual struggle for the rights of immigrants, workers, and women to be represented in the organization provides an important addition to scholarship on her. Studies on international pacifism, such as Degen's (1939), mention her leadership briefly.

Three of Spencer's books have recently been reprinted by Ayer and Hyperion Press. Her stellar leadership on behalf of women's equality, her social thought, her courageous stand on pacifism during wartime, and her role as an early sociologist point to a better future in critical thought than her current lack of analysis.

BIBLIOGRAPHY

Selected Writings by Anna Garlin Spencer

1894. "Advantages and Dangers of Organization." In *The Congress of Women*, edited by Mary Cavanaugh Oldham Eagle, pp. 170–177. Chicago: American Publishing House.

1898. *Women and Regulation.* New York: American Purity Alliance.

1899. *Bell Street Chapel Discourses.* Providence, RI: Journal of Commerce Co.

1911. "The New Center of Gravity in Philanthropy." In *Theodore Parker*, no editor, sponsored by the Free Religious Association, The Congress of Religion, the National Federation of Religious Liberals, and a Local Committee of One Hundred, pp. 51–58. Chicago: Unity Publishing.

1913a. "The Social Function of the Church." In *Social Ideals of a Free Church*, edited by Elmer S. Forber, pp. 13–24. Boston: Unitarian Association.

1913b. *Woman's Share in Social Culture.* Philadelphia: J. B. Lippincott. Rev. ed., 1925; reprinted, New York: Ayer, 1972.

1913c. "The Scarlet Woman." *Forum* 49 (March): 276–289.

1913d. "The Age of Consent and Its Significance." *Forum* 49 (May): 406–420.

1913e. "State Regulation of Vice and Its Meaning." *Forum* 49 (May): 587–601.

1913f. "Josephine Butler and the English Crusade, Part I." *Forum* 49 (June): 703–716.

1913g. "Josephine Butler and the English Crusade, Part II." *Forum* 50 (July): 77–81.

1913h. "A World Crusade." 50 *Forum* (August): 182–195.

1915. "Women and War." *The Independent* 81 (January 25): 121–124.

1919. "Social Education of Women." *Papers and Proceedings of the American Sociological Society* 13: 11–28.

1922. "Feminist Wild Oats." *Standard* 8 (January): 139–142.

1923. *The Family and Its Members.* Philadelphia: J. B. Lippincott. Reprinted, Westport, CT: Hyperion, in Pioneers of the Woman's Movement Series, 1976.

1925. *For What Do Social Hygiene Associations Stand?* New York: American Social Hygiene Association.

1927. "Constructive Pacifism." *Survey* 43 (January 10): 387.

1928a. "A Mile-Stone Meeting: The Family Life Conference in Buffalo, New York." *Journal of Social Hygiene* 14 (January): 76–80.

1928b. "A Memorial of a Great Woman." *Journal of Social Hygiene* 14 (April): 198–205.

1928c. "Social Hygiene Outline for Churches." *Journal of Social Hygiene* 14 (June): 376–378.

1930. "Summary of the Symposium of Problems of Family Relations." *Journal of Social Hygiene* 16 (March): 149–155.

1931. "Should Married Women Work Outside the Home?" *Eugenics* 4 (January): 21–25.

Coauthored Work

Spencer, Anna Garlin, and R. C. Dexter. 1931. *Special Reading List on the Minister and the Family*. Boston: American Unitarian Association.

Coedited Work

Spencer, Anna Garlin, and Charles Wesley Birtwell, eds. 1983. *The Care of Dependent, Neglected and Wayward Children*. Chicago: International Congress of Charities, Correction and Philanthropy; Baltimore: Johns Hopkins University Press, 1894. Reprinted, New York: Ayer, 1974.

Studies About Anna Garlin Spencer and Supplemental References

Addams, Jane. 1922. *Peace and Bread in Time of War*. New York: Macmillan.

Andrews, Benjamin R. 1932. "Anna Garlin Spencer and Education for the Family." *Journal of Social Hygiene* 18 (April): 183–189.

"Anna Garlin Spencer, 1851–1931." 1931. Obituary. *Journal of Social Hygiene* 17 (March): 129–130.

Deegan, Mary Jo. 1981. "Early Women Sociologists and the American Sociological Society: Patterns of Exclusion and Participation." *American Sociologist* 16 (February): 14–24.

———1987. "An American Dream: The Historical Connections Between Women, Humanism, and Sociology." *Humanity and Society* 11 (August): 553–565.

Degen, Mary Louise. 1939. *The History of the Woman's Peace Party*. Baltimore: Johns Hopkins University Press.

Eaves, Lucile. 1919. "Discussion of 'Social Education of Women.' " *Papers and Proceedings of the American Sociological Society* 13: 28–33.

Elliot, Captain Thomas D. 1919. "Discussion of 'Social Education of Women.' " *Papers and Proceedings of the American Sociological Society* 13: 36–37.

"Ford Hopes Troops Will Start a Strike." *New York Times* (November 30, 1915), 1, col. 5; 6, cols. 2–5.

Keyes, Edward L. 1931. "Anna Garlin Spencer, Patroness." *Journal of Social Hygiene* 17 (April): 208–209.

Kraditor, Aileen, ed. 1968. *Up from the Pedestal*. Chicago: Quadrangle Press.

Mercer, L. P. ed. 1893. *Review of the World's Religious Congresses*. Chicago: Rand, McNally.

"Personal Notes." 1931. Obituary. *American Journal of Sociology* 37 (July): 139.

Radest, Howard B. 1969. *Toward Common Ground: The Story of the Ethical Societies in the United States*. New York: Ungar.

Ross, Mary. 1934. "Spencer, Anna Garlin." In *Encyclopaedia of the Social Sciences*, vol. 14, edited by E. R. A. Seligman and Alvin Johnson, pp. 294–295. New York: Macmillan.

Sinclair, Andrew. 1965. *The Better Half*. New York: Harper & Row.

Talbot, Marion. 1919. "Discussion of 'Social Education of Women.' " *Papers and Proceedings of the American Sociological Society* 13: 34–36.

Zeublin, Charles. 1913. "Review of *Woman's Share in Social Culture.*" *Survey* 30 (June 28): 437.

Unpublished Material

Leaming, Hugo Prosper. 1951. "The Teaching of Social Ethics at the Meadville Theological School, 1844–1944." B. Divinity diss., Federated Theological Faculty, Chicago.

MARY JO DEEGAN

IRENE B. TAEUBER (1906–1974)

Irene B. Taeuber was a demographer and practical statistician of the highest rank and ability. Extremely prolific, her numerous personal and professional contributions reflect her intellectual industriousness as well as her varied capabilities: premiere editor of *Population Index*; nurturer of the evolution of demography within sociology; her role as a feminine humanist; her influential international population studies; and her expertise on demography in the East and Southeast Asia.

BIOGRAPHY

Irene B. Taeuber was born in Meadville, Missouri, on December 25, 1906. She was the second of four children (two girls and two boys) born to Lily (Keller) and Ninevah C. Barnes. Her father earned a living by alternating between farming and barbering, and he also served for many years as a justice of the peace. He was somewhat of a restless person and once left the family for more than a year. She was very close to both her mother and her maternal grandparents. Against her father's wishes, but with the support and encouragement of her mother, she pursued a higher education and supported herself through scholarships and various types of employment.

She received her bachelor's degree at the University of Missouri in 1927, where she majored in sociology. During her time there she was strongly influenced by a biology professor, W. C. Curtis. Irene earned a master's degree in anthropology at Northwestern University in 1928 and pursued her doctorate at the University of Minnesota.

While working on her doctorate she met Conrad Taeuber, a fellow graduate student in sociology, and they were married in 1929. While she attended the

University of Minnesota, she was influenced by other social scientists such as Stuart Chapin, Lowry Nelson, and Pitirim Sorokin.

Conrad and Irene worked as research assistants for J. H. Kolb at the University of Wisconsin while they completed their dissertations. From this experience they gained practical knowledge in statistics and rural demography that would be highly useful during both of their careers. Irene completed her doctorate in 1931. She can be thought of as a "pure scholar," as she was known for being totally committed to scientific research.

Irene was family-oriented as well as a dedicated scholar and researcher. She is remembered as someone who always put the family first. In the early years of raising a family she worked primarily part-time, at a time when few part-time positions were available, because it was important to her to be home when her boys came home from school. Even though she was able to devote only part-time hours to her employer, the Office of Population Research, they felt that her productivity was greater than that of an average full-time scholar.

Irene and Conrad Taeuber raised two boys, Richard Conrad and Karl Ernst. Both of their children pursued careers in fields related to their parents' interests—Richard in statistics and econometrics, Karl in demography and sociology.

In 1931 both Irene and Conrad received appointments in the department of economics and sociology at Mount Holyoke College, Irene as an instructor and Conrad as an assistant professor. Irene taught at the college from 1931 to 1934 until she became involved in a project with the Population Association of America, which would become her life's work.

In 1934 Irene and Conrad went to Washington after his acceptance of a research appointment with the Federal Emergency Relief Administration. Conrad had a distinguished career as an administrator, statistician, and demographer with the Department of Agriculture, the Food and Agriculture Organization of the United Nations, and the U.S. Bureau of the Census.

Early in 1935 Irene (hereafter referred to as Taeuber) prepared and edited *Population Literature*, a periodic bibliography of recent and current articles on population for Frank Lorimer, secretary of the newly organized Population Association of America. On the departure of Lorimer to work for the National Resources Committee, the biographical work was relocated at Princeton University's Office of Population Research. The Office of Population Research was established in 1936 under the direction of Frank W. Notestein, and Taeuber became a staff member as well as coeditor of *Population Index*, which was the successor to the publication that she had worked on with Frank Lorimer.

The Office of Population Research published the first volume of *Population Index* in 1937. As its premiere editor, Taeuber was primarily responsible for the success of this useful periodical guide to demographic literature. Although she shared the title of editor with Dr. Louise K. Kiser, the main responsibility from 1937 through 1954 was hers. The *Population Index* was a direct expression of her scholarship, imagination, and intellectual capabilities. She also wrote most of the *Current Items*, the articles on demographic topics at the front of *Population*

Index. At that time it was the only regular publication in the field of demography in the United States.

During World War II Taeuber produced a number of articles, for *Current Items*, on the demographic situation of the nations involved that are still relevant today. These studies, based on in-depth research, covered the population of the country in question, furnished general knowledge and explanations, presented its particular demographic situation, and discussed various effects of the war. This provided an additional source of information concerning the war as well as a sociological and demographical perspective.

After seventeen years of dedication and direct involvement with the *Population Index*, she asked to be relieved to devote more time to some of her own research. She had been a research associate at the Office of Population Research from 1936 to 1961, and senior research demographer from 1962 until her retirement from that office in 1973.

At the same time that she was editing *Population Index*, writing the *Current Items*, and raising her family, she accomplished many other projects—the Census Library Project, a book on the population of the United States, numerous articles on demography as well as other varied topics, and her magnum opus *The Population of Japan* (1958a). She was an extremely accomplished researcher and a highly prolific author during the course of her lifetime. She was known worldwide by her professional contributions, intellectual interests, personal associations, and accomplishments.

As well as these other activities, she directed the Bureau of the Census from 1941 to 1944. She also acted as a consultant on international statistics for both the Bureau of the Census (1940–1950) and the Manpower Panel of the Research and Development Board, Department of Defense (1947–1953). She was visiting professor of the School of Hygiene and Public Health of The Johns Hopkins University from 1962 to 1964.

Taeuber served as a consultant or as a member of committees for more than a dozen agencies—private foundations, international organizations, and governmental and academic institutions in the United States and abroad. The groups included specialized topics, such as service as chairs of the Standing Committee on Population of the Pacific Science Association, of the Committee on Social Demography of the American Sociological Association, of the Subcommittee on Vital and Health Statistics, U.S. National Committee on Vital and Health Statistics, and of a U.N. review committee on the Center for Latin American Demographic Studies in Santiago, Chile.

She served as the president of the Population Association of America from 1953 to 1954, as vice-president of the International Union for the Scientific Study of Population from 1961 to 1965, as secretary of the American Sociological Society in 1945, and was a fellow of the American Association for the Advancement of Science, the American Sociological Association, the American Statistical Association, and the American Academy of Arts and Sciences.

Taeuber received numerous awards for her excellent work. She received honorary degrees from Smith College in 1960 and the Western College for Women in 1965. The University of Missouri gave her its Award of Distinction in 1964 and the Centennial Honors Award in 1967. She received the Regents Award for Distinguished Achievement in 1967 from the University of Minnesota, and the District of Columbia Sociological Society chose her for the Stuart A. Rice Merit Award in 1972.

Even with the vast array of acknowledgments and awards that she received, it must be remembered that Taeuber was a woman in a male-oriented profession at a time when traditional roles and expectations were difficult to break. Although she never openly emphasized the hardships or obstacles of working in a man's world, she did think that she was not treated equally by her male colleagues at the Office of Population Research. She believed that she did not receive as much clerical and research assistance as they did. This may have been simply because she was a woman.

Irene Barnes Taeuber died at the height of her creative powers in the midst of conducting research of the high quality she was known for and at the sustained pace that had been characteristic of her remarkable career. She died quickly of pneumonia complicated by advanced emphysema in her home on February 24, 1974. At the time of her death she was working on a bibliography on the demography of China, which was published in her honor.

Her profound loss was felt by her family, her friends, the staff of Princeton University's Office of Population Research, her close colleagues in Washington as well as in Japan; along with the sociological, educational, and demographic community. She was greatly loved and admired for her many outstanding works, her professional attainments, and her warm human qualities.

Her friends and colleagues remember her honesty, her loyalty, her generosity, and her courage. She was helpful to her students, whether with personal or scholarly problems, no matter how much time it took or what action it required. She was someone who could be relied on in any situation, and she cared deeply for humanity.

A colleague of Taeuber's at Princeton, Clyde V. Kiser, felt that her work was distinguished by her interest in the social, economic, and cultural determinants of population trends. This concern can be seen in her efforts to visit rural villages and to establish ties with local residents. She was highly sensitive to the emotions of people in the various cultures that she visited and worked in. She was a good friend and confidant to many of the foreign students and young Japanese that she met throughout her lifetime.

MAJOR THEMES

One of Taeuber's most important contributions was in the area of demography as it existed as a science within sociology. Many aspects of research in the area of demography were influenced by her. She had a great deal to do with the focus and growth of the science of demography during the 1930s and 1940s. During its developmental years she nurtured it as a science and played a major role in guiding its growth in scientific objectivity within the context of a humanitarian value system. Consequently demography, as a science, remains relatively objective and value-free. It has maintained its scientific and scholarly standards and focus even through its dynamic growth.

She approached the science of demography in a meticulous and thorough manner. Rather than making use of generalizations and theory construction, she made use of imaginative and careful analysis. Taeuber was a demographer during a time when the emphasis was not placed on mathematical models or theory, but rather on the analysis itself. She applied strict social science methodology to her pursuit of knowledge in the area of demography.

She was trained according to the tradition of data-oriented empiricists. This was combined with her earlier anthropological perspective that she developed during her educational years. The result of this combination was a researcher who united a knowledge of people with a strong scientific base.

Her concerns with the basic demographic issues of fertility, mortality, migration, and marital patterns were approached from the perspective of the individual. She always was aware of the constant interaction between the forces that drive both these patterns and the individual, as well as the results of that interaction.

Demography, in this way, could be viewed as an ongoing dynamic process in which the individual played an important role. She placed herself and her family in the same perspective, and in this way she was able to understand their concerns as individuals and, as a result of the various social factors, to influence them. Her underlying values were clearly humanistic, even though her research reflected her devotion and commitment to scientific objectivity.

Taeuber can be viewed as a feminine humanist. This perspective achieved popularity in the United States before World War II and disappeared, for the most part, during the 1940s and 1950s. It reemerged in the feminism of the 1970s. As a feminine humanist, she pursued the understanding of culture and humanity for her research and for herself. She went out of her way to investigate and research areas that she felt were critical to her knowledge and the understanding of the culture.

In many instances, she tried to adapt the perspective of the people in the culture she was studying to get the most accurate information. This can be seen in her friendships in the cultures that she studied and the types of activities that she participated in during her lifetime.

While working at the Office of Population Research she began to study Asian populations. After the war she embarked on a study of Japan and made several trips there, fostering a great love for the Far East. She visited the hospitals in the famine areas of West Java after the second "police action"; she accompanied the visiting tuberculosis nurses in the slums of war-shattered Tokyo, and gossiped with the natives of China, India, Pakistan, and the Philippines as if she were one of them.

There has been no other demographer who has ever written such a large volume of research articles on so many diverse countries and subjects. Some of the countries that Taeuber studied were as small as the islands of Micronesia and as large as China. She wrote about countries in Africa, Europe, Latin America, Southeast Asia, the Pacific Islands, the United States, and Japan. Her subjects varied from "Hereditary Factors in Mental Disease" to "Manchuria as a Demographic Frontier." However, from 1940 on she published almost exclusively in the area of demography.

Irene Taeuber was the author, joint author or editor of eighteen books and monographs and more than 250 articles and contributions to books, many of which she authored exclusively. Even with this level of productivity, it was not until 1961 that she was promoted to senior research demographer at the Office of Population Research.

International population studies were greatly influenced by her work. She brought an international and comparative perspective to demography at a time when the majority of the research being done in the United States was only about the United States.

Overall, Taeuber was especially interested in the demography of East and Southeast Asia, particularly Japan and China. In her later years a great deal of her research was devoted to Chinese demography. The most outstanding example of her Asian research is her magnum opus *The Population of Japan* (1958a).

The Population of Japan is a demographic survey of Japan from the start of the literate period until 1955. It is the most detailed study available today of the demographic consequences of Western material culture being introduced into an Eastern society. It also is the only professional study of its kind written in a Western language. The study itself was so valued and respected by the Japanese that it was translated into Japanese in celebration of its ten years of interest in the field of demography.

Taeuber also coauthored major works on the United States with her husband, Conrad, who was employed at the Bureau of the Census. Some of these are *The Changing Population of the United States* (1958) and *People of the United States in the Twentieth Century* (1971).

The Changing Population of the United States examines the changes that have occurred in the U.S. population over a 160-year period. It covers topics such as population growth and distribution, social characteristics of the population, the role of natural increases, and the connections between immigration, spatial distribution patterns, and natural increases.

These are only a few of Taeuber's outstanding works. All her accomplishments display the notable characteristics of her success, her intelligence, and her careful preparation throughout her work.

CRITIQUES OF IRENE B. TAEUBER

Irene Taeuber's legacy to sociology takes several paths. Her role in the development of the *Population Index* is of major importance in demography. Her longtime coeditor, Frank Notestein, points out:

Population Index is peculiarly Dr. Taeuber's intellectual child. Although she shared the title of Editor with Dr. Louise K. Kiser and the writer, she carried the main responsibility for the bibliography from 1937 through 1954. She also wrote most of the Current Items. (1974, 3)

This institutional role is one of her major contributions.

Her training of "hundreds of students around the world" (Notestein 1974, 5) is another major, often invisible contribution. Her tables often are cited in studies, thereby building a foundation of information that does not easily lend itself to analytical discussions of Taeuber's work. Finally, her sons, Richard Conrad and Karl Ernst, have become noted demographers, and they were surely influenced in this occupational choice by their parents.

Taeuber's foundational role in demography is noted in Vance's historical overview of the field (1959), but a more recent statement on her contributions is clearly needed. Taeuber has left a major intellectual and empirical heritage that has yet to be fully explored.

BIBLIOGRAPHY

Selected Writings by Irene B. Taeuber

1943. *General Censuses and Vital Statistics in the Americas*. U.S. Bureau of the Census and U.S. Library of Congress, Census Library Project. Washington, DC: Government Printing Office.

1949. *The Population of Tanganyika*. Lake Success, NY: United Nations Publications.

1952. "The Future of Transitional Areas." In *World Population and Future Resources*, edited by Paul Hatt, pp. 25–38. New York: American Book Company.

1956. "Population Policies in Communist China." *Population Index* 22: 261–274.

1958a. *The Population of Japan*. Princeton, NJ: Princeton University Press.

1958b. "Migration, Mobility, and the Assimilation of the Negro." *Population Bulletin* 14 (November): 127–151.

1960. "Japan's Demographic Transition Re-Examined." *Population Studies* 14 (July): 28–39.

1962. "Hawaii." *Population Index* 28 (April): 97–125.

1964. *China's Populations—Some Approaches to Research*. Princeton, NJ: Princeton University Press.

1965a. "Policies, Programs and Decline of Birth Rates: China and the Chinese Populations of East Asia." In *Population Dynamics: International Action and Training Programs*, edited by Minora Muramatsu and Paul A. Harper, pp. 99–104. Baltimore: Johns Hopkins University Press.

1965b. *Population Trends in the United States*. U.S. Bureau of the Census, Technical Paper No. 10. Washington, DC: Government Printing Office.

1972. *Population Growth and Development in Southeast Asia*. New York: Asia Society, Southeast Asia Development Group.

Coauthored Works

Balfour, Marshall C., Roger F. Evans, Frank W. Notestein, and Irene B. Taeuber. 1950. *Public Health and Demography in the Far East*. New York: Rockefeller Foundation.

Ho, Ping-Ti, and Irene B. Taeuber. 1956. *The Growth of Total Population in China, 1750–1850*. Cambridge, MA: Harvard University, Chinese Economic and Political Studies.

Lorimer, Frank, and Irene B. Taeuber, eds. 1935–1936. *Population Literature*. 2 vols. Washington, DC: Population Association of America.

Notestein, Frank W., Ansley J. Coale, Irene B. Taeuber, Kirk Dudley, and Louise K. Kiser. *The Future Population of Europe and the Soviet Union*. Geneva: League of Nations.

Notestein, Frank W., and Irene B. Taeuber, eds. 1945–1953. *Population Index*, Vols. 3–10, 20. Princeton, NJ: Princeton University, Office of Population Research.

Notestein, Frank W., Irene B. Taeuber, and Louise K. Kiser, eds. 1937–1944, 1954. *Population Index*, Vols. 11–19, 20. Princeton, NJ: Princeton University, Office of Population Research.

Taeuber, Conrad, and Irene B. Taeuber. 1958. *The Changing Population of the United States*. U.S. Bureau of the Census and the Social Science Research Council. New York: John Wiley.

Taeuber, Irene B., and Conrad Taeuber. 1971. *People of the United States in the Twentieth Century*. U.S. Bureau of the Census and the Social Science Research Council, Census Monograph Series. Washington, DC: Government Printing Office.

Wiechert, Ernst Emil. 1948. *The Poet and His Times, Three Addresses*, translated by Irene Taeuber, introduced by George Shuster. Hinsdale, IL: H. Reginery Company.

Studies About Irene B. Taeuber and Supplemental References

Coale, Ansley J. 1974. "Irene Barnes Taeuber, 1906–1974." *American Statistician* 28 (August): 109–110.

Keyfitz, Nathan. 1980. "Taeuber, Irene Barnes." In *Notable American Women: The Modern Period*, edited by Barbara Sicherman and Carol Hurd Green, pp. 672–673. Cambridge, MA: Harvard University Press, Belknap Press.

Notestein, Frank W. 1974. "Irene Barnes Taeuber, 1906–1974." *Population Index* 40 (January): 3–17.

Vance, Rupert B. 1959. "The Development and Status of American Demography." In *The Study of Population: An Inventory and Appraisal*, edited by Philip M. Hauser and Otis Dudley Duncan, pp. 286–313. Chicago: University of Chicago Press.

TAMI J. STOEHR-KREPS

JESSIE TAFT (1882–1961)

Jessie Taft was a brilliant symbolic interactionist who studied women, their view of the world, and the application of their values in various situations. A feminist, a scholar with limited academic ties to sociology, and a noted social worker, Taft worked in a professional world distinct from that of mainstream, academic men in sociology. Her incisive work has been ignored by sociologists.

BIOGRAPHY

Taft was born on June 24, 1882, when women were agitating for the right to higher education. Her parents, Amanda May Farwell and Charles Chester Taft, moved from Vermont to rural Iowa, where she was born and raised. Her father ran a prosperous wholesale business selling fruit, making this "old" American family financially comfortable, but not affluent. Jessie was the eldest of three daughters, and her mother was a traditional homemaker who suffered from progressive deafness. This disability led to increasing isolation from her children (Trowle 1960, 674). Virginia Robinson, Taft's biographer, euphemistically explained this distance between mother and daughter: "Her mother was too competent a cook herself to want the children bothering her in the kitchen" (1962, 25).

Robinson reveals little conflict or passion between Taft and her parents, or between Taft and Robinson, although these women lived together for more than forty years. Such a lifelong friendship, including adoption of two children—Everett and Martha Taft—must have generated deep ties. Passionate, work-related, long-term relationships were characteristic of early women professionals, particularly sociologists (Smith-Rosenberg 1975). The few glimpses that Taft reveals about herself in her published writings, especially in her biography of Otto Rank, reveal her intensity, generosity, and involvement with others.

In addition to her father, Taft was profoundly affected by two men, George H. Mead and Otto Rank. Rosenberg (1982), who relies heavily on the Robinson account, incorrectly assumes that Taft was primarily influenced by men in her work and social thought. But as great as the imprint left by men, Taft's life was surrounded by women: their ideas, issues, friendships, life-styles, and institutions. Her life with Robinson, her friendship with Ethel Sturgess Dummer (Deegan 1978–1979), her feminist epistemology, and her female clients and colleagues are all indicators of her woman-centered life.

Characteristically, Robinson summarizes Taft's adolescence in a few words: "Loving food, she took on weight too fast and was painfully sensitive to being overweight and outsize. In retrospect, adolescence flattened out into a long desert waste marked by evenings of boredom spent on the porch in the intense heat of an Iowa summer" (p. 26).

During Taft's late adolescence her scholarly interests were fostered by a female physician, who influenced her undergraduate training at Drake University in Des Moines, Iowa, where she earned a bachelor's degree in 1904. Jessie's father experienced the ambivalent feelings toward "educated women" characteristic of his era, but he nonetheless actively supported her choices. With this mixed background of traditional Midwestern roots and emancipatory support, Taft pursued additional academic training and a professional career.

It is possible that this professional work helped to heal some private conflicts revealed as anonymous "case studies" in her writings. For example, because we know that Taft was both overweight and befriended by a female physician, Taft's description of "a neurotic girl" with these characteristics may have been autobiographical. The "case study" analyzes the pain suffered by the child who "was clumsy, pigeon-toed, and inclined to be afraid to use her body. Her parents laughed at her attempts to walk and run and at her frequent falls. They exaggerated her timidity and encouraged her not to try any unusual feats" (1920a, 167). She was called "Fatty" by other children, and responded by overdeveloping her intellectual interests. Taft concludes "this case" by noting that "middle age finds this girl just beginning, through analysis of her own behavior, to get a legitimate self-confidence intellectually and socially and the free use of her own body, which wasn't particularly inferior after all" (1920a, 168). Clearly this case history echoes the life of Taft herself.

A more documented peek into her life is provided in another article, published in 1926, when she was thirty-eight years old. Here she discussed the joy of being a foster parent, recovering her emotional ties to children.

I can remember a world thirty years ago when I, a child in that world, found nothing attractive in the traditional picture of a woman's part in life. There was no thrill, no challenge, no promise of recognition and reward. The thought of having children, or bringing them up, or creating a family, far from presenting an alluring possibility of adventure and achieve-

ment, a field in which expert skill and knowledge might find expression, loomed before me
as a fate to be avoided if possible, the crushing end of all individual development. (1926c)

Healing the divisions between her female values and experiences and her male
intellectual interests was a lifetime process. Clearly these conflicts arose from
her biographical situation as a child in Iowa.

Whatever the stress of these early years, by 1905 Taft had moved to Chicago
and earned a bachelor of philosophy degree from the University of Chicago.
Although Taft was enrolled as an undergraduate, all her coursework was done
at the graduate level (Deegan 1989). At this time the university was an intellectual
center for the Midwest (see Marion Talbot*). Despite this vibrant life, Taft's
separation from her family and responsibilities evoked a sense of guilt (Robinson
1962, 28), and she soon returned to Des Moines. For the next four years Taft
taught Latin and algebra at West High School in Des Moines. This work and
her family situation were too limiting, however, and Taft was drawn once more
to fulfilling her broader social claims. Thus, in the summer of 1908, she went
back to the University of Chicago.

This summer became a turning point in her life. She studied with W. I.
Thomas, who was developing a number of radical ideas on women's dress,
standards of behavior, right to vote, and occupations (Deegan 1988). She also
met Virginia Robinson: together they explored ideas, friendship, and professional
commitments. Both women returned to their respective teaching positions at the
end of the summer, but longed to do more invigorating and substantial work.
When the University of Chicago offered Taft a fellowship in 1909, she eagerly
accepted it.

The years from 1909 to 1913 are crucial for understanding Taft's career in
sociology. During this time she selected George H. Mead, one of the founders
of symbolic interactionism, as her doctoral chair. She also found her first professional employment, established her deep professional and personal identification
with never-married female sociologists, and entered the women's network in
sociology that was located largely outside the academy. Taft entered the world
of professional female social scientists through her University of Chicago connections, especially through Marion Talbot. The latter helped to place Katherine
Bement Davis* in a position at the Bedford Hills Reformatory for Women in
New York (Rosenberg 1982, 118). Davis, in turn, hired Taft and Robinson to
conduct interviews on the relation between crime and "feeble-mindedness."
Thus, in 1912, the young scholars began their work with Davis that led them
away from academic sociology and ultimately to "social work."

Although Taft and Robinson criticized the statistical process they used and
their categorizing of people, they had found an exciting and promising career.
Taft returned to Chicago and, in 1913, completed her doctorate on "The Woman
Movement from the Standpoint of Social Consciousness." She wanted to become
a professor, but the academic barriers to women were nearly insurmountable.
In addition, she was partially supported by an applied sociology network with

goals and training similar to hers, but located primarily in the Midwest. Her first jobs, however, were located in an Eastern network of female social workers with different training, ideals, goals, and practices.

Taft's early professional years were marked by discouragement and interruption. Her first position, after her magna cum laude graduation from the University of Chicago (Robinson 1962, 37), was as assistant superintendent of the New York State Reformatory for Women. "[But] nothing in her education or experience had given her any preparation for institutional work nor for understanding the court-committed inmates of a reformatory, and no process of instruction to the requirements of the job could be provided" (Robinson 1962, 41). When Davis left her position as superintendent in 1915, Taft lost a vital tie to the women's applied sociology network.

Taft's view of the reformatory's work and that of the new superintendent conflicted. Taft soon left Bedford Hills without a recommendation. When Taft sought help from Mary Richmond, an eminent Eastern social worker, Taft's "qualifications apparently did not impress Miss Richmond who told her she would need training in a good casework agency under a competent supervisor" (Robinson 1962, 44). Unable to find work, this talented philosopher considered returning to her home or "living off her father."

Fortunately the director of the Mental Hygiene Committee of the State Charities Aid Association of New York resigned, and Taft filled the position ("Personals" 1916, 469). She again resigned two years later when a change in leadership occurred. She wrote Robinson of her struggles with despair: "I feel so cowardly and good for nothing. But I brace up soon. It isn't like this all the time" (Robinson, citing Taft, 1962, 51–52). By 1918 she had been searching for meaningful employment for fourteen years.

Taft's continuing commitments to sociology can be seen in her work at the American Sociological Society meetings in 1921 and 1925. Both the sessions in which she presented her work were organized by Dummer, showing again the importance of the female network in Taft's sociological career (Deegan 1978–1979). Women's extreme difficulty in finding academic employment in sociology in this era is reflected in Taft's life. Her marginal faculty appointments began in 1919 when she was hired as a part-time psychology instructor in extension courses at the University of Pennsylvania. She continued in this peripheral position for ten years. Taft literally had to "beg" for a class of regular students, and in 1929 she was finally allowed to teach advanced personality courses to vocational students (cited in Taft 1962; 194).

Despite her erratic employment in a field for which she was untrained, Taft soon became a leader in social work, first in Philadelphia and then nationally. In many ways—too numerous and complex to explore here—Taft shifted her theory, practice, and network after her charismatic encounter with Otto Rank in 1926 (Deegan 1986; Robinson 1962; Taft 1958). Taft became the director of the School of Social Work at the University of Pennsylvania in 1934, and she filled this position until her retirement in 1950. She tried to write her autobiography in the early 1950s, but she became too frustrated to complete it. She switched to writing the biography of Rank (1958). This work was both taxing and rewarding: documenting Rank's leadership in social work and his central role in Taft's life after 1926. Taft died rather suddenly in 1961, eleven years after her retirement. Robinson characterized this period as generally happy and fulfilling (1962, 345–368).

MAJOR THEMES

Taft integrated and extended a particular sociological theory, symbolic inter-actionism. This perspective explains social behavior and the development of the "self" as a function of social learning. Three major criticisms of this theory have been raised: its failure to analyze women, problems between the self and the community, and the development of emotions. These three weaknesses are directly addressed by Taft, dramatically strengthening the flexibility and applica-bility of this theory.

Taft's major statement on women is found in her dissertation (1913). In this classic analysis Taft links the symbolic interaction of Mead and Thomas to the work of women sociologists and theorists. It is the most innovative statement on feminism and symbolic interaction ever written.

Taft soon extended her theoretical ideas on women into practical issues of young girls with problems. Her therapeutic approach was supportive, nonac-cusatory, and pragmatic. To her, the young woman in trouble had a positive ability to change her life and "definition of the situation." This emphasis on constructive skills and abilities emerged from a belief in the similarity between all people and the potential for growth. She analyzed feelings as integral to behavior, defined a helping person as a coequal in a creative process, and revealed time as a living limit that is part of life and not a threat to it.

Taft systematically altered her theory, practice, and network as a result of her work with and sponsorship of Otto Rank in 1926 (Taft 1958). Her deep roots in symbolic interaction continued, but they were modified to fit a clinical focus on people with problems in daily living. Instead of looking at the women's movement or the struggles between family and social claims on a societal level, Taft studied the problematic lives of individual women. Drawing on extensive case histories of women clients, Taft developed a large corpus of feminist therapy. This large body of material could be fruitfully analyzed within the extensive, recent literature on this topic.

Taft's articles appeared in professional journals such as *The Publications of the American Sociological Society*, *Mental Hygiene*, *The American Journal of Psychiatry*, and *School and Society* as well as in popular magazines. She trans-lated two of Otto Rank's books (1936a and 1936b), wrote his autobiography (1958), and formulated her own ideas in *The Dynamics of Therapy in a Controlled Relationship* (1933a). She edited a number of texts (1939, 1943, 1944, 1946a, 1946b, and 1948), some of which were originally published as issues of *The*

Journal of Social Work Process, which she cofounded. Her eminence as a social worker eclipsed her long struggle between 1913 and 1926 to be an academic social psychologist.

CRITIQUES OF JESSIE TAFT

Taft was a woman-identified theorist whose writings in sociology have been overlooked by patriarchal professionals. Taft was initially integrated into sociology, however. W. I. Thomas, for example, cited Taft's work extensively in his book on *The Unadjusted Girl* (1923). Taft's case studies are part of his "life history documents" in his book. A broad overview of Taft's early connections to male symbolic interactionists is provided by Rosalind Rosenberg (1982). John Dollard analyzed Taft's *Dynamics of Therapy* (1933a) as a major source of life history documentation. He applied his "criteria for the life history" to her text, marking her inclusion within this important, sociological tradition (1935).

My analysis of Taft locates her feminist sociology within a gender-integrated symbolic interactionism. First, I have discussed Taft's central role in articulating the relation between society, the female self, and the women's movement (1987). Second, I have analyzed her development of clinical symbolic interactionism, especially in the analysis of young girls' problems in childhood and adolescence (1986; see also Fritz 1985). Third, I analyzed her connections to Ethel S. Dummer through their correspondence (1978–1979), and to the wider sociological milieu in which she worked (1987). Finally, I have codified and connected her writings between 1913 and 1926 in an unpublished manuscript on her life and intellectual contributions (1989).

The rationale for recognizing Taft as a significant symbolic interactionist lies primarily in her work as a feminist theorist. She articulated a brilliant political theory of feminism, socialization, and social action, powerfully combining the concepts of G. H. Mead, W. I. Thomas, and Jane Addams*. In addition, she translated and introduced Otto Rank to American social workers (Taft 1936a, 1936b, 1958; Robinson 1962) and integrated his work with her own version of Chicago sociology (Taft 1913, 1926a). This later work differed significantly from her earlier writings, emphasized here. The work published after 1926 is more recognized and accessible in social work literature, although its linkage to Chicago symbolic interactionism has seldom been noted. Taft's complex work merging neo-Freudian and symbolic interactionist concepts provides a firm theoretical basis for clinical sociology. Taft's feminist symbolic interactionism is a distinct and fundamental contribution to sociological theory.

BIBLIOGRAPHY

Selected Writings by Jessie Taft

Taft, Jessie. 1913. *The Woman Movement From the Point of View of Social Consciousness*. Ph.D. diss., Department of Philosophy, University of Chicago. Published as Philosophic Studies Issued Under the Direction of the Department of Philosophy of the University of Chicago, No. 6. University of Chicago Press, 1916; partially reprinted in *Women and Symbolic Interaction*, edited by Mary Jo Deegan and M. R. Hill, pp. 19–50. Boston: Allen & Unwin, 1987.

1918. "The Limitations of the Psychiatrist." *Mental Hygiene* 2 (October): 656–662.

1920a. "The Neurotic Girl." *Modern Medicine* 2 (February): 162–170.

1920b. "Problems of Social Case Work with Children." *Family* 1 (July): 1–8.

1921a. "Mental Hygiene Problems of Normal Adolescence." *Proceedings of the National Conference of Social Work*, pp. 355–359.

1921b. "Individualizing the Child in the School." *Family* 2 (January): 208.

1921c. "Some Problems in Delinquency—Where Do They Belong?" *Proceedings of the American Sociological Society* 15: 186–196.

1923. "Progress in Social Case Work in Mental Hygiene." *Proceedings of the National Conference of Social Work*, pp. 338–339.

1924a. "Turn Good Intentions into Channels of Objective Achievement." *School Life* 9 (January): 113–114.

1924b. "The Use of the Transfer Within the Limits of the Office Interview." *Family* 5 (October): 143–146.

1925a. "The Re-Education of a Psychoneurotic Girl." *American Journal of Psychiatry* 4 (January): 479–487.

1925b. "Sex in Children." *The World Tomorrow* 8 (October): 229–300.

1926a. "The Effect of an Unsatisfactory Mother-Daughter Relationship Upon the Development of a Personality." *The Family* 7 (March): 10–17.

1926b. "Closed Doors and the Keys to Them." *Survey* 56 (September 15): 613–616.

1926c. "What It Means to Be a Foster Parent." *Progressive Education* 3 (October–November–December): 351.

1930. "The Catch in Praise." *Child Study* (February): 133–135, 150.

1932a. "An Experiment in a Therapeutically Limited Relationship with a Seven-Year-Old Girl." *The Psychoanalytic Review* 19 (October): 361.

1932b. "The Time Element in Mental Hygiene Therapy as Applied to Social Case Work." *Proceedings of the National Conference of Social Work*, pp. 368–381.

1933a. *The Dynamics of Therapy in a Controlled Relationship*. New York: Macmillan.

1933b. "Living and Feeling." *Child Study* 10 (January): 105–109.

1936a. *Will Therapy: An Analysis of the Therapeutic Process in Terms of Relationship*, by Otto Rank, translated by Jessie Taft. New York: Alfred A. Knopf.

1936b. *Truth and Reality: A Life History of the Human Will*, by Otto Rank, translated by Jessie Taft. New York: Alfred A. Knopf.

1949. "Time as the Medium of the Helping Process." *Jewish Social Service Quarterly* 26: 190–198.

1958. *Otto Rank, a Biographical Study Based on Notebooks, Letters, Collected Writings, Therapeutic Achievements, and Personal Associations*. New York: Julian Press.

1962. *Jessie Taft: Therapist and Social Work Educator*, edited with an introduction by Virginia P. Robinson. Philadelphia: University of Pennsylvania Press.

1939. Taft, Jessie, ed. *Social Case Work with Children, Studies in Structure and Process. Journal of Social Work Process* 1, no. 3.

1943. *Day Nursery Care as a Social Service*. Philadelphia: Pennsylvania School of Social Work.

1944. *A Functional Approach to Family Case Work*. Philadelphia: University of Pennsylvania Press.

1946a. *The Role of the Baby in the Placement Process*. Philadelphia: Pennsylvania School of Social Work.

1946b. *Counseling and Protective Service as Family Case Work: A Functional Approach*. Philadelphia: Pennsylvania School of Social Work.

1948. *Family Casework and Counseling: A Functional Approach*. Philadelphia: University of Pennsylvania Press.

Studies About Jessie Taft and Supplementary References

Axinn, June. 1980. "Taft, Jessie." In *Notable American Women*, edited by Barbara Sicherman and Carol Hurd Green, pp. 675–677. Cambridge, MA: Harvard University Press, Belknap Press.

Deegan, Mary Jo. 1978–1979. "The Taft-Dummer Correspondence." *Journal of the Otto Rank Association* 13 (Winter): 55–60.

———. 1986. "The Clinical Sociology of Jessie Taft." *Clinical Sociology Review* 4 (December): 30–45.

———. 1987. "Symbolic Interaction and the Study of Women: An Introduction." In *Women and Symbolic Interaction*, edited by Mary Jo Deegan and Michael R. Hill, pp. 3–15. Boston: Allen—Unwin.

———. 1988. *Jane Addams and the Men of the Chicago School, 1892–1918*. New Brunswick, NJ: Transaction Books.

Dollard, John. 1935. *Criteria for the Life History: With Analyses of Six Notable Documents*. New Haven, CT: Yale University Press.

Faatz, Anita J. 1962. "A Complete Bibliography of the Writings of Jessie Taft." In *Jessie Taft: Therapist and Social Work Educator*, edited by Virginia P. Robinson, pp. 371–384. Philadelphia: University of Pennsylvania Press.

Fritz, Jan M., ed. 1985. *The Clinical Sociology Handbook*. New York: Garland.

"Personals." 1916. *Survey* 35 (January 15): 469.

Robinson, Virginia P. 1962. "Editor's Introductions." In *Jessie Taft: Therapist and Social Work Educator*, by Jessie Taft, edited by V. P. Robinson, pp. 11–13, 23–38, 41–55, 67–75, 121–134, 193–205, 345–368. Philadelphia: University of Pennsylvania Press.

Rosenberg, Rosalind. 1982. *Beyond Separate Spheres*. New Haven, CT: Yale University Press.

Smith-Rosenberg, Carroll. 1975. "The Female World of Love and Ritual." *Signs* 1 (Autumn): 1–29.

Thomas, William I. 1923. *The Unadjusted Girl: With Cases and Standpoint for Behavior Analysis*, foreword by Ethel Sturgess Dummer. Criminal Science Monographs, No. 4. Boston: Little, Brown. Reprinted, 1967.

Trowle, Charlotte. 1960. "In Memoriam: Jessie Taft, 1882–1960." *Social Service Review* 34 (September): 345–346.

Unpublished Materials

Deegan, Mary Jo. 1989. "The Feminist Vision of Jessie Taft."

MARY JO DEEGAN

MARION TALBOT (1858–1947)

Marion Talbot was an authority on women's higher education and the sociology of the home. As an author, the first dean of women in a coeducational institution in the United States, a cofounder of the American Association of University Women, and a charter faculty member at the University of Chicago, Talbot was a significant leader of women in sociology. Her centrality to Chicago sociology is consistently hidden in the massive literature on the men of the Chicago school.

BIOGRAPHY

The Talbots of Boston were located at the center of its intellectual and cultural life (e.g., Talbot 1938). Marion, the eldest of their six children, was born in Thun, Switzerland, on July 31, 1858. Her father, Israel Tisdale Talbot, practiced homeopathic medicine and served as the first dean of the medical school of Boston University. Her mother, Emily Fairbanks Talbot, was a leader in the struggle for women's higher education and women's work in the social sciences. She was active in establishing the Girls' Latin School in Boston, an endeavor she began partially to secure a forum for her daughter's training. Marion Talbot was always encouraged by her parents in her advocacy of women's rights in academic institutions.

Talbot was admitted to Boston University with conditional limits, yet she was still able to earn a bachelor of arts degree in 1880. After several years of social life and travel, she found, like Jane Addams,* that she wanted more than the traditional life open to women. Probably at the urging of a family acquaintance and one of the founders of human ecology, Ellen H. Richards (Clarke 1973), Marion was encouraged to study "domestic science." After several years of sporadic study, she completed a bachelor of science degree from the Massachusetts Institute of Technology in 1888.

In 1881–1882 Marion, her mother, Richards, and Alice Freeman Palmer, an early president of Wellesley (Palmer 1908), among others, cofounded the Association of Collegiate Alumnae (ACA), which later adopted the name of the American Association of University Women [AAUW]. This organization became the spearhead for educated women to leverage opportunities in the academy and the wider society. Marion was its first secretary, and its president from 1895 to 1897.

In 1890, after completing her second bachelor's degree, Talbot was appointed an instructor in domestic science at Wellesley College (when Palmer was president). Talbot worked with Mary Elizabeth Burroughs Roberts Smith Coolidge* here, and met Sophonisba Breckinridge,* who became a lifelong colleague and friend.

In March 1892 Palmer met with W. R. Harper, president of the University of Chicago, who offered her the position of dean of the women's colleges. Instead of accepting the full-time position, Palmer wanted to keep her presidency at Wellesley and work part-time at Chicago. She recommended that Talbot be offered a full-time job as her assistant. With considerable anticipation mixed with fear, Talbot joined the University of Chicago faculty in 1892 as an assistant professor in the department of sociology and anthropology, and became the first full-time women's dean in a coeducational institution.

Talbot was included within the structure, teaching, and practice of sociology at the university as the head of "women's work" throughout the institution. One of the indicators of her strong ties to sociology, a fact consistently denied in sociological annals, is her position as associate editor of *The American Journal of Sociology* from its founding in 1895 to her retirement from Chicago in 1925. Her role in the women's network of sociologists has many parallels to that of Albion Small, the chair of her department, but her centrality and negotiations as an academic leader in applied sociology have yet to be analyzed.

The institutional power of Talbot as an intellectual leader was strongly circumscribed, however, at the University of Chicago. Talbot's continuing battles to make a department with its own funding, staff, journal, fellowship, library resources, and intellectual legitimacy are outlined in her personal papers and the presidents' papers at that institution.

Talbot was a charter member of the American Sociological Association, and one of the earliest participants in the Lake Placid Conferences in Home Economics. She was active in a number of professional associations, including the American Historical Association, the American Public Health Association, the Labor Legislation Association, and the National Federation of Women's Clubs. Talbot documented the multitude of activities, often supporting the work of Hull-House women, organized by the Chicago branch of the ACA by 1917 (Talbot Ca. 1918). In 1904 Talbot was awarded an honorary doctor of law degree from Cornell College in Iowa.

Talbot lived a woman-centered existence. First, she was surrounded by female luminaries such as her mother, Julia Ward Howe, and Louisa May Alcott (Talbot 1938) during her childhood and adolescence. Then she worked with Richards, Palmer, Mary Elizabeth Burroughs Roberts Smith Coolidge* and Jane Addams. She mentored Sophonisba Breckinridge,* with whom she shared her life. (From 1908 to 1920 Breckinridge lived in the summers at Hull-House while Talbot lived at her cottage on a lake in New Hampshire. See Norton 1925.) For years they lived in women's dormitories as leaders, friends, and bulwarks against a hostile world for educated women. She built institutional structures for women and carved a place for them in the academy. She was the academic foundation for women's work at the University of Chicago, the international leader in sociology. She actively helped Katherine Bement Davis* and Jessie Taft* find their first jobs.

Talbot, like most of the early Chicago women, lived a long, full life. She continued her work for women students as dean of women at Chicago until her retirement from that position in 1925. In 1927 she served as acting president of Constantinople Women's College in Turkey for a year and then again in 1931–1932.

In 1947, at the age of ninety, Talbot wrote optimistically to her aging friend and sister feminist Alice Blackwell:

It makes me very happy as the days and years pass quietly in my comfortable home and old time happy memories flood my mind. . . . I hope you feel that the outlook for the world is more encouraging. . . . We have lived through a remarkable and tragic era. I have been very fortunate and happy. (Talbot to Blackwell, January 25, 1947; NAWSA, Library of Congress, Box 29)

Within the year Talbot's fortunes changed rapidly. Breckinridge died in December 1947, and her death was a severe blow to Talbot. Within a few months Talbot died, too. According to one obituary, her passing occurred without mourning: "She was old and frail and lonely" (Morriss, NAWSA, Library of Congress, Box 29). Her decline was rapid and occurred at the end of a very loving and productive life. She had helped to establish the AAUW, which had more than a hundred thousand members at the time of her death; saw women enter universities and college campuses across the country; and lived to see deans of women working on more than a thousand campuses. She was one of the recognized founders of home economics, although male sociologists ignored her contributions and pivotal role in the lives of early women in sociology.

MAJOR THEMES

Talbot wrote in two major areas: the sociology of the home and the sociology of education. She was particularly involved in women's education, their work in higher education, and their role as sources of knowledge. Her particular administrative innovations at the University of Chicago and her analyses of women's work in that institution are major resources for scholars studying the history of the sexual division of labor in sociology.

Talbot's sociology of the home was tied to its material reality, from its rudimentary sanitary functioning to its aesthetic creation as an environment for the self. Thus Talbot's pioneering work in women's education was complemented by her scholarly study of the application of science to the home. This latter interest was probably sparked by her association with Ellen H. Richards, a leader in the home economics field, a family friend, a teacher, and a colleague. With Richards, Talbot edited *Home Sanitation: A Manual for Housekeepers* (1887) and wrote *Food as a Factor in Student Life* (1894). The latter is a more scholarly study than the former. The authors analyzed food services in dormitory settings and how to set nutritious standards at low cost. Both books are outdated as sources of factual information, but they were crucial, beginning steps in the study of nutrition and home economics.

The Modern Household (1913), coauthored with Breckinridge, is an introductory text intended for housewives and college students to help them adapt to modern social changes that affect the home. The book covers a variety of topics ranging from the mundane care of the house to ethics in consumerism and the community. Changing households were in the vortex of modernity, a complex consumer center that was part of a larger social organization.

As one of the first deans of women in American higher education, Talbot's policies on women's role in universities laid the groundwork for similar programs throughout the country. Although not a radical, she consistently made decisions favoring equality between the sexes. For example, she and Palmer decided not to claim the dean's right to present degrees to graduates to avoid segregating the sexes. Talbot also engaged in a lengthy battle to prevent the installation of sororities at Chicago. Because she believed that women were at the university to study as colleagues to men and not as social assets, she successfully blocked their establishment. This policy has continued at Chicago until the present (Talbot 1936).

More concrete precedents favoring women emerged from her leadership of women graduate students and faculty. In a 1903 report Talbot cited a number of statistics relating to women's status at Chicago. For example, she noted that until 1901, there were only twenty-one female faculty members. With the establishment of the Chicago Institute, the number of female faculty jumped to forty-one. Clearly, the policy at Chicago was to keep women in lower-level positions, noted by Talbot by name and rank, and the founding of a "woman's department" (the Chicago Institute) accounted for a rapid increase in female faculty. In an excellent statement on scholarships Talbot clearly documented the superior achievements of women students compared with men at Chicago. More women than men also graduated Phi Beta Kappa (Talbot 1903, 139). Women doctors, although graduating in a far smaller proportion than men (35 women to 209 men), were competitive in honorary awards and achievements.

Women at Chicago built a sense of comraderie through their participation in two organizations: The Club of Women Fellows for graduate women and the Women's Union, primarily composed of undergraduate women. The former group was organized by Talbot as a mentoring mechanism to learn how to become faculty members and colleagues. "Monthly meetings were held in Kelly Hall or Green Hall; and after luncheon sitting in a large circle—for we numbered from twelve to twenty—each one told of the investigating she was carrying on and discussed general problems of education" (Talbot 1936, 86). College faculty and local community leaders also addressed the group, expanding their knowledge and professional networks. Members of this club included the female sociologists Sophonisba Breckinridge, Katherine Bement Davis, and Amy Hewes* (Talbot 1903, 122–127). These women received training and support that aided in their development of the women's network in sociology. The latter group, the Women's Union, was established in October 1901: "To unite the women of the university for the promotion of their common interests" (Talbot 1903, 137). In 1903 the group had almost 200 members (Talbot 1903, 138).

Talbot's *The Education of Women* (1910a) describes the educational opportunities available to girls and women in the United States at that time. Talbot's defense of social hygiene, exercise, and training for rational thinking were "daring" ideas that are now commonplace facts because of her arguments and those of her feminist cohort. Her emphasis on women in the home made her more "radical" ideas acceptable to a skeptical readership.

The History of the American Association of University Women, 1881–1931 written by Talbot and Lois Kimball Mathews Rosenberry (1931), is a detailed account of the committees, work, and goals of the association that Talbot cofounded. It is a gold mine of information on the work and networks of early women professionals, especially sociologists.

Anyone interested in the turbulent, innovative founding days of the University of Chicago will find Talbot's *More Than Lore* (1936) a delight to read. Talbot is forthright in her statements about discrimination against women professionals at the university.

Talbot's fascinating autobiography is one of the few accounts of the attempt to segregate the sexes at Chicago. Her battle against this policy reflects her institutional struggle for coeducation and her bittersweet humor. According to Talbot, this reactionary stance was never very successful, and appeared to fade away as a policy. What is significant, however, is that as long as it was a possibility and an issue, the university stood for the separation of the sexes, in the "best interests" of the students. The concern, particularly for the chair of sociology, Albion Small, was primarily for the protection of man against "dangerous" women (Talbot 1936, 172–175).

The most important statement on sexism at Chicago is found in her autobiography, in the chapter on "The Weaker Sex." Here Talbot recounts women's long struggle to enter institutions of higher learning. Chicago was one of the few institutions that accepted women as graduate students in 1892, and before its opening, it announced that there were to be five women faculty members and eight fellows on the new staff. "This was the situation when the University opened October 1,1892. No wonder the road ahead seemed clear. But the vision proved to be somewhat of a mirage. No new appointments of women and no promotions were made for two years" (Talbot 1903, 131). In 1895 some women had been promoted, but no woman was a full professor. The same repressive future lay ahead. Well-qualified women were available but not hired.

Despite Talbot's fights for women's equality, she still believed that women should be "ladies," polite and well bred, and that a higher education prepared women to be better wives and mothers. In this way she supported the traditional roles of women. Her writings are interspersed, though, with a sharp appreciation of women's contributions to society and the difficulty of managing a home, and these analyses sound similar to modern writings on the sociology of housewives and housework. Most clearly, her critiques of discrimination against women in academia are relevant and accurate today.

Talbot, like many other early female sociologists, critiqued "women's work" in sociology and provided a "woman's perspective" in the *American Journal of Sociology*. Unlike many of her female students, Talbot reviewed several men's books. Thus, although she found several admirable points in John Gillette's *Vocational Education*, she criticized his male viewpoint as "determining what men should be as men" (Talbot 1910b, 129). According to Talbot (1913b), Gillette, later president of the American Sociological Society, did not stress training for individuality and citizenship and falsely equated specialization with vocational training. Talbot found M. J. Rosenau's analysis of the social production of milk extremely well written. She shared his pragmatic emphasis on pasteurization and inspection (1913c; other reviews are found in 1913a).

CRITIQUES OF MARION TALBOT

Biographies and autobiographies of women from Talbot's era are fruitful sources of information on Talbot (e.g., Clarke 1973). Gwendolyn Wright's excellent analysis of the ideal home and its physical construction is an important resource for understanding Talbot's milieu and role in the tempestuous and exciting world of Chicago architecture (1980). Wright also explains Talbot's work with Ellen Richards and with some of the academic men at the University of Chicago.

Most unfortunately Talbot's central role in training and supporting women in sociology has been overlooked or denied in the vast literature on the men of the Chicago school. She is dismissed as an anomaly: a nonsociologist looking for home economics. A notable exception to this general criticism is Virginia Fish's writings (1985). Fish's excellent analysis of Talbot's autobiography and central role at the University of Chicago is an important analysis, although Fish does not stress the sociological roots of Talbot's work. Rosalind Rosenberg has written a fine account of Talbot's early life and family roots in social science (1982).

Here, too, Talbot's connections to sociology are only briefly examined. Talbot's embeddedness in the life of Sophonisba Breckinridge also is overlooked.

Ella Flagg Young, an eminent student of G. H. Mead and John Dewey, positively reviewed *The Education of Women* (1910). She found Talbot to unconsciously "take the attitude of college women toward social questions" because of Talbot's wide experience and leadership (p. 120). Frances Fenton Bernard positively critiqued *The Modern Household* (1912), particularly commending the view that both men and women needed household training and pointing to some minor disagreements she had with the text. Mary Louis Mark found the second edition of *The Modern Household* a mixed improvement. The bibliography and questions had been updated, but she thought that changes wrought by World War I were underrepresented (1921). Mark's cooler reception of this book reflects larger shifts in the definition of sociology that occurred after the war as well.

I have used Talbot's account of the segregation of the sexes in my own work on the sexual division of labor in sociology (1988a, 191–200, passim) and placed Talbot in a central role in the golden era of women in sociology (1978, 1982, 1987, 1988a, and 1988b). Her central role in the lives and careers of early women sociologists is repeatedly mentioned in several entries here. Despite these efforts, a serious evaluation of Talbot's role in sociology remains to be written.

BIBLIOGRAPHY

Selected Writings by Marion Talbot

1895. "Domestic Science in the Colleges." *Table Talk* 10 (September): 289–292.
1896a. "Sanitation and Sociology." *American Journal of Sociology* 2 (July): 74–81.
1896b. "Sanitary Science and Its Place in the University." *University Record* (Chicago) 1 (December 4): 457–458.
1897. "Present Day Problems in the Education of Women." *Educational Review* 14 (October): 248–258.
1903. "The Women of the University." In *Decennial Publication of the University of Chicago*, pp. 122–145. Chicago: University of Chicago Press. pp. 122–145.
1905. "Introduction of the Convocation Orator." *University Record* (Chicago) 9 (January): 273–274.
1909. "Moral and Religious Influences as Related to Environment of Student Life: Dormitory Life for College Women." *Religious Education* (April).
1910a. *The Education of Women.* Chicago: University of Chicago Press.
1910b. "Review of *Vocational Education*." *American Journal of Sociology* 16 (July): 128–129.
1912. *House Sanitation.* Boston: Whitcomb–Barrows.
1913a. "Review of *La Reglementation de Travail des Femmes et des enfants aux Etats-Unis*." *American Journal of Sociology* 18 (January): 579.
1913b. "The Vocational and Cultural Value of Domestic Science." *Journal of Home Economics* 5 (June): 232–236.

1913c. "Review of *The Milk Question*." *American Journal of Sociology* 19 (July): 114–115.

1918. *History of the Chicago Association of Collegiate Alumnae: 1888–1917*. Chicago: Chicago Association of Collegiate Alumnae.

1922. "The Women of the University." In *President's Report: Covering the Academic Year July 1,1920 to June 30, 1921* (Chicago), pp. 34–35. Chicago: University of Chicago Press.

1925. "The Challenge of a Retrospective." *University Record* (Chicago) 11 (April): 87–101.

1934. "The World Discovers That College Women Are People." *University of Chicago Magazine* 26 (March): 181–183.

1936. *More Than Lore: Reminiscences of Marion Talbot, Dean of Women, The University of Chicago, 1892–1925*. Chicago: University of Chicago Press.

1938. "Glimpses of the Real Louisa May Alcott." *New England Quarterly* (December): 731–738.

Coauthored Works

Richards, Ellen H., and Marion Talbot, eds. 1887. *Home Sanitation: A Manual for Housekeepers*. Boston: Ticknor & Co.

———.1894. *Food as a Factor in Student Life*. Chicago: University of Chicago Press.

Talbot, Marion, and Sophonisba Breckinridge. 1913. *The Modern Household*. Boston: Whitcomb—Barrows.

Talbot, Marion, and Lois Kimball M. Rosenberry. 1931. *The History of the American Association of University Women: 1881–1931*. Cambridge, MA: Lakeside Press.

Studies About Marion Talbot and Supplemental References

Bernard, Frances Fenton. 1912. "Review of *The Modern Household*." *American Journal of Sociology* 18 (November): 411–413.

Clarke, Robert. 1973. *Ellen Swallow: The Woman Who Founded Ecology*. Chicago: Follett Publishing Co.

Deegan, Mary Jo. 1978. "Women in Sociology: 1890–1930." *Journal of the History of Sociology* 1 (Fall): 11–34.

———. 1982. "Marion Talbot." In *American Women Writers*, vol. 4, edited by Lina Mainiero, pp. 202–203. New York: Ungar.

———. 1987. "An American Dream: The Historical Connections Between Women, Humanism, and Sociology, 1890–1920." *Humanity and Society* 11 (August): 353–365.

———. 1988a. *Jane Addams and the Men of the Chicago School, 1892–1916*. New Brunswick, NJ: Transaction Books.

———.1988b. "Transcending a Patriarchal Past: Teaching the History of Early Female Sociologists." *Teaching Sociology* 16 (April): 141–150.

Fish, Virginia K. 1985. "*More Than Lore*: Marion Talbot and Her Role in the Founding Years of the University of Chicago." *International Journal of Women's Studies* 8 (Summer): 228–249.

Hayden, Delores. 1981. *The Grand Domestic Revolution*. Cambridge, MA: MIT Press.

Leonard, John Willam, ed. 1914. "Talbot, Marion." In *Women's Who's Who of America*, p. 800. New York: American Commonwealth.

Mark, Mary Louise. 1921. "Review of *The Modern Household*." *American Journal of Sociology* 26 (January): 529–530.

Norton, Alice Peloubet. 1923. "Home Economics in Constantinople College." *Journal of Home Economics* 15 (October): 532–582.

———. 1925. "Marion Talbot." *Journal of Home Economics* 17 (September): 479–482.

Palmer, George Herbert. 1908. *Alice Freeman Palmer*. Boston: Houghton Mifflin.

Rosenberg, Rosalind. 1982. *Beyond Separate Spheres*. New Haven, CT: Yale University Press.

Storr, Richard J. 1971. "Talbot, Marion." In *Notable American Women*, vol. 3, edited by Edward T. James, Janet Wilson James, and Paul S. Boyer, pp. 423–424. Cambridge, MA: Harvard University Press, Belknap Press.

Swain, Frances L. 1949. "Our Professional Debt to Marion Talbot." *Journal of Home Economics* 41 (April): 185–186.

Wright, Gwendolyn. 1980. *Moralism and the Model Home: Domestic Architecture and Cultural Conflict in Chicago, 1873–1913*. Chicago: University of Chicago Press.

Young, Ella Flagg. 1910. "Review of *The Education of Women*." *American Journal of Sociology* 16 (July): 119–121.

Archives

Library of Congress, Washington, D. C. National American Woman's Suffrage Association (NAWSA), Box 29. Marion Talbot to Alice Blackwell, January 25, 1947. Margaret S. Morriss, "Marion Talbot: In Memoriam," *Journal of the American Association of University Women*.

MARY JO DEEGAN

DOROTHY SWAINE THOMAS
(1899–1977)

Dorothy Swaine Thomas was a noted statistician and demographer. When most women in sociology were being channeled into social work, she was on the forefront of the change that made quantitative methods the hallmark of American sociology. Although she is most known for her demographic work and studies of the Japanese-American internment of World War II, she also was a groundbreaker in the observational methods of experimental sociology. In addition, Thomas holds the distinction of being the first female president of the American Sociological Society.

BIOGRAPHY

Thomas was born October 24, 1899, in Baltimore, Maryland, and was an only child of John Knight Thomas and Sarah Elizabeth Swaine Thomas. Both parents came from prosperous, well-educated, but, in her terms, "by no means intellectual" families. Thomas was herself an intellectually precocious child. Despite her father's disapproval, an uncle taught her to read and write, do arithmetic, and solve puzzles when she was no more than three years old.

Later she was an excellent student who enjoyed school immensely. As a senior in high school she won first prize in a citywide competition for an essay titled "Shipbuilding at the Port of Baltimore." At her graduation she was to receive the prize for the essay, a medal for good grades, and a full scholarship to a local women's college. A few days before the ceremony an impertinent remark to a teacher was enough to have her denied both her high school diploma and the scholarship. Undaunted, Thomas applied for and was promptly awarded a scholarship to Barnard College. In the meantime the high school reconsidered its decision, but with Barnard's offer in hand, she considered it high time to leave Baltimore.

At Barnard, Thomas developed what she called an "impelling social conscience." As chairman of the Political and Social Discussion Club, and also of a student government committee directed at curricular reform, she was somewhat unpopular with college administrators, but she enjoyed her identity as a "young radical." Her new social conscience led her to the department of economics and sociology, chaired by William F. Ogburn.

As Thomas's first mentor, Ogburn had considerable impact on the direction her life would take. At Barnard he was diverging from the traditional sociological path of the armchair theorists by teaching that the social world could be accurately scrutinized only with precise scientific methods. When he asked Thomas what she would like to research, and she replied, "Socialism," he demanded, "Do you want to become a scientist or an actionist?" He pointed out that Thomas's obvious biases might make her less than objective. Ogburn's own bias was plain, and the young Thomas's answer was that she indeed wanted to be a scientist, but she retorted that at the same time she wanted to do research on "socially significant" problems (Thomas 1970, 219).

While still an undergraduate, Thomas coauthored two articles with Ogburn. The first, prepared for publication by Ogburn, but representing Thomas's findings, was titled "Are Inventions Inevitable?" (1922). It provided evidence for and against independence of 148 simultaneous inventions or discoveries in the histories of science. The subject of the second, titled "The Influence of the Business Cycle on Certain Social Conditions," sparked an enthusiasm in Thomas that was maintained throughout her career. Based on a theory of economic determinism, this paper demonstrated the dependency of social phenomena such as marriages, births, deaths, infant mortality, suicide, and crime on fluctuations of the business cycle in the United States between 1870 and 1920.

After graduating from Barnard in 1922 Thomas set off for the London School of Economics, which was made to order for her: its emphasis was on research, and there were no required courses. She knew precisely what she wanted to do, and immediately set to work on her thesis with the influential guidance of Professor Arthur L. Bowley and William H. Beveridge, director of the school. In only two years her dissertation was completed, and readily accepted for publication. The importance of *Social Aspects of the Business Cycle* (1925) was quickly recognized in scholarly journals, and remains a landmark in the area of demography. By the age of twenty-four Thomas had attained a doctorate in economics (1924), had been awarded the prestigious Hutchinson Research Medal, and had established herself as a leader in an important area of research.

Despite the significance of her work and her impressive publication record, when she returned to the United States in the fall of 1924, Thomas was unable to obtain a position in what she considered a first-rate university, and she refused to settle for an available job in a women's college. Although she did not identify herself as a feminist, she demonstrated the type of feminism that wanted no distinction between women and men, at least in the professional realm. Without feminist fanfare, she marched into the male academic arena as if she had a perfect right to be there. Considering superior work the strongest counterforce to disadvantages that women faced, she intended to make it in the male world on her own merits.

She worked for a year as an economic statistician at the Federal Reserve Bank, and in 1926 received a postdoctoral fellowship from the Social Science Research Council. Working on a topic involving convictions for crime in New York, she encountered difficulty obtaining data, and Professor Wesley Mitchell (a major influence on her thinking) suggested that she consult the renowned sociologist W. I. Thomas.

When she approached W. I. Thomas for help in 1926, he was looking for a statistician to assist him in a child development study. When he offered her the position, she was happy to give up her fellowship for the opportunity to work with one of sociology's founding fathers. The result of their collaboration was *The Child in America* (1928), which combined W. I. Thomas's famous situational approach with Dorothy Thomas's statistical methods. In 1935 the two Thomases were married. She was thirty-six and he was sixty-two.

Between 1927 and 1930 Thomas worked as associate professor and research associate at Columbia University's Teachers College, directing studies of the behavior of nursery school children. In 1930 she became a research associate at Yale University's Institute of Human Relation, and director of research in Social Statistics from 1935 to 1939. She took with her to Yale Alice Loomis and Ruth Arrington, who had obtained their doctorates under her direction at Columbia. Together the three continued the observational studies they had begun at Columbia, and with other associates published *Observational Studies of Social Behavior* in 1933.

Thomas's collaboration with Loomis and Arrington is indicative of the importance she placed on teaching, and on giving her students the same sort of support and acknowledgment she received from Ogburn. As a teacher, she emphasized learning by participation in research. Popular and friendly on the one hand, she also was a strict taskmaster, demanding of her students the same impeccable standards that she set for herself. A number of distinguished students is one of her greatest legacies.

An associate from the Yale period recalls Dorothy Thomas as resembling a "flapper stereotype," with short, bobbed hair, cigarette in a long holder, dressed in tailored clothes, lively in conversation, and with lots of contagious enthusiasm for her research. During the first years at Yale she lived in a Victorian house with Ruth Arrington and a research worker at the law school. The house was well managed by a maid who cooked gourmet meals for a steady stream of guests, including prominent social scientists. Thomas and Thomas were yet unmarried, but he was a regular visitor, and the two of them often were sought out to participate in formal occasions and graduate seminars.

Between 1930 and 1936 the two Thomases spent part of each year in Sweden.

With Gunnar and Alva Myrdal* they intended to undertake a study of the Swedish people similar to *The Polish Peasant in Europe and America*, the classic written by W. I. Thomas and Florian Znaniecki. Although the study didn't materialize, both Thomases embarked on research that kept their annual visits to Sweden alive for several years. Dorothy Thomas was a visiting professor at the Social Science Institute, University of Stockholm, for part of 1933, 1935, and 1936.

After a brief stint as a staff member for the Carnegie Corporation Study of the Negro in America (1939–1954), Thomas realized a major career goal: she became a full professor, with tenure, at the University of California at Berkeley (lecturer in sociology, 1940–1941; professor of rural sociology, 1941–1948). Her eight years at Berkeley are most notable for two things: her studies of the Japanese-American internment of World War II and her involvement in the establishment of the university's first sociology department.

Thomas was brought to Berkeley to teach rural sociology in the agriculture department, but also in anticipation of a new sociology department, with the virtual promise that she would be its chair (Murray 1979, 70). She was considered a prime candidate for this position because of her unique training and collaboration with Ogburn and W. I. Thomas, seminal representatives of both quantitative and qualitative sociology. However, a bitter battle involving departmental rivalries, vested interests, personality clashes, possibly sex discrimination, and a general resistance to sociology, especially to the form Thomas represented most, were to keep her from the post (see Murray 1979; Roscoe 1987). This battle was interrupted by World War II, and Thomas was awarded a Giannini Foundation grant to document the evacuation, internment, and resettlement of Japanese-Americans on the West Coast. After the war the sociology department war heated up again, and finally, in 1946, a sociology department came to be at Berkeley, but Dorothy Thomas was excluded from it, along with much of the sociological perspective she represented.

Two years later Thomas became the first woman to attain the rank of professor at the University of Pennsylvania's Wharton School. Together with Simon Kuznets, a fellow student from her Mitchell-oriented days, she embarked on a series of studies on population distribution and economic growth that was to occupy her for twenty years. She was working on the fourth volume of the massive *Population and Economic Growth* when her research was interrupted by a stroke in 1974. After compulsory retirement from the University of Pennsylvania, she continued to work as a professorial lecturer at Georgetown's Center for Population Research.

Thomas is distinguished as being the first woman to hold the office of president of the American Sociological Society (1952). In the American Sociological Society (now called the American Sociological Association), she worked closely with George Lundberg and Read Bain, pushing for the adoption of more rigorous methodology in sociology. She also was the first female board member of the Social Science Research Council and later was its director. One colleague remembers her defending academic freedom with characteristic vigor when she thought that the Council had improperly withdrawn a fellowship during the McCarthy period (Taeuber 1977). She also served as president of the Population Association of America (1958–1959) and as fellow and vice-president of the American Statistical Association. She was active in numerous other organizations as well.

Dorothy Swaine Thomas died on May 1, 1977, at the age of seventy-seven.

MAJOR THEMES

In her observational studies Thomas was among the first to pound out methodological guidelines for the study of social interaction. Studying nursery school children at Columbia and Yale, she was not so much concerned with analyzing the children's social activity as she was in perfecting methods of observation. Assuring observers' objectivity was a major difficulty. "We feel that it is more important in this field to control the observer than to control the experiment" (Thomas 1929, 21). After devising and discarding numerous methods to ensure observational reliability, Thomas and her assistants came up with the novel idea of filming social situations and returning to the laboratory for repeated observations.

Despite her contributions to experimental sociology, Thomas was frustrated by the inconclusiveness of her work in this area, and was uncertain of its significance. In comparison with her other work, she did not value it much herself. Years later, and demonstrating some of W. I. Thomas's influence, she said, "I felt, both at the time and in retrospect, that I was going down a blind alley, for I was essentially trying to quantify the 'unquantifiable' by means of mechanistic, observational techniques" (1970, 223).

Thomas's heart was clearly in her demographic work. This interest can be traced to her undergraduate days at Columbia and graduate work at the London School of Economics. In her research for *Social Aspects of the Business Cycle* she became interested in migration, and in a two-country model she correlated emigration from the United Kingdom with British business cycles and British immigration to the United States with American business cycles. Studies of various population movements and impacts of business cycles would dominate much of her career.

The theme underlying Thomas's demographic work was economic determinism, although she and Ogburn, in one of their joint publications, were quick to point out that their findings did not "necessarily prove a causal influence, that is, that the economic changes produce the social changes" (1988b, 324). At the end of her career she came to question her early commitment to economic determinism, accepting the notion that there is a link between economic and demographic change "by a continuous chain of *interdependent* variables" (1970, 226).

Some of the most widely acknowledged and frequently cited of her works are her Swedish studies. She inherited a study begun by Gunnar Myrdal that traced the interrelations between industrialization and population movements in Sweden. Her research resulted in the major work *Social and Economic Aspects of Swedish Population Movements, 1750–1933* (1941). Because no other country had demographic data as complete as Sweden's, and that covered as long a period of time, this book was seminal in demography, providing original groundwork for hundreds of other studies in the area. She set precedent by publishing much of her data in raw form, thus giving other scholars full access to the material.

It was the lack of reliable demographic data in the United States that led Thomas first to Great Britain and then to Sweden to pursue her interest in demographic research. Later, at the University of Pennsylvania with Simon Kuznets and others, she began to fill the gap of data deficiencies that had frustrated some of her research efforts in the United States. Years of massive information collection resulted in the data base of an economic-demographic history of the United States since the Civil War. This was compiled in three volumes: *Population Distribution and Economic Growth: United States, 1870–1950*. Once again Thomas's work has provided essential material for innumerable scholarly studies in years to come.

The other work for which Thomas is known is her documentation of the West Coast Japanese-American internment of World War II. She watched the rounding up, detention, and resettlement of all people of Japanese descent, regardless of citizenship, with a unique perspective rooted in her previous work: "I saw the situation initially, as just a special case of migration: unselective 'push' at origin (enforced evacuation) and selective 'pull' at destination (voluntary resettlement)" (1970, 225). Working with student assistants, some of whom were evacuees themselves, Thomas collected reams of data that consisted of day-to-day experiences and life histories of the internees. The resulting books had Thomas's characteristic stamp: they were meticulously documented, with complete statistical records. But this endeavor clearly went beyond the quantifiable. Later she said, "I shudder to think of the idiocies I might have perpetrated by way of 'premature quantification' of the essentially 'unquantifiable' had I not been associated with W. I. Thomas at this time" (1970, 225).

CRITIQUES OF DOROTHY SWAINE THOMAS

Although some critics praised Thomas for spare, graceful prose, and for providing other scholars with full access to her data (e.g., Rice 1931), a common criticism of her work was that her texts were unwieldy and dense with statistical data. A typical criticism of her observational studies, and especially of her documentation of the Japanese internment, was that although she recorded the data faultlessly, she presented bare data, and failed to analyze it or to formulate any conclusions other than in methodological issues. Referring to her observational studies, one critic points out that "the investigator who publishes bare data usually places too much hope in the reader; he hopes that the reader will analyze the data for himself'' (Fry 1934). A discussant of *The Spoilage* complains that sociological insights the authors undoubtedly gained were not shared, and another critic of the same work faults the authors for failing "to make use of their materials to combine sociological theory with empirical findings'' (Young 1947).

The Spoilage and *The Salvage* may indeed have seemed "restrained, almost cold accounts of a massive human tragedy and the efforts of a rejected people to reestablish themselves as patriotic Americans'' (Lee 1979, 764). The seemingly cold treatment of the situation was not a reflection of Thomas's attitude, however; she was outraged by the internment and sympathetic with the internees. The restrainment, instead, reflected her insistence on scientific objectivity. This treatment "was vindicated when the Supreme Court accepted her books as unbiased evidence of our crimes against our fellow Americans'' (Obituary, *ASA Footnotes*, 1977).

Thomas might have responded to some of the criticism leveled at her with reference to an article she valued highly titled "Statistics in Social Research'' (1929), in which she formulated her standpoint for research. In this article, influenced greatly by Edwin B. Wilson, she critically evaluated statistical and behavioral methods of research. She concluded it with six "inferences for procedure,'' the sixth of which remained her credo throughout her career:

Interpretations are the investigator's own business. If he has good reason to believe that the statistical analysis has given an inadequate picture of the data, he should state it clearly and unashamedly. But he should carefully avoid appeal to statistics to bolster up such interpretations if they do not simply and logically grow out of the statistics themselves. (1929: 17)

As a statistician and demographer, Thomas was one of a new breed of sociologist. Quantitative methods were being preached by only a handful of people, including William F. Ogburn, when she acquired her sociological training. As one of Ogburn's star students, she was one of the first generations of quantitative sociologists. Her work is clearly important, and yet she is seldom acknowledged in the history of sociology. One of her colleagues suggested that her obscurity might be because she did not identify so much with sociology proper as she did with demography and statistics. It is more likely that she was not identified as a sociologist because she was not allowed a position in sociology proper. Her experience at Berkeley is a case in point.

The contributions of Dorothy Swaine Thomas, both the ground she broke for other women in sociology and her work, warrant a distinguished place in the history of the discipline. Not only was she the first woman to be president of the foremost sociological organization in the country, but her ground-breaking work helped to set the methodological standards that sociology must live up to to be acknowledged a science.

BIBLIOGRAPHY

Selected Writings by Dorothy Swaine Thomas

1925. *Social Aspects of the Business Cycle*. London: G. Routledge & Sons. Ph.D. dissertation, London School of Economics, 1924.

1929. "Statistics in Social Research." *American Journal of Sociology* 35 (July): 1–17.

1931. "Some Aspects of Socio-Legal Research at Yale." *American Journal of Sociology* 37 (September): 213–221.

1936. "Internal Migrations in Sweden: A Note on Their Extensiveness as Compared with Net Migration Gain or Loss." *American Journal of Sociology* 42 (November): 345–357.

1938a. *Research Memorandum on Migration Differentials*. New York: Social Science Research Council.

1938b. "Utilization of Social Security Data for Sociological Research." *American Sociological Review* 3 (October): 718–724.

1941. *Social and Economic Aspects of Swedish Population Movements, 1750–1933*. New York: Macmillan.

1952. "Experiences in Interdisciplinary Research." ASA Presidential Address. *American Sociological Review* 17 (December): 663–669.

1970. "Contribution to the Herman Wold Festschrift." Autobiographical essay. In *Scientists at Work*, edited by Tore Dalenius, G. Karlsson, and S. Malmquist, pp. 216–227. Stockholm: Almquist & Wiksell.

Coauthored Works

Eldridge, Hope T., and Dorothy Swaine Thomas. 1966. *Demographic Analyses and Interrelations*, with an introduction by Simon Kuznets. *Population Redistribution and Economic Growth, United States, 1870–1950*, vol. 3. Philadelphia: American Philosophical Society.

Kuznets, Simon, Ann Ratner Miller, and Richard A. Easterlin. 1960. *Analyses of Economic Change*, with an introduction by Dorothy Swaine Thomas. *Population Redistribution and Economic Growth, United States, 1870–1950*, vol. 2. Philadelphia: American Philosophical Society.

Kuznets, Simon, and Dorothy Swain Thomas, directors. 1957. *Methodological Considerations and Reference Tables*, by Everett S. Lee, A. R. Miller, C. P. Brainerd, and R. A. Easterlin. *Population Redistribution and Economic Growth, United States, 1870–1950*, vol. 1. Philadelphia: American Philosophical Society.

Ogburn, William F., and Dorothy Swaine Thomas. 1922a. "Are Inventions Inevitable? A Note on Social Evolution." *Political Science Quarterly* 37 (March): 83–98.

————. 1922b. "The Influence of the Business Cycle on Certain Social Conditions." *Journal of the American Statistical Association* 18 (September): 324–340.

Thomas, Dorothy Swaine, and associates. 1929. *Some New Techniques for Studying Social Behavior*. New York: Teachers College, Columbia University.

Thomas, Dorothy Swaine, with Charles Kikuchi and James Sakoda. 1952. *The Salvage. Japanese American Evacuation and Resettlement*, vol. 2. Berkeley: University of California Press.

Thomas, Dorothy Swaine, Alice M. Loomis, and Ruth E. Arrington, with Eleanor C.
    Isbell. 1933. *Observational Studies of Social Behavior*. New Haven, CT: Institute
    of Human Relations, Yale University.
Thomas, Dorothy Swaine, and Richard S. Nishimoto. 1946. *The Spoilage. Japanese
    American Evacuation and Resettlement*, vol. 1. Berkeley: University of California
    Press.
Thomas, William I., and Dorothy Swaine Thomas. 1928. *The Child in America: Behavior
    Problems and Programs*. New York: Alfred A. Knopf. Reprinted, with a new
    introduction by Mary Jo Deegan, New Brunswick, NJ: Transaction Books, in
    preparation.

Studies About Dorothy Swaine Thomas and Supplemental References

"Dorothy S. Thomas, Sociologist, Professor at Wharton School." 1977. Obituary. *Phil-
    adelphia Enquirer*, May 3.
"Dorothy Swaine Thomas." 1977. Obituary. *Footnotes* (American Sociological Asso-
    ciation), August 12.
"Dorothy Thomas, Demographer." 1977. Obituary. *Washington Post*, May 3.
Fry, C. Luther. 1934. "Review of *Observational Studies of Social Behavior*." *Annals
    of the American Academy of Political and Social Science* 172 (March): 194–195.
Lee, Everett S. 1979. "Thomas, Dorothy Swaine." In *International Encyclopedia of the
    Social Sciences, Biographical Supplement*, vol. 18, edited by David L. Sills,
    pp. 763–765. New York: Free Press.
Murray, Stephen O. 1979. "Resistance to Sociology at Berkeley." *Journal of the History
    of Sociology* 2 (Spring): 61–84.
Rice, Stuart. 1931. "Mathematical Treatment by Dorothy Swaine Thomas of Social Data
    Arranged in Time Series." In *Methods in Social Science*, edited by Stuart Rice.
    Chicago: University of Chicago Press. pp. 566–581.
Young, Kimball. 1947. "Review of *The Spoilage*." *American Sociological Review* 12
    (June): 362–363.

Unpublished Material

Hutchinson, Edward P. 1985. Correspondence, December 21.
Isbell, Eleanor C. 1986. Correspondence, January 22, May 21.
Miller, Ann. 1985. Personal communication, November.
Roscoe, Janice S. 1987. "Dorothy Swaine Thomas and the Rise of Quantitative Soci-
    ology." Brandeis University.
Taeuber, Conrad. 1977. "Service in Honor of Dorothy Swaine Thomas." May 4.
———. 1985, 1986. Correspondence, November 6; June 2. University of California
    Archives, Bancroft Library, University of California at Berkeley.

JANICE ROSCOE

MARY VAN KLEECK (1883–1972)

Mary van Kleeck was an industrial sociologist, educator, pacifist, and social activist. She is noted for her research with the Russell Sage Foundation into the working conditions of women in New York City. Her expertise in labor and industrial relations made her a reliable adviser to political leaders and legislative committees. The slow rate of improvement in conditions for workers in the United States eventually prompted her to study industrial relations in socialist countries and to advocate Marxist reform at home.

BIOGRAPHY

Mary van Kleeck was born into a wealthy and prominent family in Glenham, New York, on June 26, 1883. She was the second daughter and the youngest of three children born to Eliza Mayer and the Reverend Robert Boyd van Kleeck. Robert van Kleeck was the descendant of early Dutch farmers who created New Amsterdam and settled Duchess County. Following his family tradition, he entered the Episcopal ministry, where he combined social reform and moral appeals. Her mother was the daughter of a founder of the Baltimore and Ohio Railroad. Despite this bourgeoisie background, van Kleeck developed an interest in industrial workers and a passion for social reform. Unlike her father, she relied not only on moral appeals to change society, but also believed in action linked with moral thought.

Van Kleeck graduated from Smith College with a bachelor's degree in 1904. The year after her graduation, as a member of the College Settlement Association, she began investigations of overtime work required of girls in New York factories. This led to a subsequent study of child labor in New York City tenements (with Florence Kelley*) and ultimately to the creation of the Alliance Employment

Bureau (AEB), a philanthropic organization for the placement of women in factories. In 1907 she became director of the AEB.

By 1908 van Kleeck was awarded a grant from the newly formed Russell Sage Foundation for "investigations into trades for women and women's lodging." In 1909 she joined the Russell Sage Foundation and supported the integration of the AEB with the Foundation. In 1910 the AEB and its staff were absorbed by the Foundation as an independent Committee on Women's Work.

Four years after beginning work with Russell Sage, van Kleeck became a full-time staff member with the New York School of Philanthropy, while simultaneously continuing her work with Russell Sage. At the school she taught an introductory course on industrial conditions for first-year students specializing in industrial research. She encouraged her students to take an active part in her work at the Russell Sage Foundation, many of whom later accepted regular positions with the Foundation.

Primarily because of the influence of van Kleeck and her associates, in 1916 the Foundation formally opened the Department of Industrial Studies, with van Kleeck as director. By 1917 her responsibilities as a teacher weighed so heavily that she resigned her teaching position to devote full attention to Russell Sage.

Involvement in World War I sparked the military's interest in the civilian work of women. Van Kleeck became a consultant for the U.S. Army, and in January 1918 she took a leave of absence from Russell Sage to join the Army's Ordnance Department as the director of the Women's Branch of the Industrial Service Section. During the same period she was a member of the War Policies Board, where she created standards for the employment of women. Her work with the Army led to her appointment as director of the Women in Industry Service of the Department of Labor in July 1918. She was so successful at organizing the department that it later became the Women's Bureau under the leadership of her former assistant, Mary Anderson.

Van Kleeck returned to Russell Sage in 1919 with renewed energy. Like many feminist leaders, she opposed an equal rights amendment because she feared loss of legislative gains made by women over the years (1919a). She was on the President's Conference on Unemployment in 1921, the Committee on Unemployment and Business Cycles in 1922 and 1923, and chair of the executive committee responsible for the creation of the National Interracial Conference in 1928. Between 1929 and 1931 she made major contributions to the National Commission on Law Observance and Enforcement, better known as the Wickersham Commission. During the two decades from 1928 to 1948 she held the position of associate director of the International Industrial Relations Institute, where she met her friend and colleague Mary Fledderus. She chaired the Program Committee for the World Social Economic Congress in 1931. In 1932 she served as president of the Second International Conference of Social Work in Frankfurt am Main, Germany. During World War II she was a member of Hospites, an organization that offered relief and employment to refugees from Nazi Germany.

To highlight her many professional accomplishments, she was awarded an honorary doctor of laws degree from St. Lawrence University in 1938.

Although she was an active supporter of Franklin Roosevelt, her support flagged when she realized that many of the changes proposed by the New Deal compromised workers. Van Kleeck was appointed by Frances Perkins to the Federal Advisory Council of the U.S. Employment Service in August 1933. She resigned after the first day, complaining of the increased power of monopolies and the abrogation of workers' rights to bargain collectively under New Deal policy.

In 1948 van Kleeck retired from the Russell Sage Foundation to enter the political arena. She actively supported Henry A. Wallace, the socialist candidate for president. During the same election van Kleeck ran for the New York state legislature on the ticket of the American Labor party, an organization later accused of being a "political front organization" for the Communist party.

In addition to her many outstanding organizational accomplishments, van Kleeck was an active member in myriad professional organizations, including the American Sociological Society, the American Association of Social Workers, the American Economic Association, the American Statistical Association (of which she was vice-president in 1932 and 1935), the National Conference of Colonial Dames of New York, the Cosmopolitan Club of New York, the Inter-Professional Association for Social Insurance (of which she was national chair), the American Civil Liberties Union, and the Women's City Club.

Mary van Kleeck died of a heart attack in Kingston, New York, two and one-half weeks before her eighty-ninth birthday. Although much of her work was controversial, there can be little doubt of her contributions to sociology and social work.

MAJOR THEMES

Mary van Kleeck's interests spanned a wide spectrum of humanitarian topics. Her initial interests in the labor relations of working women in New York City later broadened to include both men and women in both national and international settings. First an advocate of reform through the legal system—marking her as a critical pragmatist—her impatience with the direction and extent of New Deal reforms led her to investigate labor relations in the Soviet Union and integrate Marxist economic policy with American democratic principles. Her political reforms were always tempered with strong moral and religious commitments evidenced by her lifelong membership in the Episcopal League for Social Action and the Church League for Industrial Democracy. After World War II she followed the development of nuclear weaponry and became an early advocate for nuclear disarmament and reconciliation.

When van Kleeck joined the Russell Sage Foundation in 1908, three studies were under way from her work with the College Settlement Association and the

AEB. *Women in the Bookbinding Trade* (1913b), *Artificial Flower Makers* (1913a), and *A Seasonal Industry* (1917) were pioneering studies in specific women's occupations. Response to these studies for Sage resulted in her recognition as an expert on women in industry. At the same time, a fourth book was planned. *Working Girls in Evening Schools* (1914) marked a new endeavor for van Kleeck, cutting across industrial occupations and considering problems common to all working women. All four books sparked controversy that led to proposals for change in the respective industries, both in the city and in the state.

During the decade of the 1920s van Kleeck broadened her interests to include both male and female workers in industry. *Employes' [sic] Representation in Coal Mines* (Selekman and van Kleeck 1924) and many articles published during this time demonstrate her commitment to scientific analysis of workers' problems and pragmatic resolution of conflict. In the introduction to the Sage Industrial Relations Series, van Kleeck states that she is interested in discovering how effective the voice of the worker has been in determining working conditions, and whether "relations between employers and employes shall square with American ideals of democracy and brotherhood" (Selekman and van Kleeck 1924, iv).

The failure of the New Deal to adequately remedy the major problems of workers was a turning point for van Kleeck. *Miners and Management* (1934) proposed the socialization of industry. She believed that collective ownership was a democratic alternative to the monopolistic practices of the current industrial giants. In her book *Creative America* (1936) she proposed the abolition of private ownership of the means of production through the formation of worker collectives.

During the 1930s van Kleeck became increasingly interested in the Soviet commitment to socialism and the elimination of private profit. She traveled to the Soviet Union and actively participated in Soviet-American friendship societies. She published articles in *The Daily Worker*, *New Masses*, and *Soviet Russia Today*, advocating democratic socialism in the United States and proposing plans for the transfer of ownership of industry to the workers.

Van Kleeck was convinced of the interdependence of the world economic systems. She believed that the rapidly changing technology of the industrialized countries could spell disaster unless long-range economic planning took place. As a member of the International Industrial Relations Institute, she organized conferences, presented papers, gave lectures, and published books and articles. Most notable among these works were *Technology and Livelihood*, written with the Institute's director, Mary L. Fledderus (Fledderus and van Kleeck 1944), and *The Technological Basis for National Development and Its Implications for International Cooperation* (Fledderus and van Kleeck 1948). The former book analyzed the demands for labor and production brought about by technology, and the latter articulated an appeal for international labor reform.

CRITIQUES OF MARY VAN KLEECK

For the most part, van Kleeck's work was well received in the academic community, reviewed by national figures like Lucile Eaves,* Edith Abbott,* Charles A. Beard, and Susan M. Kingsbury.* Her work was seen as innovative and vital with little criticism of her methods or presentation.

The most serious technical criticism of her work within sociology was leveled against *Working Girls in Evening Schools* by her colleague Susan Kingsbury. Kingsbury criticized the study for not fulfilling its objective of building a foundation for further intensive study and planning for new types of industrial courses. She questioned van Kleeck's methodology, specifically pointing out the respondents' illiteracy as a barrier to completing survey cards and the flawed supervision of the survey by unqualified teachers rather than by trained researchers. Kingsbury also criticized the book's organization and questioned the accuracy of the conclusions. Although she found problems with the survey, she agreed with van Kleeck's suggestions for improving the schools' record-keeping systems.

Because van Kleeck advocated Marxist reform, her politics often were attacked. Her address on "Our Illusions Regarding Government," delivered at the National Conference of Social Work in Kansas City in May of 1934, drew a scathing response from politically moderate social workers who believed that the measured change of the New Deal would ultimately provide relief from the problems of the Depression. This debate ignited the discipline for years.

Van Kleeck's involvement in American-Soviet friendship leagues, her criticisms of government policy, and her active political affiliation with organizations suspected of communist influence led to scrutiny by the most powerful political entity of the time, Joseph McCarthy's House Committee on Un-American Activities. In the period from 1951 through 1956, van Kleeck was accused several times of communist affiliation by Louis Budenz, a communist professor at Fordham University (*New York Times*, August 24, 1951:10; December 21, 1952:7; June 7, 1956:15).

Although she was active in labor relations and early sociological analysis, her work is seldom cited in the discipline today. Perhaps her often controversial political stances and unflagging support of unpopular causes contribute to her academic neglect.

BIBLIOGRAPHY

Selected Works by Mary van Kleeck

1906. "Working Hours of Women in Factories." *Charities and the Commons* 17 (October 6): 13–21.
1908. "Child Labor in New York City Tenements." *Charities and the Commons* 19 (January 18): 1405–1420.

1910. "How Girls Learn the Millinery Trade." *Survey* 24 (April 16) 105–113.

1911. "Women and Children Who Make Men's Clothes." *Survey* 26 (April 1): 65–69.

1913a. *Artificial Flower Makers*. New York: Russell Sage Foundation.

1913b. *Women in the Bookbinding Trade*. New York: Russell Sage Foundation.

1914. *Working Girls in Evening Schools*. New York: Russell Sage Foundation.

1915. "Effect of Unemployment on the Wage Scale." *Annals of the American Academy of Political and Social Science* 61 (September): 90–102.

1916a. "Social Workers." *Survey* 35 (January 1): 386–389.

1916b. "For Women in Industry." *Survey* 37 (December 23): 327–329.

1917. *A Seasonal Industry*. New York: Russell Sage Foundation.

1918. "Trade Union Women." *New Republic* 17 (November): 74.

1919a. "Suffragists and Industrial Democracy." New York: National Woman's Suffrage Publications Co.

1919b. "Federal Policies for Women in Industry." *Annals of the American Academy of Political and Social Science* 81 (January): 87–94.

1921. "Women and Machines." *Atlantic Monthly* 127 (February): 250–260.

1922a. "Unemployment Ended?" *Survey* 48 (June 15): 387–388.

1923a. "What Industry Means to Women Workers." *Bulletin of the Women's Bureau, No. 31*, Washington, DC: Government Printing Office.

1923b. "Outlook for 1923." *American Economic Review* 13 (Suppl., March): 47–49.

1924. "Will Canada Find a Way?" *Survey* 53. (November 15): 202–204.

1925a. "Ten Years of the Rockefeller Plan." *Survey* 53 (February 1): 507–510.

1925b. "Employees' Representation in Steel and Coal." *New Republic* 42 (February 25): 9–12.

1925c. "Standards, Not Safeguards." *New Republic* 42 (March 11): 128.

1926. "Place of the City in Stabilizing Employment." *American City* 35 (October): 535–536.

1927. "Effect of Labor Laws Upon Women in Industry." *U.S. Bureau of Labor Bulletin, No. 429* (misc. ser.): 19–26.

1928. "Recent Gains in Industrial Relations." In *Recent Gains in American Civilization*, edited by K. Page, pp. 49–70. New York: Harcourt.

1929a. "The Negro as a Municipal Problem." *American City* 40 (February): 111–112.

1929b. "Human Relations in a Scientific Organization of Industry." *Factory and Industrial Management* 78 (October): 817–818.

1930. "At Filene's." *Survey* 63 (February 1): 517–518.

1931a. "Toward a National Employment Service." *Survey* 66 (April 15): 88–90.

1931b. "Planning and the World Paradox." *Survey* 67 (November 1): 130–133, 169, 171, 173.

1932. "Planning to End Unemployment." *Survey* 67 (March 1): 618–620+, 638–639.

1934a. *Miners and Management*. New York: Russell Sage Foundation.

1934b. "International Industrial Relations Institute," edited by Mary van Kleeck, and L. Fledderus. New York: Convici, Friede.

1934c. "Labor Under the NRA." In *Challenge to the New Deal*, edited by A. M. Bingham and S. Rodman. New York: McGraw-Hill.

1934d. "NRA from Within" (with William Ormonde Thompson). New York: International Pamphlets.

1934e. "Our Illusions Regarding Government." *Survey* 70 (June): 190–193.

1936. *Creative America*. New York: Convici, Friede.

1937. "About the Women's Charter." *Industrial Woman* 61 (March): 72–73.
1940. "Industrial Productivity and Labor Legislation." *American Labor Legislation Review* 30 (June): 76–80.
1941. "What Is Happening to Social Gains of the Last Ten Years?" *American Journal of Public Health* 31 (December): 1271–1274.
1944. "Planning and Reconstruction." In *The U.S.S.R. in Reconstruction*, edited by Harriet Moore. The Institute. New York: American Russian Institute for cultural Relations with the Soviet Union. Pp. 35–44.
1944. "Soviets and the New Technology." *Survey Graphics* 33 (February): 105–107.
1948. *The Technological Basis for National Development and Its Implications for International Cooperation* (with Mary L. Fledderus). New York: International Industrial Relations Institute.

Coauthored Works

Fledderus, Mary L., and Mary van Kleeck. 1944. *Technology and Livelihood*. New York: Russell Sage Foundation. New York: American Russian Institute for Cultural Relations with the Soviet Union. pp. 35–44.
Selekman, Ben, and Mary van Kleeck. 1924. *Employes' [sic] Representation in Coal Mines*. New York: Russell Sage Foundation.
van Kleeck, Mary, and Ada M. Matthews. 1929. "Shall We Count the Unemployed?" *Survey* 62 (April 1): 22.
van Kleeck, Mary, and Graham Romeyn Taylor. 1922. "Professional Organization of Social Work." *Annals of the American Academy of Political and Social Science* 101 (May): 158–168.
van Kleeck, Mary, Emma A. Winslow, and Ira Reid. 1931. "Work and Law Observance." *U.S. National Commission on Law Observance and Enforcement Research Report*, No. 13. New York: U.S. National Commission on Law Observance and Enforcement.

Studies About Mary van Kleeck and Supplemental References

Abbott, Edith. 1918. "*A Seasonal Industry*: A Study of the Millinery Trade in New York. By Mary Van Kleeck." *American Journal of Sociology* 23 (January): 551.
Beard, Charles A. 1934. "*Miners and Management*. By Mary van Kleeck." *American Political Science Review* 28 (August): 699.
Eaves, Lucile. 1913. "*Women in the Bookbinding Trade*. By Mary Van Kleeck" [sic]. *American Journal of Sociology* 19 (September): 247.
Glenn, John M., Lilian Brandt, and F. Emerson Andrews. 1947. *Russell Sage Foundation 1907–1946*. New York: Russell Sage Foundation.
Kingsbury, Susan M. 1915. Review of "*Working Girls in Evening Schools. A Statistical Study*. By Mary van Kleeck." *Political Science Quarterly* 30 (September): 515.
Lewis, Eleanor Midman. 1980. *Notable American Women—The Modern Period*, pp. 707–709. Cambridge, MA: Harvard University Press, Belknap Press.

"Mary van Kleeck, Social Worker Led Russell Sage Fund." Obituary. *New York Times*,
    June 9, 1972, p. 41.
Springer, Gertrude. 1934. "Rising to a New Challenge." *Survey* 70 (June): 179–180.

MICHAEL R. BALL

ROSALIE WAX (1911–)

Rosalie Wax is most recognized for her field research and for her work among interned Japanese-Americans during World War II and among native Americans in the years following. She has written extensively on field research and native American education.

BIOGRAPHY

Rosalie Amelia Hankey Wax was born on November 11, 1911, in Des Plaines, Illinois, the daughter of Richard and Anna (Orb) Hankey. As she writes in her autobiography, *Doing Fieldwork: Warnings and Advice* (1971), she and her family—two brothers, two sisters, and mother—moved to a Mexican-American slum within the city of Los Angeles in 1930. For the next eight years she solicited and did housework for wages, applied for and received public relief to help her family, worked on Works Project Administration jobs, and went to school. In 1940 she received a ''tiny'' Phoebe Hearst scholarship to the University of California at Berkeley and was graduated in 1942 with a bachelor of arts degree in anthropology.

When Pearl Harbor was attacked by the Japanese in 1941, Wax attempted to enlist in military service, anticipating becoming an officer in the WAVES. She was rejected, however, because her eyesight was not 20–20, and thus went on to do graduate work (Wax 1971).

During her first semester of graduate work she was approached by Dorothy Swaine Thomas* at the University of California at Berkeley to do some fieldwork on Japanese evacuees in the Gila Center in southern Arizona. All people of Japanese ancestry in the United States were required, in the spring of 1943, to fill out a questionnaire developed by the U.S. Army on the state of their loyalties to either the United States or Japan. In mid-July the War Relocation Authority issued a decree whereby all "disloyal" evacuees were to be removed from relocation centers and segregated in the Tule Lake Segregation Center in northern California. Wax's task was to find out how the "loyals," or "yes-yes" as they called themselves, felt about their segregation and to observe and record their behavior before, during, and after the "disloyals' " move to Tule Lake. In July of 1943 Wax started her participant observation work for Thomas with little knowledge of what was involved in this kind of research and, conversely, with little knowledge about the Japanese or Japanese-American culture (Wax 1971, 63).

As her first experience "in the field," she found the initial three months of her time at the Gila Center wracked with desperation. The lack of rapport with evacuees and feelings of failure and alienation weighed heavily on her. By late August she decided to take a different route. Instead of trying to interview "loyals" to the United States about how they felt about the situation, she decided to interview "disloyals." Slowly rapport started to build between her and the evacuees. The more they would talk with her and the more she could find out about them, the more she began (in the words of R. E. Park) to "feel the pressure of the customs and expectations of the society by which [she] was surrounded" (Wax 1971, 77).

When many of her informants were moved to the Tule Lake center, she did not hear from them for a long while. From February to April of 1944 Wax visited Tule Lake several times. During these periods she developed good working relations with more than a dozen of the segregated residents. In mid-May she moved to the Tule Lake center as a permanent resident. After a year at Tule Lake, Wax left the center when the study was ending. Wax writes that she felt a great sense of loss on the completion of the project—as if some void was now present in her life (Wax 1971, 173).

In 1946, she went to the University of Chicago, where she held a teaching assistantship in the anthropology department. A year later she started work on her dissertation and was appointed an instructor in the Social Sciences College. On March 5, 1949, she married Murray Wax, a sociology professor at the University of Chicago. In 1950 she was awarded a doctor of philosophy degree in anthropology after she completed her dissertation on "The Development of Authoritarianism: A Study of the Japanese-American Relocation Centers."

During the years spanning 1950 through 1957 Rosalie was an assistant professor in the department of anthropology at the University of Chicago. In 1956–1957 she received the Ernest E. Quantrell Prize for excellence in teaching. During the summers of 1959 and 1960 she was the director of a series of workshops on American Indian Affairs at the University of Colorado. In 1959 she and Murray moved to Miami, where Rosalie was appointed a visiting lecturer in the department of sociology and anthropology at the University of Miami at Coral Gables; the Waxes stayed in Miami until 1962.

Because of their joint interests in the educational experiences of American Indians, which were enhanced by the summer workshops, Murray Wax wrote a proposal to do fieldwork on a native American reservation. Rosalie writes that she was not particularly excited by this adventure; she had come to enjoy Florida a great deal and also did not want to "objectively" study the situation of American Indians at that time. Furthermore, her remembrance of the void feelings she had when she left Tule Lake resurfaced; thoughts of how she felt at the end of her research at the relocation centers made her anxious to think that they might happen again. The Waxes' study was funded by the department of education, and in 1962 they began the Oglala Sioux Educational Research Project on the Oglala Sioux reservation in South Dakota (Wax 1971, 178).

On the reservation they hired two native American men, both with some college education, as research assistants. One offered them his parents' home as a place to stay because of the housing shortage on the reservation. Reticently they accepted this offer, and spent the next several months "kept in the closet" by the family. Over time Rosalie and Murray discovered that they were being cloistered away so that the family they were staying with would have total control over all the information the Waxes gained. This limited their research efforts and frustrated them enormously. Eventually they moved to an abandoned schoolhouse on the reservation and finished their work there in the early part of 1963.

During the remainder of 1963 and the spring of 1964 the Waxes' entertained the idea of doing some fieldwork in Africa, but in August of 1964 Rosalie was appointed an associate professor at the University of Kansas in Lawrence, where she remained until 1969. During this period she was the associate director of the Indian Education Research Project, where she and Murray spent several months investigating Indian schoolchildren in Ottawa (from 1966 to 1967). This fieldwork caused many difficulties because of the unwillingness of Indian respondents to participate and the difficulty of working with various officials.

In 1970 she was promoted to full professor at Lawrence, and from 1973 until the present she has been on the faculty as a professor in the department of anthropology and sociology at Washington University in St. Louis. Wax is a fellow in the American Anthropological Association, the American Association for the Advancement of Science, and the Society for the Study of Social Problems. She is a fellow in the Society for Applied Anthropology and was a member of the Executive Committee of the Society for Applied Anthropology from 1959 through 1962. Wax is an associate member of the Council on Anthropology and Education and of Current Anthropology and also is a member of the Central States Anthropological Society. Spanning the years 1973 to 1974, she was a councilor of the American Ethnological Society. She was a member of the National Study Commission on Undergraduate Education and the Preparation of Teachers, funded by the U.S. Department of Education through Paul Olson at the University of Nebraska, from 1972 through 1976. She currently is professor emeritus of anthropology and education at Washington University.

MAJOR THEMES

Although Rosalie Wax has written on such diverse topics as the traditional cultures of Old World and Scandinavian countries and the meaning of "magic" (Wax 1963, 1969; Wax and Wax 1964), she is most well known and recognized for her knowledge of field methods and techniques. As she writes in *Doing Fieldwork* (1971), "fieldwork is as much a social phenomenon as an individual phenomenon." She believes that the things she learned during the fieldwork process changed her the most; the fieldwork process involved her in replacing old myths and assumptions with new, more accurate information. She writes: "The true social scientist is not the person who has undergone an educational lobotomy or a moral transformation. Instead, he [sic] is a person who does an honest and thorough job, omits no important aspect of a situation, and writes an honest, coherent and fair report" (Wax 1971, 364).

Her various themes also discuss how different statuses one occupies can differentially affect one's fieldwork experience (Wax 1979). Given any fieldwork situation, one's gender, age, or education may either help to promote solidarity with respondents or hinder it. One needs to understand the culture that one is studying to better understand how to get the information one needs, taking into account—and perhaps working around—these statuses.

Because she also has done extensive research into the realm of the education of native Americans, she has made significant contributions to knowledge concerning these issues (Wax and Wax 1971a; Wax, Wax, Dumont, Dickeman, and Petit 1969). Indeed, her recognition that native American education suffers because of the dominant society's lack of ability to understand native culture, and therefore indigenous learning processes, has significantly affected how native Americans are educated.

CRITIQUES OF ROSALIE WAX

Wax has been cited and discussed by students and researchers alike in the fields of anthropology and sociology. One will note, however, the relatively scant number of literature citations afforded to Wax. As is becoming apparent, Wax, like so many other women who have offered important contributions to the social sciences, is neither widely cited nor regarded with as much esteem as comparable male social scientists. Those who have studied her work and contributions offer the following criticisms. William Foote Whyte (1972), in his review of *Doing Fieldwork*, said Wax had done an "extraordinarily impressive job in presenting the problems and processes of field work in a way that . . . will stand up against any criticisms from fellow professionals." Whyte goes on to say that he could not take exception with a single point in her work. He found especially noteworthy her treatment of the problem of emotional involvement of the fieldworker with his or her subjects: "If you don't [sic] get really emotionally involved,'' you probably cannot be an effective participant observer, yet you also must learn how to gain detachment.

Roth et al. (1973) discuss how Wax remedied for anthropologists the task of writing a comprehensive statement about the anthropologist at work. ''She presents the problems which precipitate successes and failures in field work from her personal experiences throughout a long career'' and, by so doing, allows anthropologists the insight needed to do extensive fieldwork.

She also is cited by many other authors in terms of fieldwork as reciprocal (Hatfield 1973), how to temper ''less touchy and explosive areas'' to make them easier for elites to digest (Lundaman and McFarland 1976), and how to use a network established by an informant (Salamone 1977). For her work in *Magic and the Fate of History* she has been cited concerning the contributions made by ''traditional cultures'' like Old Scandanavia to post-Reformation societies in Europe (Wax 1972).

AUTHOR'S NOTE

Several authors have questioned the ethical nature of Wax's research at Tule Lake. Violet K. de Cristoforo has presented both written and verbal accounts of the devastation Wax's actions created for her family (de Cristoforo 1988). De Cristoforo claims that Wax ''exploited [her] trust and damaged [her] irreparably'' by revealing confidentialities to the authorities that she told Wax in private and with Wax's reassurances that she would not discuss them with anyone else. De Cristoforo claims that Wax misrepresented de Cristoforo's involvement in camp politics and has obscured facts surrounding incidents at Tule Lake. Furthermore, Wax has ruined her life because she was ''blacklisted'' because of the information Wax reported to the authorities. Peter T. Suzuki (1981, 1986) gives similar accounts of Wax's unethical behavior. Suzuki claims that Wax was an FBI informer and took the information she learned from Tule Lake residents to the authorities. Suzuki also criticizes Wax's inability to leave her values at home; indeed, she wholeheartedly claims to side with different groups of people because of her personal feelings toward individuals. For a more thorough discussion of these accusations, see the cited author's discussions.

BIBLIOGRAPHY

Selected Writings by Rosalie Wax

1942. ''California Ghosts.'' *California Folklore Quarterly* 1 (January): 155–177.
1943. ''Ghosts and Shamanism in Kwangtung.'' *California Folklore Quarterly* 2 (October): 303–308.
1952. ''Field Methods and Techniques: Reciprocity as a Field Technique.'' *Human Organization* 11 (Fall): 34–37.
1953. ''The Destruction of a Democratic Impulse: A Case Study.'' *Human Organization* 12 (Spring): 11–21.

1957b. "Twelve Years Later: An Analysis of Field Experience." *American Journal of Sociology* 58 (September): 133–142.

1958. "Free Time in Other Cultures." In *Free Time: Challenge to Later Maturity*, edited by E. Donahue, W. Hunter, D. Coons, and H. Maurices, pp. 3–16. Ann Arbor: University of Michigan Press.

1964. "Cultural Deprivation As an Educational Ideology." *Journal of American Indian Education* 3, (January): 15–18.

1965a. "The *Eta* As Outcastes and Scapegoats Among Japanese-Americans." *Kansas Journal of Sociology* 1 (Fall): 175–187.

1965b. "American Indian Education for What?" *Midcontinent American Studies Journal* 6, (Fall): 164–170.

1967a. "Oglala Sioux Dropouts and Their Problems with Educators." In *Education and School Crisis: Perspectives on Teaching Disadvantaged Youth*, edited by E. T. Keach, R. Fulton and W. E. Gardner, pp. 247–257. New York: John Wiley.

1967b. "The Warrior Dropouts." *Trans-Action* 4 (May): 40–46.

1968. "Participant Observation." In *International Encyclopedia of the Social Sciences*, vol. 11, pp. 238–240. New York: Free Press and Macmillan.

1969. *Magic, Fate and History: The Changing Ethos of the Vikings*. Lawrence, KS: Coronado Press.

1971. *Doing Fieldwork: Warnings and Advice*. Chicago: University of Chicago Press.

1976. "Fieldwork as Education." In *Forms and Formulations of Education*, edited by E. Rose, pp. 120–148. Lincoln, NE: Study Commission on Undergraduate Education and the Education of Teachers. Sponsored by the University of Nebraska.

1979. "Gender and Age in Fieldwork and Fieldwork Education: No Good Thing Is Done by Any Man Alone." *Social Problems* 26, (June): 509–523.

Forthcoming. "Resistance to Terrorism at the Tule Lake Segregation Center: An Example of Fieldwork in an Extreme Situation." In *Social Research in Extreme Situations*, edited by Felix Moos, et al. Lawrence: University Press of Kansas.

Unpublished Material by Rosalie Wax

1950. "The Development of Authoritarianism: A Study of the Japanese-American Relocation Centers." Ph.D. diss., Department of Anthropology, University of Chicago.

Coauthored Works

Wax, Rosalie, and R. K. Beardsley. 1943. "A History of the Vanishing Hitchhiker." *California Folklore Quarterly* 2 (January): 13–25.

Wax, Rosalie, and R. K. Thomas. 1961. "American Indians and White People." *Phylon* 22 (Winter): 305–317.

Wax, Rosalie, and M. L. Wax. 1962. "The Magical World View." *Journal for the Scientific Study of Religion* 1 (Spring): 179–188.

———. 1963. "The Notion of Magic," *Current Anthropology* 4 (December): 495–518.

———. 1964. "Magic and Monotheism," pp. 50–59. *Annual Proceedings* of the American Ethnological Society, edited by J. Helm.

———.1968. "The Enemies of the People." In *Institutions and the Person: Essays*

Presented to Everett C. Hughes, edited by H. S. Becker, B. Geer, D. Riesman, and R. S. Weiss, pp. 101–118. Chicago: Aldine.

———. 1971a. "Federal Programs and Indian Target Populations." In *Majority and Minority: The Dynamics of Racial and Ethnic Relations in the U.S.*, edited by N. Yetman and C. H. Steele, pp. 491–502. Boston: Allyn & Bacon.

———. 1971b. "Great Tradition, Little Tradition, and Formal Education." In *Anthropological Perspectives on Education*, edited by M. L. Wax, S. Diamond, and F. O. Gearing, pp. 3–18. New York: Basic Books.

———. 1978a. "How People Stop Smoking." *Mid-American Review of Sociology* 3 (Spring): 1–15.

———. 1978b. "Religion Among American Indians." *Annals of the American Academy of Political and Social Science* 436 (March): 27–39.

———. 1980. "Fieldwork and the Research Process." *Anthropology and Education Quarterly* 11 (Spring): 29–37.

———. Forthcoming. "Anthropological Fieldwork: Comments on Its Values and Limitations." *Journal of Thought*.

Wax, Rosalie, M. L. Wax, R. V. Dumont, Jr., M. Dickeman, and P. F. Petit. 1969. "Indian Education in Eastern Oklahoma: A Report of Fieldwork Among the Cherokee." Mimeo, Final Report of the U.S. Office of Education, Bureau of Research, Contract No. OE–6–10–260, January.

Wax, Rosalie, M. L. Wax, and R. Holyrock. 1964. *Dropout of American Indians at the Secondary Level*. Cooperative Research Report, No. S–099. Atlanta: Emory University.

Studies About Rosalie Wax and Supplemental References

American Men and Women of Science. 1976. 13th ed., Vol. 6, edited by Jaques Cattell Press, New York: R. R. Bowker.

Contemporary Authors: A Bio-bibliographic Guide to Current Authors and Their Works. 1974. Vols. 45–48, edited by C. D. Kinsman, p. 620. Detroit: Gale Research Co.

Fifth International Directory of Anthropologists. 1975. p. 412. Chicago: University of Chicago Press.

Hatfield, C. R. 1973. "Fieldwork: Toward a Model of Mutual Exploitation." *Anthropological Quarterly* 46 (January): 15–29.

Lundman, R. J., and P. McFarlane. 1976. "Conflict Methodology: An Introduction and Preliminary Assessment." *Sociological Quarterly* 17 (Autumn): 503–512.

Moone, J. R. 1973. "The Best-Laid Plans: Research Pre-Design and Field Revision." *Anthropological Quarterly* 46 (January) : 7–14.

Salamone, F. 1977. "The Methodological Significance of the Lying Informant." *Anthropological Quarterly* 50 (July): 117–124.

Suzuki, Peter T. 1981. "Anthropologists in the Wartime Camps for Japanese Americans: A Documentary Study." *Dialectical Anthropology* 6 (August): 23–60.

———. 1986. "The University of California Japanese Evacuation and Resettlement Study: A Prolegomenon." *Dialectical Anthropology* 10 (April): 189–213.

Wax, M. L. 1972. "Commentary on Weber Special Issue." *Sociological Quarterly* 13 (Spring): 278–279.

Who's Who of American Women: A Biographical Dictionary of Notable Living American Women. 1958, 1961, 1964, 1968, 1972, 1983, 1985, and 1987–1988. Wilmette, IL: Marquis Who's Who.

Whyte, William Foote, 1972. "Review of Doing Fieldwork," *Social Forces* 51 (September): 107.

Unpublished Material

de Cristoforo, Violet K. 1988. *A Victim of a Tule Lake Anthropologist*. Paper presented at the Fifth National Conference of the Association for Asian American Studies. Washington State University, Pullman, Washington, March.

SHERYL J. GRANA

BEATRICE WEBB (1858–1943)

Beatrice Webb is noted for her pioneering contributions to social research, research methodology, and social reform. One of the first British women sociologists, a founder of the London School of Economics and *The New Statesman*, Webb was a prolific researcher and writer and a committed social activist. She advocated and worked for social progress based on knowledge derived from social research. Her investigations of English social problems and social institutions, as well as her proposals and efforts for social reform, contributed to the development of the modern British social welfare system.

BIOGRAPHY

Martha Beatrice Potter was born on January 22, 1858, at Standish House in Gloucestershire, England. She was the eighth of nine daughters of Laurencina Heyworth, a woman of scholarly aspirations, and Richard Potter, a wealthy railway owner and industrial financier. Both parents encouraged the intellectual development of their daughters. Although personally frustrated and overburdened by heavy childbearing and child-rearing responsibilities, her mother preferred intellectual companionship and pursuits. According to Webb, her father was "the only man I ever knew who genuinely believed that women were superior to men and acted as if he did." (MacKenzie and MacKenzie 1982, xi).

Beatrice Potter grew up in a large and stimulating Victorian household. Except for a year spent at a small academy for girls, she was educated at home. Instruction by governesses was supplemented by independent reading and study. Her limited formal education also was enriched by extensive foreign travel and by close contact and candid discussions with her parents' many influential visitors.

Among the distinguished intellectuals who called at Standish House was Herbert Spencer. One of her parents' closest friends, Spencer became a self-appointed tutor and mentor for young Beatrice. Although Potter was considered by her parents to be a sickly child, Spencer encouraged her to study seriously, to read widely, and to engage with him in critical discourse. The "old philosopher" and the "born metaphysician," as they referred to one another, built a mutually rewarding relationship on their shared interest in philosophical and social issues. In 1887 Spencer publicly recognized Potter as his friend and protégé, when he named her as his literary executor.

Like many other young women of her era and class, Beatrice Potter at eighteen entered London society and became involved in a busy schedule of social activities. At the same time, her diary reveals that she also was privately engaged in an in-depth study of religion and social positivism. Among the sources she examined were the works of Auguste Comte and Harriet Martineau.* Potter in fact credited Martineau's writings with providing for her "a higher idea of the religion of science."

After her mother's death Potter, at twenty-four, became the manager of her father's houses and income. Although Richard Potter encouraged his daughter to become his business associate, the next year she accepted a position as a rent collector in the slums of East London. Visiting relatives in Lancashire, she also observed daily life and conditions among working-class textile workers. These vivid firsthand experiences confirmed her interest in social problems that had developed during discussions with Herbert Spencer. Potter decided thereafter to devote herself to the investigation of social life and institutions. The decision to commit her life to a vocation of sociological research was based on a belief that knowledge provides a rational foundation for social change and progress.

MAJOR THEMES

In 1886 Beatrice Potter began her life's work when she became an investigator for Charles Booth's survey of poverty in London. Over the next several years her first research articles, "Dock Life in East London" (1880a), "East End Labour" (1880b), and "Pages from a Work-Girl's Diary" (1888c), were published. She also contributed to the initial volume of Booth's seventeen-volume series, *Life and Labour of the People in London*.

Stimulated by her earlier field observations, Webb next embarked on a study of consumer cooperatives and the cooperative movement. This work, based on examinations of records, observations, and interviews conducted throughout England, resulted in the publication of her first monograph, *The Co-Operative Movement in Great Britain*, in 1891.

While engaged in her research on consumer cooperatives, Beatrice Potter met Sidney Webb, a leading Fabian socialist. Initially Webb's collectivist ideas and politics interested Potter more than the man. The next year Potter joined the Fabian Society and, despite some initial misgivings, became secretly engaged to Webb. After her father's death in 1892, the engagement was made public and the couple married.

From the beginning the partnership was both personally rewarding and professionally productive. On their honeymoon the Webbs began their first of many collaborative research efforts, a study of trade unionism. Within two years the Webbs had completed and published *The History of Trade Unionism* (1894), and begun work on a second project, which resulted in the publication of *Industrial Democracy* (1897) and *Problems of Modern Industry* (1898). Over the next several decades this remarkably congenial and prolific pair produced ten more volumes based on their monumental historical analysis of English local government.

In the 1920s the Webbs expanded the focus of their research on government to incorporate the study and advocacy of nationalism and socialism. The drafting and publication of *A Constitution for the Socialist Commonwealth of Great Britain* (1920) was followed by a monograph analyzing *The Decay of Capitalist Civilization* (1923).

In addition to producing an extensive body of joint research, Beatrice and Sidney Webb collaborated in several other notable endeavors. In 1894, using funds from a bequest to the Fabian Society, the Webbs founded the London School of Economics and Political Science, an institution devoted to the study of social issues. Over the next few years they worked together to open and develop the institution. In the early decades of the twentieth century the Webbs continued to be actively involved in serving the school. At the same time they planned and instituted publication of the respected socialist weekly journal *The New Statesman*.

Beatrice Webb was active in political as well as intellectual affairs. In 1888–1889 she presented evidence to the House of Lords' Committee on the Sweating System. From 1905 to 1909 she contributed significantly to the work of the Royal Commission on Poor Laws and Unemployment. Webb was a coauthor of the Commission's influential Minority Report. The report, based on extensive research initiated and directed by Webb, advocated a new system of social insurance for Great Britain. The publication of this best-selling report was followed by a nationwide campaign conducted by the Webbs in support of the proposal.

Webb was appointed and ably served on a number of other public commissions and political committees. She also served as a member of the Government Committee on Grants-in-Aid of Distress (1914–1915), the Statutory War Pensions Committee (1916–1917), the Reconstruction Committee (1917–1918), the Committee on the Machinery of Government (1918–1919), the War Cabinet Committee on Women in Industry (1918–1919), and the Lord Chancellor's Advisory Committee for Women Justices (1919–1920).

In middle and late adulthood Webb was recognized by several academic institutions and scholarly organizations. She received honorary degrees from Manchester University (1909), the University of Edinburgh (1924), and the

University of Munich (1926). In 1932 Beatrice Webb became the first woman elected to the British Academy. In 1938 she was named honorary president of the merged Fabian Society and Fabian Research Bureau.

Beatrice Webb apparently assumed the primary responsibility for writing the last works issued by "the partnership." Building on her earlier writings and lifelong interest in social research, the Webbs published *Methods of Social Study* in 1932. This engaging text described the methods and principles that the couple developed and used in their many research undertakings. After a pilgrimage to the Soviet Union to gather research materials in the early 1930s, the Webbs produced two final monographs that described and favorably assessed the Soviet collectivist experiment.

Throughout her adult life Webb was a dedicated diarist. For seventy years she recorded her private thoughts and observations on the ideas, events, and people she encountered. In her mid-sixties, drawing on her diaries, Webb began to write her autobiography. The first volume, *My Apprenticeship*, was printed in 1926. A second installment, *Our Partnership*, was published posthumously. Seven additional volumes based on Webb's diaries have subsequently been edited and published by scholars.

Beatrice Potter Webb died at the age of eighty-five on April 13, 1943. Four years later, in the winter after Sidney's death, the Webbs' ashes were exhumed from the garden of their country home at Passfeld Corner and buried in Westminster Abbey.

CRITIQUES OF BEATRICE WEBB

Many tributes were published after Webb's death, including lengthy obituaries in *The Times* of London and the *New York Times*. Especially noteworthy, in intellectual circles, was an influential review of Webb's life and work by R. H. Tawney, which appeared in the *Proceedings of the British Academy* (1943). According to the death notice published in *The Times Literary Supplement*, "in almost every field of what today are called the social sciences the debt to . . . Beatrice Webb is beyond estimation." (Obituary, May 8, 1943).

By all accounts, Beatrice Webb played a highly significant role in British intellectual and political affairs. Most of the editors of Webb's diaries and letters, as well as her biographers, have written their assessments of Webb's legacy. Entries describing and evaluating Webb's career and contributions also are readily available in standard biographical dictionaries and handbooks.

Webb's early research on the working poor and consumer cooperatives and her later joint studies of trade unionism, poor laws, and English local government were considered ground-breaking efforts when published, and they continue to be recognized as basic references in their field. The ten volumes on the local government system, for example, have been described as "the unsurpassed account—unequalled . . . in any other literature" (Review, *Times Literary Supplement*, June 5, 1948, p. 310).

Webb's published diaries have been characterized not only as personal journals, but also as social historical documents, providing insights into the period in which she lived as well as information about the author as a person. In the words of reviewers, Webb's autobiography, covering the period from 1858 to 1912, contains "a series of penetrating essays" and provides "a fascinating picture of a significant period of British social history."

From the turn of the century Webb was known as one of the intellectual leaders of British socialism. Her efforts for social and political reform are as well known and recognized as her social research and writing. Webb is widely acknowledged to be an architect of the British social welfare system. Her work on the Poor Law Commission and the subsequent campaign for the abolition of the poor laws constitute "one of the major sources of that system of social insurance" (Review, *Times Literary Supplement*, June 5, 1948, p. 309).

Although Beatrice Webb's place in political and intellectual history is well established, she is typically excluded from historical accounts of feminism. Historian Barbara Caine attributes this exclusion to her lack of commitment to women's issues and her failure to support women's suffrage. As a collectivist "preoccupied with problems of economic inequality," Webb was disinterested in the agenda of the women's movement, which championed individualism and voting privileges for propertied, single women (Caine 1982, 33). On the other hand, as a cultural feminist, Webb valued what she saw as women's distinctive characteristics and responsibilities in the family, and supported improved working conditions and benefits for women.

Through a long and productive career, Beatrice Webb drew on, developed, and integrated the intellectual traditions of evolutionary socialism and social positivism. For thirty years she focused her attention on the analysis of social problems and institutions. In later years she shifted her attention to the study of national government and the state. To the end of her life, Beatrice Potter Webb remained committed to the pursuit of her vision of social reform based on a solid foundation of scientific research.

BIBLIOGRAPHY

Selected Writings by Beatrice Webb

1888a. "The Dock Life of East London." *Nineteenth Century* 22 (October): 483–499.

1888b. "East London Labour." *Nineteenth Century* 24 (August): 161–183.

1888c. "Pages from a Work-Girl's Diary." *Nineteenth Century* 25 (September): 301–314.

1891. *The Co-operative Movement in Great Britain*. London: Swan Sonnenschein.

1907. "Methods of Investigation." *Sociological Papers* (Sociological Society, London) 3: 343–354.

1913. "The Awakening of Women." *New Statesman*. Special Supplement (November 1): iii–v.

1919. *The Wages of Men and Women: Should They Be Equal?* London: George Allen & Unwin.

1926. *My Apprenticeship*. New York: Longmans, Green.

1948. *Our Partnership*, edited by Barbara Drake and Margaret Cole. London: Longmans, Green.

1901. Webb, Beatrice, ed. *The Case for the Factory Acts*. London: Grant Richards.

Unpublished Writings by Beatrice Webb

1892. "How Best to Do Away with the Sweating System." Paper read at the 24th Annual Congress of Co-operative Societies, Rochdale, England, June.

Coauthored Works

Webb, Sidney, and Beatrice Potter Webb. 1894. *The History of Trade Unionism*. London: Longmans, Green.

————. 1897. *Industrial Democracy*. London: Longmans, Green.

————. 1898. *Problems of Modern Industry*. London: Longmans, Green.

————. 1903–1929. *English Local Government from the Revolution to the Municipal Corporation Act*. 11 vols. London: Longmans, Green.

————. 1910a. *English Poor Law Policy*. London: Longmans, Green.

————. 1910b. *The State and the Doctor*. London: Longmans, Green.

————. 1911. *The Prevention of Destitution*. London: Longmans, Green.

————. 1920. *A Constitution for the Socialist Commonwealth of Great Britain*. London: Longmans, Green.

————. 1923. *The Decay of Capitalist Civilization*. Westminster: Fabian Society and G. Allen & Unwin.

————. 1927–1929. *English Poor Law History*. 3 vols. London: Longmans, Green.

————. 1932. *Methods of Social Study*. London: Longmans, Green.

————. 1936. *Soviet Communism: A New Civilization?* 2 vols. New York: Charles Scribners' & Sons.

————. 1942. *The Truth about Soviet Russia*. London: Longmans, Green.

Diaries and Letters of Beatrice Webb

Cole, Margaret. 1978. *Index to the Diary of Beatrice Webb, 1873–1943*. Cambridge: Chadwyck-Healey.

Webb, Beatrice Potter. 1952. *Beatrice Webb's Diaries*. Vol. 1, *1912–1924*, edited by Margaret Cole. London: Longmans, Green.

————. 1956. *Beatrice Webb's Diaries*. Vol. 2, *1924–1932*, edited by Margaret Cole. London: Longmans, Green.

————. 1963. *Beatrice Webb's American Diary*, edited by Norman MacKenzie and Jeanne Mackenzie. Madison: University of Wisconsin Press.

————. 1982. *The Diary of Beatrice Webb*. Vol. 1, *1873–1892: Glitter Around and Darkness Within*, edited by Norman MacKenzie and Jeanne MacKenzie. Cambridge, MA: Harvard University Press.

————. 1983. *The Diary of Beatrice Webb*. Vol. 2, *1892–1905: All the Good Things of Life*, edited by Norman MacKenzie and Jeanne MacKenzie. Cambridge, MA: Harvard University Press.

———. 1984. *The Diary of Beatrice Webb*. Vol. 3, *1905–1924: The Power to Alter Things*, edited by Norman MacKenzie and Jeanne MacKenzie. Cambridge, MA: Harvard University Press.

———. 1985. *The Diary of Beatrice Webb*. Vol. 4, *1924–1943: The Wheel of Life*, edited by Norman MacKenzie and Jeanne MacKenzie. Cambridge, MA: Harvard University Press.

Webb, Sidney, and Beatrice Potter Webb. 1978. *The Letters of Sidney and Beatrice Webb*. 3 vols., edited by Norman MacKenzie. London: Cambridge University Press.

Studies About Beatrice Potter Webb and Supplemental References

Abbott, Edith. 1929. "The Webbs on the English Poor Law." *Social Service Review* 3 (June): 252–269.

"Beatrice and Sidney Webb: Social Research and English Politics." 1948. *The Times Literary Supplement* 47 (June 5): 309–310.

"Beatrice Webb." Obituary. *The Times Literary Supplement* (May 8): 218.

Caine, Barbara. 1982. "Beatrice Webb and the 'Woman Question.' " *History Workshop Journal* 14 (Autumn): 23–43.

Cole, Margaret. 1945. *Beatrice Webb*. New York: Harcourt, Brace.

———. 1968. "Webb, Sidney and Beatrice." In *International Encyclopedia of the Social Sciences*, vol. 16, edited by David L. Sills, pp 487–491. New York: Macmillan and the Free Press.

———, ed. 1949. *The Webbs and Their Work*. London: Frederick Muller.

Harris, Jose. 1984. "Beatrice Webb: The Ambivalent Feminist." London: London School of Economics and Political Science.

"Lady Passfield." Obituary. *The Times* (May 1): 6.

MacKenzie, Jeanne. 1979. *A Victorian Courtship*. New York: Oxford University Press.

"Mrs. Sidney Webb Dies in England, 85." Obituary. *New York Times* (May 1): 15.

Muggeridge, Kitty, and Ruth Adam. 1968. *Beatrice Webb: A Life, 1858–1943*. New York: Alfred A. Knopf.

Nord, Deborah Epstein. 1985. *The Apprenticeship of Beatrice Webb*. Amherst: University of Massachusetts Press.

Tawney, R. H. 1943. "Beatrice Webb, 1858–1943." *Proceedings of the British Academy* 29: 285–311.

KAY RICHARDS BROSCHART

IDA B. WELLS-BARNETT (1862–1931)

Ida B. Wells-Barnett is recognized for her significant contributions to social research and social reform. While employed as a newspaper editor and reporter, she carried out ground-breaking and myth-shattering studies of lynching. Wells's research was the first investigation of lynching based on the collection and compilation of statistical evidence. A dedicated political activist as well as a pioneer in sociological research, Wells-Barnett was the founder of the international antilynching movement. She also was an outspoken leader in the struggle for black civil rights and women's suffrage.

BIOGRAPHY

Ida Wells was born in Holly Springs, Mississippi, on July 16, 1862. She was the first of eight children born to Elizabeth (Lizzie) Bell, a woman of Indian and Afro-American parentage, and her husband, James Wells, the mulatto son of a plantation owner. At the time of Ida's birth, both of her parents were slaves. After emancipation, in addition to caring for a growing family, Lizzie Wells worked for wages as a cook, while James Wells found employment as a carpenter.

In her childhood Ida Wells lived with her parents and siblings in a single-family home built by her father. Work was plentiful for a skilled carpenter in Holly Springs, since many structures had been damaged or destroyed during the war. James Wells was an independent man and an influential and civic-minded member of the community.

Ida's mother was deeply religious. Both of her parents valued and encouraged education. "Our job was to go to school and learn all we could" (Wells-Barnett 1970, 9). In 1866, at the age of four, Ida Wells entered Rust College, a school founded by the Freedman's Aid Society and staffed by Northern missionaries and teachers. By all reports, Wells was a good student and "a voracious reader." She continued to pursue her studies at Rust through high school.

In 1878 James and Lizzie Wells and their infant son, Stanley, died suddenly in a yellow fever epidemic. Ida, at sixteen, subsequently assumed the responsibility for and care of her surviving brothers and sisters. Concealing her age, she secured a position as a teacher in a rural school to support the family.

In 1884 Wells moved to Memphis, Tennessee, where she again found employment as a teacher. Although she continued to provide financial support for her siblings, she eagerly resumed her own interrupted education by enrolling in summer classes at Fisk University and LeMoyne Institute. In addition, she joined a lyceum and became engaged in many other educational and cultural activities in the city.

In Tennessee, Wells also became involved in social activism and journalism. After a conductor forced her to leave the first-class coach of a Chesapeake and Ohio train, Wells sued the railway for damages. While she pursued this landmark civil rights case in the courts, she began to write for publication. She first published an account of the lawsuit in the *Living Way*, a religious weekly, in 1887. This article was well received, and invitations to write for this and other periodicals followed. Writing under the pen name "Iola," Wells began to regularly contribute to a number of newspapers. She subsequently became the editor and part-owner of the Memphis-based *Free Speech and Highlight*. In 1891, after she published an editorial criticizing the school board for the inferior conditions in the segregated black schools, her teaching contract was revoked, and she became a full-time journalist.

A shocking and brutal lynching of three respected black Memphis businessmen in 1892 incited Wells to further public commentary and action. In response to her frank antilynching editorials in the *Free Speech*, a mob destroyed the newspaper and called for her death. Believing that her presence in Memphis would lead to further racial violence, Wells resettled in New York, where she accepted a position as a journalist and partner at the *New York Age*.

The Memphis lynching and its aftermath spurred Wells to undertake an unprecedented systematic study of lynching. The results of this research were first published in the newspaper. An expanded version of her newspaper account was later published and distributed as a pamphlet titled *Southern Horrors: Lynch Law in All Its Phases* (1892). During this period Wells also began speaking publicly in the Northeast about lynching. These antilynching activities led to an invitation to visit Great Britain in 1893. Speaking to large and receptive audiences in Scotland and England, this trip by Wells marked "the beginning of the worldwide campaign against lynching" (Wells-Barnett 1970, 82).

In returning to the United States, Wells became embroiled in a protest over the exclusion of the contributions of black Americans from the Chicago World's Fair. In the last three months of the fair 10,000 copies of *The Reason Why the Colored American Is Not in the World's Columbian Exposition* (1893), which Wells coauthored, were printed and distributed.

After the fair closed, Ida Wells elected to remain in Chicago. She began to write for the largest Negro newspaper in the city, the *Chicago Conservator*. She also was instrumental in establishing the largest permanent organization for women in the region. Boasting a membership that exceeded 300 women, the group was subsequently named the Ida B. Wells Women's Club, in recognition of her leadership.

Wells returned to England for six months in 1894 on a second lecture tour. During this trip she agreed to serve as a correspondent for the *Inter-Ocean*, regularly publishing columns under the byline "Ida B. Wells Abroad." The English public, press, and clergy continued to be more supportive of her antilynching activities than their American counterparts. An influential Anti-Lynching Committee, which included many prominent British citizens, was formed as a consequence of this effective overseas campaign.

Wells continued her antilynching crusade for a year after she returned to America. Sharing the platform on occasion with other distinguished speakers, such as Susan B. Anthony and Frederick Douglass, she traveled from coast to coast lecturing and mobilizing public opinion against lynching. Finally returning to Chicago after this demanding campaign, in June of 1895, she married Ferdinand Lee Barnett, a prominent activist lawyer, a widower, and the father of two boys. Later that year she published findings of her research on lynching in *A Red Record: Tabulated Statistics and Alleged Causes of Lynchings in the United States, 1892–1893–1894*. In 1900 an additional report, *Mob Rule in New Orleans*, was issued.

Ida Wells-Barnett was deeply committed to her husband and family, which increased in size over a decade to include two more sons and two daughters. Nevertheless, she continued to work actively in the community. A week after her marriage, for example, she assumed control of the *Chicago Conservator*. Her responsibilities as editor of the paper and president of the Ida B. Wells Club, and a schedule of lectures occupied her until a son was born in 1896. Although her stated intention was to remain at home with her family, she soon was on the road again accompanied by her infant son and a nurse. First, the three attended the convention of the National Association of Colored Women's Clubs in Washington, D.C., and subsequently they traveled within the state of Illinois to a number of speaking engagements.

After the birth of a second child in 1897, Wells-Barnett again vowed to give up her public work and "give my attention to my children" (Wells-Barnett 1970, 250). Within a few months, however, again traveling with a nursing infant, she arrived in Washington, D.C., to call on President McKinley in protest of the lynching of a South Carolina postmaster. Despite some intermittent travel, Wells-Barnett did curtail her public activities while her children were young. She relinquished the ownership of the *Conservator* in 1897 and avoided further paid employment until her youngest children were in school.

In the early decades of the twentieth century Wells-Barnett was active in the movement for women's suffrage. She was a long-term member of the Chicago Women's Suffrage Association. In 1913 she established the Alpha Suffrage Club, the first black women's suffrage organization in the nation. The same year, over the protests of some white Southern delegates, she joined the suffragists' mass march in Washington. Ida Wells-Barnett urged women to be active in politics and to exercise their rights as citizens. Nevertheless, she only ran once for elected public office. Running as an independent candidate, Wells-Barnett was unsuccessful in her 1930 campaign for the Illinois State Senate.

Wells-Barnett was dedicated to improving opportunities and enhancing the quality of life, as well as ensuring the civil liberties, of Afro-Americans. In the early 1900s she successfully worked behind the scenes with Jane Addams* and other community leaders to block a campaign to segregate the Chicago public schools. In 1910 she established the Negro Fellowship League Reading Room and Social Center, a community-based social service center modeled after Hull-House. The center offered temporary housing, social and job counseling services, and recreational facilities for uneducated and unemployed black men and boys, many of whom were recent migrants to the city. The League provided these services until 1920 when the lack of adequate funding and competition from other agencies led to its closing.

Ida Wells-Barnett worked to protect the rights of incarcerated blacks in addition to those who were educationally or economically disadvantaged. In 1909 she successfully blocked the reinstatement of a Illinois sheriff who had failed to protect a prisoner from a lynch mob. She courageously visited riot-torn East St. Louis, Illinois, in 1918 and Little Rock, Arkansas, in 1922 in support of victims of mob violence and imprisoned rioters. Wells-Barnett served as a probation officer for the Chicago municipal court from 1913 to 1916. She involved herself in a number of cases that required the legal assistance of her husband, Ferdinand. For example, their joint investigation and defense saved the life of a Joliet prison inmate unjustly accused of murder by arson.

Throughout her life Ida Wells-Barnett continued to fight for social justice and racial equality. The antilynching movement, which she inspired, led to the creation of several other national organizations committed to the betterment of the race. She worked to organize the national Afro-American Council in 1898 and served as its secretary until 1902. She also helped to establish the National Association for the Advancement of Colored People (NAACP). Because she disagreed with the principles of accommodation and compromise subsequently advocated by these groups, she was not actively involved in either of these organizations after their initial formation.

In 1928, at the age of sixty-six, Ida Wells-Barnett began to write her autobiography, which she aptly titled *Crusade for Justice*. Unfortunately, she died of uremic poisoning on March 25, 1931, before this project was completed. Her autobiography was edited and published posthumously by her daughter, Alfreda M. Duster, in 1970.

MAJOR THEMES

Ida Wells was an outspoken and courageous journalist and a zealous advocate of women's rights and racial equality. She was a recognized leader in the social reform movements of the late nineteenth and early twentieth centuries. She was a dedicated and uncompromising champion of black civil rights. She also was active in the women's suffrage campaign and the women's club movement. Wells-Barnett helped to found and establish a number of important organizations. These include the Alpha Suffrage Club, British and American Anti-Lynching Committees, the Ida B. Wells Club, the Negro Fellowship League, the Afro-American Council, and the NAACP.

Ida Wells-Barnett has been described as the chief architect of the antilynching movement. In fact, she was almost solely responsible for creating and building a successful international antilynching crusade. The mobilization of British public opinion against lynching appears to have been a critical turning point in her campaign. At the turn of the century England was the primary market for Southern cotton. A partial boycott of Southern cotton by sympathetic British importers and textile manufacturers proved to be a powerful antilynching lever. Bending under economic pressure, Southern producers and business leaders began to publicly condemn and effectively stem the violent and barbaric practice of lynching.

Wells-Barnett's pioneering contributions to sociological research and analysis have not been as widely recognized as her contributions to social reform. Her most important publications are based on her research on lynching. They include *A Red Record* (1895), *Southern Horrors* (1892), and *Mob Rule in New Orleans* (1900). These works were reprinted in a volume titled *On Lynching* in 1969. Other especially noteworthy publications include *The Reason Why the Colored American Is Not in the World's Columbian Exposition* (1893) and "Lynching and the Excuse for It" (1901), an article reprinted in *Lynching and Rape: An Exchange of Views* in 1971.

Wells-Barnett's research on lynching is unquestionably sociological. When she set out to investigate the causes of lynching, her aims were reformist but her methods of inquiry were clearly empirical. Systematically gathering, evaluating, and analyzing information, she based her logical conclusions solidly on evidence. Wells-Barnett's analysis of lynching was the first statistical study of the problem. Her research undermined prevailing myths by comparing reliable facts about lynching with traditional beliefs and assumptions. Her findings challenged the theory that lynching was provoked by the rape of white women. In her reports she consistently demonstrated that rape was not even alleged in the vast majority of lynching cases. Furthermore, in her penetrating analysis she exposed "both the racist and patriarchal foundations of Southern society" (Aptheker 1977, 17).

CRITIQUES OF IDA WELLS-BARNETT

Scholarship on black intellectuals, particularly black women, is undeveloped and fragmentary. This problem is exacerbated for Wells-Barnett. Many of her writings, scrapbooks, and personal documents were destroyed in fires at her home. Consequently a considerable amount of scholarship on Wells-Barnett is biographical, documenting (rather than analyzing) her major public activities and writings (see, e.g., Flexner 1971; Logan 1982; Noble 1978; Schlipp and Murphy 1983; Uglow 1982). Dale Spender (1982) provides a biographical and historical view of Wells-Barnett, enriched by its accompanying of analysis of other black women leaders. Dorothy Sterling's (1979) monograph on eminent black women places her in a similar context, but it is written as a popular book for young readers.

Some recent scholarship has made the writings of Wells-Barnett—both previously published (Lerner 1973, esp. 537–540) and previously unpublished works (Sterling 1984, 479–495)—more accessible. David M. Tucker's (1971) reconstruction of Wells-Barnett editorials and her role in the infamous Memphis lynchings contributes to a fuller understanding of her work. Elliott M. Rudwick and August Meier (1965) have described the historical reasons for Wells-Barnett's sociological analysis of racism at the Columbian Exposition in 1863. Allan H. Spear (1967) has placed her in the context of racially segregated Chicago. Mary White Ovington (1914) also briefly outlines her work for the NAACP. Thomas C. Holt (1982) has provided some useful historical background information about Wells-Barnett and her relations with the black community.

Critical commentary on Wells-Barnett's sociological and intellectual influence is just beginning to emerge. Bettina Aptheker (1977) has published a scholarly analysis of the relationship between Wells-Barnett and Jane Addams, documenting how their friendship and perspectives emerged from their different life experiences and racial backgrounds. Aptheker's analysis of black scholarship and racism places Wells-Barnett historically and biographically within central debates in the black community (1982, 60–75).

Mary Jo Deegan (1988) has identified Wells-Barnett as one of a network of early women sociologists who need to be integrated into sociological teaching. My own work locates Wells-Barnett in the context of early Southern and black women in sociology and demonstrates the need for a more inclusive history of the discipline (Broschart 1987, 1989).

Ida Wells-Barnett is a significant, but largely unheralded, founding sister of sociology. She deserves recognition for her courage, intellectual acumen, and social activism as well as for her penetrating sociological research and analysis. She has the further distinction of being the first black American woman sociologist.

BIBLIOGRAPHY

Selected Writings by Ida B. Wells-Barnett

1892. "Iola's Southern Field." *New York Age*, November 19. Reprinted in *Black Women in White America*, edited by Gerda Lerner, pp. 539–540. New York: Random House, Vintage, 1973.

1892. *Southern Horrors: Lynch Law in All Its Phases*. New York: New York Age Print.

1893. "Lynch Law in All Its Phases." *Our Day* 9 (May): 333–347.

1895. *A Red Record.* Chicago: Donohue & Henneberry.

1900a. *Mob Rule in New Orleans.* N.P. (See 1969 for reprint of pamphlet.)

1900b. "Lynch Law in America." *Arena* 23 (January): 15–24.

1910. "How Enfranchisement Stops Lynching." *Original Rights Magazine.* (June): 42–53.

1913. "Our Country's Lynching Record." *Survey* 29 (February 1): 573–574.

1920. *The Arkansas Race Riot.* Chicago: Hume Job Print.

1969. *On Lynchings: Southern Horrors; A Red Record; Mob Rule in New Orleans.* New York: Arno.

1970. *Crusade for Justice: The Autobiography of Ida B. Wells,* edited by Alfreda M. Duster. Chicago: University of Chicago Press.

1984. Excerpts from Ida B. Wells-Barnett's Diary. In *We Are Your Sisters: Black Women in the Nineteenth Century,* edited by Dorothy Sterling, pp. 481–495. New York: W. W. Norton.

1991. *Selected Works of Ida B. Wells-Barnett.* Compiled and introduced by Trudier Harris. New York: Oxford University Press.

Coauthored Works

Addams, Jane, and Ida B. Wells. 1901. *Lynching and Rape: An Exchange of Views.* Rev. ed. edited by Bettina Aptheker. San Jose, CA: American Institute for Marxist Studies, 1977.

Wells-Barnett, Ida B., with Frederick Douglass, Ferdinand Barnett, and I. Garland Penn. 1893. *The Reason Why the Colored American Is Not in the World's Columbian Exposition.* Chicago: privately printed.

Studies About Ida B. Wells-Barnett and Supplemental References

Andolsen, Barbara Hilkert. 1986. *Daughters of Jefferson, Daughters of Bootblacks.* Macon, GA: Mercer University Press.

Aptheker, Bettina. 1977. "Introduction." In *Lynching and Rape: An Exchange of Views,* by Jane Addams and Ida B. Wells, edited by B. Aptheker, pp. 1–21. San Jose, CA: American Institute for Marxist Studies, 1977. Originally published 1901.

———.1982. *Woman's Legacy: Essays on Race, Sex, and Class in American History.* Amherst: University of Massachusetts Press.

Deegan, Mary Jo. 1988. "Transcending a Patriarchal Past." *Teaching Sociology* 16 (April): 141–150.

Flexner, Eleanor. 1971. "Ida B. Wells-Barnett." In *Notable American Women,* vol. 3, edited by E. T. Janes, pp. 565–567. Cambridge, MA: Harvard University Press, Belknap Press.

Hall, Nora. 1983. "Ida B. Wells-Barnett." In *Dictionary of Literary Biography.* Vol. 23, *American Newspaper Journalists, 1873–1900,* pp. 340–346. Detroit: Gale.

Holt, Thomas C. 1982. "The Lonely Warrior: Ida B. Wells and the Struggle for Black Leadership." In *Black Leaders of the Twentieth Century,* edited by John Hope Franklin and August Meier, pp. 39–62. Urbana: University of Illinois Press.

Lerner, Gerda. 1973. *Black Women in White America.* New York: Random House, Vintage.

Logan, Rayford W. 1982. "Ida Bell Wells-Barnett." In *Dictionary of American Negro Biography*, pp. 30–31. New York: W. W. Norton.

Noble, Jeanne. "Ida B. Wells-Barnett." 1978. In *Beautiful Also Are the Souls of My Black Sisters: A History of the Black Woman in America*, pp. 133–135. Englewood Cliffs, NJ: Prentice-Hall.

Ovington, Mary White. 1914. *How the National Association for the Advancement of Colored People Began*. New York: NAACP. See especially Chapter 5.

Rudwick, Elliott M., and August Meier. 1965. "Black Man in the 'White City': Negroes and the Columbian Exposition, 1893." *Phylon* 26 (Winter): 354–361.

Schlipp, Madelon, and Sharon M. Murphy. 1983. "Ida B. Wells-Barnett, Crusader." In *Great Women of the Press*, pp. 121–132. Carbondale: Southern Illinois University Press.

Spear, Allan H. 1967. *Black Chicago: The Making of a Negro Ghetto*, 1890–1920. Chicago: University of Chicago Press.

Spender, Dale. "Ida B. Wells." 1982. In *Women of Ideas and What Men Have Done to Them*, by D. Spender. pp. 357–364. London: Pandora.

Sterling, Dorothy. 1979. *Black Foremothers*. Old Westbury, NY: Feminist Press.

———, ed. 1984. *We Are Your Sisters: Black Women in the Nineteenth Century*. New York: W. W. Norton.

Tucker, David M. 1971. "Miss Ida B. Wells and Memphis Lynching." *Phylon* 32 (Summer): 112–122.

Uglow, Jennifer, ed. 1982. "Ida B. Wells-Barnett." In *The Macmillan Dictionary of Women's Biography*, p. 492. London: Macmillan.

Unpublished Material

Broschart, Kay Richards. 1987. "Reconstructing Our Past: A Study of Early Southern Women Sociologists." Paper presented at the 16th Alpha Kappa Delta Sociological Research Symposium, Richmond, Virginia.

———. 1989. "Towards a More Inclusive History of the Discipline." Paper presented at the Annual Conference of the British Sociological Association, Plymouth, England.

Thomson, Mildred. 1979. "Ida B. Wells-Barnett: An Exploratory Study of an American Black Woman." Department of History, George Washington University.

KAY RICHARDS BROSCHART

HATTIE PLUM WILLIAMS (1878–1963)

The professional life of Hattie Plum Williams unfolded on the geographically isolated Great Plains of eastern Nebraska. She is the first woman known to chair a coeducational, doctoral department of sociology, and as the author of major studies on Russian German immigrants, she made significant disciplinary contributions to sociology. As a woman caught between changing definitions of the division of labor in sociology during the 1920s, she often is characterized as a social worker, although her professional allegiance remained to sociology. Williams epitomized the first generation of professional women sociologists on the Great Plains.

BIOGRAPHY

Hattie Plum was born on August 29, 1878 in Minden, Iowa. The details of her life are sketchy (she eschewed public notoriety as an adult) but can be gleaned from a brief, unpublished biography prepared by her husband, T. F. A. Williams. The biography is found in Box 68 of the Hattie Plum Williams Collection at the Nebraska State Historical Society. Florence Brugger (1964) wrote a useful but biased account based on T. F. A. Williams's later recollections.

Hattie Plum's father was a tenant farmer from Ohio, and her mother was from Pennsylvania. She had six half brothers and sisters. She graduated at age sixteen from the Shelby, Iowa, High School in 1894, and taught in a country school for the next four years. Concurrently, she attended Iowa State University.

In June 1898 Hattie Plum married T. F. A. Williams, a young lawyer and pioneer from Lincoln, Nebraska, and she moved there to live. Before their marriage her husband attended the University of Nebraska, where he made the acquaintance of two noted sociologists, Amos G. Warner and George E. Howard, who were then on the faculty. Both Warner and Howard impressed T. F. A. with their activist, egalitarian scholarship. Thus her husband's lifelong sympathy for sociological ideas had an early foundation.

Williams continued studies at the University of Nebraska in 1899 and graduated with a bachelor's degree in 1902. She resumed her teaching career as a substitute teacher in the public schools and at the First Christian Church in Lincoln. In 1907 she taught in a "beet-sugar room" that offered special classes for the children of Russian German immigrants who worked in the Nebraska sugar beet fields during the fall harvest. In response to the social conditions faced by these children, Williams decided to document the discrimination against Russian Germans in Nebraska. Her husband noted that "Mrs. Williams decided to gather the facts" on the lives and work of the Russian Germans in Nebraska.

Her empirical interest in the Russian Germans shaped her graduate sociology work at the University of Nebraska. "In 1908," wrote her husband, "a year in which there were 10 inches of rain in one month, Mrs. Williams tramped through the mud making home visits to take the Lincoln School census of the German Russians." She wrote a thesis on the naturalization of Russian German immigrants (Williams 1906) and received her master's degree in 1909.

She began doctoral studies in sociology under George E. Howard. Her continuing research on the Russian Germans occupied the next six years. During this period she also studied with Lucile Eaves.* Williams's (1916) dissertation was titled *A Social Study of the Russian German*. Her doctorate, the first awarded in sociology at the University of Nebraska, was conferred in 1915.

On receipt of her doctorate, a major opportunity opened unexpectedly. Lucile Eaves left Nebraska in 1915 (because of inadequate salary), and Williams was offered Eaves' position—albeit at an even lower salary. With Howard's encouragement, Williams accepted the post, and thus filled "the woman's position" of practical sociologist at the University of Nebraska from 1915 until her retirement in 1945.

Williams was an effective and committed educator. "From the outset Dr. Williams has proved herself possessed of the qualities of a strong and zealous teacher" (Howard 1988, 14). Her students became "a small army" for social betterment (Pound 1916). Her courses included Introduction to Sociology, Modern Social Betterment Movements, Community Problems, Criminology, Immigration, American Race Problems, Child Welfare, and Seminar in Medical Sociology (Howard 1988, 14–15).

Emphasis on detailed field research hallmarked Williams's courses. Her students mapped the sociological patterns of eastern Nebraska, and their reports (preserved in Williams's archival papers) provide untapped data for modern analysis. The reports reflect Williams's high academic standards and chronicle her influence on waves of cohorts who passed through her courses.

Williams's faculty appointment was soon followed by the departure of her powerful and respected mentor, George E. Howard. In 1917 he retired and devoted himself to his presidency of the American Sociological Society. From 1917 to 1922, without Howard's supportive presence, Williams became increasingly isolated in the department of political science and sociology. Howard's position was not filled, and the political scientists chafed at Williams's continued tenure. Her experience was not unique, however, as women sociologists were everywhere under fire during this period (Deegan 1988, 309–317).

Williams's slide into professional obscurity took an extraordinary turn in 1923, when George E. Howard successfully urged the university to make Williams the next departmental chair. To substantiate his endorsement, Howard came out of retirement and taught full-time at half salary in 1923–1924 (Howard's support is documented in the Hattie Plum Williams Collection at the Nebraska State Historical Society and the George E. Howard papers at the University of Nebraska Archives).

Even with Howard's backing, Williams struggled with her male colleagues during her years as chair from 1923 to 1928. In 1925 sociology and political science separated. Williams continued as chair of the new department of sociology, and Joyce O. Hertzler (a male protégé of Edward A. Ross) was added to the staff. Howard's death in 1928 marked the end of Williams's rise in sociology. His egalitarianism (Williams 1929) was not institutionalized, and Williams relinquished the chair to Hertzler. Williams was assigned responsibility for a new program in "social work," and turned her attention to her students and the local community.

When Willard Waller arrived on the Nebraska campus in 1929, he judged that Williams was the "powerhouse of the department" even though Hertzler was then chair (Goode, Furstenberg, and Mitchell 1970, 33). Hertzler was passively instrumental in Waller's subsequent abrupt dismissal, however, and university administrators later subjected Williams to a year's unpaid leave of absence during a financial shortfall in the 1930s.

Before being administratively shunted aside, Williams became the first woman known to chair a coeducational, doctoral sociology program in the United States. Her chairship marked the only respite in the long saga of patriarchal control of sociology at the University of Nebraska. Not one woman was hired in a tenure track position during Hertzler's subsequent forty-year reign. A sign that patriarchal domination may be lessening at Nebraska was evidenced in 1986, when Lynn White was appointed to a three-year term as chair, and thus became the second woman to hold the chief administrative office in the Nebraska department.

Professionally, Williams became increasingly identified with the emerging field of social work. Nonetheless, Williams located her interests within sociology, not within a new and separate discipline. Although her interest in practical sociology led her in 1923 to establish a medical social work program at the University Medical College in Omaha, it was operated under the joint control of the medical college and the sociology department. This initiative resulted in controversy, and the program was terminated—much to her regret—in 1926.

Williams was pushed and pulled into a widening circle of professional social workers, in which she found the collegiality that most male sociologists denied her. Williams and Edith Abbott* (a University of Nebraska alumna) corresponded about students that Williams sent to the University of Chicago for graduate work (where Abbott was dean) and about candidates that Abbott recommended for faculty posts at Nebraska. These professional exchanges in the 1920s and 1930s (preserved in the Hattie Plum Williams Collection at the Nebraska State Historical Society) document Williams's inclusion in a national social work network.

Williams's commitment to activist research (modeled after her mentors, Howard and Eaves) distanced her in the 1920s from a new breed of male sociologists who shunned progressive political action and defined sociology as "value-free." She worked tirelessly for progressive laws, in the 1920s for child welfare legislation and in the 1930s for public assistance. Ernest Witte (1963), a student of Williams and a former director of the Nebraska Graduate School of Social Work, wrote: "During the '30s and '40s [Williams] was a frequent visitor to legislative sessions where she urged support of numerous bills in the sociology field." She also traveled extensively, including a harrowing return from war-torn England in the fall of 1938 (Williams, T. F. A. 1939).

Given her commitment to social betterment, her professional visibility at the University of Nebraska, and the lack of colleagues to share the responsibility, Williams became a clearinghouse for numerous volunteer associations in Nebraska. Her correspondence reflects the heavy load she carried as the leading social welfare activist in the state for many years. Her many organizational accomplishments included cofounding the Nebraska Welfare Association. She worked long, dedicated hours answering requests for help, information, and encouragement. She also was a frequent lecturer throughout her professional career (Williams, note on "The School as an Assimilative Agent," 1916).

Williams was honored in 1936 when she received the Distinguished Service Award from the Nebraska Conference for Social Work in 1936. Despite such well-deserved recognition and her public association with social work, Williams identified herself as a "practical sociologist." Her ties to a progressive, active vision of sociology ran deep. Hattie Plum Williams retired from the University of Nebraska in 1945. A memorial fellowship was established in her name in 1963, the year of her death.

Williams's impact on the discipline of sociology was stunted by organizational and institutional factors. She was increasingly pushed away from sociology as a profession, and her research and writing were not structurally supported by her University. She never fully flourished in either social work or sociology. She remained "betwixt and between," and forged a particular practice of sociology valued in everyday life but not in the academy. She was rewarded locally by the community for her service to Nebraska as a social worker and an educator. She inspired her students, supported people of color, and lived an active political life.

MAJOR THEMES

Williams emphasized the social processes of immigration and naturalization. "Immigration is the field of Dr. Williams' special research" (Howard 1988,

14). Williams's work is grounded in the school of thought called "critical pragmatism" (cf. Deegan 1988, 247–263, 288–295). Her ideas echo those of Edith Abbott and Lucile Eaves. Williams's concern with the adjustments made by immigrants to new social conditions dovetailed with her equally strong interest in the operation and effectiveness of social welfare agencies. As a "practical sociologist," Williams focused on themes now included under the rubric of "applied sociology."

Williams left a small, but solid body of scholarly works, of which the most important part relates to immigration and naturalization. Her master's thesis (Williams 1906) prefigured her 1915 doctoral dissertation, which appeared as *A Social Study of the Russian German* (Williams 1916). Williams (1912) published her first article, on naturalization, while in graduate school.

Williams meticulously documented the experiences of the Russian Germans in Lincoln and Nebraska. She explored their historical roots in Germany, their first dislocation to Russian control, and their subsequent migration to the United States. The poverty, isolation, speech, and customs of the German Russians set them apart from their neighbors, who did not accept them as equals. Williams's analysis mirrors her strong advocacy—and that of her immigrant subjects—for democracy and human rights.

Williams's unflinching critical insight is exemplified in her comments at the 1917 meetings of the American Sociological Society, where she was asked by George Howard to discuss the papers presented in the session on "immigration" (Williams 1918). She responded favorably to Edith Abbott's paper, but Williams critiqued the work of two male sociologists (Henry Pratt Fairchild and Arthur J. Todd) as fundamentally meaningless and lacking in imagination. With the exception of Howard, there is no evidence that her critical abilities were welcomed by her considerably more powerful male colleagues.

Williams planned further studies on the Russian Germans, but did not complete the project because of her heavy teaching load and her time-consuming commitments to civic service (cf., Williams 1919, 1920). Her preliminary work (including several unpublished papers) was collected and posthumously published as *The Czar's Germans* (Williams 1975). This noteworthy, but uneven effort suggests the direction of Williams's unrealized research agenda.

The second major category of Williams's work includes careful, pragmatically useful studies of social legislation and social welfare agencies in Nebraska. In the *Nebraska Survey of Social Resources* Williams (1936) contributed a major account of the history of social welfare legislation in Nebraska. It was "used as a reference" for many years (Witte 1963).

A Handbook of Social Agencies in Nebraska was compiled by Williams (1940) from her students' cooperative research on local organizations. This was a useful contribution but not a stimulating intellectual production. It did, however, reflect the cooperative research model advocated by Lucile Eaves (1920).

Many of Williams's writings on social legislation, often unpublished or narrowly distributed, remain in archival deposits in Lincoln. Her field reports for the national Commission on Law Observance and Enforcement (Williams 1933) are good examples. In 1931 she completed metropolitan studies of "the cost of crime" for the Commission. Her reports on Lincoln and Omaha, Nebraska, were abstracted and summarized with those of numerous researchers from across the country (National Commission on Law Observance and Enforcement 1931). The typescripts of her full "cost of crime" reports reside in the University of Nebraska Library.

CRITIQUES OF HATTIE PLUM WILLIAMS

There is little published criticism of Williams's work. Herbert A. Miller, an expert on immigration, wrote a positive review in the *American Journal of Sociology* of Williams's (1916) *A Social Study of the Russian German*. Miller's (1917, 848) major criticism was that "the study is essentially objective," a comment considered praiseworthy today. Several sociologists, including Emory Bogardus, wrote to congratulate Williams for her research in *A Study of the Russian German*.

Hill (1988a) explicates Williams's (1933) unrecognized work for the National Commission on Law Observance and Enforcement. He further explores the bureaucratic ecology of Williams's work vis a vis that undertaken for the Commission by fellow Nebraskans Edith Abbott and Roscoe Pound (Hill 1989).

Williams's role in Nebraska sociology is being documented by a small group of researchers now analyzing "the Nebraska school of sociology" (Hill 1988b; Deegan and Hill, in process). This work identifies Williams's career as representative of the ideological and organizational struggles that women faced in the discipline of sociology and the academy from 1900 to 1925. Her successful fight for recognition from the majority of her white male colleagues exemplifies the contests for control typical of the discipline in the 1920s.

The meticulous demographic data collected by Williams on German Russians in Lincoln, Nebraska, is used with frequency by the many historians and popular writers who study this ethnic group. Many of these authors use Williams's raw data but do not cite her as the source of their information. An exception to this behavior is found in John Anderson's detailed study of Lincoln, Nebraska's local election on May 4, 1909. He draws on Williams's data and writings to document the contrasting view of "Americanized settlers" versus the "foreign" element of German Russians (Anderson 1989).

Williams played a major role in local women's groups, social legislation, and teaching from 1915 to 1950. Such roles were frequently filled by other, even more obscure women sociologists throughout the Midwest, Southwest, and Great Plains. These heroic women's lives have not been documented, although they deserve attention. Frequently aligned with progressive interests, these women helped to build and shape the social infrastructure of their communities. Their ideas were rooted in applied sociology both within and outside of the academy.

Hattie Plum Williams is a Weberian "ideal type" of these forgotten women in sociology.

ACKNOWLEDGMENT

Our thanks to Mary Rabenberg, librarian and archivist at the American Historical Society of Germans from Russia, Lincoln, Nebraska, for her help on this entry on Hattie Plum Williams.

BIBLIOGRAPHY

Selected Writings by Hattie Plum Williams

1912. "The Road to Citizenship: A Study of Naturalization in a Nebraska County." *Political Science Quarterly* 28 (September): 399–427. Reprinted, *Nebraska History* 68 (Winter 1987): 166–182.

1916. *A Social Study of the Russian German*. University Studies, Vol. 16, No. 3. Lincoln: University of Nebraska. Ph.D. diss., University of Nebraska, Lincoln, 1915; reprinted, Lincoln, NE: American Historical Society of Germans from Russia, 1984.

1918. "Discussion of 'Social Control and Immigration' Papers." *Papers and Proceedings of the American Sociological Society* 12: 184–190.

1919. "The University and the Community." In *The University of Nebraska, 1869–1919*, pp. 70–73. Lincoln: University of Nebraska.

1920. "Women's Activities on the Campus." *University Journal* 16 (October): 35.

1929. "Social Philosophy of George Elliott Howard." *Sociology and Social Research* 8 (January–February): 229–233.

1936. "Chronological Outline of Social Legislation in Nebraska," and "Historical Summary of Public Welfare Administration in Nebraska." In *Nebraska Survey of Social Resources*, vol. 1, sponsored by State Child Welfare Bureau, Maud E. Nuquist (director), pp. 1–55, 56–76a. Lincoln: Nebraska Emergency Relief Administration.

1940. *Handbook of Social Agencies in Nebraska*. Lincoln: University of Nebraska, School of Social Work.

1975. *The Czar's Germans: With Particular Reference to the Volga Germans*, edited by Emma S. Haynes, P. B. Legler, and G. S. Walker. Lincoln, NE: American Historical Society of Germans from Russia.

Unpublished Works by Hattie Plum Williams

1906. "The Road to Citizenship." Master's thesis, Department of Political Science and Sociology, University of Nebraska.

1933. "Report on the Cost of Administration of Criminal Justice in Lincoln, Nebraska," and "Report on the Cost of Administration of Criminal Justice in Omaha, Nebraska." Typescript. Prepared for the National Commission on Law Observance and Enforcement. Lincoln: University of Nebraska.

Studies About Hattie Plum Williams and Supplemental References

Anderson, John. 1989. "Lincoln, Nebraska and Prohibition: The Election of May 4, 1909." *Nebraska History* 70 (Summer): 184–200.

Brugger, Florence. 1964. "Hattie Plum Williams—Her Achievements and Contributions." *Nebraska Welfare Association Newsletter* (July–September): 9–10.

Deegan, Mary Jo. 1988. *Jane Addams and the Men of the Chicago School, 1892–1918*. New Brunswick, NJ: Transaction Books.

Eaves, Lucile. 1920. "Plans for Co-operative Research." *American Journal of Sociology* 25 (March): 568–571.

Goode, William J., Frank F. Furstenberg, Jr., and Larry R. Mitchell. 1970. "Introduction: Willard Waller—A Portrait." In *Willard Waller On the Family, Education, and War*, edited by W. J. Goode, F. F. Furstenberg, Jr., and L. R. Mitchell, pp. 1–112. Chicago: University of Chicago Press.

Haynes, Emma S. 1975. "Introduction." In *The Czar's Germans: With Particular Reference to the Volga Germans*, edited by Emma S. Haynes, P. B. Legler, and G. S. Walker, pp. xi–xvi. Lincoln, NE: American Historical Society of Germans from Russia.

Hill, Michael R. 1988a. "Research by Bureaucracy: Hattie Plum Williams and the National Commission on Law Observance and Enforcement, 1929–1931." *Mid-American Review of Sociology* 13 (Winter): 69–84.

———, ed. 1988b. "The Foundations of Nebraska Sociology." Special Issue. *Mid-American Review of Sociology* 13 (Winter).

Howard, George Elliott. 1988. "Sociology in the University of Nebraska, 1898–1927." *Mid-American Review of Sociology* 13 (Winter): 3–19.

Miller, Herbert A. 1917. "Review of *A Social Study of the Russian German*." *American Journal of Sociology* 22 (May): 848.

National Commission on Law Observance and Enforcement. 1931. *Report on the Cost of Crime*. Washington, DC: Government Printing Office.

Pound, Olivia. 1916. "Hattie Plum Williams: Her Service to the Community and to the University." *University Journal* 13 (October): 20–21.

Williams, T. F. A "Lincoln Folks in London World-War Clouds." *Nebraska History* 20 (July–September): 173–174.

Unpublished Material

Deegan, Mary Jo, and Michael R. Hill. In preparation. *Frontier Dreams and Visions*.

Hill, Michael R. 1989. "Hattie Plum Williams and the Wickersham Commission, 1929–1931: A Case Study in Parallel Biography." In "Roscoe Pound and American Sociology: A Study in Archival Frame Analysis, Sociobiography, and Sociological Jurisprudence," by M. R. Hill, pp. 577–665. Ph.D. diss., Department of Sociology, University of Nebraska-Lincoln.

Witte, Ernest. 1963. "Educator Dies Here." Newspaper obituary, December 29. Hattie Plum Williams Collection, Box 68.

Archives

George E. Howard Papers. University Archives, University of Nebraska-Lincoln, Lincoln, Nebraska.

Hattie Plum Williams Collection. State Archives, Nebraska State Historical Society, Lincoln, Nebraska.

Williams, Hattie Plum. "The School as an Assimilative Agent," 1916. Archives, American Historical Society of Germans from Russia, Lincoln, Nebraska.

MICHAEL R. HILL AND MARY JO DEEGAN

APPENDIX: ADDITIONAL NOTABLE WOMEN SOCIOLOGISTS

The notable female sociologists listed below played a central role in founding the profession. For various reasons, ranging from peripheral network or organizational ties within sociology to the overrepresentation of Chicago and other U.S. citizens, they were not included in the longer entries.

Abbott, Grace
Beard, Belle Boone
Beard, Mary Ritter
Beck, Dorothy Fahs
Bernard, Frances Fenton
Blau, Zena Smith
Bosanquet, Helen
Boulding, Elise Marie
Butler, Josephine
Cartwright, Marguerite Dorsey
Cormack, Margaret
Coyle, Grace
Cussler, Margaret Thekla
Cuthbert, Marion
Dunayevskya, Raya
Eastman, Crystal
Elliot, Mabel
Firestone, Rose P.
Follett, Mary Parker
George, Zelma Watson

Glueck, Eleanor
Goldman, Emma
Gouldner, Helen Patricia
Graham, Mary
Haynes, Elizabeth Ross
Hinkle, Gisela Johanna
Jaffe, Else Von Richthofen
Jahoda, Marie
Jocher, Katherine
Karpf, Fay
Lathrop, Julia
Luxemburg, Rosa
McDowell, Mary E.
Martin, Gertrude Schorb
Mead, Margaret Fogg
Meyer, Gladys Engel
Mowrer, Harriet
Mudd, Emily
Palmer, Vivian
Paul, Alice
Perkins (Wilson), Frances
Proxiotto, Jessica
Ramabai, Pandita
Reeves, Ruby Jo
Reynolds, Bertha
Robinson, Virginia
Salmon, Lucy
Sanger, Margaret
Schreiner, Olive
Simkovitch, Mary Kingsbury
de Staël, Germaine
Stein, Edith
Strong, Anna Marie
Theodore, Athena Rentoumis
Tomah, Aida
Useem, Ruth
Washington, Margaret Murray
Weber, Marianne
Winston, Ellen Black
Wollstonecraft, Mary
Woodhouse, Chase Goeing
Wunderlick, Frieda
Young, Pauline
Zetkin, Clara (Klara)

NAME INDEX

This selected, topical name index emphasizes intellectuals, mentors, feminists, and female sociologists, particularly those born before 1927. Names of the family and friends of the entrants, critics of only one entrant, and multiple, contemporary coauthors with the entrants are not listed. Page numbers in bold refer to main entries.

SUBJECT INDEX

This is a selective list of subjects, emphasizing women, sociology, and institutions that have trained or employed sociologists. Three subjects permeate the book: *working women, women in higher education,* and *feminism.* All the entrants were working women, and almost all wrote on the sociology of working women. All were women with higher education, and their biographies contain accounts of their struggles with and careers in higher education. Only two entrants said they were not feminists, but all the biographers interpreted the women as feminists in ideas and action. Only explicit references to working women, women in higher education, and feminism are included here.

ABOUT THE CONTRIBUTORS

MICHAEL R. BALL received his doctorate in sociology from the University of Nebraska–Lincoln. He has taught there and at the University of Nebraska–Omaha. His areas of interest include the history of sociology, social inequality, popular culture, and visual sociology. Currently he is a visiting assistant professor of sociology at the University of Wisconsin–Superior.

VALERIE MALHOTRA BENTZ is an associate professor of sociology and social work at Texas Women's Christian University. She is interested in both contemporary and classical theory and the connections between rationality, therapy, emotions, and women. Her book on nontraditional female students, *Becoming Mature: Childhood Ghosts and Spirits in Adult Life*, explores these themes using a combination of several theories and methodologies.

KAY RICHARDS BROSCHART received her Ph.D. from Yale University. After teaching for ten years at Boston College, she joined the faculty at Hollins College, where she currently is an associate professor of sociology. She has published articles on women and the professions, the sociology of the family, and gender and adult development. Her research and papers on the history of women in sociology focus on the careers and contributions of women in the American South and Great Britain.

MARY JO DEEGAN is professor of sociology at the University of Nebraska–Lincoln. She specializes in theory, qualitative methodology, the history of sociology, and medical sociology. She has published more than fifty articles, including a number on the Chicago school of sociology and the work of early women sociologists. She has written or coedited six books, including *Jane*

Addams and the Men of the Chicago School, 1892–1918; *Feminist Ethics and Social Science Research*; *Women and Disability*; *Women and Symbolic Interaction*; and *American Ritual Drama*.

VIRGINIA KEMP FISH is professor emeritus at the University of Wisconsin–Stevens Point. Her research has largely focused on Edith Abbott, Grace Abbott, Sophonisba Breckinridge, Florence Kelley, Julia Lathrop, and Alice Hamilton. She calls them "the Hull-House Circle." She has studied their roles as researchers, reformers, and social activists during the founding years of the University of Chicago, and the reform organizations with which they were involved.

JAN MARIE FRITZ is on the faculty of California State University–San Bernardino. She is past president of the Clinical Sociology Association (now the Sociological Practice Association) and chair of the American Sociological Association section on Sociological Practice. She has published extensively on the history of American sociology and sociological practice, and also is the editor of the history section of the *Clinical Sociology Review*.

SHERYL J. GRANA received her doctorate in sociology from the University of Nebraska–Lincoln. Currently she is a part-time assistant professor at Doane College. Her areas of expertise are the sociology of women and stratification. Her research interests include women and both their unpaid (housework) and paid (labor force) work, women and class-consciousness issues, and women's friendships.

MICHAEL R. HILL holds doctorates in both geography and sociology from the University of Nebraska–Lincoln. His interdisciplinary work centers on theory, methodology, microspatial urban behavior, social institutions, and the sociology of sociology. Hill has published numerous articles and edited a special issue of *Mid-American Review of Sociology* on "The Foundations of Nebraska Sociology." He is the author of *Walking, Crossing Streets, and Choosing Pedestrian Routes*, and coeditor of *Women and Symbolic Interaction*. Most recently he edited the sesquicentennial edition of Harriet Martineau's *How to Observe Morals and Manners*.

CARLA B. HOWERY is the assistant executive officer of the American Sociological Association (ASA) and director of the ASA'S Teaching Services Program. She has worked to enhance the effectiveness of teaching sociology at the graduate and undergraduate levels, and in the elementary schools. At ASA she also is the managing editor of *Footnotes*, and staff liaison to the Committees on World Sociology, Status of Women in Sociology, Society and Persons with Disabilities, Membership, Teaching sections, and other special projects.

BRUCE KEITH received his doctorate in sociology from the University of

Nebraska–Lincoln. He currently is an instructor at the University of Nebraska. His academic work centers on the sociology of education, the history of sociology, and sociological methods.

MARY ANN LAMANNA is an associate professor of sociology at the University of Nebraska–Omaha. She earned her doctorate at the University of Notre Dame and specializes in gender roles and in marriage and the family. She has coauthored *Marriages and Families*: *Making Choices and Facing Change*, 4th ed., and written articles on gender-related topics. She is working on a book on Émile Durkheim and the family and on a qualitative study of teenage women's decision making on sexuality and reproduction.

IMOGENE MOYER is an associate professor of criminology and women's studies at Indiana University of Pennsylvania, Indiana, Pennsylvania. She earned her doctorate in sociology with a specialization in crime and deviance from the University of Minnesota–Columbia. She has completed several research projects in the areas of women and crime and has written numerous publications on women's prisons, police processing of women offenders, sexual abuse of children, women in academia, and women pioneers in criminology. She currently is revising her book *The Changing Roles of Women in the Criminal Justice System*: *Offenders, Victims, and Professionals*.

JANE C. OLLENBURGER is an associate professor and department head of sociology at the University of Minnesota–Duluth. She specializes in research methods, sociology of law, and the sociology of women. She has published articles on feminist ethics, sex segregation in the work force, juvenile justice, and fear of crime among the elderly. She currently is coauthoring a book on the sociology of women.

TERRI PHILLIPS earned a master's degree in sociology from the University of Nebraska–Lincoln where she is currently a doctoral student. She is particularly interested in marriage and the family.

SHULAMIT REINHARZ is an associate professor of sociology at Brandeis University. She has published widely on education, qualitative and feminist methodology, miscarriage, and aging. Her books include *On Becoming a Social Scientist*, *Psychology and Community Change*, and *Qualitative Gerontology*. She is continuing research on a neglected woman in Zionist history, Manya Wilbushewitz Shohat.

AGNES RIEDMANN attended Clarke College in Dubuque, Iowa, and received her bachelor's degree from Creighton University, Omaha, Nebraska. She earned a master's degree in sociology from the University of Nebraska–Omaha and a doctorate from the University of Nebraska–Lincoln. She has coauthored *Marriages and Families: Making Choices and Facing Change*, 4th ed.

JANICE ROSCOE is a doctoral student in sociology at Brandeis University. She lives in Longview, Washington, with her husband and two young sons.

BARBARA RYAN is an assistant professor at Widener University in Chester, Pennsylvania. She has published articles in the *American Sociologist, Sociology and Social Research, Journal of Marriage and the Family*, and *Gender and Society*. Her forthcoming book is titled *Feminism and the Women's Movement: Dynamics of Change in Social Movement Ideology and Activism*.

TAMI J. STOEHR-KREPS is a graduate student at the University of Nebraska–Lincoln. Her areas of interest include demography, gerontology, and marriage and the family.

GORDON STREIB received his Ph.D. from Columbia University. After teaching at Cornell University for twenty-six years, he joined the faculty at the University of Florida. He has published in several areas of sociology: social stratification, family, sociology of religion, and methods of research. He is now professor emeritus from the University of Florida and from Cornell University.

DEBRA WINEGARTEN, a graduate of Texas Woman's University, currently is a graduate teaching associate at Ohio State University, pursuing her master's degree in sociology. Her research interests include hunger, homelessness, social movements, and gender.